Concurrent Prolog
Collected Papers

Volume 2

MIT Press Series in Logic Programming
Ehud Shapiro, editor
Koichi Furukawa, Fernando Pereira, David H. D. Warren, associate editors

The Art of Prolog: Advanced Programming Techniques, by Leon Sterling and Ehud Shapiro, 1986

Logic Programming: Proceedings of the Fourth International Conference, edited by Jean-Louis Lassez, 1987 (Vols. 1 and 2)

Concurrent Prolog: Collected Papers, edited by Ehud Shapiro, 1987 (Vols. 1 and 2)

Concurrent Prolog
Collected Papers
Volume 2

Edited by Ehud Shapiro
The Weizmann Institute of Science

The MIT Press
Cambridge, Massachusetts
London, England

PUBLISHER'S NOTE

This format is intended to reduce the cost of publishing certain works in book form and to shorten the gap between editorial preparation and final publication. Detailed editing and composition have been avoided by photographing the text of this book directly from the authors' prepared copy.

Second printing, 1988

This book was set in TₑX by Sarah Fliegelmann
at the Weizmann Institute of Science
and printed and bound in the United States of America.

Library of Congress Cataloging-in-Publication Data

Concurrent Prolog.

(MIT Press series in logic programming)
Bibliography: v. 2, p.
Includes index.
1. Prolog (Computer program language)
2. Parallel programming (Computer science)
I. Shapiro, Ehud Y.   II. Series.
QA76.73.P76C655   1987   005.13'3   87-3288
ISBN 0-262-19255-1 (set)
ISBN 0-262-19266-7 (v. 1)
ISBN 0-262-19267-5 (v. 2)

Contents

Volume 1

Volume 2

The Authors

Curtis Abbott received his B.A. in Music and Mathematics at the University of California at San Diego in 1976 and pursued graduate studies in Computer Science at the University of California at Berkeley during 1983-1984. Currently, he works at Xerox PARC and is also affiliated with Stanford's Center for the Study of Language and Information. His address is Xerox PARC, 3333 Coyote Hill Rd., Palo Alto, CA 94304, USA.

Evyatar Av-Ron received his B.S. in Computer Science from SUNY at Stony Brook in 1980 and his M.Sc. in Computer Science from the Weizmann Institute of Science in 1984. He is presently a Ph.D. student at the Department of Computer Science, The Weizmann Institute of Science, Rehovot 76100, Israel.

Daniel G. Bobrow received his B.A. in Physics from Rensselaer Polytechnic Institute in 1957, his S.M. in Applied Mathematics from Harvard University in 1958, and his Ph.D. in Mathematics from MIT in 1964. After teaching for a year at MIT, he joined Bolt Beranek and Newman in Cambridge, Mass., where he started the Artificial Intelligence Department, and later became Vice President of the Computer Science Division. In 1972 he joined Xerox PARC where he is presently a research fellow in the Intelligent Systems Laboratory, Xerox PARC, Palo Alto, CA 94304, USA.

Takashi Chikayama received his B.E. degree in mathematical engineering in 1977 and his M.E. and D.Eng. degrees in information engineering in 1979 and 1982, respectively, all from the University of Tokyo. Since 1982, he has been a researcher at the Research Center of the Institute for New Generation Computer Technology (ICOT). His present address is Fourth Research Laboratory, Institute for New Generation Computer Technology, 4-28, Mita 1-chome, Minato-ku, Tokyo 108, Japan.

Michael Codish got his B.Sc. in Mathematics from the Ben Gurion University at Beer-Sheba in 1983 and his M.Sc. from the Weizmann Institute of Science in 1986. He is presently a Ph.D. student at the Department of Computer Science, The Weizmann Institute of Science, Rehovot 76100, Israel.

Shimon Cohen got his B.A. in Mathematics and Philosophy from Tel-Aviv University in 1977, his M.A. in Computer Science from the Weizmann Institute in 1979 and his Ph.D. in Computer Science from the Hebrew University in 1983. In 1983–84 he was a visiting professor in the Univeristy of California at Berkeley and then a research member of the Artificial Intelligence Laboratory of SPAR (Schlumberger Palo Alto Research Center). Since 1986 he is a faculty member at the Tel-Aviv University. His present address is the Department of Computer Science, Tel-Aviv University, Tel-Aviv 69978, Israel.

Michael Hirsch received his B.Sc. in Mathematics and Computer Science from the University of Cape Town in 1982, B.Sc. (Hons.) from the University of Cape Town in 1983 and M.Sc. from the Weizmann Institute of Science in 1987. He is currently a staff member at the Weizmann Institute of Science, Rehovot 76100, Israel.

Avshalom Houri received his B.Sc. in Computer Science from Jerusalem College of Technology (JCT) in 1983, and his M.Sc. in Computer Science from the Weizmann Institute for Science in 1986. He is presently working at the Department of Computer Science, The Weizmann Institute of Science, Rehovot 76100, Israel.

Kenneth M. Kahn received his B.A. in Economics from the University of Pennsylvania in 1973. He received his M.S. in 1975 and Ph.D. in 1979 from MIT in Computer Science. After teaching for a year at MIT, he became a visiting professor at the University of Stockholm and a research scientist at Uppsala University. In 1984, he joined the Intelligent Systems Laboratory of Xerox PARC, Palo Alto, CA 94304, USA.

Dan Katzenenllenbogen received his B.Sc. in Mathematics and Computer Science from Tel-Aviv University in 1983, and his M.Sc. in Computer Science from The Weizmann Institute of Science in 1987. His present address is POB 173, Kohav Yair 44864, Israel.

Jacob Levy received his B.A. in Chemistry in 1979 and his M.Sc. in Organic Chemistry in 1982, both from the Hebrew University of Jerusalem. Since 1983 he has been studying towards his Ph.D. in Computer Science at the Department of Computer Science at the Weizmann Institute of Science. His present address is the Department of Computer Science, The Weizmann Institute of Science, Rehovot 76100, Israel.

Yossi Lichtenstein got his B.Sc. in Physics and Computer Science from Bar-Ilan University in 1982. He is presently a M.Sc. student at the Department of Computer Science, The Weizmann Institute of Science, Rehovot 76100, Israel.

Mark S. Miller got his B.S. in Computer Science from Yale University in 1980. He is an alumni of the Xanadu Hypertext Project and a former researcher at the

Datapoint Technology Center. He is presently exploring marketplace mechanisms as a means for allocating resources and guiding evolution in open software systems. His present address is Xerox Palo Alto Research Center, 3333 Coyote Hill Rd., Palo Alto, California.

Toshihiko Miyazaki received his B.E. degree in Information Engineering from the University of Ohita in 1981. Since 1984, he has been a researcher at the Research Center of the Institute for New Generation Computer Technology (ICOT). His present address is Fourth Research Laboratory, Institute for New Generation Computer Technology, 4-28, Mita 1-chome, Minato-ku, Tokyo 108, Japan.

Shmuel Safra got his B.Sc. in Mathematics and Computer Science in 1984 from the Hebrew University and his M.Sc. in Computer Science in 1986 from the Weizmann Institute of Science. He is presently a Ph.D. student at the Department of Computer Science, The Weizmann Institute of Science, Rehovot 76100, Israel.

Ehud Shapiro received his B.A. in Mathematics and Philosophy from Tel-Aviv University in 1979 and his Ph.D. in Computer Science from Yale University in 1982. Since 1982 he has been a faculty member at the Weizmann Institute of Science. His address is Department of Computer Science, The Weizmann Institute of Science, Rehovot 76100, Israel.

William Silverman received his B.A. in Mathematics and Sociology from the University of Minnesota in 1960. Since 1971 he has been a member of the faculty of the Weizmann Institute of Science. His address is Department of Computer Science, The Weizmann Institute of Science, Rehovot 76100, Israel.

Leon Sterling received his B.Sc. (hons.) in Mathematics and Computer Science from Melbourne University in 1976 and his Ph.D. in Pure Mathematics from Australian National University in 1981. He spent three years at the University of Edinburgh and one year at the Weizmann Institute before joining the faculty at Case Western Reserve University in 1985. His address is Department of Computer Engineering and Science, Case Western Reserve University, Cleveland, Ohio, 44106, USA.

Akikazu Takeuchi received his B.E. and M.E. degrees in Mathematical Engineering from the University of Tokyo, in 1977 and 1979, respectively. In 1979, he joined Central Research Laboratory of Mitsubishi Electric Corporation. From 1982 to 1986 he stayed at the Research Center of the Institute for New Generation Computer Technology (ICOT). His present address is Central Research Laboratory, Mitsubishi Electric Corp., 8-1-1 Tsukaguchi-honmachi, Amagasaki, Hyogo 661 Japan.

Stephen Taylor completed an H.N.C. in Electrical and Electronic Engineering and an apprenticeship in Aeronautical Engineering with British Aircraft Corporation, Stevenage, England, in 1977. In 1982 he completed a B.Sc. in Computer

Systems at Essex University, England, and in 1984 a M.Sc. in Computer Science at Columbia University in New York. He is currently a Ph.D. student at the Weizmann Institute of Science, Rehovot 76100, Israel. His research interests are primarily parallel architectures and languages.

Eric Dean Tribble is studying computer science at Stanford University and is a member of the Vulcan Project at Xerox PARC. His present address is Intelligent Systems Laboratory of Xerox PARC, Palo Alto, CA 94304, USA.

David Weinbaum got his B.Sc. in Engineering from Tel-Aviv University in 1981. Since 1984 he has been a M.Sc. student at the Electrical Engineering faculty of Tel-Aviv University. His present address is Department of Computer Science, The Weizmann Institute of Science, Rehovot 76100, Israel.

Eyal Yardeni got his B.Sc. in Computer Science and Mathematics from Ben-Gurion University in 1982 and his M.Sc. in Computer Science from the Weizmann Institute of Science in 1987. He is presently a Ph.D. student at the Department of Computer Science, The Weizmann Institute of Science, Rehovot 76100, Israel.

The Papers

Systems Programming in Concurrent Prolog, by Ehud Shapiro, appeared as an ICOT TR-034 in 1983, in the Conference Record of the 11th ACM Symposium on Principles of Programming Languages, pp. 93–105, 1984, and in Logic Programming and Its Applications, edited by M. van Caneghem and D.H.D. Warren, pp. 50–76, Ablex. It was revised and shortened for inclusion in this book.

Computation Control and Protection in the Logix System, by Michael Hirsch, William Silverman, and Ehud Shapiro, is a revision of Weizmann Institute of Science Technical Report CS86-19.

The Logix System User Manual, Version 1.22, by William Silverman, Michael Hirsch, Avshalom Houri, and Ehud Shapiro, is also available as Weizmann Institute of Science Technical Report CS86-21.

A Layered Method For Process and Code Mapping, by Stephen Taylor, Evyatar Av-Ron, and Ehud Shapiro, is in press in the Journal of New Generation Computing, 1987.

An Architecture of a Distributed Window System and Its FCP Implementation, by Dan Katzenellenbogen, Shimon Cohen, and Ehud Shapiro, is based on the first author's M.Sc. thesis. It appeared as a Weizmann Institute Technical Report CS87-09.

Logical Secrets, by Mark S. Miller, Daniel G. Bobrow, Eric Dean Tribble, and Jacob Levy, is a revision of a paper published in Logic Programming: Proceedings of the Fourth International Conference, edited by Jean-Louis Lassez, MIT Press, pp. 704–728, 1987.

Meta Interpreters for Real, by Shmuel Safra and Ehud Shapiro, appeared in Information Processing 86, Kugler, H.J. (ed.), pp. 271–278, 1986.
Copyright © 1986, IFIP, reprinted with permission.

Algorithmic Debugging of GHC Programs and its Implementation in GHC, by Akikazu Takeuchi, is a revision of ICOT Technical Report TR-185, 1986.

Representation and Enumeration of Flat Concurrent Prolog Computations, by Yossi Lichtenstein, Michael Codish, and Ehud Shapiro, appears in this volume for the first time.

A Type System for Logic Programs, by Eyal Yardeni and Ehud Shapiro, is based on the M.Sc. Thesis of the first author, and was published as a Weizmann Institute of Science Technical Report CS87-05.

Object Oriented Programming in Concurrent Prolog, by Ehud Shapiro and Akikazu Takeuchi, is a revision of a paper with the same title that appeared in the Journal of New Generation Computing 1(1), pp. 25–49, 1983.

Vulcan: Logical Concurrent Objects, by Kenneth Kahn, Eric Dean Tribble, Mark S. Miller, and Daniel G. Bobrow, appears also in Research Directions in Object-Oriented Programming, edited by P. Shriver and P. Wegner, MIT Press, 1987.

PRESSing for Parallelism: A Prolog Program Made Concurrent, by Leon Sterling and Michael Codish, appeared in the Journal of Logic Programming 3(1), pp. 75–92, 1986.

Compiling Or-Parellelim into And-Parallelism, by Michael Codish and Ehud Shapiro, is based on the first author's M.Sc. Thesis. A shortened version of this paper appeared in The Journal of New Generation Computing 5(1), pp. 45–61, 1987, and was presented at the Third International Conference on Logic Programming, 1986, London.

Translation of Safe GHC and Safe Concurrent Prolog to FCP, by Jacob Levy and Ehud Shapiro, appeared as a Weizmann Institute Technical Report CS87-08.

Or-Parallel Prolog in Flat Concurrent Prolog, by Ehud Shapiro, is a revision of a paper that appeared in Logic Programming: Proceedings of the Fourth International Conference, edited by Jean-Louis Lassez, MIT Press, pp. 311–337, 1987.

CFL — A Concurrent Functional Language Embedded in a Concurrent Logic Programming Environment, by Jacob Levy and Ehud Shapiro, is a revision and extension of Weizmann Institute of Science Technical Report CS86-28.

Hardware Description and Simulation Using Concurrent Prolog, by David Weinbaum and Ehud Shapiro, appeared in the Proceedings of CHDL '87, pp. 9–27, Elsevier Science Publishing, 1987.

A Sequential Implementation of Concurrent Prolog Based on the Shallow Binding Scheme, by Toshihiko Miyazaki, Akikazu Takeuchi, and Takashi Chikayama, was published in the Proceedings of the IEEE Symposium on Logic Programming, pp. 110–118, 1985.
Copyright © 1985, IEEE, reprinted with permission.

A Sequential Abstract Machine for Flat Concurrent Prolog, by Avshalom Houri and Ehud Shapiro, is based on the first author's M.Sc. Thesis. It is a revision of Weizmann Institute of Science Technical Report CS86-20.

A Parallel Implementation of Flat Concurrent Prolog, by Stephen Taylor, Shmuel Safra, and Ehud Shapiro, was published in the International Journal of Parallel Programming 15(3), pp. 245–275, 1987.

Copyright © 1987, Plenum Publishing Corp., reprinted with permission.

Preface to Volume 2

This volume continues the report on a search for a general-purpose programming language for parallel computers that began in Volume 1.

Part IV, Systems Programming, investigates the use of Concurrent Prolog and Flat Concurrent Prolog as systems programming languages. It outlines a technique for a stream-based interface of I/O devices to a Concurrent Prolog system; a method for computation control and protection in a multi-tasking operating system; and a method for implementing process and code mapping in a parallel computer. These techniques were incorporated in the Logix system and in the parallel implementation of Flat Concurrent Prolog. Logix is a Flat Concurrent Prolog based operating system and programming environment, developed at the Weizmann Institute. Logix is described in this part; the parallel implementation of Flat Concurrent Prolog is described in Part VII. The control and mapping techniques draw heavily on the concepts of meta-interpretation and partial evaluation, described in Part V. The last paper in this part reports on a method for implementing secure communication in Flat Concurrent Prolog, which uses encapsulation rather than encription.

Part V, Program Analysis and Transformation, reports on research towards advanced techniques for program development. The first paper shows how meta-interpreters can be enhanced to express functions not directly available in Flat Concurrent Prolog, and how the technique of partial evaluation can eliminate the overhead of interpretation by program transformation. The second paper applies the concepts and techniques of algorithmic debugging to GHC. The third paper describes various methods for the representation of FCP computations, and a method for the exhaustive enumeration of all possible computations on a given initial goal, which is a precondition for the systematic testing of a concurrent program. The last paper describes a type system for logic programs.

Part VI, Embedded Languages, describes techniques for embedding the three major high-level programming paradigms — object-oriented, logic, and functional programming — in Flat Concurrent Prolog. It shows that from the point of view of both expressiveness and efficiency, Flat Concurrent Prolog is a feasible intermediate language for the implementation of higher-level languages. The last paper in this part reports on the use of Concurrent Prolog as a hardware description language.

Part VII, Implementations, describes a sequential implementation technique for Concurrent Prolog, and sequential and parallel implementation techniques for Flat Concurrent Prolog. The latter two form the basis of the current implementations of the language.

For further introductory material, as well as acknowledgements, the reader is referred to Volume 1.

Ehud Shapiro

July, 1987   Rehovot, Israel

Part IV

Systems Programming

Introduction

One of the main applications of the kernel language of a parallel computer is to implement its operating system. For parallel computers to substitute today's general-purpose sequential computers, their operating system should provide at least the functionality of today's operating systems, including support for resource-sharing and interactive program development.

Designing and implementing an operating system for a parallel computer poses new challenges and problems. On the face of it, it would seem that to control distributed computations and distributed resources, the future operating system would have to be an order of magnitude more complex than current ones. This is not necessarily so. The high-level machine language we envisage incorporates notions of processes, communication, and synchronization. Usually these have to be implemented from the ground up in a conventional operating system. Starting from a higher plane that already includes the basic constructs required by an operating system opens new possibilities and suggests new techniques. It is conceivable that switching simultaneously from a sequential computer to a parallel one and from a low-level sequential machine language to a high-level parallel one will result in a reduction, rather than an increase, in the complexity of the operating system. Evidence in favor of this conjecture is given in the various papers included in this part.

Chapter 19, "Systems Programming in Concurrent Prolog", by Shapiro, reports on initial investigations into the question of how to implement a complete operating system and programming environment in Concurrent Prolog. It stresses the importance of the language having a simple meta-interpreter, and suggests that many of the functions of a program development environment can be implemented by enhancing a meta-interpreter. The paper discusses the problem of interfacing to input/output devices, and suggests that by providing low-level interfaces that make each input or output device produce or consume a Concurrent Prolog stream, most of the functionality of device drivers can be implemented in Concurrent Prolog itself. The method is demonstrated by the implementation of a disk-arm scheduling algorithm. The paper also addresses the question of computation control and protection. It suggests using the guard mechanism of Concurrent Prolog to achieve this: controlled computations should be activated from within a guard. Their failure can be handled by an Or-parallel *otherwise* guard. They can be aborted by an Or-parallel guard, which succeeds when it receives a certain message from an And-parallel process. The paper further demonstrates the power of Concurrent Prolog as a systems programming language by showing a

Concurrent Prolog solution to the readers-and-writers problem, with application to shared queues, and an implementation of a manager of multiple interactive processes.

Although the overall philosophy of the paper is still valid, several things have changed since its original publication in 1983. First, Concurrent Prolog is no longer the basis of Kernel Language 1, the kernel-language of the parallel inference machine planned by the Fifth Generation Project, as stated in the paper. The current design is based on GHC instead (Fuchi and Furukawa, 1987). Second, a severe conceptual problem was uncovered in the use of guards for the protection of computations: the commitment mechanism of Concurrent Prolog required that no binding computed within a guard be visible outside of it prior to commitment. Hence a computation in the guard could not be interactive, at least if communication was to be implemented in Concurrent Prolog itself, as envisaged by the paper. The dilemma seemed to be: either computations be protected and noninteractive, or interactive, and in this case their failure would cause the failure of the entire conjunctive system of processes.

An alternative approach which neither faces this dilemma, nor relies on the guard mechanism of Concurrent Prolog, and hence is applicable to Flat Concurrent Prolog, is described in Chapter 20.

Chapter 20, "Computation Control and Protection in the Logix System", by Hirsch, Silverman, and Shapiro, describes how to specify computation control and protection using enhanced FCP meta-interpreters. Doing so achieves the desired functionality, but at the cost of a high runtime overhead. Therefore often-needed functions are implemented by source-to-source transformations, which incorporate the required functionality directly in the program. Such transformations can be carried out by a general-purpose partial evaluator, as described by Safra and Shapiro (Chapter 25), or by manually constructed program transformers, as done presently. The paper describes the different layers of control and protection employed in the Logix system and discusses their associated overheads.

It seems that neither GHC nor PARLOG can adopt the approach described in this paper: PARLOG, since it is not easily amenable to meta-interpretation, and GHC, since its meta-interpreter cannot be usefully enhanced to reflect termination and failure. Hence the two languages have adopted the approach of introducing a new language primitive, designed to support systems programming. Such a primitive, called a three-argument meta-call, is described by Clark and Gregory (1984). The three-argument meta-call accepts a goal and a command stream, and produces an event stream. The commands include *suspend*, *resume*, and *abort*. The events include reports on successful termination and failure.

That approach has several undesirable properties. First, the meta-call is a significant extension to the language, and its parallel implementation requires a fairly complex machinery. Second, being implemented in the abstract machine, rather than in the language itself, the meta-call construct is rigid. Modifications and extensions to it would probably be quite difficult compared to changing a function of Logix which is implemented entirely in FCP. For example, the meta-call proposed cannot produce a snapshot of the state of the computation, and it seems that the implementation strategies proposed for it would have great difficulties in incorporating this. On the other hand, incorporating it in an FCP specification of a meta-call, as discussed below, is easy. Third, when an explicit stand is taken on the issues of failure and termination, as done in GHC, it becomes apparent that the three-argument meta-call is a problematic extension to a language without atomic unification. The simplicity of the semantics of GHC is related to its not being able to reflect on the distributed termination of a computation, nor on its failure. With the meta-call construct, one can write a GHC program that can inspect these aspects of the behavior of another GHC program. It seems, therefore, that the semantics of GHC with a three-argument meta-call would not be as simple as that of the original language.

Chapter 20 shows how the semantics of the three-argument meta-call, augmented with the ability to snapshot a computation, can be specified in FCP. This specification does not suffer from any of the above problems. It executes on a parallel machine that implements FCP without any additional support. It is easily extendable and modifiable. And it does not affect the semantics of the language.

Chapter 21 includes "The Logix System User Manual, Version 1.21", by Silverman, Hirsch, Houri, and Shapiro. Logix is a single-user multi-tasking operating system and program development environment for FCP, written almost entirely in FCP. It is the main tool with which the Flat Concurrent Prolog applications and implementations, described in the rest of this book, were developed. By now it has been used for the teaching of several Concurrent Prolog programming courses, and for the development of altogether over 30,000 lines of FCP code. The Logix system manual describes the user's view of its functionality. Although not the last word on user interfaces, Logix is an interesting object of study in its own right. It is best viewed in conjunction with the principles underlying the implementation of the system, described in the previous two papers. In principle, Logix is portable to any FCP implementation; however it is based presently on the implementation described by Houri and Shapiro in Chapter 38.

Chapter 22, "A Layered Method for Process and Code Mapping", by Taylor, Av-Ron, and Shapiro, proposes a layered system organization for parallel computers. In this method a parallel virtual machine corresponding to the physical parallel machine is constructed at bootstrap time. On top of this virtual machine additional virtual machines and applications can run concurrently. A parallel virtual machine is capable of executing programs and supporting their process-to-processor mapping and code management, as well as spawning additional virtual machines. A virtual machine is specified by an enhanced FCP meta-interpreter, and can be implemented by the source-to-source transformation the interpreter induces. As examples, specifications of ring and torus virtual machines are provided.

Chapter 23, "An Architecture for a Distributed Window System and its FCP Implementation", by Katzenellenbogen, Cohen, and Shapiro, reports on initial work towards an FCP-based window-system. It describes how the basic problems of window systems — window management, interface to applications, input handling, and screen update — can be addressed by a distributed architecture that does not have central managers. It presents distributed algorithms for window management and caching techniques to speed up screen update and input handling. A prototype window system which is based on this architecture and which incorporates these algorithms has been implemented in FCP.

Chapter 24, "Logical Secrets", by Miller, Bobrow, Tribble, and Levy, addresses a question related to the programming of open systems in FCP. It shows that given a secure implementation of FCP, a public-key system can be implemented on top of it, using encapsulation rather than encription. As an application, the implementation of a simple banking system is shown.

Chapter 19

Systems Programming in Concurrent Prolog

Ehud Shapiro

The Weizmann Institute of Science

Abstract

Concurrent Prolog combines the logic programming computation model with guarded-command indeterminacy and dataflow synchronization. It will form the basis of the Kernel Language (Furukawa et al., 1984a) of the Parallel Inference Machine (Uchida, 1983), planned by Japan's Fifth Generation Computers Project. This paper explores the feasibility of programming such a machine solely in Concurrent Prolog (in the absence of a lower-level programming language), by implementing in it a representative collection of systems programming problems.

19.1 Introduction

The process of turning a bare von Neumann machine into a usable computer is well understood. One of the more elegant techniques to do so is to implement a cross-compiler for a systems programming language (say C) on a usable computer. Then implement in that language an operating system kernel (say Unix), device drivers, a file system, and a programming environment. Then boot the operating system on the target computer. From that stage on the computer is usable, and application programs, compilers and interpreters for higher-level languages (say Franz Lisp and C-Prolog), can be developed on it.

This paper addresses the question of turning a bare computer into a usable one, but for a machine of a different type, namely, a parallel logic programming machine. In particular, it explores the suitability of Concurrent Prolog (Shapiro,

Chapter 2) as the kernel programming language[1] of such a computer, by asking the question:

(1) Will a machine that implements Concurrent Prolog in hardware or firmware be usable as a general-purpose, multi-user, interactive computer?

Or, stated slightly differently,

(2) Is Concurrent Prolog expressive enough to be a kernel language of a general-purpose computer?

We investigate these questions only from the software, not from the hardware, side. Our concern with efficiency is limited by the assumption that the machine will execute at least as many MegaLIPS[2] as today's computers execute MIPS.

These questions are far reaching, but not purely speculative, given the Fifth Generation Computers Project's plans to design and build a parallel logic programming machine and to use Concurrent Prolog as the basis for the machine's kernel language (Furukawa et al., 1984a).

The paper attempts to give some evidence towards affirmative answers to these questions. To do so, we assume a computer that behaves like a virtual Concurrent Prolog machine, but has no other (lower-level or otherwise) programming constructs, special instructions, hardware interrupts, etc. We also assume that basic drivers for I/O devices are provided, which make each device understand Concurrent Prolog streams. This assumption is elaborated further below.

We then develop a collection of Concurrent Prolog programs that can run on such a machine, including:

•   A Concurrent Prolog interpreter/debugger.

•   A top-level crash/reboot loop, that reboots the operating system automatically upon a software (and perhaps also a hardware) crash.

•   A Unix-like shell, that handles foreground and background processes, pipelining, and an abort ("Control-C") interrupt for foreground processes.

•   A multiple-process manager *a la* MUF (Ellis et al., 1982), that manages the creation of, and communication with, multiple interactive processes.

•   Programs for merging streams, using various scheduling strategies.

•   A solution to the readers-and-writers problem, based on the concept of mon-

---

[1] The term *Kernel Language* denotes a hybrid between a machine language and a systems programming language, implemented by hardware or firmware. As far as I know it was introduced by the Fifth Generation Project (Moto-Oka et al., 1981).

[2] LIPS: Logical Inferences Per Second. In the context of Concurrent Prolog, it means process reductions per second.

itors (Hoare, 1974).

- Shared queues, and their application to implementing managers of shared resources, such as a disk scheduler.

The programs have been developed and tested using a Concurrent Prolog interpreter, written in Prolog (Shapiro, Chapter 2). They show Concurrent Prolog's ability to express process creation, termination, communication, synchronization, and indeterminacy. They suggest that a "pure" Concurrent Prolog machine is self-contained, and that it will be usable "as is", without too many extraneous features.

Even if such a machine is usable, it is not necessarily useful. For Concurrent Prolog to be a general purpose programming language, it has to solve conveniently a broad range of "real-life" problems. However, determining what is a real-life problem depends upon one's point of view. One may suggest implementing the algorithms in Aho et al. book (1974) as such a problem. Concurrent Prolog will exhibit a grand failure if such an implementation is attempted, and for a reason. The algorithms in that book (and, most other sequential algorithms) are deeply rooted in the von Neumann computer. One of the basic operations they use is destructive assignment of values to variables (including destructive pointer manipulation). This operation is cheap on a von Neumann machine, but is not available directly in the logic programming computation model, is a bit expensive to simulate, and thinking in terms of it results in an awkward programming style.

On the other hand, the operations that are cheap in Concurrent Prolog — process creation and communication — are not used in conventional sequential algorithms, almost by definition. Hence Concurrent Prolog (or any other logic programming language) is not adequate for implementing most von Neumann algorithms. One may ask: Is there anything else to implement (besides payroll programs)? Or: What is Concurrent Prolog good for, then?

Our experience to date suggests that, in contrast to von Neumann languages and algorithms, Concurrent Prolog exhibits strong affiliation with four other "trends" in computer science: Object-oriented programming, dataflow and graph-reduction languages, distributed algorithms, and systolic algorithms.

Shapiro and Takeuchi (Chapter 29) show that Concurrent Prolog lends itself very naturally to the programming style and idioms of object-oriented programming languages such as Smalltalk (Ingalls, 1978) and Actors (Hewitt, 1973). Many applications are easier to implement in this framework.

The synchronization mechanism of Concurrent Prolog — read-only variables — is a natural generalization of dataflow synchronization from functional to relational languages. The basic operation of a Concurrent Prolog program — process reduction — is basically a graph reduction operation, since a process is a DAG, and a clause can be viewed as specifying how to replace one DAG by a (possibly empty) collection of other DAGs. It is interesting to observe that the synthesis of dataflow and graph reduction mechanisms has been attempted by hardware researchers, independently of logic programming (Keller et al., 1983).

We have some experience with implementing distributed algorithms in Concurrent Prolog. The implementation of the "Lord of the Ring" algorithm (Dolev et al., 1982) in Concurrent Prolog, described by Shafrir and Shapiro (Chapter 11), exhibits a striking similarity to the English description of the algorithm, where every rule of process behavior corresponds to one Concurrent Prolog clause. That paper also reports on an implementation of a complex distributed minimum spanning tree algorithm.

An implementation of Shiloach and Vishkin's MAXFLOW algorithm (Shiloach and Vishkin, 1982b) demonstrates the ability of Concurrent Prolog to implement complex parallel algorithms without loss of efficiency (Hellerstein and Shapiro, Chapter 9).

Numerical computations are quite remote from Artificial Intelligence, the original ecological niche of logic programming. Nevertheless, we find that the natural Concurrent Prolog solutions to numerical problems have a "systolic touch" to them, and vice-versa: that implementing systolic algorithms (Kung, 1979) in Concurrent Prolog is easy. A subsequent paper (Shapiro, Chapter 7) includes Concurrent Prolog implementations of several systolic algorithms, including the hexagonal band-matrix multiplication algorithm (Kung, 1979) .

Other recent applications of Concurrent Prolog include the implementation of a parallel parsing algorithm (Hirakawa , 1983), an Or-parallel Prolog interpreter (Hirakawa et al., 1983), a hardware specification and debugging system (Suzuki, 1986), and a LOOPS-like (Bobrow and Stefik, 1983) object-oriented knowledge representation language (Furukawa et al., 1984b).

19.2 Concurrent Prolog

Concurrent Prolog is a logic programming language, in that a program is a collection of universally quantified Horn-clause axioms, and a computation is an attempt to prove a goal — an existentially quantified conjunctive statement — from the axioms in the program. The goal statement describes an input/output relation for which the input is known; a successful (constructive) proof provides a corresponding output.

The difference between Concurrent Prolog and other logic programming languages (e.g., pure Prolog) is in the mechanism they provide for controlling the construction of the proof. Prolog uses the order of clauses in the program and the order of goals in a clause to guide a sequential search for a proof and uses the cut operator to prune undesired portions of the search space. Concurrent

Prolog searches for a proof in parallel. To control the search, Concurrent Prolog embodies two familiar concepts: guarded-command indeterminacy and dataflow synchronization. They are implemented using two constructs: the commit "|" and the read-only "?" operators.

The commit operator is similar to Dijkstra's (1976) guarded command and was first introduced to logic programming by Clark and Gregory (Chapter 1). It allows a process to make preliminary computations (specified in the guard of a clause), before choosing which action to take, i.e., which clause to use for reduction. Read-only variables are the basic (and only) mechanism for process synchronization. Roughly speaking, a process that attempts to instantiate a read-only variable X? suspends until the corresponding writable variable X is instantiated by another process. The other components of concurrent programming: process creation, termination, and communication, are already available in the abstract computation model of logic programming. A unit goal corresponds to a process, and a conjunctive goal to a system of processes. A process is created via goal reduction, and terminated by being reduced to the empty (true) goal. Conjunctive goals may share variables, which are used as communication channels between processes.

More precisely, a *Concurrent Prolog program* is a finite set of guarded-clauses. A *guarded-clause* is a universally quantified axiom of the form

$$A \leftarrow G_1, G_2, \ldots, G_m \mid B_1, B_2, \ldots, B_n. \qquad m, n \geq 0.$$

where the G's and the B's are atomic formulas, also called unit goals. A is called the clause's head, the G's are called its guard, and the B's its body. When the guard is empty the commit operator "|" is omitted. Clauses may contain read-only variables, such as X?. The Edinburgh Prolog syntactic conventions are followed: constants begin with a lower-case letter and variables with an upper-case letter. The special binary term $[X|Y]$ is used to denote the list whose head (car) is X and tail (cdr) is Y. The constant $[\,]$ denotes the empty list.

Concerning the declarative semantics of a guarded clause, the commit operator reads like a conjunction: A is implied by the G's and the B's. The read-only annotations can be ignored in the declarative reading.

Procedurally, a guarded-clause specifies a behavior similar to an alternative in a guarded-command. To reduce a process A using a clause

$$A1 \leftarrow G \mid B,$$

unify A with $A1$, and, if successful, recursively reduce G to the empty system, and, if successful, commit to that clause, and, if successful, reduce A to B.

The unification of a process against the head of a clause serves several functions: passing parameters, assigning values to variables, selecting and constructing data-structures, and sending and receiving messages. The example programs below demonstrate all these uses of unification.

The reduction of a process may suspend or fail during almost any of the steps described above. The unification of the process with the head of a clause suspends if it requires the instantiation of read-only variables in A or $A1$. It fails if A and $A1$ are not unifiable. The computation of the guard system G suspends if any of the processes in it suspends and fails if any one of them fails. As in guarded-commands, at most one of the process's Or-parallel guard-systems may commit.

Prior to commitment, partial results computed by the first two steps of the reduction — unifying the process against the head of the clause and solving the guard — are not accessible to other processes in A's system. This prevents interference between sibling Or-parallel computations and eliminates the need for distributed backtracking.

This completes the informal description of Concurrent Prolog.

19.3 A Meta-Interpreter for Concurrent Prolog

One of the simpler ways to implement a programming environment for a programming language L is augmenting L's interpreter. Among the program development tools that can be implemented in this way are sophisticated debuggers (Shapiro, 1982), runtime-statistics packages, extensions to the language (Safra and Shapiro, Chapter 25), and new embedded and Shapiro, Chapter 32). The languages (Codish difficulty of implementing these tools grows with the complexity of that interpreter.

For reasons of bootstrapping and elegance, the preferred implementation language for L's programming environment is L itself, as argued eloquently by Sandewall (1978). *Hence the ease in which an L interpreter can be implemented in L is of clear practical importance, as well as a useful criterion for evaluating the expressiveness and completeness of the language*, as argued by Steele and Sussman (1978b).

Designing an expressive language with a simple meta-interpreter[3] is like solving a fixpoint equation. If the language L is too weak, then L's data-structures may not be rich enough to represent L programs conveniently. If the control constructs of L are incomplete, they cannot be used to simulate themselves conveniently.

On the other hand, if the control structures of L are awkward and unrestricted, and the data-structures are too baroque, then its interpreter becomes very large and unintelligible (e.g., *goto* cannot be used in a simple way to simulate unrestricted *goto*, but the easiest way to simulate a *while* statement is using

---

[3] Called a meta-circular interpreter by Steele and Sussman (1978b).

a *while* statement in the interpreter).

A meta-interpreter for pure sequential Prolog can be written in three Prolog clauses, and, indeed, implementing software tools and embedded languages via extending this interpreter is a common activity for Prolog programmers.

A meta-interpreter for Concurrent Prolog is described in Program 19.1. It assumes the existence of a built-in system predicate *clauses*(A, Cs), that returns in Cs the list of all clauses in the interpreted program whose head is potentially unifiable with A[4]. The constant *true* signifies an empty guard or an empty body.

```
reduce(true).
reduce((A,B)) ←
    reduce(A?), reduce(B?).
reduce(A) ←
    clauses(A,Clauses) |
    resolve(A,Clauses,Body),
    reduce(Body?).

resolve(A,[(A←Guard|Body)|Cs],Body) ←
    reduce(Guard) | true.
resolve(A,[C|Clauses],Body)←
    resolve(A,Clauses,Body) | true.
```

Program 19.1: A Meta-interpreter for Concurrent Prolog

Like any other Concurrent Prolog program, Program 19.1 can be read both declaratively, i.e., as a set of axioms, and operationally, i.e., as a set of rules defining the behavior of processes. Declaratively, *reduce*(A) states that A is true (provable) with respect to the axioms defined in the predicate *clauses*. Operationally, the process *reduce*(A) attempts to reduce the system of processes A to the empty (halting) system *true*.

Declaratively, the axioms of *reduce* read: *true* is true. The conjunction (A,B) is true if A is true and B is true. The goal A is true if there are clauses Cs with the same head predicate of A, resolving A with Cs gives B, and B is true. The predicate *resolve*$(A,[C|Cs],B)$ reads, declaratively, that resolving A with the axioms $[C|Cs]$ gives B if the clause C has head A, guard G and body B, and the guard G is true, or if recursively resolving A with Cs gives B.

Operationally, the clauses of *reduce* say that the process *true* halts. The

---

[4] In our current implementation Cs is the list of all clauses with the same head predicate as A. Better indexing mechanism can make the predicate more selective. Another possible optimization is to use the bounded-buffer technique of Takeuchi and Furukawa (Chapter 18), to generate clauses on a demand-driven basis.

process (A,B) reduces itself to the processes A and B, and that the process A, with clauses Cs, reduces itself to B if the result of resolving A with Cs is B.

The reader not familiar with logic-programming may be puzzled by this interpreter. It seems to capture the control part of the computation, but does not seem to deal at all with unification, the data component. The answer to the puzzle is that the call to the first clause of *resolve* is doing the work, by unifying the process with the head of the clause. Their unification is achieved by calling them with the same name, A.

This interpreter assumes one global program, whose axioms are accessible via the system predicate *clauses*, as in conventional Prolog implementations. In a real implementation of Concurrent Prolog, programs would be objects that can be passed as arguments, and *reduce* and *clauses* would have an additional argument, the program being simulated.

This interpreter cannot execute Concurrent Prolog programs that use built-in system predicates, such as itself (it uses the predicate *clauses*). The Prolog-based interpreter of Concurrent Prolog (Shapiro, Chapter 2) contains several (13) system predicates: metalogical predicates (*clauses* and *system*), control predicates (*otherwise* and =), interface to the underlying prolog, I/O (*read* and *write*), and arithmetic predicates (the lazy evaluator := and 5 arithmetic test predicates). To handle system predicates, the interpreter can be augmented with the clause

reduce(A) ← system(A) | A.

system(X) is a system predicate that succeeds if X is a Concurrent Prolog system predicate and fails otherwise. For example, the call *system*(*system*(X)) succeeds. The clause demonstrates the use of the *meta-variable*, a facility also available in Prolog, which allows to pass processes to other processes as data-structures. It is used extensively in the shell programs below.

One may suggest that using the meta-variable facility, a Concurrent Prolog meta-interpreter can be implemented via the clause

reduce(A) ← A.

This claim is true, except that it will be rather difficult to implement the software tools mentioned earlier as an extension to this interpreter, whereas implementing a Concurrent Prolog single stepper by extending Program 19.1 is a trivial matter.

The interpreter in Program 19.1 is 10 to 20 times slower than the underlying Concurrent Prolog implementation (Shapiro, Chapter 2). We feel that it is reasonable to pay a 10-fold slow down during the program development phase for a good programming environment. Besides, a default to the underlying Concurrent Prolog can be incorporated easily, as in the case of system predicates, so that in developing large systems only the portion of the code that is under development needs the extra layer of interpretation.

19.4 Streams

Concurrent Prolog processes communicate via shared logical-variables. Logical-variables are single-assignment: they can be either uninstantiated or instantiated, but, once instantiated, their value cannot be destructively modified. Hence the Concurrent Prolog computation model is indifferent to the distinction between a shared-memory computation model and a communication based model. A shared logical-variable can be viewed as a shared memory cell that can accept only one value, or as a communication channel that can transmit only one message.

The distinction between the "reader" and "writer" of a shared variable (or the "sender" and "receiver" of the message) is done via read-only annotations. A process $p(\ldots X?\ldots)$ cannot instantiate X. Attempts of p to reduce itself to other processes using clauses that require the instantiation of X, such as

$$p(\ldots f(a)\ldots) \leftarrow \ldots$$

suspend, until X is instantiated by some other process. If X is instantiated to $f(Y)$, then the process p can unify with that clause, even though it instantiated Y to a, since the scope of a read-only annotation is only the main functor of a term, but not variables that occur inside the term. This property enables a powerful programming technique called *incomplete messages* (Shapiro, Chapter 2).

Even though logical variables are single-assignment, two processes can communicate with each other via a single shared variable, by instantiating a variable into a term that contains both the message and another variable, to be used in subsequent communications. This programming technique gives the effect of streams.

> instream([X|Xs]) ←
>   read(X) | instream(Xs).
>
> outstream([ ]).
> outstream([X|Xs]) ←
>   write(X), outstream(Xs?).

Program 19.2: Implementing terminal I/O streams using *read* and *write*

The cleanest way to implement I/O functions in a Concurrent Prolog machine is for I/O devices to generate and/or consume Concurrent Prolog streams. The Prolog-based interpreter of Concurrent Prolog, supports only terminal I/O (the rest is done by the underlying Prolog). It implements the stream abstraction for the user terminal via two predicates, *instream*(X), which generated the stream X of terms typed in by the user, and *outstream*(X), that outputs to the screen the stream X, shown in Program 19.2. They are implemented using the underlying Prolog *read* and *write* predicates.

If we want *instream* to allow the user to signify the end of the stream, the program has to be complicated a little.

Using these programs, a "device-driver" that implements a stream interface to the terminal can be specified:

```
terminal(Keyboard,Screen) ←
    instream(KeyBoard), outstream(Screen?).
```

In a virtual Concurrent Prolog machine in which interfaces to I/O device drivers are implemented as streams, there will be no need for specialized I/O primitives.

19.5 Booting an Operating System

Assume that device drivers for a terminal (screen, keyboard and a mouse), disk, and a local network have been defined for a personal workstation. Then Program 19.3 can be used to boot its operating system[5].

```
boot ←
    monitor(KeyBoard?,Mouse?,Screen,DiskIn?,DiskOut,NetIn?,Netout),
    disk(DiskIn,DiskOut?),
    net(NetIn,NetOut?) |
    true.
boot ←
    otherwise |
    boot.
```

Program 19.3: Booting an operating system

The first clause invokes the device drivers and the monitor. The second clause automatically reboots the system upon a software crash of either the monitor or the device drivers. *otherwise* is a Concurrent Prolog system predicate that succeeds if and when all of its sibling or-parallel guards fail. Declaratively, it may read as the negation of the disjunction of the guards of the sibling clauses[6].

---

[5] We are aware of the fact that efficiency considerations may prevent the use of pure streams for devices that generate a lot of useless data, such as a mouse, and that some lower-level interface may be required.

[6] The predicate *otherwise* is not implemented correctly in the Prolog-based Concurrent Prolog interpreter (Shapiro, Chapter 2). It may succeed when it has suspended brother or-parallel

19.6 A Unix-like Shell

A shell is a process that receives a stream of commands from the terminal and executes them. In our context the commands are processes and executing them means invoking them. A simple shell can be implemented using the meta-variable facility,

> shell([X|Xs]) ←
>   X, shell(Xs?).
> shell([ ]).

This shell is batch-oriented. It behaves like a Unix-shell that executes all commands in "background" mode, in the sense that it does not wait for the completion of the previous process before accepting the next command. As is, it achieves the effect of Unix-like pipes, using conjunctive goals with shared variables as commands. For example, the Unix command

> p | q | r

can be simulated with the conjunctive system

> p(X), q(X?,Y), r(Y?).

provided that the Unix command p does not read from its primary input and q does not write to its primary output. External I/O by user programs is handled below.

Note that since the process's I/O streams have explicit names, we are not confined to linear pipelining, and any desired I/O configuration of the process network can be specified.

One of this shell's drawbacks is that it would crash if the user process X crashes, since X and *shell(Xs)* are part of the same conjunctive system, which fails if one of its members fails. This can be remedied by calling *envelope(X)* instead of X.

> envelope(X) ← X | write(halted(X)).
> envelope(X) ← otherwise | write(failed(X)).

It is easy to augment the shell to distinguish between background and foreground processes, assuming that every command X is tagged $bg(X)$ or $fg(X)$, as done in Program 19.4.

Note that in this program foreground processes are executed in the shell's guard. This allows a simple extension to the shell so it will handle an abort

---

guards, instead of suspending, and succeeding only when all such guards fail. Hence programs using it are not fully debugged.

(1) shell([ ]).
(2) shell([fg(X)|Xs]) ←
            envelope(X) | shell(Xs?).
(3) shell([bg(X)|Xs]) ←
            envelope(X), shell(Xs?).

Program 19.4: A shell that handles foreground and background
                   processes

(4) shell(Xs) ←
            seek(abort,Xs,Ys) | shell(Ys?).

     seek(X,[X|Xs],Xs).
     seek(X,[Y|Xs],Ys) ←
            X\=Y | seek(X,Xs?,Ys).

Program 19.4a: An extension to the shell that handled an *abort*
                    interrupt

('control-C' on some computers) interrupt for foreground processes. Upon the
reception of an *abort* command, the currently running foreground process (if there
is one) is aborted, and the content of the input stream past the abort command
is flushed. This is achieved by the clauses in Program 19.4a.

The program operates as follows. When an *fg(X)* command is received, the
two guards, *envelope* and *seek* are spawned in parallel, and begin to race. The
first to commit aborts the second, so if *envelope* terminates before *seek* found
an *abort* command in the input stream (most probably because the user hasn't
typed such a command yet) then the *envelope* commits, *seek* is aborted, and *shell*
proceeds normally with the next command. On the other hand, if *seek* succeeds in
finding an *abort* command before *envelope* terminates, then *envelope* is aborted,
and *shell* proceeds with the input past the *abort* command, as returned by *seek*.

A more general interrupt, *grand_abort*, that aborts all processes spawned by
shell, both foreground and background, can also be implemented quite easily:

        topshell(Xs) ←
            shell(Xs) | true.
        topshell(Xs) ←
            seek(grand_abort,Xs,Ys) | topshell(Ys?).

The distinction the shell in Program 19.4 makes between background and
foreground processing is not of much use, however, since foreground processes are
not interactive, i.e., they do not have access to the shell's input stream. One
problem with the shell giving a user program its input stream is that upon ter-

mination the user program has to return the remaining stream back, so that the shell can proceed. Since we cannot expect every interactive user program to obey a certain convention for halting (*cf.* quit, exit, halt, stop, bye, etc.), the shell has to implement a uniform command, say *exit* to "softly" terminate an interactive session with a user program (in contrast to aborting it). A filter, called *switch*, monitors the input stream to the program. Upon the reception of an *exit* command it closes the output stream to the program, returns the rest of the input stream to the shell, and terminates. A reasonable interactive user program should terminate upon encountering the end of the input stream. If it is not reasonable, an *abort* interrupt will always do the job. Program 19.4b implements this idea. Commands to interactive foreground processes are of the form $fg(P,Pi)$, where P is the process and Pi is its input stream. For example, a command to run the process $foo(X)$ with input stream X will be given as $fg(foo(X?),X)$.

(5)   shell([fg(X,Xi)|Xs]) ←
        envelope(X), switch(Xs?,Xi,Ys) |
        shell(Ys?).

      switch([exit|Xs],[ ] ,Xs).
      switch([X|Xs],[X|Ys],Zs) ←
        X\=exit | switch(Xs?,Ys,Zs).

Program 19.4b: An extension to the shell that handles interactive
                    user programs

19.7 A Manager of Multiple Interactive Processes

The shell described above can handle only one interactive process at a time, like the DEC supplied TOPS-20 EXEC. MUF (Multiple User Forks) is a popular DEC-20 program, developed at Yale university (Ellis et al., 1982), which overcomes this limitation. It can handle multiple interactive processes and has a mechanism for easy context switching. It cannot compete, of course, with the convenience of a system with a bitmap display and a pointing device.

MUF associates names with processes. It has commands for creating a new process, freezing or killing a process, resuming a frozen process, and others. Program 19.5 achieves some of this functionality.

The *muf* process is invoked with the call $muf(X?)$ where X is its input stream. It first initializes itself with the empty process list, using Clause (0), then iterates, serving user commands.

On the command *create(Pname,Process,Pi,Po)*, it creates a process *Process*, and a process *tag(Pname,Po)*, that tags the process's output stream elements

(0) muf(X) ←
       muf(X,[ ]).

(1) muf([create(Pname,Process,Pin,Pout)|Input],Ps) ←
       Process,
       tag(Pname,Pout),
       muf([resume(Pname)|Input?],[(Pname,Pin)|Ps]).

(2) muf([resume(Pname)|Input],Ps) ←
       find_process(Pname,Ps,Pin,Ps1)|
       distribute(Input?,Pin,Input1,Pin1),
       muf(Input1?,[(Pname,Pin1)|Ps1]).

(3) muf([exit|Input],[(Pname,[ ])|Ps]) ←
       muf(Input?,Ps).

(4) muf([ ],Ps) ←
       close_input(Ps).

(1) find_process(Pname,[(Pname,Pin)|Ps],Pin,Ps).

(2) find_process(Pname,[Pr|Ps],Pin,[Pr|Ps1])←
       otherwise |
       find_process(Pname,Ps,Pin,Ps1).

(1) distribute([ ],Pin,[ ],Pin).

(2) distribute([X|Input],Pin,[X|Input],Pin)←
       muf_command(X)| true.

(3) distribute([X|Input],[X|Pin],Input1,Pin1)←
       otherwise |
       distribute(Input?,Pin,Input1,Pin1).

(1) close_input([ ]).

(2) close_input([(Pname,[ ])|Ps]) ←
       close_input(Ps).

(1) muf_command(create(_,_,_,_)).

(2) muf_command(resume(_)).

(3) muf_command(exit).

Program 19.5: mini-MUF

with the process's name and displays them on the screen. It also adds a record with the process's name, *Pname*, and input stream, *Pi*, to its process list and sends itself the command *resume(Pname)*.

On the command *resume(Pname)*, *muf* uses Clause (3). It searches its process list for the input stream of the process *Pname*, and puts this process record first on the list. This is done by *find_process*. If successful, it invokes *distribute(Input?,Pin,Input1,Pin1)*, which copies the elements of the stream *Input* to the stream *Pi* (Clause 3) until it reaches the end of the stream (Clause 1), or encounters a command to *muf* (Clause 2). In that event it terminates, returning the updated streams in *Pi1* and *Input1*. *muf* itself is suspended on *Input1*.

On the command *exit*, *muf* closes the input stream of the current process and removes it from the process list (Clause 3).

When encountering the end of its input stream, *muf* closes the input streams of all the processes in its list and terminates (Clause 4).

Some of the frills of the real MUF can be easily incorporated in our mini-implementation. For example, the *freeze* command resumes the previously resumed process, without having to name it explicitly. This is implemented by the following clause:

> muf([freeze|Input],[Pr,(Pname,Pi)|Ps])←
> muf([resume(Pname)|Input?],[(Pname,Pi),Pr|Ps]).

which reverses the order of the first two process records on the process list and sends itself a *resume* command with the name of the previously resumed process. A similar default for *exit* can be added likewise.

Note that if the length of the process list is less then two, this clause would not apply, since its head would not unify with the *muf* process. Similarly, if a *resume* command is given with a wrong argument, Clause (2) wouldn't apply, since the guard, *find_process*, would fail.

muf, as defined in Program 19.5, would crash upon receiving such erroneous commands. Adding the following clause would cause it to default, in such cases, to an error-message routine:

> muf([X|Input],Ps)←
> otherwise |
> muf_error(X,Ps),
> muf(Input?,Ps).

muf_error analyses the command with respect to the process list and reports to the user the type of error he has made.

Similarly easy to implement are queries concerning the names of the processes in the process list and the identity of the currently resumed process.

19.8 Monitors and the Readers-And-Writers Problem

The Concurrent Prolog solution to the readers-and-writers problem uses this method of many-to-one communication. It is very similar, in spirit, to the idea of monitors (Hoare, 1974). A designated process (a 'monitor') holds the shared data in a local argument and serves the merged input stream of 'read' and 'write' requests ('monitor calls'). It responds to a 'read' request through the uninstantiated response variable in it ('result argument').

A schematic implementation of a monitor is shown in Program 19.6. Note that it serves a sequence of *read* requests in parallel, since the recursive invocation of *monitor* in Clause (2) is not suspended on the result of *serve*, in contrast to Clause (1).

(1) monitor([write(Args)|S], Data) ←
        serve(write(Args), Data, NewData), monitor(S?, NewData?).
(2) monitor([read(Args)|S], Data) ←
        serve(read(Args), Data, _), monitor(S?, Data).
(3) monitor([ ] ,_).

Program 19.6: A schematic implementation of a monitor

In monitor-based programming languages, a procedure call and a monitor call are two basic, mutually irreducible operations. In Concurrent Prolog, on the other hand, there is one basic construct, a process invocation, whereas a monitor call is a secondary concept, or, rather, a programming technique.

Concurrent Prolog monitors and merge operators can implement operating systems in a functional style without side-effects, using techniques similar to Henderson's (1982).

19.9 Queues

Merged streams allow many client processes to share one resource; but when several client processes want to share several resources effectively, a more complex buffering strategy is needed. Such buffering can be obtained with a simple FIFO queue: a client who requires the service of a resource enqueues its request. When a resource becomes available, it dequeues the next request from the queue and serves it.

The following implementation of a shared queue is a canonical example of Concurrent Prolog programming style. It exploits two powerful logic programming techniques: incomplete messages and difference-lists.

A shared queue manager is an instance of a monitor. *enqueue* is a 'write' operation, and *dequeue* involves both 'read' and 'write'. An abstract implementation of a queue monitor is shown in Program 19.7.

Clause (0) creates an empty queue; Clause (1) iterates, serving queue requests; and Clause (2) halts the queue monitor upon reaching the end of the requests stream.

```
(0)  queue_monitor(S) ←
         create_queue(Q),
         queue_monitor(S,Q).

(1)  queue_monitor([Request|S],Q) ←
         serve(Request,Q,Q1),
         queue_monitor(S?,Q1?).

(2)  queue_monitor([ ],Q).
```

Program 19.7: A queue monitor

The implementation of the queue operations employs difference-lists (Clark and Tärnlund, 1977). A difference-list represents a list of elements (in this context, the queue's content) as the difference between two lists, or streams. For example, the difference between $[1,2,3,4\,|X]$ and X is the list $[1,2,3,4]$. As a notational convention, we use the binary term $X\backslash Y$ (read "the difference between X and Y"), to denote the list that is the difference between the list X and the list Y. Note that this term has no special properties predefined, and any binary term will do, as long as it is used consistently.

```
create_queue(X\X).

serve(enqueue(X),Head\[X|NewTail],Head\NewTail).
serve(dequeue(X),[X|NewHead]\Tail,NewHead\Tail).
```

Program 19.7a: Queue operations

Program 19.7a includes the specific queue operations. *create_queue(Q)* states that Q is an empty difference-list. The clauses for *serve* define the relation between the operation, the old queue, and the new queue. On an *enqueue(X)* message, X is unified with the first element of the *Tail* stream, and in the new queue *NewTail* is the rest of the stream. On a *dequeue(X)* message, X is unified with the first element of the *Head* stream, and in the new queue *NewHead* is the rest of the old *Head* stream.

Operationally, the program mimics the pointer twiddling of a conventional queue program. One difference is the simplicity and uniformity of the way in which variables are transmitted into and from the queue, using unification, compared to any other method of parameter passing and message routing.

Another difference is the behavior of the program when more *dequeue* messages have arrived than *enqueue* messages. In this case the content of the difference-list becomes "negative". The *Head* runs ahead of the *Tail*, and the negative difference between them is a list of uninstantiated variables, each for an excessive dequeue message. Presumably, a process that sends such a message suspends on its variables in a read-only mode. One consequence is that excessive dequeue requests are served exactly in the order in which they arrived.

The program can be condensed and simplified, using program transformation techniques (Komorowski, 1982; Tamaki and Sato, 1983). The resulting Program 19.8 is more efficient and reveals more clearly the declarative semantics of the queue monitor. Its operational semantics, however, seem to become a bit more obscure, and it does not hide the internal representation of the queue, as Program 19.7 does.

(0) queue_monitor(S) ←
     queue_monitor(S?, X\X).

(1) queue_monitor([dequeue(X)|S]], [X|NewHead]\Tail) ←
     queue_monitor(S?, NewHead\Tail).

(2) queue_monitor([enqueue(X)|S], [Head\[X|NewTail]]) ←
     queue_monitor(S?,Head\NewTail).

(3) queue_monitor([ ] ,_).

Program 19.8: A simplified queue monitor

Declaratively, the *queue_monitor* program computes the relation *queue(S)*, which says that *S* is a legal stream of queue operations. It uses an auxiliary relation *queue_monitor(S,Dequeue\Enqueue)*, which says that *Dequeue* is the list of all elements *X* such that *dequeue(X)* occurs in *S* (Clause 1), and that *Enqueue* is the list of all elements *X* such that *enqueue(X)* occurs in *S* (Clause 2). The interface between these two relations (Clause 0) constrains the list of enqueued elements to be identical to the list of dequeued elements, by calling them with the same variable name.

19.10 Bounded-Buffer Communication

Bounded buffers were introduced into logic programming by Clark and Gregory (Chapter 1) as a primitive construct. Their principal use in logic-programming is not to utilize a fixed memory-area for communication, but rather to enforce tighter synchronization between the producer and the consumer of a stream.

Takeuchi and Furukawa (Chapter 18) have shown how to implement bounded-buffers in Concurrent Prolog, hence it need not be considered a primitive. Their implementation represents the buffer using a difference-list, difference-list and uses incomplete messages to synchronize the producer and the consumer of the stream.

19.11   An Implementation of the SCAN Disk-Arm Scheduling Algorithm

The goal of a disk-arm scheduler is to satisfy disk I/O requests with minimal arm movements. The simplest algorithm is to serve the next I/O request which refers to the track closest to the current arm position. This algorithm may result in unbounded waiting — a disk I/O request may be postponed indefinitely. The SCAN algorithm tries to minimize the arm movement, while guaranteeing bounded waiting. The algorithm reads as follows:

"*While there remain requests in the current direction, the disk arm continues to move in that direction, serving the request(s) at the nearest cylinder; if there are no pending requests in that direction (possibly because an edge of the disk surface has been encountered), the arm direction changes, and the disk arm begins its sweep across the surface in the opposite direction*" (from Holt et al., 1979, p. 94).

The disk scheduler in Program 19.9 has two input streams — a stream of I/O requests from the user(s) of the disk and a stream of incomplete messages from the disk itself. The scheduler has two priority queues, represented as lists: one for requests to be served at the upsweep of the arm, and one for the requests to be served at the downsweep. It represents the arm state with the pair (*Track, Direction*), where *Track* is the current track number, and *Direction* is *up* or *down*.

The disk scheduler is invoked with the goal:

disk_scheduler(DiskS?, UserS?)

where *UserS* is a stream of I/O requests from the user(s) of the disk, and *DiskS* is a stream of partially determined (incomplete) messages from the disk controller. I/O requests are of the form *io(Track, Args)*, where *Track* is the track number and *Args* contain all other necessary information.

The first step of the scheduler is to initialize itself with two empty queues and the arm positioned on track 0, ready for an upsweep; this is done by Clause (0). Following the initialization, the scheduler proceeds using three clauses:

- Clause (1) handles requests from the disk. If such a request is ready in the disk stream, the scheduler tries to dequeue the next request from one of the queues. If successful, that request is unified with the disk request, and the scheduler iterates with the rest of the disk stream, the new queues, and the new arm state. The dequeue operation fails if both queues are empty.

- Clause (2) handles requests from the user. If an I/O request is received from the user, it is enqueued in one of the queues, and the scheduler iterates with the rest of the user stream and the new queues.

(0) disk_scheduler(DiskS, UserS) ←
        disk_scheduler(DiskS?, UserS?, ([ ], [ ]), (0, up)).

(1) disk_scheduler([Request|DiskS], UserS, Queues, ArmState) ←
        dequeue(Request, Queues, Queues1, ArmState, ArmState1) |
        disk_scheduler(DiskS?, UserS, Queues1, ArmState1).

(2) disk_scheduler(DiskS,[Request|UserS], Queues, ArmState) ←
        enqueue(Request, Queues, Queues1, ArmState) |
        disk_scheduler(DiskS, UserS?, Queues1, ArmState).

(3) disk_scheduler([io(0, halt)| _], [ ], ([ ],[ ]), _).

(1) dequeue(io(T,X), ([io(T,X)|UpQ],[ ]), (UpQ,[ ]), _, (T,up)).

(2) dequeue(io(T,X), ([io(T,X)|UpQ],DownQ), (UpQ,DownQ), (_,up),
        (T),up)).

(3) dequeue(io(T,X), ([ ], [io(T,X)|DownQ]), ([ ] ,DownQ), _, (T,down)).

(4) dequeue(io(T,X), (UpQ,[io(T,X)|DownQ]), (UpQ,DownQ), (_,down),
        (T,down)).

(1) enqueue(io(T, Args), (UpQ, DownQ), ([io(T, Args)|UpQ], DownQ),
        (T, down)).

(2) enqueue(io(T, Args), (UpQ, DownQ), (UpQ,[io(T, Args)|DownQ]),
        (T, up)).

(3) enqueue(io(T, Args), (UpQ, DownQ), (UpQ1, DownQ), (T1, Dir)) ←
        T>T1 | insert(io(T, Args), UpQ, UpQ1, up).

(4) enqueue(io(T, Args), (UpQ, DownQ), (UpQ, DownQ1), (T1, Dir)) ←
        T<T1 | insert(io(T, Args), DownQ, DownQ1, down).

(1) insert(io(T, X), [ ], [io(T,X)],_).

(2) insert(io(T, X), [io(T1, X1)|Q], [io(T, X), io(T1, X1)|Q], up) ←
        T<T1 | true.

(3) insert(io(T, X), [io(T1, X1)|Q], [io(T, X), io(T1, X1)|Q], down) ←
        T>T1 | true.

(4) insert(io(T, X), [io(T1, X1)|Q], [io(T1, X1)|Q1], up) ←
        T≥T1 | insert(io(T, X), Q, Q1, up).

(5) insert(io(T, X), [io(T1, X1)|Q], [io(T1, X1)|Q1], down) ←
        T≤T1 | insert(io(T, X), Q, Q1, down).

Program 19.9: The SCAN disk-arm scheduler

- Clause (3) terminates the scheduler, if the end of the user stream is reached and if both queues are empty. Upon termination, the scheduler sends a 'halt' message to the disk controller.

The *dequeue* procedure has clauses for each of the following four cases:

- (1): If *DownQ* is empty, then it dequeues the first request in *UpQ* and changes the new state to be upsweep, where the track number is the track of the I/O request.

- Clause (2): If the arm is on the upsweep and *UpQ* is nonempty, then it dequeues the first request in *UpQ*. The new state is as in Clause (1).

- Clauses (3) and (4): Are the symmetric clauses for *DownQ*.

Note that no clause applies if both queues are empty, hence in such a case the *dequeue* procedure fails. Since the disk scheduler invokes *dequeue* as a guard, it must wait in this case for the next user request, and use Clause (3) to enqueue it. If such a request is received and enqueued, then in the next iteration the disk request can be served.

The *enqueue* procedure also handles four cases. If the I/O request refers to the current arm track, then according to the SCAN algorithm it must be postponed to the next sweep. Clauses (1) and (2) handle this situation for the upsweep and downsweep cases. If the request refers to a track number larger than the current track, then it is inserted to *UpQ* by Clause (3); otherwise it is inserted to *DownQ* by Clause (4).

The insertion operation is a straightforward ordered-list insertion. More efficient data-structures, such as 2-3-trees, can be used if necessary.

To test the disk scheduler, we have implemented a simulator for a 10-track disk controller shown in Program 19.10. The controller sends a stream of partially determined I/O requests, and, when the arguments of the previous request become determined, it serves it and sends the next request.

```
(0)  disk_controller([io(Track, Args)|S]) ←
         disk_controller(Track?, Args?, S, [0, 0, 0, 0, 0, 0, 0, 0, 0, 0]).

(1)  disk_controller(Track, Args,[io(Track1, Args1)|S],D) ←
         disk(Track, Args, D, D1) | disk_controller(Track1?, Args1?, S, D1).

(2)  disk_controller(_, halt,[ ], _).

(1)  disk(_, (_, false),[ ],[ ]).
(2)  disk(0, (read(X), true), [X|D], [X|D]).
(3)  disk(0, (write(X), true), [_|D], [X|D]).
(4)  disk(N, IO, [X|D], [X|D1]) ←
         N>0 | N1:=N−1, disk(N1?, IO, D, D1).
```

Program 19.10: A simulator of a 10-track disk controller

When invoked with a stream S, the controller initializes the disk content and sends the first request using Clause (0). It then iterates with Clause (1), serving the previous I/O request and sending the next partially determined request, until a *halt* message is received, upon which it closes its output stream and terminates, using Clause (2).

The disk simulator assumes that the arguments of an I/O request are pairs (*Operation, ResultCode*), where the operations are *read*(X) and *write*(X). On *read*(X) Clause (2) unifies X with the content of the requested track number. On *write*(X) Clause (3) replaces the requested track content with X. The *ResultCode* is unified with *true* if the operation completed successfully (Clauses (2) and (3)) and with *false* otherwise (Clause (1)). An example of an unsuccessful completion is when the requested track number exceeds the size of the disk.

19.12 Conclusion

We have provided some evidence that a machine that implements Concurrent Prolog in hardware or firmware will be self-contained, usable, and useful, without much need to resort to reactionary concepts and techniques.

The next logical step is to build it.

Acknowledgements

This research was supported in part by IBM Poughkeepsie, Data Systems Division. Part of it was carried out while the author was visiting ICOT, the Institute for New Generation Computer Technology.

The paper benefited from a critical survey of an earlier paper, written by David Gelernter (1984).

Chapter 20

Computation Control and Protection in the Logix System

Michael Hirsch, William Silverman and Ehud Shapiro

The Weizmann Institute of Science

Abstract

A *computation* is a sequence of process reductions starting from some initial process. A method for defining and implementing computation control and protection in an abstract and machine independent way is described. The method has been incorporated in the Flat Concurrent Prolog based Logix system. Computation control in Logix is analogous to process control in conventional operating systems. Layers of control are defined via enhanced meta-interpreters and implemented via the source-to-source transformation each interpreter induces. Although Logix is at present a single-processor multi-process single-user system, it is indicated how the method would scale with Logix both to multi-processor and to multi-user.

Four layers of execution are defined in Logix — *trusted*, *failsafe*, *interruptible* and *controlled*. In addition, an *interpreted* layer is provided to accommodate user and system defined meta-interpreters and debuggers. The transformation each interpreter induces is explained via examples, and its resulting runtime overhead is measured.

The structure of the Logix compiler, which implements these transformations, is outlined, and the compile-time overhead associated with each transformation is measured.

20.1 Introduction

In multi-process computer systems, the system must be protected from failure of a process and processes must be provided with mechanisms to monitor and control the execution of their sub-processes. The standard single-processor solution offers hardware memory protection mechanisms and interrupts (usually trapped by the operating system) on failure. The extension of these solutions to multi-processors is not trivial.

Some existing languages provide the programmer with special constructs to enable the trapping of program exceptions. PL/I allows the user to set conditions with *ON* statements and to signal them with *SIGNAL* statements (ANSI PL/I, 1976). In CLU, statements may have statically bound *except* clauses (Liskov et al., 1981). In Ada, exception handlers may be attached to a subprogram body, a package body or a block, after the keyword *exception* (U.S. Dept. of Defense, 1980). Blocks in Mesa, too, may have exception handlers attached to them, and much thought was devoted to the interaction between exceptions and monitors (Hoare, 1974; Lampson and Redell, 1980). In Multilisp, exception handlers are bound to the execution of a sub-computation by *catch*, and they are activated by signalling an exception from the sub-computation with *throw* (Halstead and Loaiza, 1985).

PARLOG (Clark and Gregory, Chapter 3) provides the ability to *suspend*, *continue* or *stop* a subcomputation in the three-argument metacall (Clark and Gregory, 1985). The termination of the subcomputation is also signalled. However, the metacall is a primitive in the language.

Synchronizing Resources (SR) (Andrews, 1981, 1982; Andrews and Olsson, 1985) is an experimental language to which failure handling has been added (Schlichting and Purdin, 1985). The construct *event* was added. An event may be simple (one of *up, down, restart or crash*) or complex (allowing existential and universal quantification of events). Events may be dynamically bound to recovery operations using a *bind* statement. Stable storage of variables is provided at the language level to facilitate the program-controlled restarting of resources.

Implementations do not usually provide the user with much of a meta-level control mechanism. Usually compiled code may be aborted but to examine the execution state, one must run under a debugger. For example, Berkeley implementations of Unix provide a universal process control mechanism in the form of *signals*. Processes may be stopped, restarted, hung, interrupted, quit, killed, run in background (with special signals for tty input/output) or in foreground, and so on. To examine the state of a process, however, a dump of the executing program must be forced and examined with the aid of a debugger.

The problems have thus been approached from the directions of language design and operating system design, but nevertheless the solutions are language

dependent or machine dependent. In this paper we present general, machine independent solutions to both problems for single and multi-processor systems. We
show how these solutions are implemented in the framework of Flat Concurrent
Prolog (FCP) (Mierowsky et al., 1985) and Logix (Silverman et al., Chapter 21),
an operating system and programming environment written in FCP. The novelty
of our approach is that we solve the problems totally within a high-level language
using source-to-source transformations.

Our model of a process is somewhat unconventional. Processes are light-
weight and in general short-lived. Process spawning is so cheap that it has replaced
procedure calling (cf. Mesa, Lampson and Redell, 1980, where light-weight process
spawn has only extended procedure call). At any given instant, there may be
thousands of processes in the system, some of them active, the rest suspended on
events. (For example, compiling a hundred lines of source code using the Logix
compiler generates about 10,000 processes. When Logix is idle, it consists of
about 800 suspended processes.) There are too many processes for each to be
referred to by a conventional name, too many to be controlled in a conventional
manner.

A *computation* is a sequence of process reductions starting from some initial
goal. The *resolvent* of a computation is a multi-set of processes, all the currently
existing offspring of the initial goal, all cooperating to accomplish this goal. Our
aim is to afford the user a measure of control over his computations and a measure
of insulation between them. A computation is a suitable object of control since
it represents a set of processes co-operating to accomplish a given task, and there
are relatively few computations initiated by a user at any given time.

A *meta-interpreter* is an interpreter for a language written in the language.
If a meta-interpreter is *enhanced* (written with augmented functionality), the semantics of the interpreted programs appear enhanced. This is called the behavior
induced by the enhanced meta-interpreter.

The layers of control and protection of Logix (introduced below) are defined
by a sequence of meta-interpreters for FCP with monotonically increasing functionality. The bottom layer is plain and provides no user controls. It is called
trusted since its computations are trusted not to diverge (loop indefinitely) or
fail. Failure of a trusted process causes the FCP abstract machine to fail. The
second layer is called *failsafe*. The failure of a process is reported and the abstract machine does not fail, but the user may not intervene. User intervention
is introduced in the *interruptible* layer. In addition to the reporting of process
failure, a computation may be temporarily suspended or it may be aborted. The
top layer, *controlled*, goes further. Termination of the computation is detected,
the computation may be inspected and its state (resolvent) may be editted.

The *interpreted* layer could be thought of as a fifth layer. This layer provides
support for debuggers, profilers, and user defined meta-interpreters, allowing exe-

cution of one reduction at a time and permitting total control (and full inspection) even of the process scheduling.

A (general-purpose) *partial evaluator* (Jones et al., 1985; Safra, 1986; Safra and Shapiro, Chapter 25) for a language is a program which takes a program and its partial input and produces a residual program which is the original program specialized for the known part of the input. In general, if provided sufficient input, non-trivial partial evaluators produce residual programs which are more efficient than the original programs.

We have two possible uses for a partial evaluator. Firstly, if the input program is an enhanced meta-interpreter and its partial input is a user's program, then the output is a program which behaves like the user's program, but has the enhanced behavior induced by the meta-interpreter. An experimental partial evaluator capable of doing this is described by Safra (1986). The problem with this approach is its large compile-time overhead.

Secondly, if the input program is the partial evaluator itself and its partial input is an enhanced meta-interpreter, then the output is a compiler, which, given a user's program, produces an equivalent program with the required induced behavior. This is the most promising approach, but at present we lack a partial evaluator which can partially evaluate itself.

Each layer may be viewed as a semantic extension to FCP. These extensions are defined by enhanced meta-interpreters. In view of the current difficulties with partial evaluation explained above, a more direct approach is taken. The meta-interpreter for each layer is used as an operational specification for a source-to-source transformation. The transformer for each layer is constructed manually. The correspondence between the meta-interpreters and the transformers is justified informally.

Any operating system in FCP which aims at being multi-user, or even single-user and perpetual, must address the problem of preventing any process from failing. This may be done either by verifying that no process can fail or by rewriting each procedure so some clause will succeed in reduction with any process. The former is the approach taken in the system code of Logix itself (for efficiency), while the latter is the approach suggested in this paper for user programs.

20.2 The Logix System

Logix is an experimental high-level language environment/operating system for FCP written totally in FCP. The Logix user is supplied with a module system and a remote procedure call mechanism for intermodule communication. On this base, a compiler, a debugger, an interactive shell, and basic terminal and file access have been built. The compiler produces code which runs at a peak rate of about 5KLIPS on a Sun 3/50. This is acceptable performance compared with commercially available Prolog compilers.

The module system and remote procedure call mechanism are orthogonal to the issues presented in this paper and are discussed further by Hirsch (1986). Research is underway to implement Logix on multi-processors (Taylor et al., Chapter 39; Shapiro, Chapter 7). This paper represents the first step towards making Logix multi-user.

Logix currently runs as an application under Berkeley 4.2 Unix. The user is provided with interfaces to the terminal and file input/output of the underlying operating system. Each user has a multi-process, single-processor virtual machine.

20.3 Flat Concurrent Prolog

Flat Concurrent Prolog is a logic programming language, in that a program is a collection of universally quantified Horn-clause axioms, and a computation is an attempt to prove a goal — an existentially quantified conjunctive statement — from the axioms in the program. The goal statement describes an input/output relation for which the input is known; a successful (constructive) proof provides a corresponding output.

Flat Concurrent Prolog (FCP) is introduced by Shapiro (Chapter 5). This section reviews meta-interpreters and introduces the FCP programming techniques which are used to implement the control and protection mechanisms.

20.3.1 Meta-interpretation

A meta-interpreter is a program in a language which interprets programs in the language. Program 20.1 is the simplest meta-interpreter for FCP and consists of three clauses:

```
reduce(true).                    % 1
reduce((A, B)) ←                 % 2
    reduce(A?),
    reduce(B?).
reduce(A) ←                      % 3
    A ≠ true, A ≠ (_,_) |
    clause(A?, Body),
    reduce(Body?).
```

Program 20.1: A plain FCP meta-interpreter

Declaratively, the three axioms are read as follows. The truth of a goal *true* is asserted (1); the truth of a conjunct is implied by the combined truth of its conjuncts (2); and the truth of a unit goal is implied by the truth of the body of a clause whose head is unifiable with the goal and whose guard is true (3) (see below).

Operationally, the three clauses correspond to the three primitive control operations of FCP. Respectively, the process *true* terminates (1); a conjunct causes spawning of the conjunctive processes (2) and a unit goal reduces (3).

The call to *clause(A, Body)* is actually the reduction. For each clause in the original program

$$H \leftarrow G \mid B.$$

there is a clause

$$clause(H, B) \leftarrow G \mid true.$$

Thus the call *clause(A, Body)* attempts to unify A with a head H and to solve the guard G corresponding to the head, returning the corresponding body B as an argument. This call succeeds, suspends or fails exactly as a real reduction of the goal with the original clause would have succeeded, suspended or failed respectively. However, the body goals are not spawned as independent And-parallel goals. Instead, they are returned as data for further meta-interpretation.

The plain meta-interpreter above interprets the program exactly as it would have run. This meta-interpreter is nicknamed "vanilla", implying its lack of flavour.

Enhancing meta-interpreters is an interesting and easy way to extend and to experiment with extensions to the semantics of a language. To gain the induced functionality in such a simple way, however, there is a price to be paid, the cost of an extra level of interpretation. Execution is slowed between 5 and 10 times, depending on the extra mechanics of the meta-interpreter. As mentioned above, there are, however, two techniques to preserve (almost all) the efficiency of the original program while inducing on it flavoured behavior, viz., partial evaluation and source-to-source transformation.

20.3.2 Programming techniques

Three FCP programming techniques are used in this paper to accomplish the tasks of broadcasting computation control messages, detecting termination and communicating failure.

A logical variable may have at most one writer, but it may have several readers. In other words, it is naturally suited to broadcast. The writer instantiates the variable to a list cell with the message in its head. The tail of the list cell is a logical variable and is used for the next broadcast. Readers wait for the logical variable to be instantiated to a list cell, read the message in its head and act upon it, and then wait for the tail to be instantiated. In this manner, a stream of messages may be sent by one process to any number of recipients. This programming technique is referred to as a *signals stream* below, indicating its use here as a medium for broadcasting signals.

The reverse situation of many-to-one communication also arises. For this, we use a *channel* (Tribble et al., Chapter 17). A channel is a generalization of a stream which allows multiple writers to communicate with multiple readers.

A *short-circuit* in FCP is a programming technique for detecting the termination of a set of processes (Takeuchi, 1983). The analogy is to an electrical circuit. Every active element is threaded into a circuit in series by sharing a wire with each neighbor. Whenever an element terminates, it joins its pair of wires, effectively connecting its neighbors with each other directly and removing itself from the circuit. An element may replace itself by a string of new elements as long as the circuit remains connected in series through all elements. Any element may detect if it is alone by testing the resistance on the circuit. If each element in the circuit forwards pulses, any pulse will eventually return to its originator after passing through every element.

Processes are the elements of the FCP short-circuit. The links of the circuit are variables held in common by adjacent processes. Each process carries two extra arguments, called its *left* and *right circuit variables*, as its ends in the circuit. When a process terminates, it unifies its circuit variables, connecting its neighbors and shorting itself out of the circuit. When new processes are spawned, they are threaded into their parent's circuit by the creation of new links between the newly spawned processes. Any process (in particular the process monitoring the computation) can detect termination by comparing its two variables for identity. Special messages querying the state of the computation can circulate on the circuit, reaching every process.

20.4 The Method

The (meta-)interpreters presented below are written in Concurrent Prolog rather than in FCP. There are two reasons for this. Firstly, meta-interpreters written in Concurrent Prolog are more amenable to partial evaluation using the transformations described by Safra (1986) and secondly, the interpreters for FCP thus defined are more concise, clearer to read and easier to explain and understand. The essential difference between the interpreters is the way in which the *clause* procedure is called. The Concurrent Prolog interpreter may call it from a guard and thus be protected from failure at the call. The FCP meta-interpreter must spawn the call as a sibling process and explicitly wait for the result. The clause procedure must then trap failure (once this is required), and the meta-interpreter must check the result before proceeding.

20.4.1 The different layers

Trusted

Trusted processes run with no protection at all. They are, in general, integral parts of Logix and are failure-proofed and divergence-proofed by author. This layer is to Logix what assembly language is to Unix.

A meta-interpreter for this layer is the vanilla meta-interpreter, and source and transformed code are one and the same.

Failsafe

Failure of a goal is trapped and reported. This layer is used for system interfaces.

A meta-interpreter which traps failure (Program 20.2) has an extra clause and an extra variable. The extra clause checks for failure, and the extra variable is used to communicate the failure.

```
reduce(true, _).                      % terminate
reduce((A, B), Channel) ←             % spawn
      reduce(A?, Channel),
      reduce(B?, Channel).
reduce(Goal, Channel) ←               % reduce
      clause(Goal?, Body) |
      reduce(Body?, Channel).
reduce(Goal, Channel) ←               % fail
      otherwise |
      write(failed(Goal), Channel, _).
```

Program 20.2: The meta-interpreter defining the failsafe layer

The key to trapping failure in this layer is the fourth clause of the *reduce/2* predicate (*fail*). The guard predicate *otherwise* is defined to succeed when the reduction with every other (textually previous) clause has failed.

A channel is used in this layer to communicate failure. If the interpreted process would have failed, this fact is written on the channel (using the procedure *write/3*).

There are potentially multiple writers of the channel but only one reader, a process monitoring the progress of the computation. Since the channel is never closed, the monitor process cannot detect the termination of the computation. The best it can do is "failure has not yet occurred", and if failure never occurs (the norm) it will suspend forever. Once the computation has terminated, however, no active process will have a reference to the channel (the monitor is suspended). Since garbage collection copies exactly everything reachable from the active processes, the redundant monitor will eventually be collected.

The source-to-source transformations on any procedure are equally straight-forward. The head and each body predicate of every clause is rewritten with an extra, common variable as the channel. An extra clause of the form

$$p(X_1, X_2, \ldots, X_n, \text{Channel}) \leftarrow$$
$$\quad otherwise \mid$$
$$\quad \text{write}(\text{failed}(p(X_1, X_2, \ldots, X_n)), \text{Channel}, \_).$$

is appended to each procedure. Since the X_i are variables, if this clause is ever tried, the unification with the head will succeed.

By the definition of *otherwise* above, this clause succeeds when all the other clauses have failed, i.e., when the original procedure would have failed. In other words, this clause detects failure (depending entirely on *otherwise* for this) and communicates the fact on the channel.

Interruptible

In general, this is the lowest layer in which a user program may run. The user is provided with the added ability to interrupt computations in order to suspend or abort them.

Failure is still detected, and in addition a signals stream is polled every reduction to check that no signal has arrived. Thus the process monitoring the computation may now interrupt the computation simply by writing on the signals stream. This process cannot, however, inspect the state of the computation (i.e., the resolvent).

Program 20.3 is the meta-interpreter defining the interruptible layer. The main loop is formed by the recursion of the procedure *reduce/3*, which deals with termination, spawning, reduction, failure-detection and interruption in its five clauses respectively.

Use is made of the sequential semantics of *otherwise* (Codish and Shapiro, Chapter 32). The *otherwise* in the failure-detecting clause (*fail*) succeeds if all the previous clauses have failed, i.e., if the reduction of the process would have failed. If, however, there were suspensions (but no successes), then the otherwise suspends and the reduction suspends on the signals stream as well (in the final clause *interrupt*).

The guard predicate *unknown/1* succeeds if the value of its argument is still unknown, i.e., not instantiated. If its argument is instantiated, it eventually fails. The guard predicate *known/1* suspends until its argument has been instantiated to a non-variable term, allowing suspension until the occurrence of an interrupt. A guard predicate *unknown/1* is added to ensure that reduction eventually ceases after interruption (*reduce*) and that interruption is not confused with failure (*fail*).

The procedure *interrupt_server/3* inspects the signals stream for a messages (from a monitor process) and acts accordingly. The *abort* interrupt causes the

reduce(*true*, _, _).   % terminate
reduce((A, B), Signals, Channel) ←   % spawn
    reduce(A?, Signals, Channel),
    reduce(B?, Signals, Channel).
reduce(Goal, Signals, Channel) ←   % reduce
    unknown(Signals),
    clause(Goal?, Body) |
    reduce(Body?, Signals, Channel).
reduce(Goal, Signals, Channel) ←   % fail
    otherwise, unknown(Signals) |
    write(failed(Goal), Channel, _).
reduce(Goal, Signals, Channel) ←   % interrupt
    known(Signals) |
    interrupt_server(Signals?, Goal, Channel).

interrupt_server([abort | Signals], Goal, Channel) ←   % abort
    write(aborted(Goal), Channel, _).
interrupt_server([suspend | Signals], Goal, Channel) ←   % suspend
    interrupt_server(Signals?, Goal, Channel).
interrupt_server([resume | Signals], Goal, Channel) ←   % resume
    reduce(Goal?, Signals, Channel).

Program 20.3: The meta-interpreter defining the interruptible layer

process to terminate. A *suspend* causes it to remain in the interrupt server (suspended). A *resume* allows reduction to proceed.

The source-to-source transformations reflect the added work required in each reduction. Active reduction proceeds until the arrival of an interrupt, but if the reduction suspends, then suspension is on the signals stream as well. The head and each body predicate of every clause is rewritten with two extra, common variables as the signals stream and channel and an extra guard predicate *unknown/1*. Each procedure is augmented by two clauses, one to trap failure and the second to catch interrupts.

As an example, the transformations on naive reverse are shown. The original *rev/2*:

    rev([ ], [ ]).
    rev([X | Y], Z) ← rev(Y?, Z1), append(Z1?, [X], Z).

and the transformed procedure:

    rev([ ], [ ], Signals, Channel).
    rev([X | Y], Z, Signals, Channel) ←

```
        unknown(Signals) |
            rev(Y?, Z1, Signals, Channel), append(Z1?, [X], Z, Signals, Channel).
    rev(X, Y, Signals, Channel) ←
        otherwise, unknown(Signals) |
            write(failed(rev(X, Y)), Channel, _).
    rev(X, Y, Signals, Channel) ←
        known(Signals) |
            interrupt_server(Signals?, rev(X, Y), Channel).
```

The interrupt server differs in one subtle point from that above. It can no longer resume a computation by calling the meta-interpreter, and so has a subsidiary table to restart processes.

```
    interrupt_server([resume | Signals], Goal, Channel) ←
        interrupt_restart(Goal?, Signals, Channel).
```

The extra procedure *interrupt_restart/3* has an entry for every procedure p/n:

```
    interrupt_restart(p(X_1, X_2, ..., X_n), Signals, Channel) ←
        p(X_1, X_2, ..., X_n, Signals, Channel).
```

Controlled

The controlled layer allows the suspending and aborting of computations and, in addition, allows the user to inspect (and possibly alter) the state of the computation.

The essence of the meta-interpreter defining the controlled layer (Program 20.4) is the same as that for the interruptible layer. In addition to a signals stream and channel, each process executing in this layer carries a short-circuit.

In this layer, the short-circuit is used to detect termination of the computation and to circulate special computation control messages. Each message circulating on the short-circuit has the property that it reaches every process in turn. The interrupt server shows how this property is used effectively. On receipt of the message *show_state/1* on the left branch, a process forwards the message to the next process via its right branch, after adding its own goal (*show*). Once the message *show_state/1* has circulated completely, it has visited every process and has collected the whole resolvent. The message *kill/1* circulates on the circuit (using the *forward* clause) until its argument unifies with the goal of a process (*kill*).

The source-to-source transformations associated with this layer of control are similar to those associated with the previous layer, interruptible. The head and each body predicate of every clause is given a signals stream and a channel and the guard predicate *unknown/1* is added. In addition, the short-circuit is added. If there is no body, the short-circuit is closed (the variables are unified) since any process reducing with such a clause would terminate. If the body consists

reduce(*true*, Signals, Close, Close, Channel).   % terminate
reduce((A, B), Signals, L, R, Channel) ←   % spawn
    reduce(A?, Signals, L?, M, Channel),
    reduce(B?, Signals, M?, R, Channel).
reduce(Goal, Signals, L, R, Channel) ←   % reduce
    unknown(Signals),
    clause(Goal?, Body) |
    reduce(Body?, Signals, L, R, Channel).
reduce(Goal, Signals, Close, Close, Channel) ←   % fail
    otherwise, unknown(Signals) |
    write(failed(Goal), Channel, _).
reduce(Goal, Signals, L, R, Channel) ←   % interrupt
    known(Signals) |
    interrupt_server(Signals?, Goal, L?, R, Channel).

interrupt_server([abort | Signals], Goal, Close, Close, Channel) ← % abort
    write(aborted(Goal), Channel, _).
interrupt_server([suspend | Signals], Goal, L, R, Channel) ←   % suspend
    interrupt_server(Signals?, Goal, L, R, Channel).
interrupt_server([resume | Signals], Goal, L, R, Channel) ←   % resume
    reduce(Goal?, Signals, L, R, Channel).
interrupt_server(Signals, Goal, [show_state(X) | L],
      [show_state([Goal| X]) | R], Channel) ←   % show
    interrupt_server(Signals, Goal, L?, R, Channel).
interrupt_server(Signals, Goal, [kill(Goal) | Close],
    [killed | Close], Channel).   % kill
interrupt_server(Signals, Goal, [X | L], [X | R], Channel)←   % forward
    otherwise | interrupt_server(Signals, Goal, L?, R, Channel).

Program 20.4: The meta-interpreter defining the controlled layer

of one predicate, then it inherits the head's short-circuit variables. Otherwise, the short-circuit is threaded through the body predicates. For example, given a procedure

$$p(T_1, T_2, \ldots, T_n).$$
$$p(T_1, T_2, \ldots, T_n) \leftarrow$$
$$q_1(T_{1,1}, T_{1,2}, \ldots, T_{1,m_1}),$$
$$q_2(T_{2,1}, T_{2,2}, \ldots, T_{2,m_2}),$$
$$\vdots$$
$$q_k(T_{k,1}, T_{k,2}, \ldots, T_{k,m_k}).$$

it would be rewritten as

$$p(T_1, T_2, \ldots, T_n, \text{Signals}, \text{Close}, \text{Close}, \text{Channel}),$$
$$p(T_1, T_2, \ldots, T_n, \text{Signals}, \text{Left}, \text{Right}, \text{Channel}) \leftarrow$$
$$q_1(T_{1,1}, T_{1,2}, \ldots, T_{1,m_1}, \text{Signals}, \text{Left}, \text{Bridge}_1, \text{Channel}),$$
$$q_2(T_{2,1}, T_{2,2}, \ldots, T_{2,m_2}, \text{Signals}, \text{Bridge}_1, \text{Bridge}_2, \text{Channel}),$$
$$\vdots$$
$$q_k(T_{k,1}, T_{k,2}, \ldots, T_{k,m_k}, \text{Signals}, \text{Bridge}_{k-1}, \text{Right}, \text{Channel}).$$

with the extra clauses

$$p(X_1, X_2, \ldots, X_n, \text{Signals}, \text{Close}, \text{Close}, \text{Channel}) \leftarrow$$
$$\textit{otherwise}, \text{unknown}(\text{Signals}) \mid$$
$$\text{write}(\text{failed}(p(X_1, X_2, \ldots, X_n)), \text{Channel}, \_).$$
$$p(X_1, X_2, \ldots, X_n, \text{Signals}, \text{Left}, \text{Right}, \text{Channel}) \leftarrow$$
$$\text{known}(\text{Signals}) \mid$$
$$\text{interrupt\_server}(\text{Signals}?, p(X_1, X_2, \ldots, X_n),$$
$$\text{Left}, \text{Right}, \text{Channel}).$$

Two extra clauses are added per procedure, as before. The first, which detects failure, now closes the short-circuit. The second, which detects interrupts and calls the interrupt server, includes the short-circuit as arguments in the call.

The interrupt server is similar to that used in the meta-interpreter. As before, it needs an auxiliary table to restart processes. Additionally, it watches for any messages on the short-circuit.

The interpreted layer

The functionality of the controlled layer is subsumed in the interpreted layer. In addition, procedures in the interpreted layer are debuggable. This layer supplies a *clause/3* predicate for use in user-provided or system-provided meta-interpreters. Using this predicate, sophisticated debuggers (Shapiro, 1982), run-time statistics packages, language extensions (as above) and new embedded languages can be built. Reduction of processes in this layer is by meta-interpretation.

The *clause/3* predicate is similar to the *clause/2* predicate explained previously. The third argument is used to return a result to the caller. If the reduction succeeded, the third argument is instantiated to true, otherwise it is used to return the failed goal. This explicit result returned in the third argument may be used to detect failure in FCP meta-interpreters. If the interpreters for the failsafe, interruptible and controlled layers had been written in FCP, they would have used the *clause/3* predicate for its third argument.

Below is an example of the source-to-source transformations resulting in the clause predicate itself. Given a procedure

$$p(T_1, T_2, \ldots, T_n).$$
$$p(T_1, T_2, \ldots, T_n) \leftarrow$$
$$\quad g(T_1, T_2, \ldots, T_m) \mid q(T_1, T_2, \ldots, T_m).$$

it would be rewritten as

clause($p(T_1, T_2, \ldots, T_n)$), *true, true*).
clause($p(T_1, T_2, \ldots, T_n)$, $q(T_1, T_2, \ldots, T_m)$, *true*) $\leftarrow$
    $g(T_1, T_2, \ldots, T_m) \mid$ *true*.
clause($p(X_1, X_2, \ldots, X_n)$, $_-$, failed($p(X_1, X_2, \ldots, X_n)$)) $\leftarrow$
    otherwise|*true*.

20.4.2 Computations and layers

When a request to start a computation is initiated in Logix, it is initiated with a signals stream, a short-circuit and a channel. A computation may span modules compiled in different layers (Hirsch, 1986). All controlled and interpreted processes in the computation are threaded in the short-circuit and share the signals stream and channel. The same signals stream and channel are shared by all interruptible processes. All failsafe processes have access to the same channel. This was a fundamental design decision of the module system. The concept is shown in Figure 20.1.

20.4.3 A computation monitor

The computation monitor is a process which monitors a computation. Its functionality is comparable to that of the three-argument metacall of PARLOG (Clark and Gregory, 1985). The monitor accepts a stream of commands and produces a stream of events. Independently of the commands, the monitor may receive indications of failure of processes of the computation. These are forwarded on the events stream.

Program 20.5 is an example computation monitor. *Signals*, *Left*, *Right* and *Channel* are computation controls. *Command* is a stream of commands from the user and *Events* is a stream of events generated by the computation. The question of starting a computation and its monitor is part of the module system and the question of addressing the monitor is part of the user interface. Neither of these topics is dealt with here.

Commands from the user lead to their equivalents being sent to the computation. This example is simplified. In reality, the computation and monitor themselves are part of a larger computation and the monitor interprets the signals sent to it by the outer computation.

monitor(Command, Signals, Left, Right, Channel, Events) ←
    serialize(Channel?, Stream),
    monitor(Command?, Stream?, Signals, Left, Right, Events, running).

monitor([abort|_], _, [abort|_], _, _, [aborted], _).
monitor([suspend|Command], Stream, Signals, Left, Right, [suspended|Events],
        Status) ←
    suspend(Status?, Signals, Signals1),
    monitor(Command?, Stream?, Signals1, Left, Right, Events, suspended).
monitor([resume|Command], Stream, Signals, Left, Right, [resumed|Events],
        Status) ←
    resume(Status?, Signals, Signals1),
    monitor(Command?, Stream?, Signals1, Left, Right, Events, running).
monitor([state(State)|Command], Stream, Signals, Left, Right, Events,
        Status) ←
    suspend(Status?, Signals, Signals1),
    Left = [show_state([ ])|Left1],
    Right? = [show_state(State)|Right1],
    monitor(Command?, Stream?, Signals1, Left1, Right1, Events, suspended).
monitor([kill(Goal)|Command], Stream, Signals, Left, Right,
        [kill(Response)|Events], Status) ←
    suspend(Status?, Signals, Signals1),
    Left = [kill(Goal)|Left1],
    Right? = [Response|Right1],
    monitor(Command?, Stream?, Signals1, Left1, Right1, Events, suspended).
monitor(_, _, _, Left, Right, [terminated], _) ←
    Left? = Right? |
    true.
monitor(Command, [failed(Goal)|Stream], Signals, Left, Right,
        [failed(Goal)|Events], Status) ←
    monitor(Command, Stream, Signals, Left, Right, Events, Status).

suspend(running, [suspend|Signals], Signals).
suspend(suspended, Signals, Signals).

resume(suspended, [resume|Signals], Signals).
resume(running, Signals, Signals).

Program 20.5: An example computation monitor

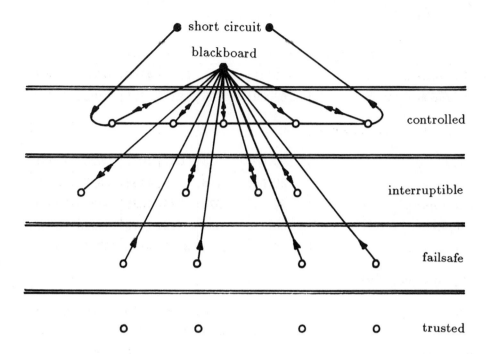

Figure 20.1: Layers, the blackboard and the short-circuit

20.4.4 Performance

In Table 20.1 *allqueens* calculates all solutions to the 8 queens problem; *append* appends a list of 400 elements to a list of 40 elements, 15 times; *deriv* calculates derivatives symbolically; *qsort* sorts 375 numbers using quicksort; *rev* is naive $O(n^2)$ reverse of 1000 elements; and *tak* is a common benchmark program applied to the numbers 18, 12 and 6.

Each time is the average of 10 runs, excluding garbage collections. The overhead for failsafe code is around 8%, a very acceptable price for trapping failure within the language. Interruptible code carries a penalty of about 25%, while controlled code carries a penalty of about 52%. Interpreted code runs more than 4 times slower than trusted code.

It appears that much of the price to be paid is in the size of the object code produced. Failsafe code is on average 25% larger than trusted code. Interruptible code carries a 62% penalty, and controlled code carries over a 100% penalty.

program:	allqueens	append	deriv	qsort	rev	tak
# reductions	108431	6143	6834	4796	502586	63694
# process creations	62009	66	831	771	1022	47727
CPU time (in milliseconds)						
trust	29760	415	661	1081	29268	19581
failsafe	30962	458	718	1188	33070	20459
interrupt	32326	574	784	1386	41815	22014
control	38211	664	918	1679	49223	25607
interpret	85823	2013	3301	4843	167450	59765
code size (in bytes)						
trust	1868	3548	2636	3176	1368	1228
failsafe	2504	4052	3320	3584	1888	1564
interrupt	3384	4776	4272	4176	2624	2076
control	4512	5820	5472	5172	3664	3024
interpret	3384	4964	4216	4664	2808	2692

Table 20.1: Performance results

20.4.5 Compilation overhead

Compilation in Logix is pipelined. The tokenizer, parser, and a pre-processor (all written in FCP) do syntactic and simple semantic checking. Their output is input to filters which do the source-to-source transformations. The output of these filters is pipelined to the encoder, which is followed by an assembler.

The compilation overhead associated with the different filters is small relative to the whole compilation process. However, the various filters add control mechanisms to the original programs. The encoder and assembler run in time roughly proportional to the size of the program to be encoded and assembled respectively. Since this program now contains the control mechanisms, the encoder and assembler can require up to twice as long to encode and assemble a control-layer program than the same trust-layer program. Over all, compilation times can double.

20.5 Extensions

The major research interest in Logix is to extend it to multiple processors and multiple users.

The ideas presented in this paper scale to assist in making Logix multi-user. We have shown a method to isolate the multiple distributed computations of a single user from each other. The same method isolates the distributed computations of multiple users from each other. We have shown that adding (system-controlled) streams and variables to a computation by source-to-source transformations adds acceptable execution overhead. The same method allows a distributed computation to be tied to the physical terminal or logical device of a particular user. We have yet to develop a method to perform memory management in a multi-user environment.

Since Logix is written entirely in FCP, it will run as a program directly on a distributed implementation. As an operating system, though, Logix must be extended to implement some process-to-processor mapping scheme and to handle distributed code and memory management. There is also a bootstrap problem which needs to be solved in conjunction with the implementation. Present research in this direction follows the initial work described by Taylor et al. (Chapter 22).

In general, an exception is a parameterized failure. The method used to trap failure can thus be extended to the general case by allowing for this parameterization. This could be done with an *otherwise* with a parameter.

20.6 Conclusions

Within the high level formalism of concurrent logic programming, we have shown a method to trap failure of processes in a distributed computation. We have defined and implemented various layers of control for distributed computations in a machine independent way. We have indicated how this could be extended to exceptions in general.

The methods used scale to a multi-processor implementation of FCP. We have indicated how our methods can be used to allow multiple users.

The feasibility of these methods was shown by incorporating them into the Logix system.

Chapter 21

The Logix System User Manual Version 1.21

William Silverman, Michael Hirsch, Avshalom Houri
and Ehud Shapiro

The Weizmann Institute of Science

21.1 Introduction

Concurrent Prolog (Shapiro, Chapter 2) is a logic programming language designed for concurrent programming and parallel execution. It is a process oriented language, which embodies dataflow synchronization and guarded-command indeterminacy as the basic control mechanisms. Flat Concurrent Prolog (FCP) (Mierowsky et al., 1985), was identified as a practical and efficient subset of Concurrent Prolog, which supports most of its programming techniques. The reader is referred to (Shapiro, Chapter 5) for a survey of the language and its programming techniques, and an extensive bibliography.

The purpose of this manual is to serve as a concise specification for Logix users, as well as to document the various aspects of the system which are of interest to the research community. It is not necessarily the best starting point for someone not familiar with concurrent logic programming.

Logix is a programming environment written in Flat Concurrent Prolog (FCP) which allows the development and testing of concurrent logic programs. Logix includes a compiler, which compiles FCP programs into an FCP abstract machine instruction set, and an emulator, written in C, which emulates these instructions.

Logix is not a conventional programming environment. Although presently a single user, single processor system, its basic design scales to a multiprocessor, multiuser system. As such it may be overdeveloped for the casual user in certain respects (e.g., its multitasking capabilities), underdeveloped in others (e.g., interactive help facilities, "friendliness", etc.).

Logix is organized around three types of objects: computations, modules, and servers. A computation is the unit of execution, control and debugging in Logix; a module is the unit of compilation; a server provides access to facilities and capabilities of the underlying system; for example the screen and the file system. Several computations may proceed in parallel under Logix. A computation may span many modules; several concurrent computations may execute code in the same module and employ the services of the same server.

A computation occurs in time. It starts with an initial process, typically specified interactively by the user. At each point in time a computation consists of a multiset of processes; it terminates when this becomes empty. A computation proceeds by processes performing actions. A process may terminate, fork, or change state. While doing so, it may assign values to variables by unification, thus achieving the effect of communication in general, and output construction in particular. On a multiprocessor Logix, a computation could span several processors.

A module is a unit of compilation. It consists of a set of procedures, preceded by an optional module declaration. A procedure may call and be called by procedures in other modules using remote procedure calls. Modules are loaded automatically when called and compiled automatically as needed.

Remote procedure calls between modules are implemented via the stream communication capabilities of FCP. In a parallel implementation of Logix, different modules may reside in different processors, and remote procedure calls may cross processor boundaries.

A Logix user is provided with an initial set of services, which are accessed via remote procedure calls. These include a screen server, a file server, and a compilation server, among others. In addition, a module server is created for each active module, to serve remote procedure calls addressed to it.

In a parallel implementation of Logix, different services may reside in different processors. One of the services on each processor may include links to adjacent processors (Taylor et al., Chapter 22).

The compilation technique used in the Logix system, as well as the underlying abstract machine, are described by Houri and Shapiro (Chapter 38). The techniques for specifying and implementing the layers of protection and control in Logix are explained by Hirsch et al. (Chapter 20).

The rest of the manual is organized as follows. Section 21.2 informally defines Flat Concurrent Prolog. Section 21.3 contains an annotated session with Logix, demonstrating some of its capabilities. Section 21.4 explains the user interface. Section 21.5 details the notions of computation, event, and the commands for manipulating and inspecting computations. Section 21.6 introduces the notion of modules and explains their compilation and manipulation. Section 21.7 explains the notion of systems and services and reviews some of the system services provided by Logix. Section 21.8 explains the debugger. Section 21.9 shows how to implement FCP meta-interpreters under Logix. Section 21.10 lists some utilities, and Section 21.11 reports on some Logix bugs.

21.2 Flat Concurrent Prolog

The following definition of Flat Concurrent Prolog attempts to be self-contained. However, it is intended for a reader already familiar with the concepts of logic programming and sequential Prolog. For a more tutorial introduction the reader is referred to other papers on Concurrent Prolog, such as (Shapiro, Chapter 5).

21.2.1 Syntax and terminology

We generally follow the Edinburgh Prolog syntactic conventions. A *term* is either a constant, a variable, or a compound term. A *constant* is an *integer*, such as 0, 1, 999, –512, a *real*, such as 9.0, 3.1415, 0.003, or a string. A *string* is any sequence of characters; it may be written within single quotes if there is a possibility of confusion with other symbols, such as integers and variables. A *variable* is distinguished by an initial capital letter or character "_". Example of variables are X, *Value*, *A1*, *_3*, and *_Result*.

A *compound term* is either a tuple of the form $\{T_1, T_2, \ldots, T_n\}$, $n > 0$, where each T_i is a term, or a list of the form $[X|Xs]$, where X and Xs are terms. The standard Prolog syntax for terms, $f(T_1, T_2, \ldots, T_n)$, where f is a string, is equivalent to $\{f, T_1, T_2, \ldots, T_n\}$. Prefix, infix, and postfix notation is supported. The list of predefined operators appears in Appendix 21.1. [ ] (read *nil*) denotes the empty list. $[X|Xs]$ is a list whose head (car) is X and tail (cdr) is Xs. The term $[a,b,c]$ is equivalent to $[a|[b|[c|[\;]]]]$, and $[a,b|Xs]$ is equivalent to $[a|[b|Xs]]$.

A *goal* is a term of the form $p(T_1, T_2, \ldots, T_n)$, where p is a string, called the *predicate name*, and $n \geq 0$ is the predicate's *arity*.

A *guarded clause* is a term of the form

$$A \leftarrow G_1, G_2, \ldots, G_m \mid B_1, B_2, \ldots, B_n. \qquad m, n \geq 0$$

where A, the G_i's and the B_i's are goals. A is called the clause's *head*, G's are its *guard*, and the B's its *body*. "←", read *if*, denotes implication, and "|" is called the *commit* operator. If the guard is empty the clause is written as

$$A \leftarrow B_1, B_2, \ldots, B_n.$$

and the commit operator is omitted. If the body is empty and the guard is not the clause is written as

$$A \leftarrow G_1, G_2, \ldots, G_m \mid true.$$

and if both are empty the clause is called a *unit clause*, and is written simply as

$$A.$$

A clause whose body includes exactly one goal is called an *iterative clause*.

A *flat guarded clause* is a clause whose guard predicates are in the set of predefined guard test predicates. The set of FCP guard test predicates is in Section 21.2.4.

A Flat Concurrent Prolog *procedure* is a list of flat guarded clauses whose heads have the same predicate name and arity.

A *program module*, or *module*, for short, is a set of procedures.

A module may begin with an optional *module declaration*, whose format is specified in Section 21.6.3.

An example of a module is shown below:

```
– export([isort/2]).
– author(bill).

isort([X|Xs],Ys) ← isort(Xs?,Zs), insert(X?,Zs?,Ys).
isort([ ],[ ]).

insert(X,[Y|Ys],[X,Y|Ys]) ← X ≤ Y | true.
insert(X,[Y|Ys],[Y|Zs]) ← X > Y | insert(X,Ys?,Zs).
insert(X,[ ],[X]).
```

21.2.2 Read-only unification

The read-only variable is Concurrent Prolog's basic process synchronization mechanism. We assume two types of logical variables: *writable variables*, and *read-only variables*.

The *read-only operator*, denoted *?*, maps a writable variable to a read-only variable. If X is a writable variable, then $X?$ is called the read-only variable *corresponding* to X. Intuitively, a read-only variable can only be read from, but not written upon. It receives a non-variable value only when its corresponding writable variable receives a non-variable value.

The read-only operator has no effect when applied to a term other than a writable variable.

A *substitution element* is a pair of the form *Variable=Value*. A *substitution* is a set of substitution elements $\{V_1 = T_1, V_2 = T_2, \ldots, V_n = T_n\}$ such that $V_i \neq V_j$ if $i \neq j$, and V_i does not occur in T_j for any i and j.

The application of a substitution θ to a term S, denoted $S\theta$, is the term obtained by replacing every occurrence of a variable V by the term T, for every substitution element $V = T$ in θ.

A substitution θ *unifies* terms T_1 and T_2 if $T_1\theta = T_2\theta$. Two terms are *unifiable* if they have a unifying substitution. If two terms T_1 and T_2 are unifiable, then there exists a unique (up to renaming variables) substitution θ, called *the most general unifier* (mgu for short) of T_1 and T_2, with the following property: for any other unifying substitution θ_1 of T_1 and T_2, $T_1\theta_1$ is an instance of $T_1\theta$.

For example, the mgu of X and a is $\{X=a\}$. The mgu of X and Y is $\{X=Y\}$ (or $\{Y=X\}$). The mgu of $f(X,X)$ and $f(A,b)$ is $\{X=b,\ A=b\}$, and the mgu of $g(X,X)$ and $g(a,b)$ does not exist.

Intuitively, a unification that attempts to assign a read-only variable to a non-variable term suspends until the variable gets a value.

For example, the unification of $X?$ with a suspends; of $f(X,Y?)$ with $f(a,Z)$ succeeds, with unifier $\{X=a,\ Z=Y?\}$; of $g(X,f(X?))$ with $g(a,Z)$ succeeds with unifier $\{X=a,\ X?=a,\ Z=f(a)\}$. Considering the sort program above, the unification of $isort(In?,Out)$ with both $sort([X|Xs],Ys)$ and $isort([\ ],[\ ])$ suspends. However, as soon as $In?$ gets instantiated to $[3|In1]$, for example, by another process which has a writable occurrence of In, the unification of the $isort$ goal with the head of the first clause succeeds, and with the second clause fails.

Definition. A substitution θ *affects* a variable X if it contains a substitution element $X=T$.

Definition. Let T_1 and T_2 be two terms. We say that T_1 and T_2 are *read-only unifiable* if they have an mgu which does not affect any read-only variable. Let θ be such an mgu. The *read-only mgu* of T_1 and T_2 is obtained by adding to θ the substitution element $X?=T?$ for every substitution element $X=T$ in θ.

We say that the read-only unification of T_1 and T_2 *succeeds* if T_1 and T_2 have a read-only mgu. It *suspends* if T_1 and T_2 unify, but every mgu of them affects some read-only variable. It *fails* if T_1 and T_2 have no mgu.

Note that the definition of unifiability prevents a unification attempt to assign read-only variables. However, once the unification is successful, the read-only mgu is augmented to assign a read-only variable whose corresponding writable variable was assigned.

21.2.3 Processes, reductions, and computations

The basic active FCP object is a process. An FCP *process* is represented by a term of the form

$$p(T_1, T_2, \ldots, T_n).$$

A process can perform one basic operation, called *reduction*. A reduction is effected using a clause, called the *reducing clause*. To reduce with a clause, a copy of the clause with new variable names is made. The process unifies with the head of the reducing clause, solves its guard, and becomes the processes specified by its body. The unifying substitution is applied to the global environment and may affect values of variables also occurring in other processes. Depending on the type of the reducing clause, the reduced process terminates, changes its state, or, in the general case, forks into several parallel processes. A unit clause specifies termination, an iterative clause (with one goal in the body) a state change, and a general clause (with multiple goals in the body) specifies process forking.

A reduction of a process using a clause is *enabled* if reduction as defined above can proceed unhindered. It is *suspended* if the unification is suspended, or if it succeeds and any of the instantiated guard tests suspend. It *fails* if the process and the clause head do not unify, or if they unify and any of the guard tests fails.

A process is *enabled* if it has an enabled reduction. It is *suspended* if none of its reductions are enabled and at least one reduction is suspended. It *fails* if all of its reductions fail. If a process is continuously enabled, then eventually it will be reduced.

A process may share variables with other processes. A suspended process may become enabled when a read-only variable is assigned a value by some other process reduction. Similarly, a process reduction may enable other processes by assigning values to variables shared with them.

An FCP *computation* is a sequence of process reductions, starting from an initial process (or processes). A computation occurs in time. The current set of processes of a computation is called the *resolvent*. A computation *terminates* when the resolvent is empty. A computation is *suspended* when all the processes in the resolvent are suspended.

A computation may share variables with other computations and can thus interact with its environment. Hence a suspended computation may be resumed if some of its variables are assigned from outside.

21.2.4 Guard test predicates

Below is the list of guard test predicates of FCP. Logix implements several additional guard predicates for system interface purposes.

Unification:

X = Y	X and Y unify.
X ≠ Y	X and Y fail to unify.
X =?= Y	X and Y are identical (unify without assigning variables).

Type checking:

integer(X)	X is an integer.
real(X)	X is a real number.
number(X)	X is a number (either an integer or a real).
string(X)	X is a string.
constant(X)	X is a constant (either a number or a string or nil).
tuple(X)	X is a tuple.
list(X)	X is a list.
compound(X)	X is compound (either a tuple or a list).

Arithmetic:

X =:= Y	Arithmetic comparison of numeric expressions.
X > Y	ditto.
X >= Y	ditto.
X < Y	ditto.
X =< Y	ditto.

Term comparison:

X @< Y	X is less then Y according to the canonical ordering: numbers @< strings @< [ ] @< lists @< tuples. Variables are incomparable, so for two different variables X and Y tests X @< Y, $X \neq Y$ and $X=?=Y$ suspend. Strings are ordered lexically, tuples are ordered according to arity.

Meta-logical:

unknown(X)	the value of X is unknown.
known(X)	the value of X is known.

Control:

true	succeeds.
otherwise	succeeds when it is detected that all textually previous clauses fail.

Note: A test predicate suspends if it does not succeed but may succeed later.

21.2.5 Primitive procedures

The following are predefined FCP procedures.

Arithmetic:

X:=E   Evaluate the arithmetic expression E and unify the result with X. Provided operators: $+$, $-$, $*$, $/$, *mod*, *max*, *min*, *abs*, *integer*, *real*, *round* and bitwise *and*, *or*, *not*.

Term inspection:

arity(T,A)   The arity of the compound term T is unified with A (the arity of a list is 2 and of a constant is 0).

arg(N,T,A)   The N'th argument of a compound term T is unified with A (for a list $[X|Xs]$, X is its first argument and Xs is its second).

string_length(S,L)   The length of the string S is unified with L.

nth_char(S,N,C)   The N'th character of string S is unified with C.

string_hash(S,H)   The integer-valued hash-code of string S is unified with H.

Term creation:

make_tuple(N,T) T is a new tuple of arity N.

copy_skeleton(T,T1)   *T1* is a copy of the top level of the compound term T.

Type conversion:

string_to_dlist(String,ListOfAscii,E)   Convert characters of string *String* into an incomplete list of integers with tail E and unify it with *List*.

list_to_string(ListOfAscii,String)   Convert a list of integers to a string.

tuple_to_dlist(Tuple,List,E)   Convert a tuple to a difference-list *List* with tail E.

list_to_tuple(List,Tuple)   Convert a list to a tuple.

convert_to_integer(Value,Integer)   Convert a string or a number to an integer.

convert_to_real(Value,Real)   Convert a string or a number to a real.

convert_to_string(Value,String)   Convert a string or a number to a string.

A numeric value is converted to/from its visual representation as a string.
Note that *arity*, *arg*, and *copy_skeleton* are polymorphic: they work for lists and tuples.

21.2.6 Arithmetic expressions

Integer and real numbers may be mixed freely in arithmetic expressions, except that the arguments of the *mod* function must both be integers. The result of an operation is real if any of its arguments is real and integer if all arguments are integer. Division truncates its result if both arguments are integer.

The function *real(I)* may be used to convert an integer expression to a real value. The functions *integer(R)* and *round(R)* convert their argument to integer, either truncated toward zero or rounded away from zero; both fail in case of overflow of the integer range.

Guard arithmetic expressions may not include the operators *min*, *max*, *abs*, and *round*.

21.3 Getting Started with Logix

The basic cycle of program development under Logix is similar to other systems:

> Compose a program
> Repeat
> > Test the program
> > Modify the program
> Until the program works to your satisfaction.

For example, assume that we want to compose a program for reversing a list. Initially we compose the following program, using a text editor, and save it in the file *rev.cp*.

```
reverse([X|Xs],Ys) ←
      reverse(Xs?,Zs), append(Zs?,X,Ys).
reverse([ ],[ ]).

append([X|Xs],Ys,[X|Zs]) ←
      append(Xs?,Ys,Zs).
append([ ],Ys,Ys).
```

We start Logix, which prompts us with '@'. To test *append/3*, we issue to Logix the command:

>   @rev#append([1,2,3],[4,5],L1)

The module *rev* is compiled automatically, and following a successful compilation the computation of the goal starts:

⟨*1*⟩ *started*
⟨*1*⟩ *ended*
@

When computation ⟨*1*⟩ ends, and Logix is idle, it prompts again. Variable bindings are kept through the interaction with Logix. To see the result of the computation, i.e., the value of *L1*, we use the command:

@L1↑
$L1 = [1, 2, 3, 4, 5]$

Variables in the goal can be marked with ↑, to indicate that their value should be printed when available, as in:

@rev#append([a,b,c|Xs1],[d,e],L2↑)
⟨*2*⟩ *started*
$L2/1 = a$
$L2/2 = b$
$L2/3 = c$

which prints the stream of elements of *L2* as they are produced. The values of goal variables can be provided incrementally, for example:

@Xs1=[f,g,h|Xs2?]
$L2/4 = f$
$L2/5 = g$
$L2/6 = h$

@Xs2=[ ]
$L2/7 = d$
$L2/8 = e$
$L2/ = [\ ]$
⟨*2*⟩ *ended*
@

We turn to test *reverse*. For the goal:

@rev#reverse([a,b,c],L3↑)

we get the response:

⟨*3*⟩ *started*
⟨*3*⟩ *failed(append(c, b, _))*

which indicates that the specified *append* goal has failed. The goal has failed since no clause unifies with it. *append* expects a list as its first argument. A look at the code shows that *reverse* called *append* with the wrong arguments. To fix the *rev* module, we give the command:

@edit(rev)

which indicates to Logix that we plan to edit this file, suspends Logix, and brings us back to Unix, where we enter our favorite text editor and edit *rev.cp*. We fix the recursive clause of *reverse* to be:

reverse([X|Xs],Ys) ←
    reverse(Xs?,Zs), append(Zs?,[X],Ys).

return to Logix, and retry the program:

@rev#reverse([a,b,c|Xs3],L3↑)
⟨*4*⟩ *started*

we do not get any output, since *reverse* starts producing its output only after the input list is completed. However, we can inspect the current state of the computation, i.e., the resolvent:

@resolvent
⟨*4*⟩*goal-1 = reverse(_?, _)*
⟨*4*⟩*goal-2 = append(_?, [c], _)*
⟨*4*⟩*goal-3 = append(_?, [b], _)*
⟨*4*⟩*goal-4 = append(_?, [a], _)*
@

which suspends the computation and shows that there are three *append* processes and one *reverse* process suspended. If we wish to observe parts of the computation in greater detail, we can do that. The command

@debug(1)

invokes the debugger for process number 1. We can supply it with further input:

@Xs3=[d,e|Xs4?]

Inspecting the resolvent causes a computation to suspend. The command

@resume

resumes it and initiates the following debugging session:

⟨*4*⟩ *rev#reverse([d, e| _?], _) ←*
    reverse([e| _?], _), append(_?, [d], _)?
⟨*4*⟩ *rev#reverse([e| _?], _) ←*
    reverse(_?, _), append(_?, [e], _)?
@

The computation is blocked. We can close the input stream now:

@Xs4=[ ]

L3/1 = e

⟨*4*⟩ *rev#reverse*([ ], [ ]).

⟨*4*⟩ *rev#append*([ ], [*e*], [*e*]).

⟨*4*⟩ *rev#append*([*e*], [*d*], [*e*| _]) ←
     append([ ], [*d*], _)?

L3/2 = d

L3/3 = c

L3/4 = b

L3/5 = a

⟨*4*⟩ *rev#append*([ ], [*d*], [*d*]).

L3/ = [ ]

⟨*4*⟩ *ended*

@.

21.4 The User Interface

21.4.1 Interacting with Logix

Commands are typed to a command interpreter. A prompt '@' appears whenever the system becomes idle. A command may be typed when the system is not idle — a prompt is prefixed to the echoed command to indicate that the system is responding.

Several commands may be entered on a single line, separated by commas. To continue a command over several lines, end each line except the last with "%".

There are several ways to exit from Logix:

⟨control⟩ Z
> Suspend Logix and return to the Unix shell.

⟨control⟩ C
> Abort Logix.

⟨control⟩ G
> Graceful shut-down. Deadlocked processes appear in the post-mortem dump, and some useful statistics are printed.

⟨control⟩ \
> Unconditional termination. All active and suspended processes appear in the post-mortem dump.

21.4.2 The binding environment

The scope of symbolic variable names entered interactively (or input from a file — see the input command in Section 21.7.5) is an entire session. In other words, a variable name used more than once, even in different commands, represents the same term. An exception is the anonymous variable name "$-$", which is unbound (and unique) for each use.

The following commands relate to the binding environment:

X↑	Display the current value of variable X. Variables annotated with ↑ can occur inside commands with the same effect.
↑	Display the current values of all variables used so far.
unbind(X)	Unbind variable X.
unbind	Discard all variable bindings.

21.4.3 Line editing

Logix supports many of the line-editing features of *tcsh* shell under Unix. They are documented in Appendix 21.3.

21.5 Computations

A computation is the basic unit of execution, control, and debugging in Logix. A computation can be started, suspended, resumed, aborted, and inspected. Furthermore, pieces of the computation can be debugged: they can be stepped through, can be set with breakpoints, etc.

Each computation is numbered; its number is displayed in angled brackets, e.g., ⟨3⟩.

21.5.1 Events

A computation can go through a sequence of events, which are described in its events stream. Possible events include:

started
    The computation has started. The first event in a computation.
suspended
    The computation has been suspended.
resumed
    The suspended computation has been resumed.
aborted
    The computation has been aborted. A terminal event.
ended
    The computation ended successfully. A terminal event.
failed(Module#Goal,ErrorCode)

Goal in *Module* has failed, due to error *ErrorCode*. The failed process is extracted from the computation, and the computation is suspended. The computation (without the failed process) can then be resumed or aborted at the user's discretion.

21.5.2 Computation management

The following commands relate to computation management. Their description uses the following conventions. Output arguments of commands are annotated with a postfix ↑. Arguments are assumed to be omitted from the right. If an output argument is omitted, its value is displayed on the screen.

The *No* argument refers to computation ⟨*No*⟩. If a *No* input argument is omitted, the current (most recently started) computation is assumed.

The *Module* argument refers to a module name. If it is omitted, the current (most recently mentioned) module name is assumed.

The constant *all* can be given instead of a number argument to affect all computations or all processes, as appropriate.

The full version of the commands is used mainly from inside computations via the shell server, as explained in Section 21.7 on system services; most output and default arguments are omitted in interactive use.

Invocation:

> start(Module#Goal,No↑,Events↑,Ok↑)
>> Start a computation of *Goal* in *Module* (modules are explained below), unify *No* with its number, and unify *Events* with its stream of events.
>
> Module#Goal
>> Same as above, where ⟨*No*⟩ and *Events* are displayed on the screen.
>
> #Goal
>> Same as above, where the current *Module* is assumed.

Inspection:

> state(No,Goal↑,Events↑,Ok↑)
>> Unify *Goal* with the initial goal of computation ⟨*No*⟩, which includes values assigned so far to its output variables.
>>
>> Unify *Events* with the list of events of the computation so far.
>
> events(No,Events↑,Ok↑)
>> Unify *Events* with the stream of events of the computation.
>
> resolvent(No,Resolvent↑,Ok↑)
>> Suspend computation ⟨*No*⟩, and unify *Resolvent* with a snapshot of its resolvent.

Manipulation:

    suspend(No,Ok↑)

        Suspend computation ⟨*No*⟩.

    resume(No,Ok↑)

        Resume suspended computation ⟨*No*⟩.

    abort(No,Ok↑)

        Abort computation ⟨*No*⟩.

        "suspend", "resume", and "abort" without arguments affect the current computation.

    extract(ProcessNo,No,(Module#Goal)↑,Ok↑)

        Extract *Goal* in *Module* with serial number *ProcessNo* from computation ⟨*No*⟩. Process numbers can be extracted by inspecting the resolvent.

    add(Module#Goal,No,Ok↑)

        Add *Goal* in *Module* to computation ⟨*No*⟩.

Debugging:

    debug(Module#Goal,No↑,Events↑,Ok↑)

        Start a computation of *Goal* in *Module* under the debugger, unify *No* with its number.

    debug(ProcessNo,No,Ok↑)

        Debug process number *ProcessNo* in computation ⟨*No*⟩.

        Process numbers can be extracted by inspecting the resolvent.

        debug(ProcessNo) debugs *ProcessNo* in the current computation.

Performance:

    time(Module#Goal,Timing↑,No↑,Events↑,Ok↑)

        Unify *Timing* with timing information about the computation of *Goal* in *Module*.

        Interactive computations cannot be timed with this command.

    rpc(Module#Goal,Rpc↑,No↑,Events↑,Ok↑)

        Provides a crude measure of the parallelism in a computation, which is the average number of process reductions in one emulator cycle.

        The measure is crude since there could be dependencies between reductions in the same cycle, which may prevent their true parallel execution.

    profile(Module#Goal,Profile↑,No↑,Events↑,Ok↑)

        Unify Profile with profiling information about the computation of *Goal* in *Module*.

Environment:

    The current computation and module can be queried and set.

computation(New,Old↑)

    ⟨*Old*⟩ used to be the current computation.

    Set the current computation to be ⟨*New*⟩.

    (The current computation can be found with the command "computation(X,X)", or just "computation").

service(New,Old↑)

    Old used to be the current module (or, in general, service. See Section 21.7 on system services).

    Set the current module to be *New*.

21.6 Modules and Their Compilation

A module is the basic unit of compilation in Logix. A module is a set of procedures. As a convention, the source of a module *foo* resides in the file *foo.cp*. When compiled, the binary form of that module is saved in the file *foo.bin*.

A module source text may begin with an optional module declaration, whose format is explained below. The procedures in a module can be in any order. Clauses of a procedure should be grouped together. A module is self-contained in the sense that it defines all procedures that it calls, with the exception of remote procedure calls and primitive procedures. Primitive procedures were listed in Section 21.2.5.

21.6.1 Remote procedure calls

A remote procedure call is a goal in the body of a clause of the form

    ModuleName#Goal

For example, to reduce the process *isort(In?,Out)* defined in module *sort*, use the call:

    sort#isort(In?,Out).

This call indicates that *isort(In,Out)* is executed with the procedure defined in module *sort*. Undefined and multiply defined procedures in a module cause compilation errors. Undefined remote procedure calls cause runtime errors.

The special call *merge(Stream)* is explained in Section 21.7. Two special remote procedure calls *clause(A,B)* and *execute(A)* are used for writing meta-interpreters, as explained in Section 21.9.

21.6.2 Module management

The following commands relate to module management.

compile(Module,Options,OK↑)
> Invalidate the current binary of *Module*, if it exists, and (re)compile it.

edit(Modules)
> *Modules* can be a module name or a list of module names.
> Invalidate the current binaries of *Modules*, and suspend
> Logix. The modules are recompiled next time they are called.

lint(Module,Options,OK↑)
> Performs various checks on *Module*.

reload(Module,Options,OK↑)
> Reload the binary of *Module*.
> Options are for the compiler if no binary is available.

If the *Options* argument is omitted, default options are used.

If the *Module* argument is omitted, the current module is used.

Note that if a module that was not mentioned in an *edit* command is edited, it must be compiled explicitly to keep its binary consistent with the source.

21.6.3 The module declaration

The compiler can be directed using a module declaration to achieve various tradeoffs between functionality, compile time, and runtime performance.

A module can begin with declarations, identified by a prefix '–':

– AttributeName(Value).

The list of attributes of module *ModuleName* can be found by executing the remote procedure call:

ModuleName#attributes(List).

The following are meaningful attributes:

The *export* attribute

– export(ExportList).

where *ExportList* is a list of *Name/Arity*. The export attribute indicates the procedures in a module that can be called from the outside. If *ExportList*='all', or the attribute is omitted, then all procedures are exported. If the attribute is present, the compiler detects dead code (procedures that are not reachable from the exported procedures) and undefined exported procedures.

The *mode* attribute

– mode(Mode).

where *Mode* is one of [*interpret, control, interrupt, failsafe, trust*]. The default mode is *interpret*. A process executing interpret-mode code is responsive to all the commands mentioned above: it can be inspected, debugged, suspended, resumed, aborted, and if it fails it announces this and suspends the computation. In addition, procedures in an interpret-mode module can be meta-interpreted, as explained in Section 21.9.

Modules can be compiled in modes other than *interpret* to increase performance, at the expense of control, as follows.

control
> Pros: 3 times faster in runtime than interpreted.
> Cons: Processes cannot be debugged or interpreted.

interrupt
> Pros: 5% to 10% faster in runtime than controlled.
> Cons: In addition, the state of a process cannot be inspected.

failsafe
> Pros: 10% to 20% faster in runtime than controlled.
> Cons: In addition, a process cannot be suspended or aborted.

trust
> Pros: 10% to 30% faster in runtime than controlled.
> Cons: In addition, the failure of a process aborts Logix.

There is also a significant improvement in compilation time and code size for the less-controlled modes of execution.

The *include* attribute

– include(ListOfModuleNames).

where *ListOfModuleNames* is a list of module names. This indicates to the compiler to include in the current module all procedures in *ListOfModuleNames* reachable from the exported procedures of this module. Note that a module can export procedures defined in included modules, and that all procedures are compiled in the mode of the current module.

The result of the inclusion is that remote procedure calls between the current module and the modules in *ListOfModuleNames* become local procedure calls. A remote procedure call is much slower then a local procedure call. Hence the extra overhead in compile time is justified when runtime performance is necessary.

<u>Other attributes</u>

The compiler adds two attributes automatically:

       – path(AbsolutePathOfSource).
       – date(DateOfSource).

They can be queried using the *attributes* call and used to verify the validity of the binary with respect to the source. Other attributes can be included, without affecting the compiler, for example:

       – name(ModuleName).
       – author(AuthorName).

21.7 System Services

The Logix system is a collection of communicating servers. The system is connected to a directory. All modules residing in the connected directory are implicitly defined services of the system. They are opened dynamically when called. If the binary of a module that is called is available, then it is loaded and activated, or else the module is compiled.

A *Request* from *Service* is called:

    Service#Request.

As is apparent from the syntax, a module is in fact a kind of a server, which serves requests to execute procedures which it exports, or interpret procedures which it defines.

To send a stream of calls *Stream* to a service *ServiceName*, use the call

    system#ServiceName#merge(Stream).

The following are services provided by Logix.

21.7.1 System

The system server maintains the set of services available. It can serve the following requests:

    system#services(Services↑)
        Unify *Services* with the set of services available.
    system#open_service(Name,Stream,Options,Ok↑)
        Define a service with name *Name*.
        Route requests to it to *Stream*, according to *Options*.
        For casual users *Options*=[ ].

system#rename_service(Old,New,Ok↑)
> Rename service *Old* to be *New*.

system#close_service(Service,Ok↑)
> Close the stream to *Service*, and remove it from the system. Processes which have obtained access to the service previously can still use it.

21.7.2 Shell

The shell server accepts commands that can be given interactively.

shell#Request
> Where *Request* is any command that can be given interactively, except binding environment commands.

The shell understands several other commands:

X=Y	Unify *X* with *Y*.
X:=Y	Evaluate the arithmetic expression *Y*, unifying the result with *X*.
hi	The Logix system user-friendliness facility. The shell responds with *hello*.
macros	Add the commands defined via macros in file *shellrc.cp* to the list of shell commands. See Appendix 21.4 for macros format.

21.7.3 Screen

The screen server can serve the following requests:

screen#display(Term,Options)
> Display *Term* on the screen, according to *Options*.

screen#display_stream(TermsStream,Options)
> Display *TermsStream*, one term per line as they become available, according to *Options*.

screen#ask(Term,Answer↑,Options)
> Display the query *Term*, according to *Options*, and read *Answer*.

The *Options* argument can be omitted, and then the default options are assumed. *Options* is a list of terms of the form *Control*(*Arguments*) or *Attribute*(*Value*). *Attributes* are in [*type,read,depth,length*].
Default values of attributes can be inspected and modified with the request:

screen#option(Attribute,New,Old↑)
> Modify default option *Attribute* from *Old* to *New*.

Control options are used to control the time and format of display. *Controls* are:

known(X)
>   Wait until *X* is assigned a non-variable value before printing.

close(L,R)
>   After printing, unify *L* and *R*.

prefix(T)
>   Print the term *T* before (each) *Term*, separated by one space.

list
>   Treat (each) Term as a list of terms to be printed without separation — no automatic final line-feed is added.

Values of option attributes are described below. The format of their description is:

>   *Attribute*
>   >   *Value*
>   >   >   *Meaning.*

The *type* attribute determines the mode of display of variables.

type
>   freeze
>   >   Variables are printed as "_",
>   >   read-only variables as "_?".
>
>   ground
>   >   The term is printed after it is ground.
>
>   namevars
>   >   The term is frozen and variables are printed by name or, if anonymous, numbered as *_Xnnn* or *_Xnnn?*. Identical variables are given identical names.
>
>   (default is "freeze").

The *read* attribute is relevant to queries only. It specifies what input is read by the query, and what is returned to answer.

read
>   char
>   >   One character is read from input (the keyboard) and converted to a string.
>
>   string
>   >   One line is read from input, returned as a string ending with the line-feed character (*ascii⟨lf⟩*).
>
>   chars
>   >   One line is read from input, returned as a difference list of *ascii* characters (small integers) followed by *ascii* characters

$\langle space \rangle$, ".", $\langle lf \rangle$.
(default is char).

Terms are printed only to a limited depth, after which the arity of the term is printed, and the sub-terms are not examined. Lists are inspected only to a given length. Only a few head and tail elements are printed, along with the number of omitted elements if the whole list was examined. The attributes which control this are:

depth
>integer (default is 8)
>>depth of nesting of tuples/lists.

length
>integer (default is 20)
>>maximum length of list examined.

21.7.4 File

The file server interfaces to the Unix file system. It provides the basic file utilities needed by the user.

At any given time the server is connected to one directory, called the current directory. Initially the current directory is the directory the user was connected to when invoking Logix.

The file server can serve the following requests:

file#cd(New,Old↑)
>Change connected directory from *Old* to *New*.

file#get_file(Name,Contents,Options,Ok↑)
>Read the file *Name* and return the string *Contents*.
>*Ok* becomes "true" or "not_found".
>*Options* currently is [ ].

file#put_file(Name,Contents,Options,Ok↑)
>Write the *Contents* into the file *Name*.
>*Ok* becomes "true" or "write_error" when writing completes.
>*Contents* can be a constant or a stream of constants.
>*Options* is currently [ ].

21.7.5 Keyboard

The keyboard server maintains access to the keyboard input stream. It serves the request:

keyboard#input(Object,Option)
>If *Option=file*, treat the contents of the file with name *Object* as if

it was typed from the keyboard.

If *Option=string*, treat the string *Object* as if it was typed from
the keyboard.

In both cases wait until Logix is idle before processing the next
command line.

If the *Option* parameter is omitted, the default is *Option=file*.

This service is useful for driving Logix during long performance analysis runs or
for canned demonstrations.

The file *.logix* is automatically input when Logix starts.

21.8 The Debugger

The debugger is a meta-interpreter which prints its goals as it reduces them
and asks for directions on how to continue.

Commands for invoking the debugger were shown in Section 21.5.2.

The debugger displays each reduction and prompts the user for a one character response:

User response	Action
a	abort the computation;
b	prompt for spy-points (see below);
h	help;
s	skip, i.e., debug the derived goals but don't display their reductions;
x	execute the derived goals without debugging;
u	unleash the trace — execute and print reductions, but don't query;
⟨lf⟩	suspend the computation;
other	step this goal (including ⟨*space*⟩, etc.).

Skip and unleash are bounded by a debugger parameter that can be set. Initially
it is 25.

After typing a *b* response, the user is prompted ... : *debugger?* – reply with
one or more of the following requests:

Name+Arity	Set a spy-point on the procedure *Name* with arity *Arity*.
Name–Arity	Stop spying procedure *Name* with arity *Arity*.
list	List all procedures for which spy-points are set.
skip(New,Old↑)	Change the skip/unleash parameter from *Old* to *New*.

The user may enter several requests in response to one prompt, separating them with commas; e.g., the response *project+2*, *on+2*, *not–1*, *list* sets spy-points on *project/2* and *on/2*, clears the spy-point on *not/1*, and lists the resultant set of spy-points.

Whenever the debugger reduces a spied goal, it prints a message and waits for a response, even if the goal would otherwise be skipped or traced.

21.9 Meta-Interpreters

Several parts of the Logix system, notably the debugger and the profiler, are written as enhanced FCP meta-interpreters. Logix supports user defined meta-interpreters as well. A plain FCP meta-interpreter is shown below:

```
reduce(Module,true).
reduce(Module,(A,B)) ←
    reduce(Module,A?),
    reduce(Module,B?).
reduce(Module,Module1#A) ←
    reduce(Module1?,A?).
reduce(Module,A) ←
    otherwise |
    Module#clause(A,B),
    reduce(Module,B?).
```

Each module (compiled in interpret mode, which is the default) serves the *clause(A,B)* request, whose meaning is: Goal *A* can be reduced using the clause $A \leftarrow G|B$ in *Module*. If *A* is reduced by a unit clause, then *B* is *true*.

Other services serve *clause(A,B)* with meaning: Goal *A* can be reduced by an exported procedure of the service, and *B* is true.

In order to resume normal (uninterpreted) execution of non-exported procedures, use the remote procedure call *Module#execute(Goal)*.

21.10 Utilities

Logix provides several utilities, which can be accessed via remote procedure calls.

21.10.1 Stream

This module provides access to the fast multi-way merge and to the indexed distribute. It exports the procedures *merger/2* and *distributor/2*.

```
stream#merger(In,Out)
```

Each term which appears on the *In* stream is copied to the *Out* stream, except for the term *merge(OtherIn)*. In that case terms from the *OtherIn* stream are also copied to the *Out* stream.

The merger remains open until all merged in-streams are closed (end-of-stream is reached) — then the *Out* stream is closed.

Each service in the system has a merger filter in front of it, hence can serve a merge request.

stream#distributor(In,Tuple)

Tuple is an *n*-tuple or a list of *n* output streams.

In is a stream of requests of the form:

   I # Term

For each such request, *Term* is copied to the *I*'th stream (where *I* is an integer between 1 and *n*). When *In* is closed, all of the output streams are closed.

21.10.2 Utils

This module is a general utilities package. It exports seven procedures — *chars_to_lines/2*, *append_strings/2*, *evaluate/2*, *freeze_term/3*, *ground/2*, *ground_stream/2*, *integer_to_dlist/3*.

chars_to_lines(Chars,Lines)

Splits the ascii stream *Chars* into strings which are returned in the list *Lines*. A new string is started at each ascii $\langle lf \rangle$ or $\langle cr \rangle$ in the character stream.

append_strings(Strings,String)

Strings is a list of strings, which are concatenated and returned in *String*.

evaluate(Expression,Result)

Evaluate the arithmetic term *Expression*, returning integer *Result*.

ground(X,Y)

Wait until *X* is ground and then unify *X* and *Y*.

ground_stream(X,Y)

Treat *X* as a stream, doing a "ground" for each element in turn, unifying the element with the corresponding element in *Y*.

integer_to_dlist(I,List,Tail)

Convert the integer *I* to a list of ascii characters in *List*, ending with *Tail*.

21.11 Bugs

Several features in this manual are not fully implemented, or are implemented differently than specified. A list of such mismatches is provided with the Logix system release. Some deeper problems are mentioned below.

Guard calls in a clause are executed from left to right, rather then in parallel. This makes a difference only when the unification guard predicate $=/2$ is used, since it is the only one which may produce bindings.

A more serious problem is caused by a guard test predicate that attempts to suspend on an argument of a structure in the head. In case the structure is unified with a goal variable, its arguments are local. If a guard suspends on one of them, the reduction with this clause is not enabled, therefore the binding to the goal variable is not done; but in that case the guard would have no variables to suspend upon. This situation causes a *suspension on a local variable* error. There exists a solution to this problem, but it is not yet implemented.

Some system services (particularly those which are not documented in this report) are fragile, and fail, failing the entire system, if they receive unexpected messages or parameters.

A process which fails while executing in a trusted module aborts the entire system. The symptom is a post-mortem dump which begins:

Process Failed
Process: .... .

The ellipsis represents the process which failed, including its arguments, followed on subsequent lines by further post-mortem information which may be useful in debugging the failure. Goals which appear in the post-mortem dump include the expanded code and additional arguments produced by the compiler.

When some process becomes an orphan (independent of all active processes), post-mortem information appears following normal termination, beginning with the diagnostic:

Suspended Procedures:
scanning the heap at *xxxxxx* ...
scanned the heap, *ppp* processes found, *mmm* processes missing!

The processes that were found are printed on subsequent lines. The missing processes were orphaned and were subsequently garbage collected.

The system garbage collector, a part of the emulator, announces its activity by temporarily suspending all other activity, writing (GC) to the screen and when it has finished, erasing the message. This may have a peculiar looking effect if it happens near the end of a line which is being printed.

The overall capacity of the heap can be exceeded. This is diagnosed, and the system terminates.

To run with a larger heap, you may enter the command:

  logix −h*number*

where *number* is the size of storage needed in kilo-bytes. The maximum possible size of storage is a Unix system parameter.

Tokenizing rules for sequences of special characters are based on Edinburgh Prolog conventions and may disagree with intuition. Appendix 21.1 presents the rules for token production and some common mistakes which are detected by the parser.

Constants beginning with underscore '_' are reserved for system use.

Variables in a call to := can be bound at runtime to integers but not to general arithmetic expressions. To evaluate arithmetic expressions generated at runtime, use the utility *evaluate*.

Dynamic remote procedure calls (where the module name is a compiler-time variable) are extremely inefficient. To write serious meta-interpreters, it is advisable to merge a stream into the interpreted module and send *clause* requests explicitly.

Acknowledgements

The Logix system was developed, and is being developed, by many contributors, both members of the project and visitors. We would like to thank Erez Altschueler, Eli Biham, Michael Codish, Jim Crammond, Nir Friedman, Jacob Levy, Yossi Lichtenstein, Tony Kusalik, Norm McCain, Colin Mierowsky, Shmuel Safra, Daniel Szoke, Steve Taylor, Phil Thrift, David Weinbaum and Iraj Yaacobian for their contribution.

Appendix 21.1: Token Rules

The following (modified) BNF specifies the rules for token production in FCP. The full grammar of FCP is based on these rules.

        ⟨token⟩ ::= ⟨variable⟩ |
            ⟨number⟩ |
            ⟨string⟩
        ⟨variable⟩ ::= ⟨upper_case_letter⟩ |
            ⟨variable⟩ ⟨letter_or_digit⟩⟩
        ⟨upper_case_letter⟩ ::= _ A ... Z
        ⟨lower_case_letter⟩ ::= $ a ... z
        ⟨letter_or_digit⟩ ::= ⟨letter⟩ |

⟨digit⟩ |
⟨letter⟩ ::= ⟨upper_case_letter⟩ |
⟨lower_case_letter⟩
⟨digit⟩ ::= 0 ... 9
⟨string⟩ ::= ⟨named_string⟩ |
⟨operator_string⟩ |
⟨quoted_string⟩
⟨named_string⟩ ::= ⟨lower_case_letter⟩ |
⟨named_string⟩ ⟨letter_or_digit⟩
⟨operator_string⟩ ::= ⟨self_delimiting_operator⟩ |
⟨multi_graph_operator⟩
⟨self_delimiting_operator⟩ ::= (,) [|] { } ¯ ! ↑ * +
⟨multi_graph_operator⟩ ::= ⟨concatenating_operator⟩ |
⟨multi_graph_operator⟩ ⟨concatenating_operator⟩
⟨concatenating_operator⟩ ::= < = > / − \ : ; . ? @ # &
⟨operator⟩ ::= ⟨self_delimiting_operator⟩ |
⟨concatenating_operator⟩
⟨quoted_string⟩ ::= ' ⟨single_quotable⟩ ' |
" ⟨double_quotable⟩ "
⟨single_quotable⟩ ::= ⟨not_single_quote⟩ |
⟨single_quotable⟩ ⟨ not_single_quote⟩
⟨not_single_quote⟩ ::= " |
" |
⟨not_quote⟩
⟨double_quotable⟩ ::= ⟨not_double_quote⟩ |
⟨double_quotable⟩ ⟨not_double_quote⟩
⟨not_double_quote⟩ ::= ' |
"" |
⟨not_quote⟩
⟨not_quote⟩ ::= ⟨letter_or_digit⟩ |
⟨operator⟩ |
⟨space⟩.
⟨number⟩ ::= ⟨integer⟩ | ⟨real⟩
⟨integer⟩ ::= ⟨digit⟩ | ⟨integer⟩⟨digit⟩
⟨real⟩ ::= ⟨integer⟩ · ⟨integer⟩

The rules relating to the comment operators %, /*, */ have been omitted.
Note that ⟨space⟩ separates tokens, except within a quoted string.

⟨concatenating_operators⟩ which are not separated by ⟨space⟩ produce a ⟨multi_graph_operator⟩, which may not parse.

Some common mistakes which produce parsing diagnostics:

A?\B   is tokenized   [A , ?\ , B]
I--J   is tokenized   [I , -- , J]
X:=-7+Y   is tokenized   [X , :=- , 7 , + , Y].

These should be re-written:

A? \ B   or   (A?)\B
I - -J   or   I-(-J)
X:= -7+Y   or   X:=(-7)+Y   or   X:=(-7+Y).

Appendix 21.2: List of Operators

Operator	Position	Meaning	Priority	Associative
←	infix	if	1200	no
|	infix	commit/cons	1100	right
;	infix		1100	right
,	infix	argument/goal separator	1000	right
@	infix		720	left
#	infix,prefix		710	right
:=	infix	arithmetic assignment	700	no
=?=	infix	recursive equality	700	no
≠	infix	recursive inequality	700	no
=:=	infix	arithmetic equality	700	no
==	infix	top level equality	700	no
\=	infix	top level inequality	700	no
#<	infix	canonical ordering	700	no
=	infix	unify	700	no
<	infix	less	700	no
>	infix	greater	700	no
≤	infix	less or equal	700	no
≥	infix	greater or equal	700	no
+	infix,prefix	plus	500,220	left
−	infix,prefix	minus	500,220	no
↑	suffix		500	no
*	infix	times	400	left
/	infix	divide	400	no
div	infix	divide	400	no
\/	infix	bit or	250	left
/\	infix	bit and	240	left
\	infix	mod	300	no

mod	infix	mod	300	no
~	prefix	bit complement	220	no
∧	suffix	display	210	no

Note ≠ is represented by the tri-graph =\=.

Appendix 21.3: Line Editing Commands

In the following, "point" refers to the position in a line represented by the left edge of the keyboard cursor. It is always between characters, never on them.

Back-Space	(or Delete) deletes the character to the left of point.
⟨control⟩ D	deletes the character to the right of point.
⟨control⟩ A	moves point to the beginning of a line.
⟨control⟩ E	moves point to the end of a line.
⟨control⟩ U	kills all input to the left of point.
⟨control⟩ K	kills all input to the right of point.
⟨control⟩ B	moves point left one character in a line.
⟨control⟩ F	moves point right one character in a line.
⟨control⟩ T	swaps the characters just to the left and right of point.
⟨control⟩ R	re-display the line; point is unaffected.

In addition to the intra-line editing functions described above, Logix remembers up to 20 lines and up to 10 partial lines. Remembered lines can be recalled by:

⟨control⟩ P	recalls the previous line (circularly); repeat to step backward.
⟨control⟩ N	recalls the next line (circularly); repeat to step forward.
⟨control⟩ I	clears the remembered line record.
⟨control⟩ X ⟨control⟩ P	recalls previous killed partial line (circularly); (repeat ⟨*control*⟩ *P* to step backward); see ⟨*control*⟩ *K*, ⟨*control*⟩ *U*.
⟨control⟩ X ⟨control⟩ N	(repeat ⟨*control*⟩ *N* to step forward) recalls next killed partial line (circularly) —
⟨control⟩ X ⟨control⟩ I	clears the remembered partial line record.

Appendix 21.4: Initial *shellrc.cp*

```
/* User Shell default macros */
    - export([expand/2]).
```

```
/*
    expand/2
```

Expands macro commands.

```
    expand(Goal, Commands\Commands1) ←
        Goal is a command.
        Commands\Commands1 is a difference list of commands to the
        system-macro processor and the user shell.
```

Goals which are not expanded here are forwarded for system-macro expansion
and user shell processing.
```
*/
```

```
    expand(hi, Commands\Commands) ←
        screen#output(shell, hello).
```

```
    expand(macros,[reload(shellrc)|Commands]\Commands).
    expand(Goal, [Goal|Commands]\Commands) ←
        otherwise | true.
```

Appendix 21.5: An Example of Defining and Using a Monitor

We show how a *counter* monitor can be defined and implemented.

```
/*
 * counter_monitor.cp
 *
 * maintain a named value.
 */
-export([counter/1]).
-mode(interrupt).
-author('     $Author: mh $').
-revision('    $Revision: 1.1 $').
-rcs_date('    $Date: 86/07/04 13:50:16 $').
-rcs_source('  $Source: /users/mh/RCS/counter_monitor.cp,v $').
```

```
counter(In) ← counter(In?,0).

counter([attributes(   [ name(counter),
                         author(mh),
                         monitor,
                         export([up/1,down/1,value/1])
                       ])
              |In,]
              Value).
counter([up(N)|In],Value) ←
       Value1 := Value + N,
       counter(In?,Value1).
counter([down(N)|In],Value) ←
       Value1 := Value – N,
       counter(In?,Value1).
counter([ ],_Value).
counter([value(Value)|In],Value) ←
       counter(In,Value).
counter([X|In],Value) ←
       otherwise |
       error#error(counter,dont_understand,X),
       counter(In?,Value).
```

To start counter 'first':

```
counter_monitor#counter(CounterInput1?)
system#open_service(first,CounterInput1,[ ],true)
```

To start counter 'second':

```
counter_monitor#counter(CounterInput2?)
system#open_service(second,CounterInput2,[ ],true)
```

Using monitors:

Example Command	Explanation
first#up(5)	– add 5 to counter 'first'
first#down(1)	– decrement 'first' by 1
second#value(X)	– read value of counter 'second'
second#up(17)	– add 17 to counter 'second'

Chapter 22

A Layered Method for Process and Code Mapping

Stephen Taylor, Evyatar Av-Ron and Ehud Shapiro

The Weizmann Institute of Science

Abstract

The mapping problem has been shown to be computationally equivalent to the graph isomorphism problem; as such it is unlikely that a polynomial time algorithm exists for its solution. Practical algorithms of general applicability and low computational complexity have not been found and are unlikely to appear.

This paper describes a layered method to support specialized process and code mapping strategies. The method separates the task of mapping a problem to a virtual machine from the task of mapping a virtual machine to a physical machine. It allows multiple virtual machines to execute concurrently and many applications to run on a single virtual machine.

The method is in use on a parallel implementation of Flat Concurrent Prolog which runs on an Intel iPSC Hypercube; for concreteness the description is based on this implementation.

22.1 Background

The usefulness of parallel architectures has been limited by the lack of a practical methodology for mapping computational structures into the physical machine. Two major problems, partitioning and assignment, have received considerable attention in the literature. The partitioning problem involves specifying the set of processes which implement an algorithm, on a specific architecture, in the most efficient manner. The assignment, or mapping problem, involves assigning processes to physical processors; it is complicated by the need to make tradeoffs in the organization of communication.

Bokhari (1981) has shown that the mapping problem is computationally equivalent to the graph isomorphism problem; as such it is unlikely that a polynomial time algorithm exists for its solution. Stone (1977) and Stone and Bokhari (1978) have described methods for formulating the assignment problem as a network flow problem; an assignment is obtained by maximizing the flow through the network. The techniques are appropriate to small numbers of processors and assume that execution and communication costs are known a priori.

A comprehensive study of the mapping problem for SW-Banyan networks has been conducted by DeGroot (1981). Analytical solutions are given for some simple specific computational structures (e.g., broadcast tree, pipeline) but heuristic methods are suggested for more general structures. The latter methods, termed partitioning and node grouping, are of limited practicality; the former can be applied to a restricted class of structures while the latter appear to be NP-complete. Lint and Agerwala (1981) describe a number of algorithms for partitioning based on the notions of clustering and computation-communication tradeoffs. Heuristic assignment algorithms are described which are based on iterative improvement of communication costs. The results indicate that using communication costs as a guideline improves efficiency for some algorithms but it is unclear if this is a general maxim.

A more general technique has been developed by Steele (1985). Partitioning of an application into a set of communicating processes is assumed to be carried out by the programmer. Static physical placement of processes to processors is achieved by simulated annealing. This technique is a variation of iterative assignment which generates trial mappings and examines their *cost*; mappings with low cost are accepted. The process continues according to an *annealing schedule* until all trials are of higher cost than the best currently achieved. The method produces reasonably good solutions for a variety of logical to physical graph embeddings; it requires considerable computational cost and appears most suitable for programs which need be compiled infrequently. The method does not appear suited to applications which are irregular or highly dynamic; algorithms for dynamic process structures have not been studied extensively.

Algorithms to solve the mapping problem which are of general practicality and low computational complexity have not evolved and seem unlikely to appear. The advantage of a general purpose strategy is that it relieves the programmer of a supposedly difficult task; unfortunately it also removes the ability to use application specific information and thus may produce less efficient solutions. Since mapping algorithms are generally viewed as part of the compiler, important decisions are hidden from the user. An alternative approach is to provide simple,

versatile and efficient support for specialized mapping strategies; these provide
the opportunity to optimize performance by variations in the mapping strategy.

22.2 Concepts

This paper provides a layered method to construct practical mapping schemes
based on the familiar notions of *virtual machine* and *shell*. The layers that can
be identified when mapping a problem to a physical machine are shown in Figure
22.1.

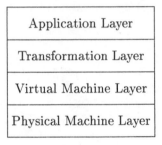

Figure 22.1: System layers

Application layer

The application layer provides a user interface for programming. It consists
of a process oriented language which includes some form of mapping construct
or annotation. The mapping constructs provide a mechanism to map processes
to processing elements in some convenient virtual machine structure. The user is
responsible for problem partitioning.

Transformation layer

The transformation layer exists to transform mapping constructs in the language into messages in the virtual machine. For efficiency we prefer this transformation to be carried out at compile time.

Virtual machine layer

The virtual machine layer exists to simplify the task of algorithm design.
The virtual machine is a computational structure which is suitable for expressing
a particular problem. The virtual machine layer maps this structure into the
structure of the physical machine. It is desirable that many virtual machines of
different organizations may run concurrently on the same physical architecture.

Additionally, it should be possible to execute many applications on a single virtual machine concurrently.

A virtual machine may be viewed as a set of processing elements (PE's). Each PE is represented by a monitor which encapsulates its logical communication channels. In the absence of global communication, a computation must begin at some PE; thus it is necessary to break the symmetry of the system. This can be achieved by running a shell process on the virtual machine; use of the virtual machine is achieved via a command stream to its associated shell. One of the commands which can be sent to a shell is *create a virtual machine*; this allows hierarchies of virtual machines to be constructed. The practical significance of this facility is illustrated below.

Physical machine layer

The physical structure of the machine is only of importance when designing the virtual machine layer which maps to it. The machine structure may vary in the number and organization of physical devises, connection topology etc.

A layered organization separates a number of difficult activities:

(1) Mapping a problem to a convenient computational structure; this can be carried out at the application layer by use of mapping constructs.

(2) Mapping processes in an application to computational structures; this can be carried out at the transformation layer by transforming processes with mapping constructs into messages.

(3) Mapping the code for a problem to a computational structure. This can be carried out at either the application layer or the virtual machine layer; at the former by spawning processes whose purpose is to carry code or at the latter by simply loading code modules from the underlying system.

(4) Mapping a computational structure into a physical structure; this can be carried out at the virtual machine layer using programming techniques.

The benefit of this separation is that each of the mappings can be reasoned about individually and optimized effectively. Figure 22.2 shows the system structure and the organization of virtual machines at run time. An initial virtual machine which mirrors the physical machine is created; other virtual machines can then be bootstrapped onto the initial machine.

The hierarchical layering is prevalent only at the time of bootstrapping a virtual machine. After bootstrapping is complete, the virtual machine created has new and completely independent logical communication channels; these are multiplexed directly on the physical communication channels with those of other existing machines.

Although the method is applicable to any convenient programming language

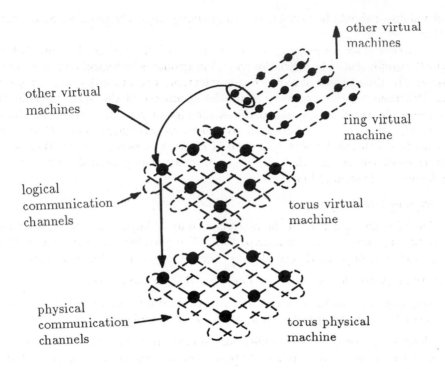

Figure 22.2: System structure

for concreteness, the paper will illustrate it using an actual implementation. The implementation is in use on a parallel system using the logic programming language Flat Concurrent Prolog (FCP) (Mierowsky et al., 1985). The implementation described illustrates the method but should not be viewed as a general solution; many tradeoffs can be made in order to optimize performance.

FCP is a simple, process oriented, single assignment language whose semantics is based on non-deterministic process reduction. Processes may either terminate, fork or reduce; computation is achieved by execution of reductions. Communication is achieved via shared logical variables and list structures are used to implement streams. Data-flow synchronization is achieved by read-only occurrences of variables; processes suspend if they attempt to bind a variable via a read-only occurrence of a variable. Dynamic process and code allocation is used. This subsumes static methods without loss of efficiency; static mapping can be achieved by structuring algorithms as distinct spawn and execute phases. All the layers described in this paper are implemented in the language itself without additional constructs; this allows the functionality of the system to be provided without complicating the semantics of the language.

The physical machine used is an Intel iPSC Hypercube. This machine consists of a set of processors, each connected in a binary n-cube topology. Each processor can communicate directly with a host machine which has access to I/O devices. There is no shared memory; each processor has local memory and may communicate to a small number of neighbors by message passing.

22.3 Virtual Machine Layer

Recall that a virtual machine represents a computational structure (e.g., ring, binary tree, torus) and is a collection of processing elements (PE's). Each PE is represented by a monitor which encapsulates its logical communication channels. A monitor may communicate with the underlying virtual machine to access services which are not provided explicitly by a virtual machine (i.e., system calls). A virtual machine is simply a program and as such it may execute on top of another virtual machine.

22.3.1 A ring virtual machine

Assume that some mechanism exists to provide each monitor with the necessary logical communication channels; how this is achieved will be described later. Figure 22.3 shows the organization of one monitor in a ring virtual machine.

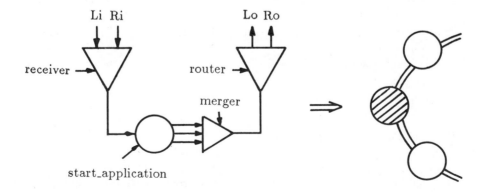

Figure 22.3: A ring link monitor

The monitor has four logical communication channels; one input and one output to each neighbor in the ring (i.e., *Li*, *Lo*, *Ri*, *Ro*). It comprises four

processes; *receiver*, *start_application*, *merger* and *router*. The receiver merges
all requests arriving on logical input channels into a single stream; this stream is
passed to a process responsible for starting execution of applications. Applications
are partitions of the user program and as such they may make requests for remote
process reductions via a set of output streams. These streams are merged into a
single stream; messages on the stream are distributed to the appropriate logical
output communication channel by a routing process.

Program 22.1 implements the link monitor for a ring virtual machine which
executes on top of some other virtual machine. Communication with the virtual
machine below is carried out by calls of the form *P@system* which is read as:
"execute process *P* at the underlying system"; the mechanics of these calls will
be explained later.

```
links(Li,Lo,Ri,Ro) ←
     receiver(Li?,Ri?,Ins),
     start_application(Ins?,Outs),
     merger(Outs?,Os1),
     router(Os1?,Lo,Ro).

receiver(I1,I2,Os) ← merger([merge(I1),merge(I2)],Os).

start_application([reduce(P,C) | Is],[merge(Os1) | Os]) ←
     run(reduce(P?,C?),C?,Os1)@system,            % run application
     start_application(Is?,Os).
start_application([ ],[ ]).

router([send(fwd,P,C) | Os],[reduce(P,C) | Lo],Ro) ←      % send forward
     router(Os?,Lo,Ro).
router([send(bwd,P,C) | Os],Lo,[reduce(P,C) | Ro]) ←      % send backward
     router(Os?,Lo,Ro).
router([send(system,Msg) | Os],Lo,Ro) ←                   % send system
     Msg@system,
     router(Os?,Lo,Ro).
router([ ],[ ],[ ]).
```

Program 22.1: A ring link monitor

The *receiver* process simply merges requests arriving on the input channels
into a single stream (*Ins*). The *start_application* process is responsible for loading
and executing applications. This action is performed when a process arrives from
a remote processing element using a system call to the underlying machine (i.e.,
run(P,C,Os) – run process *P* on code module named *C* with output stream *Os*).
The *merger* process is used to merge output requests from applications into a
single stream to the router. The *router* process puts remote process activations

from applications onto the appropriate logical output channel; it directs system calls made by the application to the underlying virtual machine.

The structure of the ring monitor is simple and can be understood independently of the rest of the system.

22.3.2 A torus virtual machine

A slightly more complex structure is necessary to implement a torus virtual machine. In designing the torus, we will assume that it performs code management and traps system calls. Each PE in the torus will have a direct connection with a host machine which has facilities for code storage and interactive terminal I/O. Some simple examples of messages which may be sent to the host are: *get_module(C,M)* which returns the compiled code module *M* with symbolic name *C* or *output*; *(M)* which causes message *M* to be displayed on the host screen. Each monitor in the virtual machine encapsulates a total of ten streams; input and output streams to each of four neighbors and a host.

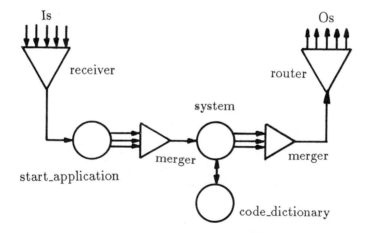

Figure 22.4: A torus link monitor

The structure of the torus monitor shown in Figure 22.4 and Program 22.2 is very similar to that of the ring described previously. The five directions on the torus are termed *north, east, south, west* and *host*. The *receiver* must now receive five input channels and the *router* must distribute messages on five output channels. System calls are filtered out of the remote requests made by applications and simply executed by a *system* process. Since this layer in the hierarchy executes system calls, applications are invoked by sending a system call directly to the

links(Is,Os) ←
    receiver(Is?,Is1),
    start_application(Is1?,Os1),
    merger(Os1?,Os2),
    system(Os2?,Os3,Dic),
    code_dictionary(Dic?),
    merger(Os3?,Os4),
    router(Os4?,Os).

receiver(In,Ie,Is,Iw,Ih,Os) ←
    merger([merge(In),merge(Ie),merge(Is),merge(Iw),merge(Ih)],Os).

start_application([reduce(P,H,C) | Is],
    [merge(Os1),send(system,run(reduce(P,H,C),C,Os1)) | Os]) ←
    start_application(Is?,Os).
start_application([],[]).

router([send(north,P,H,C) | Is], [reduce(P,H,C) | On],Oe,Os,Ow,Oh) ←
    router(Is?,On,Oe,Os,Ow,Oh).
router([send(east,P,H,C) | Is], On,[reduce(P,H,C) | Oe],Os,Ow,Oh) ←
    router(Is?,On,Oe,Os,Ow,Oh).
router([send(south,P,H,C) | Is], On,Oe,[reduce(P,H,C) | Os],Ow,Oh) ←
    router(Is?,On,Oe,Os,Ow,Oh).
router([send(west,P,H,C) | Is], On,Oe,Os,[reduce(P,H,C) | Ow],Oh) ←
    router(Is?,On,Oe,Os,Ow,Oh).
router([send(host,Msg) | Is], On,Oe,Os,Ow,[Msg | Oh]) ←
    router(Is?,On,Oe,Os,Ow,Oh).
router([],[ ],[ ],[ ],[ ],[ ]).

system([send(system,output(M)) | Is], [send(host,output(M)) | Os],Dic) ←
    string(M) |
    system(Is?,Os,Dic).
system([send(system,run(P,C,Os1)) | Is], [merge(Os2) | Os],
    [find(C,Os2,M) | Dic]) ←
    boot_module(P?,M?,Os1),
    system(Is?,Os,Dic).
system([send(D,P,H,C) | Is], [send(D,P,H,C) | Os],Dic) ←
    system(Is?,Os,Dic).
system([ ],[ ],[ ]).

boot_module(P,M,Os) ←
    module(M),
    activate(M,[P],Os) |
    true.

Program 22.2: A torus link monitor

```
code_dictionary(Is) ← dictionary(Is?,[ ]).

dictionary([find(A,Os,M) | Is],L) ←
    search(A?,M,L?,L1,Os),
    dictionary(Is?,L1?).
dictionary([ ],_).

search(A,M,[A,M | R],[A,M | R],[ ]).                              % found
search(A,M,[ ],[A,M],[send(host,get_module(A,M))]).              % not found
search(A,M,[A1,M1 | R],[A1,M1 | R1],Os) ←                        % looking
    A ≠ A1 |
    search(A?,M,R?,R1,Os).
```

Program 22.2: (Continued)

system server rather than the underlying machine. A *code_dictionary* is used to provide code management.

A simple system server can be constructed to trap the two system calls *run* and *output* as shown in Program 22.2. The run call causes a message to be sent to the host to obtain compiled code, then runs a goal on the code. This is accomplished using an FCP kernel predicate *activate(M,Is,Os)* which runs a goal *boot(Is,Os)* on a code module M; *Is* and *Os* are the inputs and output streams to the module and the module includes a server procedure *boot(Is,Os)* ← ... by convention. Output system calls are simply forwarded to the host.

Program 22.2 provides code sharing by allowing the *system* process to communicate with a code dictionary which stores loaded modules. This feature is not required on certain classes of simple systolic programs but is necessary when a large number of modules are in use or process structures wrap around the torus.

The *dictionary* process receives a stream of requests to find a module M with name C and has an output stream to the router. The dictionary is searched for the module specified. If it cannot be found, a request is sent to the host to obtain the module and it is entered into the dictionary with its name.

In performing code allocation, various tradeoffs are possible. It is possible to have a dedicated virtual machine for each application; this would prevent the need for code sharing at the expense of creating additional virtual machines. If a large number of modules are in use, a more sophisticated dictionary for code sharing could be used. Obviously the granularity of the computation performed by a remote process must be sufficiently large to offset the cost of spawning and dictionary lookup. Considerable investigation remains to quantify these tradeoffs.

22.4 Transformation Layer

The transformation layer is responsible for transforming processes annotated with a suitable mapping construct into messages in the virtual machine. This can be achieved by extending the semantics of the language to include the mapping construct; the extension can be defined by a meta-interpreter. This strategy allows process mapping to be achieved while maintaining a simple language semantics. An additional benefit is that specialized meta-interpreters may be developed for a particular application. The transformation layer interfaces to the application layer via mapping constructs and to the virtual machine layer via input and output streams to the link monitor.

22.4.1 Mapping processes onto a ring

Consider the following process mapping construct which can be used to dynamically map processes around a ring virtual machine. Each process has a position within the virtual machine which it inherits from the process which invoked it. A process P may be annotated to include a direction D, e.g., $P@D$ (read: "execute P at D"). Possible directions are *fwd* (clockwise) or *bwd* (counter-clockwise) in the ring.

When a process is annotated as $P@fwd$, it is clear that the message which should result over the logical communication channels is of the form $reduce(P,C)$ (i.e., reduce process P with code named C). To enable the router in the monitor described previously to discern this action, it must be sent a message of the form $send(fwd, reduce(P,C))$. Thus the necessary transformations from mapping constructs to messages are:

$$P@fwd \implies send(fwd, reduce(P,C))$$

$$P@bwd \implies send(bwd, reduce(P,C))$$

$$P@system \implies send(system, P)$$

Program 22.3 shows a meta-interpreter for FCP programs augmented with a direction mapping construct.

The meta-interpreter mimics the execution of the underlying FCP implementation by providing process termination, process forking and process reduction. In addition, it allows processes annotated with a direction to be remotely executed.

Execution of a mapping construct, i.e., *fwd* or *bwd* causes a process P and its associated code name C to be sent on the output stream to the link monitor. The link monitor on receipt of these messages routes them to the appropriate logical channel in the virtual machine. Execution of a system call is routed to the underlying virtual machine.

```
reduce(true,_,[ ]).                              % terminate
reduce((P1,P2),C,[merge(Os1) | Os]) ←           % fork
    reduce(P1?,C?,Os1),
    reduce(P2?,C?,Os).
reduce(P@D,C,Os) ←                               % turtle program
    execute(P?,C?,D?,Os).
reduce(P,C,Os) ←                                 % process reduction
    P ≠ true, P ≠ (_,_), P ≠ (_@_) |
    clause(P?,B),
    reduce(B?,C?,Os).

execute(P,C,fwd,[send(fwd,P,C)]).                % send forward
execute(P,C,bwd,[send(bwd,P,C)]).                % send backward
execute(P,_,system,[send(system,P)]).           % send to system
```

Program 22.3: A mapping meta-interpreter for a ring

22.4.2 Mapping processes onto a torus

Mapping processes over a torus is slightly more complex than on a ring. Consider the following process mapping mechanism based on LOGO turtle programs (Shapiro, Chapter 7). Each process has a position and heading within the virtual machine. A process P may be annotated to include a Turtle program T, e.g., $P@T$ (read: "execute P at T"). Initially the position and heading of a process P is inherited from the process that invoked it. Its final position and heading are determined by executing its associated turtle program T. The process executes on the processor at its final position. The turtle commands *fwd* and *bwd* cause movement of the process forward or backward one processor. The commands *left* and *right* cause the heading to change by 90 degrees to the left or right. Thus the following call causes *process*(...) to be executed two processors away in the current direction:

process(...)@(fwd,left,left,bwd,right,right)

The transformation layer for this mapping construct on a torus virtual machine can be described by the meta-interpreter in Program 22.4.

The underlying FCP implementation is simulated in a similar manner to that of the ring but passes the process heading when processes are forked or spawned during reduction. Reducing a process with an attached turtle program causes the turtle program to be executed; this corresponds to process mapping.

Program 22.4 produces the necessary transformation from mapping constructs to messages. Execution of a process at the *fwd* processor causes the process to be sent in the direction of the current heading with the same heading.

```
reduce(true,_,_,[ ]).                              % terminate
reduce((P1,P2),H,C,[merge(Os1) | Os]) ←           % fork
    reduce(P1?,H?,C?,Os1),
    reduce(P2?,H?,C?,Os).
reduce(P@T,H,C,Os) ←                               % turtle program
    execute(P?,T?,H?,C?,Os).
reduce(P,H,C,Os) ←                                 % process reduction
    P ≠ true, P ≠ (_,_), P ≠ (_@_) |
    clause(P?,B),
    reduce(B?,H?,C?,Os).

execute(P,fwd,H,C,[send(H,P,H,C)]).                % send forward
execute(P,bwd,H,C,[send(To,P,H,C)]) ←              % send backward
    go_backward(H?,To).
execute(P,left,H,C,Os) ←                           % change heading left
    go_left(H?,NewH),
    reduce(P?,NewH?,C?,Os).
execute(P,right,H,C,Os) ←                          % change heading right
    go_right(H?,NewH),
    reduce(P?,NewH?,C?,Os).
execute(P,system,_,[send(system,P)]).              % send to system
execute(P,(TP1,Rest),H,C,Os) ←                     % concatenation
    execute(P@Rest?,TP1?,H?,C?,Os).

go_backward(north,south).                          % lookup for going backward
    :

go_left(west,south).                               % lookup for going left
    :

go_right(west,north).                              % lookup for going right
    :
```

Program 22.4: A mapping meta-interpreter for a torus

Execution of a process at the *bwd* processor causes the process to be sent in the reverse direction of the current heading with the same heading; the new direction is obtained by lookup. Changes in heading simply cause the process to be reduced with a heading obtained by lookup. System calls are sent to the underlying virtual machine. Conjunctive turtle programs are solved recursively.

22.5 The Application Layer

The application layer consists of a programming language which includes a process mapping construct. Program 22.5 illustrates the use of the direction annotation on a ring virtual machine and implements insertion sort.

```
sort([X | Xs],Ys) ←
      insert(X,Zs?,Ys),              % insert X into sorted Zs
      sort(Xs?,Zs)@fwd.              % sort the rest
sort([ ],[ ]).

insert(X,[Y | Ys],[Y | Zs?]) ←      % still looking
      X > Y |
      insert(X,Ys?,Zs).
insert(X,[Y | Ys],[X,Y | Ys]) ←     % place found
      X ≤ Y |
      true.
insert(X,[ ],[X]).                   % not found
```

Program 22.5: Insertion sort on a ring

The *sort* program spawns a linearly connected sequence of *insert* processes around the ring by virtue of the *@fwd* annotation in the first clause. One process is spawned for each element of the input stream. The last insert process is spawned with the empty input stream due to the last sort clause. At this time processes begin propagating data backwards starting from the last process. Each process copies its ordered (or empty in the case of the last process) input stream, inserting its local number in the output stream so that the latter remains ordered.

The turtle mapping constructs described earlier can be used to compute matrix multiplication on a torus.

Program 22.6 forms a matrix Z which is the result of multiplying a matrix X by a transposed matrix Y. A grid of *ip* processes are spawned each of which computes the inner-product of two vectors. Notice that the *vm* (vector multiply) processes are spawned at right-angles to the direction in which *mm* (matrix multiply) processes are spawned. The *vm* processes effectively create the path for spawning *ip* processes. The turtle construct thus causes processes to dynamically migrate between processors in the virtual machine. The virtual machine used by the program is a torus; wrap around allows processes to spawn on a seemingly infinite processing surface.

The careful reader will note that the complexity of these programs is very poor; sorting requires time $O(n^2)$ and matrix multiplication requires time $O(n^3)$ using $O(n)$ processors. Analysis and improved algorithms are presented by Taylor

```
mm([Xv | Xm],Ym,[Zv | Zm]) ←                % matrix multiply
    vm(Xv,Ym?,Ym1,Zv)@left,
    mm(Xm?,Ym1?,Zm)@fwd.
mm([ ],Ym,[ ]).

vm(Xv,[Yv | Ym],[Yv1 | Ym1],[Z | Zv]) ←      % vector multiply
    ip(Xv?,Xv1,Yv?,Yv1,Z),
    vm(Xv1?,Ym?,Ym1,Zv)@fwd.
vm(Xv,[ ],[ ],[ ]).

ip(Xv,Xv1,Yv,Yv1,Z) ←
    ip1(Xv?,Xv1,Yv?,Yv1,0,Z).                % inner product

ip1([X | Xv],[X | Xv1],[Y | Yv],[Y | Yv1],Z0,Z) ←
    Z1 := (X * Y) + Z0,
    ip1(Xv?,Xv1,Yv?,Yv1,Z1,Z).
ip1([ ],[ ],[ ],[ ],Z,Z).
```

Program 22.6: Matrix multiplication on a torus

et al. (Chapter 39). A selection of other parallel algorithms expressed using process mapping constructs was given by Shapiro (Chapter 7).

22.6 Partial Evaluation

The meta-interpreters shown previously would generally incur a loss of efficiency which is approximately an order of magnitude. However the layer of interpretation is only of importance in specification; it may be removed at compile-time by partial evaluation. Program 22.7 was generated using a working prototype partial evaluator (Safra, 1986). The inputs were the parallel matrix multiplication, Program 22.6, and the meta-interpreter which defines the mapping strategy, Program 22.4.

There are a number of interesting aspects to this program. The layer of interpretation and mapping constructs have been completely removed. When execution can cause remote spawning of a process to a remote processor, the appropriate messages are already entered onto the output stream. These messages replace execution of the mapping constructs which occurred in the meta-interpreter. The first inner product differs from subsequent ones since it does not depend on previous calculations; thus it is open coded to a separate routine (i.e., *ip0*) which performs less arithmetic. The transformation was obtained fully automatically and demonstrates the power of the technique.

```
mm([Xv | Xm],Ym,[Zv | Zm],
        [merge(Os),send(east,mm(Xm?,Ym1?,Zm),east,mm)]
) ←
        vm(Xv?,Ym?,Ym1,Zv,Os).
mm([ ],Ym,[ ],[ ]).

vm(Xv,[Yv | Ym],[Yv1 | Ym1],[Z | Zv],
        [merge(Os),send(north,vm(Xv1?,Ym?,Ym1,Zv),north,mm)]
) ←
        ip0(Xv?,Xv1,Yv?,Yv1,Z,Os).
vm(Xv,[ ],[ ],[ ],[ ]).

ip0([X | Xv],[X | Xv1],[Y | Yv],[Y | Yv1],Z), [merge(Os1) | Os]) ←
        :=(Z1,X,Y,Os1),
        ipN(Xv?,Xv1,Yv?,Yv1,Z1?,Z,Os).
ip0([ ],[ ],[ ],[ ],0,[ ]).

ipN([X | Xv],[X | Xv1],[Y | Yv], [Y | Yv1],Z0,Z,[merge(Os1) | Os]) ←
        :=(Z1,X,Y,Z0,Os1),
        ipN(Xv?,Xv1,Yv?,Yv1,Z1?,Z,Os).
ipN([ ],[ ],[ ],[ ],Z,Z,[ ]).

:=(Z,X,Y,[ ]) ← Z := X * Y | true.

:=(Z,X,Y,Z0,[ ]) ← Z := (X * Y) + Z0 | true.
```

Program 22.7: Partial evaluation of Program 22.4 with respect to
             Program 22.6

Although the above transformation is impressive, it should be pointed out that methods shown in this paper do not rely on the availability of a working partial evaluator. For any specific meta-interpreter it is possible to define a transformation which effectively produces a specialized compiler (Codish and Shapiro, Chapter 32; Hirsch et al., Chapter 20). This compiler does not perform additional optimizations such as the open coding shown in the above example but does remove the layer of interpretation. Thus the method stands as a practical technique even in the absence of a working partial evaluator.

22.7 Bootstrapping

There are two problems of interest:

(1) How to bootstrap virtual machines on top of each other.

(2) How to bootstrap an initial virtual machine onto the hardware.

22.7.1 Constructing hierarchies of virtual machines

Assume the existence of a virtual machine in the hierarchy; to generate the next machine in the hierarchy, simply write a program using the mapping annotations of the existing machine which traverses it and generates a new virtual machine.

We will adopt the convention that every virtual machine has an associated shell process; communication with the virtual machine is achieved by sending messages to the shell via a command stream. Additionally we adopt the convention that shells may accept a command of the form:

vm(CommandStream,Shell,SpawnCode)

which causes a virtual machine to be spawned. The new virtual machine is constructed by loading and executing the code named *SpawnCode*. On top of the new virtual machine the shell process described by the code named *Shell* is executed; this shell may accept commands via the *CommandStream*. Using this convention, it is possible to spawn a new virtual machine on an existing virtual machine; the command stream used in the call can then be used to access the new virtual machine via its command stream.

Consider mapping a ring containing $2n^2$ virtual processing elements on top of an $n \times n$ torus virtual machine. (The size and organization of the ring were chosen to simplify the programs involved.) Each monitor in the ring is precisely that described in a previous section. The ring virtual machine can be constructed by the mapping described in Figure 22.5.

A ring of n loops of PE's are created in the horizontal direction; the right end of each loop is connected to the left end of the next loop. Each loop contains $2n$ PE's and is created by spawning two ring PE's per torus PE in the vertical direction. As the loops are created, adjacent PE's share channels and the last two PE's in a loop share a common channel. To ensure that when sending messages forward around the ring the correct direction is maintained, the channels to PE's on the right of a loop must be created in the direction opposite to those on the left. The first PE in the ring is designated as a special PE; the shell process for the ring virtual machine will run on top of this PE.

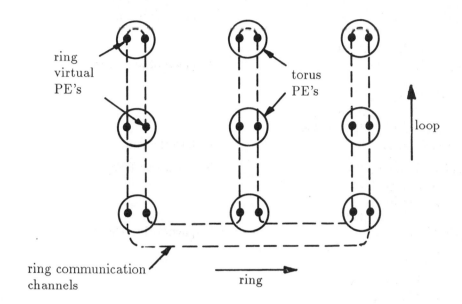

Figure 22.5: Mapping a ring onto a torus

The application Program 22.8, run on a torus virtual machine, creates the ring virtual machine recursively when invoked with the goal:

ring(n,1,L,L,shell(Cmds),Shell).   % ring of size $2n^2$

The ring and loop clauses create the ring as described earlier. When each PE is initiated, it unifies each of its streams with a pair or streams; the result is two streams between each PE, one for input and one for output. The special PE (i.e., *vpe*) is started by placing a process to reduce on its left input stream; this process is the shell process from the original call. Thus the program generates a ring and starts a shell process running on it.

Notice that Program 22.8 executes on top of a virtual machine only to spawn the new virtual machine. The new virtual machine has completely independent logical channels and can obtain direct access to the system call layer by stream cashing if necessary. Thus the new virtual machine effectively runs directly on the physical machine; its communication channels are multiplexed with those of other virtual machines on the physical communication channels.

The shell process in Program 22.9 is very simple; its purpose is to receive processes to be run on its associated virtual machine.

The shell module, by virtue of running on top of the ring, has an output

```
ring(N,1,Lc,Rc,P,C) ←                       % spawn first loop
    loop(N?,1,Lc,Mc,P,C)@left,
    ring(N?,2,Mc,Rc)@fwd.
ring(N,M,Lc,Rc) ←                           % spawn other loops
    M < N,
    M1 := M + 1 |
    loop(N?,1,Lc,Mc)@left,
    ring(N?,M1?,Mc,Rc)@fwd.
ring(N,N,L,L).                              % close the ring

loop(N,1,Lc,Rc,P,C) ←                       % spawn two PEs
    vpe(Lc,M1,P,C),
    vpe(M2,Rc),
    loop(N?,2,M1,M2).
loop(N,M,Lc,Rc) ←                           % spawn other PEs
    M < N,
    NewM := M + 1 |
    vpe(Lc,M1),
    vpe(M2,Rc),
    loop(N?,NewM?,M1,M2)@fwd.
loop(N,N,L,L).                              % close the loop

vpe({Li,Lo},{Ro,Ri},P,C) ←                  % special shell PE
    links([reduce(P,C) | Li?],Lo,Ri,Ro).
vpe({Li,Lo},{Ro,Ri}) ←                      % normal virtual PE
    links(Li?,Lo,Ri?,Ro).
```

Program 22.8: Spawning a ring on a torus

```
shell([reduce(P,C) | Is],[merge(Os) | Ro]) ←        % run process
    run(P,C,Os)@system,
    shell(Is?,Ro).
shell([vm(Cmds,Shell,SC) | Is],[merge(Os) | Ro]) ←  % run virtual machine
    run(vm(Cmds,Shell,SC),SC,Os)@system,
    shell(Is?,Ro).
shell([ ],[ ]).                                      % terminate
```

Program 22.9: The shell process

stream directly to the rings router process (defined in the link monitor). When the shell receives a *reduce* command, the associated process is run on the appropriate module via a *run* system call. Since the reduction is to be executed on the ring, if the module makes any remote process calls they need to be sent to the ring router. This is achieved by merging requests from the module output stream into the shell output stream. Exactly the same principle is used to activate a new virtual machine on receipt of a virtual machine (i.e., *vm*) command; a virtual machine is just an application that runs on the ring.

22.7.2 Bootstrapping an initial virtual machine

An initial virtual machine must be created on top of the physical machine to provide access to the physical communication channels. This virtual machine mirrors the structure of the physical machine but has logical channels instead of physical ones. It provides the ability to bootstrap other virtual machines on top of it.

Stream-based communication is available in FCP via shared logical variables; manipulation of streams is conducted in the underlying implementation. The details of parallel execution of FCP (Taylor et al., Chapter 39) are beyond the scope of this paper; it suffices to say that only a single occurrence of a variable exists at run time and all other occurrences are simply local or remote references to it. The parallel algorithm ensures that the correct operations are carried out when variables are manipulated and prevents deadlock.

The problem of bootstrapping an initial virtual machine corresponds to establishing a state where adjacent processors share logical variables; one processor holding the actual variable and the others holding remote references to it. This configuration can be achieved simply by a common agreement among all processors at bootstrap time; each processor writes a known configuration of variables and remote references onto its memory and hands this configuration to the upper levels of the implementation. Figure 22.6 illustrates the technique by creating two logical variables shared by two processors, one for input and the other for output.

A simple algorithm which uses the PE number can be used to ensure that each PE writes remote references on its local memory that refer to the appropriate places on remote memories. An initial process (i.e., *boot(Is,Os)*) is created at bootstrap time which has access to the logical variables on the memory. It also has access to an initial module which may contain code which uses these logical variables, e.g.,

```
boot(Is,Os) ←
    consumer(Is?),
    producer(Os).
```

The input stream can be used for consuming values from the remote proces-

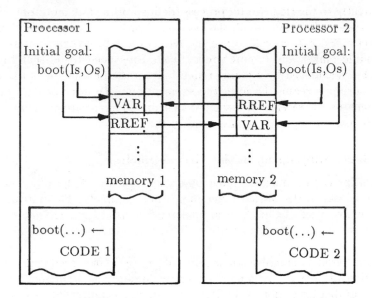

Figure 22.6: Creating initial logical streams

sor while the output stream is used for producing values needed by the remote processor. Since nodes do not receive messages until their local bootstrapping phase is over, bootstrapping can be carried out asynchronously.

Now consider bootstrapping a torus virtual machine onto a torus physical machine. Assume that an initial module can be downloaded to every PE at bootstrap time; let this initial module contain the torus link monitor described earlier. The initial process activated at bootstrap time contains logical variables corresponding to the physical channels as shown above. If a shell process is now activated on top of the torus, bootstrapping is complete.

It is now possible to bootstrap completely independent and concurrently executing virtual machines on top of the initial virtual machine by sending commands to the initial shell.

22.8 The Host Process

To illustrate how the facilities to create virtual machines can be used, consider the following simple host process. The host may use facilities for code storage, terminal I/O, etc., via an output stream to a system process. An input stream from the system allows it to accept commands from users.

At bootstrap time input channels from all processors in the initial virtual machine are merged into a single stream to the host. The host also has a stream to a distributor process. The distributor accepts two message forms:

(1) *vm(Shell,SC,VM,N)* – adds a command stream *Cmd* to the distributor for a new virtual machine, sends a message *vm(Cmd,Shell,SC)* to virtual machine shell specified by *VM* and returns the number *N* allocated to the new command stream.

(2) *send(V,N)* – sends value *V* on stream *N* of the distributor.

Using these four streams a simple host process can be defined as shown in Program 22.10.

```
host(Si,[Msg | So],[Msg | Cis],VMs) ←
    host(Si?,So,Cis?,VMs).
host([vm(Shell,SC,VM) | Si],[vm(N) | So],Cis,
    [vm(Shell,SC,VM,N) | VMs]) ←
    host(Si?,So,Cis?,VMs).
host([run(Process,VM) | Si],So,Cis, [send(Process,VM) | VMs]) ←
    host(Si?,So,Cis?,VMs).
host([ ],[ ],[ ],[ ]).
```

Program 22.10: A host process

If the host receives a system call (e.g., *get_module(C,M)*) on the input stream from the torus, it passes it to the system. The host may receive a request to spawn a virtual machine on top of some virtual machine *VM*. In this case a *vm* message is sent to the distributor which causes it to spawn a new virtual machine and retain a stream to its shell. If the host receives a command to run a process on a virtual machine, the process is sent to the virtual machine via the distributor. When all input streams are closed, all output streams are closed and the host terminates.

Additional functionality can obviously be added to the host.

22.9 Conclusion

This paper has demonstrated a method to support specialized process and code mapping strategies. The method allows multiple virtual machines to be bootstrapped onto the physical machine and run concurrently; additionally, many applications may execute on a specific virtual machine concurrently. The method allows a number of difficult problems to be separated and attacked individually:

(1) Mapping of a problem to a suitable virtual machine.

(2) Mapping a virtual machine to a physical machine.

(3) Managing and accessing code.

The sample programs illustrated in this paper serve only as examples and should not be viewed as general solutions in themselves. They demonstrate the simplicity and versatility of the general method. Practical use of the method may involve various tradeoffs and may use different architectural topologies, different device organizations, methods for separating applications into a number of modules, and loading only specific code into individual machines, etc. Since in general only a small number of virtual machines form the basic set required for programming, they can be provided as libraries for programmers; the programmer need only be concerned with mapping the problem to a convenient computational structure. The libraries may then be used as a basis to be modified and improved when optimizing a particular program.

The method described can be applied in any convenient programming formalism. The simplicity and elegance of its definition in FCP is largely due to the power of the logical variable and the uniformity of the logic programming formalism. These aspects of the language allow uniform dynamic manipulation of streams and processes.

Acknowledgements

This research was partially supported by Intel Scientific Computers, Portland, Oregon.

The authors wish to acknowledge Shmuel Safra for many helpful discussions and for the ideas and methods related to partial evaluation.

Chapter 23

An Architecture of a Distributed Window System and its FCP Implementation

Dan Katzenellenbogen, Shimon Cohen and Ehud Shapiro

The Weizmann Institute of Science

Abstract

An architecture for a distributed window system is presented, which is suitable for a distributed network of computers, each with multiple processors. A distributed algorithm for managing windows is described. The algorithm does not depend on a central window manager or a locking mechanism thereby making it suitable for implementation on a distributed network of processors. We discuss the complexity of the algorithm and describe the implementation of the architecture in FCP.

23.1 Introduction

23.1.1 Motivation

Modern programming environments allow user tasks to be carried out on separate sections of the screen. Each such section is called a window and individual tasks are associated with it. Within a window, clients are allowed to interact, producing output and receiving information (input or otherwise) supplied by the window.

In a distributed system there are multiple processes distributed over a network of processors. Each client process may wish to read or write to one or more windows. There is a need to cater for the distributed nature of these operations.

In addition, we would like to take advantage of the possibilities of performing window operations in parallel.

Most window systems which support distribution of processes are server-based (Sun Microsystems, 1986; Gettys et al., 1986). This means that requests to the window system are serialized before being processed. The server itself is a single process that serves client requests sequentially. In a distributed environment the window system should be able to concurrently process client requests. Otherwise, the server becomes a bottleneck in the network.

23.1.2 Review of major issues

The task of a window system is to share resources between a collection of processes (Pike, 1983; Adobe Systems, 1985). The processes wish to access devices and services concurrently. It is the window system's task to arbitrate in cases of dispute. The two main resources are the screen and the input devices.

Screen handling

Two main paradigms of organizing the screen exist, namely *tiling* and *overlapping* (Hopgood et al., 1986). In the tiling paradigm the screen is divided into non-overlapping rectangles, each of which is owned by some process. The overlapping paradigm is best described with the desktop metaphor. The desk (screen) is covered with a pile of papers (windows). Papers can be pulled from anywhere in the pile and placed anywhere on the desk. Papers may be shuffled thereby changing the face of the desk.

The tiling paradigm views user requests as hints as to how to perform operations. It does not guarantee successful satisfaction of requests. The window manager determines the layout of windows based on user hints and architecture restrictions. The system might restrict windows to be of certain width or height.

The overlapping paradigm is more general and allows the user greater flexibility in constructing his working environment. It does, however, demand more of the window manager. The tiling paradigm imposes restrictions on the layout of windows but simplifies the algorithms needed to control the screen. Tiling advocates argue that experienced users divide their screen into a non-overlapping state and then begin to work making the support for overlapping redundant.

There is an interesting classification of window systems relating to the way in which the window is layed out or *composed* (Nelson, private communication). It is defined in terms of operators called *composers*. There are X, Y, and Z composers. A composer is an operator that takes a set of VAT's (Visibly Active Things) and composes an image according to some rule. An X composer takes a sequence of VATs all of the same height and displays them in a row. A Y composer takes a sequence VAT's all of the same width and displays them as a column. Complexities arise in negotiation between the parts and the whole for allocation of screen space. For example, the user may reshape the Y composer to half their original height. The Y composer then asks each of its parts to reshape to half of its height, but one may refuse (because of other constraints).

A Z composer composes VAT's on the Z axis. The task of the Z composer is to compose the images of its parts into its own image while occluding according to Z order. In order for the Z composer itself to be a nestable VAT, it needs to respond to the VAT protocol (which is the same protocol it demands of its parts). The Z composer conforms partially to the overlapping paradigms. In the overlapping paradigm the window may overlap in one level. Each of the windows, however, may be constructed as an X, Y, or Z composer. If each of the windows is composed as a Z composer the system is called a full Z composer. A window system that allows overlapping of windows but where each of the windows is composed of non-overlapping subwindows is a limited Z composer.

In an overlapping window system, not all portions of a window are exposed on the screen. Thus, there is a need for a mechanism that will restrict windows to paint the screen only where they are exposed. This task is performed by the window manager. Most current window systems use a centralized window manager. A centralized window manager is a single process that communicates with each of the windows. Window requests and instructions are serialized by the manager. When the window manager permits a window to write on the screen it disallows all other windows from doing so, thereby *locking* the screen. When the screen is locked all write operations by windows are suspended until the screen is unlocked by the window manager.

Another issue concerning screen output is the responsibility for screen updates. Two alternatives exist. The first is to enable the window system to retain each window's bitmap. If the window's image becomes damaged it is the responsibility of the window manager to refresh the screen. The second alternative is to request the client program to supply the window manager with information on how to refresh the screen. Some systems argue that the client program (which constructed the window's bitmap in the first place) will have sufficient knowledge of how to reconstruct the window, making the window system's bitmap redundant. Others argue that when optimizing for performance it is best to retain the window's bitmap. We feel that in a distributed network reconstructing the window by the client places a heavy burden on the communication channels while memory considerations are less significant. However, in the case of resizing windows most window systems agree that the client should be responsible for refreshing the window. This is since the window system can only guess how the client wants its window contents resized while the client should have specific knowledge.

Some systems view the window manager as a server (Gettys et al., 1986; Morris et al., 1986). The window system serves client requests and notifies the clients owning windows of events that occur within the window's bounds. Client requests are generated anywhere in the network but are serialized by the server. A typical interaction is as follows: a client asks the server to open a window. The window is created but not displayed on the screen since the client did not request that. The client then requests the window to be displayed. If the window becomes damaged, the client is notified and is expected to refresh the window itself. An input event is sent to the client only if it specifically requested it. A minimal amount of information is kept by the server making it fast and reliable.

Input

Another major concern of window systems is input distribution. Again, two alternatives exist. The more restrictive method is to assign a selected window as the *fixed listener*. The fixed listener accepts all input until the window system assigns a new fixed listener window. The cursor may be placed anywhere on the screen without affecting the selected window. A new listener is usually found by placing the cursor on top of some window and clicking the mouse. The more general method is the *cursor dependent listener* method which distributes input events to the window located where the cursor is placed. Shifting the cursor across window boundaries changes the selected window.

The fixed listener method is simpler to implement, but causes some confusion as to where events are directed (the mouse might be pointing at a window which is not the listener). The usual method to overcome this problem is to signal (by a highlighted bar, for instance) the listener window.

The cursor dependent listener method introduces problems known as type ahead or mouse ahead. A common problem occurs when creating a window and immediately proceeding with typing characters before the window actually appeared on the screen. The question is: where should these character events go? to the new window which has been created but perhaps not yet displayed or to the window currently exposed. These types of questions should be addressed by the window system. There is no right or wrong way to go, rather there are practical issues that determine which method is chosen. If the system is commonly slow then type ahead becomes annoying and a fixed listener will suffice. If the system is quick to respond then the general method may be considered.

When the system does not respond quickly enough, mouse-ahead and type-ahead cause another problem: Imagine a menu appearing on the screen and the user clicks the appropriate item but the screen does not respond. The user then clicks again causing an error in the interpretation of input events since the user produced a non-intentional sequence of events.

23.1.3 Issues related to a distributed implementation

Problems related to screen update become considerably more complicated in a distributed system. The processes producing output on windows might be placed on remote processors. A remote process is able to create, close, or move windows while window processes could be placed on separate processors. The task of allocating resources on a distributed network has to take into consideration the parallel nature of these window operations, the location of the resources, and the location of the clients.

The server based solution in a distributed environment was discussed in the previous section. It should be noted, however, that the implication of serializing requests is that a lot of the parallelism of the application is lost. In a distributed window system, it is undesirable to have a centralized window manager that will lock and suspend all other windows on every window operation. If we do lock and suspend we get a bottleneck in the parallel execution that could lead to no parallel speedup. Serializing client requests performs even worse in a system with multiple input and output devices since those should be activated in parallel.

23.1.4 Other window systems

SunWindow

The SunWindows window system (Gossling, 1986) uses an overlapping approach to windowing. Windows seem to be written on concurrently. It is possible to write on a hidden portion of a window.

SunWindow achieves these desired effects by *clipping* and *locking*. Clipping allows a window to write only within clipping bounds that are parameters of the window while anything which is outside the clipping bounds is ignored. Locking allows a window to gain exclusive access to the output device. Getting hold of the lock means forbidding any other window from getting this lock until the lock is released. Locking is a routine that blocks a request if the lock is not currently available and issues the lock if it is free.

A window which has access to the lock is managed (as other windows) by the window manager. The window manager will check to see if the window has been damaged lately, i.e., have portions of the window been written on by other windows or by a foreign process. If this is the case then some updating will be done on the tables and the window manager will then permit the window to proceed with I/O operations. Updating is important since the window has to be sure its attributes are correct. Otherwise it might be writing outside its bounds.

SunWindows keeps a list of currently exposed portions of the window and a list of damaged portions. A damaged portion of a window is one that for some reason has been either covered or uncovered by other windows. Before a window process reads or writes to the screen it must satisfy several conditions:

(a) Obtain exclusive use of the display hardware.

(b) Disallow other windows from changing their window coordinates.

(c) Update current list of visible subportions.

(d) Confine I/O activities to those portions.

The first three are due to locking while the last means that we have to clip to the size of the window.

The following systems are based on a *server* approach. A server is a process that clients communicate with. Most distributed window systems use the server approach.

Andrew

Andrew (Morris et al., 1986) is a distributed personal computing environment developed at Carnegie Mellon University.

In Andrew each window is attached to a process. This process is not aware of the existence of other windows in the system. Each window on the other hand must be prepared at all times to redisplay its contents. The window manager (server) communicates with multiple client processes. When a window needs to be redrawn, the client is notified. It is then the responsibility of the client to request the window coordinates and invoke the low level calls to the window manager to accomplish the redrawing. In Andrew a centralized window manager is responsible for the maintenance of current window coordinates.

Andrew chose a tiling paradigm to arrange windows on the screen. The screen is divided vertically and within each column windows can be of any height (in Nelson's terminology this window system is a Y composer). The empty part of the screen is kept at the bottom of the column and is denoted by a grey background color. The window system confines the task of allocating space for windows to a user specified column. Since there is no overlapping, the window system simply creates a window within a column at the bottom of the screen. Creating, destroying, or altering the size of the window does not effect windows outside this column in the system. Creation and enlargement is confined to vacated (grey) areas of the screen while deleting a window causes the remaining windows to be moved upwards. These design decisions, though greatly improving performance, limit the user.

The X window system

X-windows (Gettys, et al., 1986) is a network-transparent window system developed at MIT. At the heart of X lies a server whose task is to distribute input events and to serve output requests from various client programs. The programs can be located either on the server's machine or elsewhere in the network. X does not manage the contents of the windows. If a window is damaged then the client program is notified. The client should be prepared to regenerate the contents of the window, otherwise it may be lost. A client program has to notify the server that it is interested in accepting events. The server never sends a client events it did not ask for.

The server is a centralized controller of clients' requests. Servers work well in a network where each node is a sequential computer. The approach cannot, however, utilize the internal parallelism of future parallel computers.

23.1.5 Overview

The paper defines a window management algorithm for managing windows in a distributed network of processors. It introduces a method for distributed resource allocation that supports parallel output and distribution of input. The system, which is implemented in FCP, has the following capabilities:

(1) Concurrent write operations are allowed on multiple windows.

(2) Concurrent screen access is possible.

(3) Window requests are served concurrently.

(4) Window movement and reshape operations can be done without centralized control.

(5) A variety of window flavors (attributes) and facilities for user defined flavors are provided.

(6) A simple interface to application processes is provided.

Section 23.2 describes the proposed architecture. Section 23.3 introduces a new distributed window management algorithm. Section 23.4 focuses on the I/O problem.

23.2 System Architecture

23.2.1 Introduction

The architecture is designed for a distributed network of computers, each with multiple processors. Every effort was made to eliminate central managers. The architecture allows for the distributed management of windows where windows are not aware of the existence of each other. Windows update the screen by caching output channels to the screen with no centralized control. Input distribution to the windows is incorporated into the system.

Window systems have to solve three basic problems: how to arrange windows on the screen, how to display the contents of the windows on the screen, and how to direct input events to the windows.

Arranging windows on the screen in the proposed architecture conforms to the overlapping paradigm. The window system is a Z composer. Windows are ordered in the Z axis and no two windows have the same Z coordinate.

The design allows the window system to be a nestable Z composer, which means windows may be composed of subwindows conforming to the Z composer protocol. However, the current implementation does not support subwindowing.

The architecture allows windows to cache output channels to the screen. This output is filtered so as not to damage other windows. There is no central control of the filters and their update is done concurrently with the execution of other tasks in the system.

The architecture conforms to the fixed listener paradigm for input handling. It was felt that this paradigm is more suitable for a distributed environment than the general input distribution paradigm, since windows may perform window operations spontaneously without centralized control. In a distributed network there is no clear semantics to a window being exposed. A window might be exposed currently, but in the system there are already messages being propagated that will shortly change its state.

23.2.2 The window system architecture

The window system is a set of communicating processes. Figure 23.1 describes the top level system architecture. *Windows* represent the window processes in the system. These are nameless objects communicating with each other in order to determine resource sharing. Windows in the system interact with window *clients* which are said to own the window. A client instructs its window to perform window operations (move, close, resize, refresh, receive input etc.). A window process outputs its image on the *I/O cache* channel to a *pane* process which displays the update on the screen. Each pane process owns a distinct portion of the screen which enables it to write on the screen without fear of damaging other windows. A pane process acts as a filter of output requests ensuring that no window output is written outside the window's exposed bounds. Pane processes can therefore write on the screen concurrently.

The I/O process communicates with the panes in order to determine a listener window or in order to update the panes. The window system allows any interested window to accept input events, even if it is not the listener window (but this is in addition to the listener window).

Window operations result in instructions as to how to update the set of pane processes. When panes are being updated, the screen is consequently updated. The I/O process coordinates between pane updates and the determination of a new listener window.

There are several types of processes in the system. Figure 23.2 describes the layout of processes in the system.

(1) A *window* process represents the window structure.

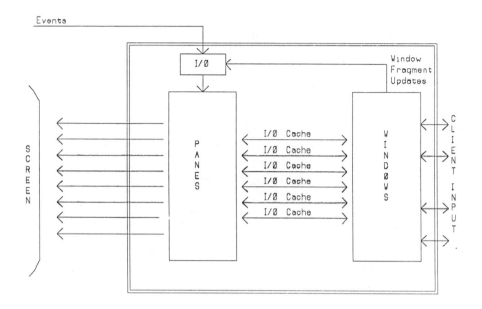

Figure 23.1: The top level window system architecture

(2) A *flavor* process represents the window's interface.

(3) A *pane* process represents a rectangular portion of a window which is exposed on the screen.

(4) The *I/O* process handles screen layout updates and input events.

(5) An *event* process creates a stream of input events.

We list a number of points which should be noted about the system architecture:

- Windows are ordered in the Z axis. Two special windows always exist namely *TOP* and *BOTTOM*. These are pseudo windows which implement the top and bottom of the Z hierarchy of windows. In addition, the *BOTTOM* window represents the background color. A window which overlaps a lower window will obscure the intersecting portion of the lower window.

- Windows are connected by channels (Tribble et al., Chapter 17). Each window is connected to its two neighboring windows (in the Z axis).

- Each window process has an associated flavor process connected to it by a

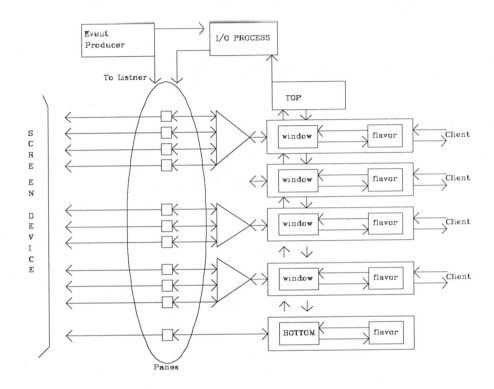

Figure 23.2: The window system architecture

channel.

Channels between flavors and windows are used to control the contents of the window and initiate a display action. A client request from the window system to open a window results in the spawning of a window process and a flavor process connected to it.

- Each window has a *client* process. The client process is the process that requested the window system to open the window. The client process supplies the flavor with input and receives output from it.

- Each window is connected via a channel to a number (perhaps zero) of pane processes representing its currently exposed rectangular fragments.

- A window caches output to the screen via its panes. A pane has direct access to the screen.

Each pane holds a channel to its window. This channel is used to pass input events to the appropriate window.

- Output from *TOP* (which is output from the windows) is directed to the I/O process so as to update the current pool of panes.

- The event producer produces a stream of events which are read by one of the panes (the *listener pane*).

- Input events are forwarded from the listener pane to the *listener window*.

- A special event whose meaning is to change the listener window is passed to the I/O process.

23.2.3 The algorithms

The first algorithm we introduce deals with window management (window movement, creation, deletion etc.). The second algorithm deals with input distribution to windows. Update of window contents is supported by the first algorithm using additional features.

A window is created by spawning a window process with its associated flavor process. The window process has to be placed within the Z order of windows. Once the window process is inserted it begins to function like any other window process in the system, which means it may write output to the screen, interact with that client process and assist in sharing resources. But, even when the window is inserted, it is not yet displayed. For the window to be displayed the system has to recognize if and where the window is exposed on the screen. The knowledge of which parts of a window are exposed is computed in a distributed fashion. It is the system in general that gains the knowledge, not just a single process.

A window wishing to display itself sends a message to that affect to the window above it. The message contains the rectangular coordinates of the window and the appropriate part of the window's bitmap. This message propagates up through every window above the sending window. Each window clips off the rectangle the part which it obscures. Eventually the rectangle is clipped to a set of sub-rectangles which represent the exposed portion of the window.

For each such sub-rectangle a pane process is spawned with which the window (that originated the display action) can communicate in order to display output on the screen. The pane process owns a rectangular portion of the screen and acts as a clipping region for the window's output.

A similar algorithm is executed when a window is closed. The closing window sends a message to the window below it requesting it to reconstruct the vacated portion of the screen. The message contains the rectangular coordinates of the window. The message propagates down to every window below the sending window. Each of the windows checks which portion of itself the rectangle covers. That portion is sent up for display as described above. The portion is clipped off the rectangle which is passed to the next window down. Eventually the rectangle will be clipped to zero size or will reach the bottom-most window which sends up a message to display the background color.

Problems might seem to arise when one of the windows that has already clipped its size of the rectangle is moved, for instance, to another location. The resulting set of panes is no longer correct. However, this type of problem is dealt with correctly by the algorithm with no special additional mechanisms.

We show in Section 23.3 that these algorithms allow a window to perform operations concurrently with other windows. A window performing an operation does not need to suspend until the operation is completed. In addition, windows that are affected by a window operation are also not suspended and may write output and receive input and perform any other window operation.

The second algorithm determines how input events are distributed. Input distribution depends on an invariant holding for the set of pane processes existing at any one time in the system. The invariant states that the set of panes is always a non-overlapping cover of the screen. Using this invariant we can safely determine that an input event occurring at an (X,Y) location has one and only one pane process that has the (X,Y) location within its bounds. We use the panes to determine input ownership. The mouse click associated with the change of a listener is tested against all panes in the system in order to determine a new listener.

Finally windows refresh their contents by writing to pane processes connected to them. Since these panes represent the exposed fragments of the window, the window may write freely to the screen being sure that no other windows are damaged in the process.

23.2.4   The window process

A window process is created as a result of a request to the window system to open a window and remains alive until the window is closed. The window process contains all the information needed to determine its position relative to other windows and some facts about its internal contents. The window process has three channels that are used to pass messages to the two neighboring window processes (in the Z order of windows) and to its associated flavor. In addition the window has a further channel on which window output may be sent directly to the screen via its pane processes.

A window process has the form:

```
window(
      XLocation
      YLocation
      Form
      TopChannel
      BottomChannel
      FlavorChannel
      ToPanes)
```

Figure 23.3 describes a window process.

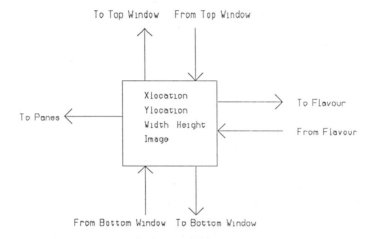

Figure 23.3: Window process

- *XLocation* and *YLocation* define the location (top-left) of the window.

- *Form* is of the form: {*frame*(*Width,Height*),*Image*} where *Width* and *Height* are the width and height of the window and *Image* is a pointer to the bitmap representing the window contents.

- *TopChannel* is a channel to the next highest window process.

- *BottomChannel* is a channel to the next lowest window process.

- *FlavorChannel* is a channel to the associated flavor process.

- *ToPanes* is the window output channel to its current set of panes.

A window communicates with its neighboring windows, its flavor and its panes concurrently. Communication with neighboring windows is a result of win-

dow movement in the system. Communications with the flavor are initiated by
the flavor which requires the window to update its image. Lastly, communications with the pane processes are aimed at producing output on the screen. For
instance, a window process receiving a message to move to a new (X, Y) location
will produce a number of messages on its output channels achieving the desired
effect and then recursively call itself with its *Xlocation* and *YLocation* as X and
Y respectively. Thus the perpetual process representing the window has new
locations for further processing. Program 23.1 serves a *move* request. The code
will become apparent in Section 23.3.

```
window_serve(move(X1,Y1),

        X,
        Y,
        form(frame(W,H),Image),
        link(FromTop,
                [display(X1,Y1,W,H,Image) | ToTop]),
        link([reconstruct(X,Y,W,H)) | ToBottom],
            FromBottom),
        FlavorChannel,
        ToPanes
    ) ←
        window(X1,
                Y1,
                form(frame(W,H),Image),
                link(FromTop,ToTop),
                link(ToBottom,FromBottom),
                FlavorChannel,
                ToPanes).
```

Program 23.1: Moving a window

23.2.5 Window flavors

Not all windows function in the same way. Some windows are little bars
that display some information while others are as powerful as another terminal.
However, it is desirable to keep the same data structure for all windows. This
is true since however powerful the window is, it has a lot in common with less
powerful windows. For the window manager which has to lay the windows on the
screen all windows are the same regardless of their functionality. As a result the
functionality of the windows are drawn away from the window structure. The
functionality is implemented by the window's *flavor*.

Example: A window move operation

A window flavor is the process that controls the contents of the window. The flavor receives two channels of messages that are either input events or requests from the window's client process. The flavor interprets the messages and directs the window process to act accordingly. Windows with different flavors may respond differently to identical messages. This scheme enables the user to define classes and subclasses of interfaces (as in Smalltalk).

A flavor process has the form:

```
flavor(
    EventStream,
    ClientChannel,
    WindowChannel,
    Info)
```

Figure 23.4 describes a flavor process.

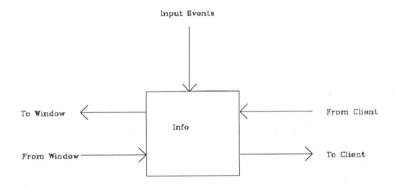

Figure 23.4: Flavor process

- *EventStream* is a stream of input events from the keyboard and the mouse directed to this window.

- *ClientChannel* is the window's communication channel with the client.

- *WindowChannel* is a channel to the associated window.

- *Info* is a logical term of the form: *info*(. . .) which encapsulates information regarding the flavor and the window.

For example, the *Info* variable has the following structure:

```
info(
     Width
     Height
     CurrentX
     CurrentY
     Font
     InputOnOff)
```

- *Width* and *Height* represent the size of the corresponding window.

- *CurrentX* and *CurrentY* represent the current cursor location within the bitmap.

  The four variables are needed so that the flavor can calculate where a character or string is to be printed within a bitmap or when to start a new line and when to start scrolling the window. Note that the flavor knows only the relative positions of characters. The actual position is calculated by the associated window process.

- The *Font* variable has the form: *font(FontTable,W,H)*. The *Font* variable is used to determine the font for writing on the window's bitmap and to advance the cursor the correct number of pixels when moving a character forward or moving to a new line.

- *InputOnOff* gives the flavor an indication if input events should be passed to the client or not.

  This is only an example. Windows can have flavors that do not allow writing characters at all (e.g., an icon) or allow graphics only.

  The flavor is input-driven. Messages originating in the *event* process or in the window's client process trigger a response. On receiving such messages, the flavor responds by sending an appropriate message to the connected window process and/or to the associated client process. Clients express an interest in input events by requesting the flavor to turn on the *InputOnOff* variable.

Example: A shell flavor

Program 23.2 describes how a keyboard input character is handled by a shell flavor. The shell flavor allows echoing of characters on the window. The flavor, upon receiving a keyboard character event on its *EventStream* (% *S1*), performs two operations simultaneously: A message is sent to the associated window requesting it to print a character at the appropriate place on the window's bitmap (% *S3*), and since the input mode is *on*, a message is sent to the client process presenting it with the next keyboard character (% *S2*). The flavor then recursively calls itself with its *Info* variable containing the new cursor location.

The guard tests come to ensure that the cursor is advanced by the width

```
shellflavor([Char | EventStream],                          % S1
    link([Char | ToClient],FromClient),                    % S2
    link(FromWindow,
        [print_char(Char?,Cx,Cy,Font)| ToWindow]),         % S3
    info(W,H,Cx,Cy,font(Font,Wf,Hf),on)
) ←
    char(Char),
    Cx1 := Cx + Wf,
    Cx1 < W|
    shellflavor(EventStream?,
        link(ToClient,FromClient),
        link(FromWindow,ToWindow),
        info(on,W,H,Cx1,Cy,font(Font,Wf,Wh),on)).
```

Program 23.2: Character input handling by a shell flavor

of a single character of the associated font. It also checks that no writing is done beyond the window's bitmap bounds. The font for writing on the window's bitmap is taken from the *Info* variable.

A flavor responds only to what is defined in its procedures. In the example above the procedure deals with a single input character. There are also procedures dealing with a string of characters or control characters. It should be noted, however, that users may open their window with a user defined flavor which enables a client to control the contents of the window in any other fashion.

23.2.6 The pane process

The pane process represents a rectangular portion of some window which is exposed on the screen. A pane process is spawned by the *I/O* process which recognizes that some portion of the window is exposed. The process has two tasks: to control screen update and to support input distribution.

A pane process has the form:

```
pane(
    X,Y,W,H,
    FromIO,
    FromWindow,
    ToFlavor,
    ScreenDevice)
```

- *X, Y, W, H* represent the location and size of the pane in absolute screen co-ordinates.

- *FromIO* is a channel from the I/O process to the pane.

- *FromWindow* is used by the connected window to cache output to the pane.

- *ToFlavor* is a channel to the flavor process from which the window is able to read input events.

- *ScreenDevice* is a pointer to the screen's bitmap. It is used by the pane process to write bitmaps on the screen.

  A pane process can become a listener pane process by adding two channels:

- *EventStream* is a stream of events produced by the event process.

- *Return* is used to return the event stream to the I/O process.

  Figure 23.5 describes a pane and a listener pane process.

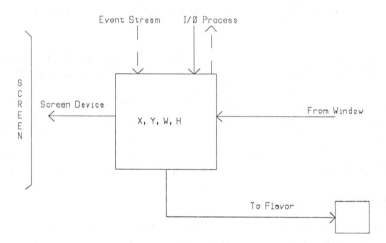

Figure 23.5: A pane and a listener pane

Pane processes form a non-overlapping collection of rectangles that completely cover the screen. A window is connected to a number of pane processes representing its currently exposed rectangular fragments. Each pane is connected via a channel to its window flavor's process. If a window process has a number of exposed fragments then for each of these there is one pane. The window places output requests on the channel to its panes. The channel is read by all panes connected to that window which in turn perform the actual screen update.

Panes allow windows in the system to write concurrently to the screen (when it is supported by the hardware). Each pane is an independent process that reads requests from its window and writes to the screen device. Since the panes are non-overlapping there is no danger of windows writing outside their exposed bounds.

Since the set of panes are kept as a non-overlapping cover of the actual screen, it is possible to determine for each event which pane *owns* it. In our system we do not determine for each event who owns it, rather, only special mouse events that are aimed at changing the listener window are checked. Still, the same architecture can support the general paradigm of input distribution.

23.2.7 The I/O process

The I/O process synchronizes between the two tasks of determining a listener pane and updating the panes. Special input events are trapped by the I/O process. An I/O process has the form:

> io(
> > FromTop
> > EventStream
> > ToPanes
> > Signals)

- *FromTop* reads output from the *TOP* window. These are messages that are aimed at updating the window layout on the screen.

- *EventStream* are special input events produced by the low level interface.

- *ToPanes* is a channel on which the I/O process notifies panes of updates.

- *Signals* is a channel of interrupts produced by the low level interface.

Figure 23.2 (and Figure 23.13) describe the I/O process.

The I/O process has access to all the panes via the *ToPanes* channel. It is able to instruct all panes to take some update measure by writing on the channel. The I/O process produces a channel of pane updates or listener change requests. The channel is read concurrently by all pane processes. Section 23.4 describes how and why all panes receive a correct channel of requests and how it is assured that a correct listener is always found.

The I/O process receives only input events on the *EventStream* channel which are aimed at changing the listener window.

Screen update requests received on the *FromTop* channel are passed to the panes so as to update them. However, if there is an *update_listener* mouse click, the I/O process gives preference to handling the new listener request. This is done since it is assumed that the *update_listener* mouse click is related to the state of the screen which is currently displayed and not to the one that is about to be displayed after the pane update. Even though this architecture does not handle input events immediately, it is assured that the division of the screen among the windows does not change before an event is processed. Thus, input events are always directed to the window which was the listener at the time the event took place.

23.3 A Distributed Window Management Algorithm

This section introduces the concept of window self-management. We describe a distributed algorithm for managing windows conforming to the Z composer protocol presented in Section 23.1. The algorithm is dependent upon two basic operations which are its building blocks.

23.3.1 Two building blocks

We introduce the following definitions. All coordinates in this section are in absolute screen coordinates (integers). The top-left corner of the screen is $(0,0)$.

Window rectangle

With each window we associate a *rectangle* defined by a 4-tuple (X,Y,W,H) where X and Y are the window's top-left corner, W is the width of the window and H is the height of the window.

Window fragment

Let rectangle $R_1 = (X_1,Y_1,W_1,H_1)$ and $R_2 = (X_2,Y_2,W_2,H_2)$ be two rectangles. R_2 is a *fragment* of R_1 if:

$$X_2 \geq X_1,$$
$$Y_2 \geq Y_1,$$
$$X_1 + W_1 \geq X_2 + W_2,$$
$$Y_1 + H_1 \geq Y_2 + H_2.$$

Intersecting rectangle

Let R_1 and R_2 be two rectangles. The *intersecting rectangle R* of R_1 with R_2 is the maximal fragment of R_1 which is also a fragment of R_2.

Overlapping function

An *overlapping function* is defined as:

overlap: Rect $\times$ Rect $\Longrightarrow$ Boolean.

Given two rectangles the function returns a *True* if the two rectangles intersect and *False* otherwise.

Cover

A set of rectangles $\{R_1 \cdots R_n\}$ is said to *exactly cover* a rectangle R if:

(1) The union of the rectangles $R_1 \cdots R_n$ is R.

(2) $\forall i,j \in [i \cdots n]$ R_i and R_j do not intersect.

Relaxing the second condition produces a *cover*.

Outersecting rectangles

Let R_1 and R_2 be two intersecting rectangles, with an intersecting rectangle R. A set OR of rectangles are *outersecting rectangles* of R_1 w.r.t. R_2 if:

(1) The set of rectangles in OR exactly cover $R_1 - R$.

(2) The set of rectangles OR is minimal in the number of rectangles.

Intersection function

$$\text{intersect: Rect} \times \text{Rect} \implies (\text{Rect} \times \text{ListofRects})$$

Given two rectangles R_1 and R_2 the *intersect function* returns a pair $\langle IR, OR \rangle$ where IR is the *intersecting rectangle* (perhaps empty) and OR are the *outersecting rectangles* of R_1 w.r.t. R_2.

Display messages

When a window or window fragment wishes to display itself it sends a message to that effect to the window above. Windows that are below the requesting window should not affect the resulting real screen so that we need only concern ourselves with windows that are above this window. The message a window sends requesting to be displayed is called a *display* message. A *display* message is of the form:

$$display(X, Y, W, H, Image)[1]$$

- (X, Y, W, H) is a window fragment.

- *Image* is either the window's bitmap or a window's fragment bitmap.

Receiving a *display* message from below

When a window receives a *display* message from below, it acts as follows:

- Applies an overlapping function on its own window coordinates and the rectangle specified in the *display* message.

---

[1] The message contains some other arguments that are not relevant to the discussion at hand

- If the overlapping function returns *False* then the window is not obscuring any portion of the rectangle specified by the *display* message and therefore the message is propagated on to the next window up.

- If the returned value is *True* then the window applies the intersection function to the rectangle specified in the message w.r.t. the window's coordinates in order to produce an intersecting rectangle and a list of outersecting rectangles. There is exactly one intersecting rectangle and zero or more outersecting rectangles. Each of the outersecting rectangles is a window fragment.

  The intersecting rectangle is the portion of the rectangle specified in the message that the window obscures. The outersecting rectangles are the remaining rectangles that are not obscured by the window. As for the obscured portion, the window simply does nothing but for each of the outersecting rectangles a new *display* message is constructed and is passed to the next window up.

Example

Assume two windows denoted by *A* and *B* that overlap each other as in Figure 23.6(a).

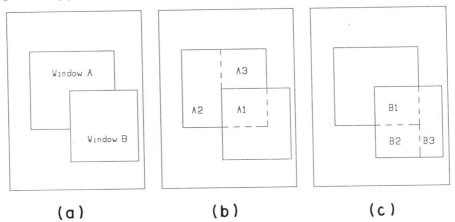

(a)   **(b)**   **(c)**

Figure 23.6: Before and after application of intersection function

Suppose window *A* wishes to be displayed. Using the mechanism described it will send a *display* message to *B*. *B* upon receiving the message applies the overlapping function. Since there is an overlap *B* applies the intersection function of *A* w.r.t. *B*.

The intersecting rectangle is *A1* and the outersecting rectangles are *A2* and *A3* (Figure 23.6(b)). Since *B* obscures *A1*, this fragment is discarded. However

A2 and *A3* are not obscured by *B* and therefore for each of the fragments (*A2*, *A3*) a new *display* message is constructed and is passed on from *B* up.
The new *display* messages look like this:

$$display(A2\text{'s coordinates},A2\text{'s bitmap})$$

$$display(A3\text{'s coordinates },A3\text{'s bitmap})$$

In this example two *display* messages were filtered up. Each of these messages is received by the next window up and may filter more *display* messages further up. Eventually some of the messages propagate as far as the top-most window *TOP*. When *TOP* receives a *display* message it interprets the message to mean: display this fragment on the real screen. The fragment's bitmap will be displayed on the screen and this reflects that at some point in the past this fragment was highest within the *Z* order at that location. In the system, however, there may be other messages that are about to cover that screen location.

Reconstruct messages

The purpose of a *reconstruct* message is to reconstruct a portion of the screen that needs updating. For example, when a window moves from one location to another the vacated area should be reconstructed.

A *reconstruct* message is syntactically similar to a *display* message but whereas a *display* message is sent up the *reconstruct* message is sent down. The message is of the form:

$$reconstruct(X,Y,W,H)$$

- (*X,Y,W,H*) is a window rectangle or fragment.

Receiving a *reconstruct* message from above

A window receiving a *reconstruct* message from above does the following:

- Applies the overlapping function on its window coordinates and the coordinates specified in the *reconstruct* message.

  - If the overlapping function returns *False* then the window does not overlap the reconstructed area. The window can not help in the reconstruction process and therefore passes the message further down.

  - If the overlapping function returns *True* then the window applies the intersection function of the specified coordinates in the *reconstruct* message w.r.t. the window's coordinates. The intersecting rectangle is the fragment that should be reconstructed with the window's bitmap. As for the outersecting rectangle, those fragments are yet to be reconstructed and should therefore be sent further down.

The intersecting fragment is sent up by the window as a *display* message. This is because it has just been discovered to be an exposed region of the screen. As for each of the outersecting fragments, those are possibly exposed as well but we have not yet found which window is situated there. Thus for each of the outersecting fragments a *reconstruct* message is sent down.

Example

Consider again the two windows in Figure 23.6(a).

Suppose now that window B wants to reconstruct its location (for instance, if it has been deleted and the space it occupied needs to be reconstructed). To this purpose it sends a *reconstruct* message down to A. A upon receipt of this message applies the overlapping function of B and A. Since there is an intersection A applies the intersection function of B w.r.t. A and determines that $B1$ is the intersecting rectangle and that $B2$ and $B3$ are the outersecting rectangles (Figure 23.6(c)). Window A then produces the following messages:

reconstruct(*B2's coordinates*)

reconstruct(*B3's coordinates*)

display(*B1's coordinates, A1's bitmap*)

The first two messages are sent by A further down and the third message is sent by A back up (which is not necessarily to B since this window may have been deleted since).

A reconstructed fragment is tested for emptiness. If it is empty it is not processed further. The reconstruction process terminates when either all fragments have been found to be empty or all non-empty fragments have reached the dummy *BOTTOM* window. The *BOTTOM* window will treat each *reconstruct* message as stating that the background has to be displayed where the fragment is situated. Therefore, it sends a *display* message back up.

Note that the *BOTTOM* window does not assume the background should be displayed since this is a distributed system and anything may have happened to the windows in the system in the meantime. It simply initiates a request to display the background at the fragment's coordinates. If no window has moved since the first *reconstruct* message was sent then eventually the background will be displayed.

With these basic *display* and *reconstruct* operations we can proceed to describe how a new window is created, moved, reshaped, and closed.

23.3.2 Window operations

Creating a new window

To create a new window, a new window process is spawned and inserted into the linked list of window processes. The window process transmits a *display* message to the window above it requesting to display itself. This message is dealt with by the receiving message as described above. The desired effect will be achieved since all non-obscured fragments will eventually be filtered to the dummy *TOP* window while all obscured fragments will be absorbed by one of the windows above the new window.

Closing a window

To close a window, we delete the window process from the linked list of window processes. The closing window, as a last operation before terminating, sends a *reconstruct* message down requesting to reconstruct the vacated area. The effect achieved is that the vacated region (where the closing window resided) will eventually be reconstructed. Note that the closing window may have been partially or wholly obscured by other windows. This should not worry us since any attempt to display a fragment that is not exposed will be absorbed by the lowest obscuring window.

Moving a window

Moving a window is only a slightly more complex operation, and is implemented by the create and close operations (*display* and *reconstruct*) above. A window can be requested to move to another location. This operation may be viewed as closing the window in the old location and creating it in the new one. The window will therefore send *display* and *reconstruct* messages up and down respectively (Program 23.1). Sending a *display* message has the same effect as creating a new window in the new location. Sending a *reconstruct* message is like closing the window in the old location. As an optimization the reconstruction need only be done in the outersecting rectangles of the old location w.r.t. to the new location since the rest of the area is known to be beneath the window's new location.

Hiding and exposing windows

Hiding a window is the same as closing the window in the one location and then re-opening it in the same location as the bottom-most window. Closing the window is implemented by deleting the window process from the *Z* order of windows and sending a *reconstruct* message with the coordinates of the closing window down. Re-opening the window is implemented by sending a message to the *BOTTOM* window requesting it to reopen the window. *BOTTOM* will initiate a *display* message that will attempt to display the window as the lowest

Z order window.

Exposing a window is the same as closing the window in one location and re-opening it as the top-most window in the same location. Closing in this case is implemented by deleting the window from the *Z* order of windows and requesting *TOP* to re-open the window as the top-most window. There is no need to reconstruct since the window will be exposed in at least as many fragments as it was before the operation. There will not be new fragments appearing on the screen other than the ones belonging to that particular window. *TOP*, when opening a window does so by inserting the window just below itself and by sending a *display* message up (which is usually immediately received by *TOP*).

Reshaping a window

Reshaping a window is similar to moving a window. We close the window in the old location and reopen the window in the new location with its new size. The window system assumes the client will re-arrange the contents of the window.

23.3.3 A detailed example

Many aspects of this algorithm should be inspected carefully. It is not altogether apparent that a correct behavior is achieved by this method. The distributed nature of this algorithm causes many operations to take place concurrently so that it is necessary to prove that ultimately the desired effect is achieved. A formal proof can be found in (Katzenellenbogen, 1987). In this section we present an example which illustrates some of the issues involved.

The problematic aspect of the algorithm may be demonstrated by the following case: what happens when two windows wish to perform a window operation simultaneously. Since both of these window operations produce a series of *display* and *reconstruct* messages, all of which are in existence in the system simultaneously, it may be the case that the resulting screen is not the required one. It should therefore be proved that the desired screen (and this will be defined) is reached while at the same time the complexity of the algorithm is reasonable.

We first present a test case on which we illustrate the issues involved. Suppose two windows are being moved simultaneously. The windows overlap as in Figure 23.7 before they respond to the move request.

Suppose the two windows are adjacent and that *B* is above *A*. Suppose for simplicity that the two windows are the only windows residing in the system. There are three possible cases:

(1) The two windows are moved simultaneously which means they send out *display* and *reconstruct* messages at the same time.

(2) *B* moves before *A*.

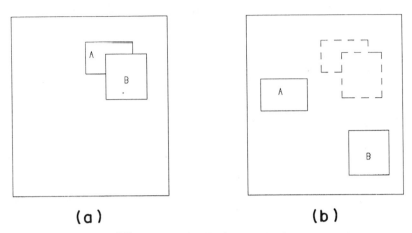

Figure 23.7: Before and after

(3) *A* moves before *B*.

<u>Case 1</u> (Figure 23.7)

- *B* sends a *display* message up to *TOP*. This will display *B* on the screen at the new location.

- *B* requests *A* to reconstruct *B*'s vacated area. Since *A*'s new location does not intersect *B*'s old location the *reconstruct* message will be passed on down to *BOTTOM*. This will eventually cause the background color to be displayed on *B's* vacated area of the screen.

- *A* sends a *display* message up to *B*. This will eventually cause *A* to be displayed on the screen at the new location since *B*'s new location does not obscure *A*'s new location.

- *A* requests *BOTTOM* to reconstruct its vacated area. This will eventually cause the background color to be displayed on the vacated area of the screen.

<u>Case 2</u> (Figure 23.8)

B moves first:

- *B* sends a *display* message up to *TOP*. This will cause *B* to be displayed on the screen at the new location.

- *B* requests *A* to reconstruct *B*'s vacated area. Since *A* is still in its old location there is some area of *A* which perhaps should be printed. Therefore a *display* message is sent with respect to *A1* (the intersecting rectangle). The *display* message is sent to *B*, and since *B* is in the new position the

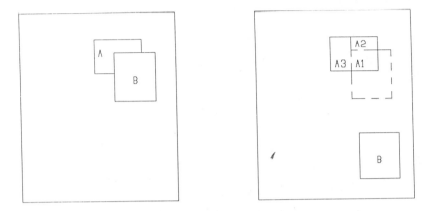

Figure 23.8: B in new location A still in old location

fragment is not affected by *B* and will therefore eventually get displayed. This erroneous display is temporary and will be corrected by later display messages.

The other two fragments of *B* will be sent further down in order to reconstruct those areas. The two messages reach *BOTTOM* which subsequently sends up messages requesting to display the fragments with the background color. The background will be displayed regardless of *A*'s current position.

A moves:

- *A* sends a *display* message with respect to its new location. The message is received by *B* and since *B* does not affect the area it simply passes the message on to *B*'s top-window *SCREEN* which will display window *A* on the screen.

- *A* sends a *reconstruct* message with respect to its old location. This results, eventually, in *A1,A2* and *A3* being displayed as the background color.

The algorithm in this case will print *A* and *B* in their new locations and refresh *A*'s and *B*'s old location once only with the exception of *A1* which is displayed twice (once by *A*'s *reconstruct* message and once by *B*'s *reconstruct* message).

Case 3 is very similar to Case 2 and is therefore omitted.

23.3.4 Complexity analysis

It may seem that in the worst case the number of messages is exponential in the number of windows created in the system, but a closer look at the analysis will reveal that the worst-case complexity is actually $O(N^3)$ where N is the number of windows. Suppose there are N windows in the system. Let $X_1 \cdots X_{k1}$ be the set of points along the X-axis where there is a corner of some window. Note that $k1 \leq 2N$. Suppose similarly that $Y_1 \cdots Y_{k2}$ is the set of points along the Y-axis with the same property. Note too that $k2 \leq 2N$. The number of rectangles produced by drawing vertical and horizontal lines across the plane is $4N^2$. We will refer to these rectangles as atomic rectangles. We claim that the number of *display* messages that can be produced as a result of a single *display* message is always less than the number of atomic rectangles.

A message can be broken up to a number of other messages each representing one or more atomic rectangles. But, once a message represents a single atomic rectangle it can no longer be broken and all that it may do is to propagate up to the *TOP* window.

We will analyze the case of window creation. The system begins in a stable state. The created window invokes a *display* message sent from itself up. The message can be broken up to no more than $4N^2$ messages each of which can propagate $O(N)$ steps to the *TOP* window. Thus, the complexity of a window creation is $O(N^3)$.

Generally of course the number of messages will be far smaller since:

(1) There is a trade off between the $O(N^2)$ required to maximally split the screen to atomic rectangles and the $O(N)$ a message will have to travel until it gets to *TOP*. The more windows needed to split the message, the less distance the window will have to travel to the top.

(2) Windows are generally created closer to *TOP* than to *BOTTOM*, thus a maximal division is not required.

(3) Windows are usually layed with little overlap between them, thus again a maximal split is not $O(N^2)$.

23.4 Input/Output

Section 23.1 surveyed some of the issues related to I/O in window systems in general and distributed window systems in particular. This section focuses on possible solutions to these problems and presents our solution.

Several alternative designs were considered with respect to the I/O components. The simplest design demanded no additions to the system presented in the previous section. When a window wishes to display a part of its bitmap (echo a character, for instance) it sends a *display* message upwards. Eventually, if the fragment is exposed, it will be displayed. Similarly an input event could be sent from the top most window *TOP* downwards until some window recognizes the event is within its bounds. Though simple, the performance of this method is not acceptable. A window low down in the hierarchy pays a heavy overhead for display, and waits a long time for input events.

These consideration led us to adopt a caching mechanism that enables windows to cache streams to the screen and enables an input process to cache an input events stream to the listener windows.

The architecture we chose is described in Figure 23.9. We chose a fixed listener input paradigm though the architecture allows for cursor dependent listener paradigm.

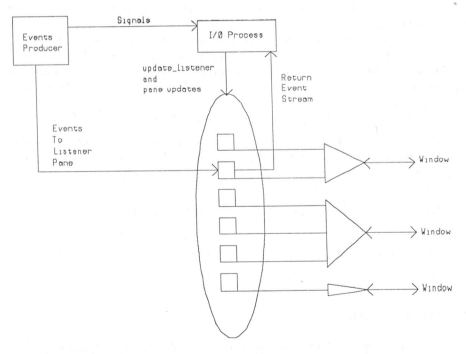

Figure 23.9: Input/Output in the model

In the proposed architecture it might happen that a window which is not exposed will receive the input stream but that is still consistent with the general philosophy since one can not definitely say which window is exposed even if it is currently exposed on the screen. Another window higher in the Z axis could be in the process of exposing itself.

In the proposed architecture the screen is viewed as a pool of non-overlapping panes, each of which represents an exposed window fragment at some location on the screen. Each pane is a process that is connected to one of the windows. Each window is connected to zero or more such pane processes (representing its exposed fragments). Panes are able to copy bitmaps to the screen device. In addition since the panes are non-overlapping they are used to determine event ownership.

A special perpetual process, namely the I/O process, is constructed in order to synchronize between input events and screen updates. The need for such a process arose since we wanted to use the pane mechanism (which determines what gets displayed on the screen) for determining which is the listener' window. Since the panes are the most updated processes reflecting the state of the screen it is natural to use them for input distribution. When a mouse triggers an *up-date_listener*(X, Y) event the fastest way of checking which is the exposed window at location (X, Y) is by querying the panes. The windows themselves do not know whether they are exposed. The I/O process gives greater priority to assigning a new listener than to update the pool of panes.

The I/O process then has four tasks:

(1) Informing pane processes of how to update themselves.

(2) Spawning new pane processes.

(3) Giving priority to *update_listener* events over pane updates.

(4) Distributing event streams to the various pane processes.

23.4.1 Output

The caching method we introduce allows window processes to write directly to the screen disregarding other windows. The mechanism allows a window to send out write requests without blocking and with no fear of damaging other windows. Assuming the hardware is capable of executing parallel output, the system can exploit this feature allowing parallel output from the windows.

Pane processes are able to write directly to the screen. Windows write to the screen by sending their panes a write request in the form of an image and a location. Panes belonging to the same window consume the same channel so that the window need write only once. Each pane determines which part of the image to display by clipping the image's bitmap to the size of the pane. The pane acts as a clipping region. For small bitmaps (characters, for instance) there would normally be only one such pane. The clipped portion is written on the screen.

So long as the windows are static (meaning there are no movements of windows in the system) this scheme works smoothly. When there is a window operation, internal messages begin to propagate in the system, some of which propagate as far as *TOP*. When this happens a new window fragment should be displayed on the screen reflecting the new relative positioning of windows. The pool of panes has to be updated in order to reflect the screen division correctly.

The dummy window *TOP* outputs messages of the form:

display(X,Y,W,H,ToFlavor,FromWindow)

Its meaning is: There is a new exposed window fragment at location (X, Y) with size (W,H). The pane (if and when constructed) should pass input events (when its window becomes the listener) via the *ToFlavor* channel, and the window should send output to the screen on the *FromWindow* channel.

Program 23.3 performs pane creation and update. The I/O process has access to each of the panes in the pool. It is able, given a new *display* message, to update the pool of panes by sending them messages. A new pane process is appended to the set while existing panes are instructed to update.

```
io([display(X,Y,W,H,ToFlavor,FromWindow) | FromTop],     % S1
    Events,
    [clip(X,Y,W,H)| ToPanes],                             % S2
    ScreenPointer,
    Signal
) ←
    unknown(Signal) |                                     % S3
    pane(X,Y,W,H,
        ToPanes?,
        FromWindow?,
        ToFlavor,
        ScreenPointer)
    io(FromTop?,
        Events,
        ToPanes
        ScreenPointer
        Signal).
```

Program 23.3: A pane update

When the *I/O* process receives a *display*$(X, Y, W, H, \ldots)$ (% *S1*) message and there are no signals (% *S3*), an instruction to all currently existing panes to clip (X,Y,W,H) off their coordinates is sent (% *S2*). A pane process is added to the pool of panes with the appropriate coordinates. The pane receives subsequent messages from the I/O process on the *ToPanes?* variable.

When a pane process receives an instruction to update (in the form of a $clip(X,Y,W,H)$ message) it acts as follows: If it intersects with the clipping rectangle, it is either deleted (if the clipping rectangle totally covers it) or split (if it partially covers it).

Pane processes give priority to serving instructions from the I/O process over instructions from their windows as will be explained. This priority is essential since otherwise, it may be the case that the new pane which has been spawned will refresh its window's image before existing panes have been updated. If this happens an existing pane might write over a location owned by the new pane. To achieve this priority, panes are connected via a short circuit. The I/O process sends a message (the clipping instruction) to the first pane and waits for the last pane to acknowledge. The I/O process will only spawn the new pane process after all existing panes have updated.

It is important to notice that windows never stop writing to the output device. A window may continue to send messages on its output cache channel to its panes in order to output to the screen. The panes themselves may halt temporarily in order to update, but they immediately continue to output, while disregarding other panes in the system.

This scheme assures us that each pane receives an identical series of instructions. When the new pane is added, the pool of updated panes together with the new pane again become a non-overlapping cover of the screen. The instructions may be processed by the panes at different times, but the set of panes accepting an instruction X will always form the non-overlapping cover for the screen. This invariant is important since it assures that the I/O process is able to find a window residing at a specified location by querying the panes and receiving as a reply one and only one pane which resides at that specified location.

We are now in a position to examine Program 23.1 more closely. The moving window in Program 23.4 sends a *display* message on its new location (% *S1*) and a *reconstruct* message on its old location (% *S2*). The *display* message contains the *ToFlavor* channel on which panes are able to send input events to the window and the *ToPanes1* variable on which subsequent output requests will be sent to the panes. The existing panes are notified of this new caching channel (% *S3*).

If a window is damaged by some foreign process and a client wants to refresh the window or refresh the screen the window should be instructed to simply write on its cache channel an instruction to display the contents of the window. Each connected pane clips the window and prints only the exposed portions of the window. In order to refresh the entire screen the client would have to request all windows to display themselves on their output cache channels.

```
window_serve(move(X1,Y1),
    X,
    Y,
    form(frame(W,H),Image),
    link(FromTop,
        [display(X1,Y1,W,H,Image,ToFlavor,ToPanes1?) | ToTop]),      % S1
    link([reconstruct(X,Y,W,H)) | ToBottom],                         % S2
        FromBottom),
    link(ToFlavor,FromFlavor),
    [new_stream(ToPanes1)]                                           % S3
) ←
    window(X1,
        Y1,
        form(frame(W,H),Image),
        link(FromTop?,ToTop),
        link(ToBottom,FromBottom),
        link(ToFlavor,FromFlavor),
        ToPanes1).
```

Program 23.4: Moving a window

23.4.2 Input handling

An important issue that the window system has to solve is how to pass input events to the client process and how to maintain the order in which events occur. This section describes how input events are passed to the window and how screen updates are synchronized with input events. The design we introduce is a consequence of the distributed nature of the system.

Since we chose the fixed listener paradigm, mouse movement events are meaningless and hence filtered. We assume a special purpose processor is tracking the mouse and echoing its image on the physical output device. Only character events and mouse clicks are trapped and passed to the windows. One mouse click is designated to change the listener window. Other mouse clicks are passed to the window which interprets them using the window flavor.

The I/O process gives greater priority to the *update_listener* mouse click over pane updates since it is assumed that events occur with respect to what is displayed on the screen at the time the event took place. If a new pane will be created after a mouse click occurred, it is possible that a wrong pane would be found when querying the panes.

A low-level interface produces a stream of events. We call the low level routine the *producer*. The producer creates a stream of events which is consumed by the

```
io(FromTop,
    [update_listener(X,Y) | Events],              % S1
    [new_event_stream(X,Y,Events,Return) | ToPanes],   % S2
    ScreenPointer,
    [signal | Signal]                             % S4
) ←
    io(FromTop,
        Return?,
        ToPanes,
        ScreenPointer,
        Signal?).
```

Program 23.5: Distributing an event stream

I/O process or by a listener pane (a listener pane is a pane that is selected by an *update_listener* mouse click). In addition, the producer is able to signal the I/O process that an *update_listener* event has occurred by placing a *signal* message on its *Signal* variable. This is important since we would like the I/O process to halt pane updates as soon as the *update_listener* mouse click occurs. Signalling the I/O process is as if we allowed the I/O process to look ahead into the stream of input events and detect the mouse click. Program 23.5 presents the code for this scheme.

The I/O process does no pane updates while its *Signal* variable is instantiated (% *S4*). In addition the I/O process does not attempt to determine a new listener window so long as the previous pane listener has not finished copying events to the appropriate window.

When the I/O process reads an *update_listener* event it sends a message to all panes: *new_events(X,Y,Events,Return)*. One of the panes succeeds in finding (X,Y) to be within its bounds (Program 23.6). The pane process begins to function as a pane listener by copying events from *Events* to its associated window. The pane does this until it reads a new *update_listener(X,Y)* event (Program 23.7). When the pane reads that event it unifies [*update_listener(X,Y)* | *Events*] with *Return* thus returning the event stream to the I/O process that, in turn, will find a new pane listener.

The *I/O* process waits for further signals on the *Signal* variable, thus if there have not been any *update_listener* events the I/O process may continue to update panes.

Pane processes write to their associated window flavor using a specialized multiple-writer stream-of-streams mechanism (Tribble et al., Chapter 17). A writing pane might have to skip through a limited number of list cells before it can

```
pane(X,Y,W,H,
    [new_event_stream(X1,Y1,Events,Return) | FromIO],
    FromWindow,
    ToFlavor,
    ScreenDevice
) ←
    (X1,Y1) ∈ (X,Y,W,H) |
    listener_pane(X,Y,W,H,
        FromIO,
        FromWindow,
        Events?,
        ToFlavor,
        Return,
        ScreenDevice).
```

Program 23.6: Accepting an event stream

```
listener_pane(X,Y,W,H,
    FromIO,
    FromWindow,
    [update_listener(X,Y) | Events],
    ToFlavor,
    [update_listener(X,Y) | Events],
    ScreenDevice
) ←
    pane(X,Y,W,H,
        FromIO,
        FromWindow,
        ToFlavor,
        ScreenDevice).
```

Program 23.7: Returning an event stream

begin to write on its own stream. This number is determined by the number of listener pane switches and this number is thought to be insignificant.

It should be noted that windows do not stop writing to the screen while there is an input event. In fact, windows may still perform any window operation they wish. Internal messages continue to propagate in the system. Only pane update is suspended. The panes themselves continue to serve their window's write requests.

We have shown that when a window moves it does not block write requests even if the window operation has not been fulfilled yet. Now we have shown that input events do not block output.

23.4.3 Optimizations

One of the problems facing the pane method of updating the screen is that the number of panes grows continuously. Every time a pane receives an instruction to clip, the number of pane process spawned as a result is between 0 and 4. In addition, the I/O process adds a new pane process to the pool. It is possible that after some window operations there are panes belonging to the same window that could be joined into one pane. It is desirable to minimize the number of panes since a window's write requests are processed by all its existing panes. We introduce two methods for overcoming this problem.

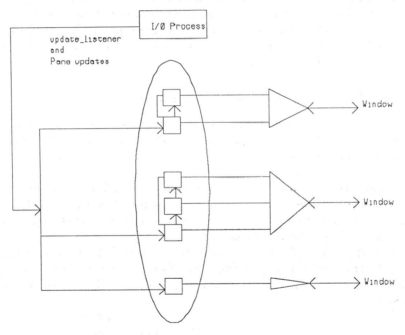

Figure 23.10: Panes in a cluster model

The first method is to garbage collect the panes following some fixed number of pane creations. This is done by sending a message from the top-most window down declaring the intention. Windows then halt output and close their old output cache channels thereby terminating the connected pane processes. A second message immediately follows from the top-most window down in order to reconstruct the entire screen. Windows then attempt to display their exposed portions thus creating a new minimal set of pane processes. In the process of garbage collection it is necessary to lock input to the system since temporarily the pool of panes might not be a cover for the screen.

An alternative which does not lock the windows in the system in any way is to introduce an optimized method of connecting panes. The idea is to cluster pane processes belonging to the same window. This could be easily done by each pane containing a signature of the window associated with it in the form of a logical variable. The cluster of panes is kept, always, at a minimal number of panes (the cluster is minimal when no two panes may be joined). A new pane is added to the pool of panes by adding it to its appropriate cluster and updating the remaining panes. Each pane in the cluster is serially checked with the new pane for a possibility of joining the two panes. If a join was possible then the joint pane is checked for a possibility of joining itself with each of the remaining panes. The algorithm minimizes the number of panes and is of quadratic complexity in the number of panes. Checking for a possible join of two panes $(X1,Y1,W1,H1)$ and $(X2,Y2,W2,H2)$ is equal to four integer comparisons: $(X1=X2$ and $W1=W2)$ or $(Y1=Y2$ and $H1=H2)$.

23.5 Implementation and Performance

This section discusses the implemention of the window system and its performance. The architecture is implemented in FCP. The basic architecture which initializes the system and defines the processes interface is about 1500 lines of code.

Low-level kernels which perform *bitblt* operation and initialize the screen are implemented in C. The low-level graphics package is Sun-Core which conforms to the ACM standard for graphics. The system may be ported to any machine which runs FCP by adapting the kernels.

The performance of system is measured by the FCP emulator (Houri and Shapiro, Chapter 38) running on Sun 3-50. The system has not yet been ported to a multiprocessor. The following tables give some indication of the system's performance:

Operations	CPU Time	Process Reductions
Open a first window	1.78 sec.	1511
Open a second window	1.26 sec.	1067
Open a third (bottom) window	2.1 sec.	1797
expose the second window	1.1 sec.	897
hide the top window	2.0 sec.	1676
print string on top window	0.6 sec.	424
print string on hidden window	0.4 sec.	299
move a hidden window	4.1 sec.	3528

The system is quite slow at present. Using better compilation techniques (Kliger, 1987), a uniprocessor speedup of at least 10 is achievable. Such a speedup will bring the system closer to being practical.

23.6 Discussion

We have described an architecture for a distributed window system. The architecture is influenced by the requirement that no central managers exist. Central managers may cause execution bottlenecks since every service granted by it is serialized. In addition the system architecture is influenced by the object oriented paradigm (Hewitt, 1973; Shapiro and Takeuchi, Chapter 29; Kahn et al., Chapter 30). The system is constructed of objects (perpetual processes) communicating with each other by message passing. The system is written almost entirely in FCP except for a limited number of low level primitives that control I/O devices.

The significance of this work is in showing novel approach to designing a fully distributed window system. The properties listed in Section 23.1.5 make this system unique in its capabilities.

We have found FCP a suitable programming language for implementing the window systems. Since FCP is very high level and intended for distributed applications, implementations need not consider low level problems concerning, for example, mutual exclusion and communication. We used FCP as a specification language for the proposed architecture. The specification is also the executable implementation.

Although presently not implemented, the architecture can be implemented as a full Z composer of windows by controlling the contents of every window recursively by the same architecture. This means that subwindows write their output to panes that access, instead of the screen, the parent window's bitmap. If the contents of every window is controlled by the proposed architecture then the screen can be viewed as just a special kind of a window.

An important point to consider is the question of process mapping. Clients, window processes, pane processes and the I/O devices may be spread over the network in many fashions. In the one end of the scale all processes except the client can be placed on one processor. In the other extreme all processes can reside anywhere in the system. In the middle, window and pane processes can be placed near the client process. Another alternative is to place window processes near the client while pane processes can be placed at the processor devoted to I/O. The tradeoff depends on the overhead of communication, the network architecture, the number of input devices, the number of output devices, and the application itself. The tradeoff will have to be determined by experimentation.

Chapter 24

Logical Secrets

Mark S. Miller, Daniel G. Bobrow, Eric Dean Tribble

Xerox Palo Alto Research Center

Jacob Levy

The Weizmann Institute of Science

Abstract

Public-key systems implement a set of abstract security and authentication operations. These abstract operations are generally useful in a world of mutually mistrusted but cooperating agents. Cryptography is only necessary for implementing these operations in the absence of a mutually trusted secure substrate. Concurrent logic programming languages provide such a substrate for embedded computations, and indeed may be a foundation for secure multi-user systems. We present an implementation of a public-key system in Flat Concurrent Prolog which derives security from encapsulation rather than encryption. An implementation of a banking system is then presented as an example of its use.

24.1 Introduction

Computer security concerns generally arise in the domains of operating systems and data communications. Achieving secure systems in these domains has enabled the use of computation in many aspects of society, such as electronic funds transfer, publicly accessible databases, and time-sharing services. Security has rarely been an issue in programming language design. However, concurrent logic programming languages have been proposed as a foundation for secure distributed multi-user operating systems (Shapiro, Chapter 2). In this paper we examine the ability of these languages to express some of the security constructs that these previous systems have provided.

Security may also be important for artificial intelligence. A tradition in AI is to investigate systems of loosely-coupled cooperating agents. These agents might be computations in an open system (Hewitt, 1985; Stefik, 1986), heuristics cooperating while exploring different parts of a search space (Kornfeld and Hewitt, 1981), or intelligent agents participating in a society of mind (Minsky, 1985). The interactions between components within these systems can create overwhelming complexity. Trust is a form of dependency between entities; by reducing dependencies the modularity of a system is increased. This is particularly important if Eurisko-like systems (Lenat, 1983) are to be robust — the system must be able to survive the introduction of the potentially arbitrary code resulting from free experimentation. Thus, the degree of cooperation possible among mutually mistrusted agents is one measure for how viable a language is in supporting the "systems of agents" tradition.

Two of the issues in security are secrecy and authentication. Capability operating systems and languages with strict encapsulation already provide this for two-party interactions. Providing secure three-party communication is more demanding. Three-party secrecy is the ability to pass a message through an untrusted intermediary to an intended recipient in such a way that only the intended recipient may read the message. Three party authentication is the ability to pass a message through an untrusted intermediary to an intended recipient so that the message contents cannot be faked while preserving the appearance of the original authorship. This corresponds to human signatures, and can be expected to be used for similar purposes. In particular, authenticated messages constitute proof to third parties that some transaction occurred. Both types of three-party security will be demonstrated by the banking system at the end of this paper.

The operations provided by a public-key system (Rivest et al., 1978) satisfy these requirements. These are usually associated with cryptography, which is indeed the only known solution when the underlying medium is insecure. Cryptography has a high overhead for communication intensive computations, though. We describe an implementation in Flat Concurrent Prolog (FCP) using encapsulation to implement this functionality without the overhead of encryption. Unlike encryption, the resulting security does not rely on probability or complexity considerations.

We depend on the shared underlying implementation of FCP to preserve the security properties guaranteed by the language semantics. This can be done without encryption when there is secure shared hardware (as with a single machine or site). However, to preserve FCP's security properties in a distributed implementation will require encryption, so we gain little in this case. The point of this work is to achieve the functionality of public-key systems among mutually *mistrusted* software entities residing on mutually *trusted* hardware without the overhead of encryption. Therefore, the FCP (and Logix) implementation should be considered the equivalent of a secure operating systems kernel, hosting belligerent processes as "users".

This work does not depend upon the logical aspect of logic programming, since Actors (Clinger, 1981) also have the same capabilities. The security features which are crucially important to the current approach are: strict encapsulation (the ability to provide a service based on access to private data while denying that access to one's clients), capability security, and non-forgeable unique identifiers.

24.2 Public-Key Communication

Public-key security is based on unique pairs of keys that can be used for sealing and unsealing data. *Sealing* and *unsealing* are the abstract operations corresponding to encrypting and decrypting. The two keys of a pair are inverses with respect to the sealing and unsealing operations: data sealed with the first key can only be unsealed with the second, and vice-versa. Security arises from the constraint that the inverse of a key cannot be determined from the key itself.

Since the keys are independent, one of the keys can be publicly known. The inverse of a *public key* is called a *private key*. Secure data can be transmitted to the owner of the private key by sealing the data with the public key. The sealed data can then only be accessed using the private key.

Authentication is the complementary operation. If an agent seals something with his private key, other agents with access to his public key can examine the data, with the guarantee that only the owner of the private key could have so sealed the data. This is equivalent to signing a message. In diagrams, the public key is represented with a hollow letter (as shown in Figure 24.1).

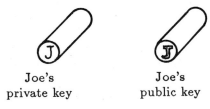

Joe's
private key

Joe's
public key

Figure 24.1

As an example, Joe and Sam wish to communicate over an insecure channel. They each generate a key pair. Both make one of their keys public and keep the other as their private key. For Joe to send a private message to Sam, and guarantee that the message is from Joe, Joe seals the message with his private key (to sign the message), and seals the result with Sam's public key (locking it so only Sam can read it). This is shown in Figure24.2.

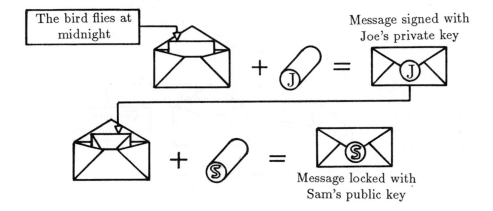

Figure 24.2

The result is then transmitted to Sam. Sam unseals the message with his private key (as in Figure 24.3), and unseals the result with Joe's public key (as in Figure 24.4). The success of this latter operations verifies that Joe authored the message.

24.2.1 FCP specification

The Flat Concurrent Prolog operations for implementing a public-key security system are:

keyPair(Key1, Key2)

The *keyPair* operation returns two unique keys which are each other's only inverses. This is the only operation that can create a key.

seal(Key, Msg, SealedMsg, Ok)

Msg is the data to be sealed. *SealedMsg* is an entity that can be passed to *unseal* with the inverse of *Key* to return *Msg*. *Ok* is *true* if the *seal* operation succeeds, *false* if it fails, and uninstantiated if it suspends.

unseal(Key, SealedMsg, Msg, Ok)

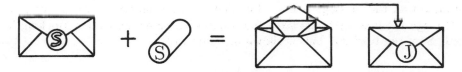

Sam unlocks the envelope using his private key
revealing the message signed by Joe

Figure 24.3

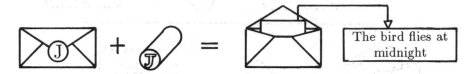

Sam verifies & removes Joe's signature
using Joe's public key, revealing ...

Figure 24.4

SealedMsg comes from a *seal* operation. *Msg* is the contents that were sealed using the inverse of *Key*. *Ok* is the same as for *seal*. *Msg* will not be bound if *Key* is not the correct key for unsealing *SealedMsg*. The *Ok* flag indicates success rather than simply the binding of *Msg* so that uninstantiated variables can be transmitted as messages.

The public-key mechanism can be used to set up a secret authenticated channel by transmitting a message stream (including the uninstantiated tail). Once this channel is set up, it can be used securely without further public-key operations. This is analogous to the cryptographic practice of employing public-key systems to transmit keys for non-public-key encryption schemes. Once these other kinds of keys have been securely distributed (using public-key encryption) they may be used to engage in further secure communication without further invocation of the public-key system.

The above operations must satisfy the following properties:

(1) Communications property:

        For all Msg :
        (keyPair(Key1, Key2) ∨ keyPair(Key2, Key1)) ⇔
           (seal(Key1, Msg, SealedMsg, true) ⇔
           unseal(Key2, SealedMsg, Msg, true))

In other words, *Key1* and *Key2* are inverse keys iff any data sealed with *Key1* unseals with *Key2*, and only data sealed with *Key1* successfully unseals with *Key2*.

(2) Secrecy property:

Given that *SealedMsg* was produced using *Key1* and *Msg*, and that *Key2* is the inverse of *Key1*, if one has access to *SealedMsg* and *Key1*, but not to *Key2* or *Msg*, there is no way to gain access to either *Key2* or *Msg*. Given access to *SealedMsg*, *Key1*, and *Msg*, one cannot gain access to *Key2* (this is known as resisting the "known plaintext attack", i.e., that one cannot crack the key even with before & after samples).

(3) Authentication property:

The only way for an *unseal(Key, SealedMsg, Msg, true)* to succeed is to provide it with a *SealedMsg* which was sealed using the inverse of *Key*. Without access to the inverse of *Key*, there is no way to create an object that will let the above operation succeed.

(4) Privacy property:

Performing any of the above operations must not result in the granting to any party access to any object. This rules out the initially appealing implementation of having the *Keys* be perpetual processes consuming streams, and having these operations be performed by these *Key* processes in response to corresponding requests on these streams. Suppose that we were using this technique. Then when Joe is supposed to send his public key to Sam, he can instead send a stream to a perpetual process of his own making. As long as this process is behaviorally equivalent, Sam can't tell the difference. When Sam then seals a *Msg* by sending a seal request on this stream, Joe could have arranged to immediately see this *Msg*, despite the fact that Sam intended to not yet transfer it to Joe. These same considerations rule out implementations in which *Msgs* or *SealedMsgs* are perpetual processes which implement these operations.

24.3 Implementation in FCP

The technique used in this paper is to have a table for each key associating data to be sealed (*Msgs*) with unique tokens returned as the *SealedMsgs*. Sealing data with a key involves creating a new *SealedMsg* token, and storing the association between this token and the data in the table for this key. Unsealing looks up the *SealedMsg* in the table associated with the *inverse* of the supplied key, returning the associated data. These two tables are shared in an object called a

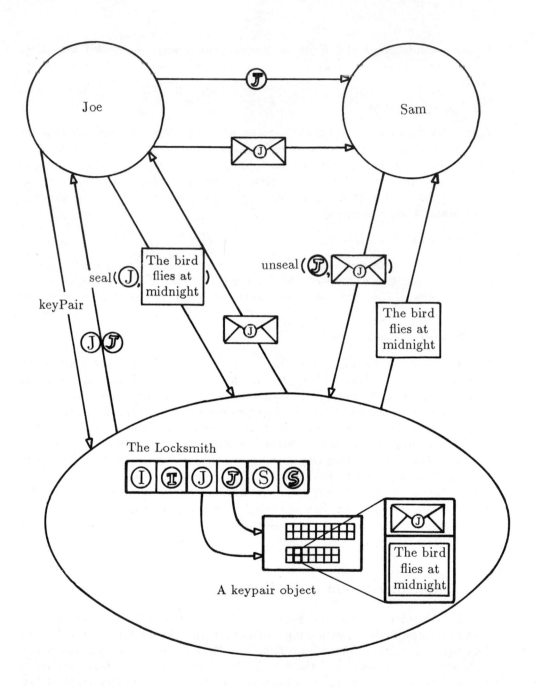

Figure 24.5

keyPair. This approach critically depends on the ability of FCP to realize encapsulated mutable objects. These are implemented by perpetual processes as described in (Shapiro and Takeuchi, Chapter 29) and (Kahn et al., Chapter 30). The *keyPair* consumes two streams, one for each key.

A global *locksmith* object creates unique keys and their associated *keyPair* objects. It also remembers the association between the unique keys and the corresponding streams. The reliance on secure access to a shared global locksmith is a potential weakness. This will be discussed in more detail in the last section.

The current implementation uses read-only variables as the unique tokens. The read-only variables are required so that nothing elsewhere in the system can forge an already existing key. Each token also has a unique integer in it to make incorrect comparisons of tokens fail instead of merely suspend. This is discussed in more detail later.

Figure 24.5 shows the flow of information among Joe, Sam, and the Locksmith that results from Joe sending a message to Sam which is signed by Joe.

24.3.1 The locksmith

Everyone is assumed to possess a private stream to the locksmith object. The above operations are performed by sending them as requests to this locksmith object. The operation

locksmith(SmithStream)

makes *SmithStream* into a stream of messages to a new locksmith object. Entities employing the same locksmith object are able to communicate with each other coherently. If the locksmith operation is performed multiple times, it results in mutually disjoint (unintelligible) public-key communication worlds. In the Logix operating system (Silverman et al., Chapter 21) — an operating system written in FCP — we can install this stream as a server known by the name *locksmith*. Logix provides syntactic sugar for sending messages to installed servers. For example, to send a keyPair message to the locksmith server, we would write:

locksmith#keyPair(Key1, Key2).

To understand in detail how the name locksmith is resolved, see Silverman et al. (Chapter 21). We assume that this name resolution is done in a sufficiently secure fashion for the purpose of using this syntactic sugar in this paper.

The only public predicate in the locksmith is *locksmith/1*, which implements the above specified locksmith operation. All the other public operations are implemented by sending them as requests on the stream returned by this operation.

```
-export(locksmith/1)

locksmith(SmithStream) ←
    emptyTable(KeyTable),
    stream#merger(SmithStream?, Self),
    locksmith(Self?, KeyTable).
```

stream#merger(SmithStream?, Self) invokes a Logix primitive for performing a non-deterministic fair merge of all the elements on *SmithStream* onto *Self* in constant time for each element of *SmithStream* (Shapiro and Safra, Chapter 15). By putting a *stream#merger* process in front of our services, we give them the ability to accept requests to merge a new stream into their input stream. The semantics of *stream#merger* (but not its performance) is equivalent to the following code:

```
merger([merge(In1) | In], Out) ←
    merge(In1?, In?, Out1),
    merger(Out1?, Out).

merger([Msg | In], [Msg | Out]) ←
    Msg =\= merge(Ignore) |
    merger(In?, Out).
```

This locksmith contains an (initially empty) table associating keys with streams. The *keyPair* request creates two new keys and a single *keyPair* object consuming a stream for each key. The locksmith remembers (in the *KeyTable*) the association between each key and its corresponding *keyStream*. Tables (presented in detail later) are perpetual processes that respond to requests to store data indexed by an id, to look up the data indexed by an id, and (assuming that the indexed data is a stream) to send a message on the stream indexed by an id (and as a result redefining the tail of the stream to be the data now indexed by the id).

```
locksmith([keyPair(Key1?, Key2?) | Self], KeyTable) ←
    newId(Key1),
    newId(Key2),
    keyPair(Key1Stream?, Key2Stream?),
    KeyTable = [store(Key1?, Key1Stream),
        store(Key2?, Key2Stream) | NewKeyTable?],
    locksmith(Self?, NewKeyTable).
```

We provide an additional operation, *keyStream* (defined below), which returns a new stream that is merged into the stream associated with the supplied key. This may result in an important performance enhancement, as the client can perform successive operations on that key without further involving the locksmith object (by just sending directly on this stream). The locksmith object will be less of a serial bottleneck if clients cache the stream associated with a key. Note that one should never believe that a stream sent from a mistrusted entity is a valid key stream. Only keys themselves should be considered safe. This necessitates a *keyStream* operation to the locksmith whenever keys need to be transmitted between mutually mistrusted entities.

> locksmith([keyStream(Key, KeyStream, Ok) | Self], KeyTable) ←
>   KeyTable = [send(Key, merge(KeyStream?), Ok) | NewKeyTable?],
>   locksmith(Self?, NewKeyTable).

None of the messages sent on other key streams merged into the stored key stream are visible from this *KeyStream*.

The *seal* and *unseal* requests are performed by the *keyPair* object associated with the *Key* being used, so this forwards those requests to the appropriate stream.

> locksmith([seal(Key, Msg, SealedMsg, Ok) | Self], KeyTable) ←
>   KeyStream = [seal(Msg, SealedMsg)],
>   locksmith([keyStream(Key, KeyStream?, Ok) | Self], KeyTable).

> locksmith([unseal(Key, SealedMsg, Msg, Ok) | Self], KeyTable) ←
>   KeyStream = [unseal(SealedMsg, Msg, Ok1)],
>   locksmith([keyStream(Key, KeyStream?, Ok2) | Self], KeyTable),
>   andOks(Ok1?, Ok2?, Ok).

andOks(true, true, true).
andOks(false, Ignored, false).
andOks(Ignored, false, false).

24.3.2 KeyPair objects

A *keyPair* object has two incoming streams corresponding to the two keys which it represents. It contains two tables, each records the correspondence between a *Msg* sealed with this key, and the resulting *SealedMsg*. Every time a new *seal* request comes in, a new *SealedMsg* is generated, and this correspondence is added to the table for this key. Every time an *unseal* request comes in, we look up the message corresponding to the given *SealedMsg* in the *opposite* table. This results in the two keys being inverses with respect to the *seal* and *unseal* operations.

> /∗ Create a *keyPair* object. ∗/
> keyPair(Key1Stream, Key2Stream) ←
>   emptyTable(Key1Table),
>   emptyTable(Key2Table),
>   stream#merger(Key1Stream?, Key1In),
>   stream#merger(Key2Stream?, Key2In),
>   keyPair(Key1In?, Key2In?, Key1Table, Key2Table).

keyPair(Key1In, Key2In, Key1Table, Key2Table) ←
    Key1In? = [seal(Msg, SealedMsg?) | NewKey1In] |
    newId(SealedMsg),
    Key1Table = [store(SealedMsg?, Msg) | NewKey1Table?],
    keyPair(NewKey1In?, Key2In, NewKey1Table, Key2Table).

keyPair(Key1In, Key2In, Key1Table, Key2Table) ←
    Key2In? = [seal(Msg, SealedMsg?) | NewKey2In] |
    newId(SealedMsg),
    Key2Table = [store(SealedMsg?, Msg) | NewKey2Table?],
    keyPair(Key1In, NewKey2In?, Key1Table, NewKey2Table).

keyPair(Key1In, Key2In, Key1Table, Key2Table) ←
    Key1In? = [unseal(SealedMsg, Msg, Ok) | NewKey1In] |
    Key2Table = [lookup(SealedMsg, Msg, Ok) | NewKey2Table?],
    keyPair(NewKey1In?, Key2In, Key1Table, NewKey2Table).

keyPair(Key1In, Key2In, Key1Table, Key2Table) ←
    Key2In? = [unseal(SealedMsg, Msg, Ok) | NewKey2In] |
    Key1Table = [lookup(SealedMsg, Msg, Ok) | NewKey1Table?],
    keyPair(Key1In, NewKey2In?, NewKey1Table, Key2Table).

24.3.3 Unique identifiers

Unique identifiers are used for keys and for sealed messages.

newId(Id)

creates and returns a new unique identifier such that two references to the same unique identifier are testably the same, but a unique identifier will not test the same as any other object.

sameId(Id1, Id2, Ok)

If *Id1* and *Id2* refer to the same unique identifier then *Ok* is instantiated to *true*. Otherwise, it is either instantiated to *false*, or not instantiated (because of infinite suspension).

Using read only variables to represent unique identifiers, we can implement these operations as:

newId(Id?).

sameId(Id1, Id2, true) ←
    Id1 =?= Id2 | true.

This relies on the predicate =?= which is read "is identical to". This succeeds if the two arguments unify without introducing any new bindings. If it is known that the two will never unify, this fails. Otherwise it waits until new bindings introduced elsewhere are sufficient to resolve this into one of these two cases. When both arguments are variables that will never be instantiated, this succeeds only if both arguments refer to the same variable.

$$\text{sameId(Id1, Id2, false)} \leftarrow$$
$$\text{Id1} =\backslash= \text{Id2} \mid \text{true.}$$

The predicate $=\backslash=$ is read "is not identical to". It is the complement of $=?=$. This predicate also waits until equality can be resolved without introducing new bindings.

This satisfies the specification. One problem is that the *sameId* operation on two different unique ids will infinitely suspend. We would prefer it to complete, binding *Ok* to *false*. If we have a source of unique ground terms, we can remedy this as follows:

$$\text{newId(id(SerialNumber, RealId?))} \leftarrow$$
$$\text{gensym\#newSerialNo(SerialNumber).}$$

As the specification of *sameId* allows it to infinitely suspend, a forged coincidence of *SerialNumbers* would not be fatal. Unique *SerialNumbers* can be generated without the generator becoming a serial bottleneck (Nelson, 1981). The purpose of this change is simply to avoid unnecessary suspended processes. An infinite suspension would only result from a malicious attack, and would be its only negative consequence. An open question is how to guarantee both termination and unforgeability. We have explored the possibility of using $==$ and $\backslash==$ (like the above except they fail if they cannot immediately succeed), but found that we lose essential dataflow synchronization. Without this synchronization, an attempt to *unseal* a message may fail simply because it occurred before its *SealedMsg* got registered. It may be desirable in the future to introduce a unique unforgeable identifier as a new data type, but this paper examines what can be done without such extensions.

We are not depending on the existence of read-only variables to provide testable uniqueness. Regular logic variables (together with the $=?=$ and $=\backslash=$ predicates) are sufficient to provide this. However, if an agent makes a writable logic variable his public key, anyone may disable it by instantiating it. It seems essential that the ability to write on a variable be a dynamic *capability* as in FCP.

24.3.4 Association tables

The following operations provide the abstraction of tables of associations between unique ids and arbitrary values:

$$\text{emptyTable(TableStream)}$$

TableStream is a stream to a table object containing no associations. Tables respond to three requests:

    store(Id, Value)

All succeeding lookups should find this *Value* associated with this *Id*, unless overridden by a succeeding *store* for this same *Id*.

    lookup(Id, Value, Ok)

If there is an association in *Table* for *Id*, instantiate *Value* to it, and instantiate *Ok* to *true*. Otherwise, *Ok* is either instantiated to *false* or not at all (because of infinite suspension), and *Value* is definitely not instantiated. Declaratively, *Value* is the same as the *Value* of the most recent *store* on this stream for this *Id*.

    send(Id, Message, Ok)

Assuming that the *Value* associated with *Id* is a stream, send the message on this stream, instantiate *Ok* to *true*, and associate the tail of the stream with *Id*.

These can be naively implemented in terms of linear lists as follows:

–export(emptyTable/1)

emptyTable(TableStream) ←
    table(TableStream?, [ ]).

table([store(Id, Value) | Self], Table) ←
    table(Self?, [entry(Id, Value) | Table]).

table([lookup(Id, Value, false) | Self], [ ]) ←
    table(Self?, [ ]).

table([lookup(Id, Value, true) | Self], Table) ←
    Table = [entry(Id1, Value) | Ignored],
    sameId(Id1, Id, true) |
    table(Self?, Table).

table([lookup(Id, Value, Ok) | Self], Table) ←
    sameId(Id1, Id, false) |
    Table = [Ignored | Table1],
    table([lookup(Id, Value, Ok)], Table1),
    table(Self?, Table).

table([send(Id, Message, Ok) | Self], Table) ←
    table([lookup(Id, [Message | Value], Ok), store(Id, Value, Ok?) | Self],
        Table).

table([store(Id, Value, true) | Self], Table) ←
    table([store(Id, Value) | Self], Table).

table([store(Id, Value, false) | Self], Table) ←
    table(Self?, Table).

table([ ], Ignored).

(**Note:** This is not quite a valid FCP implementation because *sameId* is not a valid guard predicate. Given the above implementation of *sameId* though, we can simply replace *sameId(Id1, Id, true)* above with *Id1 =?= Id*. This does result in loss of modularity, though.)

This implementation satisfies its specification, but it does have some problems:

The suspension problem is inherited from the suspension problem of *sameId*. If someone sends a key with a forged serial number they can disable further use of this locksmith. This is a severe problem for open systems. A topic for further research is how to avoid this problem with the tools provided in FCP.

The linear list results in average $O(n)$ lookup time. This can be improved by building an efficient data structure (such as a balanced 2–3 tree or hash table) based on the value of the *SerialNumbers* inside the *Ids*.

Old associations should be removed once they are overridden by a new association for the same *Id*.

An association should also be removed after its *Id* is not otherwise accessible. One might normally provide a "remove" operation which constitutes a promise that this *Id* will not be used in further lookups. As we are generally assuming lack of trust, we are not in a position to believe such a promise. In the T language, *weak tables* (Rees and Adams, 1982) are a type of association table such that associations for keys that are otherwise garbage collectable are garbage collected (along with these keys). Weak tables could be provided in FCP as a primitive type of perpetual process that exactly implements the above program. This corresponds to the methodology followed in (Shapiro and Safra, Chapter 15).

24.4 Banking Example

Instead of attempting to represent cash, we can create a bank in which one can have accounts with associated quantities of money. The owners of those accounts can transfer the money by writing and signing checks, sending them to each other, and depositing them. The external representation of an account is a public key. When a check is deposited, the bank authenticates the signature by unsealing with this public key, and cancels the check to prevent it from being re-deposited. This cancellation serves to indicate to all those with access to the check (at least the author and the depositor) whether the check cleared or bounced. Because of the above suspension problems, an attempt to deposit a forged check may also suspend forever.

An individual bank represents an individual currency (in this sense our *bank* is like a new federal reserve bank of a new country). To effect a transfer between banks either requires trust between those banks or mutual trust of some other bank, and is beyond the scope of this paper.

When a bank is created, it is initialized with one account which already contains some specified amount of currency. This is necessary in order to introduce currency into the system. As anyone can create a new bank, anyone can mint a new currency. Between the currencies established by different banks one may expect the eventual rise of exchange rates.

bank(BankStream, InitialAcct, InitialBalance, BankPublicKey)

establishes a new bank serving requests arriving on *BankStream*. The bank starts with an account containing *InitialBalance*, and with the public key *InitialAcct* used to identify this account. It is the responsibility of the owner of an account to keep his private key private. The bank itself never needs access to anyone's private key.

BankPublicKey is the public key others can use to authenticate data which is signed by the bank. The bank itself is the only entity with access to the corresponding private key.

The bank responds to two requests, a request to deposit a signed check, and a balance inquiry.

deposit(SignedCheck, ToAcct, Cancellation)

The representation of a signed check is:

signedCheck(SealedCheck, FromAcct)

where *SealedCheck* unseals with *FromAcct* to yield check data. The representation of check data is:

checkData(Amount, Cancellation)

If the *SignedCheck* is a properly signed uncancelled check, the bank attempts to transfer the amount of money specified by the check from *FromAcct* to *ToAcct*. If the target account doesn't already exist, it is established. As with standard banking practice, one does not have to have permission of the owner of the account into which the money is being transferred.

Notice that the check does not itself specify the *ToAcct* the money is to be transferred to. Anyone possessing a reference to a properly signed uncancelled check may deposit it to any account he chooses. This corresponds to a "bearer note" (one which says "Pay to the bearer..."). If the author of a check wishes only a certain party to be able to deposit it, he can *seal* the signed check with the public key of this party.

If the check bounces or clears, it is cancelled to indicate this to all those with access to it. This cancellation is signed by the bank itself (using the bank's private key). The valid values for *Cancellation* are:

> an unbound, writable variable (uncancelled check),
> a receipt that the check cleared, or
> an indication that the check bounced.

A receipt that the check cleared is a *SealedMsg* that unseals (with the bank's public key) to: *cleared(SealedCheck, ToAcct)*. A bounce indication is a *SealedMsg* that unseals (with the bank's public key) to: *bounced(SealedCheck)*. These cancellations contain the *SealedCheck* so that they will be specific to this check. Otherwise, one could take a signed cancellation from one check and insert it into another check (to falsify a cancelled check for use as a forged receipt).

When the check clears, the *FromAcct* is debited immediately. In other words, once a client finds that the check is cancelled, those funds are guaranteed not to be available from the *FromAcct*. However, these funds are not yet guaranteed to be available from the *ToAcct*. Once the *ToAcct* in the receipt is instantiated, then the funds are guaranteed to be available from the *ToAcct*. This interval corresponds to a "hold" on the check.

One should only believe that a check was cancelled as a result of *this* deposit operation if the *Cancellation* parameter of this deposit request becomes instantiated. Without this safeguard, two concurrent attempts to deposit the same check may fool both into thinking that their deposit succeeded.

The owner of an account must also be able to inquire about its balance. The operation provided is:

> balance(Acct, Balance)

Where *Balance* is a *SealedMsg* that unseals with *Acct* to yield an unbound variable. This variable is then filled in with a record of the current balance signed by the bank. The signed statement is proof to third parties that this money actually was present at some time in the history of this account.

24.4.1 Implementing the bank

A bank object contains a table associating *Acct* identifiers with streams to account objects. The bank also remembers its own keys so that it can sign receipts, etc.

```
—export(bank/4)

bank(BankStream, InitialAcct, InitialBalance, BankPubKey?) ←
    locksmith#keyPair(BankPubKey, BankPrivKey),
    Keys = keys(BankPrivKey?, BankPubKey?),
    account(AcctStream?, InitialAcct, InitialBalance, Keys?),
    emptyTable([store(InitialAcct, AcctStream) | Accounts?]),
    stream#merger(BankStream?, Self),
    bank(Self?, Accounts, Keys?).
```

The *acctStream* operation (defined below) returns the stream associated with a given *Acct*. If the account doesn't already exist, a new one is created with a zero balance. As with the locksmith and *keyPair* objects, clients which expect to make frequent use of an account can cache a stream to it. This prevents the bank from becoming as much of a serial bottleneck.

```
bank([acctStream(Acct, AcctStream) | Self], Accounts, Keys) ←
    Accounts = [send(Acct, merge(AcctStream?), Ok) | NewAccounts?],
    makeAccount(Ok?, Acct, AcctStream, NewAccounts, NewAccounts1),
    bank(Self?, NewAccounts1, Keys).

makeAccount(true, Ignore1, Ignore2, NewAccounts, NewAccounts).

makeAccount(false, Acct, AcctStream, NewAccounts, NewAccounts1) ←
    account([merge(AcctStream?) | AcctStream1?], Acct, 0, Keys),
    NewAccounts = [store(Acct, AcctStream1) | NewAccounts1? ].
```

The bank handles the *deposit* and *balance* operations by forwarding them on to the appropriate account object.

```
bank([deposit(Check, ToAcct, Cancellation?) | Self], Accounts, Keys) ←
    check(SealedCheck, FromAcct) = Check,
    FromStream = [transfer(SealedCheck, ToStream, Cancellation)],
    NewSelf = [acctStream(FromAcct, FromStream) | NewSelf1],
    NewSelf1 = [acctStream(ToAcct, ToStream) | Self?],
    bank(NewSelf?, Accounts, Keys).

bank([balance(Acct, Balance) | Self], Accounts, Keys) ←
    FromStream = [balance(Balance)],
    bank([acctStream(FromAcct, FromStream) | Self?], Accounts, Keys).
```

An account object contains *Acct* — the identifier for this account, *Balance* — the balance in this account, and the keys of the bank this is an account in. The accounts carry these keys since the most of the work of the bank is performed by the accounts.

account([Request | Self], Acct, Balance, Keys) ←
    transfer(SealedCheck, ToStream, Cancellation) = Request |
    locksmith#unseal(Acct, SealedCheck, CheckData, true),
    checkData(Amount, Cancellation) = CheckData,
    Keys = keys(BankPrivKey, Ignore),
    transfer(Balance?, Amount?, NewBalance, ToStream,
        Cancellation, SealedCheck, BankPrivKey),
    account(Self?, Acct, NewBalance?, Keys).

transfer(Balance, Amount, NewBalance, ToStream,
        Cancellation?, SealedCheck, BankPrivKey) ←
    Balance ≥ Amount |
    ToStream = [credit(CreditRequest?)],
    NewBalance := Balance − Amount,
    Cleared = cleared(SealedCheck?, ToAcct?),
    locksmith#seal(BankPrivKey, Cleared?, Cancellation, true),
    Credit = credit(Amount?, ToAcct?),
    locksmith#seal(BankPrivKey, Credit?, CreditRequest, true).

transfer(Balance, Amount, Balance, Ignore,
        Cancellation?, SealedCheck, BankPrivKey) ←
    Balance < Amount |
    Bounced = bounced(SealedCheck?),
    locksmith#seal(BankPrivKey, Bounced?, Cancellation, true).

The read only annotation on *Cancellation* in the head insures that only an uncancelled check may be cancelled. If the check clears, this account asks the target account to credit this amount (i.e., to increment its balance by this amount). The target account instantiates the *ToAcct* field of the *credit* request in order to indicate that succeeding *deposit* (and *balance*) requests to this account will find the funds to be available.

The *ToAcct* field is also used to insure that an individual *CreditRequest* cannot be used more than once. (It is left as an exercise to discover how a user may gain access to a signed *CreditRequest*, and why this does not constitute a security problem.)

account([credit(CreditRequest) | Self], Acct, Balance, Keys) ←
    Keys = keys(Ignore, BankPubKey),
    locksmith#unseal(BankPubKey, CreditRequest?, Credit, true),
    credit(Amount, Acct) = Credit,
    NewBalance := Balance + Amount.
    account(Self?, Acct, NewBalance?, Keys).

As only the owner of an account may inquire about its balance, *BalanceReq* must be a variable signed by the owner. This variable is filled in with a balance statement signed by the bank.

account([balance(BalanceReq) | Self], Acct, Balance, BankPrivKey) ←
    Bal = balance(Acct?, Balance),
    locksmith#seal(BankPrivKey, Bal?, SignedBalance, true),
    locksmith#unseal(Acct, BalanceReq, SignedBalance, true),
    account(Self?, Acct, Balance, BankPrivKey).

This banking code does not deal properly with the issue of failure. A correct bank would have to reject arbitrary nonsense messages and continue to provide service. In general, dealing with this problem correctly is a difficult issue in concurrent logic programming languages. The declarative semantics of a service responding to a stream of requests is a set of constraints on the allowable form of this stream. Operationally, concurrent logic programming languages allow these constraints to be expressed only at the price of failure of the service if the constraints are not met. A fail-proof service would be left with the vacuous declarative reading of allowing any stream whatsoever. The service itself would have meaning only in the operational realm. Miller (1987) presents a solution to this in FCP that once again depends upon the properties of read-only variables.

24.5 Discussion

Virtually all programming languages are as powerful as a Universal Turing Machine. As a result, it would seem they are all formally equivalent. This would be unfortunate as it wouldn't allow us to distinguish between them on formal grounds.

Despite the Turing-equivalence of (virtually) all programming languages, they can nevertheless differ formally and absolutely in their ability to provide for security. How can this be if we can write an interpreter for a secure language in an insecure one? To make this distinction we have to ask not "what functions can be computed?", but "given that I am a computational entity, what is my relationship to an already populated computational world?". Let us call the computational entities that exist at my level (including myself) *base level entities*, and those which exist on top of base level interpreters *interpreted entities*. If I am embedded in an insecure programming language, and I write an interpreter for a secure one, then the interpreted entities are protected from each other, but none are protected from the other base level entities. Any base level entities can reach up through the interpreter I've written to wreck havoc on my interpreted entities.

We choose to implement this public-key system in a concurrent logic programming language (as opposed to other programming languages with encapsulation) for several reasons. Most of the languages thought to provide encapsulation, for example Smalltalk, also provide ways to violate this encapsulation. This is generally provided in order to allow for programming environment features such as debuggers. Recognizing that programming environment views are better considered meta-level views of the program, some have proposed reflexive systems (e.g., 3-Lisp by Smith, 1982) as a principled way of gaining access to this view. However, the ability of entities *within a computation* to view the system in which they are embedded from the point of view of their interpreter destroys the security of the encapsulation boundaries between these entities.

A methodology being pursued in the concurrent logic programming community is to provide programming environment facilities through enhanced meta-interpreters (Safra and Shapiro, Chapter 25; Hirsch et al., Chapter 20). Given that I am a base level entity operating in a secure system, if I run a computation under a meta-interpreter, the interpreted entities are protected from each other, and I (together with this interpreted world which I have created) am protected from the other base level entities.

I can even provide the ability for my interpreted entities to participate safely in activities taking place at my level. This is easy when the meta-interpreter is written in such a way that logic variables and terms of the interpreted level are mapped onto identical logic variables and terms of the base level (as is typical practice). As communication among encapsulated entities is performed by instantiating logic variables to terms, such communication can cross levels transparently.

Debugging is supported as follows: Processes of the interpreted level are mapped onto terms of the base level. Processes are the mechanism for providing encapsulation, but the interpreter views these processes as terms, so the interpreter has a non-encapsulated view of the computation. The terms representing the processes of the interpreted system are themselves encapsulated within the processes making up the interpreter, and so the interpreted objects are still encapsulated with respect to the base level entities outside this interpreter.

We choose Flat Concurrent Prolog in particular, because read-only variables provide us with several essential abilities we don't know how to achieve in the other concurrent logic programming languages. Ground terms do not provide for unforgeable unique identifiers. We use unbound logic variables for this purpose. A variable would loose this ability were it to be instantiated. We need to give access to these unique identifier to entities that must therefore not be allowed to instantiate them. FCP's read-only variables meet these criteria perfectly. It is an open question whether the power of public-key systems can be fully realized in other concurrent logic programming languages.

A critical security assumption in this paper is that any party can gain a secure stream to the locksmith (and the bank), via a mechanism which does not already employ three-party security. A possible approach is to have all processes run under a meta-interpreter which contains the locksmith, and which provides the public-key operations as language primitives to the processes being interpreted.

This is in effect what we are doing by employing the Logix remote procedure call mechanism. The procedure calls are only messages-sent-to-objects at the meta-level. Therefore, by installing the locksmith as a Logix service, it is running at a meta-level with respect to the processes employing it. However, depending on the Logix module system to be the kind of secure meta-interpreter discussed above may be unrealistic currently, as this mechanism is embodied in a large amount of code which wasn't designed to be secure, and is not known to satisfy any formal semantics from which one could derive security. In particular, there are many operations available in Logix for manipulating the name space, and gaining access to the stream corresponding to a named service. One would have to examine all these operations carefully. Redesigning the Logix module system to be secure is an important open research question.

Another approach relies on the constraint that a process has no choice about trusting its ancestor process. Given that a process always trusts its ancestor processes, but not its descendants or siblings, we could establish the following convention: each process has an extra argument which is a stream to the locksmith. Whenever a process spawns a set of child processes, it passes each a new stream. The streams passed to the child processes are merged together into the stream passed to the parent. This is easily accomplished by a source to source transformation. It may also result from partially evaluating the secure meta-interpreter discussed above.

24.6 Conclusions

The concurrent logic programming languages promise to be a viable foundation for distributed intelligent systems based on the metaphor of loosely coupled cooperating agents. An extreme in loose-coupling is mistrust. Public-key systems have defined a set of abstract operations for use among mistrusting agents. The implementation of these operations by encryption is merely an artifact of assumed insecure hardware foundations. If we assume secure hardware (and language) foundations, then this same functionality can be provided much more cheaply. We have shown an implementation in Flat Concurrent Prolog, and an example of its use for secure banking.

Acknowledgements

We would like to thank Curtis Abbott, Peter Deutsch, K. Eric Drexler, Carl Hewitt, Kenneth Kahn, Ehud Shapiro, and Terry Stanley, for having helped us form both this paper and its ideas.

Part V

Program Analysis and Transformation

Introduction

High-level languages are more suitable for human expression than low-level ones. At least as important, and perhaps in the long run even more important, is their greater amenability to systematic analysis and transformation. This part reports on initial work on algorithms for the analysis and transformation of concurrent logic programs, which may form the basis of future advanced program development environments.

Chapter 25, "Meta-Interpreters for Real", by Safra and Shapiro, describes the theoretical foundations of the approach to systems programming reported in Part IV. It describes how enhanced meta-interpreters can be used to enhance the functionality of a language; and how partial evaluation of an enhanced meta-interpreter with respect to a program can produce a new program that inherits the enhanced functionality from the interpreter, but not its overhead. Several enhanced Concurrent Prolog meta-interpreters are described, and their partial evaluation is demonstrated. The same approach can be used to compile an embedded language, given an interpreter for it, a topic discussed in Part VI.

A program transformer (or compiler) may be derived from each meta-interpreter by partially evaluating the partial evaluator itself with respect to that meta-interpreter. However, the Concurrent Prolog partial evaluator used was not able to partially-evaluate itself, hence the program transformers needed for the Logix system (Chapter 20) were constructed manually, based on the meta-interpreters specifying their functionality.

Chapter 26, "Algorithmic Debugging of GHC and its Implementation in GHC", by Takeuchi, reports on the application of the method of algorithmic debugging to the concurrent logic programming language GHC. Previously, algorithmic debugging has been applied to Prolog. Concurrent logic programming languages have, in addition to bugs in their logical component, synchronization bugs which may result in erroneous deadlock or failure. The significance of this work is in showing that if the semantics of the concurrent programming language is defined appropriately, then the same technique of algorithmic debugging used for sequential languages applies. A semantics which captures part of the concurrent aspects of a GHC program is proposed. Using this semantics, algorithms which can diagnose termination with incorrect answer and erroneous deadlock are developed and implemented in GHC.

Chapter 27, "Representation and Enumeration of Flat Concurrent Prolog Computations", by Lichtenstein, Codish, and Shapiro, contains initial investigations into the semantics and the structure of FCP computations. Several representations of the meaning of an FCP program are proposed, based on a simple operational semantics. The relation between these representations is investigated using the concept of abstract interpretation. In particular, it is shown that the standard semantics of logic programs is the most abstract amongst the representations studied. A technique for enumerating all possible computations of an FCP program on a given goal is given. It seems to be a precondition for systematic testing of FCP programs.

In general, further substantial progress in program analysis and transformation depends on a clearer understanding of the language semantics.

Chapter 28, "A Type System for Logic Programs", by Yardeni and Shapiro, defines the notion of a type for logic programs based on the concept of tuple-distributivity. It defines a notion of type-inference, which is a form of abstract interpretation of a logic program. It suggests using the class of regular unary logic programs for specifying types and describes a type checking algorithm. Although the theory is stated in terms of general logic programs, it is, of course, applicable to concurrent logic programming languages in general, and to FCP in particular. The development of a type system for FCP based on this theory and its incorporation in the Logix system is a subject of current research.

Chapter 25

Meta Interpreters for Real

Shmuel Safra and Ehud Shapiro

The Weizmann Institute of Science

Abstract

Enhanced meta-interpreters can be used to add functionality to a program without the need to include this functionality in the language semantics. Partial evaluation can remove unnecessary layers of interpretation; thus it can be used to incorporate the functionality of a meta-interpreter into the model of execution without overhead. The result of partially evaluating an enhanced meta-interpreter with respect to a program is a new residual program. This program behaves as the original program but is enhanced to include the functionality of the meta-interpreter. The method is demonstrated using program examples and is argued to retain the program's efficiency.

25.1 Introduction

Enhanced meta-interpreters can be used to add functionality to a program without the need for this functionality to be included in the language semantics. Operating systems can be extended using enhanced meta-interpreters to achieve layers of control, debugging tools (Shapiro, 1982) or other system facilities; expert systems can also be designed by enhanced meta-interpreters (Sterling, 1984; Shapiro, 1983b). Adding a layer of interpretation to a computation results in a run-time slow-down of an order of magnitude. Composing different meta-interpreters to achieve a combination of functionalities is beneficial for simplicity but results in a slow-down which is exponential in the number of interpreters combined. We would like to use meta-interpreters to achieve functionality but want our programs to run rather than crawl.

Partial evaluation can remove unnecessary layers of interpretation; thus it can be used to incorporate the functionality of a meta-interpreter without overhead. Partially evaluating a meta-interpreter with respect to a known program results in a new program that inherits the meta-interpreter functionality but not its overhead (Gallagher, 1983, 1986; Takeuchi and Furukawa, 1986).

Partial evaluation was studied before as a program transformation technique. It originates from Kleene's (1952) S-m-n theorem which arises in recursive function theory. It was argued (Futamura, 1971; Beckman et al., 1976; Turchin, 1980; Ershov, 1977; Jones et al., 1985) that it can be used to automatically derive a compiler from a given interpreter. We show in this paper the use of partial evaluation to remove the part of an interpreter which performs analysis of the program structure leaving only the execution of its simulation to be carried out at run-time.

The following process of development to achieve general functionalities is proposed. An enhanced meta-interpreter is written that adds some functionality to a computation while simulating a program. This meta-interpreter is partially evaluated with respect to a program which need not contain this functionality. The result of the partial evaluation process is a program that contains the original program behavior but includes the meta-interpreter functionality.

The method is demonstrated using program examples, and it is argued that the program efficiency is restored. The resulting programs, with the added functionality, introduce an acceptable slow-down compared to the original program.

25.2 Overview

25.2.1 Partial evaluation

Partial evaluation is a process of specializing a program with respect to a partially known input at compile-time. The process produces, as a result, a new residual program which is semantically equivalent to the original program under the known input.

Given a partial evaluator PE^L for the language L, a program P_L written in L and partly known input to it C

$$\text{PE}^L(\text{P}_L(\text{Known, Unknown}), \text{C}) = \text{P}'_L(\text{Unknown})$$

$$\text{P}'_L(\text{Unknown}) \equiv \text{P}_L(\text{C, Unknown}).$$

This condition can be achieved trivially but vacuously if the residual program simply calls the original program with the known input, i.e., P'_L is the following program:

P$'_L$(Unknown)
begin
     P$_L$(C, Unknown)
end.

The goal of a nontrivial partial evaluator is to produce a "better" program. In the context of this paper "better" refers to run-time efficiency.

Given an interpreter $I_L^{L_I}$ written in the language L which interprets the language L_I and a program P_{L_I} in the language L_I such that

$$I_L^{L_I}(P_{L_I}, \text{Input}) \equiv P_{L_I}(\text{Input}).$$

Partially evaluating the interpreter $I_L^{L_I}$ with respect to a given program, P_{L_I} produces:

$$PE^L(I_L^{L_I}(\text{Prog, Input}), P_{L_I}) = P_L(\text{Input})$$

such that

$$P_L(\text{Input}) \equiv I_L^{L_I}(P_{L_I}, \text{Input}).$$

Note that this process, given an interpreter, produces for each program in L_I a program in L with the same behavior; thus it compiles programs in L_I into programs in L. If the partial evaluator is an autoprojector (i.e., it is written in the same language it analyses) this compilation process can be specialized, given an interpreter $I_L^{L_I}$, to produce a compiler $C_L^{L_I}$.

$$PE^L(PE_L^L(\text{Int, Prog}), I_L^{L_I}) = C_L^{L_I}(\text{Prog})$$

such that

$$C_L^{L_I}(\text{Prog}) \equiv PE_L^L(I_L^{L_I}, \text{Prog}).$$

$C_L^{L_I}$ is a compiler from L_I into L corresponding to the interpreter $I_L^{L_I}$.

Thus partial evaluation can be used as a method for generating compilers (Futamura, 1971; Jones et al., 1985).

Given a meta-interpreter I_L^L such that

$$I_L^L(P_L, \text{Input}) \equiv P_L(\text{Input})$$

and given a program P_L in L, partially evaluating I_L^L with respect to P_L produces:

$$PE^L(I_L^L(\text{Prog, Input}), P_L) = P'_L(\text{Input})$$

such that

$$P'_L(\text{Input}) \equiv I_L^L(P_L, \text{Input}) \equiv P_L(\text{Input}).$$

Thus a non-trivial partial evaluator can remove the overhead encountered by the layer of interpretation.

An enhanced meta-interpreter is a meta-interpreter with added functionality. It interprets a language L^+ with the same syntax as L but some added semantic functionality.

Given an enhanced meta-interpreter $I_L^{L^+}$ and a program P in L, partially evaluating the enhanced meta-interpreter $I_L^{L^+}$ with respect to the program P produces:

$$PE^L(I_L^{L^+}(\text{Prog}, \text{Input}), P) = P'_L(\text{Input})$$

such that

$$P'_L(\text{Input}) \equiv P_{L^+}(\text{Input}).$$

The resulting program is a program in L but with the added functionality inherited from the enhanced meta-interpreter $I_L^{L^+}$.

The practical implication of the above transformation is that partial evaluation can be used to improve run-time efficiency of a program interpreted by a meta-interpreter. It allows the functionality of the meta-interpreter to be added to that of the program without the unnecessary overhead incurred by a layer of interpretation.

25.2.2 Specification

Interpreters are constructed from two components which perform:

(1) Analysis of the program structure to determine its meaning.

(2) Execution of the operations required by the meaning.

It is obvious that if the program is known during partial evaluation there is no need to carry out the structural analysis at run-time.

Execution time of logic programming languages is loosely proportional to the number of reductions performed; thus the important part of partial evaluation is compile-time reduction (Safra, 1986). Partially evaluating a meta-interpreter with respect to a program will perform reductions involved in the analysis of the program structure at compile-time.

25.2.3 Concurrent Prolog

A Concurrent Prolog program is a set of guarded Horn clauses of the form:

$$H \leftarrow G \mid B.$$

where H is the head predicate; G (guard) and B (body) are sets of procedure calls. Procedure calls may be solved in any order and thus may be viewed as a system of parallel processes. A program may be viewed as a set of rewrite rules to be applied nondeterministically to the processes. A process may be rewritten to a clause body if it unifies with the clause head and the clause guard can be solved. Processes are synchronized using data flow synchronization via read-only occurrences of variables. A read-only occurrence of a variable is an occurrence that was previously annotated read-only (i.e., *X?*). A procedure is a set of clauses each of which has the same head predicate. Two forms of nondeterminism exist: process selection and clause selection. They correspond to two forms of parallel execution: And-parallel and Or-parallel.

Flat Concurrent Prolog (FCP) is the subset of Concurrent Prolog in which the guards are system defined test predicates and the nondeterministic clause selection can be simulated by sequential execution. The practicality of the language has been demonstrated on a number of sizable applications which includes a compiler (Houri and Shapiro, Chapter 38), programming environment and sections of an operating system (Shapiro, Chapter 5; Silverman et al., Chapter 21). Partial evaluation may generate a FCP program from a Concurrent Prolog program provided that the guard computation is bounded.

Consider the Concurrent Prolog meta-interpreter in Program 25.1. It takes as input a program to simulate and a process to solve with respect to this program. If the process is *true*, execution terminates; if it is a conjunction of processes, the meta-interpreter calls itself recursively in parallel to interpret both conjuncts with respect to the same program. If the process is a general call, the meta-interpreter calls the procedure *clause* to analyze it with respect to the program. The *clause* call returns the body from the reduction and the meta-interpreter calls itself recursively to solve this body.

```
reduce(Program, true).                    % halt
reduce(Program, (A, B)) ←                 % fork
    reduce(Program?, A?),
    reduce(Program?,B?).

reduce(Program, Goal) ←                   % reduce
    Goal ≠ true,Goal ≠ (A,B),
    clause(Goal?,Program?,Body) |
    reduce(Program?, Body?).

clause(Goal, [C | Cs], B) ←               % a clause
    new_copy(C?, (H, G, B)),
    Goal = H, G | true.

clause(Goal, [C | Cs], B) ←               % the rest
    clause(Goal, Cs?, B) | true.
```

Program 25.1: A Concurrent Prolog meta-interpreter

The *clause* procedure produces for each clause a *new_copy* which is a variant of the clause with new variables. It tries to unify the process with the head of the copied clause and to call the clause guard. If both succeed, the procedure returns the body of the copied clause. Different program clauses are tried in different Or-parallel environments and thus do not affect each other. Any clause that succeeds can commit and return its body.

Compile-time reduction can be carried out to reduce both the *clause* call in the guard and the recursive calls for *reduce* in the body. This effectively removes the overhead of the meta-interpreter which is involved in the analysis of the program structure; only the execution remains to be carried out at run-time.

25.3 Meta-Interpreters

The following section describes Concurrent Prolog and Prolog enhanced meta-interpreters and their use. The meta-interpreters are shown to add functionality to the execution model without the need to incorporate this functionality into the model. Partially evaluating these meta-interpreters with respect to a given program will produce a program that inherits the meta-interpreter's functionality but not its overhead.

25.3.1 Process abortion

The model of execution of Concurrent Prolog does not provide any mechanism to artificially stop computations. A computation terminates only when all its processes are solved; an infinite computation cannot be terminated. When considering a multi-tasking operating system, a mechanism to abort specific computations should be provided. The mechanism should not abort all the running computations but only the one being interrupted. This mechanism can be provided within the model by an enhanced meta-interpreter. It accepts an extra argument which, when assigned a value, stops the computation being simulated. The resulting enhanced meta-interpreter is composed of the plain meta-interpreter with an extra *Abort* argument and an additional clause. This clause corresponds to the process halting when the *Abort* argument is assigned.

The semantics of the language do not specify any priority or fairness in clause selection. To prevent the execution from repeatedly selecting the reduction clause after the *Abort* argument is assigned, the *unknown* (Safra, 1986) system call is used. This call eventually fails if its argument has a value; the computation will not be able to proceed in reduction and will halt due to the abortion clause. The body of any clause is finite; thus there is no need to protect the clause performing conjunctive analysis from being repeatedly taken.

```
reduce(P, true, Abort).              % halt
reduce(P, (A, B), Abort) ←           % fork
    reduce(P?, A?, Abort?),
    reduce(P?,B?,Abort?).
reduce(P, Goal, Abort) ←             % reduce
    Goal ≠ true,Goal ≠ (A,B),
    unknown(Abort?),
    clause(Goal?,P?,Body) |
    reduce(P?, Body?, Abort?).
reduce(P, A, abort).                 % abort
```

Program 25.2: An abortable Concurrent Prolog meta-interpreter

25.3.2 Termination detection

The model of execution of Concurrent Prolog does not provide any means to detect the termination of a specific computation. Different computations may run in parallel on a parallel machine and distributed termination must be detected. The following meta-interpreter provides this functionality using the short circuit technique (Takeuchi, 1983). Two chains are given to the initial process; one is assigned to a constant and the other is waited upon. When a process halts, it closes the circuit by unifying both its chains. When the process forks, the chain is divided into two chains sharing the middle connection; these two chains are passed to the two forked processes. When a process is reduced to some body, the chain is passed to the body. When all the processes terminate, the constant of the initial process is assigned to the initial free chain and the meta-interpreter can announce the termination of the computation.

```
reduce(P, true, Chain–Chain).        % halt
reduce(P, (A, B), Left–Right) ←      % fork
    reduce(P?, A?, Left–Middle),
    reduce(P?,B?, Middle–Right).
reduce(P, Goal, Left–Right) ←        % reduce
    Goal ≠ true,Goal ≠ (A,B),
    clause(Goal?,P?,Body) |
    reduce(P?, Body?, Left–Right).
```

Program 25.3: A termination detecting meta-interpreter

The initial left chain passed to the meta-interpreter is *done*. Unification of both the chain connections is performed upon termination. The chain is broken into two chains sharing the *Middle* when forking. It is passed on upon reduction.

25.3.3 Snapshot

The abortable meta-interpreter shown above allows a computation to be aborted. The computation may be infinite and thus needs to be aborted. If the computation runs for some time, it may be finite but just long. A snapshot meta-interpreter is suggested to inspect the execution. When the computation is required to show its state, it produces a list of all processes active in some relative time frame.

```
reduce(P, true, Chain–Chain).              % halt
reduce(P, (A, B), Left–Right) ←            % fork
    reduce(P?, A?, Left? –Middle),
    reduce(P?,B?, Middle? –Right).
reduce(P, Goal, Left–Right) ←              % reduce
    Goal ≠ true,Goal ≠ (A,B),
    unknown(Left?),
    clause(Goal?,P?,Body) |
    reduce(P?, Body?, Left? –Right).
reduce(P,Goal,[shot(Ps) | Left] –
       [shot([Goal | Ps]) | Right]) ←      % shot
    reduce(P?, Goal?, Left? –Right).
```

Program 25.4: A snapshot meta-interpreter

Each process simulation accepts an interrupt stream from its left neighbor and sends an interrupt stream to its right neighbor. When a *shot* message appears on the left stream, the process adds its state to the snapshot and passes it to the right. When all the processes handle their interrupt streams, the first element of the rightmost stream is assigned to a list of all the processes' states.

The *shot* message that appears on the left chain contains the processes to the left of the circuit. The *shot* message which is passed to the right contains also the current process. Execution proceeds with the tail of both interrupt streams.

25.3.4 Deadlock detection

A Concurrent Prolog computation may be deadlocked; all the processes are suspended waiting for some variables to be assigned. A mechanism to detect deadlock can be provided by meta-interpretation. Deadlock detection in this context is similar to the termination detection problem which has been investigated in the literature. An algorithm for termination detection is given by Dijkstra et al. (1983) and can be adopted here. The processes are connected in a circuit of interrupt streams as shown above. When deadlock needs to be detected, a *first* message is passed starting from the left side of the circuit. A process that receives the message and is able to reduce sends *no-deadlock* message to its right; if it is unable to reduce, it passes the message on to its right and waits for the *second* message. When the first message appears on the right side of the circuit, it is tested; if it is *no-deadlock*, this is announced; if it is the *first* message — the *second* message is sent on the left side.

Any process that is able to reduce after handling the *first* message sends a *no-deadlock* message to its right; otherwise the *second* message is passed on. If *no-deadlock* appears on the right side of the circuit, there is no deadlock; if the *second* message appears, then deadlock occurred.

The above algorithm requires that the language semantics provide a method to analyze a program and detect if a process is able to reduce. This functionality requires the language to provide meta-predicates to test the state of terms, which is undesirable; moreover, incorporating these into the distributed execution algorithm for the language is non-trivial.

25.3.5 Interrupt handling

Overlaying meta-interpreters on top of each other produces a combination of their functionalities, e.g., the abortable meta-interpreter can interpret the snapshot meta-interpreter. The result is a computation which is abortable and can be snapshot. Each of these meta-interpreters uses different arguments to incorporate its functionality. These functionalities can be combined more concisely by presenting a meta-interpreter that handles a general interrupt stream. This stream may contain messages like *abort*, *suspend* or *resume*. These messages result in computation abortion, snapshot of state, or suspension until resume. This structure produces a controlled mode of execution which allows computations to be interrupted to provide system functionalities.

25.3.6 Debugging

Enhanced meta-interpreters can be used for debugging. The meta-interpreter in Program 25.5 can form the basis of a parallel debugger. It builds up a representation of the execution tree while simulating a program. Another process interfaces with the programmer and shares with the meta-interpreter the tree of execution. The meta-interpreter prevents the control processes from running too far down in the execution tree. A process running in control mode is given a number of reductions which it is allowed to execute. When the process exhausts this number of reductions, it waits for the interface process to provide the next command. The interface process may give it another number of reductions to execute or change its mode to *raw*; this allows the process to continues without debugging.

When the number of reductions the process is allowed to perform is zero,

```
reduce(P, true, Time, halted).                    % halt
reduce(P, (A, B), Time, (Ta?, Tb?)) ←            % fork
    reduce(P?, A?, Time?, Ta),
    reduce(P?, B?, Time?, Tb).
reduce(P, G, Time, (G ← Tbody)) ←                % reduce
    Time > 0, New_t := Time − 1,
    G ≠ true, G ≠ (A, B),
    clause(G?, P?, Body) |
    reduce(P?, Body?, New_t?, Tbody).
reduce(P, G, 0, what_now(Mode)) ←                % wait
    G ≠ true, G ≠ (A, B) |
    next(P?, G?, Mode?).

next(P, G, debug(Time, Tree)) ←                  % debug
    reduce(P?, G?, Time?, Tree).
next(P, G, raw) ← G.                             % raw
```

Program 25.5: A parallel debugger

the meta-interpreter sends a message to the interface process to give the next command and calls *next* to wait for it. If the command is *debug* with some number, the meta-interpreter is called to perform these reductions and to produce the tree of execution; if the command is *raw*, the raw procedure is called and execution proceeds without interpretation. Note that when the *raw* mode is needed, a meta-call is performed to execute *G*. The semantics of the language do not allow meta-calls but partial evaluation will assign *G* to the needed call and no meta-call will exist in the resulting program.

25.3.7 Uncertainties

Execution of a Prolog program searches an And-Or tree for an appropriate solution. A program can be augmented with a certainty factor attached to each clause. The meta-interpreter in Program 25.6 (Shapiro, 1983b) computes the certainty of the result while executing the computation.

The certainty of *true* is one; the certainty of a conjunction is the minimum of the certainties of the conjuncts. The certainty of a reduction is the certainty of the clause multiplied by the certainty of the body.

```
reduce(Program, true, 1).
reduce(Program, (A, B), C) ←
    reduce(Program, A, C_of_a),
    reduce(Program,B, C_of_b),
    min(C_of_a, C_of_b, C).
reduce(Program, Goal, C) ←
    clause(Goal,Program,Body, Cr),
    reduce(Program, Body, C_of_body),
    C := Cr * C_of_body.
```

Program 25.6: A meta-interpreter computing uncertainties

25.4 For Real

The following section presents the results of applying partial evaluation to the enhanced Concurrent Prolog meta-interpreters with respect to a known program. The results were produced using the Concurrent Prolog partial evaluator of Safra (1986). The examples demonstrate the effectiveness of the process and shows that the layer of interpretation can be removed using the method; the resulting programs contain the added functionality without the overhead. Each program was tested on the FCP compiler (Houri and Shapiro, Chapter 38) and produced an acceptable run-time slow-down compared to the raw program without the added functionality. The examples show partial evaluation of different meta-interpreters with respect to the program naive reverse.

The meta-interpreters that were used to produce the results are slightly different from these shown above. When reducing a process to a clause whose body is *true*, execution halts; no recursive call to reduce the *true* body is performed.

The naive reverse program accepts a list and produces another list whose elements are in the reverse order of the original list. The procedure *reverse* calls itself recursively for the tail of the list to produce the reversal; an *append* call is made to append the head of the list to the end of the reversal of the tail.

```
reverse([X | Xs], Ys) ←
    reverse(Xs?, Zs),
    append(Zs?, [X?], Ys).
reverse([ ], [ ]).

append([X | Xs], Ys, [X | Zs]) ←
    append(Xs?, Ys?, Zs).
append([ ], Ys, Ys).
```

Partially evaluating this program produces a specialized version of the *append* predicate called with a single *X?* instead of a singleton list [*X?*] in the second

argument. The *append* procedure assigns [*Ys*] instead of *Y* to the third argument
if the first argument is [ ]; thus the global behavior of the program is maintained.

```
reverse([X | Xs], Ys) ←
    reverse(Xs?, Zs),
    append(Zs?, X?, Ys).
reverse([ ], [ ]).

append([X | Xs], Ys, [X | Zs]) ←
    append(Xs?, Ys?, Zs).
append([ ], Ys, [Ys]).
```

Partially evaluating the plain meta-interpreter with respect to the above resulting
program produces, as a result, the same program. We use the resulting program
to demonstrate the results of applying other meta-interpreters with respect to it.
Using the original naive reverse produces the same results.

25.4.1 Abortable meta-interpreter

The abortable meta-interpreter is called with the procedure call *reverse* and
additional argument *Abort*:

```
reduce(⟨Reverse⟩, reverse(Xs?, Ys), Abort?).
```

The resulting program:

```
reverse([X | Xs], Ys, Abort) ←
    unknown(Abort?) |
    reverse(Xs?, Zs, Abort?),
    append(Zs?, X?, Ys, Abort?).
reverse([ ], [ ], Abort).
reverse(Xs, Ys, abort).

append([X | Xs], Ys, [X | Zs], Abort) ←
    unknown(Abort?) |
    append(Xs?, Ys?, Zs, Abort?).
append([ ], Ys, [Ys], Abort).
append(Xs, Ys, Zs, abort).
```

The transformation adds an additional argument to each of the procedures — the
Abort variable — and checks for it to be *unknown* upon reduction. In addition
another clause is added that halts the execution if the *Abort* argument is assigned.

25.4.2 Termination detecting meta-interpreter

The termination detecting meta-interpreter is called with the *reverse* procedure call and the circuit chain. The left connection is *done* and the right connection is free. The form of the call:

reduce(⟨Reverse⟩, reverse(Xs?, Ys), done–Done).

The resulting program is:

```
reverse([X | Xs], Ys, Done) ←
    reverse(Xs, Zs, Rev_Done),
    append(Zs?, X?, Ys, Rev_Done?, Done).
reverse([ ], [ ], done).

append([X | Xs], Ys, [X | Zs], Left, Right) ←
    append(Xs?, Ys?, Zs, Left, Right).
append([ ], Ys, [Ys], Chain, Chain).
```

Upon termination each process unifies its two connections of the circuit. When one recursive call is executed, both connections are passed on to the call. When more then one recursive call is performed, the chain is split and the parts are divided with the appropriate connection between the recursive calls. The left chain of the reverse process is always *done*; thus it is omitted by part of the partial evaluator algorithm called renaming (Safra, 1986). Only the right connection is passed and is assigned to *done* upon termination.

25.4.3 Snapshot meta-interpreter

The snapshot meta-interpreter is called with two interrupt streams: an input stream and an output stream. Both streams are unknown at partial evaluation time. The call:

reduce(⟨Reverse⟩, reverse(Xs?, Ys), Left? – Right).

The resulting program:

```
reverse([X | Xs], Ys, Left, Right) ←
    unknown(Left?) |
    reverse(Xs, Zs, Left?, Middle),
    append(Zs?, X?, Ys, Middle?, Right).
reverse([ ], [ ], Chain, Chain).
reverse(Xs, Ys, [shot(Ps) | Left],
        [shot([reverse(Xs, Ys)| Ps]) | Right]) ←
    reverse(Xs, Ys, Left?, Right).

append([X | Xs], Ys, [X | Zs], Left, Right) ←
```

```
            unknown(Left?) |
            append(Xs?, Ys?, Zs, Left?, Right).
    append([ ], Ys, [Ys], Chain, Chain).
    append(Xs, Ys, Zs, [shot(Ps) | Left],
            [shot([append(Xs,Ys,Zs) | Ps]) | Right]) ←
        append(Xs, Ys, Zs, Left?, Right).
```

The last clause of each procedure is invoked when a *shot* message appears on the left interrupt stream. It puts *reverse* or *append* with the corresponding arguments on the shot stream and passes it to the right; then execution proceeds with the same process.

25.5 Conclusion

The resulting examples shown above are almost as efficient as the raw programs without the functionality. The programs contain the functionality but do not produce a significant overhead.

The method suggests a simple automatic mechanism to incorporate functionality into programs. A specific functionality need not be encoded into the program but, ultimately, a compiler will be derived automatically from a meta-interpreter specifying it. When a program is required to run in some *mode*, it will be compiled by the corresponding compiler produced from the interpreter.

Meta-interpreters can be used for real!

Acknowledgements

The authors wish to acknowledge the encouragement of Kenneth Kahn in using partial evaluation. The idea of applying this technique to meta-interpreters which led to the research reported in this paper was communicated to us by Akikazu Takeuchi. We also wish to thank Steve Taylor for comments and discussions while reviewing this paper.

Chapter 26

Algorithmic Debugging of GHC Programs and Its Implementation in GHC

Akikazu Takeuchi

Institute for New Generation Computing Technology

Abstract

An intended interpretation of a GHC program which formalizes how a program is expected to behave is given. Based on this, a debugging algorithm for two major errors of GHC programs, termination with incorrect answer and incorrect deadlock, is presented. It can search for a bug efficiently over a computation tree using the divide and query strategy. The implementation of the debugger in GHC is also given.

26.1 Introduction

As parallel computers become widely used, the debugging of parallel programs will become an important software development technology. Even in sequential computers, debugging programs which are written in parallel languages or languages with extended control such as coroutining is a large obstacle for software development. In fact, it has been said that debugging of these programs is a very hard task, compared with the debugging sequential programs. The reasons why this is the case are that conceptually several computations are executed in parallel, these computations may interact with each other, and there are new types of bugs such as deadlock.

In conventional debugging methods, a programmer tries to find a bug by observing the execution trace. If an incorrect behavior is found at some place, then the bug is detected in its neighborhood. For this style of debugging, it is assumed that a programmer has complete knowledge of program behavior, and it is required that the execution trace is displayed in a structured way in order for the programmer to recognize easily the flow of computation and to compare the trace with his knowledge. The flaw with this style of debugging is its complexity, which increases as a program becomes complicated. As the complexity of the program increases, both the size of the execution trace and the amount of knowledge a programmer must have increase, so that the programmer faces the danger of misjudging. Concerning parallel programs, because of the reasons mentioned in the first paragraph, the complexity of a program is surmised to increase. Therefore we suspect that debugging parallel programs using execution traces will face serious problems.

In general, we should distinguish between debugging and understanding program behavior. It is essential to clearly display what happens in a computer in order for a programmer to understand the data and the control flow of a program. Monitoring the program's behavior will help finding a bug, but it forces a programmer to understand this behavior. It is better if a programmer could debug a program only with more abstract knowledge such as input and output specification of component modules.

Generally speaking, a logic program has two different aspects, logic and control. The logic aspect of a program directly relates to its declarative semantics and the control aspect to its procedural semantics. Owing to these two aspects, a program can be read declaratively and procedurally. This is also true for debugging, that is, debugging can be done declaratively and/or procedurally. Conventional debugging corresponds to debugging using the procedural meaning of a program. Debugging using declarative meaning is known as algorithmic debugging and was first investigated by Shapiro (1982). In algorithmic debugging, a bug is detected by observing the result of computation such as input/output history, a rather static information compared with the dynamic behavior of the program. There are several algorithms for locating a bug. Each algorithm guarantees that the debugger can find a bug within a finite session of question-answerings. Each question issued by the debugger is isolated, that is, it concerns itself with the correctness of the result of a procedure. Therefore answering each question is easy no matter how complicated a program is, although the number of questions depends on the complexity of the program. Therefore algorithmic debugging is a steady and efficient way of debugging and is a promising method for the debugging of parallel programs.

The pioneering work of algorithmic debugging is due to Shapiro (1982). Several researchers investigated algorithmic debugging of logic programs further (Ferrand, 1985; Pereira, 1986; Lloyd, 1986). Algorithmic debugging of functional languages was investigated by Takahashi and Ono (1985).

In this paper, we present algorithmic debuggers for a parallel logic programming language, GHC (Ueda, Chapter 4). The debuggers with different debugging strategies, "single-stepping" and "divide-and-query", are shown with their implementation in GHC. The formal framework of our debuggers is investigated in the subsequent paper (Lloyd and Takeuchi, 1986).

Readers are assumed to be familiar with parallel logic programming and algorithmic debugging.

26.2 GHC

A GHC program is a finite set of guarded clauses. A guarded clause has the form:

$$H \leftarrow G_1, \ldots, G_n \mid B_1, \ldots, B_m.$$

where H, $G_1, \ldots, G_n$ and $B_1, \ldots, B_m$ are called the head, the guard part and the body part of the clause, respectively.

For simplicity, the algorithm developed in this paper only deals with body parts of GHC clauses. Therefore we will restrict our attention to Flat GHC programs, which are only allowed to have system predicates in the guard.

26.3 A Framework for Algorithmic Debugging of GHC Programs

We summarize the framework of algorithmic debugging of GHC programs following Lloyd and Takeuchi (1986).

In order to debug a buggy program, the abstract meaning of a program, which is called the intended interpretation of the program, is required. Shapiro's system uses the least model obtained from the program as its intended interpretation. In our system, the intended interpretation of a program has the following definition.

Definition 1. Given a program S, *Msuc* and *Msus* are defined to be the following two sets.

$$Msuc = \{A : \text{there exists a derivation from } \leftarrow A \text{ which succeeds} \\ \text{without further instantiation of } A\}$$

$$Msus = \{A : \text{there exists a derivation from } \leftarrow A \text{ which suspends} \\ \text{without further instantiation of } A\}$$

We call *Msuc* and *Msus* together the "intended interpretation" of the program S. ∎

The debugging algorithms are applied to a computation tree of a given goal $\leftarrow A$. The computation tree is a proof tree of the goal and is also a final And-tree, to which all the substitutions made during the computation have been applied. The advantage of using a final And-tree is that computations in disjoint subtrees can be regarded as independent computations.

Definition 2. We say a node $\leftarrow A$ in the computation tree has been *executed incorrectly* if:

(a) $\leftarrow A$ succeeds in the tree, but $A \notin Msuc$, or
(b) $\leftarrow A$ suspends in the tree, but $A \notin Msus$.

Otherwise a node is said to be *executed correctly*. ▮

Two major errors of GHC programs are considered in this paper and are defined as follows.

Definition 3. A result of a computation is called *termination with incorrect answer* if the computation has terminated with incorrect answer. A result of a computation is called *incorrect deadlock* if the computation deadlocks where it should not deadlock. ▮

Two major bugs corresponding to the two major errors are *incorrect clause instance* and *buggy suspension*.

Definition 4. We say that a clause instance,

$$H \leftarrow G_1, \ldots, G_n \mid B_1, \ldots, B_m.$$

invoked at some node in the computation tree is *incorrect* if H has been incorrectly executed, but each goal B_j has been correctly executed, for $j = 1, \ldots, m$. We say a goal $\leftarrow A$ invoked at some node in the computation tree is a *buggy suspension* if $\leftarrow A$ immediately suspends, but $A \notin Msus$. ▮

Buggy suspension indicates that there is a missing clause in the definition called by the goal. The correlation between errors and bugs are shown in Table 26.1.

Errors\Bugs	Incorrect Clause	Buggy Suspension
Incorrect Answer	○	×
Incorrect Deadlock	○	○

○   indicates that an error is invoked by a bug.

×   indicates that an error is not invoked by a bug.

Table 26.1: Relation between errors and bugs

We assume that a programmer knows what literals are included in *Msuc* and
what literals in *Msus*, as declarative debuggers of pure Prolog assume. Therefore,
when it is necessary to know whether a node $\leftarrow A$ in a computation tree has
been executed correctly or not, a query is issued to the programmer. The query
is called an *oracle query* and has two forms depending on the context of the node
in the computation tree.

> *succeeded(A)?*   if $\leftarrow A$ succeeds in the computation tree.
>   Meaning: $A \in Msuc$?
>
> *suspended(A)?*   if $\leftarrow A$ suspends in the computation tree.
>   Meaning: $A \in Msus$?

26.4 Implementation

There are several strategies for locating a bug. Shapiro (1982) proposed two
strategies, "single stepping" and "divide and query". Pereira (1986) proposed
dependency directed strategy. In Lloyd (1986), Lloyd and Takeuchi (1986), the
top-down strategy was adopted. In this paper, we present GHC implementation
of the debuggers based on "single stepping" and "divide and query" strategies. In
Section 26.4.1, the debugger for termination with incorrect answer adopting the
"single stepping" strategy is presented. Section 26.4.2 presents the debugger for
the same error based on the "divide and query" strategy. In Section 26.4.3, the
debugger handling both termination with incorrect answer and incorrect deadlock
based on the "divide and query" strategy is presented.

26.4.1 A single stepping algorithm for termination with incorrect answer

When a program terminates with an incorrect answer, it can be concluded
that there is at least one incorrect clause instance.

The algorithm to find such clause is specified as follows:

Algorithm 1.

> Input: A goal G that terminates with an incorrect answer.
>
> Output: An incorrect clause instance.

Simulate the execution of G; whenever a subgoal Q terminates with Q', check,
using an oracle query, whether Q' has been executed correctly. If not, return the
clause invoked there as an incorrect clause instance.   ∎

The point of this algorithm is that by confirming the result of a computation
whenever a goal terminates, we can find a clause instance invoked at some node

in the computation tree that generates an incorrect answer, but all its body goals have been executed correctly. It is clear that such a clause is an incorrect clause instance. The query complexity (the maximum number of queries issued by the debugger) of this algorithm is proportional to the number of goal reductions. A GHC implementation of this algorithm is shown in Program 26.1.

single_stepping(Goal,IncClsIns) ←
    Given *Goal*, it returns an incorrect clause instance at *IncClsIns*.

single_stepping(Goals,IncClsIns) ← true | tree(Goals,IncClsIns,_).

tree(Goals,IncClsIns,Ctr) ←
    Given *Goals*, it returns an incorrect clause instance at *IncClsIns*.
    Ctr is used to abort irrelevant computation.

tree(_,_,abort) ← true | true.
tree(true,X,_) ← true | X=ok.
tree(A,X,_) ← ghcsystem(A) | X=ok, call(A).
tree((A, B),X,C) ← true |
    tree(A,Xa,Ca), tree(B,Xb,Cb), and(Xa,Ca,Xb,Cb,X,C).
tree(A,X,C) ← clause(A,Body) |
    tree(Body,X1,C), reduction(X1,(A←Body),X,C).

reduction(X1,Clause,X,Ctr) ←
    reduction corresponds to reduction of a goal to a body part.
    Clause is an instance of the clause used for the reduction.
    X and *X1* are used to send an incorrect clause instance to the
    head and to receive it from the body part, respectively.

reduction(ok,(P←Q),X,_) ← true |
    query(P,Ans), react(Ans,(P←Q),X).
reduction((P←Q),_,X,_) ← true | X=(P←Q).
reduction(_,_,_,abort) ← true | true.

and(_,Ca,_,Cb,_,abort) ← true | Ca=abort, Cb=abort.
and((P←Q),_,_,Cb,X,_) ← true | Cb=abort, X=(P←Q).
and(_,Ca,(P←Q),_,X,_) ← true | Ca=abort, X=(P←Q).
and(ok,_,Xb,_,X,_) ← true | Xb=X.
and(Xa,_,ok,_,X,_) ← true | Xa=X.

react(yes,_,Ans) ← true | Ans=ok.
react(no,(P←Q),Ans) ← true | Ans=(P←Q).

Program 26.1: A single-stepping debugger of an incorrect answer *ghcsystem*(*A*) is a system predicate checking whether *A* is a system predicate or not. *clause*(*A,Body*) is also a system predicate which, given a goal *A*, returns a body part of the clause, the head and the guard of which have been successfully solved. *tree* simulates execution of the goal; at the same time it forms a computation tree as the network of *reduction* and *and*.

When *reduction*(*X1*,(*P←Q*),*X*,*Ctr*) receives *ok* at *X1* from the body part, it means that the body goals *Q* have been executed correctly. Then it asks a programmer whether *P* has been executed correctly or not by the predicate *query*(*P,Ans*). If answer is *yes*, then it returns *ok* on *X*. If the answer is *no*, it means that *P←Q* is an incorrect clause instance. Hence it is returned on *X*. When *X1* is already instantiated to some clause, it means that an incorrect clause instance has been already found. Such a clause is passed on *X*.

and processes make the intelligent communication network for *reduction* processes in the form of the binary tree. They carry the information about correctness of reductions to their parent reductions. At the same time, they send *abort* messages to appropriate *reduction* processes in order to kill irrelevant computation.

Conceptually the single-stepping debugger has two phases. In the first phase, it forms the computation tree as a tree of *reduction* processes inter-connected by *and* processes. In the second phase, for each reduction from leaves to the root, the result of the reduction is confirmed using oracle queries. In actual execution, these two phases are appropriately overlapped.

Example 1. Debugging of a program terminating with incorrect answer by single-stepping algorithm.

```
qsort(Xs, Ys) ← qsort(Xs, Ys, [ ]).

qsort([X|Xs], Ys0, Ys2) ←
    % part(Xs, X, S, L), qsort(S, Ys0, [X|Ys1]), qsort(L, Ys1, Ys2).
    part(Xs, X, S, L), qsort(S, Ys0, Ys1), qsort(L, Ys1, Ys2).
qsort([ ], Ys, O) ← true | O=Ys.

part([X|Xs], A, S, L) ← A < X | L=[X|L1], part(Xs, A, S, L1).
part([X|Xs], A, S, L) ← A ≥ X | S=[X|S1], part(Xs, A, S1, L).
part([ ], _, S, L) ← true | S=[ ], L=[ ].
```

Program 26.2: An incorrect Quicksort

Program 26.2 contains a buggy Quicksort which returns [ ] with *[3,1,2]* as input.

```
| ?– ghc single_stepping(qsort([3,1,2],P),L).
succeeded(part([ ],3,[ ],[ ])) ? (yes/no) y.
succeeded(part([2],3,[2],[ ])) ? (yes/no) y.
```

succeeded(part([1,2],3,[1,2],[ ])) ? (yes/no) *y*.
succeeded(part([ ],1,[ ],[ ])) ? (yes/no) *y*.
succeeded(part([2],1,[ ],[2])) ? (yes/no) *y*.
succeeded(qsort([ ],-57,-57)) ? (yes/no) *y*.
succeeded(part([ ],2,[ ],[ ])) ? (yes/no) *y*.
succeeded(qsort([ ],-57,-57)) ? (yes/no) *y*.
succeeded(qsort([ ],-57,-57)) ? (yes/no) *y*.
succeeded(qsort([2],-57,-57)) ? (yes/no) *n*.
succeeded(qsort([ ],[ ],[ ])) ? (yes/no) *y*.

L = qsort([2],[ ],[ ])←part([ ],2,[ ],[ ]), qsort([ ],[ ],[ ]), qsort([ ],[ ],[ ]),
P = [ ]

yes ∎

26.4.2 A divide-and-query algorithm for termination with incorrect answer

Using the divide-and-query strategy, we can improve the query complexity of the algorithm. The basic idea is to perform a binary search for an incorrect clause instance over the computation tree spawned by reduction processes. Before specifying the algorithm, we first define the weight of a reduction in the computation tree.

Definition 5. Let G be a goal reduced in a reduction R, and M a set of goals.

(a) $weight(R)=0$ if G is in M.

(b) $weight(R)=1+\sum_{i=1}^{n} weight(R_i)$ if R invokes n reductions, $R_1,\ldots,R_n$.   ∎

The weight of a reduction reflects the size of the subtree rooted at that reduction.

Algorithm 2.

Input: A goal G that terminates with an incorrect answer and a (possibly empty) subset M' of *Msuc* ∪ *Msus*.

Output: An incorrect clause instance.

Simulate the execution of G, compute w, the weight of the reduction of G modulo M'. If w is 1, then the clause invoked at the root is returned. Otherwise, it finds the heaviest node Q in the computation tree whose weight is less than or equal to $\lceil w/2 \rceil$ and queries oracle whether the goal G_Q reduced at Q has been executed correctly. If the oracle answers *yes*, then the algorithm is applied to the same computation tree with $M' \cup \{G_Q\}$ as new M'. If the oracle answers *no*, then the algorithm is applied to the computation tree rooted at Q with the same M'.   ∎

It is known that the maximum number of the queries of this algorithm is $O(\log N)$, where N is the number of reductions.

A GHC implementation of this algorithm is shown in Program 26.3. The predicates similar to those in the single stepping algorithm have the same names.

divide&query(Goal,IncClsIns) is a top level procedure, which invokes three subgoals, *tree*, *cursor* and *oracle*. Roughly speaking, *tree* simulates the computation of the goal *Goal* and forms the computation tree by spawning *reduction* processes which correspond to reductions. *cursor* points two important nodes in the tree, the root and the middle nodes, and can communicate with them. *cursor* is also an interface between these two nodes and *oracle*. *oracle* is the manager of oracle queries.

omerge processes makes the intelligent communication network for *reduction* processes in the form of a binary tree.

The tree formed by the network of *reduction* and *omerge* processes computes the weights, finds the middle point of the tree and updates the tree and the weights according to oracles.

The middle point of the computation tree is determined in the following way. First *reduction* at the root of the computation tree receives a *down* message. Let w be the current weight of the root. Then it computes $\lceil w/2 \rceil$, sends it downward as a *new* message and waits for the reply (3). On receiving a *new* message, *reduction* sends it downward, if its current weight is greater than the value (4). Otherwise *reduction* changes to *middle* and returns the clause invoked there, with its current weight and input/output streams as a *middle* message (5). On receiving a *middle* message, *reduction* processes which are waiting for reply pass it upwards (7). In this algorithm, more than one *middle* processes are created. However, *omerge* processes select one which has the greatest weight and the rest of the *middle* processes change back to *reduction* processes (11).

cursor is an interface between the root, the middle point of the tree and *oracle*. Initially *cursor* only points at the root of the tree as the middle point and waits for a *down* message (see the definition of *divide&query*). The message initiates the computation of the middle point.

Whenever *cursor* receives the new middle point of the tree, it sends the goal reduced in the middle point to *oracle*. *oracle* replies *down* or *up* to *cursor*, depending on whether the goal has been executed correctly or not. On receiving the *down* message from *oracle*, *cursor* sends the *down* message to the middle point in order to examine the subtree rooted at the middle point and to discard the rest of the tree. That message initiates the computation of the new middle point of the new tree. On receiving the *up* message, *cursor* sends the *terminal* message to the middle point in order to discard the subtree rooted at the middle point and to examine the rest of the tree. That message initiates the computation of the new middle point of the updated tree.

divide&query(Goal,IncClsIns) ←
    true |
        tree(Goal,W,I/O),
        cursor([down|In],Out,top($\_,\_$),mid(O,I)),
        oracle(Out,In,[ ],IncClsIns).

tree(Goals,Weights,Input/Output) ←
    Given *Goals*, *tree* simulates the computation of *Goals* and forms
    the computation tree as a network of *reductions*. *Weights* is the
    sum of the initial weights of reductions of *Goals*. *Input* and
    Output are streams from and to the outside, respectively.

tree((A,B),Wab,I/O) ←
    true |
        tree(A,Wa,I/Oa), tree(B,Wb,I/Ob),
        Wab := Wa+Wb, omerge(Oa,Ob,O).
tree(A,Wa,I/O) ←
    ghcsystem(A) |
        Wa=0, call(A), O=[ ].
tree(A,Wa,I/O) ←
    clause(A,Body) |
        tree(Body,Wb,Ob/Ib),
        Wa := Wb+1,
        reduction(I,O,Ib,Ob,Wa,(A←Body)).

omerge([middle((Ra,Wa),Ca)|X],[middle((Rb,Wb),mid(I,O))|Y],Z) ←
    Wa≥Wb | Z=[middle((Ra,Wa),Ca)|ZZ], O=[ ], omerge(X,Y,ZZ).
omerge([middle((Ra,Wa),mid(I,O))|X],[middle((Rb,Wb),Cb)|Y],Z) ←
    Wa<Wb | Z=[middle((Rb,Wb),Cb)|ZZ], O=[ ], omerge(X,Y,ZZ).
omerge([A|X],Y,Z) ← A\=middle($\_,\_$) | Z=[A|ZZ], omerge(X,Y,ZZ).
omerge(X,[A|Y],Z) ← A\=middle($\_,\_$) | Z=[A|ZZ], omerge(X,Y,ZZ).
omerge([ ],Y,Z) ← true | Y=Z.
omerge(X,[ ],Z) ← true | X=Z.

reduction(I,O,Ib,Ob,W,Clause) ←
    Clause is an instance of the clause invoked there. *I* and *O* are
    streams from and to the preceding reduction, respectively. *Ib* and
    Ob are streams from and to the reductions of the body goals.
    W is the weight. Initial weights are computed when the
    computation tree is formed by *tree*.

reduction([ ],Op,$\_$,Oc,$\_,\_$) ←   (1)
    true |
        Oc=[ ], Op=[ ].

Program 26.3: A divide-and-query debugger of an incorrect answer

reduction([down|Mi],Mo,Ic,Oc,1,Clause) ←   (2)
      true |
            Mo=[answer(Clause)], Oc=[ ].
reduction([down|Mi],Mo,Ic,Oc,Wa,Clause) ←   (3)
      NBD := (Wa+1)/2, Wa=\=1 |
            Oc=[new(NBD)|Oc2],
            reduction2(Mi,Mo,Ic,Oc2,Wa,Clause).
reduction([new(NBD)|Ip],Op,Ic,Oc,Wa,Clause) ←   (4)
      Wa>NBD |
            Oc=[new(NBD)|Oc2],
            reduction2(Ip,Op,Ic,Oc2,Wa,Clause).
reduction([new(NBD)|Ip],Op,Ic,Oc,Wa,Clause) ←   (5)
      Wa≤NBD |
            Op=[middle((Clause,Wa),mid(Mo,Mi))|Op2],
            middle(Mi,Mo,Ip,Op2,Ic,Oc,Wa,Clause).
reduction(Ip,Op,[update(Wb,_)|Ic],Oc,Wa,Clause) ←   (6)
      true |
            Wa1 := Wa–Wb, Op=[update(Wb,Wa1)|Op2],
            reduction(Ip,Op2,Ic,Oc,Wa1,Clause).
reduction2(Ip,Op,[middle(M,C)|Ic],Oc,Wa,Clause) ←   (7)
      true |
            Op=[middle(M,C)|Op2],
            reduction(Ip,Op2,Ic,Oc,Wa,Clause).

middle(Mi,Mo,Ip,Op,Ib,Ob,Weight,Clause) ←
      A variant of *reduction(Ip,Op,Ib,Ob,Weight,Clause)* which locates
      in the middle point of the computation tree. *Mi* and *Mo* are
      streams from and to *cursor*.

middle([terminal],Mo,Ip,Op,Ic,Oc,Wa,Clause) ←   (8)
      true |
            Op=[update(Wa,0)|Op2], Mo=[ ], Oc=[ ],
            reduction(Ip,Op2,_,_,0,Clause).
middle([down|Mi],Mo,Ip,Op,Ic,Oc,1,Clause) ←   (9)
      true |
            Mo=[answer(Clause)],Oc=[ ],Op=[ ].
middle([down|Mi],Mo,Ip,Op,Ic,Oc,Wa,Clause) ←   (10)
      NBD := (Wa+1)/2, Wa=\=1 |
            Oc=[new(NBD)|Oc2], Op=[ ],
            reduction2(Mi,Mo,Ic,Oc2,Wa,Clause).

Program 26.3: (Continued)

middle([ ],Mo,Ip,Op,Ic,Oc,Wa,Clause) ←   (11)
    true |
        Mo=[ ], reduction(Ip,Op,Ic,Oc,Wa,Clause).

cursor(In,Out,top(Ti,To),mid(Mi,Mo)) ←
    cursor points at two important *reduction* processes in the computation tree, the root and the middle nodes, and can communicate with them. *Ti* and *To* are streams from and to the root, and *Mi* and *Mo* are streams from and to the middle point, respectively.

cursor([down|In],Out,top(Ti,To),mid(Mi,Mo)) ←   (12)
    true |
        Mo=[down|Mo2], To=[ ],
        cursor2(In,Out,top(Mi,Mo2)).
cursor([up|In],Out,Top,mid(Mi,Mo)) ←   (13)
    true |
        Mo=[terminal],
        cursor2(In,Out,Top).
cursor2(In,Out,top([answer(Clause)|Ti],To)) ←   (14)
    true |
        Out=[answer(Clause)],To=[ ].
cursor2(In,Out,top([middle(Mid,MChan)|Ti],To)) ←   (15)
    true |
        Out=[middle(Mid)|Out2],
        cursor(In,Out2,top(Ti,To),MChan).
cursor2(In,Out,top([update(_,W)|Ti],To)) ←   (16)
    NBD:=(W+1)/2 |
        To=[new(NBD)|To2],
        cursor2(In,Out,top(Ti,To2)).

oracle(In,Out,QDB,IncClsIns) ←
    oracle receives a goal from the input stream *In* and queries the programmer whether the goal has been executed correctly or not. If the reply from the ghc programmer is *yes*, then the message *up* is sent through the output stream *Out*. Otherwise the message *down* is sent. The queries already asked and their answers are stored in *QDB*. *QDB* is used to suppress asking the same query twice.

oracle([middle(((P←Q),W))|In],Out,S,IncClsIns) ←
    true |
        member(P,S,R), branchonr(R,Out,In,P,S,IncClsIns).

Program 26.3: (Continued)

oracle([answer((P←Q))],Out,S,IncClsIns) ←
    true |
        IncClsIns=(P←Q).
branchonr(yes,Out,In,Query,S,IncClsIns) ←
    true |
        Out=[up|Out2], oracle(In,Out2,S,IncClsIns).
branchonr(no,Out,In,Query,S,IncClsIns) ←
    true |
        Out=[down|Out2], oracle(In,Out2,S,IncClsIns).
branchonr(unknown,Out,In,Query,S,IncClsIns) ←
    query(Query,Ans) |
        branchonr2(Ans,Out,In,[fact(Query,Ans)|S],IncClsIns).
branchonr2(yes,Out,In,S,IncClsIns) ←
    true |
        Out=[up|Out2], oracle(In,Out2,S,IncClsIns).
branchonr2(no,Out,In,S,IncClsIns) ←
    true |
        Out=[down|Out2], oracle(In,Out2,S,IncClsIns).

Program 26.3: (Continued)

26.4.3 A divide-and-query algorithm for both errors

A debugging algorithm for a program which deadlocks incorrectly can be obtained by slightly extending the debugger in Program 26.3.

First the top level procedure is changed to *divide&query(Goal,BUG,DL)* where *DL* is a *deadlock flag* which is uninstantiated during the computation of the *Goal* and is instantiated externally to *deadlock* when the computation deadlocks. It is impossible to implement such a deadlock detecting mechanism in GHC itself. Discussion of the implementation of such a mechanism is beyond the scope of this paper and we assume that there is such a mechanism. *divide&query* invokes three subgoals, *tree*, *cursor* and *oracle*, where *tree* and *oracle* are extended and *cursor* is unchanged.

The basic idea of the extension in Program 26.4 is to make the computation tree include suspended goals upon deadlocking. Once the computation tree including suspended goals is formed, the debugging algorithm used so far can be applied as before.

The last clause defining *tree* handles the suspended goals when the entire computation deadlocks. It creates *reduction* with *susp(A)* instead of the clause used in the reduction.

In order to distinguish between a reduction which at least one of its de-

divide&query(Goal,BUG,DL) ←

    Given *Goal*, it returns an incorrect clause instance or
    buggy suspension at *BUG*.

divide&query(Goal,BUG,DL) ←
    true |
        tree(Goal,W,I/O,H–[ ],DL),
        cursor([down|In],Out,top(_,_),mid(O,I)),
            oracle(Out,In,[ ],BUG).

tree(Goals,Weights,Input/Output,H\ T,DL) ←

    Given *Goals*, *tree* simulates the computation of *Goals* and forms the com-
    putation tree as a network of *reductions*. If the simulation deadlocks
    and DL is then instantiated (it is detected from the outside to be
    deadlocked), the suspended goals are included in the computation tree.
    Weights is the sum of the initial weights of reductions of *Goals*.
    Input and *Output* are streams from and to outside, respectively.
    H\ T is the difference list of the goals which are included in *Goals*
    and have not terminated upon deadlocking.

tree((A,B),Wab,I/O,H\T,DL) ←
    true |
        tree(A,Wa,I/Oa,H\T1,DL), tree(B,Wb,I/Ob,T1\T,DL),
        Wab := Wa+Wb, omerge(Oa,Ob,O).
tree(A,Wa,I/O,H\T,DL) ←
    ghcsystem(A) |
        call(A,Res,Ctr), filter(Res,A,H\T,DL,Ctr),
        O=[ ], Wa=0.
tree(A,Wa,I/O,H\T,DL) ←
    clause(A,Body) |
        tree(Body,Wb,Ob/Ib,H1\[ ],DL),
        Wa := Wb+1, switch(H1,H\T,A),
        check_termination(H1,I,O,Ib,Ob,Wa,(A←Body)).
tree(A,Wa,I/O,H\T,deadlock) ←
    true |
        H=[susp(A)|T], Wa=1, reduction(I,O,_,_,1,susp(A)).

filter(Res,A,H\ T,DL,Ctr) ←
    filter examines the result *Res* of the evaluation of the system
    predicate and unifies *H* with *T* if it is *success*. Otherwise, upon
    deadlocking, *susp(A)* is registered in the difference list *H–T*.

Program 26.4: A divide-and-query debugger for incorrect answer
                and deadlock

filter(success,_,H\T,_,_) ←
    true |
        H=T.
filter(Res,A,H–T,deadlock,Ctr) ←
    true |
        Ctr=stop, H=[susp(A)|T].

switch(H1,H\T,A) ←
    switch examines the difference list *H1*\[ ] and registers *open(A)* in
    H\T if there is at least one element. Otherwise it unifies *H* with *T*.

switch([ ],H\T,_) ←
    true |
        H=T.
switch([_|_],H\T,A) ←
    true |
        H=[open(A)|T].
check_termination([ ],Ip,Op,Ic,Oc,Weight,Clause) ←
    true |
        reduction(Ip,Op,Ic,Oc,Weight,Clause).
check_termination([A|B],Ip,Op,Ic,Oc,Weight,Clause) ←
    true |
        reduction(Ip,Op,Ic,Oc,Weight,open(Clause)).
oracle([middle((susp(P),W))|In],Out,S,BUG) ←
    true |
        member(suspended(P),S,R), branchonr(R,Out,In,suspended(P),S,BUG).
oracle([middle((open((P←Q)),W))|In],Out,S,BUG) ←
    true |
        member(open(P),S,R), branchonr(R,Out,In,open(P),S,BUG).
oracle([middle(((P←Q),W))|In],Out,S,BUG) ←
    true |
        member(P,S,R), branchonr(R,Out,In,P,S,BUG).
oracle([answer(Clause)],Out,S,BUG) ←
    true |
        BUG=answer(Clause).

Program 26.4: (Continued)

scendants suspends and a reduction which all of its descendants terminate, *check_termination* is introduced. It creates *reduction* with *open(Clause)* for the former and *reduction* with *Clause* for the latter.

oracle is extended to handle the new terms such as $susp(P)$ and $open(C)$.

Example 2. Debugging Program 26.2 by the divide-and-query algorithm.

| ?– ghc divide&query(qsort([3,1,2],P),DL).
succeeded(qsort([2],[ ],[ ])) ? (yes/no) *n*.
succeeded(part([ ],2,[ ],[ ])) ? (yes/no) *y*.
succeeded(qsort([ ],[ ],[ ])) ? (yes/no) *y*.

answer((qsort([2],[ ],[ ])←part([ ],[ ],[ ]), qsort([ ],[ ],[ ]), qsort([ ],[ ],[ ])

DL = _78,
P = [ ]

yes

Since the simulation of the goal does not deadlock in this example, it is not necessary to instantiate externally *DL*. ∎

qsort(Xs, Ys) ← qsort(Xs, Ys, [ ]).

qsort([X|Xs], Ys0, Ys2) ←
        part(Xs, X, S, L), qsort(S, Ys0, [X|Ys1]), qsort(L, Ys1, Ys2).
qsort([ ], Ys, O) ← true | O=Ys.

% part([X|Xs], A, S, L) ← A < X | L=[X|L1], part(Xs, A, S, L1).
part([X|Xs], A, S, [X|L1]) ← A < X | part(Xs, A, S, L1).
part([X|Xs], A, S, L) ← A ≥ X | S=[X|S1], part(Xs, A, S1, L).
part([ ], _, S, L) ← true | S=[ ], L=[ ].

Program 26.5: A deadlocking Quicksort

Example 3. Debugging Program 26.5, which incorrectly deadlocks, by the divide-and-query algorithm. The program deadlocks for given input [*3,1,2*].

| ?– ghc divide&query(qsort([3,1,2],P),DL).

%% It is assumed that *DL* is instantiated externally to
%% *deadlock* upon deadlocking of the simulation of the goal.

suspended(qsort([1,2],_57,[3])) ? (yes/no) n.
suspended(part([2],1,_1452,_1453)) ? (yes/no) n.

answer(susp(part([2],1,_1452,_1453)))

DL = deadlock,
P = _57

yes

The answer indicates that $part([2],1,\_1452,\_1453)$ is the buggy suspension and that there is a missing clause in the definition of *part*.   ∎

26.5 Concluding Remarks

We have presented debugging algorithms for two major errors of GHC programs, termination with incorrect answer and incorrect deadlock, together with their GHC implementations.

A subsequent paper by Lloyd and Takeuchi (1986), gives a formal framework for algorithmic debugging of GHC. It is proved there that the debugger can always find a bug under certain conditions. The handling of buggy failure is also presented in that paper.

Although we concentrate on a debugger for GHC programs, the technique developed here are applicable to other parallel logic programming languages such as PARLOG (Clark and Gregory, Chapter 3) and Concurrent Prolog (Shapiro, Chapter 2).

The following types of bugs can be treated by our debugger with appropriate augmentation:

- Infinite loop

- Bugs in the guard part.

The following types of bugs are difficult to handle in our framework:

- Bugs which do not reappear because of GHC's nondeterminism

- Bugs caused by unfairness of scheduling such as starvation

- Termination with correct answer but incorrect behavior.

Acknowledgement

We would like to thank Kazuhiro Fuchi, Koichi Furukawa and all the other members of ICOT, both for help with this research and for providing a stimulating place in which to work.

Yossi Lichtenstein assisted in editing this paper.

Chapter 27

Representation and Enumeration of Flat Concurrent Prolog Computations

Yossi Lichtenstein, Michael Codish and Ehud Shapiro

The Weizmann Institute of Science

Abstract

Concurrent systems cannot be characterized only by their input-output behaviors, but should be viewed as reactive systems with time-dependent behavior. This paper examines the reactive aspects of the concurrent logic programming language Flat Concurrent Prolog. A notion of a Flat Concurrent Prolog computation is defined by labeled transition operational semantics. A hierarchy of four abstractions of computations is presented. Three of these are of reactive nature and the fourth is the standard representation for logic program computations. The structure of the hierarchy is discussed in the context of abstract interpretation.

Given a Flat Concurrent Prolog initial goal with an input and a program, it is useful to be able to enumerate some or all possible computations of the goal. For example, such a construction seems to be a precondition for an algorithmic debugger for Flat Concurrent Prolog. In this paper an enumeration method which constructs all possible computations of a goal is shown and an example interpreter is described.

27.1 Introduction

Reactive systems are systems which cannot be described only as a relation between initial and final states. The description of a component in such a system must refer to its continuous interaction with other components (Harel and Pnueli,

1985). A component in a concurrent system should be viewed as a reactive component. This is because, typically, a component in a concurrent system maintains a reactive interaction with the other components in the system. Consequently, if we want to view a full system in the same way we view its components, as seems to be recommended by any compositional approach, we find ourselves viewing all concurrent systems as reactive (Pnueli, 1986).

This paper is concerned with the representation and construction of Flat Concurrent Prolog (FCP) computations. FCP is a concurrent logic programming language described by Shapiro (Chapter 5). The classical approach to the semantics of logic programming languages is inadequate to capture the reactive aspects of concurrent logic programming languages.

Substitutions provide the declarative understanding of the desired output of a logic program and goal (Lloyd, 1984). In FCP as well as in other concurrent logic programming languages, substitutions by themselves are insufficient to describe the desired reactive nature of a program-component. A representation based on an ordered series of substitutions is needed to reflect temporal behavior of these programs. We suggest the notion of *behaviors* in this context. The least Herbrand model is regarded as the intended meaning of a logic program (Lloyd, 1984). This also is an insufficient concept with which to capture the meaning of concurrent logic programming languages. We suggest a representation consisting of an augmented Herbrand universe.

In the classical approach to the semantics of logic programming the meaning of a program is viewed as a set of ground goals; the relation between Herbrand models and least fixpoints is established, and soundness and completeness theorems for SLD-resolution are proved. The development of a similar theory for concurrent (reactive) logic programming languages is an important and much needed step. In such a theory one may consider behaviors instead of substitutions, time-stamped ground goals instead of ground goals and concurrent resolution instead of SLD-resolution. In this paper we do not give such a theory — it is a subject of ongoing research. However, behaviors and labeled goals, even with weaker semantic claims, are useful in system specification and debugging. They provide a precise way for specifying the intended temporal behavior of a program and a tool for debugging synchronization errors.

This paper is organized as follows: The next section, 27.2, surveys related work: scenarios, abstract interpretation and enumeration of computations in parallel logic programming languages. Section 27.3 defines FCP computations and presents four abstractions of this notion. Three of these (*traces*, *behaviors* and *labeled goals*) are of reactive nature and the fourth (*goals*) is the standard, non-temporal representation. Section 27.4 describes the relationship between the different representations in terms of abstract interpretation. We demonstrate how these abstractions form a hierarchy by showing how goals can be defined as an abstraction of labeled goals. Section 27.5 demonstrates how to enumerate FCP computations and Section 27.6 describes some example interpreters.

27.2 Related Work

Scenarios

Scenarios were defined to overcome incompleteness in history relations for non-determinate network computations (Brock and Ackerman, 1981). In the course of a network computation, each input port receives and each output port transmits a sequence of values. The relation mapping input sequences into output sequences is called a *history relation*. History relations are inadequate to specify non-determinate networks. This is demonstrated by taking two networks with the same history relations and showing that they are not substitutable as components of a larger network. History relations are incomplete because they lack causality information. A *scenario* is a history relation augmented with a partial ordering which specifies the causality constraints on input/output events.

As a simple example consider two processes A and B each with an input port (*in*) and an output port (*out*). Process A outputs immediately data items which appear on its input port, process B waits to get two inputs before it transmits these items on its output port. The history relations of the two processes are identical (e.g., $history_A(i.j)=history_B(i.j) = i.j$), but their behavior as part of a larger network may be very different. The scenario sets for these processes capture the difference between A and B through constraints on the order of port events. Namely $scenarios_A$ and $scenarios_B$ contain the linearly ordered scenario (*in = i, in = j, out = i, out = j*), but only $scenarios_A$ contains the scenario (*in = i, out = i, in = j, out = j*). In this paper we use linearly ordered scenarios which are referred to as *behaviors*.

Scenarios have been suggested in the context of parallel logic programming languages also by Saraswat (1985) and recently by Takeuchi (unpublished memorandum).

Abstract interpretation

Abstract interpretation is a formal framework for the static analysis of programs (Cousot and Cousot, 1977). It provides a method for gathering information about specific, finitely computable, aspects of a program's behavior. The potentially infinite computational domain of a program (the *concrete* domain) is approximated by partitioning it into (generally, a finite number of) equivalence classes (referred to as the *abstract* domain). The simulation of the program over the abstract domain is terminating (under appropriate conditions) and may reveal information about certain aspects of the original program's behavior.

An intuitive example taken from Cousot and Cousot (1977) concerns the domain of arithmetic expressions over integers. In this example we wish to gather information about the possible sign of the value of an arithmetic expression. A typical abstract domain may contain the following three elements: the class of negative integers $(-)$, the class of positive integers $(+)$ and zero (0). The standard operation of multiplication is replaced by an abstract multiplication operator '$*$' which is actually the rule of signs: $(+)*(+) = (+)$; $(+)*(-) = (-)$ etc. Interpretation in this abstract domain enables us for example to determine the sign of a multiplication without actually computing the result.

A unique approach in which abstract interpretation is not applied to the analysis of programs but rather to formalize nondeterminism in dataflow networks can be found in Panangaden (1984). In this work the standard (infinite) domain is taken as the abstract domain and the nonstandard domain is defined as a concretization. The elements of the standard domain are streams of tokens. These are enriched with special τ tokens which represent timing information. Elements (streams) of the new domain typically contain data values interspersed with these tokens. Computations in the concrete domain are deterministic, in contrast with the nondeterministic computations of the standard domain.

In this paper we use abstract interpretation in a similar way: the standard domain of goals is the abstract domain, while the concrete domain is a new one containing timing information.

Enumeration of computations

The enumeration of computations in parallel logic programming languages has been investigated in different contexts (Clark and Gregory, 1985; Hirakawa et al., 1984; Ueda, 1987). Enumeration is relevant because there are different possibilities to compute a given task. This is due to the nondeterminism of the underlying computational models. Previous research was motivated by the need to obtain *all-solutions* for a given goal. For this reason only the Or-nondeterminism of the languages was considered. In this paper we consider also And-nondeterminism and provide a method to enumerate all the computations of a given goal. This is of both theoretical and practical importance. For example, enumeration is a prerequisite for algorithmic debugging of some synchronization errors in parallel logic programming languages.

27.3 Computations and Abstractions

This section defines the notion of a Flat Concurrent Prolog computation and considers various abstractions of this notion which capture the reactive nature of programs behaviors. The syntax of FCP programs and an informal operational semantics are defined by Shapiro (Chapter 5). In this paper we restrict ourselves to an interleaving semantics of FCP, although it seems that some aspects of the language are not captured by this approach. Ongoing research attempts to better capture the nondeterminism and concurrency of FCP using a notion similar to refusals (Hoare, 1985). The semantics given in this paper is designed with compositionality in mind, however a fuller treatment of the semantics is yet to be provided.

A *trace* is defined as an abstraction of a computation obtained by considering the labels of a computation, ignoring the intermediate states which are not externally observable. We then define *behaviors* as a further abstraction of traces. Section 27.3.2 defines the notion of *time-stamped computations* and its abstraction to *time-stamped goals*. The relation between the various abstractions is discussed in the next section.

In this paper we consider FCP programs without guards. Guards can be added by extending the read-only most-general-unifier ($mgu_?$) to include their evaluation. The $mgu_?$ is the FCP analog to the standard most-general-unifier of logic programming (roughly speaking it is an mgu that does not bind read-only variables; see Shapiro, Chapter 5).

Definitions.

- A *state* is a tuple $\langle R,\theta \rangle$ where R is a multiset of atoms (referred to as *resolvent*) or one of the special symbols *fail* or *deadlock*; θ is a substitution.

- An *initial state* $I(G)$ for an atom system G, is a state $\langle G,\{\ \} \rangle$ in which the substitution is the identity substitution.

- A *terminal state* is a state $\langle R,\theta \rangle$ where R is empty, *fail* or *deadlock*.

- A *communication* is a substitution or one of the symbols *fail* or *deadlock*, annotated as input (I) or output (O).

- An *event* is a tuple $(r,c,comm)$ where r and c are integers and *comm* is a communication. The choice of the goal is specified by r and c specifies the clause which is used to reduce that goal. For transitions, where no goal and no clause are used, r and c are both zero.

States are transformed by the application of transition rules. The application of a transition rule produces an event. It is denoted by $S_1 \xrightarrow{e} S_2$ (which reads "S_1 is transformed into S_2 producing the event e"). Transition rules cannot be applied to terminal states.

Let P be a program. The transition rules are:

(1) <u>Reduce</u>
   Let $(H \leftarrow B_1,\ldots,B_k)$ be the jth clause in the procedure H in P, and e be $(i,j,(\theta_2)^O)$ then

$$\langle (A_1,\ldots,A_i,\ldots,A_n),\theta_1 \rangle \underset{e}{\rightrightarrows}$$
$$\langle (A_1,\ldots,A_{i-1},B_1,\ldots,B_k,A_{i+1},\ldots,A_n).\theta_2,\ \theta_1.\theta_2 \rangle$$
If $\exists \theta_2 = mgu_?(A_i,H) \neq fail$.

(2) <u>Fail</u>

Let e be $(i,0,(fail)^O)$ then
$$\langle (A_1,\ldots,A_i,\ldots,A_n),\theta \rangle \underset{e}{\rightrightarrows} \langle fail,\theta \rangle$$
If $\forall\ (H \leftarrow B)\ in\ P\ mgu(A_i,H) = fail$.

(3) <u>Input</u>

Let e be $(0,0,(\theta_1)^I)$ then
$$\langle R,\theta \rangle \underset{e}{\rightrightarrows} \langle R.\theta_1,\theta.\theta_1 \rangle.$$

(4) <u>Abort</u>

Let e be $(0,0,(fail)^I)$ then
$$\langle R,\theta \rangle \underset{e}{\rightrightarrows} \langle fail,\theta \rangle.$$

(5) <u>Deadlock</u>

Let e be $(0,0,(deadlock)^O)$ then
$$\langle R,\theta \rangle \underset{e}{\rightrightarrows} \langle deadlock,\theta \rangle.$$
If R is not empty and the rules *Reduce* and *Fail* cannot be applied.

Definition. A *computation* is either a finite sequence $I(G) \underset{e_0}{\rightrightarrows} S_1 \underset{e_1}{\rightrightarrows} \cdots \underset{e_{n-1}}{\longrightarrow} S_n$ $\underset{e_n}{\rightrightarrows} S$ or an infinite sequence $I(G) \underset{e_0}{\rightrightarrows} S_1 \underset{e_1}{\rightrightarrows} S_2 \cdots$ where G is an atom system, e_i are events, S_i are states and (in the finite case) S is a terminal state.

27.3.1 Traces and behaviors

Two abstractions of computations are presented in this section: A *trace* is the sequence of labels of a computation. A *behavior* is the sequence of communications of a trace.

The transitive closure of the application of transition rules is denoted by $S_1 \underset{T}{\overset{*}{\rightarrow}} S_2$, where T is a trace.

Definition. The *trace* of a computation $C = I(G) \underset{e_0}{\rightrightarrows} S_1 \underset{e_1}{\rightrightarrows} S_2 \underset{e_2}{\rightrightarrows} \cdots$ is the sequence $Tr(C) = e_0,e_1,e_2,\ldots$.

For an atom system G and a program P, the set of all traces is denoted by $TR_P[G]$:

$$TR_P[G] = \{ T \mid \exists \text{ terminal state } S \text{ s.t. } I(G) \underset{T}{\overset{*}{\rightarrow}} S \} \cup \{ Tr(C) \mid C \text{ is infinite} \}$$

Definitions.

- A *behavior* is a series of communications.

- The function *bhv*: events $\rightarrow$ communications is defined as follows:
  $bhv(\ (r,c,comm)\ ) = comm$.

- A behavior of a computation C with the trace $e_0, e_1, e_2, \ldots$ is the series $b_0, b_1, b_2, \ldots$ such that $b_i = bhv(e_i)$ for all i.

- An *input behavior* is a behavior in which all communications are input annotated substitutions.

27.3.2 Labeled goals

In the previous sections we have described representations which capture reactive aspects of computations (traces, behaviors). These involve additional semantic entities independent to the standard output of the computation (i.e., substitutions). Below we present a different approach in which the Herbrand Universe itself is augmented. As in Levi and Palamidessi (1985) terms are labeled, but here labels contain concrete data concerning the computation.

Definition. A *Labeled Herbrand Universe* is a Herbrand Universe of a first order theory with an alphabet of the following form:

- Constants and functions are replaced by *labeled constants* and *labeled function symbols*.

- A *labeled constant* is a triplet $\langle c, t, io \rangle$ where c is referred to as the constant, t as its time and io as its I/O label. A *labeled function symbol* is a triplet $\langle f, t, io \rangle$ where f is referred to as the function symbol, t as its time and io as its I/O label.

- Variables, predicates, connectives, quantifiers and punctuation symbols have the usual form.

The t elements in the triplets defined above denote the time in which a variable is instantiated. Time labels are integers as we assume discrete time, however other domains (e.g., reals) may be considered. The io elements denote whether the instantiation was done in an input or output transition. For example "$\langle f, 1, I \rangle (\langle a, 3, O \rangle, B)$" is a labeled term which corresponds to the term "$f(a, B)$". In this example a variable (say X) was assigned as input to $f(A, B)$ at time 1 and A was assigned as output to a at time 3.

The operational semantics for FCP computations over a labeled Herbrand universe is defined as follows.

Definitions.

- A *state* is a triplet $\langle R, \theta, t \rangle$ where R is a multiset of atoms (the resolvent) or one of the special symbols *fail* and *deadlock*, θ a substitution (over the labeled Herbrand universe) and t an integer (referred to as time).

- An *initial state* $I(G)$ for an atom system G, is a state $\langle G, \{\ \}, t_0 \rangle$ for some t_0.

- A *terminal state* is a state $\langle R,\theta,t \rangle$ where R is empty, *fail* or *deadlock*.

- A *labeled read-only most general unifier* (denoted by $mgu_?[t,io]$) is constructed as follows:
  Let (A,B) be labeled terms, $mgu_?(A,B)$ be $\{R_1,\ldots,R_n\}$, V_i and X_i denote variables and $\langle c_i,t_i,io_i \rangle$ denotes a labeled constant or function symbol;
  then $mgu_?[t,io](A,B)$ is $\{S_1,\ldots,S_n\}$ such that $\forall\ 1 \le i \le n$:
  $$S_i = \begin{cases} V_i/X_i & \text{if } R_i \text{ is } V_i/X_i; \\ V_i/\langle c_i,t,io \rangle & \text{if } R_i \text{ is } V_i/\langle c_i,t_i,io_i \rangle \end{cases}$$
  (i.e., $mgu_?[t,io]$ ignores the t_i and io_i elements in R_i replacing it with t and io).

- Let θ be $\{R_1,\ldots,R_n\}$, V_i and X_i denote variables and $\langle c_i,t_i,io_i \rangle$ denote a labeled constant or function symbol;
  then $in(\theta,t)$ is $\{S_1,\ldots,S_n\}$ such that $\forall\ 1 \le i \le n$:
  $$S_i = \begin{cases} V_i/X_i & \text{if } R_i \text{ is } V_i/X_i; \\ V_i/\langle c_i,t,i \rangle & \text{if } R_i \text{ is } V_i/\langle c_i,t_i,io_i \rangle \end{cases}$$

States are transformed by the application of transition rules. An application of a transition rule is denoted by $S_1 \rightarrow S_2$ (where the state S_2 is the state S_1 after applying the transition rule). The transitive closure of an application of transition rules is denoted by $S_1 \overset{*}{\longrightarrow} S_2$. Transition rules cannot be applied to terminal states.

Let P be a program. The transition rules are:

(1) <u>Reduce</u>
   Let $H \leftarrow B_1,\ldots,B_k$ is in P then
   $\langle (A_1,\ldots,A_i,\ldots,A_n),\theta_1,t \rangle \rightarrow \langle (A_1,\ldots,A_{i-1},B_1,\ldots,B_k,A_{i+1},\ldots,A_n).\theta_2,\ \theta_1.\theta_2,$
   $t+1 \rangle$
   If $\exists \theta_2 = mgu_?[t,o](A_i,H) \ne fail$.

(2) <u>Fail</u>
   $\langle (A_1,\ldots,A_i,\ldots,A_n),\theta,t \rangle \rightarrow \langle fail,\theta,t+1 \rangle$
   If $\forall (H \leftarrow B) \in P\ mgu(A_i,H) = fail$.

(3) <u>Input</u>
   $\langle R,\theta,t \rangle \rightarrow \langle R.in(\theta_1,t),\theta.in(\theta_1,t),t+1 \rangle$.

(4) <u>Abort</u>
   $\langle R,\theta,t \rangle \rightarrow \langle fail,\theta,t+1 \rangle$

(5) <u>Deadlock</u>
   $\langle R,\theta,t \rangle \rightarrow \langle deadlock,\theta,t+1 \rangle$
   If R is not empty and the rules *Reduce* and *Fail* cannot be applied.

Definition. A *labeled computation* is either a finite series $I(G) \to S_1 \to \cdots \to S_n \to S$ or an infinite series $I(G) \to S_1 \to S_2 \cdots$ where G is an atom system, S_i are states and (in the finite case) S is a terminal state.

For an atom system G and a program P, the set of all finitely computable results of labeled computations is denoted by $O_P[G]$:

$$O_P[G] = \{\, G.\theta \mid \exists \text{terminal state } S = \langle R,\theta,t \rangle \text{ s.t. } I(G) \xrightarrow{*} S \,\}.$$

27.4 The Hierarchy of Abstractions

In this section we describe the relationship between the various abstractions defined. These can be formally described in terms of abstract interpretation. Each of the three reactive representations can be expressed as a *concretization* of the standard *goals* representation.

First we describe the information captured by the various abstractions and explain the differences between them. Then we examine the relationship between *goals* and *labeled goals* and demonstrate how this relationship can be expressed in terms of abstract interpretation.

Traces

FCP provides two types of nondeterminism. *And-nondeterminism* — the choice of goal from the resolvent, and *Or-nondetermism* — selection of a matching clause. A trace records both nondeterminstic decisions for each step of a computation. Thus, given a trace and a goal it is possible to uniquely reconstruct the computation from which the trace was abstracted.

Behaviors

Behaviors ignore some details of a computation. A simple example shows a behavior which may be a result of two different traces (or schedules), representing two different computations. Consider the program:

```
p(X) ← q(X), r(X).
q(a).
r(a).
```

There are two possible traces for a goal $p(X)$: one in which $q(X)$ is reduced before $r(X)$ (i.e., $(1,1,\{\ \}),(1,1,\{X/a\}^0),(1,1,\{\ \})$); and the other in which $r(X)$'s reduction precedes (i.e., $(1,1,\{\ \}),(2,1,\{X/a\}^0),(1,1,\{\ \})$). However, only the behavior $\{X/a\}^0$ exists for the goal $p(X)$, thus ignoring the order information which is recorded in the two possible traces.

Labeled goals

A labeled goal ignores some details which a behavior captures: variable to variable substitutions are absent in labeled goals. Again, a simple example demonstrates the difference in the level of detail captured by behaviors and by labeled goals. For the sake of simplicity we use only output events. Consider the program:

p(X,Y) ← q(X,Y), r(X,Y).
q(a,a).
r(X,X).

There are two possible behaviors for the goal $p(X, Y)$: one in which X and Y become bound to a by the reduction of $q(X, Y)$ and only then the reduction of $r(X, Y)$ (i.e., $(X/a, Y/a)^O$); and the second behavior in which X becomes bound to Y and then both becomes bound to a by first reducing $r(X, Y)$ (i.e., $(X/Y)^O, (Y/a)^O$).

The set of labeled goals $\{p(\langle a,0,O\rangle, \langle a,0,O\rangle), p(\langle a,1,O\rangle, \langle a,1,O\rangle) \dots \}$ is the set of possible solutions (in the labeled Herbrand universe) for the $p(X,X)$ goal. An argument is labeled only when it is bound to a non-variable so the two behaviors are projected into identical labeled goals.

Goals

Finally, a goal is the standard way to represent the result of a computation. It captures the computation's result through its substitution, ignoring all reactive details.

27.4.1 Abstracting labeled goals to goals

In this section we examine the relationship between goals and labeled goals defined above. This relationship is described in terms of abstraction and concretization functions of abstract interpretation (α and γ). The goals are described as an abstraction of labeled goals or, alternatively, labeled goals as a concretization of goals.

Let P be a program; L_Term is the domain of labeled terms over P; $Term$ is the domain of terms over P. The concrete domain is the power-domain of L_Term and the abstract domain is the power-domain of $Term$.

$$\alpha: 2^{L\_Term} \to 2^{Term}$$
$$\gamma: 2^{Term} \to 2^{L\_Term}$$

Informally, α and γ are defined as follows: $\alpha(\{l\_term\})$ removes the labels of l_term giving a term. $\gamma(\{term\})$ is the set of all possible labeled terms which can be constructed from $term$. Both definitions are naturally extended to sets.

One primitive operation on 2^{Term} is the natural extension of unification to sets s_unify. The corresponding operation on labeled terms is Ls_unify.

$$\text{s\_unify}(S_1,S_2) = \left\{ \; s \; \middle| \; \begin{array}{l} \exists s_1 \in S_1 \wedge \exists s_2 \in S_2 \text{ s.t.} \\ \text{mgu}_?(s_1,s_2) = \theta \wedge s = s_1\theta = s_2\theta \end{array} \right\}$$

$$\text{l\_s\_unify}[t,\text{io}](S_1,S_2) = \left\{ \; s \; \middle| \; \begin{array}{l} \exists s_1 \in S_1 \wedge \exists s_2 \in S_2 \text{ s.t.} \\ \text{mgu}_?[t,\text{io}](s_1,s_2) = \theta \wedge s = s_1\theta = s_2\theta \end{array} \right\}$$

The consistency of the abstract interpretation with the concrete one results from three conditions on α, γ and the primitive operations of the interpretations (Cousot and Cousot, 1977). In our context these can be stated as follows:

(1) α and γ are monotonic with respect to set inclusion (i.e., $S_1 \subseteq S_2$ implies $\alpha(S_1) \subseteq \alpha(S_2)$ and $A_1 \subseteq A_2$ implies $\gamma(A_1) \subseteq \gamma(A_2)$).

(2) $\alpha(\gamma(A)) = A$ and $S \subseteq \gamma(\alpha(S))$.

(3) $\forall \, t, \forall \, io \in \{i,o\}$
$\alpha(l\_s\_unify[t,io](S)) \subseteq s\_unify(\alpha(S)) \wedge$
$l\_s\_unify[t,io](\gamma(A)) \subseteq \gamma(s\_unify(A))$.

These conditions can be verified using the definitions given in this section. In the standard use of abstract interpretation, the consistency conditions imply the soundness of the interpretation in the abstract domain. In our case, the standard interpretation is the abstract one and this result is obvious. However, abstract interpretation provides a convenient way to formalize the various representations of FCP computations using the standard representation as a basis.

A formalism for the abstract interpretation of parallel logic programming is the subject of ongoing research. Such a formalism differs from abstract interpretation of sequential logic programming languages, in considering the reactive nature and temporal behavior of parallel programs.

27.5 Enumeration

The first part of the paper has dealt with the representation of FCP computations. This provides a framework in which to discuss the enumeration of the different computations of a goal. In this section we show how to enumerate all possible computations of a goal with a given input behavior. An enumeration tree is defined in which every path represents a computation (or a trace); each node represents the nondeterministic choice of a goal from the resolvent and of a clause to match it. If all of the computations of a goal are finite then the enumeration tree is also finite. If a goal has an infinite computation then the enumeration tree has an infinite path and may be of unbounded degree.

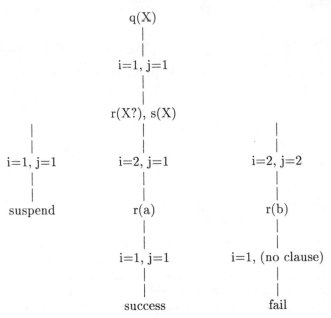

Figure 27.1: An enumeration tree of $q(X)$

Definition. An *enumeration tree* is constructed as follows:
Let P be a program and G a goal,

(1) Each node of the tree is a resolvent, *fail*, *suspend* or *success*.

(2) The root node is G.

(3) The only descendent of an empty resolvent is the node *success*.

(4) Let $A_1,\ldots,A_k$ be a node (for $k > 0$). The descendents of this node are divided into k groups.

    (a) If $\forall\,(H \leftarrow B) \in P\ mgu(A_i,H) = fail$, then the ith group has the single node *fail*.

    (b) If $\exists(H \leftarrow B) \in P\ mgu(A_i,H) \neq fail$, then in the ith group there is a descendent for each clause $(H_j \leftarrow B_j)$ in P such that $mgu(A_i,H_j) \neq fail$. The jth descendent is

       —   *suspend*, if $\exists mgu(A_i,H_j) \neq fail$ and $\neg\exists mgu_?(A_i,H_j)$.

       — $\leftarrow (A_1,\ldots,A_{i-1},C_1,\ldots,C_q,A_{i+1},\ldots,A_k)\theta$ if B_j is $C_1,\ldots,C_q$ and $\theta = mgu_?(A_i,H_j)$.

        – $\leftarrow(A_1,\ldots,A_{i-1},A_{i+1},\ldots,A_k)\theta$, if B_j is *true* and $\theta = mgu_?(A_i,H_j)$.

(5) Nodes which are *fail*, *suspend* or *success* have no descendents.

As an example consider this program:

        q(X) ← r(X?), s(X).
        r(a).
        s(a).
        s(b).

The goal $q(X)$ with the empty input behavior results in the enumeration tree shown in Figure 27.1.

27.6 Interpreters

We have described the notion of FCP computations and considered various abstractions of this notion. The standard FCP interpreter (Shapiro, Chapter 5) computes the *goals* abstraction. For interpretation of the more concrete layers it is necessary to define more concrete interpreters.

In order to construct traces, programs are transformed in such a manner that Or-nondeterminism may be controlled by the interpreter. A sufficient tool for controlling nondeterministic choice of clauses is provided by associating a unique identifier with each clause.

Then an interpreter for the trace level is realized by sequential interpretation of a goal, modeling the interleaving semantics. At each computation step the interpreter records which goal is taken from the resolvent and which clause is used to reduce it. Using the trace interpreter, an enumeration tree may be built by enumerating the sequences of the goals and clause numbers. In the behavior level the goals and clause numbers are ignored and only substitutions are recorded.

To support labeled interpretation each FCP program is transformed into a *labeled program*. Each constant and function symbol is transformed into a triplet containing the symbol and new time and I/O variables. Using an interleaving interpretation (as for traces) and a time-stamped read-only unification (as defined in Section 27.3.2) an interpreter for time-stamped goals is achieved.

27.7 Conclusions

A hierarchy of four abstractions of FCP computations has been suggested. Three of these include temporal information and capture various reactive aspects of FCP computations. The fourth is the standard representation for logic program computations. We have demonstrated that the relationship between these representations can be formally expressed in terms of abstract interpretation. Using these representations the enumeration of the computations of a goal becomes feasible. The enumeration algorithm presented is a prerequisite for investigations of properties of FCP computations. Debugging synchronization errors and testing of reactive programs are central examples of this and are subjects of ongoing research.

Acknowledgments

The operational semantics of FCP included in this paper was inspired by the work of Ran Ever-Hadani. We wish to thank the Vulcan group from Xerox PARC, Fernando Pereira from SRI, and Jacob Levy, Daniel Szoke and Eyal Yardeni from the Weizmann Institute for their helpful remarks on an earlier version of this paper.

Chapter 28

A Type System for Logic Programs

Eyal Yardeni and Ehud Shapiro

The Weizmann Institute of Science

Abstract

A theory for a type system for logic programs is developed. A type is a
recursively enumerable set of ground atoms, which is tuple distributive. The
association of a type to a program is intended to mean that only ground atoms
that are elements of the type may be derived from the program. A declarative
definition of well-typed programs is formulated based on an intuitive approach
related to the fixpoint semantics of logic programs. Whether a program is well-
typed is undecidable in general. We define a restricted class of types, called regular
types, for which type-checking is decidable. Regular Unary Logic (RUL) programs
are proposed as a specification language for regular types. The existence of regular
types that can well-type nonredundant programs is shown. An algorithm for type-
checking a logic program with respect to a regular type definition is described and
its complexity is analyzed. Finally the practicality of the type system is discussed
and some examples are demonstrated.

28.1 Introduction

Type-checking within the framework of logic programming is useful for several
reasons:

- Type declarations and compile time type-checking provide a measure of con-
  fidence in the correctness of a program.

- Typing a program makes it clearer and more readable.

- Errors in logic programs tend to fall into several broad categories. One of these is bad interfacing between predicates. This can be caused by incorrect ordering of arguments in a call, by an incorrect type of argument being passed, or by misspelling variable names. The detection of the first two errors is especially beneficial in a system which allows separate compilation of modules, as in Logix (Silverman et al., Chapter 21).

This paper attempts to formulate a type theory for pure logic programs and to develop a type-checking algorithm. From this basic theoretical model we intend to develop type systems for concrete logic programming languages. For this purpose, a new interpretation of types is introduced, and a novel method for performing type-checking is developed.

Three aspects of the type system are introduced; type declaration, type inference and type-checking. Firstly, a formal definition of type declaration is given. The paper defines the class of regular types and a subclass of logic programs, called regular unary logic programs, and shows the equivalence between them. The syntax of regular types is defined by a BNF-notation, and instances of regular types can be implemented by Deterministic Finite Automata (DFA). The incarnation of regular types as DFA is useful for showing inclusion, union and equivalence of regular types.

By type inference we mean the relation of the notion of type to the semantics of logic programs. A type may be associated with any logic program, given by a fixpoint of a function. This is an abstraction of the usual fixpoint semantics of logic programs, and corresponds to the intuition that every atom in the type is inferable from the program. This leads to a definition of well-typing.

In general, the question of whether a program is well-typed according to our definition is undecidable. However any particular computation can be checked not to violate well-typing by run-time check, although this check could be expensive. For regular types, well-typing is decidable. A compile-time type-checking algorithm is developed for regular types, and its complexity is considered.

The significance of this work is in the formalization of a type theory for logic programs based on a sound mathematical foundation. The approach taken here is declarative in nature, as opposed to the type systems developed in the past, which were based on an operational approach. Thus, the well-typing of a program can be discussed without reference to any specific type-checking algorithm.

28.1.1 Related work

Bruynooghe (1982) suggests adding types and modes (input or output) to a logic program. In this system each argument has a mode annotation and using this knowledge he develops an algorithm for type-checking. The algorithm is not described within any theoretical framework, but is only shown to work on several programs.

Two other approaches to constructing type systems for Prolog have been suggested. Mishra (1984) presents a scheme by which the type of the program can be inferred. Mishra represents types by *regular trees* (RTs) which themselves denote (possibly) infinitely many trees that represent terms. He first defines the syntax of *ground regular trees* (GRTs). Then he defines *parameterized* RTs, which contain type variables to denote sets of GRTs. He also defines the notion of *tuple distributivity* and *tuple distributive closure* (these will be formally defined in Section 28.2). Intuitively, the tuple distributive closure of a set of terms is the set of all terms constructed by permuting each argument position among all terms that have the same functor/arity combination. For example, the closure of $t(a,b)$ and $t(c,d)$ is $\{t(a,b), t(a,d), t(c,b), t(c,d)\}$. He finds that if he describes GRTs by DFA, then the union of the two regular languages that represent the GRTs will create a language that represents the tuple distributive closure of the two GRTs.

The type inference system assumes that each argument position of the procedure has a type. Then for each clause $A \leftarrow B_1,\ldots,B_n$ in the program he derives "inclusion inequations" over RTs by derivation rules that follows this logic: A conforms to the type provided that every atom in the body conforms to the type of the corresponding procedure. Then he develops an algorithm that solves and finds the least constrained solution of these inequations yielding the type of the procedures.

The type that is inferred is a superset of the meaning of the program, so if a procedure is found to be ill-typed it will always fail. In general, the type inference system does not deal with polymorphic predicates. Some simple polymorphic predicates can be analyzed by an ad-hoc extension to the standard algorithm, by simply assuming that type-variables in RTs can be treated as constants. For example consider the program:

```
plus(0,Y,Y).
plus(s(X),Y,s(Z)) ←
    plus(X,Y,Z).
```

According to Mishra the inferred type is

$$\left\{ plus(X,\beta,Z) \,\middle|\, \begin{array}{l} X \in \{0,s(0),s(s(0)),\ldots\} \\ Z \in \{\beta, s(\beta), s(s(\beta)),\ldots\} \end{array} \right\}$$

where β is a type variable.

Mycroft and O'Keefe (1983) adopt the outlook of Milner (1978) that well-typed programs cannot go wrong. They treat Prolog as a procedural or an applicative language — each procedure and each function call conforms to the type declaration of that object. First they define typing a program as an association of a type to each symbol in every clause, which they call "the typed premise".

Then they specify derivation rules to determine when a variable, a term, an atom, and a clause are well-typed with respect to the typed premises. The program is well-typed with respect to the typed premises if each clause is well-typed and if its top level goal is. In practice the derivation rules guarantee that each symbol that occurs in a clause conforms to the declaration. They also define a resolvent to be well-typed if each atom in the resolvent is well-typed. Afterwards they prove that well-typed programs (described in first order logic) including the goal, have the properties:

(1) The resolution at each step of the computation is well-typed.

(2) The variables of the top level goal can only be instantiated to values having types as dictated by the typed premises.

Consider, again, the previous program:

$$\leftarrow \text{plus}(A,B,C)$$
$$\text{plus}(0,D,D).$$
$$\text{plus}(s(X),Y,s(Z)) \leftarrow$$
$$\text{plus}(X,Y,Z).$$

The program is well-typed by the typed premises $\{plus^{\beta,\beta,\beta},\ s^{\beta\rightarrow\beta},\ A^{\beta},\ B^{\beta},\ C^{\beta},\ D^{\beta},\ X^{\beta},\ Y^{\beta},\ Z^{\beta}\}$ (the associated type is written as a superscript) where β is used as shorthand for the set $\{0,s(0),s(s(0)),...\}$. The difference between Mishra's scheme and this framework is that the second argument is restricted to be 0 or a successor of 0.

Mycroft and O'Keefe have suggested that if symbols of the program are allowed to be overloaded then the typed premises should contain more than one type associated with any given functor or predicate symbol. But then, the evaluation of the top level goal may be instantiated to a value that violates the typed premises. For example, consider the program:

$$\leftarrow \text{p}(X).$$
$$\text{p}(a).$$
$$\text{p}(b).$$

The typed premises are $\{p^{a},\ p^{b},\ X^{a}\}$. Although this is a well typing of the program, X could be instantiated to b.

It seems that by requiring types to be tuple-distributive, the properties Mycroft and O'Keefe proved to hold could be restored for overloading as well. If the well-typed program is augmented by adding the typed premises as restrictions on the values that each variable can obtain, then the typed premises denote a superset of the meaning of this program.

Finally Mycroft and O'Keefe suggest how to extend their type system to deal with higher order objects of Prolog.

Mishra deals mainly with the aspect of automatic type inference, while Mycroft and O'Keefe concentrate on type checking. Our approach gives a single formal framework which includes type declaration, inference and checking.

We believe that knowing and checking the top level goal statically is too restrictive since the top-level goal is usually not known at compile time, and the goal of type-checking is to perform as much checking as possible at compile time. The above type systems have a procedural orientation and ours has a declarative one, in the sense that being well-typed is defined as a fixpoint of some operator. The type of a program that is well-typed in our system is not necessarily a superset of the meaning of the program, so the resolvent may not conform to the type declaration. The rationale behind the definition of well-typing is presented in the next section. There is a certain amount of similarity between our scheme and that of Mishra's; both represent regular types by DFA and both use tuple distributive closure for types.

28.2 Type Declaration

We define the notion of types and then introduce a subset of types that can be represented by DFA. Later we define Regular Unary Logic programs (RUL programs). RUL programs are unary logic programs that obey certain syntactic rules. In a way, we use RUL programs to simulate DFA in order to represent regular sets of terms. We have chosen RUL programs instead of DFA in order to achieve a more readable representation of types. In addition, RUL programs can be incorporated in general logic programs to achieve a form of runtime type-checking. Finally we present a BNF syntax of a typed-program.

28.2.1 General overview

Definition. Let S be a set of ground atoms and P a program. The *signature* of S, $sig(S)$, is the set that contains all predicate symbols, function symbols and constants that appear in S. Similarly we define the *signature* of P, $sig(P)$.

Note. To facilitate meta-programming, we assume one set of symbols for both functions and predicates.

Let L be a union of a set of constant symbols and a set of function and predicate symbols. The *Herbrand universe* and the *Herbrand base* are defined as usual. A logic program P defines a signature. We use the symbol B_P as a synonym for $B_{sig(P)}$ to denote the Herbrand base of P.

Notation. $A \ll B$ means that A is a ground instance of a term B.

Definition. Let B_P be the Herbrand base of a program P. Define the mapping $T_P : 2^{B_P} \to 2^{B_P}$ as follows: Let I be a Herbrand interpretation. Then

$$T_P(I) = \{A \in B_P \mid A \leftarrow B_1, \ldots, B_n \ll C \in P, \text{ and } B_1, \ldots, B_n \in I\}.$$

Van Emden and Kowalski (1976) prove that the meaning of a program, which is the intersection of all Herbrand models for P, is equal to $T_P \uparrow \omega$, where ω is the first infinite ordinal. We denote by $M[P]$ the meaning of a program P.

28.2.2 Tuple distributivity

The notion of tuple-distributivity is due to Mishra (1984).

Definition. With each term t we associate a labeled tree, which we refer to as the *associated tree* of t. The edges and the leaves of the tree are labeled according to the following construction rules:

(1) If t is a constant or a variable, then make a leaf and label it with the string t.

(2) If $t = f(t_1, t_2, \ldots, t_n)$, f is of arity n, then:

    (a) make a new node associated with t.

    (b) for all $i \in [1..n]$ construct recursively the subtree associated with t_i, and draw an edge, labeled $f(n,i)$, from the new node to the root of the subtree.

Definition. Let t be a term. A *path* in t is the sequence of labels between the root and a leaf of the tree associated with t. The set of all paths of the associated tree of t is denoted by $paths(t)$. A *node* in t is the node of the associated tree of t. The set of all paths between a node and the leaves in the associated tree of t is called *paths of the node* of t. A path is *ground* if it does not end in a variable symbol.

Definition. Let S be a set of ground terms. Define

-    $paths(S) = \bigcup\limits_{t \in S} paths(t)$.

-    The *tuple-distributive closure* of S is denoted by

$$\alpha(S) = \{t \mid t \text{ is a term and } paths(t) \subseteq paths(S)\}.$$

-    S is *tuple-distributive* if $\alpha(S) = S$.

Example. If $S = \{f(a,b), f(c,d)\}$ then $paths(S) = \{f(2,1)a, f(2,2)b, f(2,1)c, f(2,2)d\}$ and $\alpha(S) = \{f(a,b), f(a,d), f(c,b), f(c,d)\}$.

Remark. α is idempotent i.e., $\alpha(\alpha(S)) = \alpha(S)$ for all sets of ground terms S.

Definition. Let p/n be a predicate in a program P. Then

$$M_{p/n}[P] = \{p(t_1,\ldots,t_n) \mid p(t_1,\ldots,t_n) \in M[P]\}.$$

We extend the notions of paths and tuple-distributivity to include atoms.

Claim. Let P be a program with different predicates $p_1,\ldots,p_n$. Then $\alpha(M[P]) = \alpha(M_{p_1}[P]) \cup \cdots \cup \alpha(M_{p_n}[P])$.

The claim is true since an atom can be built from $paths(M[P])$ only if all its paths have the same prefix of the predicate name.

Definition. A *type* is a recursively enumerable (r.e.) tuple distributive set of ground atoms with a finite signature.

28.2.3 Regular types and their properties

Definition. Let S be a type or a program. Define

$$\Sigma_S = \{f(n,i) \mid f/n \in sig(S), i = 1..n\} \cup \{c \mid c \in sig(S) \text{ is a constant}\}.$$

Definition. A set of ground terms S with a finite signature is *regular* iff there exists a regular language $L \subseteq \Sigma_S^*$ s.t. for every term t, $t \in S$ iff $paths(t) \subseteq L$.

Remark. It is clear from the definition that every regular set of terms is tuple-distributive.

Example. The set of terms $S = \{t(X,X) \mid X = s(s(s\ldots(s(0)\ldots))\}$ is not regular.

Assume that S is a regular set of terms. Then there exists a regular language L for S, which satisfies the condition of the definition. That means that L contains paths '$t(2,1)0$' and '$t(2,2)s(1,1)0$' which belong to the terms $t(0,0)$ and $t(s(0),s(0))$. But, then $t(0,s(0)) \in S$ which contradicts the definition of S.

Definition. A logic program P is *regular* if $M[P]$ is regular.

Claim. The intersection of regular sets of terms is regular.
Proof. Trivial, by the fact that the intersection of regular languages is regular. ∎

Example. Union of regular sets is not necessarily regular. Let

$$S1 = f(a,b)$$
$$S2 = f(c,d)$$

then

$$S3 = S1 \cup S2 \text{ is not regular.}$$

Explanation.

$$paths(f(a,b)) = \{f(\emptyset,1)a \,,\, f(\emptyset,\emptyset)b\}.$$
$$paths(f(c,d)) = \{f(2,1)c \,,\, f(2,2)d\}.$$

Assume that *S3* is regular. Then there exists a regular language L, s.t. $t \in S3$ iff $paths(t) \subseteq L$. Clearly L contains $paths(f(a,b)) \cup paths(f(c,d))$. But then $f(a,d)$ is also in *S3*. Contradiction.

If S is a regular set of terms then we know that there exists a regular language L s.t. $t \in S$ iff $paths(t) \subseteq L$. The following lemma shows that $paths(S)$ is an example of a regular language fitting this definition.

Lemma 1. For every regular set of terms S, $paths(S)$ is regular.
Proof. The proof is done by constructing the automaton that corresponds to S and proving by induction that for every word s that the automaton accepts there exists a term $t \in S$ s.t. s is a path of t. ∎

Definition. Let S be a regular set of terms. Define $L(S)$ to be the minimal language s.t. $t \in S$ iff $paths(t) \subseteq L(S)$.

Claim. $L(S)$ is well defined and regular.
Proof. By Lemma 1, $paths(S)$ is the minimal regular language that is wanted. ∎

Theorem 1. Let S_1 and S_2 be regular sets of terms. Then

$$S_1 \subseteq S_2 \text{ iff } L(S_1) \subseteq L(S_2).$$

Proof. By Lemma 1 and the above claim. ∎

28.2.4 RUL programs

Definition. A *Regular Unary Logic (RUL)* program P is a logic program satisfying the following syntactic rules:

(1) Every predicate in P is unary.

(2) The head argument of no clause in P is a variable.

(3) No two head arguments of clauses of the same predicate have the same functor/arity combinations, i.e., they are top level pairwise not unifiable.

(4) Every body goal of every clause in P is of the form $p(X)$, where p is a predicate name and X is a variable.

(5) Every variable in a clause occurs exactly once in its head and once in its body.

(6) The arguments of facts (clauses with empty bodies) are ground terms (implied by rule 5).

Example. The following is a RUL program:

> type(merge_all(Xs,Ys)) ←
>   list_of_nat_lists(Xs),
>   list_of_nat_lists(Ys).
>
> nat_list([ ]).
> nat_list([X|Xs]) ←
>   natural(X),
>   nat_list(Xs).
>
> list_of_nat_lists([ ]).
> list_of_nat_lists([X|Xs]) ←
>   nat_list(X),
>   list_of_nat_lists(Xs).

Definition. Let p be a predicate in a unary logic program P. Define $M[P]/p$ to be the set $\{t \mid p(t) \in M[P]\}$.

Theorem 2.

(1) RUL programs are regular.

(2) For every regular set of terms S there exists a RUL program P with a predicate p such that $S = M[P]/p$.

Proof. The proof can be found in (Yardeni, 1987). ∎

28.2.5 Regular type definitions

In this subsection we show how to declare the type of a program by a RUL program. Then we introduce a BNF notation as a convenient syntax for RUL programs.

If we define *type/1* to be a distinguished predicate that can be applied to predicates, then we can define a type by making a RUL program Q, s.t. $M[Q]/type$ is the desired type.

Example. <u>Isomorphism of binary trees with labeled nodes.</u>

The type definition by a RUL program:

> natural(0).
> natural(s(X)) ←
>   natural(X).
>
> binary_tree(void).

```
binary_tree(tree(X,Y,Z)) ←
    natural(X),
    binary_tree(Y),
    binary_tree(Z).

type(isotree(Y,Z)) ←
    binary_tree(Y),
    binary_tree(Z).
```

BNF-notation for the above type definition:

We use BNF derivation rules to define a type.

$Natural \implies 0 \; ; \; s(Natural).$

$Binary\_tree \implies void \; ; \; tree(Natural, Binary\_tree, Binary\_tree).$

The code of the program:

The start symbol is *type*. We use the shorthand *type isotree(Binary_tree,Binary_tree)* to represent the derivation rule *type* $\implies$ *isotree(Binary_tree, Binary_tree)*.

```
type isotree(Binary_tree,Binary_tree).
isotree(void,void).
isotree(tree(X,Left1,Right1),tree(X,Left2,Right2)) ←
    isotree(Left1,Left2),
    isotree(Right1,Right2).
isotree(tree(X,Left1,Right1),tree(X,Left2,Right2)) ←
    isotree(Left1,Right2),
    isotree(Right1,Left2).
```

The example above shows a type definition, its BNF definition, and the program with a type declaration, which is well-typed by those definitions. The isomorphism between the RUL type definition and the BNF definition is trivial. The syntax for type definitions has the following form:

$$A_1 \implies \alpha_{1,1}; \alpha_{1,2}; \ldots; \alpha_{1,m_1}.$$
$$A_2 \implies \alpha_{2,1}; \alpha_{2,2}; \ldots; \alpha_{2,m_2}.$$
$$\vdots$$
$$A_n \implies \alpha_{n,1}; \alpha_{n,2}; \ldots; \alpha_{n,m_n}.$$

type β_1.
Code of procedure β_1

type β_2.
Code of procedure β_2

$$\vdots$$

type β_m.
Code of procedure β_m

where:

- The A_i's are variables, and the $\alpha_{i,j}$'s are non-variable terms.

- For every $1 \leq i \leq n$, $1 \leq j < k \leq m_i$, $\alpha_{i,j}$ and $\alpha_{i,k}$ are top level not unifiable.

- The β_i's are atoms which have different predicate names (functor/arity).

The derivation rule is the same as in BNF. The starting symbol is *type* where it can derive each of the β_i's (*type* β_m is a shorthand for *type* $\Longrightarrow$ β_m). The ';' symbol is used instead of the '|' symbol in BNF.

28.2.6 Results

If types are defined by RUL programs then:

(1) Determining intersection can be done by intersecting the corresponding automata and building a new RUL program from the intersected automaton.

(2) Determining inclusion of two regular sets of terms can be done by checking the inclusion of the minimal regular languages that represent them. Algorithms for inclusion, intersection and union of regular languages are well known (Aho et al., 1974)

28.3 Type Inference

This section is based on the semantics of logic programs described by van Emden and Kowalski (1976) and by Lloyd (1984).

A formal definition of well-typing is given below. Here we would like to provide some intuition for our approach.

We define a rule of type-relative inference by a program P with respect to a type S. We say that a ground atom $A \in S$ is *inferred by P relative to S* if there exists a clause C in P and atoms $B_1, B_2, \ldots, B_n \in S$ such that $A \leftarrow B_1, \ldots, B_n$ is an instance of C. In addition, any atom in the tuple-distributive closure of atoms inferred by this rule is also defined to be inferred by P relative to S.

We would like the type declaration S to be an approximation to the set of values that the program can infer from the assumption that these values are in the meaning of P. So we define that a program in our system is *well-typed by S* if it infers S relative to S. In addition, we require that all clauses in the program are useful, i.e., each clause can infer at least one atom in S relative to S.

In general the type S is not a subset or a superset of the meaning of the program it well-types, but it is in some sense a fixpoint of the program. This leads to the idea that the well-typing notion of a program can be stated declaratively — a fixpoint of some operator (to be defined below). This is opposed to the other type systems reviewed (Bruynooghe, 1982; Mishra, 1984; Mycroft and O'Keefe, 1983) where this notion is stated operationally via an algorithm or derivation rules.

Usually a programmer has in mind the type of arguments that a procedure is to be used with, but in fact the program actually written accepts larger types. For example consider the program:

```
plus(0,Y,Y).
plus(s(X),Y,s(Z)) ←
    plus(X,Y,Z).
```

This program is well-typed, according to our definition, by the set

$$\{plus(X,Y,Z) \mid X,Y,Z \in \{0,s(0),s(s(0)),\ldots\}\}.$$

The second argument of this procedure could be of any type. Hence, declaration of the type of the second argument adds more information to the program. In this example we see that the type declaration is neither a superset nor a subset of the meaning. Although the set

$$\{plus(X,Y,Z) \mid X,Y,Z \in \{0,s(0)\}\}$$

is also legal as a type declaration for the program, as the level of detail in the type declaration increases, more information is available to the type checker and better type checking can be done.

The information that is given by the type declaration can either be used to type-check the program, without having to change its semantics, or can be added to the program restricting its meaning to be a subset of the type. In the second case the program will not only be type-checked statically but also be checked at run-time.

28.3.1 Abstract interpretation

A program denotes computations in some universe of objects. Abstract interpretation of programs uses that denotation to describe computations in another universe of abstract objects, so that the computation in the abstract domain is effective and yields some information about the standard denotation (Cousot and Cousot, 1977).

Our notion of well-typing is defined below in terms of abstract interpretation. We show that types can be viewed as an abstraction of meanings. We show interesting properties that relate the concrete domain to the abstract domain and the type system. We describe an interpreter that operates in the abstract domain and is an abstraction of the well known interpreter for logic programs.

Let L be a first order language and B_L be its Herbrand base. We define an abstract interpretation of logic programs as follows: The concrete domain is 2^{B_L}, and the abstract domain is the set of all tuple distributive sets in 2^{B_L}.

The abstraction function, $\alpha(S) = \{t \mid t$ is a term and $paths(t) \subseteq paths(S)\}$, was defined in the previous section. The concretization function γ is the identity function.

We define a new operator, which is an approximation to T_P and operates on the abstract domain.

Definition. Let P be a program. Define T_P^α, the abstraction function of T_P, to be:

$$T_P^\alpha(X) = \alpha\left(\left\{ A \in B_P \;\middle|\; \begin{array}{l} A \leftarrow B_1,B_2,\ldots,B_n \ll C,\ C \in P, \\ \text{and } B_1,B_2,\ldots,B_n \in X \end{array} \right\}\right).$$

From the definition of *paths* we see that every tuple distributive set can be represented uniquely by its paths. The above function is equivalent to:

$$T_P^{\alpha'}(paths(X)) = \left\{ paths(A) \subseteq paths(B_P) \;\middle|\; \begin{array}{c} A \leftarrow B_1,B_2,\ldots,B_n \ll C,\ C \in P, \\ \text{and} \\ paths(\{B_1,\ldots,B_n\}) \subseteq paths(X) \end{array} \right\}.$$

Definition. Let L be a complete lattice, ordered by the inclusion relation.

- Let $X \subseteq L$. X is *directed* if every finite subset of X has an upper bound in X.

- Let $T : L \to L$ be a function. T is *continuous* if $T(lub(X)) = lub(\{T(I) \mid I \in X\})$, for every directed subset X of L.

Lemma 2. T_P^α is continuous over the set of tuple distributive elements in 2^{B_P}.
Proof. Let X be a directed subset of tuple distributive elements in 2^{B_P}. We have to prove that $T_P^\alpha(lub(X)) = lub(\{T_P^\alpha(I) \mid I \in X\})$.

$$A \in T_P^\alpha(lub(X))$$

iff there exists

$$A_1 \leftarrow B_{(1,1)},B_{(1,2)},\ldots,B_{(1,n_1)} \ll C_1,\ C_1 \in P,$$
$$A_2 \leftarrow B_{(2,1)},B_{(2,2)},\ldots,B_{(2,n_2)} \ll C_2,\ C_2 \in P,$$
$$\vdots$$
$$A_k \leftarrow B_{(k,1)},B_{(k,2)},\ldots,B_{(k,n_k)} \ll C_k,\ C_k \in P,$$
$$\text{s.t. } B_{(1,1)},B_{(1,2)},\ldots,B_{(k,n_k)} \in lub(X), \text{ and } A \in \alpha(A_1,\ldots,A_k)$$

iff there exists

$$A_1 \leftarrow B_{(1,1)}, B_{(1,2)}, \ldots, B_{(1,n_1)} \ll C_1, \; C_1 \in P,$$
$$A_2 \leftarrow B_{(2,1)}, B_{(2,2)}, \ldots, B_{(2,n_2)} \ll C_2, \; C_2 \in P,$$
$$\vdots$$
$$A_k \leftarrow B_{(k,1)}, B_{(k,2)}, \ldots, B_{(k,n_k)} \ll C_k, \; C_k \in P,$$
$$\text{s.t. } B_{(1,1)}, B_{(1,2)}, \ldots, B_{(k,n_k)} \in I \text{ for some } I \in X \text{ and } A \in \alpha(A_1, \ldots, A_k)$$

iff

$$A \in T_P^\alpha(I), \text{ for some } I \in X$$

iff

$$A \in lub(\{ T_P^\alpha(I) \mid I \in X \}). \quad \blacksquare$$

Result. Let P be a logic program. Then the least fixpoint of T_P^α is $T_P^\alpha \uparrow \omega$, and is denoted by $M^\alpha[P]$.

Proof. By Tarski (1955) we know that if $T : L \longrightarrow L$ is continuous where L is a complete lattice, then $lfp(T) = T \uparrow \omega$. $\quad \blacksquare$

28.3.2 The abstract interpreter

We present an interpreter (Figure 28.1) that recognizes goals that are in $M^\alpha[P]$. The resolvent contains a set of ground paths. The interpreter nondeterministically finds a successful execution path if one exists.

Input: A logic program P
                   A ground goal G

Output: *true* if $G \in M^\alpha[P]$

Interpreter:
                   Initialize the resolvent to be $paths(G)$

                   While the resolvent is not empty do
                       Choose a path ξ from the resolvent and
                       choose $A \leftarrow B_1, \ldots, B_n \ll C$, $C \in P$ s.t. $\xi \in paths(A)$
                       Remove ξ from and add $paths(\{B_1, \ldots, B_n\})$ to the resolvent.

                   If the resolvent is empty output *true*.

Figure 28.1: The abstract interpreter

Lemma 3. $G \in M^\alpha[P]$ iff the above interpreter has an execution path that outputs *true*.

Proof. $\Longrightarrow$ If $G \in M^\alpha[P]$ then there exists n, s.t. $G \in T_P^\alpha \uparrow n$. The proof is by induction on n. If $n = 1$ then $paths(G) \subseteq paths(\{X \mid X$ is a fact in $P\})$.

Since the body of facts is empty, then every iteration of the interpreter reduces a path from the resolvent and that implies that it will be empty after $|paths(G)|$ iterations. Assume true for $n\text{--}1$ and prove for n. There exist

$$A_1 \leftarrow B_{(1,1)}, B_{(1,2)}, \ldots, B_{(1,n_1)} \ll C_1,\ C_1 \in P,$$
$$A_2 \leftarrow B_{(2,1)}, B_{(2,2)}, \ldots, B_{(2,n_2)} \ll C_2,\ C_2 \in P,$$

$$\vdots$$

$$A_k \leftarrow B_{(k,1)}, B_{(k,2)}, \ldots, B_{(k,n_k)} \ll C_k,\ C_k \in P,$$
$$\text{s.t. } B_{(1,1)}, B_{(1,2)}, \ldots, B_{(k,n_k)} \in T_P^\alpha{\uparrow}(n\text{--}1) \text{ and } G \in \alpha(\{A_1, \ldots, A_k\}).$$

After $|paths(G)|$ iterations the resolvent can contain exactly $paths(\{B_{(1,1)}, \ldots, B_{(k,n_k)}\})$. By the induction hypothesis each of the $B_{(i,j)}$ is "provable" by the interpreter. Hence, after a finite number of iterations the interpreter answers *true*.

$\Longleftarrow$ In this part we prove that if the resolvent is initialized to a set S and the interpreter outputs *true* then $S \subseteq paths(M^\alpha[P])$. This implies the lemma. The proof is by induction on the number, n, of iterations that the interpreter does. If $n = 0$ then $\phi = S \subseteq paths(M^\alpha[P])$. Assume true for $n\text{--}1$ and prove for n iterations. Also assume that ξ is the first path chosen in the first iteration and that $A \leftarrow B_1, \ldots, B_m \ll C,\ C \in P$ is the chosen clause s.t. $\xi \in paths(A)$. By the induction hypothesis

$$S_1 = ((S \setminus \{\xi\}) \cup paths(\{B_1, \ldots, B_m\})) \subseteq paths(M^\alpha[P])$$

If we apply $T_P^{\alpha'}$ which is monotonic to both sides of the inclusion we get that

$$\xi \in paths(A) \subseteq T_P^{\alpha'}(S_1) \subseteq paths(M^\alpha[P])$$

Finally, we get that

$$S \subseteq (S_1 \cup \{\xi\}) \subseteq paths(M^\alpha[P]). \quad \blacksquare$$

Example. Let P be the following program:

> q(e) ← p(a,d).
>
> p(a,b).
> p(c,d).

Then

$$M[P] = \{p(a,b), p(c,d)\}.$$
$$\alpha(M[P]) = \{p(a,b), p(a,d), p(c,b), p(c,d)\} = \alpha(T_P{\uparrow}1) = T_P^\alpha{\uparrow}1$$
$$M^\alpha[P] = \{p(a,b), p(a,d), p(c,b), p(c,d), q(e)\} = T_P^\alpha{\uparrow}2$$

One should note that $M^\alpha[P]$ is not always $\alpha(M[P])$ nor always a fixpoint of T_P, but it is always true that $M[P] \subseteq \alpha(M[P]) \subseteq M^\alpha[P]$.

28.3.3 Well-typing

Definition. Let P be a program and S a type. Define P_S to be the result of replacing each clause of the form $A \leftarrow B_1,\ldots,B_n$ by $A \leftarrow type(A),B_1,\ldots,B_n$ where *type* is a distinguished predicate that verifies that $A \in S$. A logic program defining this predicate, which uses a distinct set of predicate symbols, is added to P_S.

Note. A program for *type/1* exists since S is r.e.

Example. Let P be the following program and let $S = \{s^i(0) \mid i$ is a natural number$\}$.

        plus(0,X,X).
        plus(s(X),Y,s(Z)) ←
            plus(X,Y,Z).

Then the transformed program P_S is:

        plus(0,X,X) ←
            type(plus(0,X,X)).
        plus(s(X),Y,s(Z)) ←
            type(plus(s(X),Y,s(Z))),
            plus(X,Y,Z).

        type(plus(X,Y,Z)) ←
            natural(X),
            natural(Y),
            natural(Z).

        natural(0).
        natural(s(X)) ←
            natural(X).

Definition. Let B_L be the Herbrand base of L. Let P be a program whose signature is in L and let $S \subseteq B_L$.

$T_P : 2^{B_L} \rightarrow 2^{B_L}$ is defined as follows:

$$T_P(S) = \alpha \left(\left\{ A \in S \;\middle|\; \begin{array}{l} A \leftarrow B_1,B_2,\ldots,B_n \ll C,\ C \in P, \\ \text{and } B_1,\ldots,B_n \in S \end{array} \right\} \right).$$

Definition. Let S be a set of atoms and let C be a clause in a program P. Define:

- $M_C^\alpha(S) = \alpha(\{A \in S \mid A \leftarrow B_1,\ldots,B_n \ll C \text{ and } B_1,\ldots,B_n \in S\})$.

- We say that $M_C^\alpha(S)$ *is inferred from C relative to S.*

- We say that $T_P(S)$ *is inferred from P relative to S.*

- A clause C is *useless relative to* S if $M_C^\alpha(S)$ is the empty set.

Definition. Let P be a program and let S be a type. Then

- P is *weakly well-typed by* S if $\mathcal{T}_P(S) = S$ i.e., S is a fixpoint of $\mathcal{T}_P$.

- P is *well-typed by* S if it is weakly well-typed by S and it does not contain useless clauses relative to S.

Alternatively, we can define a program P to be weakly well-typed by S as follows: Let Q be the the subprogram that is added to P getting P_S. Then P is weakly well-typed by S if $T_{P_S}^\alpha(S \cup M[Q]) = S \cup \alpha(M[Q])$. This definition is equivalent to the first one and relates well-typing to abstract interpretation.

Remark. If Q is a RUL program then $S \cup M[Q]$ is a fixpoint of $T_{P_S}^\alpha$.

In the following theorem we prove that a program P is weakly well-typed by the empty set, by the tuple distributive closure of the meaning of the program, and in fact by the tuple distributive closure of any power of T_P.

Theorem 3. Let P be a program. Then

(1) P is weakly well-typed by the empty set.

(2) P is weakly well-typed by $\alpha(M[P])$.

(3) For every natural number n, $\alpha(T_P{\uparrow}n)$ well-types P.

(4) If S is a fixpoint of T_P then $\alpha(S)$ is a fixpoint of $\mathcal{T}_P$.

Proof.

(1) Trivial from the definition.

(2) Although we do not prove it, $\alpha(M[P])$ is r.e. Clearly, for every tuple-distributive set U, $\mathcal{T}_P(U) \subseteq U$. To complete the proof we have to show that $\mathcal{T}_P(\alpha(M[P])) \supseteq \alpha(M[P])$. It is easy to verify that $\mathcal{T}_P$ is monotonic, and that $M[P] \subseteq \alpha(M[P])$. It is enough then to prove that $\mathcal{T}_P(M[P]) \supseteq \alpha(M[P])$:

$$\alpha(M[P]) =$$
$$\alpha(T_P(M[P]))=$$
$$\alpha\left(\left\{\, A \in B_P \;\middle|\; \begin{array}{l} A \leftarrow B_1, B_2, \ldots, B_n \ll C,\ C \in P \\ \text{and } B_1, B_2, \ldots, B_n \in M[P] \end{array} \right\}\right) =$$
$$\mathcal{T}_P(M[P]).$$

(3) As in the previous step it is enough to prove that $\mathcal{T}_P(T_P{\uparrow}n) \supseteq \alpha(T_P{\uparrow}n)$ for $n \geq 1$. This is easy to verify from the definition and the fact that $T_P{\uparrow}n \supseteq T_P{\uparrow}(n{-}1)$.

(4) Exactly like 2.

Yardeni (1987) proves that if $U = \bigcup\limits_{\substack{S \text{ is a} \\ \text{fixpoint of } \mathcal{T}_P}} S$ then $gfp(\mathcal{T}_P) = \alpha(U) = U$.

The following example shows that $gfp(\mathcal{T}_P)$ may be different from $\alpha(M[P])$.

Example. Let P be the program:

> q(a) ← p(a,d).
>
> p(a,b).
> p(c,d).

Then

$$M[P] = \{p(a,b),\ p(c,d)\}$$
$$\alpha(M[P]) = \{p(a,b),\ p(a,d),\ p(c,b),\ p(c,d)\}$$

Another fixpoint of $\mathcal{T}_P$ is $\{p(a,b),\ p(a,d),\ p(c,b),\ p(c,d),\ q(a)\}$.

28.3.4 Examples

In this section we present some programs and explanation on their well-typing. We use the term "infer" as a shorthand for "infer a set from a clause or from a program relative to a type".

> plus(0,X,X).
> plus(s(X),Y,s(Z)) ←
>   plus(X,Y,Z).

When we constructed the program *plus/3*, we had in mind the fact that all its arguments are 0 or successors of 0, where $s^i(0)$ represents the natural number i. From the first clause we see that the first argument can only be 0 and the other two can be anything, including natural numbers. From the second clause we see that its first argument can only be a successor of anything, especially a successor of a natural number. Its second argument can be anything, and its third also a successor of anything, so it is possible to restrict "anything" to be a natural number. Combining the facts from the two clauses we get that its first argument is 0 or a successor of a natural number, i.e., a natural number. The other two do not have any restrictions so we can take them to be natural numbers. Let $S_1 = \{plus(X,Y,Z) \mid X,Y,Z \in \{0,s(0),s(s(0)),\ldots\}\}$. S_1 is a well-typing of the program above because: From the first clause we see that the set

$$\{plus(0,X,Y) \mid X,Y \in \{0,s(0),s(s(0)),\ldots\}\}$$

is inferred. From the second clause we see that we can infer the set

$$\{plus(s(X),Y,s(Z)) \mid X,Y,Z \in \{0,s(0),s(s(0)),\ldots\}\}$$

which is equivalent to the set

$$\left\{ \; plus(X,Y,Z) \; \middle| \; \begin{array}{l} Y \in \{0,s(0),s(s(0)),\ldots\} \\ X,Z \in \{s(0),s(s(0)),\ldots\} \end{array} \right\}.$$

If we take the tuple distributive closure of their union we get S_1 back, which implies that the program is well-typed by S_1.

It is worthwhile to note that the set

$$\left\{ \; plus(X,any,Z) \; \middle| \; \begin{array}{l} X \in \{0,s(0),s(s(0)),\ldots\} \\ Z \in \{any,s(any),s(s(any)),\ldots\} \end{array} \right\}$$

is also a well-typing of the program. This shows the tolerance of the type system.

Now we add to the above program two more clauses that will enable us to multiply two natural numbers:

```
plus(0,X,X).
plus(s(X),Y,s(Z)) ←
    plus(X,Y,Z).

times(0,Y,0).
times(s(X),Y,Z) ←
    times(X,Y,Z1),
    plus(Z1,Y,Z).
```

When we wrote the *times/3* predicate we had in mind that all its three arguments can be natural numbers.   Let $S_2 = \{times(X,Y,Z) \mid X,Y,Z \in \{0,s(0),s(s(0)),\ldots\}\}$. This program is well-typed by $S_1 \cup S_2$ since: From the first two clauses we can infer S_1 exactly the same as in the previous example. From the third clause we infer the set $\{times(0,Y,0) \mid Y \in \{0,s(0),s(s(0)),\ldots\}\}$. If we look at the body of the last clause, we observe that all the variables can obtain all natural numbers, that means that the set

$$\left\{ \; times(X,Y,Z) \; \middle| \; \begin{array}{l} X \in \{s(0),s(s(0)),\ldots\} \\ Y,Z \in \{0,s(0),s(s(0)),\ldots\} \end{array} \right\}$$

is inferred. Now, taking the tuple distributive closure of these last two sets yields S_2. So we conclude that $S_1 \cup S_2$ is a well-typing of the program above.

The last example is to find a natural number in an ordered labeled tree s.t. for every node, each label of a node in the left subtree is always less than the label of this node and all labels of nodes in the right subtree are bigger than the label of this node.

```
0 < s(Y).
s(X) < s(Y) ←
    X < Y.

member(X,t(X,L,R)).
member(X,t(V,L,R)) ←
    X < V,
```

```
        member(X,L).
    member(X,t(V,L,R)) ←
        V < X,
        member(X,R).
```

Since we are used to the fact that '<' in many languages compares between two numbers we would like to say that the types of its arguments are natural numbers. But if we look at the code we see that 0 cannot be inferred for the second argument.

Let us define the set that can be derived using a BNF-notation:

$Natural \implies 0;\ s(Natural).$

$Binary\_tree \implies void\ ;\ t(Natural, Binary\_tree, Binary\_tree).$

Let *Nat* be the set that can be derived starting with the variable *Natural*, and let *Btree* be the set that can be derived starting with *Binary_tree*. Define

$$S_3 = \{X < s(Y) \mid X, Y \in Nat\}$$
$$S_4 = \{member(X, t(V, L, R)) \mid X, V \in Nat,\ R, L \in Btree\}.$$

$S_3 \cup S_4$ is a well-typing of the program. From the first clause we infer S_3 and from the second clause we can infer the set $\{X < Y \mid X, Y \in \{s(0), s(s(0)), \ldots\}\}$ which is a subset of S_3. In a similar way we verify that S_4 is inferred concluding that the program above is well-typed by $S_3 \cup S_4$.

Following are some interesting properties that will be used in the rest of the paper:

- Any r.e. fixpoint of T_P^α well-types P.

- It is easy to verify that $T_P^\alpha \uparrow n$ well-types P for every natural number n.

28.4 Type Checking

Type-checking determines whether a program is well-typed by a type declaration. In general, type-checking in our framework is undecidable since it would require to intersect types of two occurrences of a logical variable, and finding the intersection of two r.e. sets may not be computable. Therefore we investigate regular types, for which type-checking is decidable. We show that regular types are strong enough for type declarations. We suggest an algorithm for type-checking and analyze its complexity.

Definition. The *meaning* of a clause C in a program P is the set

$$\{A \in B_P \mid A \leftarrow B_1, \ldots, B_n \ll C,\ B_1, \ldots, B_n \in \boldsymbol{M}[P]\}$$

Example. The meaning of a ground fact is the set that contains only the ground fact.

Definition. A clause is *nonredundant* with respect to a program if its meaning is nonempty. It is *redundant* if its meaning is empty.

Definition. A program is *nonredundant* if all its clauses are nonredundant.

In general, it is undecidable whether a program is nonredundant but we will see that for RUL programs this problem is decidable.

Claim. For every logic program P, there exists a nonredundant logic program Q s.t. $M[P] = M[Q]$.
Proof. Trivial. ∎

28.4.1 Any nonredundant program can be well-typed by a regular type

In this subsection we show that if a program is nonredundant, then there exists a regular type that well-types it.

Lemma 4. If S is a regular type and C is a clause in a program P then $\alpha(\{A \in B_P \mid A \leftarrow B_1, \ldots, B_n \ll C, B_1, \ldots, B_n \in S\})$ is regular.
Proof. The proof is straightforward since B_P is regular. ∎

Lemma 5. If P is a program, then for every natural number n, $T_P^\alpha \uparrow n$ is regular.
Proof. It can be shown by induction on n that $T_P^\alpha \uparrow n$ is regular using the facts that:

- The tuple distributive closure of a finite union of regular sets of terms is a regular set.

- Lemma 4 guarantees that at each iteration of T_P^α we get a regular set. ∎

Theorem 4. Every nonredundant program P can be well-typed by a regular type.
Proof. Since P is nonredundant, for each clause C in P there exist atoms $A, B_1, \ldots, B_n \in M[P]$ s.t. $A \leftarrow B_1, \ldots, B_n \ll C$. If for each clause we take one instance and find the union of all atoms that appear in these instances, we will get a finite set S s.t. P does not have useless clauses with respect to S. Since S is finite and in $M[P]$, there exists a natural number n, s.t. $S \subseteq T_P \uparrow n$. But $S \subseteq T_P \uparrow n \subseteq T_P^\alpha \uparrow n$. So $T_P^\alpha \uparrow n$ is a regular type that well-types P. ∎

Note that the type computed by Theorem 4 is rather interesting.

Example. Let P be the following program:

```
plus(0,Y,Y)
plus(s(X),Y,s(Z)) ←
```

plus(X,Y,Z).

Then

$$T_P^\alpha \uparrow 1 = \{plus(0,Y,Z) \mid Y,Z \in \{0,s(0),s(s(0)),\ldots\}\}$$
$$T_P^\alpha \uparrow 2 = \{plus(X,Y,Z) \mid X \in \{0,s(0)\}, \; Y,Z \in \{0,s(0),s(s(0)),\ldots\}\}$$

$T_P^\alpha \uparrow 2$ well-types P.

An interesting open question is to determine the minimal n for which a nonredundant program is well-typed by $T_P^\alpha \uparrow n$ (in the above example $n = 2$).

28.4.2 Decidability of nonredundancy for RUL programs

Here, we present an algorithm for finding redundant clauses of RUL programs. The algorithm is used to transform a redundant RUL program to an equivalent nonredundant RUL program.

The algorithm

Let P be a RUL program.

(1) Label all facts in P as *nonredundant* and call this group A_0.

(2) Let $S_0 = \{p \mid p$ is a predicate name of a fact in $P\}$.

(3) Let S_i be the last set that was computed and define A_{i+1} and S_{i+1}:

$$A_{i+1} = \left\{ \; C \in P \; \middle| \; \begin{array}{l} C = p(\;) \leftarrow b_1(\;),\ldots,b_n(\;) \text{ unlabeled} \\ \text{and } b_1,\ldots,b_n \in S_i \end{array} \right\}$$

$$S_{i+1} = S_i \cup \{p \mid p \text{ is a predicate name that appears in } A_{i+1}\}$$

(4) Label all clauses in P that appear in A_{i+1} as *nonredundant*.

(5) If $S_i = S_{i+1}$ then stop else go to 3.

Claim. All the clauses that were not labeled by the above algorithm are redundant. Those that were labeled are nonredundant.
Proof. The proof is straightforward. Details can be found in Yardeni (1987).

28.4.3 A type checking algorithm

We describe an algorithm that type-checks a program whose type is declared with a regular type declaration.

Let P be a program and S be a regular type. We check whether P is well-typed by S as follows: For each clause in P we find the maximal set of atoms that can be inferred relative to S. Then we find the union of all these sets and check if it equals S. This implicitly means that for every node of each goal in S we check that the value of this node can be obtained by some clause in P, that is, there is a ground instance of a clause in P whose head has this value at this node, and whose head and body are in S.

The type checker should also report on clauses that might be useless, i.e., if there is no ground instance of the clause that is constructed from the type.

We would like to remind the reader of the notation

$$M_C^\alpha(S) = \alpha(\{A \in S \mid A \leftarrow B_1,\ldots,B_n \ll C \text{ and } B_1,\ldots,B_n \in S\}).$$

$M_C^\alpha(S)$ denotes the set of atoms in S that are inferred from C relative to S.

The key idea in focusing on regular types, which are represented by DFA, is that it is possible to infer the maximal set of values that a node of a term can obtain with respect to the type declaration S and hence the maximal set of values that a variable can assume (we call this *the type of the variable*).

We want to show that we can find $paths(M_C^\alpha(S))$. For each node in the clause C where a variable appears, we can find the maximal set of values that it can obtain. If B is an atom in C and Y is some node of B then we can find the path from the root to Y in the associated tree of B, and run this path on the DFA that represents S getting to some state q. The set of all strings that lead from q to a final state represent the maximal set of values that Y can obtain with respect to S. All nodes in C that have the same logical variable must be intersected to obtain its type. If there is a variable in C that has an empty type or there is a ground path of some atom in C that is not in $paths(S)$ then $M_C^\alpha(S) = \phi$, else we can build the automaton for $paths(M_C^\alpha(S))$ from the head of the clause and the types that were found for the variables in the clause C.

The algorithm

For each clause C in P do:

    For each variable Y that appears in C do:

        For each occurrence of Y in C do:

            Infer the maximal set of values that this occurrence can obtain.

        Intersect all the above sets getting the variable's type.

    Construct $M_C^\alpha(S)$ using the type of the variables.

    If $M_C^\alpha(S) = \phi$ then print a warning that clause C may be useless.

Find the tuple-distributive closure of the union of the $M_C^\alpha(S)$'s computed. If the result is equal to S and no clause was suspected to be useless then *succeed* else *fail*. ∎

Claim. Let S be a regular type. Then P is well typed by S iff the above algorithm succeeds.

Proof. We have to prove that $T_P(S) = S$ iff the algorithm succeeds.

$$T_P(S) = \alpha\left(\left\{ A \in S \;\middle|\; \begin{array}{l} A \leftarrow B_1,B_2,\ldots,B_n \ll C, \ C \in P, \\ \text{and } B_1,\ldots,B_n \in S \end{array} \right\}\right)$$

$$= \alpha \left(\bigcup_{C \in P} \{A \in S \mid A \leftarrow B_1,\ldots,B_n \ll C \text{ and } B_1,\ldots,B_n \in S\} \right)$$

$$= \left\{ X \;\middle|\; paths(X) \subseteq \bigcup_{C \in P} paths(M_C^\alpha(S)) \right\}$$

So we get that $T_P(S) = S$ iff $\bigcup_{C \in P} paths(M_C^\alpha(S)) = paths(S)$. We have shown above that finding $M_C^\alpha(S)$ is possible. The union of the $M_C^\alpha(S)$'s is simply the union of DFA getting possibly a NDFA.   ∎

In our implementation we transform the NDFA that was constructed to a DFA, which may take exponential time, and then by an equivalence algorithm which is known to be almost linear we do the last step of the algorithm.

28.4.4 Complexity analysis

We now consider the complexity of the above algorithm. We show that the complexity is exponential in the maximal number of clauses that belong to the same procedure and is exponential in the maximal number of occurrences of a variable in a clause.

Assume that:

- N_P is the number of clauses.

- N_V is the maximal number of all occurrences of a variable in a clause of P.

- L_C is the maximal length of a clause in P.

- N_p is the maximal number of clauses of the same predicate.

- N is the number of states in the DFA that represents the type.

Then

- Inferring the maximal possible set of values of a variable occurrence in a clause requires finding the right state in the DFA, which can be done in time $O(N \cdot L_C)$.

- Intersection of the regular sets to get the type of a variable takes $O(N^{N_V})$.

- Constructing $M_C^\alpha(S)$ can be done in $O(L_C \cdot N^{N_V})$.

- Uniting two DFA's and transforming their union into an equivalent DFA takes $O(N^2)$. So uniting the $M_C^\alpha(S)$'s to get a DFA takes $O(N_P \cdot L_C^{N_p} \cdot N^{N_V \cdot N_p})$.

- The equivalence of the DFA that represents the type and the DFA that was constructed is almost linear. So the overall complexity of the algorithm is

$$O(N_P \cdot L_C^{N_p} \cdot N^{N_V \cdot N_p}).$$

In practice, the number of intersections in a clause is small and in most applications that do not involve databases the number of clauses in a procedure is small. In all programs that appear in this paper the number of occurrences of the same logical variable does not exceed four. The intersection of these occurrences does not take an exponential time because they all lead to the same state in the DFA that represents the type. Although in the water jug problem in the next section there are procedures that contain six clauses, the union of the corresponding DFA is done in linear time since the arguments have the same type.

If we have to deal with a large database of ground facts then the algorithm takes polynomial time.

It is possible to define a subset of logic programs for which the algorithm has polynomial time complexity:

(a) N_V is bounded by a constant.

(b) If h and h' are heads of the same predicate then for all i, if arg_i is the ith argument of h and arg'_i is the ith argument of h' then arg_i and arg'_i are top level not unifiable.

It seems that (a) is a reasonable demand but (b) is too restrictive, as it excludes most nondeterministic and many other programs.

28.5 Examples

Three more examples that are long enough and use a non trivial variety of data structures are presented, demonstrating the ease of well-typing. Additional examples can be found in the appendix.

Example. The towers of Hanoi problem (Adapted from H. Yasukawa).

Given three pegs labeled a, b and c. The problem is to move a tower of n disks from peg a to peg c, with the help of peg b. Only one disk can be moved at a time, and a larger disk can never be placed on top of a smaller disk.

> *Natural* $\implies$ *0* ; *s(Natural)*.
>
> *Moves* $\implies$ *(Moves,(Peg,Peg),Moves)* ; *(Peg,Peg)*.
>
> *Peg* $\implies$ *a* ; *b* ; *c*.
>
> *type hanoi(Natural)*.
> hanoi(N) ←
>   hanoi(N,X).
>
> *type hanoi(Natural,Moves)*.

```
hanoi(N,X) ←
    hanoi(N,a,c,X).
```

type hanoi(Natural,Peg,Peg,Moves).
```
hanoi(0,From,To,(From,To)).
hanoi(s(N),From,To,(Before,(From,To),After)) ←
    free(From,To,Free),
    hanoi(N,From,Free,Before),
    hanoi(N,Free,To,After).
```

type free(Peg,Peg,Peg).
```
free(a,b,c).
free(a,c,b).
free(b,a,c).
free(b,c,a).
free(c,a,b).
free(c,b,a).
```

Example. Priority queue

The program is adapted from Shapiro (Chapter 2).

In the following example a priority queue is represented as a list of pairs (X,P), where X is the element and P is its associated priority. On *enqueue(X,P)* the queue process inserts X into the list according to its priority; on *dequeue(X)* it moves X from the head of the list.

Natural $\Longrightarrow$ *0 ; s(Natural).*

Enqueue $\Longrightarrow$ *[ ] ; [enqueue(any,Natural)|Enqueue].*

Dequeue $\Longrightarrow$ *[ ] ; [dequeue(any)|Dequeue].*

Queue $\Longrightarrow$ *[ ] ; [(any,Natural)|Queue].*

type Natural $\leq$ *Natural.*
```
0 ≤ Y.
s(X) ≤ s(Y) ←
    X ≤ Y.
```

type Natural $<$ *s(Natural).*
```
X < s(Y) ←
    X ≤ Y.
```

type queue(Enqueue,Dequeue).
```
queue(Es,Ds) ←
    queue(Es,Ds,[ ]).
```

type queue(Enqueue,Dequeue,Queue).

```
queue(Es,[dequeue(X)|Ds],[(X,P)|Q]) ←
    queue(Es,Ds,Q).
queue([enqueue(X,P)|Es],Ds,Q) ←
    insert((X,P),Q,Q1),
    queue(Es,Ds,Q1).
queue([ ],[ ],Q).
```

type insert((any,Natural),Queue,[(any,Natural)|Queue]).
```
insert((X,P),[(X1,P1)|Q],[(X,P),(X1,P1)|Q]) ←
    P ≤ P1.
insert((X,P),[(X1,P1)|Q],[(X1,P1)|Q1]) ←
    P1 < P,
    insert((X,P),Q,Q1).
insert((X,P),[ ],[(X,P)]).
```

Example. The water jug problem

The problem and the code are adapted from Sterling and Shapiro (1986).

There are two jugs, of capacity 8 and 5 liters with no markings, and the problem is to measure out exactly 4 liters from a vat containing 20 liters (or some other large number). The possible operations are filling up a jug from the vat, emptying a jug into the vat, and transferring the contents of one jug to another until either the pouring jug is emptied completely, or the other jug is filled to capacity.

Natural $\Longrightarrow$ *0 ; s(Natural).*

Jug $\Longrightarrow$ *1 ; 2.*

State $\Longrightarrow$ *jugs(Natural,Natural).*

States $\Longrightarrow$ *[ ] ; [State|States].*

Move $\Longrightarrow$ *fill(Jug) ; empty(Jug) ; transfer(Jug,Jug).*

Moves $\Longrightarrow$ *[ ] ; [Move|Moves].*

Capacity $\Longrightarrow$ *s(s(s(s(s(0))))) ; s(s(s(s(s(s(s(s(0)))))))).*

type s(Natural) > Natural.
```
s(X) > 0.
s(X) > s(Y) ←
    X > Y.
```

type plus(Natural,Natural,Natural).
```
plus(0,X,X).
plus(s(X),Y,s(Z)) ←
    plus(X,Y,Z).
```

type nat_minus(Natural,Natural,Natural).
nat_minus(0,X,0).
nat_minus(X,0,X).
nat_minus(s(X),s(Y),Z) ←
    nat_minus(X,Y,Z).

type initial_state(jugs,jugs(0,0)).
initial_state(jugs,jugs(0,0)).

type final_state(State).
final_state(jugs(s(s(s(s(0)))),V2)).
final_state(jugs(V1,s(s(s(s(0)))))).

type move(State,Move).
move(jugs(V1,V2),fill(1)).
move(jugs(V1,V2),fill(2)).
move(jugs(V1,V2),empty(1)) ←
    V1 > 0.
move(jugs(V1,V2),empty(2)) ←
    V2 > 0.
move(jugs(V1,V2),transfer(2,1)).
move(jugs(V1,V2),transfer(1,2)).

type update(State,Move,State).
update(jugs(V1,V2),empty(1),jugs(0,V2)).
update(jugs(V1,V2),empty(2),jugs(V1,0)).
update(jugs(V1,V2),fill(2),jugs(C1,V2)) ←
    capacity(1,C1).
update(jugs(V1,V2),fill(2),jugs(V1,C2)) ←
    capacity(2,C2).
update(jugs(V1,V2),transfer(2,1),jugs(W1,W2)) ←
    capacity(1,C1),
    plus(V1,V2,Liquid),
    nat_minus(Liquid,C1,Excess),
    adjust(Liquid,Excess,W2,W1).
update(jugs(V1,V2),transfer(1,2),jugs(W1,W2)) ←
    capacity(2,C2),
    plus(V1,V2,Liquid),
    nat_minus(Liquid,C2,Excess),
    adjust(Liquid,Excess,W2,W1).

type adjust(Natural,Natural,Natural,Natural).
adjust(Liquid,0,Liquid,0).
adjust(Liquid,Excess,V,Excess) ←

Excess > 0,
nat_minus(Liquid,Excess,V).

type legal(State).
legal(jugs(V1,V2)).

type capacity(Jug,Capacity).
capacity(1,s(s(s(s(s(s(s(s(0)))))))))).
capacity(2,s(s(s(s(s(0)))))).

type not_member(State,States).
not_member(State,[ ]).
not_member(State,[State1|States]) ←
    diff(State,State1),
    not_member(State,States).

type diff(State,State).
diff(jugs(V1,V2),jugs(W1,W2)) ←
    V1 > W1.
diff(jugs(V1,V2),jugs(W1,W2)) ←
    W1 > V1.
diff(jugs(V1,V2),jugs(W1,W2)) ←
    V2 > W2.
diff(jugs(V1,V2),jugs(W1,W2)) ←
    W2 > V2.

type solve_dfs(State,States,Moves).
solve_dfs(State,History,[ ]) ←
    final_state(State).
solve_dfs(State,History,[Move|Moves]) ←
    move(State,Move),
    update(State,Move,State1),
    not_member(State1,History),
    solve_dfs(State1,[State1|History],Moves).

type test_dfs(jugs,Moves).
test_dfs(Problem,Moves) ←
    initial_state(Problem,State),
    solve_dfs(State,[State],Moves).

28.6 Discussion

From our experience it seems that a regular type can be constructed naturally for every program we have tried. The one who writes the program knows the type that each of its variables can obtain and therefore it makes it quite easy to declare types. When we use large databases it may be cumbersome to declare all the values that an argument can obtain, since the list would be a long declaration. However, even in this case the declaration is still conceptually easy.

Our type system deals only with pure logic programs that are self contained. This is the basic theoretical model from which we would like to build type systems for concrete logic programming languages such as FCP or Prolog. In such languages there are system predicates, services and remote procedure calls like *append/3*, which appends two lists that may contain any sort of data. We should also note that a module of a program that is not self-contained cannot be well-typed, since the fixpoint requirement is violated. Another construct that other languages have are basic types like integers, strings, atoms, etc., which are a necessity in type systems. This implies that:

- Adding type variables to type declarations is a necessary tool which should extend the existing type system.

- The theory should be extended to deal with modules and basic types.

The relation between type-checking, well-typing and type-inference deserves further investigation. However, in Section 28.4.1 there is a hint on how an impractical automatic type inference system can be built — begin with the empty set, and at each iteration infer the next type from of the previous step, which weakly well-types P. Furthermore, we show that for all nonredundant logic programs regular types can be inferred by this approach. However, if the program has a redundant clause, this may not be a practical approach, since the termination condition cannot be fulfilled unless the meaning is a finite set.

Several topics touched upon in this paper remain open research directions:

- The type system developed here should be extended to allow parametrized types, but perhaps in a restricted way so as to preserve decidability.

- To apply the type system to working programming languages such as Prolog or FCP.

- A type-checking algorithm for a wider class of type declarations could also be constructed. However, as mentioned above, all nonredundant logic programs can be well-typed by regular types, and construction of regular types is very intuitive. Therefore the need for this direction still has to be demonstrated.

- Development of a more usable approach to automatic type inference is also a subject of further research. Such an approach should be based on a type system which allows parameterized types.

Acknowledgements

We thank John Gallager, who contributed greatly to the conceptual organization of this paper and to the clarity of the presentation.

Appendix 1: Examples of Well-Typed Programs

Arithmetics

> *Natural* $\Longrightarrow$ *0* ; *s(Natural)*.
>
> *type Natural $\leq$ Natural*.
> $0 \leq Y$.
> $s(X) \leq s(Y) \leftarrow$
> $X \leq Y$.
>
> *type Natural $\geq$ Natural*.
> $X \geq Y \leftarrow$
> $Y \leq X$.
>
> *type s(Natural) > Natural*.
> $s(X) > Y \leftarrow$
> $X \geq Y$.
>
> *type Natural < s(Natural)*.
> $X < s(Y) \leftarrow$
> $X \leq Y$.
>
> *type plus(Natural,Natural,Natural)*.
> plus(0,Y,Y).
> plus(s(X),Y,s(Z)) $\leftarrow$
>   plus(X,Y,Z).
>
> *type mult(Natural,Natural,Natural)*.
> mult(0,Y,0).
> mult(s(X),Y,Z) $\leftarrow$
>   mult(X,Y,T),
>   plus(Y,T,Z).
>
> *type factorial(Natural,Natural)*.
> factorial(0,s(0)).
> factorial(s(N),F) $\leftarrow$
>   factorial(N,F1),
>   mult(s(N),F1,F).

type div(Natural,s(Natural),Natural).
div(X,Y,0) ←
    X < Y.
div(X,s(Y),s(Z)) ←
    X > Y,
    plus(W,s(Y),X),
    div(W,s(Y),Z).

type mod(Natural,s(Natural),Natural).
mod(X,Y,X) ←
    X < Y.
mod(X,s(Y),Z) ←
    X > Y,
    plus(W,s(Y),X),
    mod(W,s(Y),Z).

Merge sort

Natural $\Longrightarrow$ *0 ; s(Natural).*

Nat_list $\Longrightarrow$ *[ ] ; [Natural|Nat_list].*

Special_list $\Longrightarrow$ *[ ] ; [[Natural]|Special_list].*

List_of_nat_lists $\Longrightarrow$ *[ ] ; [Nat_list|List_of_nat_lists].*

type mergesort(Nat_list,Nat_list).
mergesort(Xs,Ys) ←
    convert(Xs,Xs1), msort(Xs1,[Ys]).

type convert(Nat_list,Special_list).
convert([ ],[ ]).
convert([X1|Xs],[[X1]|Ys]) ←
    convert(Xs,Ys).

type msort(List_of_nat_lists,List_of_nat_lists).
msort([ ],[ ]).
msort([X],[X]).
msort([X1,X2|Xs],Zs) ←
    merge_all([X1,X2|Xs],Ys),
    msort(Ys,Zs).

type merge_all(List_of_nat_lists,List_of_nat_lists).
merge_all([ ],[ ]).
merge_all([X],[X]).
merge_all([X1,X2|Xs],[Y|Ys]) ←

```
        merge2(X1,X2,Y),
        merge_all(Xs,Ys).
```

type merge2(Nat_list,Nat_list,Nat_list).
```
merge2([ ],X,X).
merge2(X,[ ],X).
merge2([X|Xs],[Y|Ys],[X|Zs]) ←
        X ≤ Y,
        merge2(Xs,[Y|Ys],Zs).
merge2([X|Xs],[Y|Ys],[Y|Zs]) ←
        X > Y,
        merge2([X|Xs],Ys,Zs).
```

Prime numbers

Adapted from Shapiro (Chapter 7).

Natural ⟹ *0 ; s(Natural).*

Nat_list ⟹ *[ ] ; [Natural|Nat_list].*

type primes(Natural,Nat_list).
```
primes(N,Ps) ←
        integers(2,N,Ns),
        sift(Ns,Ps).
```

type sift(Nat_list,Nat_list).
```
sift([ ],[ ]).
sift([P|In],[P|Out]) ←
        filter(In,P,Out1),
        sift(Out1,Out).
```

type filter(Nat_list,Natural,Nat_list).
```
filter([ ],P,[ ]).
filter([N|In],P,[N|Out]) ←
        mod(P,N,M),
        M > 0,
        filter(In,P,Out).
filter([N|In],P,Out) ←
        mod(P,N,0),
        filter(In,P,Out).
```

type integers(Natural,Natural,Nat_list).
```
integers(To,To,[ ]).
integers(From,To,[From|Is]) ←
        To > From,
```

    plus(1,From,From1),
    integers(From1,To,Is).

List handling

Any_list $\Longrightarrow$ [ ] ; [*any*|*Any_list*].

type rev(Any_list,Any_list).
rev([X|Xs],Ys) ←
    rev(Xs,Zs),
    append(Zs,[X],Ys).
rev([ ],[ ]).

type append(Any_list,Any_list,Any_list).
append([X|Xs],Ys,[X|Zs]) ←
    append(Xs,Ys,Zs).
append([ ],Xs,Xs).

Part VI

Embedded Languages

Introduction

The goal of identifying a fundamental high-level machine language should not be confused with the goal of designing high-level programming languages suitable for human expression. It seems that there is no one single language which is uniformly better than all other languages for all purposes. Furthermore, the aspiration towards higher and higher level languages does not seem to diminish, which ensures that the programming languages we use will continue to evolve in the forseeable future.

Although presently considered a high-level programming language, Flat Concurrent Prolog might not be the most convenient programming language for many applications even today. Some applications require no expression of concurrency: for those, the specification of synchronization by the programmer is just a burden. Some applications are best described by a set of communicating objects, exchanging messages. Those might find the use of unification to express message passing too unstructured, and the syntax of tail recursive processes too verbose. Some applications are best specified using functional or equational notation. For those, the relational syntax might prove cumbersome.

Therefore, even if Flat Concurrent Prolog is to be used as the general-purpose machine language of parallel computers, it cannot be its sole programming language and hence should be capable of implementing other high-level languages effectively. Presently, there are three major approaches to high-level languages, each with its own basic computational model, growing family of language designs and implementations, and avid community — object-oriented programming, functional programming, and logic programming. It seems that each of these approaches has a justification for its existence: a domain of excellence, in which its solutions seem to perform better than those of any other approach. It seems that all three have strong affinity with parallelism in that their basic computation models are inherently concurrent, or can be easily rephrased as such.

Assuming that all three approaches will remain viable in the future, a question arises: will we need a different type of computer architecture, implementation technology, and operating system, to support each of the three computation models? This part of the book attempts to answer this question in the negative. It suggests that, as a parallel machine language, Flat Concurrent Prolog can support all three models of computation effectively; that on a single architecture, using a single low-level implementation technology and a single operating system, concurrent languages from all three families can co-exist and be used effectively.

Of course a compiler and a computer architecture can be optimized for a single language, application, or even program. Furthermore, crossing layers of abstraction may also provide performance gains, especially if these layers are ill-defined. However, it seems that the cost-effectiveness of general purpose architectures, and the compelling conceptual and organizational power of strict abstractions are such that it might not be necessary or fruitful to specialize architectures or cross layers of abstraction for quite some time.

The time to do this may come when both "silicon compilers" and general-purpose partial evaluators become a reality. With these tools one may be able to partially evaluate a specification of a computer architecture written in a high-level hardware description language with respect to a compiler for a high-level programming language and a program written in this language, to produce a specification of an architecture specialized just to run this program. Until such a day comes, it seems that the more mundane implementation techniques reported in this part may be of use.

This part shows how object-oriented, functional, and logic programming languages can be translated efficiently to Flat Concurrent Prolog, and how this language can be used for hardware description and simulation. Church's thesis states that any reasonably rich computation model can simulate any other computation model effectively; its refinements state that this can always be done in polynomially more time and space. Hence it should not be surprising that Flat Concurrent Prolog can implement, in principle, other languages and computation models. However, the evidence provided in this part is of a different quality. We find the simplicity and clarity of the transformations compelling, and the resulting performance convincing. Furthermore, we find that the attempt to translate another computation model into the concurrent logic programming model usually sheds new light on the original model, and results in a clean and consistent design, as shown below for both object-oriented and functional programming.

The results suggest that Flat Concurrent Prolog has succeeded in striking a very desirable balance. On the one hand Flat Concurrent Prolog is rich enough to allow fairly direct embeddings of other computation models; on the other hand its generality does not seem to carry a significant performance penalty. It is simple enough to be implemented efficiently, so that its use as an intermediate language for high-level languages, even on conventional sequential computers, is practical.

Object-oriented programming

The first two chapters in this part investigate object-oriented programming.

Chapter 29, "Object Oriented Programming in Concurrent Prolog", by Shapiro and Takeuchi, suggest that Concurrent Prolog can express the main concepts of object-oriented programming rather directly. It shows that object creation and termination, message sending, receiving and delegation can be expressed naturally in Concurrent Prolog, although none of these concepts is included explicitly in its formal computation model. It suggests incomplete messages as a new and powerful object-oriented programming technique, and describes its use in simplifying communication protocols and in managing shared resources. The paper also describes a Concurrent Prolog implementation of a toy window system, which exemplifies some of these techniques.

Chapter 30, "Vulcan: Logical Concurrent Objects", by Kahn, Tribble, Miller, and Bobrow, takes these ideas further. It claims that although Concurrent Prolog provides good computational support for object-oriented programming in the sense described above, it also provides poor linguistic support. Object-oriented programs in Concurrent Prolog are verbose and sensitive to small errors. To exploit the computational model of Concurrent Prolog for object-oriented programming but avoid its verbosity a new programming language, Vulcan, is defined. Vulcan programs are expressed in terms of classes and methods, and provide concise expressions for common Concurrent Prolog object-oriented cliches. The semantics of Vulcan, as well as its implementation, are defined in terms of its translation to (Flat) Concurrent Prolog.

It is interesting to note that the desire to support transparent forwarding of communication channels between objects in Vulcan led to the formalization of the channels concepts, described in Chapter 17.

Logic programming

The following four papers investigate the translation of logic programming languages.

Chapter 31, "PRESSing for Parallelism", by Sterling and Codish, reports on experience with translating a complex Prolog program for equation solving, PRESS, into Concurrent Prolog, and further into Flat Concurrent Prolog. The results suggest that even for hard-core AI applications, Concurrent Prolog and Flat Concurrent Prolog, although lower level than Prolog in many ways, may serve as reasonable implementation languages. The techniques developed for these translations were the basis for defining Safe Concurrent Prolog and its translation to Flat Concurrent Prolog, reported in Chapter 32.

Chapter 32, "Compiling Or-Parallelism Into And-parallelism", by Codish and Shapiro, describes how a language with both Or-parallelism and And-parallelism can be compiled into a language with only And-parallelism, such as Flat Concurrent Prolog. The language Safe Concurrent Prolog is defined. An interpreter for Safe Concurrent Prolog in Flat Concurrent Prolog is shown. The transformation induced by this interpreter is identified with the help of a Concurrent Prolog partial evaluator (Safra, 1986). An interpreter for Prolog programs whose mode of unification is known can be written in Safe Concurrent Prolog. Hence by partially evaluating the two layers of interpretation, such Prolog programs can be translated into Flat Concurrent Prolog. The performance of the resulting FCP programs was found acceptable in comparison with the original Prolog programs. Safe Concurrent Prolog and the translation scheme described are the basis for the GHC-to-FCP compiler, described in Chapter 33.

Chapter 33, "Translating Safe GHC and Safe Concurrent Prolog to Flat Concurrent Prolog", by Levy and Shapiro, describes an implementation of the safe subset of GHC by translation to FCP. The translation involves two stages: first, a Safe GHC program is translated into Safe Concurrent Prolog. Then, an optimized version of the translation from Chapter 32 is employed, to translate SCP into FCP. One of the main improvements in the translation is the use of an indexing mechanism. The indexing mechanism and the theory behind it are also presented. The translation technique used is applicable to translating the single-solution subset of PARLOG to FCP as well. It is not, of course, applicable to the implementation of the all-solutions subset of PARLOG in FCP. This is the subject of the following paper.

Chapter 34, "Or-Parallel Prolog in Flat Concurrent Prolog", by Shapiro, described an Or-parallel execution algorithm for Prolog and its implementation in Flat Concurrent Prolog. The algorithm is most suitable for implementation on non shared-memory parallel computers. The performance of an interpreter-based FCP implementation of the algorithm is compared with the C-Prolog interpreter on a uniprocessor and is found acceptable. Several extensions of the algorithm, including the implementation of parallel cut, demand-driven search, and dynamic load balancing are discussed, and their implementations are shown.

Together, these four papers show that FCP can be used both as a high-level programming language for AI applications and as a target implementation language for all the other major logic programming languages proposed so far.

Functional programming

Chapter 35, "CFL — A Concurrent Functional Programming Language Embedded in a Concurrent Logic Programming Environment", by Levy and Shapiro, describes an experimental embedding of a rich functional language in FCP. CFL is a lexically-scoped nondeterministic concurrent functional language, which contains higher-order functions and both "upward" and "downward" lexical closures. It is not a toy language, yet its translation to FCP is quite straightforward. Its performance is surprising: using the standard compiler of Logix (Houri and Shapiro, Chapter 38) it achieves performance similar to compiled Franz Lisp on a uniprocessor. Using the experimental native code compiler for FCP (Kliger, 1987), it is about ten times faster than Franz Lisp.

Hardware description

Chapter 36, "Hardware Description and Simulation in Concurrent Prolog", by Weinbaum and Shapiro, shows how the parallelism of hardware is expressed naturally in Concurrent Prolog, and how using the recursive and hierarchical structure of Concurrent Prolog, highly abstract, comprehensible, and compact descriptions of complex hardware systems are obtained. These descriptions are executable Concurrent Prolog programs. Two phases are identified in their execution: structural reduction, in which a hierarchical and recursive description is decomposed into a network of primitive components, and functional simulation, in which these components exchange messages simulating the execution of the hardware described. The paper reports on a hardware simulator, implemented in FCP, which can inspect and control the execution of such descriptions.

Chapter 29

Object Oriented Programming
in Concurrent Prolog

Ehud Shapiro

The Weizmann Institute of Science

Akikazu Takeuchi

Institute for New Generation Computer Technology

Abstract

It is shown that the basic operations of object-oriented programming languages — creating an object, sending and receiving messages, modifying an object's state, and forming class-superclass hierarchies — can be implemented naturally in Concurrent Prolog. In addition, a new object-oriented programming paradigm, called incomplete messages, is presented. This paradigm subsumes stream communication, and greatly simplifies the complexity of programs defining communication networks and protocols for managing shared resources. Several programs are presented, including a multiple-window manager. All programs have been developed and tested using the Concurrent Prolog interpreter described by Shapiro (Chapter 2).

29.1 Introduction

Concurrent Prolog introduces an operational semantics of parallel execution to logic programs, thus allowing them to express concurrent computations. Concurrent Prolog can specify process creation, termination, communication, synchronization, and indeterminacy. This paper focuses on the object-oriented aspects of Concurrent Prolog. It is shown that the language lends itself naturally to the programming idioms and techniques of Actors (Hewitt, 1977) and Smalltalk (XEROX, 1981).

The paper is structured as follows. Section 29.2 surveys the elements of object-oriented logic programming. Section 29.3 studies in detail a non-trivial Concurrent Prolog program: a toy multiple-window system. The system is operational on the DEC-20 and VAX-11 for a VT-100 terminal. Section 29.4 compares traditional object-oriented programming to object-oriented logic programming, and identifies two important programming techniques not easily available in the former: incomplete messages, and constraint propagation.

29.2 Object Oriented Programming in Concurrent Prolog

Concurrent Prolog is capable of expressing modern programming concepts, including object-oriented programming. The concept of objects in Concurrent Prolog has a close resemblance to that of Actor systems (Hewitt, 1977), in that a computation is performed via the cooperation of distributed objects. First we present a general scheme for object-oriented programming in Concurrent Prolog, then explain how object are created, and how they can cooperate in a computation. We then introduce a Concurrent Prolog programming technique, called *filters*, which achieves the effect of hierarchical definition of objects and property inheritance, a useful tool in other object-oriented programming languages. In addition to the usual object-oriented features, Concurrent Prolog provides two new features that stem from the power of logical variables and unification. One of them is computation by incomplete messages and the other is implicit activation of objects, which is similar to a constraint network (Steele, 1980; Borning, 1981; Sussman and Steele, 1980).

29.2.1 Objects

Our view of objects is based on Hewitt's (1977) Actor model of parallel computation.

An object can be thought of as an active process that receives messages and performs actions on its internal state according to the received message. During the computation, an object can send messages to other objects.

The general properties of objects are as follows:

(1) An object is a process that has an internal state. It becomes active when it receives a message.

(2) The internal state of an object can be operated upon from the outside only by sending it a message, which specifies the operation to be performed.

(3) An object can exchange messages with other objects during its computation.

(4) Any number of object-instances can be generated from a definition of an object.

29.2.2 Realization of objects

First we show how Concurrent Prolog realizes objects.

(1) A (perpetual) object is a process that calls itself recursively and holds its internal state in unshared arguments.

The state of an object corresponds to the arguments of a process. Its internal state corresponds to arguments not shared by other processes. An object acts by reducing itself to other objects. A perpetual object survives by reducing itself to itself. A perpetual object changes its state by calling itself recursively with different arguments.

(2) Objects communicate with each other by instantiating shared variables.

Since parallel processes are realized by And-parallelism, they can be linked by shared variables. These variables are used as communication channels among objects. Message passing is performed by instantiating a shared variable to a message. Because a shared variable can be referred to by multiple processes, a message can be sent to multiple objects at once. Successive communication is possible by the stream communication technique, that is, by instantiating a channel variable to the binary term $[\langle message \rangle | X]$ where $\langle message \rangle$ is a message to be sent and X is a new variable to be used in the next communication.

(3) An object becomes active when it receives a message, otherwise it is suspended.

The synchronization mechanism forces a process to suspend when it tries to instantiate read-only variables to non-variable terms. Since objects peek into their input stream in read-only mode, they are suspended if the next message is not available yet.

(4) An object-instance is created by process reduction.

An object instance B is created when an object A is reduced via a clause $A \leftarrow \ldots B \ldots$.

(5) Response to a message.

When an object sends a message which requires a response, the response cannot be sent through the same shared variable, since logical variables are single-assignment. There are two techniques for sending a response to a message. One is to prepare another shared stream variable, in which the communication flows in the opposite direction. Another uses a technique called incomplete messages, which is explained more fully in Section 29.4.1. In this technique the sender sends a message that contains an uninstantiated variable, and then examines that variable in a read-only mode, which causes it to suspend until this variable gets instantiated to the response by the recipient of the message. For example, a message *show* which asks a target object about its internal state is implemented by the message *show(State)*, where the variable *State* is used as a communication channel that carries the response from the target object back to the sender. The sender will get the response in this variable sometime in the future, when the message is received and processed. So the sender must wait until the response variable is instantiated if it needs to refer to the response.

29.2.3 The *counter* example

A simple example of how to describe an object is shown in Program 29.1.

```
counter([clear|S],State) ←
    counter(S,0).
counter([up|S],State) ←
    plus(State,1,NewState), counter(S?,NewState?).
counter([down|S],State) ←
    plus(Newstate,1,State), counter(S?,NewState?).
counter([show(State)|S],State) ←
    counter(S,State).
counter([ ],State).
```

Program 29.1: A counter process

The object *counter* has two arguments, one is an input stream and the other is its internal state. When receiving a *clear* message, it resets the state to *0*. When receiving *up* and *down* messages, it increments or decrements its state by *1*, respectively. The process $plus(X,Y,Z)$ suspends until at least two of its arguments are instantiated, then instantiates the third so that they satisfy the constraint $X+Y=Z$. If this constraint cannot be satisfied, *plus* fails. The implementation of *plus* is described in Section 29.4.2.

When receiving a $show(X)$ message, *counter* unifies the variable X with the internal state *State*. The last clause terminates the *counter* process, upon encountering the end of the input stream. Note that the stream variable is used recursively. In every reduction it is instantiated to a pair: the message and a new variable, to be used in the next communication.

29.2.4 Object-instance creation

Object-instance creation is accomplished by And-parallel process forking. A new instance of an object *counter* may be created by executing the following code;

terminal(X), use_counter(X?,C1), counter(C1?,0)

where *terminal* is an object that generates the stream of commands produced by a user at a terminal. Program 29.2 defines *use_counter*. It is an object that receives commands from the terminal and passes them to the object *counter*, except for the *show* command. In response to a *show* command, *use_counter* passes it to *counter*, waits for its *counter*'s response, and outputs the response to the screen. Note that the first argument of *use_counter* and the second argument of the object *counter* are treated as read only variables, because they are used only as input.

use_counter([show(Val)|Input],[show(Val)|Command]) ←
    use_counter(Input?,Command), wait_write(Val).
use_counter([X|Input],[X|Command]) ←
    X≠show(Y) | use_counter(Input?,Command).
use_counter([ ],[ ].

wait_write(X) ← known(X) | write(X).

Program 29.2: Using a counter

known(X) is a Concurrent Prolog system predicate which is suspended if X is not instantiated, and succeeds if it is. X≠Y is a system predicate that succeeds if and when it can determine that X and Y are different (i.e., not unifiable). Note that the stream variable is used as an object-instance name. Message passing is performed against the stream variable and not against the target object itself, because there are no global names in Concurrent Prolog, and the only information about an object that is accessible from the outside are the communication channels to it.

As described before, a new object-instance is created using a definition in the program. However, object-instances created from the same definition are different, and can be distinguished by the names of their communication channels. The example below demonstrates this. The object *use_many_counters* shown in Program 29.3 is similar to *use_counter*. It receives a command stream from the terminal. When it receives a *create(Name)* message, it creates a new object *counter* and saves its name and a communication channel to it in its internal state. Other messages must be of the form (*Name,Command*), where *Name* specifies the name of an object *counter* to which the message *Command* should be sent.

The object *use_many_counters* has two arguments, one an input stream from the terminal and the other a list of (*Name,channel*) where *Name* is an identifier

use_many_counters([create(Name)|Input],List_of_counters) ←
    counter(Com?,0),
    use_many_counters(Input?,[(Name,Com)|List_of_counters]).
use_many_counters([(Name,show(Val))|Input],List_of_counters) ←
    send(List_of_counters,Name,show(Val),NewList) |
    use_many_counters(Input?,NewList), wait_write(Val).
use_many_counters([X|Input],List_of_counters) ←
    X≠create(Y), X≠show(Y),
    send(List_of_counters,Name,X,NewList) |
    use_many_counters(Input?,NewList).

send([(Name,[Message|Y])|List],Name,Message,[(Name,Y)|List]).
send([C|List],Name,Message,[C|L1]) ← send(List,Name,Message,L1).

Program 29.3: Using many counters

of the object *counter* given by the *create* command and *Channel* is the communication channel to that object. The object *send* takes four arguments, the first argument is the same as the second argument of *use_many_counters*. The second and the third arguments are an identifier of the object *counter* and a message to be sent respectively. The fourth argument is the updated list of counters. Figure 29.1 shows the situation after three *create* command have been processed. Note that since there are no global variables in Concurrent Prolog, an object must keep channel variables associated with other objects in order to send messages to them.

use_many_counters(In?,[ ])

   ↓   In = [create(c1) | In1]

use_many_counters(In1,[(c1,X1)]) , counter(X1?,0)

   ↓   In1 = [create(c2) | In2]

use_many_counters(In2,[(c2,X2),(c1,X1)]) , counter(X2?,0)

   ↓   In2 = [create(c3) | In3]

use_many_counters(In3,[(c3,X3),(c2,X2),(c1,X1)]) , counter(X3?,0)

Figure 29.1: Multiple object-instantiation

The multi-window system described in Section 29.3 uses a similar technique to create processes and to associate windows and communication channels with them.

29.2.5 Default programming, filters, and object hierarchies

Some object-oriented languages, such as Smalltalk (XEROX, 1981), associate a hierarchy with objects. This hierarchy supports a very convenient form of default programming. Methods for responding to a message can be associated with an object high in the hierarchy, and an object-instance, receiving a message which it does not know how to respond to, can default to an object higher in the hierarchy to respond to the message. In addition to increasing the brevity of programs, such a mechanism also increases modularity, since code associated with a class of objects occurs only in the definition of the class. This mechanism also encourages the programmer to identify useful abstractions.

Concurrent Prolog does not have special hard-wired mechanisms to support object hierarchies. However, a certain programming technique, called filters, together with the Concurrent Prolog construct *otherwise* achieves a very similar effect. The resulting programs exhibit an Actor-like cooperative behavior.

Consider the following hierarchy of objects: a rectangular-area; a window-frame, which is a rectangular-area with four border-lines; a window-with-label, which is a window-frame with a label at the bottom of the window. These can be defined by a class-superclass hierarchy (see Figure 29.2).

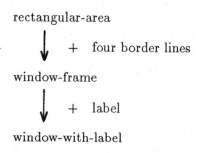

Figure 29.2: Class-superclass hierarchy

In a language that supports such hierarchies directly, the functionality of a rectangular-area is inherited by the window-frame, and the functionality of a window-frame is inherited by a window with a label. Operationally, an object that receives a message checks whether it knows how to respond to it. If it does not, then it defaults to its parent in the hierarchy. In this sense every object in the hierarchy functions like a filter on a stream of messages, and this is precisely how object hierarchies are implemented in Concurrent Prolog.

Every object in a hierarchy must have at least one designated input stream and one designated output stream, except the top-most object, which may have an input stream only. The hierarchical structure of the objects is reflected by the structure of the communication network that they form. An object *A* lower in the hierarchy has its output stream connected to the input stream of an object *B* next in the hierarchy. If *A* receives a message that it cannot respond to, it simply defaults to *B*, by passing the message to it.

The following Concurrent Prolog implementation of the window hierarchy demonstrates this technique. First a rectangular-area is defined in Program 29.4.

```
rectangular_area([clear|M],Parameters) ←
    clear_primitive(Parameters),
    rectangular_area(M?,Parameters).
rectangular_area([ask(Parameters)|M],Parameters) ←
    rectangular_area(M?,Parameters).
```

Program 29.4: Rectangular area

Parameters is a data structure consisting of four parameters (*Xpos, Ypos, Width, Height*), where *Xpos* and *Ypos* are the coordinates of the upper-left corner of the area, and *Width* and *Height* are the size of the area. *clear_primitive* is a system defined primitive predicate which clears the screen area specified in its arguments.

From this *rectangular_area* object, a window-frame can be defined. The *frame* object shown in Program 29.5 can be viewed as a filter on the input stream of a *rectangular_area*. It filters two types of message, on which it knows how to respond: *draw* and *refresh*.

```
create_frame(M,Parameters) ←
    rectangular_area(M1?,Parameters),
    frame(M,M1).
frame([draw|M],[ask(Parameters)|M1]) ←
    draw_lines(Parameters?),
    frame(M?,M1).
frame([refresh|M],[clear|M1]) ←
    frame([draw|M],M1).
frame([X|M],[X|M1]) ←
    X≠draw, X≠refresh |
    frame(M?,M1).
```

Program 29.5: Frame

The first clause specifies the initialization procedure, which creates a *rectangular_area* object by passing the parameters and an original *frame* object with the communication channel to the *rectangular_area*. The rest of the clauses specify a method for interpreting each message. On receiving a *draw* message, it asks the *rectangular_area* about the dimensional parameters and then draws four border lines. On receiving a *refresh* message, it sends two messages, *clear* and *draw*, to the *rectangular_area* and self respectively. On receiving other messages, it passes them to the *rectangular_area*.

To support default programming, we use the Concurrent Prolog construct *otherwise*. An *otherwise* goal that occurs in a guard succeeds if and when all previous Or-parallel guards fail. Given the other clauses for *frame*, the last clause is equivalent to:

> frame([X|M],[X|M1]) ←
>   otherwise | frame(M?,M1).

It is not difficult to see that if all clauses for an object have empty guards, then *otherwise* can be implemented via a preprocessor that expands it to an appropriate sequence of calls to $X \neq Y$. If the guards are not empty, then *otherwise* can be implemented via a negation-as-failure primitive. In this sense *otherwise* does not increase the expressive power of Concurrent Prolog more than the addition of negation as failure does. However, an efficient implementation of *otherwise* requires modifications to the Concurrent Prolog interpreter.

> create_window_with_label(M,Label,Parameters) ←
>   create_frame(M1?,Parameters),
>   window_with_label(M?,Label,M1).
> window_with_label([change(Label)|M],OldLabel,M1) ←
>   window_with_label(M?,Label,M1).
> window_with_label([show|M],Label,[ask(Parameters)|M1]) ←
>   show_label_primitive(Label?,Parameters?),
>   window_with_label(M?,Label,M1).
> window_with_label([refresh|M],Label,[refresh|M1]) ←
>   window_with_label([show|M],Label,M1).
> window_with_label([X|M],Label,[X|M1]) ←
>   otherwise |
>   window_with_label(M?,Label,M1).

Program 29.6: Window with label

A window frame with a label is defined in Program 29.6. The first clause defines the initialization procedure which creates the object *frame* with the parameters and a *window_with_label* with a communication channel to the object *frame*. The rest of the clauses define the methods to interpret messages. On receiving a *change* message, it changes the label. On receiving a *show* message, it asks the object *frame* about its parameters and displays the label in the appropriate position in the window, using the predefined predicate *show_label_primitive*.

On receiving a *refresh* message, it sends two messages, *refresh* and *show*, to the *frame* and self respectively. On receiving other messages, it passes them to the *frame*.

In the class-superclass hierarchy, a message which cannot be processed by an object is passed to its superclass. In Concurrent Prolog such a hierarchy is simulated by a network of objects connected via communication channels, through which unprocessable messages are sent. A system like Flavors (Weinreb and Moon, 1980) and Smalltalk-80 (XEROX, 1981) can permit objects to access instance variables of their superclass. However, in Concurrent Prolog, since a superclass of an object is also an object, such direct access to states of other objects is not possible. Instead, an object has to send a message asking about the state to the object that fills the role of its superclass.

Table 29.1 shows the relation between objects and acceptable messages.

Objects	Messages	Process
rectangular area	1 clear	clear the area
	2 ask(X)	instantiate X to parameters
frame	3 draw	draw four lines
	4 refresh	$= 1 + 3$
	clear	send to rectangular area
	ask(X)	send to rectangular area
window_with_label	5 change(Label)	change the label
	6 show	display the label
	draw	send to frame
	refresh	send to frame
	clear	send to frame
	ask(X)	send to frame

Table 29.1: Objects and Acceptable Messages

In the case of *window_with_label*, there are two kinds of methods, one is an own method and the other is a so-called generic method. Generic methods are invoked by sending messages to objects which play the role of a superclass.

In our cooperating objects approach, there is no difference between the class-superclass hierarchy and the part-whole relation. In other words, the role of an object in a group of cooperating objects is not determined from a structural

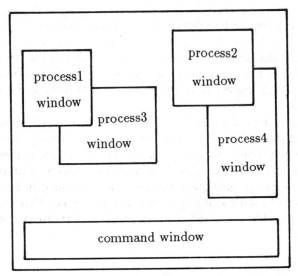

Terminal Screen

(a) A Sample Screen of the Multi-Window System

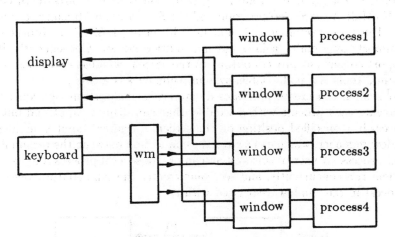

(b) Total View of the Multi-Window System

Figure 29.3: Multi-window system

description (such as superclass declaration and part declaration), but from a be-havioral description in the form of a communication network. From this point of view, a *rectangular_area* can be seen both as a superclass of a *frame* and as a part of a *frame*. The essential point, however, is the behavioral role of the *rectangular_area* with respect to the *frame*, and in this sense we are close to the Actor formalism.

The internal states of an object can never be operated upon directly from a user of the object. All a user can do is send a message that specifies the operation to be performed. So the encapsulation of internal states is established. Also, there is no way to access directly component objects of an object from the outside, except by using incomplete messages, as explained in Section 29.4.1. So the encapsulation of component objects is also established. Using these properties of objects, it is possible to construct complicated objects from simpler objects in a modular way.

29.3 A Toy Multi-Window System

As a powerful and expressive example, we show a Concurrent Prolog im-plementation of a toy multi-windows system. The system is architectured after the MUF (Multi User Forks) program and the SM (Session Manager) program of the Yale Tools programming environment (Ellis et al., 1982). The Tools environ-ment supports only multi-tasking but not multi-windows. Consequently, it does not support concurrent process output to the screen, whereas ours does. On the other hand, Tools is a real, usable, system while ours is a toy[1].

Our system can create processes dynamically, make them run concurrently and associate each process with a window that can display input and output of the process in a specified position on the screen. Terminal input is managed by the window manager, which can switch the connection between the terminal and a specified process. A user of this system can create several processes dynamically, make them run concurrently, and see concurrently the input-output behavior of each process in the window associated with it.

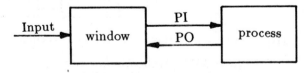

Figure 29.4: A window object

---

[1] See Katzenellenbogen et al. (Chapter 23) for further work on this subject.

A window consists of a rectangular area, four border lines and a label field like a *window_with_label*, defined above. It also has a text string as its internal state. A window has two modes. In normal mode it can fill the region with its text string, append a new string and display it by scrolling up if the window is full. In another mode which is called session manager mode, "sm" mode for short, all the history of the input and the output since the window was created is displayed according to the commands the window receives, by scrolling up and down. In both modes, a window can also move to somewhere else on the screen and change its size and so on. First we show the structure of the window object.

window((Input,PI,PO),State,normal)   in *normal* mode
window((Input,PI,PO),State,sm)   in *sm* mode

The first argument of *window* is three communication channels: *Input* is input from the window manager, and *PI* and *PO* are output to the associated process, and input from this process, respectively. The second argument, *State*, must be a data structure which represents the window's internal state: geographical parameters, contents (text string), and label. In the current implementation, it is represented as $((X0,Y0,W,H),Y,Contents,Label)$ where $X0$ and $Y0$ are the coordinate of the upper-left corner of the window, W and H are width and height of the window respectively and Y denotes the current cursor position. The form of *Contents* is $(Tof,Top,Tail,Last)$, where *Tof*, *Top* and *Tail* point to the top of file (all the string), the head of the text currently displayed in the screen and end of text respectively. *Last* is used when entering the *sm* mode to save the current *Top*, which will be restored upon exit from *sm* mode. Text strings are represented as a bi-directionally linked list of lines, which can be constructed easily by unification with no occur-check. The variable *Label* is the label of the window. The fourth argument of *window* indicates the current mode of the window and must be *sm* or *normal*. The window's behavior is defined in Program 29.7.

On receiving an *erase* message, it erases the area specified in the *State* parameter, including border lines and label field. On receiving a $move(X,Y)$ message, it erases the current area and appears in the new position, the *xy*-coordinate of the upper-left corner, which is specified by X and Y. $set\_parameters(xy,(X,Y),State,State1)$ is a primitive method which changes the *xy* parameter (*xy*-coordinates of a window) of *State* to X and Y and returns new window parameters *State1*. On receiving a $grow(W,H)$, it erases the current area and appears again in the same position with new size specified by the new width W and the new height H. It can become wider, narrower, longer or smaller according to W and H. On receiving a *show* message, it redisplays itself in the same position with the same size.

On receiving an *sm* message in *normal* mode, it enters *sm* mode. On receiving any other message, which must be a message to the associated process, it appends

```
window(([erase|In],PI,PO),State,Mode) ←
     erase_window(State) |
     window((In?,PI,PO),State,Mode).
window(([move(X,Y)|In],PI,PO),State,Mode) ←
     erase_window(State), set_parameters(xy,(X,Y),State,State1) |
     window(([show|In],PI,PO),State1,Mode).
window(([grow(W,H)|In],PI,PO),State,Mode) ←
     erase_window(State), set_parameters(wh,(W,H),State,State1) |
     window(([show|In],PI,PO),State1,Mode).
window(([show|In],PI,PO),State,Mode) ←
     show(State) |
     window((In?,PI,PO),State,Mode).
window(([sm|In],PI,PO),State,normal) ←
     enter_sm(State) |
     window((In?,PI,PO),State,sm).
window(([X|In],[X|PI],PO),State,normal) ←
     fill_input(X,State,State1) |
     window((In?,PI,PO),State1,normal).
window((In,PI,[X|PO]),State,normal) ←
     fill_output(X,State,State1) |
     window((In,PI,PO?),State1,normal).
window(([up|In],PI,PO),State,sm) ←
     show_up(State,State1) | window((In?,PI,PO),State1,sm).
window(([down|In],PI,PO),State,sm) ←
     show_down(State,State1) | window((In?,PI,PO),State1,sm).
window(([exit|In],PI,PO),State,sm) ←
     exit_sm(State,State1) |
     window(([show|In],PI,PO),State1,normal).
window(([X|In],PI,PO),State,sm) ←
     window((In?,PI,PO),State,sm).
```

Program 29.7: The window

the message to the current contents, displays it and passes it to the associated
process. On receiving a message from the associated process, it also appends the
message to the current contents and displays it.

On receiving *up* and *down* messages in *sm* mode, it scrolls up and down the
screen respectively. On receiving an *exit* message, it exits from *sm* mode and
returns to *normal* mode.

The window manager, *wm* for short, has two arguments.

wm(Input,ListOfChannels)

The first argument is the input command stream to the window manager, and the second argument is a list of pairs of a window label and an output channel to the associated process.

```
wm([create(Label,Process,(PI,PO),(X0,Y0,W,H))|Input],Processes) ←
    window(((([show|In],PI,PO?),
        ((X0,Y0,W,H),Y0,(C,C,C,C),Label),normal),
    Process,
    wm(Input?,[(Label,In)|Processes]).
wm([resume(Label)|Input],Processes) ←
    find_process(Label,Processes,PI,Processes1) |
    distribute([show|Input],PI,Input1,PI1),
    wm(Input1?,[(Label,PI1)|Processes1]).
wm([close|Input],[(Label,[ ])|Processes]) ←
    wm(Input?,[(Label,_)|Processes1]).
wm([],Processes) ← close_input(Processes).

distribute([X|Input],PI,[X|Input],PI) ←
    member(X,[resume(_),close,create(_,_,_,_)]) | true.
distribute([X|Input],[X|PI],Input1,PI1) ←
    otherwise | distribute(Input?,PI,Input1,PI1).
distribute([ ],PI,[ ],PI).

find_process(Label,[(Label,PI)|Processes],PI,Processes).
find_process(Label,[PD|Processes],PI,[PD|Processes1]) ←
    find_process(Label,Processes,PI,Processes1).

close_input([ ]).
close_input([(_,[ ])|Processes]) ← close_input(Processes).
```

Program 29.8: The window manager

The window manager can accept three kinds of messages. On receiving *create(Label,Process,(PI,PO),(X0,Y0,W,H))* message, it creates a process *Process*, and a window with label *Label* monitoring the process's input and output, and sends a *show* message to the window. *PI* and *PO* are variables representing the primary input and primary output channels of the process respectively, and may appear in the goal *Process*. *X0*, *Y0*, *W* and *H* are window parameters. On receiving the *resume(Label)* message, it finds the input channel to the process with a name *Label* from the list of processes *Processes* and connects the input stream of the window manager and the input channel of the process by creating the object *distribute*. At the same time, it picks up the process and places it at the top of the list of processes. On receiving a *close* message, it closes the input channel of the process currently resumed. On reaching the end of the input stream, the window manager closes all the input channels of the processes and terminates.

The object *distribute* has four arguments. The first argument is an input channel from the terminal. The second and the third arguments are output channels to the window associated with the process currently resumed and to the window manager respectively. The fourth argument returns the updated input channel of the window when the connection is cut. The *distribute* object peeks ahead into the input, and if the input is a window manager command, then it returns the input stream and the window's input channel to the window manager and terminates. Otherwise it passes the input to the window process (Figure 29.5).

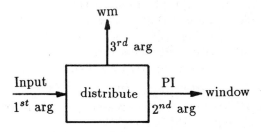

Figure 29.5: A *distribute* object

29.4 New Object-Oriented Programming Techniques in Concurrent Prolog

Concurrent Prolog supports several powerful object-oriented programming techniques not available easily in Actor system and other object-oriented languages. These techniques depend heavily on properties of unification.

In object-oriented languages, a message is sent by specifying the name of the target objects. However, in Concurrent Prolog, objects are connected by shared variables and a message is sent by instantiating a shared variable to it. Therefore the name of the target object does not necessarily appear in the message passing phase and furthermore broadcasting becomes quite simple, because a message is sent to all the objects that share the variable at once. Generally, shared variables are created at the moment when a process creates a new system of processes, as in the following clause:

$$p(X) \leftarrow q(X,Y), r(Y?).$$

In the example above, Y is created and used as a communication channel from q to r. Shared variables can also be made dynamically by sending a variable as a part of a message. This means that a communication channel can be made dynamically and it can be sent to other objects also. A message that contains variables is called an incomplete message. Section 29.4.1 explains this concept.

As described before, information can be sent implicitly to any number of objects without knowing who are the receivers by simply instantiating a shared variable to it. This can be seen also as if the sender and the receivers of a message do not know each other beyond knowing that the variable is shared with some objects. All that the sender has to do is to instantiate a variable as soon as possible, and all that the receivers have to do is to wait until the variable becomes instantiated. This kind of implicit communication is useful for constructing a dependency network like Constraints (Steele, 1980; Borning, 1981; Sussman and Steele, 1980), as explained in Section 29.4.2.

29.4.1 Incomplete messages

The concept of incomplete messages is a new, encompassing programming paradigm, which includes the basic communication mechanism between objects, pipelined processing on stream data, and yields new object-oriented programming techniques. As in the Actor system, Concurrent Prolog is a model of parallel computation, and provides communication methods based on message passing through shared variables. A message is sent by instantiating a shared variable. A message that contains a variable is called an incomplete message. It makes a new variable shared between the sender and the receiver of the message, that is, it creates a new communication channel. Since once a variable is instantiated it will never be rewritten, it can carry only one message. In order to enable subsequent communications, generally a shared variable is instantiated to a pair of a message and a variable which will be used in a next communication, which gives the effects of a stream. Although pipelined processing on stream data usually requires adding new constructs to a language, it is subsumed naturally by the paradigm of the incomplete message.

As in the case of a *show*(X) message to a counter object presented in Section 29.2.3, when a message requires a response it is sent with a variable which will be instantiated by the receiver to the response. This is also an example of an incomplete message. However, this use of incomplete messages is different from streams, because the object that instantiates the variable in the message is the receiver of the message, not the sender. Once a message is sent to an object, the sender and the receiver run independently as long as they can. If the response variable is not instantiated yet by the receiver when the sender refers to it, then the sender suspends.

This programming technique is extremely useful when implementing managers of shared resources. The following implementation of a queue manager demonstrates this. The queue manager handles the messages *enqueue(X)* and *dequeue(X)*, which represent requests to append X at the end of the queue and to return an element positioned at the head of the queue respectively. The predicate *qm* takes three arguments, the first argument is an input channel of requests from users and the second and the third arguments are pointers to the head of the queue and the tail of the queue respectively. To ensure that the *qm* is invoked with an empty queue, these two pointers must be the same variable in the first invocation. For example, the situation where there are two user processes accessing the queue manager is described as follows.

user1(X), user2(Y), merge(X?,Y?,Z), qm(Z?,Q,Q)

user1 and *user2* are user processes sending requests to the queue. Those two request streams are merged into one stream by the object *merge* and the resulting stream is sent to the queue manager. The *merge* program is:

merge([A|Xs],Ys,[A|Zs]) ← merge(Xs?,Ys,Zs).
merge(Xs,[A|Ys],[A|Zs]) ← merge(Xs,Ys?,Zs).

The queue manager program is:

qm([dequeue(X)|S],[X|Head],Tail) ← qm(S?,Head,Tail).
qm([enqueue(X)|S],Head,[X|Tail]) ← qm(S?,Head,Tail).

On receiving a *dequeue(X)* message, it instantiates X to the top element of the queue. On receiving *enqueue(X)* message, it inserts X at the end of the queue. The behavior of *qm* is quite interesting when the queue is empty and the queue manager receives a *dequeue(X)* message. It never returns a negative response to the sender of the message. It only unifies the variable X with a variable which is located at the top of the queue. This variable will be instantiated to a queue element sometime in the future, when the *qm* will receive an *enqueue* message. After the unification, *qm* tries to serve the next request from the input stream. The point is that the interaction between the *qm* and the sender of a *dequeue* message is completed at the moment of the unification. The sender will not need to send another messages to *qm* whether X is instantiated or not, and *qm* will never send any additional message to the sender. The response will be conveyed indirectly by instantiating X to an enqueued element when *qm* will receive an *enqueue* message.

The behavior of the *qm* is also interesting when it receives the message *enqueue(X)* with X uninstantiated. As in the case above, it unifies the variable X with the tail element of the queue and finishes the processing of the request. The object which will send *dequeue* message in the future will receive the variable X

if the object sending *enqueue(X)* will not have instantiated X at that time as in the case above. From the point of view of the sender of a *dequeue* message, the situation is the same as in the above example, and it will have to wait for the value of X when it will need to refer to it. The situation can be seen as the object sending *enqueue(X)* reserves the place to which it will really enqueue something only later (Figure 29.6).

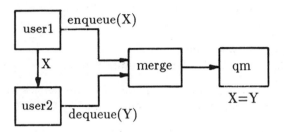

Figure 29.6: The queue manager

From these observations, it is clear that the behavior of the object *qm* is only to connect logically the arguments of *dequeue* and *enqueue* messages, in their arrival order, and real information is sent from the enqueueing object to the dequeueing object directly. However the important point here is that this logical connection cannot be seen by the users of *qm*. All they can see is the *qm* object. This reduces the overhead on the resource manager because the manager will never be locked and requests will never be refused. Using incomplete messages, we can create dynamically a new information path, which is hidden from the objects taking part in the message passing. This cannot be expressed in other object-oriented languages as simply as in Concurrent Prolog. This use of incomplete messages reduces message exchanging overhead and gives great expressive power to Concurrent Prolog.

29.4.2 Constraints

A constraint specifies a dependency relation among properties of objects. It is associated with procedures for satisfying it and can determine properties of objects if enough information about other properties of the objects are determined. There is no static input and output relation among the properties of objects; rather, which property is input and which is output is determined dynamically, in an indeterminate way.

For example, the constraint *plus(X,Y,Z)* specifies the relation,

$$X + Y = Z$$

where X, Y and Z are properties of some objects. Because the degree of freedom of this relation is two, it can find the value of an unknown property when two of the arguments are determined.

plus(2,3,Z) → instantiate Z to 5.
plus(2,Y,5) → instantiate Y to 3.
plus(X,3,5) → instantiate X to 2.

A constraint becomes active only when a sufficient number of its arguments are determined. Otherwise it is suspended.

plus(X,3,Z) → suspended
plus(X,3,5) → active and instantiates X to 2.

Constraints can form a dependency network over properties of objects. In the case of the *plus* constraints, it can represent simple equation systems, like:

plus(X,A,5)   X + A = 5
    &
plus(Y,1,X) $\implies$ Y + 1 = X
    &
plus(Y,5,Z)   Y + 5 = Z

In this network, each *plus* node plays the role of propagating values of properties of objects. For example, if the network receives *1* for *A*, it instantiates *X*, *Y*, *Z* to *4*, *3*, *8* respectively, and if it receives *4* for *X*, it instantiates *A*, *Y*, *Z* to *1*, *3*, *8* respectively, and so on.

Generally the representation of a constraint consists of methods to satisfy the relation. The constraint *plus* is defined in Concurrent Prolog simply as shown in Program 29.9.

plus(X,Y,Z) ← known(X), known(Y) | Z := X+Y.
plus(X,Y,Z) ← known(Y), known(Z) | X := Z–Y.
plus(X,Y,Z) ← known(Z), known(X) | Y := Z–X.

Program 29.9: A *plus* constraint

"$X := Y$" is a system predicate that evaluates an arithmetic expression Y and unifies the result with X. This definition shows that indeterminate computation is realized by Or-parallelism, and that the activation of a constraint is specified by *known* predicates in guards. A dependency network of constraints can be formed by And-parallel processes with shared variables. For example, the equation system above is represented as follows.

plus(X,A,5), plus(Y,1,X), plus(Y,5,Z)

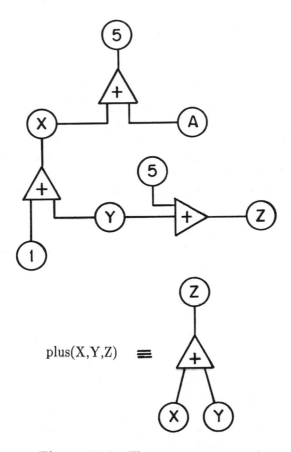

Figure 29.7: The constraint network

The behavior of this network is —

    Initially: All constraints are suspended

    A is instantiated to *1* externally
    then *plus(X,A,5)* becomes active and instantiates *X* to *4*
    then *plus(Y,1,X)* becomes active and instantiates *Y* to *3*
    then *plus(Y,5,Z)* becomes active and instantiates *Z* to *8*

    The current implementation of constraints does not treat the methods to update values of properties because logical variables are single assignment and can never be rewritten, and the dependency network cannot find the solution, even if there exists a unique solution, when the network contains some circular dependency, for example $plus(X,Y,5),plus(X,1,Y)$.

29.5 Conclusion

When designing a logic programming language, one tries to find a control regime over logic programs that achieves a desired behavior. One is constrained by the requirements that any result of the computation must be a logical consequence of the axioms in the program, and that the control regime is both expressive and simple, to make the efficient implementation of algorithms in the language possible without inducing too much runtime overhead. Sequential Prolog (side-effects excluded) is an example of such a logic programming language, designed to run efficiently on a von Neumann machine. Concurrent Prolog is another example.

Having these constraints in mind, we did not have much freedom in choosing the target programming style when designing Concurrent Prolog. Hence it was an experimental finding, almost a surprise, that Concurrent Prolog lends itself most naturally to a very specific concurrent programming style, namely object-oriented programming. This paper has attempted to convey this finding via programming examples.

These examples show that the basic operations of object-oriented programming languages — creating an object, sending and receiving messages among objects, modifying an object's state, and forming class-superclass hierarchies — all correspond naturally to Concurrent Prolog programming techniques, rather than to specialized programming language constructs. We believe that showing that a programming technique in one language subsumes specialized constructs in another language is among the strongest types of evidence for the expressive power of a programming language.

In addition, we have presented a new object-oriented programming paradigm, unique to concurrent logic programming language, called incomplete messages. This technique subsumes stream communication, and greatly simplifies the complexity of communication networks and the communication overhead usually associated with managing shared resources.

In this paper we have only provided a glimpse of the potential of Concurrent Prolog in implementing constraint systems. The ability to determine dynamically the inputs and outputs of an object seems to be an invaluable asset for this task.

Acknowledgements

We thank Dan Ingalls for suggesting the problem of implementing a multi-window system as a generic object-oriented programming problem.

We would also especially like to thank Kazuhiro Fuchi, Director of ICOT Research Center, Koichi Furukawa, Chief of second research laboratory of ICOT Research Center, and all the other members of ICOT, both for help with this research and for providing a stimulating place in which to work.

Part of this research was carried while Ehud Shapiro was visiting ICOT, the Institute for New Generation Computer Technology.

Chapter 30

Vulcan: Logical Concurrent Objects

Kenneth Kahn, Eric Dean Tribble, Mark S. Miller
and Daniel G. Bobrow
Xerox Palo Alto Research Center

Abstract

Concurrent logic programming languages support object-oriented programming with a clean semantics and additional programming constructs such as incomplete messages, unification, direct broadcasting, and concurrency synchronization (Shapiro and Takeuchi, Chapter 29). While they provide excellent computational support, we claim they do not provide good notation for expressing the abstractions of object-oriented programming. We describe a higher-level language, Vulcan, that remedies this problem. Vulcan is then used as a vehicle for exploring new variants of object-oriented programming which become possible in this framework.

30.1 Introduction

The concurrent logic programming languages cleanly build objects with changeable state out of purely side-effect-free foundations. As in physics, a causal chain of events with enough coherence over time can be viewed as an object with state.

The resulting system has all the fine-grained concurrency, synchronization, encapsulation, and open-systems abilities of Actors (Hewitt, 1973). In addition, it provides unification, logic variables, partially instantiated messages and data, and the declarative semantics of first-order logic.

Abstract machines and corresponding concrete implementations support the computational model of these languages, providing cheap, light-weight processes, fast unification, and parallel architectures. The implementations provide the equivalent of tail recursion optimization, so objects built on these foundations have the same complexity measure as objects implemented directly.

Since objects with state are not taken as a base concept, but are built out of finer-grained material, many variations on traditional notions of object-oriented programming are possible. These include object forking and merging, direct broadcasting, message stream peeking, prioritized message sending, and multiple message streams per object.

In exploring these issues, we found that the implementation of objects was extremely verbose and fraught with sensitivity to small mistakes. We remedy this by creating a higher-level language with a syntax which succinctly captures the cliches used for object-oriented programming in concurrent logic programming languages. We call the resulting language "Vulcan" because Vulcan is a fictional place characterized by a community of Actors behaving logically.

30.2 Support for a Programming Style

Object-oriented programming is a programming style in which operations are grouped together with structured objects. Descriptions of operations and structure are collected together in classes which share operations and structural descriptions with their super-classes. The support a programming system gives to a programming paradigm includes linguistic, semantic, execution, and environmental support.

30.2.1 Linguistic support

The linguistic expression of a program should correspond well with the intentions of the programmer. The system should support clear and concise expression. Common programming cliches should be supported.

As we argue in this paper, Concurrent Prolog provides very poor linguistic support for object-oriented programming. Object-oriented programs in Concurrent Prolog are verbose and syntactically delicate. Slight deviations from the complex pattern used in writing these programs produces subtle bugs. One of the main purposes in building Vulcan is to overcome this shortcoming of object-oriented programming in Concurrent Prolog. Class definitions in Vulcan provide a more declarative means of defining creation and initialization methods. Common cliches such as inheritance and method specialization are supported.

30.2.2 Clear semantics

The basic constructs supporting a paradigm should have a simple clean semantics. The underlying semantics should be well-suited for both human understanding of programs and machine analysis and transformation of programs.

The semantics of object-oriented programs in Concurrent Prolog is simple and clean. The declarative semantics of Concurrent Prolog is on a sound footing (Shapiro, Chapter 2). The programs can be viewed as logical axioms and the execution viewed as controlled deduction. The semantics of perpetual processes is an active area of research and does not appear problematic. The Concurrent Prolog predicate defining a class of objects is a collection of Horn clauses which define the permissible histories an instance can have.

The operational and declarative semantics of Vulcan programs is given in terms of their translation to Concurrent Prolog. So long as this translation is straight-forward, Vulcan is able to exploit the clean semantics of Concurrent Prolog.

30.2.3 Execution support

The system must be able to execute programs in the paradigm efficiently. A programmer should not be penalized unnecessarily for programming in a good style.

Object-oriented programs perform well on sequential implementations of Concurrent Prolog. There are no side-effects in Concurrent Prolog, but due to tail-recursion optimizations, there are no performance penalties for this. The programs can be compiled so that the costs of processing messages, creating instances, and sending messages are comparable to existing object-oriented systems. The performance should be very good on parallel implementations of Concurrent Prolog.

The performance of Vulcan is comparable with Concurrent Prolog since Vulcan programs are translated directly into Concurrent Prolog. In a few places there is some extra overhead that can be avoided with simple declarations.

30.2.4 Environmental support

The system should support the debugging of programs at the level of abstraction of the programming paradigm. For example, if a system supports object-oriented programming, then the tracing, editing, and browsing of programs should be in terms of objects, methods, messages, classes, and instance variables and not the underlying implementation constructs.

The environmental support of Vulcan has yet to be developed but no fundamental obstacles are expected. Normally it is difficult to debug the execution of translated programs (e.g., debugging compiled programs) since the program being executed is so different from its source. The declarative information in the Vulcan class definitions is lacking in the Concurrent Prolog programs and is necessary for good browsing tools. Tracing can be accomplished by having Vulcan leave behind extra code in methods that saves or prints the relevant state. More relevant error messages such as "message not understood" can be produced by automatically generating for every class a final clause to catch the error. Declarative debugging systems (Shapiro, 1982) should be modifiable to provide an object-oriented view.

In summary, Concurrent Prolog does well in providing semantic and execution support for object-oriented programming and Vulcan builds upon Concurrent Prolog in a way that preserves those capabilities. Concurrent Prolog does *not* provide good linguistic or environmental support, while Vulcan was designed to alleviate these shortcomings.

30.3 Object-Oriented Programming

Most attempts to integrate object-oriented programming with logic have ignored some very important properties. The first is that objects have encapsulated, changeable state. Changeable state conflicts with the declarative semantics of logic programming languages. This conflict is sometimes resolved by making each change of state create a new object with the updated state. This approach does not support sharing of objects with state.

Encapsulation is the property that linearizes the development curve of large object-oriented applications. Without it, large programs develop many more hidden dependencies because module boundaries are violated. The ability to define the protocol of an object independent of its implementation removes much mental overhead.

When addressing parallelism, encapsulation takes on new facets. Without a known controlled interface, conceptualizing the activity of a truly concurrent system rapidly overwhelms the programmer. With specific protocols protecting the state of a program, the relations between concurrent processes can be established. This leads to the final important property: the ability to synchronize asynchronous state changes and accesses. Fortunately, all this can be expressed in a system that retains the formal power of logic programming.

Hewitt (1985) correctly points out that Prolog is poorly suited for supporting concurrent changes in shared state. Concurrent Prolog, on the other hand, does support this well. Consider a bank system where there are several users of a bank account. If there is only $10 in the account, and both users try to withdraw $10, only one will succeed. The situation is inherently a non-deterministic race. The response of the bank account to any one user will be not only a function of that user's input, but also of its own internal state which is subject to modification as a result of interaction with the other users. A capable system has to be able to deal with this, even when the number and identity of the users change as the system runs.

30.4 Object-Oriented Programming in Concurrent Prolog

Shapiro and Takeuchi (Chapter 29) present Concurrent Prolog and a set of programming cliches for programming in an object-oriented style. Here we summarize their findings and in the following sections evaluate and extend their work. We use Concurrent Prolog since it is a typical example of a concurrent logic programming language. Most of the ideas presented apply equally well to other concurrent logic programming languages (GHC, PARLOG, etc.).

The ephemeral processes of Concurrent Prolog hardly possess the permanence and identity of objects. We can associate the identity of an object in the execution of a Concurrent Prolog program with a communication channel carrying messages for consumption by an ephemeral process. A sender of a message uses a communication channel to send a message and a new communication channel. When the process receives a message, it reduces to other processes. For object-like behavior, one of the processes has the same functor as the original and attempts to read more messages from the new communication channel. This process is often called the tail-recursive process because it is recursive and can be optimized in a manner similar to functional tail-recursion optimization. Concurrent Prolog programs written in this cliche represent state changes by incarnating the tail-recursive process with the new state instead of the old. Such continually reincarnated processes are called *perpetual processes*. The communication channels passed along from process to process provides the identity of a perpetual process.

The communication channels of Concurrent Prolog are simply shared logical variables. Since logical variables cannot be reset once they are set (instantiated), a communication variable is instantiated to a pair of the message transmitted and a new logical variable for further messages. A process waiting for a message suspends on the communication variable (via read-only annotations) until it becomes instantiated to such a pair, then executes the method appropriate to the first element of the pair. Once the pair contains a message, the new variable (second in the pair) must be used for further communication because the message part cannot be reset. This write-once property requires the recursive process creation scheme described above. Furthermore, multiple suppliers cannot put messages onto the same stream without special provisions because one process would instantiate the message before the second. The second process would fail attempting to unify its message and the first message. This problem will be dealt with later.

Since a communication channel identifies an object, the logic variable representing the channel is often treated and referred to as the pointer to the object. This engenders our variable naming convention: we name channel variables for the kind of process interpreting the message stream. We add the prefix 'New' to the name of the variable representing the future messages to an object (typically the variable used in the recursive call). Whenever examples include two different variables with the same name, numbers will be appended to their names to distinguish them.

Consider the example Concurrent Prolog Program 30.1. It implements a simple bank account defined to respond to the messages *deposit*, *withdraw*, and *balance*.

account([deposit(Amount) | NewAccount], Balance, Name, ...) →
    /* *Increase the balance by Amount* */
    NewBalance := Balance + Amount,
    account(NewAccount?, NewBalance?, Name, ...).
account([balance(Balance) | NewAccount], Balance, Name, ...) →
    account(NewAccount?, Balance, Name, ...).
account([withdraw(Amount) | NewAccount], Balance, Name, ...) →
    /* *Subtract Amount from the balance unless the balance is too low.* */
    Balance ≥ Amount |
    NewBalance := Balance – Amount,
    account(NewAccount?, NewBalance?, Name, ...).
account([withdraw(Amount) | NewAccount], Balance, Name, ...) →
    /* *Leave balance untouched and report attempt to overdraw* */
    Balance < Amount |
    reportOverdrawn(Name, Balance, Amount, ...),
    account(NewAccount?, Balance, Name, ...).

Program 30.1: A bank account in Concurrent Prolog

The *deposit* clause increases the *Balance* by the given amount. The second clause simply instantiates the argument to the current *Balance*. The third clause can only commit if the account contains at least *Amount* in it. Otherwise the fourth clause reports the attempt to overdraw the account. The first two clauses each correspond to a method in an object-oriented programming system. The third and fourth clauses together correspond to a single method. All the clauses have the same arguments. The first represents the input message stream. When the message stream of an *account* instantiates, it attempts unification with the first argument from each clause. Since all methods have the form [*MessagePattern*

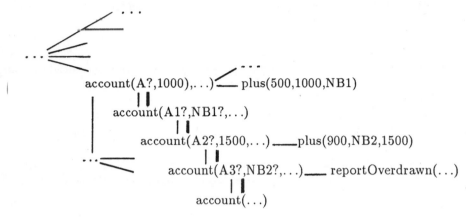

Figure 30.1: A part of the process spawning tree. We identify the path indicated by bold lines with a particular bank account

| *Variable*], the actual *MessagePattern* determines which clause will successfully unify, so the message dispatches properly. *MessagePattern* can be any logical term and may include variables. Often those variables get used to return values, as in the *balance* clause.

> account(A?,1000, ...),
> A = [deposit(500), balance(B), withdraw(800) | NewAccount].

The *account* process immediately suspends if it tries to run. The second process runs, instantiating *A* to [*deposit(500), balance(B), withdraw(800) | NewAccount*]. Now the first process proceeds, unifying [*deposit(500), ...*] with the first argument of the first clause (none of the others can succeed). It reduces, leaving the following processes:

> plus(1000,500,NewBalance1),
> account([balance(B), withdraw(800) | NewAccount],NewBalance1?, ...).

Taking the most pathological route, assume that *account* keeps being reduced. The balance message drops out immediately. It succeeds, and the argument will be instantiated when the *plus* process completes. If any concurrent operation attempts to use the value of that variable, it will suspend because the variable is read-only. Such is the case with the *withdraw* message. It unifies with the correct clause, but the guard tries to compare an uninstantiated variable with a number, so the comparison suspends. The *account* process that looks at *NewAccount* also suspends. Therefore the *plus* process will run since it is the only remaining active process. It computes the new balance. The process doing the withdrawal compares that balance to discover that the withdrawal is legal, and so finally withdraws the money.

This sequence of reductions demonstrates the pipelining ability and the power of the simple read-only annotations.

The declarative semantics of a perpetual process is peculiar. Each clause can be read declaratively as stating constraints on possible histories of messages and the corresponding state. The first clause of *account*, for example, can be read as "a history of messages beginning with one matching *deposit(Amount)* is a valid balance history if the remainder of the history is valid in the state where the *Balance* is the sum of the previous balance and the *Amount*".

This peculiar declarative semantics can be a useful basis of a debugger which keeps a pointer to the history of messages and provides a convenient way to browse the message history.

30.4.1 Special features of Concurrent Prolog objects

Shapiro and Takeuchi claim that Concurrent Prolog realizes objects in the sense of Hewitt's Actor model (Clinger, 1981). Concurrent Prolog objects have internal state, can be operated upon only by message sending, and can exchange arbitrary messages. Any number of instances can be created from a definition of an object. Unlike Smalltalk, Flavors, Loops and the like, Concurrent Prolog objects are not based upon call/return message passing. Concurrent Prolog objects have the full control generality of Actors. Call/return is just a particular pattern of message passing (Hewitt, 1977).

In addition to the full generality of actors, Concurrent Prolog objects have special features not found in other object-oriented programming systems. The streams and processes of Concurrent Prolog are side-effect free. Perpetual processes seem to change because a process terminates and causes a similar but different one to be created. This lack of side-effects leads to a simpler, clearer declarative semantics. The explicit manipulation of streams is more flexible than the system-supported message queues of actor systems (Clinger, 1981). Several objects can share a stream of messages, enabling direct broadcasting. A stream can be held onto to provide a message history to inspect. A stream of incoming messages is available for peeking ahead. A perpetual process can read from multiple streams, differing in capability or priority.

30.4.2 Concurrency

The underlying model and motivation for Concurrent Prolog is based upon large-scale concurrency and simple, yet adequate, synchronization primitives. Concurrent Prolog defaults to concurrency. It achieves sequencing and synchronization with the commit operator and read-only annotations. Shapiro (Chapter

2) has shown Concurrent Prolog to be adequate for solving classical synchronization problems like multiple readers and writers and addressing issues like starvation, fairness, and deadlock. Unification and commit are atomic transactions.

Unlike Smalltalk and similar languages, Concurrent Prolog objects are *active*. They can execute continually, though by convention they normally suspend when there are no messages to process. Like serialized actors, Concurrent Prolog objects process messages one at a time, though unlike serialized actors the typical Concurrent Prolog object processes messages in a pipeline fashion. The body of the clauses for an object by convention creates a new process to receive subsequent messages. This process is normally spawned concurrently with some of the method computation. Consider the first clause of *account*.

> account([deposit(Amount) | NewAccount], Balance, Name, . . .) ←
> NewBalance := Balance + Amount,
> account(NewAccount?, NewBalance?, Name, . . .).

When a *deposit* message is in the front of the stream of incoming messages, this clause commits and spawns a process to add *Amount* to *Balance* and a process to receive more messages. If the new *account* process receives a message before the *plus* process has terminated, then the *Balance* will be the uninstantiated variable *NewBalance*. Since *NewBalance* is read-only, it can only be instantiated by the *plus* operation that runs concurrently with the recursive call. When another process actually tries to use *NewBalance*, it will suspend until *plus* finishes. This resembles futures in actor systems (Baker and Hewitt, 1977).

30.4.3 Logic variables

The usefulness of the logic variable has been repeatedly demonstrated in both Prolog and Concurrent Prolog programming. Unbound variables in logic programming are "first class objects" in that they can be passed around and embedded in structures. In object-oriented programming in Concurrent Prolog, this is frequently exploited by a technique called *incomplete messages*. Messages are sent which contain variables and typically the recipient binds those variables. This is the most common way of sending a message and getting a reply. The second clause of account is an example of this.

> account([balance(Balance) | NewAccount], Balance, Name, . . .) ←
> account(NewAccount?, Balance, Name, . . .).

The sender of a *balance* message requests the current *Balance* of an object. Unlike call/return message sending, the sender does not wait for a reply. Frequently the users of the response from an incomplete message have read-only annotations to prevent those parts of the computation from using the uninstantiated variables of the response before the recipient fills them in.

Another use of logic variables in Concurrent Prolog objects is to leave some state variables uninstantiated. We saw how this could occur naturally in the pipeline style of message processing. It is also possible to create objects with parts left uninstantiated. The following processes create an *account* with an unknown *Balance* and use a *balance* message to initialize it to 300.

    account(A?, X, joe, ...),
    A=[balance(300) | A1].

This technique may be useful in creating objects which need complex initialization.

30.4.4 Verbosity

The major shortcoming of object-oriented programming in Concurrent Prolog is its verbosity. Each method must at the very least repeat the names of the state variables in both the head of the method and in the tail recursive call. Each method must explicitly fetch the next method from the stream and then recur on the stream of remaining messages. Such tedious repetition easily results in subtle mistakes. The tail-recursive call requires a read-only annotation on the stream of remaining messages, for example. Without it, the process does not suspend, so unification non-deterministically applies a clause (anything unifies with a variable), setting the first element of the stream to the message for that clause, then executing its body. Logically, we queried, "What sequence of messages could objects of this class have, starting from the current state, and what would be the new state?" Later message sends to the object would likely fail because they would try to unify different message terms. All this from leaving out one question mark!

Shapiro and Takeuchi (Chapter 29) address the inconvenient necessity of repeating the state variables by packaging up the entire state into a single term and using special predicates to access or create modified versions. Consider the differences between the following two ways of writing a move method for a window.

```
/* Version with multiple state variables */
window([move(NewX,NewY)|NewWindow],X,Y,Width,Height,Contents) ←
    eraseRegion(X,Y,Width,Height) |
    window([show|NewWindow],NewX,NewY,Width,Height,Contents).
/* Version with one state variable */
window([move(NewX,NewY)|NewWindow],State) ←
    eraseRegion(State),
    setWindowState(xy,NewX,NewY,State,NewState) |
    window([show|NewWindow],NewState).

/* the relevant part of the definition of setWindowState */
setWindowState(xy,NewX,NewY,windowState(X,Y,Width,Height,Contents),
```

windowState(NewX,NewY,Width,Height,Contents)).

Without sophisticated compile-time optimizations, packaging requires significantly more time and space. Also, *setWindowState* and *getWindowState* clauses must be defined for each collection of state variables.

30.5 A Higher-Level Language Solution

The verbosity of object-oriented programming in Concurrent Prolog can be avoided by using a higher level language that translates into Concurrent Prolog. The language discussed here is called Vulcan. Its exact syntax is covered in Appendix 30.1. Vulcan provides concise expressions for the Concurrent Prolog programming cliches. Vulcan programs are defined in terms of classes and methods. For example,

class(window,[X,Y,Width,Height,Contents]).

declares that all windows have five instance variables (*X*, *Y*, ...). A message can be sent to an instance using the syntax *Awindow : Message*. It also allows the following syntax within a method to create a window instance

window : make([X,Y,Width,Height,Contents],Window)

Method definitions use the class declarations to expand into operations invoked by particular messages to the object. A method for getting the position of a window can be defined as

window :: position(X,Y).

Vulcan recognizes references to the variables declared in the class, and generates code appropriately. The obvious expansion shown below directly unifies the arguments of the message with the appropriate state variables, just as the Vulcan code indicated.

window([position(X,Y)|NewWindow],X,Y,Width,Height,Contents) ←
     window(NewWindow?,X,Y,Width,Height,Contents).

Since *position* has no body to expand, the clause just contains the head and the tail-recursive call. The preprocessor would actually generate unique names for variables rather than names like *NewWindow* that might conflict with programmer defined variables. These examples use the simpler names for readability.

Vulcan introduces the *new* operator rather than a kind of assignment statement because in a relational language, the assignment could apply to any argument. As an example exploiting the generality of the *new* operator, consider a rectangle defined as follows:

   class(rectangle, [Length, Width, LowerLeft]).

We can define a method to adjust its upper right corner, using the *gridDistance* method defined for points in the appendix as follows:

   rectangle :: moveUpperRight(ToPoint) →
     LowerLeft : gridDistance(ToPoint, new Length, new Width).

which expands to:

rectangle([moveUpperRight(ToPoint) | NewRectangle],
  Length
  Width,
  [gridDistance(ToPoint, NewLength, NewWidth) | NewLowerLeft]) →
    rectangle(NewRectangle, NewLength?, NewWidth?, NewLowerLeft).

Vulcan permits the use of the infix operator *is* for expressing arithmetic. This is similar to the *is* of Prolog and the ":=" of Concurrent Prolog. It expands to calls to the appropriate arithmetic predicates. It can be used in conjunction with the *new* operator. Consider the following method for moving a window:

   window :: moveBy(DeltaX,DeltaY) →
     new X is X + DeltaX,
     new Y is Y + DeltaY.

It expands to:

window([moveBy(DeltaX,DeltaY) | NewWindow], X,Y,Width,Height,Contents) →
  plus(X,DeltaX, Result1),
  plus(Y, DeltaY, Result2),
  window(NewWindow?, Result1?, Result2?, Width,Height,Contents).

30.5.1 Message sending

  The body of a method can be thought of as a collection of requests to queue messages to objects. The queuing is concurrent, except that messages to the same object reference (same variable name) are queued in the order that they appear within the method. Communication channels are purely asynchronous, so only the order of messages on a particular stream is preserved. Messages transmitted on different streams are not synchronized at all.

  Within the execution of a method, the pseudo-variable *Self* refers to the object that received the message. Methods can treat *Self* just like any other pointer except that a message to *Self* could reference or change any state variable. These changes must be reflected to other references within the method, so the order of *send-Self requests* and state changes must be maintained. The ordering mechanism supplied by Concurrent Prolog is message sending, so state

variable references translate to (private) messages whenever they might conflict
with normal sends to *Self*. Messages to *Self* are actually implemented by pre-
setting the tail-recursive call with the messages to be interpreted before messages
already on the stream. Adding erasure and redisplay of the window to the above
definition of *moveBy* exemplifies these principles:

> window :: moveBy(DeltaX, DeltaY) →
>   Self : erase,
>   new X is X + DeltaX,
>   new Y is Y + DeltaY.
>   Self : show.

translates to:

> window([moveBy(DeltaX,DeltaY) | NewWindow],
>   X,Y,Width,Height,Contents) ←
>   X2 := X1 + DeltaX,
>   Y2 := Y1 + DeltaY,
>   window([erase, getX(X1), getY(Y1), setX(X2?), setY(Y2?), show |
>   NewWindow?], X,Y,Width,Height,Contents).

The get messages are necessary because the erase message might change the value
of X or Y; the set messages because show might need to use the new values of
X and Y. This technique can be optimized in several ways. For common set/get
combinations, a single message could retrieve and change more than one variable.
For variable references before any send to *Self*, the new values can be recurred
on normally without sending any messages for them.

30.5.2 Intricacies of message sending

In most object-oriented systems, mutable and immutable objects are programmed in a uniform manner. To get the first element of a list, one sends the
list the same message independent of whether it is immutable or not. Concurrent Prolog preserves this interchangeability and code-sharing between different
implementations of an object when computing with perpetual processes.

Logical terms, however, are not interchangeable with streams to perpetual
processes. Logical terms are created and accessed by unification. They are much
simpler and more efficient than Concurrent Prolog mutable objects. Logical terms
can be incrementally filled in since they can contain logical variables to be instantiated later. Terms cannot, however, be the basis of object-oriented programming
since they are immutable. A term can represent a window of a particular size and
location but cannot continue to represent that window as it moves and grows.
For uniformity, message sending must be extended to work with terms.

We have been sending messages to objects in Concurrent Prolog by simply open-coding a unification of the message stream with the message and a new tail. In order to generalize message sending to apply to terms as well, we introduce a send predicate:

> send([Message | NewObject], Message, NewObject).

A call to *send*

> send(Window, move(3,42), NewWindow)

is equivalent to

> Window = [move(3,42) | NewWindow].

The definition must be extended to handle terms with:

> send(Term, Message, Term) ←
> otherwise |
> sendToTerm(Term, Message).

This relies upon the special guard literal *otherwise* of Flat Concurrent Prolog which succeeds if all lexically preceding clauses fail. Declaratively, *otherwise* operates as the conjunction of negative literals corresponding to guards and unifications of the preceding clauses. This clause will succeed if none of the earlier clauses applies.

sendToTerm actually does the requisite operations, rather than just queueing messages. Suppose we have both immutable and mutable line segments in a graphics package. Immutable line segments are terms of the form *line(StartPoint,EndPoint)* while mutable line segments are defined by:

> class(line, [StartPoint,EndPoint]).

A method for displaying mutable lines is:

> line :: display → drawLine(StartPoint, EndPoint).

Extending send in Concurrent Prolog to display immutable lines is done by:

> sendToTerm(line(StartPoint,EndPoint), display) ←
> drawLine(StartPoint,EndPoint).

The Vulcan version is:

> line(StartPoint,EndPoint) :: display → drawLine(StartPoint,EndPoint).

Thus, the same syntax defines methods for both mutable objects and immutable terms.

Terms can be used anywhere objects are used. Unfortunately, Concurrent Prolog objects cannot be used where terms are used. Unification of Concurrent

Prolog objects is problematic since there are no pointers to the objects. Unification between streams to Concurrent Prolog objects simply constrains the streams to have the same messages. Also, low-level primitives for arithmetic and the like deal only with terms.

30.5.3 Class inheritance

Vulcan can implement inheritance in at least two ways. The first is the description copying semantics corresponding to subclassing. The second is inheritance by delegation to parts.

For subclassing, class declarations include the superclasses as the third argument. The subclass is then created with source copies of all methods and instance variables inherited from its superclasses. The superclasses field can be a single class or a list of classes for multiple inheritance.

> class(labeledWindow, [Label], window).

makes the preprocessor expand all window methods with respect to *labeledWindow*. Below, the source from the *moveBy* method of window is copied to *labeledWindow*:

> labeledWindow :: moveBy(DeltaX,DeltaY) →
>   Self : erase,
>   new X is X + DeltaX,
>   new Y is Y + DeltaY,
>   Self : show.

expands to:

> labeledWindow([moveBy(DeltaX,DeltaY) | NewLabeledWindow],
>   X,Y,Width,Height,Contents) ←
> plus(X1, DeltaX, X2),
> plus(Y1, DeltaY, Y2),
> labeledWindow([erase, getX(X1), getY(Y1),
>   setX(X2?), setY(Y2?), show | NewLabeledWindow?],
>   X,Y,Width,Height,Contents).

If the programmer defines a new *moveBy* method for *labeledWindow*, it overrides the automatically generated one. As in Smalltalk, an overriding method can access the inherited version. *Super : Message* tells the translator to expand the inherited method definition inline. (When the message matches more than a single method, the relevant methods can be copied with a unique predicate name, and a call to that predicate substituted inline.) The *show* message from *moveBy* is a good example of the use of *send super*. It must show the label, then do whatever windows do to show their contents. The *show* definitions for the two classes:

> window :: show →
>   Contents : displayAt(X,Y).
>
> labeledWindow :: show →
>   Super : show,
>   Self : displayLabel.

combine for *labeledWindow* to give:

> labeledWindow :: show →
>   Contents : displayAt(X,Y),
>   Self : displayLabel.

which expands to:

> labeledWindow([show | NewLabeledWindow],
>   X,Y,Width,Height,Contents,Label) ←
>   send(Contents, displayAt(X,Y), NewContents),
>   labeledWindow([displayLabel | NewLabeledWindow?],
>   X,Y,Width,Height,NewContents?,Label).

30.5.4 Inheritance by delegation to parts

Shapiro and Takeuchi achieve the sharing of methods and structure common in systems with class inheritance by using delegation to parts. A *labeledWindow* contains a window as a part, rather than being a kind of window. For delegation, the definition of *labeledWindows* is:

> class(labeledWindow, [Window, Label]).

A message not defined for labeledWindows is *delegated* to the contained window (referenced through a state variable) with a method of the form:

> labeledWindow([Message | NewLabeledWindow], Window, Label) ←
>   otherwise | /* *no earlier methods were applicable* */
>   send(Window, Message, NewWindow),
>   labeledWindow(NewLabeledWindow?, NewWindow?, Label).

This is the same as simply sending the same message to the contained window. The execution of *moveBy*, for example, would only erase and redraw the window, not the label (as discussed by Bobrow, 1985). Since the *labeledWindow* is conceptually executing the method, the message to *Self* should be sent to it, not just to the window. Separating the reference to *Self* from specific objects in the delegation solves this problem. It requires that a stream representing *Self* be passed in the delegation message (Snyder, 1986; Lieberman, 1986). The new default method is:

labeledWindow([Message | NewLabeledWindow], Window, Label) ←
   otherwise | /* no earlier methods were applicable */
   send(Window, handle(Message, Self, NewLabeledWindow), NewWindow),
   labeledWindow(Self?, NewWindow?, Label).

Normally, the *labeledWindow* would recur on *NewLabeledWindow*. Here, it recurs on *Self* so that any messages to *Self* in the delegation will arrive before those sent externally (just as in send to *Self*). The handle method must eventually make *NewLabeledWindow* a tail of *Self* (*Self* = [*Msg1,Msg2,...* | *NewLabeledWindow*]).

   The delegation equivalent of send to *Super* explicitly delegates a message. The delegation version of the *show* method for *labeledWindow* is just:

     labeledWindow :: show →
       delegateTo(Window, show),
       Self : displayLabel.

This translates to:

labeledWindow([show | NewLabeledWindow], Window, Label) ←
   send(Window, handle(show, Self, [displayLabel | NewLabeledWindow]),
     NewWindow),
   labeledWindow(Self?, NewWindow?, Label).

Sending a message to an object to handle an embedded message for itself is equivalent to sending the embedded message to the object but it entails the overhead of the indirection (Snyder, 1986). Instead of implementing send as delegation, we translate each Vulcan method into two clauses: one for handling normal messages and another for handling delegation messages.

   Properly demonstrating that the Concurrent Prolog code described above actually supports reentrant, state changing delegation involves quite long and complicated examples, and so lies beyond the scope of this paper. Classical inheritance and delegation are compatible, allowing selection of an inheritance scheme suited to the problem.

30.5.5 Variations on the notion of an object

   The streams consumed by perpetual processes are ordinary Concurrent Prolog terms. As such it is possible for several perpetual processes to be consuming the same stream. When a message is put on the stream, it is directly broadcast to all the objects sharing that stream. To be able to send to both individuals and groups, the stream being consumed can be split into a shared broadcasting stream and a private stream. The following clause for making windows maintains the shared stream called *Ether*.

makeWindow(InitValues, Ether, PrivateNewObject) ←
    make(window, InitValues, NewObject),
    merge(PrivateNewObject?, Ether?, NewObject).

The caller of *makeWindow* gets a private channel to the newly created object which is consuming a stream which is the merger of the *Ether* and the private channel. *InitValues* contains initial values for the state variables.

One can broadcast on the *Ether* by sending messages just like any other message sending. For example,

    send(Ether, redisplay, NewEther)

will cause all windows to redisplay themselves. If the message is incomplete, for example,

    send(Ether, positions(Positions), NewEther)

then one can arrange to get the bag of responses by using "open-ended" lists. Open-ended lists are lists whose last tail is always an uninstantiated variable. If one is interested in just the first answer, then one waits for just the head of the list. If one is interested all the elements, the short-circuit technique of Takeuchi (1983) described by Shapiro and Safra (Chapter 15) can be used to tell when they are all present.

A useful ability that few object-oriented systems support is the ability of an object to change its class. This is straightforward in Vulcan. Consider a rectangle class which changes its instances to instances of square when the length and width are equal.

    rectangle :: setWidth(Length) →
      square : make([Length], new Self).

expands to

    rectangle([setWidth(Length) | NewRectangle], Length, Width) ←
      square(NewRectangle?, Length).

Various object-oriented programming systems support features such as meta-classes and method combination (Bobrow, 1986). These features can be incorporated into the Vulcan framework. Given some support for naming of processes (e.g., the module feature of Logix, Silverman et al., Chapter 21), it is possible to support classes as objects. If the Vulcan preprocessor itself was built in an object-oriented fashion, then different meta-classes could process class and method specifications differently. Method combination is normally implemented as a define-time process. The Vulcan preprocessor could be extended to combine pieces of methods and expand the combinations into ordinary Concurrent Prolog clauses.

There are some unique capabilities of objects in Concurrent Prolog because the communication channels are explicit. A method can, for example, peek ahead in the message stream to see if some particular message is pending. The following method does nothing if there is an undo message of the same sort pending. The example is inspired by the time warp system for discrete simulations (Jefferson, 1982). Since Vulcan does not support some experimental extensions yet, the examples have a bit of Concurrent Prolog flavor.

```
timeWarpObject :: do(X) →
    pendingMessage(undo(X), Self) |
    true.
timeWarpObject :: do(X) →
    otherwise |
    <do large computation and save old state>
```

where *pendingMessage* is defined as

```
pendingMessage(Message, Stream) ←
    unknown(Stream) | false.
pendingMessage(Message, Stream) ←
    Stream? = [Message|Msgs] | true.
pendingMessage(Message, Stream) ←
    Stream? = [OtherMessage|Msgs],
    Message ≠ OtherMessage | pendingMessage(Message, Msgs).
```

Since message channels are just terms, an object can have more than one. The messages responded to on the streams can be different, leading to capability streams, private streams, etc.

The objects of Concurrent Prolog are really sequences of process reductions that we choose to view as an object with identity and permanence. By convention, a process representing an object reduces to a collection of processes one of which has the same predicate and the same state variable values unless they have been explicitly changed. It is worthwhile exploring the usefulness of occasionally breaking this convention. An object can become several objects which perhaps share some state or channels.

30.6 Comparisons with Other Work

There have been several approaches to combining the logic programming and object programming paradigms. Components of the logic programming paradigm are: terms, clauses, goals, logic variables, unification, etc. Components of the object programming paradigm are: objects, classes, methods, messages, message sending, instance variables (slots, acquaintances), object references, continuations, inheritance, etc. The different approaches to combining these paradigms can be roughly categorized according to how they draw correspondences between their respective components.

A straightforward way to embed objects in Prolog is for an object to consist of a set of unit-clauses asserted in the database. Consider:

```
name(sym0003,bob).
species(sym0003,human).
age(sym0003,24).
mother(sym0003,sym0002).
parent(X,Y) ← mother(X,Y).
parent(X,Y) ← father(X,Y).
```

In object-oriented terminology, *sym0003* is an object reference to an object with instance variables *name*, *age*, etc., and that responds to the message *parent*. Each unit clause stating a property of such an identifier serves as the storage for an instance variable of that object. In this framework, the user makes no distinction between stored and computed values, i.e., between instance variables and methods. It is also natural in this scheme to have methods defined on individuals, or on classes whose membership is based on some computed quality (e.g., all humans with a parent named fred). The approach taken by Gullichsen (1985) is essentially similar to this.

There are disadvantages to this approach. One is its heavy reliance on the non-logical assert and retract: they must be used to change the value of instance variables, and even to create new instances (something that is pure in most other systems). Because these objects exist as assertions in the database, garbage collecting them is also hard. Also there is no encapsulation, so any program can inspect or update the state of an object without sending it a message. Distributed implementations require something like database transaction handling.

LM-Prolog (Kahn and Carlsson, 1984), CommonLog (a logic programming extension to CommonLoops (Bobrow, 1986)), Tao (Takeuchi et al., 1986), and Uniform (Kahn, 1981) directly support employing user-defined objects as terms. Unification of primitive term types like symbols and list-cells is handled primitively as in any Prolog. Unification of user-defined objects causes unification messages to be sent, so that the objects can unify according to their abstract properties. This supports the abstraction power of object-oriented languages. In contrast, standard Prologs only support unification of syntactic representations. If these user-defined objects also have changeable state (as in CommonLog, LM-Prolog, and Tao), then the declarative semantics of unification are lost. This approach does not merge the notions of changeable state and logic programming, it just allows them to co-exist uneasily.

Prolog-with-Equality (Kornfeld, 1983) represents a similar approach in which regular Prolog syntactic terms are able to serve as user defined objects. When the Prolog interpreter fails to syntactically unify terms *A* and *B*, it instead attempts to satisfy the goal *equals*(*A,B*). If this goal succeeds, then the two terms are considered to be unified, with the bindings introduced by the equality proof in effect. In this approach, the clauses defined for *equals* correspond to unify methods, and functors of terms typically correspond to classes. This approach also deals only with object-oriented abstraction, and not with changeable state.

Several people have suggested the following approach for dealing with changeable state within the logic framework: A term corresponds to the state of an object at a given moment in time. An object consists of the list of such states, representing the object's history. An object reference consists of a pointer into this list. The current state of the object is the state immediately before the currently uninstantiated tail of this list. Any state changes to the object are represented by further instantiating the object's history list. From the logic point of view, the object's state is not being changed, more of its history is being discovered. This could avoid actual search if implemented primitively. The semantics of this approach is suspect since a memory cell is being simulated by using the meta-logical *var* predicate to reveal the otherwise hidden side-effect in unification. This approach also does not support object encapsulation.

Mandala (Furukawa et al., 1984b) is perhaps most similar in approach to Vulcan. Mandala objects are also perpetual processes consuming streams, built on a concurrent logic programming language. Unlike Vulcan, all object references are indirect by name through a name server object, which binds names to streams. The individual Mandala object contains its own set of clauses, which are processed meta-interpretively when the object processes a message. This meta-interpretive set of clauses is reminiscent of Logix modules. There are as yet unresolved efficiency issues with this approach: the name server is a central bottleneck in the system, and garbage collection is hard since all objects are referred to by name. It is hoped that the interpretive overhead can be removed through partial evaluation.

30.7 Directions for future research

Although research groups in Japan, Israel, England, and other countries have been actively programming in an object-oriented style in Concurrent Prolog and related languages, there is no experience yet with using Vulcan for a serious application. This experience is necessary to evaluate the system and to discover its strengths and weaknesses.

The Vulcan language provides at least as much basic functionality as most object-oriented programming languages do. Exploring new functionality such as message stream peeking, direct broadcasting, multiple streams per object (for capabilities and perspectives), and object forking looks very exciting. Also trying to absorb the ideas of multi-methods and meta-objects of CommonLoops (Bobrow, 1986) into Vulcan may be worthwhile.

The current implementation of Vulcan automatically generates calls to split streams to achieve sharing. Our more recent work on channels (Tribble et al., Chapter 17) provides a communication mechanism in FCP which is more flexible, better suited for multiple readers and writers, and permits the expression of more concurrency than stream-based communication. We are redesigning Vulcan to exploit these capabilities of channels.

A promising avenue of research being pursued in the logic programming context is to provide language extensions by writing extended meta interpreters and use partial evaluation to remove the cost of the extra layer of interpretation. Vulcan implementation was not conceived of as an interpreter written in Concurrent Prolog, but instead as a translator to Concurrent Prolog. The meta-interpreter approach combined with partial evaluation provides a means of experimenting with variants of Vulcan without paying a performance penalty.

The expansion of Vulcan code, when read declaratively in the underlying logic programming language, is a description of the permissible history of the object's behavior. In this, the expansion of a Vulcan program resembles the actor semantics (Clinger, 1981) of an actor program. This leads to the interesting possibility that Vulcan is a good representation language for reasoning about, and proving properties of, programs with side effects. The Concurrent Prolog interpreter itself or a Concurrent Prolog partial evaluator (being sound, though incomplete, theorem provers) might serve as the proof engine.

30.8 Summary

Concurrent Prolog is a suitable base for object-oriented programming. Unadorned, it suffers some syntactic problems of awkwardness and verbosity. We have presented a design for Vulcan, a syntactic sugaring for Concurrent Prolog that remedies these problems. The result is a language in which logic programming and object-oriented programming are smoothly integrated. The language supports, in addition to the usual object-oriented constructs, concurrency, unification, and incomplete messages. This framework facilitates the exploration of variations on object-oriented programming including message stream peeking, direct broadcasting, and multiple streams.

Acknowledgements

This is a major revision of "Objects in Concurrent Logic Programming Languages" which appeared in the proceedings of the ACM Object-oriented Programming, Systems, Languages and Applications Conference, Portland, Oregon, September 1986 and is a minor revision of the paper of the same name in *Research Directions in Object-Oriented Programming*, edited by B. Shriver and P. Wegner.

The authors would like to thank Curtis Abbott, Peter Deutsch, Carl Hewitt, Stan Lanning, Ehud Shapiro, and Mark Stefik for their comments on earlier drafts.

Appendix 30.1: A User's Guide

The following is a description of Vulcan from a programmer's point of view.

<u>Syntax</u>

Following Prolog, an identifier beginning with a lower case letter is a constant. Those with an initial upper case letter are variables. In describing the syntax below, italics is used to indicate a part of a template which users are to fill in. Completely upper case italic items are to be filled in with variables, lower case with constants, and identifiers starting with a capital letter followed by some lower case letters with any kind of term.

Defining classes: Defining classes in Vulcan is not very different from most object-oriented languages.

class(*name*, [*VAR₁*, *VAR₂*, ..., *VARₙ*])

For example,

       class(point, [X, Y]).

defines a class named *point* with instance variables X and Y.

class(*name*, [*VAR₁*, *VAR₂*, ..., *VARₙ*], *superClassName*)

For example,

       class(colorPoint, [Color], point).

defines a class named *colorPoint* with instance variables X, Y and *Color*.

class(*name*, [*VAR₁*, *VAR₂*, ..., *VARₙ*],
    [*superClassName₁*, ..., *superClassNameₙ*])

For example, given

       class(movingPoint, [Velocity], point).

we can define

> **class**(movingColorPoint, [ ], [movingPoint, colorPoint]).

which defines a class named *movingColorPoint* with instance variables X, Y, *Color* and *Velocity*.

Note: We are planning to generalize variable names in class declarations to include initial values, type restrictions, documentation, etc.

Sending messages

Object : Message

The above form queues *Message* for *Object* to process sometime later. For example,

> Window3 : goTo(position(X,Y)).

Puts on the queue of *Window3* the message *goTo(position(X,Y))*.

Object : Message$_1$: Message$_2$: ... : Message$_n$

The above form queues *Message$_1$* through *Message$_n$* for *Object* in order. E.g.,

> Window3 : goTo(position(X,Y)) : display.

guarantees the *goTo(position(X,Y))* message will be processed by *Window3* before the *display* message.

Messages can be any term. A term is either a constant, a variable, or a constructed term. The general form of a constructed term is

functor(Term$_1$, Term$_2$, ..., Term$_n$)

where *functor* is any constant.

Note: Vulcan needs a convention for which parts of a message are typically input and which are output. We follow the convention that the first parts of the message are the inputs followed by the outputs. This is a common convention in logic programming.

Making instances

className : **make**([*Value$_1$*, *Value$_2$*, ..., *Value$_n$*], *NEWOBJECT*)

creates an instance of *className* and binds it to *NEWOBJECT*. The number and order of initial values should correspond to the instance variables given in the class definition.

For example,

colorPoint : make([1,4,red], Point33)

binds *Point33* to an instance of *colorPoint* with X being *1*, Y being *4*, and *Color* being red.

Defining methods: There are two forms for defining methods.

className **::** *MessagePattern*.

If an instance of *className* receives a message unifying with *MessagePattern*, then such a method may be applied. If it is the only method that is applicable, it will be applied when the instance processes the message.

For example,

point :: x(X).

defines a method for accessing the value of a point's X. It can be invoked as follows.

Point33 : x(X33)

which will bind *X33* to the current value of *Point33*'s instance variable named X.

An assignment operator *new* preceding a variable name means that the value of the variable is to be updated. This is mostly used to update instance variables as in the following example:

point :: setX(new X).

defines a method for replacing the value of a point's X.

className **::** *MessagePattern* → *Body*.

where the *Body* is a collection of sends separated by commas. If an instance of *className* processes a message that unifies with *messagePattern* then, as in the case of a bodyless method, we say that the method is *applicable*. If there is more than one applicable method, one is chosen non-deterministically. If there are no applicable methods, an error is signaled.

When a method with a body is chosen, the statements of the body are executed concurrently. Messages sent in a method may arrive in any order except for messages sent to the same variable, which arrive in the order sent. The assignment operator for these purposes is treated as a message to *Self*.

point :: moveBy(Dx, Dy) →
    new X is X+Dx,
    new Y is Y+Dy.

defines a *moveBy* method on points which increment their X and then their Y values. The implementation may execute this by concurrently performing two additions and updates.

Consider a *moveBy* method for visible points which are displayed on their Window instance variable.

visiblePoint :: moveBy(Dx, Dy) →
    Window : erasePoint(X, Y),
    new X is X+Dx,
    new Y is Y+Dy,
    Window : drawPoint(X, Y).

Because messages are sent to the same variable *Window*, the *erasePoint(X, Y)* will be received before the *drawPoint(X, Y)*. The values of X and Y will typically be different in the two messages.

The previous example could have been written as follows.

visiblePoint :: moveBy(Dx,Dy) →
    Self : erase,
    new X is X+Dx,
    new Y is Y+Dy,
    Self : draw.

visiblePoint :: erase →
    Window : erasePoint(X, Y).

visiblePoint :: draw →
    Window : drawPoint(X, Y).

A visible point receiving a *moveBy* message will then receive an *erase* and *draw* message before any other messages. The *erase* message will be processed with the old values of X and Y, while the *draw* message will have the same values as *new X* and *new Y*.

If a message is sent to a variable before its value has been computed, the transmission suspends until the variable gets a value. For example,

point : make([27,12],P1),
P1 : x(X1).

may try to execute *P1 : x(X1)* before *P1* is created. In any case *P1* will become a point and *X1* will become *27*.

Unification or Matching

The main workhorse of Vulcan is unification. Messages are unified with the message patterns of methods. The basic rules of unification are:

(1) unbound variables unify with anything (even another unbound variable) and bind to the corresponding term,

(2) a bound variable behaves identically as the term it is bound to,

(3)   two constants unify only if they are the same,

(4)   two constructed terms unify only if their functors are the same, the number of arguments of each are the same, and corresponding arguments unify

(5)   otherwise the unification fails.

Notice that it is therefore possible, and useful, to "return" answers that contain variables that are being computed concurrently.

For example,

> point :: gridDistance(AnotherPoint, HorizontalDistance,
>   VerticalDistance) →
>   AnotherPoint : x(OtherX),
>   AnotherPoint : y(OtherY),
>   HorizontalDistance is X – OtherX,
>   VerticalDistance is Y – OtherY.

The execution of the following

> Point27 : gridDistance(Point5, H,V), Total is H + V

might begin the sum before both *H* and *V* are computed.

Methods on terms

When dealing with immutable entities, it is often more convenient to implement them as terms. Terms can be thought of as concise light-weight immutable objects. Message sending is defined as with objects as

Term : Message
Term : Message$_1$: ... : Message$_n$

and methods are defined on terms with the same syntax as methods on classes.

Term :: MessagePattern.
Term :: MessagePattern → Body.

For example, a position could add with another position as follows:

> pos(X1,Y1) :: add(pos(X2, Y2), pos(XSum, YSum)) →
>   XSum is X1 + X2,
>   YSum is Y1 + Y2.

Terms corresponding to lists are denoted using the Prolog notation

[Element$_1$, Element$_2$, ..., Element$_n$]
[Element$_1$, Element$_2$, ... | Tail]

For example, a method for a list to append on the end another list can be written as

> [First | Rest] :: append(AnotherList,[First | RestOfBoth]) →
>   Rest : append(AnotherList,RestOfBoth).
>
> [ ] :: append(AnotherList,AnotherList).

Expressions

Expressions are a syntactic sugar for writing in a functional notation. They currently mean the same as ":=" in Concurrent Prolog, i.e., a macro which expands to the appropriate calls to arithmetic predicates. We are considering changing it as follows to show user extensions and have a message sending semantics.

Expression$_1$ is *Expression$_2$*

can be thought of as evaluating *Expression$_1$* and *Expression$_2$* and unifying the results. It really works by transforming the expressions into a collection of sends. For example,

> Rho is squareRoot(X*X + Y*Y)

is shorthand for

> X : internalTimes(X, Temp1),
> Y : internalTimes(Y, Temp2),
> Temp1 : internalPlus(Temp2,Temp3),
> Temp3 : squareRoot(Rho)

Users can extend *is* by declaring how to transform a term to a send.

isMacro(*Expression, Value, Target : Message*).

where *Target : Message* computes *Value* for Expression. E.g.,

> isMacro(fact(N), Answer, N : factorial(Answer)).

where

> 0 :: factorial(1).
> N :: factorial(Answer) -default→
>   Answer is N*fact(N–1)).

The factorial message can be written in a more normal style using conditionals.

As another example, the *gridDistance* method above could have been written as follows:

> point :: gridDistance(AnotherPoint, HorizontalDistance, VerticalDistance) →
>   HorizontalDistance is X – AnotherPoint : x,
>   VerticalDistance is Y – AnotherPoint : y.

> isMacro(SomePoint : x, Value, SomePoint : x(Value)).

isMacro(SomePoint : y, Value, SomePoint : y(Value)).

Conditionals

Because conditionals are common we provide the following syntactic sugar
for them:

BooleanExpression **ifTrue** TrueBody
BooleanExpression **ifFalse** FalseBody
BooleanExpression **ifTrue** TrueBody **ifFalse** FalseBody
BooleanExpression **ifFalse** FalseBody **ifTrue** TrueBody

TrueBody and *FalseBody* are just like bodies of methods. *BooleanExpression* is
an expression (i.e., is acceptable on either side of an *is* statement) and should
evaluate to *true* or *false*. A missing *TrueBody* or *FalseBody* does nothing.

For example,

number :: maximum(AnotherNumber, Max) →
    Self > AnotherNumber
        ifTrue Max=Self
        ifFalse Max=AnotherNumber.

This definition of maximum is syntactic sugar for

number :: maximum(AnotherNumber, Max) →
    Boolean is Self > AnotherNumber,
    Boolean : maximumPrivate(Self, AnotherNumber, Max).

true :: maximumPrivate(Max, AnotherNumber, Max).
false :: maximumPrivate(Self, Max, Max).

where *maximumPrivate* is a private method.

Factorial could be defined using conditionals as

number :: factorial(Answer) →
    Self = 0 ifTrue Answer=1 ifFalse Answer is N*fact(N–1).

Explicit unification

$Term_1 = Term_2$

This boolean expression explicitly unifies $Term_1$ and $Term_2$. It is frequently used
as a degenerate conditional where no *ifTrue* or *ifFalse* expression is given. In
these cases it is used to make bindings and not to answer the question of whether
two terms unify. For example, a stack can be defined as follows:

class(stack,[Elements]).

stack :: push(X) → new Elements = [X|Elements].

> stack :: pop(X) → Elements = [X|new Elements] ifFalse ⟨report error⟩.

Send super

One can send a message to the next superclass with an applicable method by sending to *Super*. For example, if *labeledWindow* has *window* as a superclass, the following displays the *Label* and does whatever windows do when displayed.

> labeledWindow :: display →
>   Label : display,
>   Super : display.

Note: We think we have a way of constructing a reference to *Super* if someone wanted to pass out a reference, so it can be used like any other instance variable.

Delegation

delegateTo(*Proxy, Message, Client*)

This sends *Message* to *Proxy* with *Self* bound to *Client*.

Note that *delegateTo*(*X, M, X*) is behaviorally equivalent to *X : M*.

delegateTo(*Proxy, Message*)

is shorthand for

delegateTo(*Proxy, Message, Self*)

Default methods

className Or Term **::** *MessagePattern* **-default**→.
className Or Term **::** *MessagePattern* **-default**→ *Body*.

A default method for an object will not be selected until it has been determined that all the other methods have been found to be inapplicable. For example, a re-routable transparent forwarder can be implemented as follows:

> class(forwarder, [Contents]).
>
> forwarder :: rerouteTo(new Contents).
>
> forwarder :: Message -default→ Contents : Message.

All messages to a *forwarder* (except the *rerouteTo* message) are sent along to the *Contents*.

Chapter 31

PRESSing for Parallelism:
A Prolog Program Made Concurrent

Leon Sterling and Michael Codish

The Weizmann Institute of Science

Abstract

We describe the translation of a nontrivial program for solving equations from Prolog to Concurrent Prolog, and further to Flat Concurrent Prolog. The translation from Prolog to Concurrent Prolog required understanding of the program but was straightforward. The translation from Concurrent Prolog to Flat Concurrent Prolog was more amenable to implementation via automatic procedures. The different styles of translation used are illustrated with examples from the three equation solving programs. The gain in speed by performing computations in parallel is discussed.

31.1 Introduction

An ideal of logic programming is to free the programmer from worrying about control. The task of the programmer according to this ideal is to compose the logical axioms which specify the relationship the program is to compute. How to use the axioms in a particular computation is left to the interpreter of the logic program.

The reality of logic programming using current languages is otherwise. Languages such as Prolog and Concurrent Prolog have well-defined operational semantics which must be understood and exploited to write practical programs. In particular, there are control-related primitives specific to the language whose use must be mastered. The set is minimal; consisting of clause and goal order and the cut in Prolog, and commit and the read-only annotation in Concurrent Prolog. However their correct use is crucial.

Programming techniques continue to evolve based on the operational behavior of the languages. The techniques are collected and abstracted into programming paradigms. Examples are generate and test for problem solving in Prolog, and message passing in Concurrent Prolog. The techniques are passed into the folklore, handed down, and determine the applications for which the languages are used.

It is an interesting, largely unstudied question how techniques in different logic programming languages correspond. More generally, how and whether programs written in the natural paradigms of one logic programming language can be translated to another. This paper concerns these questions.

We translated part of the Prolog program PRESS (Bundy and Welham, 1981; Sterling et al., 1982) to gain insight into the relationship between the languages. PRESS is a program developed at the University of Edinburgh for solving symbolic equations. It has evolved into a significant piece of software combining different styles of programming: deterministic algorithms, heuristic rules and Prolog utilities. Our Concurrent Prolog version is CONPRESS.

The evolution from PRESS to CONPRESS required basic common sense. The translation is straightforward for procedures of the program using don't-care nondeterminism. Procedures which depend on the sequential nature of Prolog use the synchronization capabilities of Concurrent Prolog to achieve the same effect. The message passing features of Concurrent Prolog were exploited in some places to save unnecessary computation.

Implementing the Or-parallel part of Concurrent Prolog efficiently is difficult, due to the maintenance of separate guard environments. This has suggested the language Flat Concurrent Prolog (FCP), which is essentially the And-parallel subset of Concurrent Prolog (Houri and Shapiro, Chapter 38; Mierowsky et al., 1985). Many Concurrent Prolog programs are readily translated to Flat Concurrent Prolog (Bloch, 1984), but evaluations of the expressive power of the languages are still being made. We further successfully translated CONPRESS into FCPRESS, an equivalent version of the equation solver in Flat Concurrent Prolog to gain insight into the expressiveness of the language.

The translation from CONPRESS to FCPRESS was more systematic than from PRESS to CONPRESS. Three standard approaches were identified for removing the Or-parallel sections of CONPRESS. The first is running the guards in And-parallelism and using a mutual exclusion variable to decide which guard would be chosen. The second is the compilation of the guards into if-then-else structures. The third approach involves writing specialized predicates. The approaches are connected. More details on translating Concurrent Prolog code to FCP can be found in (Codish and Shapiro, Chapter 32).

Our experience shows that all three languages are suitable for writing symbolic equation solvers. However the style of programming is slightly different in each case. PRESS is the least explicit but the most general. It uses Prolog's backtracking, and exploits unpredictable interactions to solve difficult equations. CONPRESS, and more especially FCPRESS, demand a more explicit elaboration of conditions.

There is an interesting underlying issue of composing parallel algorithms. Since Prolog executes programs sequentially while Concurrent Prolog and FCP execute programs concurrently, the translation of a Prolog program to Concurrent Prolog or to FCP involves the development of a parallel algorithm from a sequential one. This approach is potentially very powerful. Shapiro (Chapter 7) demonstrates that powerful systolic algorithms appear from naive translation to Concurrent Prolog of pure logic programs. Our translation of PRESS is not the ultimate in parallel equation solvers, and the form of CONPRESS is a direct result of the form of PRESS. Nonetheless there was a considerable speed-up in some examples due to performing part of the computation in parallel.

The outline of the paper is as follows. The next section gives a brief overview of PRESS to make the paper somewhat self-contained. The equation solving methods themselves are not described: the reader is referred to the papers on PRESS (Bundy and Welham, 1981; Sterling et al., 1982; Bundy and Silver, 1981) or to Sterling and Shapiro (1986) for details. The research in this paper is based on a simplified version of PRESS. It has been partially reconstructed and cleaned up from the original to allow easier comparison with CONPRESS and FCPRESS. The complete code of the three programs used in this paper can be found in Appendix 31.1.

Section 31.3 describes the translation process from Prolog to Concurrent Prolog. The process is illustrated with examples from PRESS and CONPRESS. Similarly Section 31.4 uses examples from CONPRESS and FCPRESS to discuss translation from Concurrent Prolog to FCP. The next section presents statistics on the speed-up achieved by using a parallel language, while finally some conclusions are given.

Knowledge of all three languages is assumed.

31.2 Meet the PRESSes

The top level of the equation solver is a collection of axioms defining methods. Abstractly, a method can be split into two parts: a condition, called the *entrance condition*, determining whether the method is applicable, and the application of the method itself. An entrance condition is *binding* if its success guarantees that the equation will be solved correctly.

The clause below is an abstracted prototypical clause at the top level of PRESS. The basic predicate is *solve_equation(Equation,X,Solution)*. The predicate is true if *Solution* solves equation *Equation* in the unknown X. The predicate *condition(Equation,X)* determines whether the equation satisfies the entrance condition for the method, while *method(Equation,X,Solution)* applies the method to solve the equation.

> solve_equation(Equation,X,Solution) ←
> condition(Equation,X), method(Equation,X,Solution).

Instances of this clause will be given as examples in the following sections. Four equation-solving methods were translated to provide the comparison: Factorization, Isolation for solving equations with a single occurrence of the unknown, a suite of polynomial methods, and a general form of change of unknown called Homogenization.

All these methods apart from Homogenization have binding entrance conditions. Since PRESS has backtracking, nonbinding entrance conditions are no problem. In CONPRESS and FCPRESS a condition sufficient to distinguish Homogenization from the other methods was used.

Syntactically the top level of PRESS and CONPRESS look similar. Operationally they are different. PRESS attempts the methods in the order: Factorization, Isolation, Polynomial and Homogenization. CONPRESS attempts the entrance conditions of the methods in parallel, and the first to succeed commits the equation solver. The top level of FCPRESS explicitly shows the behavior of CONPRESS.

31.3 PRESSing in Parallel

Syntactically any pure Prolog program is a Concurrent Prolog program. However an arbitrary Prolog program will usually behave incorrectly when run as a Concurrent Prolog program. In this section we give examples of the changes necessary to Prolog programs so that they behave correctly as Concurrent Prolog ones.

We concentrate our discussion on control issues. The goal and clause order of Prolog programs convey implicit control information, particularly when cuts are present. This control information generally must be made explicit in the translation. The basic tools for expressing control information in Concurrent Prolog are the commit operator and the read-only annotation.

Let us consider the task of placing a commit operator. For each clause we must define a condition, the guard, which will enable commitment to this clause from the other possible choices. This condition should be as concise as possible to reduce the amount of unnecessary computation and speed up execution.

The simplest guard is the empty guard, possible if unification successfully determines the correct choice of clause. Otherwise one must determine the appropriate test whose satisfaction establishes that the correct clause has been chosen. This is not difficult in general. The worst case is when the condition for commitment is the success of the whole body. As a guarded clause the guard is then the whole body, and the body is empty. Examples of the two extremes can be seen in Programs 31.2 and 31.4.

Shapiro (Chapter 2) argues that Concurrent Prolog incorporates indeterminacy but not nondeterminism, whereas Prolog supports both. In Kowalski's (1979) terms don't-care nondeterminism can be expressed easily, but not don't-know nondeterminism. This is reflected in our translation. Those parts of PRESS incorporating don't-care nondeterminism were the most easily and elegantly translated. More generally, code written 'nondeterministically' where clause and goal orders are not important can be translated immediately.

Elegant translation is exemplified by the several parsing procedures in PRESS. Parsing procedures typically make the correct choice of clause depending on the success of unification. Such code is almost identical when naively translated to Concurrent Prolog. Generally the translated clauses have empty guards. A few of the clauses have simple guards easily defined as in the Prolog code.

As an example we give the predicate *is_polynomial*(*X,Term*) true if *Term* is a polynomial in *X*. Program 31.1 is the version in PRESS, while Program 31.2 is the equivalent code in CONPRESS.

The commit operator is concerned with the choice of the correct clause to use in a computation. In a less clean way, cuts also indicate the correct choice of clause. During the translation process cuts are simply removed from the Prolog code. However their placement in well-written code should not be ignored. It can suggest an appropriate positioning of commit operators. Note that this is true for Programs 31.1 and 31.2.

An example of a predicate less elegantly translated is *position*(*Sub,Term,P*) which computes a position list *P* of a subterm *Sub* occurring in a term *Term*. The PRESS code appears as Program 31.3.

The translation of Program 31.3 to CONPRESS is given as Program 31.4. The two clauses of *position/3* are neatly translated. The clauses of *position/4* have an immediate naive translation, but are less pleasing as Concurrent Prolog code due to the complex nature of the guards. Essentially all subterms of the term are searched in parallel. We do not know the correct branch in advance and this is reflected in the code. (Better versions of *position* can be written in Concurrent Prolog. In fact *position* was rewritten in the context of FCPRESS.)

Cuts are often used in Prolog to achieve implicit negation. Care is needed when translating clauses in a procedure appearing after a clause with a cut. Con-

is_polynomial(X,X) ← !.
is_polynomial(X,Term) ←
    free_of(X,Term), !.
is_polynomial(X,Term1+Term2) ←
    !, is_polynomial(X,Term1), is_polynomial(X,Term2).
is_polynomial(X,Term1−Term2) ←
    !, is_polynomial(X,Term1), is_polynomial(X,Term2).
is_polynomial(X,Term1*Term2) ←
    !, is_polynomial(X,Term1), is_polynomial(X,Term2).
is_polynomial(X,Term1/Term2) ←
    !, is_polynomial(X,Term1), free_of(X,Term2).
is_polynomial(X,Term↑N) ←
    !, integer(N), $N \geq 0$, is_polynomial(X,Term).

Program 31.1: Recognizing polynomials in PRESS

is_polynomial(X,X).
is_polynomial(X,Term) ←
    free_of(X,Term) | true.
is_polynomial(X,Term1+Term2) ←
    is_polynomial(X,Term1), is_polynomial(X,Term2).
is_polynomial(X,Term1−Term2) ←
    is_polynomial(X,Term1), is_polynomial(X,Term2).
is_polynomial(X,Term1*Term2) ←
    is_polynomial(X,Term1), is_polynomial(X,Term2).
is_polynomial(X,Term1/Term2) ←
    is_polynomial(X,Term1), free_of(X,Term2).
is_polynomial(X,Term↑N) ←
    integer(N), $N \geq 0$, is_polynomial(X,Term).

Program 31.2: Recognizing polynomials in CONPRESS

position(Term,Term,[ ]).
position(Sub,Term,Path) ←
    compound(Term), functor(Term,_,N), position(N,Sub,Term,Path), !.

position(N,Sub,Term,[N|Path]) ←
    N > 0, arg(N,Term,Arg), position(Sub,Arg,Path).
position(N,Sub,Term,Path) ←
    N1 is N−1, N1 > 0, position(N1,Sub,Term,Path).

Program 31.3: *Position* in PRESS

```
position(Term,Term,[ ]).
position(Sub,Term,Path) ←
    compound(Term) | functor(Term,_,N),

position(N,Sub,Term,Path).
position(N,Sub,Term,[N|Path]) ←
    N > 0, arg(N,Term,Arg), position(Sub,Arg?,Path) | true.
position(N,Sub,Term,Path) ←
    N1 := N–1, N1 > 0, position(N1?,Sub,Term,Path) | true.
```

Program 31.4: *Position* in CONPRESS

ditions that were omitted because of the cut may have to be explicitly written. This is true for the top-level equation solving clauses.

A binding entrance condition for Isolation is that there be a single occurrence of the unknown in the equation. In PRESS, the entrance condition for Homogenization, which was checked after Isolation, assumed that there were multiple occurrences of the unknown in the equation. When writing the entrance condition for Homogenization in CONPRESS, multiple occurrences of the unknown had to be specified.

Several parts of the equation solver implement deterministic algorithms. In contrast to the nondeterministic code where the translation effort concerns mainly the placement of commit operators, algorithmic code must worry about synchronization.

To implement deterministic algorithms where the order of steps is important, the read-only annotation is necessary. There are two uses of read-only annotations. The first is *consumer protection*. In a clause whose body has goals with a shared variable, such as

$$a ← p(X), q(X).$$

the goal which instantiates the value of X, $p(X)$ say, is the *producer* of X, while the goal which then uses the value, $q(X)$, is the *consumer*. In Prolog, one uses goal order in a rule to ensure that the producer is called before the consumer. In Concurrent Prolog, one needs to synchronize the computation so that the consumer goal waits on values from the producer goal. This is done by annotating the occurrence of the variable in the consumer goal, i.e., $q(X?)$ in the above clause. If q is a recursive procedure consuming a stream, then the recursive calls of q will have to protect the tail of the stream with a read-only annotation as well.

A typical example of deterministic code is the algorithm for Isolation, the method for solving equations with a single occurrence of the unknown. The algorithm is described by Bundy and Welham (1981). Its top level implementation

```
solve_equation(Equation,X,Solution) ←
    single_occurrence(X,Equation), !,
    position(X,Equation,[Side|Position]),
    maneuver_sides(Side,Equation,Equation1),
    isolate(Position,Equation1,Solution).
```

Program 31.5: Solving equations by *isolation* in PRESS

in PRESS is given in Program 31.5. The entrance condition, which is binding, is *single_occurrence/2*.

The necessary synchronization to translate the program in Program 31.5 to CONPRESS is straightforward. The algorithm proceeds by calculating a position list locating the single occurrence of the unknown in the term in predicate *position/3*. The head of the position list is used by *maneuver_sides/3* to ensure that the unknown occurs in the left hand side of the equation, reversing the equation if necessary. The tail of the position list is used by *isolate/3* to know how to apply the appropriate rewrite rules. Also *isolate/3* must wait for the equation produced by *maneuver_sides/3*. All the necessary read-only annotations are of the consumer protection type. The transformed code is given in Program 31.6.

```
solve_equation(Equation,X,Solution) ←
    single_occurrence(X,Equation) |
    position(X,Equation,[Side|Position]),
    maneuver_sides(Side?,Equation,Equation1),
    isolate(Position?,Equation1?,Solution).
```

Program 31.6: Solving equations by *isolation* in CONPRESS

The second use of read-only annotations is *producer protection* where the producer goal is responsible for protecting the incomplete part of the structure under construction (Hellerstein and Shapiro, Chapter 9). Occurrences of a variable in the head of the clause are annotated, and thus passed on with protection. Producer protection is necessary when a structure in the head of a clause is being partially built by a goal G in the clause body. Commitment to that clause may occur before G has finished executing, and the partially built structure communicated to the rest of the computation. To avoid other goals incorrectly instantiating the value, the value is marked as read-only in the head of the clause. An example clause is:

```
a(B,f(X?)) ← b(X).
```

An example of the use of producer protection read-only annotation comes in the implementation of an algorithm for adding polynomials. Polynomials are converted to a *polynomial normal form* which is a list of tuples of the form (A_i, N_i), where A_i is the coefficient of X^{N_i}. In this normal form terms with zero coefficients are eliminated. The polynomial manipulation routines assume polynomials in normal form.

The predicate *add_polynomials(Xs, Ys, Zs)* adds the polynomials *Xs* and *Ys* in normal form to give a polynomial *Zs* in normal form. The PRESS code is given in Program 31.7.

```
add_polynomials([ ],Poly,Poly).
add_polynomials(Poly,[ ],Poly).
add_polynomials([(Ai,Ni)|Ps], [(Aj,Nj)|Qs],[(Ai,Ni)|Rs]) ←
     Ni > Nj, !, add_polynomials(Ps,[(Aj,Nj)|Qs],Rs).
add_polynomials([(Ai,N)|Ps],[(Aj,N)|Qs],[(A,N)|Rs]) ←
     !, A is Ai+Aj, add_polynomials(Ps,Qs,Rs).
add_polynomials([(Ai,Ni)|Ps],[(Aj,Nj)|Qs], [(Aj,Nj)|Rs]) ←
     Ni < Nj, !, add_polynomials([(Ai,Ni)|Ps],Qs,Rs).
```

Program 31.7: Adding polynomials in PRESS

The adaptation to CONPRESS is given in Program 31.8. The interesting point is the read-only annotation of *A* in the fourth clause of the program. This prevents *A* from being instantiated by other goals in the computation. The bug caused by its omission was discovered by experience.

```
add_polynomials([ ],Poly,Poly).
add_polynomials(Poly,[ ],Poly).
add_polynomials([(Ai,Ni)|Ps], [(Aj,Nj)|Qs],[(Ai,Ni)|Rs]) ←
     Ni > Nj | add_polynomials(Ps,[(Aj,Nj)|Qs],Rs).
add_polynomials([(Ai,N)|Ps],[(Aj,N)|Qs],[(A?,N)|Rs]) ←
     A := Ai+Aj, add_polynomials(Ps,Qs,Rs).
add_polynomials([(Ai,Ni)|Ps],[(Aj,Nj)|Qs], [(Aj,Nj)|Rs]) ←
     Ni < Nj | add_polynomials([(Ai,Ni)|Ps],Qs,Rs).
```

Program 31.8: Adding polynomials in CONPRESS

The examples of code so far in this section have been essentially literal translations. All the translation involved was the correct modification of the control. Better translations are sometimes possible if features of the new language are taken into account. We demonstrate two changes here which were possible due to the use of streams and the message-passing capabilities of Concurrent Prolog.

Several of the equation solving methods perform problem reduction. The equation to be solved is reduced to simpler equations. It seems sensible to solve the subproblems in parallel. There are several different ways of handling separate solutions or multiple solutions in the original PRESS. For example a disjunction operator, treated specially in the various methods, indicates alternative solutions. When translating from PRESS to CONPRESS, we decided to make the handling of multiple equations uniform. The natural technique in Concurrent Prolog is to use streams.

If the input to the equation solver is a stream of equations, it is necessary to associate with each equation a specific unknown. For this reason we regard an equation in CONPRESS as a tuple (*Equation, Unknown*). The top level of CONPRESS is changed to be a predicate *solve_equation(Equations, Solution\Ss)* where *Equations* is a stream of tuples of equations and the unknown the equation is solved for, and *Solution\Ss* is a queue, represented as a difference-list of the solutions. A queue is used so that the order of solutions corresponds to the order of the equations. Using streams rather than a single equation means that *solve_equations* becomes a tail-recursive process.

Streams in Concurrent Prolog correspond to lists in Prolog. It transpired that the extension to PRESS to solve lists of equations was natural. Our modified version of PRESS is actually written this way. Other predicates where streams were useful were filtering processes, for example Program 31.17 in the next section.

```
solve_equations([(Equation,X)|Eqns],Solution–Solns) ←
    single_occurrence(X,Equation), !,
    position(X,Equation,[Side|Position]),
    maneuver_sides(Side,Equation,Equation1),
    isolate(Position,Equation1,Solution\Ss),
    solve_equations(Eqns,Ss\Solns).
```

Program 31.9: The modified top level rule for isolation

Program 31.9 gives the appropriate modification of Program 31.5 for solving an equation with a single occurrence of the unknown, which uses streams. Since the isolation procedure can give multiple solutions, it must update the queue.

Our next example of translation exploits the message-passing features of Concurrent Prolog. A useful relationship when solving equations is the number of times one term appears as a subterm of another. Examples are determining how many times an unknown appears in an equation, whether a term is free of appearances of an unknown and whether there is more than one occurrence of an unknown in an equation.

This kind of relation is called an *occurrence relation*. PRESS and CONPRESS use the predicates *occurrences(Subterm, Term, Occs)* defining the relation that there are *Occs* occurrences of *Term* in *Subterm*, *free_of(Subterm, Term)* defining the relation that *Term* is free of occurrences of *Subterm*, and the predicates *single_occurrence(Subterm, Term)* and *multiple_occurrence(Subterm, Term)* with similar definitions.

The code for the occurrence predicates was rewritten for CONPRESS to take advantage of the message-passing capabilities of Concurrent Prolog. Neater code than the immediate 'naive' translation from PRESS resulted.

```
free_of(Subterm,Term) ←
    occurrences(Subterm,Term,N), N=0.
single_occurrence(Subterm,Term) ←
    occurrences(Subterm,Term,N), N=1.
multiple_occurrence(Subterm,Term) ←
    occurrences(Subterm,Term,N), N>1.
```

Program 31.10: Defining occurrence relations

We could use *occurrences(Subterm,Term,Occs)* to define all occurrence relations as in the three clauses in Program 31.10. This is a clean declarative definition which uniformly expresses occurrence relations in terms of *occurrences*. Procedurally these are not the best definitions in Prolog. Instead of counting all the occurrences of the subterm in the term, *free_of* could fail upon encountering the first occurrence. Similarly in *multiple_occurrences* it is sufficient to locate just two occurrences of the subterm in the term.

In Prolog there is no obvious way to define these predicates capturing both efficiency and conciseness. To achieve efficient Prolog code, each of these predicates must be rewritten. Indeed this happened in PRESS. The original version of *free_of* had the clean declarative definition, which was later replaced by a more efficient version written by Richard O'Keefe with a structure similar to that of *occurrences*. They differ in their response to occurrences of the *Subterm*, *occurrences* counts these, *free_of* will fail if one is encountered. The code is illustrated in Program 31.11.

In Concurrent Prolog the situation is different and definitions similar to those in Program 31.10 can be given capturing both clarity and efficiency. All the occurrence relations can be defined in terms of the *occurrences* predicate. Correct communication between the goals will enable success or failure once there is sufficient information, eliminating excess computations.

In CONPRESS the *occurrences* predicate has been modified and is defined as a relation *occurrences(Subterm,Term,Pulses,H)*. *Pulses* is an output stream which is used to pass on information about occurrences of *Subterm*. Each time an occurrence of *Subterm* is encountered a signal is sent along this communication channel. The fourth argument is used by *multiple_occurrences* to signal *occurrences* that it already has enough information to succeed so that *occurrences* can terminate.

The definitions of the occurrence relations in CONPRESS using communi-

```
free_of(Kernel,Kernel) ←
    !, fail.
free_of(Kernel,Expression) ←
    atomic(Expression), !.
free_of(Kernel,Expression) ←
    functor(Expression,_,Arity), !, free_of(Arity,Kernel,Expression).

free_of(0,Kernel,Expression) ← !.
free_of(N,Kernel,Expression) ←
    arg(N,Expression,Argument),
    free_of(Kernel,Argument),
    !, N1 is N−1,
    free_of(N1,Kernel,Expression).
```

Program 31.11: An efficient version of *free_of*

```
free_of(Sub,Term) ←
    occurrences(Sub,Term,Pulses,_), no_pulse(Pulses?).
single_occurrence(Sub,Term) ←
    occurrences(Sub,Term,Pulses,_), single_pulse(Pulses?).
multiple_occurrence(Sub,Term) ←
    occurrences(Sub,Term,Pulses,H), multiple_pulse(Pulses?,H).

no_pulse([ ]).
single_pulse([pulse]).
multiple_pulse([pulse,pulse|Ps],halt).
```

Program 31.12: Occurrence relations in CONPRESS

cation are given by Program 31.12. The predicate *no_pulse* fails as soon as one pulse is sent, causing the failure of *free_of*. Similarly *single_occurrence* fails as soon as two pulses have been sent.

31.4 PRESSed Flat

The task of translating Concurrent Prolog into Flat Concurrent Prolog is different in essence from that of translating Prolog into Concurrent Prolog. Flat Concurrent Prolog, as a powerful subset of Concurrent Prolog, inherits most of the latter's programming techniques and styles. The problem then is the technical issue of re-expressing the logic of a program in terms of And-parallelism.

The resulting code simulates explicitly the operational behavior of Concurrent Prolog when executing the original program. The techniques used for flattening Concurrent Prolog are automated more easily (see Bloch, 1984 and Codish and Shapiro, Chapter 32) than those for making Prolog concurrent.

We present three different approaches used to flatten CONPRESS. The first is illustrated by the top level of FCPRESS. An extra level of reasoning has been added with the clauses

```
solve_equations([EqVar|EqVars],Ss\Ss1) ←
    choose(EqVar,Method),
    solve_by_method(EqVar,Method?,Ss\Ss2?),
    solve_equations(EqVars?,Ss2\Ss1?).
solve_equations([ ],Ss\Ss).
```

The predicate *choose* calls a conjunction of goals derived from the predicates which appeared as guards in the top level of CONPRESS. It uses a mutual exclusion variable to convey to the *solve_by_method* predicate the name of a method which can be applied to the given equation. A *mutual exclusion variable* is a variable that several processes are concurrently trying to instantiate. Successful instantiation by one of the processes renders the continuation of the others irrelevant. The definition of *choose* is given in Program 31.13. Note the use of the control primitive *otherwise* to achieve the effect of if-then-else in *condition_factorize*.

Predicates called by *choose* of necessity must be altered. Each will contain a copy of the mutual exclusion variable, *Method*. Guards must be treated differently. Those that previously would succeed causing the computation to commit must now succeed and instantiate the mutual exclusion variable, resulting in a simulation of commitment. Guards that previously would fail now *quit*, that is do not fail, but rather succeed without affecting the rest of the computation. The code is also altered to accept abort messages. When one of the goals called by *choose* succeeds in instantiating the mutual exclusion variable, computation of all the others is aborted.

In Program 31.13 *choose* calls a condition for each of the four methods implemented. The first condition to succeed instantiates *Method* with the name of the method which is to be applied. An exception is Homogenization, the condition for which is that a multiple offenders set, *MOS*, has been identified in the equation. Application of the method itself involves a computation based on *MOS*. When this is the first condition to succeed, *Method* is instantiated to the multiple offenders set.

In flattening CONPRESS, more structure has been added to the program. The computation of a goal is now clearly divided into two stages. In terms of equation solving, a clear distinction is made between choosing a method and

solve_equations([EqVar|EqVars],Ss\Ss1) ←
    choose(EqVar,Method),
    solve_by_method(EqVar,Method?,Ss\Ss2?),
    solve_equations(EqVars?,Ss2\Ss1?).
solve_equations([],Ss\Ss).

choose(EqVar,Method)←
    condition_factorize(EqVar,Method),
    condition_isolation(EqVar,Method),
    condition_polynomial(EqVar,Method),
    condition_homogenization(EqVar,Method).

condition_factorize((Lhs=0,_),Method) ←
    mulbag(Lhs,Method).
condition_factorize(_,Method) ←
    otherwise | true.

condition_isolation((Eq,Var),Method) ←
    single_occ(Var,Eq,Method).

condition_polynomial((Lhs=Rhs,Var),Method)←
    is_polynomial(Var,Lhs–Rhs,Method).

condition_homogenization(EqVar,Method) ←
    multiple_offender_set(EqVar,Method).

Program 31.13: Choosing a method

applying it. This is a major change from the original style of PRESS code.

The first style of translation could be generalized into a method for flattening Concurrent Prolog programs. For general applications there are several problems to be solved. The guards of a Concurrent Prolog procedure are executed in separate environments and different guards could instantiate a common variable to different values. Only when a guard commits are the local values of the variables broadcast to the rest of the computation. A generalization of this method would have to make separate copies of any common structures instantiated by the guards themselves to simulate this aspect of Concurrent Prolog's execution of Or-parallelism. Copying structures is an expensive operation. Another problem to be solved is ensuring consistency between a copied variable and an instance of the original variable (Bloch, 1984). In our application the guards being flattened did not instantiate variables, and so these problems were avoided. A general solution to both these problems was given by Codish and Shapiro (Chapter 32).

How (or even whether) to simulate commitment by aborting the computation of other guards is a question of efficiency, not of correctness. At one extreme, the program would be correct even if unnecessary computations were not aborted, but rather continued uselessly. At the other extreme, too many additional halting variables and too much insistence on handling abort messages could result in efforts being diverted from the subject of solving equations to that of simulating commitment. There is a tradeoff between clarity and efficiency.

Two versions of the predicate *multiple_offender_set* are given in Programs 31.14 and 31.15 respectively. The predicate parses an equation to determine if it contains at least two offenders. This predicate can abort when some other goal instantiates *Method*. Program 31.14 is a more efficient version. When an abort message is received, it is propagated to all the processes spawned by the top level process. This introduces an additional halting variable in each of these processes as well as code to handle abort messages (not shown here). In Program 31.15 only the top level will respond to an abort message, leaving its spawned processes computing undisturbed without affecting the main computation.

```
multiple_offender_set((Eq,Var),Method) ←
    unknown(Method) |
    parse(Eq,Var,Offs,Method),
    remove_duplicates(Offs?,Foffs,Method),
    mult_members(Foffs?,Method).
```

Program 31.14: More abortable code

```
multiple_offender_set((Eq,Var),Method) ←
    unknown(Method) |
    parse(Eq,Var,Offs),
    remove_duplicates(Offs?,Foffs),
    mult_members(Foffs?,Method).
```

Program 31.15: Less abortable code

The second approach to flattening Concurrent Prolog code is to compile the guarded commands into if-then-else structures. This is done by adding an extra argument to each guard predicate. This argument returns the result of the guard's execution — whether it succeeded or failed. This approach is a special case of the previous one when the procedure being flattened contains a single guard, which is not already a Flat Concurrent Prolog kernel guard predicate.

Program 31.16 shows an example of a parsing predicate in FCPRESS. A term *Term* is parsed to check if it is a polynomial in *Var*. In CONPRESS *free_of* appeared in the guard of a clause (Program 31.2). In FCPRESS *free_of* is called in conjunction with a continuation predicate which waits on the result of *free_of*, giving the effect of an if-then-else structure.

is_polynomial(Var,Term,Method)←
    is_polynomial(Var,Term,Method,H).

is_polynomial(_,_,_,H) ←
    H =?= halt | true.
is_polynomial(_,_,M,halt) ←
    nonvar(M) | true.
is_polynomial(Var,Term1+Term2,Method,H) ←
    is_polynomial(Var,Term1,M1,H),
    is_polynomial(Var,Term2,M2,H),
    poly_merge_results(M1,M2,Method,H).
is_polynomial(Var,Term1−Term2,Method,H) ←
    is_polynomial(Var,Term1,M1,H),
    is_polynomial(Var,Term2,M2,H),
    poly_merge_results(M1,M2,Method,H).
is_polynomial(Var,Term1*Term2,Method,H) ←
    is_polynomial(Var,Term1,M1,H),
    is_polynomial(Var,Term2,M2,H),
    poly_merge_results(M1,M2,Method,H).
is_polynomial(Var,Term↑N,Method,H) ←
    N ≥ 0 | is_polynomial(Var,Term,Method,H).
is_polynomial(Var,Var,polynomial,H).
is_polynomial(Var,Term,M,H) ←
    otherwise | free_of(Var,Term,Ans), base_is_polynomial(Ans?,M).

base_is_polynomial(yes,polynomial).
base_is_polynomial(_,_) ←
    otherwise | true.

poly_merge_results(_,_,_,H) ←
    H =?= halt | true.
poly_merge_results(M1,M2,polynomial,H) ←
    M1 =?= polynomial, M2 =?= polynomial | true.
poly_merge_results(_,_,_,halt) ←
    otherwise | true.

Program 31.16: Recognizing polynomials in FCPRESS

In this method, as in the previous one, we have ensured that none of the predicates fail. They either succeed, returning a negative answer, or just quit. Goals in the bodies of these predicates have also been altered so as not to fail. One of these predicates could give a negative answer (or quit) as soon as one of the goals spawned by it did so. To gain efficiency we could add communication between brother goals to enable one to abort the others when possible. As before this involves a trade off between clarity and efficiency. The price of increased efficiency is performing the explicit communication.

Two extra variables are used for communication in Program 31.16. There is an instance of the mutual exclusion variable *Method*, for communication with other predicates for choosing a method, and an additional halting variable *H* to halt all processes spawned by *is_polynomial* as soon as one of these discovers a non-polynomial subterm of *Term*. An additional predicate is required by *is_polynomial* to merge the results of its subgoals. The predicate *poly_merge_results(M1,M2,Method,H)* defines *Method* to be *polynomial* if and only if both *M1* and *M2* are *polynomial*.

The third approach to translation is writing specialized definitions for those predicates which appear in the guards. A typical example is specializing *member*. Programs 31.17 and 31.18 respectively show the Concurrent Prolog and the Flat Concurrent Prolog versions of the predicate *remove_duplicates*, which filters duplicates from a stream. In the Concurrent Prolog version *member* appears in the guard. In Program 31.18 the predicate *remove_duplicates_1* is a specialized version of *member*, which has been optimized to gain parallelism.

remove_duplicates(In,Out) ← remove_duplicates(In,[ ],Out).

remove_duplicates([ ],_,[ ]).
remove_duplicates([X|Xs],Acc,Out) ←
    member(X,Acc) | remove_duplicates(Xs?,Acc,Out).
remove_duplicates([X|Xs],Acc,[X|Out]) ←
    otherwise | remove_duplicates(Xs?,[X|Acc],Out).

Program 31.17: *remove_duplicates* in CONPRESS

remove_duplicates(In,Out) ← remove_duplicates(In,[ ],Out\[ ]).

remove_duplicates([X|Xs],Acc,Out\Out1) ←
    remove_duplicates_1(X,Acc,Acc1,Out\Out2),
    remove_duplicates(Xs?,Acc1?,Out2\Out1).
remove_duplicates([ ],_,Out\Out).
remove_duplicates_1(A,[ ],[A],[A|Out]\Out).
remove_duplicates_1(A,[S|Ss],[S|Ss1],Out) ←
    S ≠ A | remove_duplicates_1(A,Ss?,Ss1,Out).
remove_duplicates_1(A,[S|Ss],[S|Ss],Out\Out) ←
    S =?= A | true.

Program 31.18: *remove_duplicates* with specialized member in
                       FCPRESS

The third approach is a generalization of the second. Instead of modifying the guard to return *yes* or *no*, and writing code to handle each answer, the guard is modified to return a more general result, which reflects the behavior of the original program.

The question of using these and related approaches to translate Concurrent Prolog programs to FCP are discussed by Codish and Shapiro (Chapter 32). A general automated method based on partial evaluation is described there. The three approaches described in this section are handled in a uniform way.

31.5 Parallel Speed-up

It is a controversial issue in AI whether a machine which allows true parallel programming will make a significant difference in our ability to write intelligent programs (Bobrow and Hayes, 1985). This section describes the (theoretical) gain in speed obtained in the domain of equation solving by being allowed to perform calculations in parallel. We compare the performance of PRESS, CONPRESS and FCPRESS in solving equations.

There are two levels where latent parallelism has been exploited in our translation. At the top level, the various entrance conditions can be checked in parallel in both CONPRESS and FCPRESS. Also, independent equations, arising for example from factorization, can be solved in parallel. At a lower level some of the algorithms used in solving equations have been made parallel. Of particular note are the parsing and filtering algorithms.

We collected statistics on the number of logical inferences performed by the three programs in solving equations. Appropriate meta-interpreters were written. The process of collection favours the parallel languages Concurrent Prolog and FCP. The communication costs of the parallelism are ignored, for example.

The equation we use as the basis for comparison is

$$2^{2x} - 5 \cdot 2^{x+1} + 16 = 0$$

There are three stages to solving this equation. The first is homogenizing the equation to produce the equation

$$y^2 - 10 \cdot y + 16 = 0 \text{ where } y = 2^x$$

The second stage is solving the quadratic equation for y, producing two solutions. Solving the two resultant equations for x is the third stage.

The performance of the three programs during the three stages is summarized in Table 31.1. The column for PRESS is the total number of reductions (or logical inferences) needed to solve the equation. This number includes the 'unnecessary calculations,' for example testing the entrance conditions of methods which are not in fact applicable. The columns for CONPRESS and FCPRESS have the form $r_t/r_s/c$ where r_t is the total number of reductions performed, r_s is the total number of reductions in the successful computation path and c is the number of cycles in the whole computation, where a cycle is one reduction of all active processes.

Stage	PRESS	CONPRESS	FCPRESS
1	500	243/144/21	238/120/26
2	460	114/61/15	138/100/21
3	140	207/150/24	215/143/26
Total	900	564/355/56	591/365/67

Table 31.1: Comparing logical inferences

The different figures for CONPRESS and FCPRESS represent different measures of potential speed-up. The total number of reductions indicates how the program performs on a single processor. Parallelism is simulated by sharing among the processes equally. This type of speed-up has been discussed in the context of cryptarithmetic puzzles by Kornfeld (1983).

In trying to estimate how fast programs would run, the comparative speeds of the interpreters for the languages should be taken into consideration. C-Prolog on a Vax, which was used for this research, runs at approximately 1000 Lips for Prolog, 300 Lips for Concurrent Prolog and 500 Lips for FCP.

The number of cycles is a measure of how fast a parallel program can perform with as many processors as needed, and ignoring communication time. An equation requires at least the number of cycles to be solved. In contrast to the number of reductions, the number of cycles in the total is less than the sum of the numbers of cycles in the three stages. This is true because some of the calculation can be interleaved. For this example the interleaving is between 5 and 10%.

The number of cycles is less for CONPRESS than FCPRESS. This is due to the difference between And-parallelism and Or-parallelism in the way statistics are collected. In FCPRESS which only has And-parallelism all reductions are counted with the exception of guard kernel predicates which are considered part of unification. In CONPRESS however all guards are counted as one cycle, even if they are complex. To avoid the same problem with the reductions, we estimated the number of reductions separately.

The number of successful reductions is the basis of the estimate of the amount of parallelism possible at the lower level of equation solving. The measure is provided by the quotient of the number of reductions by the number of cycles.

The table shows a factor of approximately 5 for each stage. This factor is also a lower bound on the number of processors needed to achieve maximum speed-up.

The quotient of the total number of reductions by the number of cycles is another estimate of the number of processors needed for maximum speed-up. The figure, approximately 10 from the table, is an average over the whole computation. The maximum number of processes actively reducing at one time was over 20.

An interesting quotient is the number of reductions in PRESS by the number of cycles in FCPRESS. This estimates the actual gain in speed under best circumstances. The speed-up for Homogenization is 900/67, approximately 14. Table 31.2 compares the speed-up for the different methods. These can be calculated from our example since polynomial methods are used to solve the second stage, and isolation is used to solve the two equations from the third stage.

Method	Speed-up
Isolation	3.5
Polynomial	20
Homogenization	15

Table 31.2: Speed-up for different methods

The different methods reflect different features. The principal reason why Isolation has the lowest speed-up is that it is the first method tested for in PRESS. Testing whether an equation can be factorized is trivial.

31.6 Conclusions

We were successful in translating a Prolog program to Concurrent Prolog, and further to Flat Concurrent Prolog. The cleaner parts of PRESS corresponding to pure logic programs were the easiest to translate. Both Prolog and Concurrent Prolog are good for don't-care nondeterminism, with Concurrent Prolog being more correct logically, insisting that all conditions are made explicit. PRESS code which relies heavily on don't-know nondeterminism is not translated efficiently to Concurrent Prolog, resorting occasionally to the simulation of Or-parallel Prolog in the guard system. In such cases a new algorithm is desirable. When this was overlooked while translating Prolog to Concurrent Prolog, it had to be solved later when translating to Flat Concurrent Prolog.

General translation of Prolog programs into Concurrent Prolog seems to require basic common sense and understanding of the semantics of the program.

No technique emerged which was suitable as the basis for automatic translation. In contrast, the techniques used for translating Concurrent Prolog programs into Flat Concurrent Prolog represent a promising step towards general translating methods, which have been successfully developed by Codish and Shapiro (Chapter 32).

Acknowledgements

This work was supported by a Dov Biegun postdoctoral fellowship to the first author and a Weizmann studentship to the second author. Helpful suggestions were made by Ehud Shapiro and anonymous referees. The use of computing facilities at the Weizmann Institute, supported by a Digital Equipment External research grant, and at Case Institute of Technology, are gratefully acknowledged.

Appendix 31.1: Code For Press[1]

I. The top level

```
slve_eqns(EqVars,Ss?) ← solve_eqns(EqVars,Ss\[ ]).

slve_equation(Eq,Var,Ss) ← solve_equation(Eq,Var,Ss\[ ]).

solve_eqns([(Eq,Var)|EqVars],Ss\Ss1) ←
    solve_equation(Eq,Var,Ss\Ss2?),
    solve_eqns(EqVars,Ss2\Ss1?).
solve_eqns([ ],S\S).
```

/* *Case for factorization* */

```
solve_equation(Lhs=Rhs,Var,Ss) ←
    zero(Rhs), mulbag(Lhs), !,
    factorize(Lhs,Var,Factored_eqns),
    solve_eqns(Factored_eqns,Ss).
```

/* *Case for isolation* */

```
solve_equation(Eq,Var,Ss) ←
    single_occurrence(Var,Eq), !,
    position(Var,Eq,[Side|Position]),
    maneuver_sides(Side,Eq,Eq1),
    isolate(Position,Eq1,Ss).
```

---

[1] modified version of a subset of Press

/* *Case for polynomials* */

solve_equation(Lhs=Rhs,Var,Ss) ←
    is_polynomial(Var,Lhs−Rhs), !,
    solve_polynomial_equation(Lhs=Rhs,Var,Ss),

/* *Case for homogenization* */

solve_equations(Eq,Var,Ss) ←
    mult_off_set(Eq,Var,OffendersSet),
    homogenize(Eq,Var,OffendersSet,Eq1,Var1),
    solve_homo_equation(Eq1,Var1,Var,Ss),

II. The methods

/* *Predicates for factorization* */

% An equation, $A*B*\cdots*C=0$, is factorized into non trivial, non redundant
% equations, $A=0, B=0, \ldots, C=0$

factorize(Lhs,X,Feqs) ← factorize(Lhs,X,[ ],Feqs).
factorize(A*B,X,Sofar,Feqs) ← !,
    factorize(B,X,Sofar,NewSofar),
    factorize(A,X,NewSofar,Feqs).
factorize(A,X,Sofar,Sofar) ←
    free_of(A,X), !.
factorize(A,X,Sofar,Sofar) ←
    member((A=0,X),Sofar), !.
factorize(A,X,Sofar,[(A=0,X)|Sofar]).

/* *Predicates for isolation* */

isolate([ ],Equation,[Equation|Eqs]\Eqs) ← !.
isolate([N|Position],Equation,IsolatedEquation) ← !,
    isolax(N,Equation,Equation1),
    isolate(Position,Equation1,IsolatedEquation).

maneuver_sides(1,Lhs = Rhs,Lhs = Rhs) ← !.
maneuver_sides(2,Lhs = Rhs,Rhs = Lhs) ← !.

% Some axioms to isolate unknown, sufficient for our tests

isolax(1,−Lhs = Rhs,Lhs = −Rhs) ← !.
isolax(1,Term1+Term2 = Rhs,Term1 = Rhs−Term2) ← !.
isolax(2,Term1+Term2 = Rhs,Term2 = Rhs−Term1) ← !.
isolax(1,Term1−Term2 = Rhs,Term1 = Rhs+Term2) ← !.
isolax(2,Term1−Term2 = Rhs,Term2 = Rhs+Term1) ← !.
isolax(1,Term1*Term2 = Rhs,Term1 = Rhs/Term2) ←

```
       non_zero(Term2), !.
isolax(2,Term1*Term2 = Rhs,Term2 = Rhs/Term1) ←
       non_zero(Term1), !.
isolax(1,Term1/Term2 = Rhs,Term1 = Rhs*Term2) ←
       non_zero(Term2), !.
isolax(2,Term1/Term2 = Rhs,Term2 = Term1/Rhs) ←
       non_zero(Rhs), !.
isolax(1,Term1↑Term2 = Rhs,Term1 = Rhs↑(−Term2)) ← !.
isolax(2,Term1↑Term2 = Rhs,Term2 = log(base(Term1),Rhs)) ← !.
```

% *position*(*Subterm,Term,Position*), *Position* of *Subterm* in *Term*

```
position(Term,Term,[ ]).
position(Term,Expression,Path) ←
       compound(Expression),
       functor(Expression,_,N),
       position(N,Term,Expression,Path), !.
position(N,Term,Expression,[N|Path]) ←
       N > 0,
       arg(N,Expression,Arg),
       position(Term,Arg,Path).
position(N,Term,Expression,Path) ←
       N1 := N − 1,
       N1 > 0,
       position(N1,Term,Expression,Path).
```

/* *Predicates for polynomials* */

% Check if *Expression* is a polynomial

```
is_polynomial(X,X) ← !.
is_polynomial(X,Term) ← free_of(X,Term), !.
is_polynomial(X,Term1+Term2) ←
       !, is_polynomial(X,Term1), is_polynomial(X,Term2).
is_polynomial(X,Term1−Term2) ←
       !, is_polynomial(X,Term1), is_polynomial(X,Term2).
is_polynomial(X,Term1*Term2) ←
       !, is_polynomial(X,Term1), is_polynomial(X,Term2).
is_polynomial(X,Term↑N) ←
       !, integer(N), N ≥ 0, is_polynomial(X,Term)
```

% Solving polynomials

```
solve_polynomial_equation(Lhs=Rhs,X,Solution) ←
       polynomial_normal_form(Lhs−Rhs,X,Poly),
```

poly_method(X,Poly,Solution).

% Polynomial method for quadratic equations (the only method included)

poly_method(X,Poly,Solution) ←
    quadratic(Poly), !,
    find_coefficients(Poly,A,B,C),
    discriminant(A,B,C,Discriminant),
    roots(X,A,B,C,Discriminant,Solution).

quadratic([(_,2)|_]).

find_coefficients([(A,2)|Poly],A,B,C) ← find2(Poly,B,C).
find2([(B,1),(C,0)],B,C) ← !.
find2([(B,1)],B,0) ← !.
find2([(C,0)],0,C) ← !.
find2([ ],0,0) ← !.

discriminant(A,B,C,Discriminant) ← Discriminant := B*B–4*A*C.

roots(X,A,B,_,0,[X = Root|Rs]\Rs) ←
    !, Root := –B/(2*A).
roots(X,A,B,C,Discr,[X = Root1, X = Root2|Rs]\Rs) ←
    Root1 := (–B + sqrt(Discr))/(2*A),
    Root2 := (–B – sqrt(Discr))/(2*A).

% Polynomials are converted to a normal form consisting of a list of the form
% (*Ck,Nk*), ..., (*C0,0*). Terms with zero coefficients are removed

polynomial_normal_form(Polynomial,X,NormalForm) ←
    polynomial_to_list(X,Polynomial,List),
    remove_zero_terms(List,NormalForm).

polynomial_to_list(X,X,[(1,1)]) ← !.
polynomial_to_list(X,X↑N,[(1,N)]) ← !.
polynomial_to_list(X,Term,[(Term,0)]) ← free_of(X,Term), !.
polynomial_to_list(X,Poly1+Poly2,List) ← !.
    polynomial_to_list(X,Poly1,List1),
    polynomial_to_list(X,Poly2,List2),
    add_polynomials(List1,List2,List).
polynomial_to_list(X,Poly1–Poly2,List) ← !.
    polynomial_to_list(X,Poly1,List1),
    polynomial_to_list(X,Poly2,List2),
    subtract_polynomials(List1,List2,List).
polynomial_to_list(X,Poly1*Poly2,List) ← !.
    polynomial_to_list(X,Poly1,List1),

```
        polynomial_to_list(X,Poly2,List2),
        multiply_polynomials(List1,List2,List).
polynomial_to_list(X,Poly↑N,List) ← !.
        polynomial_to_list(X,Poly,List1),
        binomial(List1,N,List).

add_polynomials([ ],Poly,Poly) ← !.
add_polynomials(Poly,[ ],Poly) ← !.
add_polynomials([(C1,N1)|Ps],[(C2,N2)|Qs],[(C1,N1)|Rs]) ←
        N1 > N2, !,
        add_polynomials(Ps,[(C2,N2)|Qs],Rs).
add_polynomials([(C1,N)|Ps],[(C2,N)|Qs],[(C,N)|Rs]) ←
        !, C := C1+C2, add_polynomials(Ps,Qs,Rs).
add_polynomials([(C1,N1)|Ps],[(C2,N2)|Qs],[(C2,N2)|Rs]) ←
        add_polynomials([(C1,N1)|Ps],Qs,Rs).

subtract_polynomials(Poly1,Poly2,Poly) ←
        multiply_single(Poly2,(-1,0),Poly3),
        add_polynomials(Poly1,Poly3,Poly).

multiply_polynomials([ ],_,[ ] ) ← !.
multiply_polynomials([(C,N)|Ps],Qs,Rs) ←
        multiply_single(Qs,(C,N),Rs1),
        multiply_polynomials(Ps,Qs,Rs2),
        add_polynomials(Rs1,Rs2,Rs), !.

multiply_single([ ],_,[ ]) ← !.
multiply_single([(C1,N1)|Ps],(C,N),[(C2,N2)|Qs]) ←
        N2 := N+N1, C2 := C*C1,
        multiply_single(Ps,(C,N),Qs).

binomial(_,0,[(1,0)]) ← !.
binomial(Bag,1,Bag) ← !.
binomial(Sbag,N,Ebag) ← !,
        eval(N-1,N1),
        binomial(Sbag,N1,Ebag1),
        multiply_poly(Sbag,Ebag1,Ebag).

remove_zero_terms([ ],[ ]) ← !.
remove_zero_terms([(0,N)|Ps],Qs) ← !,
        remove_zero_terms(Ps,Qs).
remove_zero_terms([(C,N)|Ps],[(C,N)|Qs]) ←
        remove_zero_terms(Ps,Qs).
```

/* *Predicates for homogenization* */

% Check if equation has multiple offenders. Offenders are located by *parse*
% and duplicates are removed before checking if there are multiple many

mult_off_set(Eq,X,Foffs)←prse(Eq,X,Offs),
    remove_duplicates(Offs,Foffs),
    mult_list(Foffs).

prse(E,X,L)←parse(E,X,L\[ ]).

parse(A∗B,X,L1\L2)← !, parse(A,X,L1\L3),parse(B,X,L3\L2).
parse(A–B,X,L1\L2)← !, parse(A,X,L1\L3),parse(B,X,L3\L2).
parse(A+B,X,L1\L2)← !, parse(A,X,L1\L3),parse(B,X,L3\L2).
parse(A=B,X,L1\L2)← !, parse(A,X,L1\L3),parse(B,X,L3\L2).
parse(A↑B,X,L)←integer(B), !, parse(A,X,L).
parse(X,X,[X|L]\L) ← !.
parse(A,X,L\L)←free_of(X,A), !.
parse(A,X,[A|L]\L) ← !.

remove_duplicates(Set,Fset) ←
    remove_duplicates(Set,[ ],Fset).
remove_duplicates([A|As],Sofar,Bs)←
    member(A,Sofar), !,
    remove_duplicates(As,Sofar,Bs).
remove_duplicates([A|As],Sofar,[A|Bs]) ← !,
    remove_duplicates(As,[A|Sofar],Bs).
remove_duplicates([ ],_,[ ]).

% A list is *multiple* if it contains at least two elements *mult_list*([_,_|_]).
% The Equation in X is homogenized to *NewEquation* in *Subterm*

homogenize(Eq,X,Offs,NewEq,Subterm)←
    reduced_term(Eq,X,Offs,Type,Subterm),
    rewrite(Offs,Type,Subterm,Substitutions),
    substitute(Substitutions,Eq,NewEq).

% *reduced term* is defined only to serve our tests and is not implemented

reduced_term(_,_,[2↑(2∗x),2↑(x+1)],expo,2↑ x).
reduced_term(_,_,[2↑(x+1),2↑(2∗x)],expo,2↑ x).

rewrite([Term|Rest],Type,Subterm,[Term=Rw|Rws])←
    rewrite_rule(Term,Type,Subterm,Rw),
    rewrite(Rest,Type,Subterm,Rws).
rewrite([ ],_,_,[ ]).

rewrite_rule(A↑(N∗X),expo,A↑X,(A↑X)↑N).
rewrite_rule(A↑(−X),expo,A↑X,1/(A↑X)).
rewrite_rule(A↑(X+B),expo,A↑X,A↑B∗A↑X).

substitute(Subs,A=B,NewA=NewB) ← !,
    substitute(Subs,A,NewA),
    substitute(Subs,B,NewB).
substitute(Subs,A∗B, NewA∗NewB) ← !,
    substitute(Subs,A,NewA),
    substitute(Subs,B,NewB).
substitute(Subs,A/B,NewA/NewB) ← !,
    substitute(Subs,A,NewA),
    substitute(Subs,B,NewB).
substitute(Subs,A+B,NewA+NewB) ← !,
    substitute(Subs,A,NewA),
    substitute(Subs,B,NewB).
substitute(Subs,A−B,NewA−NewB) ← !,
    substitute(Subs,A,NewA),
    substitute(Subs,B,NewB).
substitute(Subs,A↑B,NewA) ←
    integer(B), !,
    substitute(Subs,A,NewA).
substitute(Subs,A,NewA) ← !,
    ground_substitute(Subs,A,NewA).

ground_substitute(Subs,A,NewA) ←
    member(A=NewA,Subs), !.
ground_substitute(Subs,A,A) ← !.

% The substituted equation is solved for intermediate results, which are then
% solved against the substitution to give the final results

solve_homo_equation(Eq,Subterm,X,Ss) ←
    slve_equation(Eq,Subterm,S),
    filter_eqns(S,X,NewEqs),
    solve_equations(NewEqs,Ss).

% This filter takes nonredundant intermediate results and packages them as
% equations in the original unknown

filter_eqns(InterResults,X,NewEqs) ←
    filter_eqns(InterResults,X,[ ],NewEqs).
filter_eqns([S|Ss],X,Sofar,Feqs)←
    member(S,Sofar), !,

```
filter_eqns(Ss,X,Sofar,Feqs).
filter_eqns([S|Ss],X,Sofar,Feqs) ←
    !,filter_eqns(Ss,X,[S|Sofar],[(S,X)|Feqs]).

filter_eqs([ ],_,_,[ ]).
```

III. Occurrence predicates

```
free_of(Kernel,Kernel) ← !, fail.
free_of(Kernel,Expression) ← indecomposable(Expression), !.
free_of(Kernel,Expression) ←
    functor(Expression,_,Arity), !,
    free_of(Arity,Kernel,Expression).
free_of(0,Kernel,Expression) ← !.
free_of(N,Kernel,Expression) ←
    arg(N,Expression,Argument),
    free_of(Kernel,Argument), !,
    N1 := N–1,
    free_of(N1,Kernel,Expression).

single_occurrence(Kernel,Expression) ←
    occurrence(Kernel,Expression,1).

multiple_occurrence(Kernel,Expression) ←
    occurrence(Kernel,Expression,N), !,
    N > 1.

occurrence(SubTerm,Term,Occurrences) ←
    occurrence(SubTerm,Term,0,Times), !,
    Occurrences = Times.
occurrence(SubTerm,Term,Accumulator,Total) ←
    Term == SubTerm, !,
    Total := Accumulator+1.
occurrence(SubTerm,Term,Total,Total) ←
    indecomposable(Term), !.
occurrence(SubTerm,Term,SoFar,Total) ←
    functor(Term,Functor,Arity), !,
    occurrence(Arity,SubTerm,Term,SoFar,Total).
occurrence(0,SubTerm,Term,Total,Total) ← !.
occurrence(N,SubTerm,Term,Accumulator,Total) ←
    arg(N,Term,Arg),
    occurrence(SubTerm,Arg,Accumulator,Accumulator1), !,
    N1 := N – 1,
    occurrence(N1,SubTerm,Term,Accumulator1,Total).
```

IV. Utilities

zero(0).

non_zero(A) ← A≠0.

mulbag(A∗B).

indecomposable(Term) ← var(Term).
indecomposable(Term) ← atomic(Term).
indecomposable(Term) ← rational(Term).

Appendix 31.2: Code for CONPRESS

I. The top level

solve_eqns([(Eq,Var)|EqVars],Ss\Ss1) ←
      solve_equation(Eq,Var,Ss\Ss2?),
      solve_eqns(EqVars,Ss2\Ss1?).
solve_eqns([ ],S\S).

/∗ *Case for factorization* ∗/

solve_equation(Lhs=Rhs,Var, Ss) ←
      zero(Rhs), mulbag(Lhs) |
      factorize(Lhs,Var,Factored_eqns),
      solve_eqns(Factored_eqns? ,Ss).

/∗ *Case for isolation* ∗/

solve_equation(Eq,Var,Ss) ←
      single_occ(Var,Eq) |
      position(Var,Eq,[Side|Posn]),
      maneuver_sides(Side?,Eq,Eq1),
      isolate(Posn?,Eq1,Ss).

/∗ *Case for polynomials* ∗/

solve_equation(Lhs=Rhs,Var,Ss) ←
      is_polynomial(Var,Lhs–Rhs) |
      solve_polynomial_equation(Lhs=Rhs,Var,Ss).

/∗ *Case for homogenization* ∗/

solve_equation(Eq,Var,Ss) ←
      mult_off_set(Eq,Var,Offs) |
      homogenize(Eq,Var,Offs,NewEq,Subterm),

solve_homo_eqn(NewEq?,Subterm?,Var,Ss).

II. The methods

/* *Predicates for factorization* */

% An equation, $A*B*\cdots*C=0$, is factorized into nontrivial, nonredundant
% equations, $A=0, B=0, \ldots, C=0$

factorize(Lhs,X,Feqs) ← factorize(Lhs,X,[ ],Feqs).
factorize(A*B,X,Sofar,Feqs) ←
    factorize_1(B?,X,Sofar,NewSofar,Feqs1),
    factorize(A?,X,NewSofar?,Feqs2),
    merge(Feqs1?,Feqs2?,Feqs).
factorize(A,X,Sofar,Feqs) ←
    A ≠ _*_ |
    factorize_1(A,X,Sofar,_,Feqs).
factorize_1(A,X,[So|Far],[So|Far1],Feqs1) ←
    A ≠ So |
    factorize_1(A,X,Far?,Far1,Feqs1).
factorize_1(A,X,[So|Far],[So|Far],[ ]) ←
    A =?= So | true.
factorize_1(A,X,[ ],[ ],[ ]) ←
    free_of(X,A) | true.
factorize_1(A,X,[ ],[A],[(A=0,X)]) ←
    otherwise | true.

/* *Predicates for isolation* */

isolate([ ],Equation,[Equation|Eqs]\Eqs).
isolate([N|Position],Equation,IsolatedEquations) ←
    isolax(N,Equation,Equation1),
    isolate(Position,Equation1?,IsolatedEquations).

maneuver_sides(1,Lhs = Rhs,Lhs = Rhs).
maneuver_sides(2,Lhs = Rhs,Rhs = Lhs).

% Some axioms to isolate unknown, sufficient for our tests

isolax(1,–Lhs = Rhs,Lhs = –Rhs).
isolax(1,Term1+Term2 = Rhs,Term1 = Rhs–Term2).
isolax(2,Term1+Term2 = Rhs,Term2 = Rhs–Term1).
isolax(1,Term1–Term2 = Rhs,Term1 = Rhs+Term2).
isolax(2,Term1–Term2 = Rhs,Term2 = Term1–Rhs).
isolax(1,Term1*Term2 = Rhs,Term1 = Rhs/Term2) ←
    Term2 ≠ 0 | true.

isolax(2,Term1∗Term2 = Rhs,Term2 = Rhs/Term1) ←
    Term1 ≠ 0 | true.
isolax(1,Term1/Term2 − Rhs,Term1 = Rhs∗Term2) ←
    Term2 ≠ 0 | true.
isolax(2,Term1/Term2 = Rhs,Term2 = Term1/Rhs) ←
    Rhs ≠ 0 | true.
isolax(1,Term1↑Term2 = Rhs,Term1 = Rhs↑(−Term2)).
isolax(2,Term1↑Term2 = Rhs,Term2 = log(base(Term1),Rhs)).

% *position*(*Sub,Term,Position*), the *Position* of *Sub* in *Term*

position(Term, Term, [ ]).
position(Term, Exp, Path) ←
    compound(Exp) |
    functor(Exp, _, N),
    position(N, Term, Exp, Path).
position(N, Term, Exp, [N|Path]) ←
    N > 0,
    arg(N,Exp,Arg),
    position(Term, Arg?, Path) | true.
position(N, Term, Exp, Path) ←
    M := N−1,
    M > 0,
    position(M?, Term, Exp, Path) | true.

/∗ *Predicates for polynomials* ∗/

% To determine if equation is a polynomial

is_polynomial(X,X).
is_polynomial(X,Term) ←
    free_of(X,Term) | true.
is_polynomial(X,Term1+Term2) ←
    is_polynomial(X,Term1?), is_polynomial(X,Term2?).
is_polynomial(X,Term1−Term2) ←
    is_polynomial(X,Term1?), is_polynomial(X,Term2?).
is_polynomial(X,Term1∗Term2) ←
    is_polynomial(X,Term1?), is_polynomial(X,Term2?).
is_polynomial(X,Term↑N) ←
    integer(N), N ≥ 0, is_polynomial(X,Term?).

% Solving polynomials

solve_polynomial_equation(Lhs=Rhs,X,Solution) ←
    polynomial_normal_form(Lhs−Rhs,X,Poly),

poly_method(X,Poly?,Solution).

% Polynomial method for quadratic equations (the only polynomial method
% currently implemented)

poly_method(X,Poly,S) ←
    quadratic(Poly) |
    find_coefficients(Poly,Coeffs),
    discriminant(Coeffs?,Discriminant),
    roots(X,Coeffs?,Discriminant?,S).

quadratic([(_,2)|_]).

find_coefficients([(A,2)|Poly],(A,B?,C?)) ←
find2(Poly?,B,C).
find2([(B,1),(C,0)],B,C).
find2([(B,1)],B,0).
find2([(C,0)],0,C).
find2([ ],0,0).

discriminant((A,B,C),Discriminant?) ←
    Discriminant := B*B–4*A*C.

roots(X,(A,B,_),0,[X = Root?|Rs]–Rs) ←
    Root := –B/(2*A).
roots(X,(A,B,C),Discr,[X = Root1?,X = Root2?|Rs]–Rs) ←
    Discr ≠ 0 |
    Root1 := (–B + sqrt(Discr))/(2*A),
    Root2 := (–B – sqrt(Discr))/(2*A).

% Polynomials are converted to a normal form consisting of a list of the form
% (*Ck,Nk*),...,(*C0,0*). Terms with zero coefficients are removed

polynomial_normal_form(Polynomial,Var,NormalForm) ←
    polynomial_to_list(Var,Polynomial,List),
    remove_zero_terms(List?,NormalForm).
polynomial_to_list(Var,Var,[(1,1)]).
polynomial_to_list(Var,Var↑N,[(1,N)]).
polynomial_to_list(Var,Poly1+Poly2,List) ←
    polynomial_to_list(Var,Poly1,List1),
    polynomial_to_list(Var,Poly2,List2),
    add_polynomials(List1?,List2?,List).
polynomial_to_list(Var,Poly1–Poly2,List) ←
    polynomial_to_list(Var,Poly1,List1),
    polynomial_to_list(Var,Poly2,List2),
    subtract_polynomials(List1?,List2?,List).

polynomial_to_list(Var,Poly1∗Poly2,List) ←
    polynomial_to_list(Var,Poly1,List1),
    polynomial_to_list(Var,Poly2,List2),
    multiply_polynomials(List1?,List2?,List).
polynomial_to_list(Var,Poly↑N,List) ←
    polynomial_to_list(Var,Poly,List1),
    binomial(List1?,N,List).
polynomial_to_list(Var,Term,[(Term,0)]) ←
    free_of(Var,Term) | true.

add_polynomials([ ],Poly,Poly).
add_polynomials(Poly,[ ],Poly).
add_polynomials([(C1,N1)|Ps],[(C2,N2)|Qs],[(C1,N1)|Rs]) ←
    N1 > N2 |
    add_polynomials(Ps,[(C2,N2)|Qs],Rs).
add_polynomials([(C1,N)|Ps],[(C2,N)|Qs],[(C?,N)|Rs]) ←
    C := C1+C2, add_polynomials(Ps,Qs,Rs).
add_polynomials([(C1,N1)|Ps],[(C2,N2)|Qs],[(C2,N2)|Rs]) ←
    N1 < N2 |
    add_polynomials([(C1,N1)|Ps],Qs,Rs).

subtract_polynomials(Poly1,Poly2,Poly) ←
    multiply_single(Poly2,(−1,0),Poly3),
    add_polynomials(Poly1,Poly3?,Poly).

multiply_polynomials([ ],_,[ ]).
multiply_polynomials([(C,N)|Ps],Qs,Rs) ←
    multiply_single(Qs,(C,N),Rs1),
    multiply_polynomials(Ps,Qs,Rs2),
    add_polynomials(Rs1?,Rs2?,Rs).

multiply_single([ ],_,[ ]).
multiply_single([(C1,N1) |
Ps],(C,N),[(C2?,N2?)|Qs]) ←
    N2 := N+N1, C2 := C∗C1,
    multiply_single(Ps,(C,N),Qs).

binomial(_,0,[(1,0)]).
binomial(Bag,1,Bag).
binomial(Sbag,N,Ebag) ←
    N > 1 |
    N1 := N−1,
    binomial(Sbag,N1?,Ebag1),
    multiply_polynomials(Sbag,Ebag1?,Ebag).

remove_zero_terms([ ],[ ]).
remove_zero_terms([(0,N)|Ps],Qs) ←
    remove_zero_terms(Ps?,Qs).
remove_zero_terms([(C,N)|Ps],[(C,N)|Qs?]) ←
    C ≠ 0 |
    remove_zero_terms(Ps?,Qs).

/* *Predicates for homogenization* */

% Check if equation has multiple offenders. Offenders are located by *parse* and
% duplicates are removed before checking if there are multiple many

mult_off_set(Eq,X,Foffs?)←
    prse(Eq,X,Offs),
    remove_duplicates(Offs?,Foffs),
    mult_list(Foffs?).

prse(E,X,L) ← parse(E,X,L\[ ]).

parse(A∗B,X,L1\L2) ← parse(A?,X,L1\L3), parse(B?,X,L3\L2).
parse(A/B,X,L1\L2) ← parse(A?,X,L1\L3), parse(B?,X,L3\L2).
parse(A–B,X,L1\L2) ← parse(A?,X,L1\L3), parse(B?,X,L3\L2).
parse(A+B,X,L1\L2) ← parse(A?,X,L1\L3), parse(B?,X,L3\L2).
parse(A=B,X,L1\L2) ← parse(A?,X,L1\L3), parse(B?,X,L3\L2).
parse(A↑B,X,L) ← integer(B) | parse(A?,X,L).
parse(X,X,[X|L]\L).
parse(A,X,L\L) ← free_of(X,A) | true.
parse(A,X,[A| L]\L)←otherwise | true.

remove_duplicates(As,Bs) ←
remove_duplicates(As,[ ],Bs).
remove_duplicates([A|As],Acc,Outs) ←
    remove_duplicates_1(A,Acc,Acc1,Out1),
    remove_duplicates(As?,Acc1?,Out2),
    merge(Out1?,Out2?,Outs).
remove_duplicates([ ],_,[ ]).
remove_duplicates_1(A,[ ],[A],[A]).
remove_duplicates_1(A,[S|Ss],[S|Ss1],Out) ←
    S ≠ A |
    remove_duplicates_1(A,Ss?,Ss1,Out).
remove_duplicates_1(A,[S|Ss],[S|Ss],[ ]) ←
    S =?= A | true.

% A list is multiple if it contains at least two elements

mult_list([_|Xs]) ← mult_list_2(Xs?).

mult_list_2([_|_]).

% The equation in *X* is homogenized to a new equation in *Subterm*

homogenize(Eq,X,Offs,NewEq?,Subterm?) ←
    reduced_term(Eq,X,Offs,Type,Subterm),
    rewrite(Offs,Type?,Subterm?,Substitutions),
    substitute(Substitutions?,Eq,NewEq).

% *reduced_term* is defined only to serve our tests and isn't implemented

reduced_term(_,_,[2↑(2∗x),2↑ (x+1)],expo,2↑x).
reduced_term(_,_,[2↑(x+1),2↑ (2∗x)],expo,2↑x).

rewrite([Term|Rest],Type,Subterm,[Term=Rw?|Rws?]) ←
    rewrite_rule(Term,Type,Subterm,Rw),
    rewrite(Rest,Type,Subterm,Rws).
rewrite([ ],_,_,[ ]).

rewrite_rule(A↑(N∗X),expo,A↑X,(A↑X)↑N).
rewrite_rule(A↑(−X),expo,A↑X,1/(A↑X)).
rewrite_rule(A↑(X+B),expo,A↑X,A↑B∗A↑X).

substitute(Subs,A=B,(NewA?)=(NewB?)) ←
    substitute(Subs,A,NewA),
    substitute(Subs,B,NewB).
substitute(Subs,A∗B, (NewA?)∗(NewB?)) ←
    substitute(Subs,A,NewA),
    substitute(Subs,B,NewB).
substitute(Subs,A/B,(NewA?)/(NewB?)) ←
    substitute(Subs,A,NewA),
    substitute(Subs,B,NewB).
substitute(Subs,A+B,(NewA?)+(NewB?)) ←
    substitute(Subs,A,NewA),
    substitute(Subs,B,NewB).
substitute(Subs,A−B,(NewA?)−(NewB?)) ←
    substitute(Subs,A,NewA),
    substitute(Subs,B,NewB).
substitute(Subs,A↑B,NewA?) ←
    integer(B) |
    substitute(Subs,A,NewA).
substitute(Subs,A,NewA?) ←
    otherwise |
    ground_substitute(Subs,A,NewA).

ground_substitute(Subs,A?,NewA) ←

```
            member(A=NewA,Subs) | true.
ground_substitute(Subs,A?,A) ←
    otherwise | true.
```

% The substituted equation is solved for intermediate results, which are then
% solved against the substitution to give the final results

```
solve_homo_eqn(Eq,Subterm,X,Ss) ←
    slve_equation(Eq,Subterm,S),
    filter_eqns(S?,X,NewEqs),
    solve_eqns(NewEqs?,Ss).
```

% This filter takes nonredundant intermediate results and packages them as
% equations in the original unknown

```
filter_equations(InterResults,X,NewEqs?) ←
    filter_equations(InterResults,X,[ ],NewEqs).
filter_equations([S|Ss],X,Sofar,Feqns) ←
    filter_equations_1(S,X,Sofar,NewSofar,Feqns1),
    filter_equations(Ss?,X,NewSofar?,Feqns2),
    merge(Feqns1?,Feqns2?,Feqns).
filter_equations([ ],_,_,[ ]).
filter_equations_1(S,X,[ ],[S],[(S,X)]).
```

```
filter_equations_1(S,X,[More|Sofar],[More|Sofar1],Feqns) ←
    S ≠ More |
    filter_equations_1(S,X,Sofar?,Sofar1,Feqns).
filter_equations_1(S,X,[More|Sofar],[More|Sofar],[ ]) ←
    S =?= More | true.
```

III. Occurrence Predicates

```
free_of(Sub,Term) ←
    occs(Sub,Term,Ps,_),
    no_pulse(Ps?).
```

```
single_occ(Sub,Term) ←
    occs(Sub,Term,Ps,_),
    single_pulse(Ps?).
```

```
no_pulse([ ]).
```

```
single_pulse([pulse]).
```

```
occs(_,_,_,H) ←
    H=?=halt | true.
occs(Sub,Term,[ ],H) ←
```

Term ≠ Sub, indecomposable(Term) | true.
occs(Sub,Term,[pulse],H) ←
    Term=?=Sub |true.
occs(Sub,Term,Ps,H) ←
    compound(Term) |
    functor(Term,F,A),
    occs(A?,Sub,Term,Ps,H).
occs(_,_,_,_,H) ←
    H=?=halt | true.
occs(0,Sub,Term,[ ],H) ← true.
occs(N,Sub,Term,Ps,H) ←
    N>0 |
    M := N−1, arg(N,Term,Arg),
    occs(Sub,Arg?,Ps1,H),
    occs(M?,Sub,Term,Ps2,H),
    haltable_merge(Ps1?,Ps2?,Ps,H).

IV. Utilities

zero(0).

mulbag(A∗B).

indecomposable(Exp) ← var(Exp) | true.
indecomposable(Exp) ← atomic(Exp) | true.
indecomposable(Exp) ← rational(Exp) | true.

% merge with halt variable, *H*

haltable_merge(_,_,_,H) ← H=?=halt | true.
haltable_merge([X| Xs],Ys,[X| Zs?],H) ←
    haltable_merge(Ys,Xs?,Zs,H).
haltable_merge(Xs,[Y| Ys],[Y| Zs?],H) ←
    haltable_merge(Xs,Ys?,Zs,H).
haltable_merge([ ],Ys,Ys,_).
haltable_merge(Xs,[ ],Xs,_).

Appendix 31.3: Code for FCPRESS

I. The top level

slve_equations(EqVars,Ss?) ← solve_equations(EqVars,Ss\[ ]).
solve_equations([EqVar|EqVars],Ss\Ss1) ←

```
        choose(EqVar,Method),
        solve_by_method(EqVar,Method?,Ss\Ss2?),
        solve_equations(EqVars?,Ss2\Ss1?).
solve_equations([ ],Ss\Ss).

solve_by_method((Lhs=0,Var),factorize,Ss) ←
        factorize(Lhs,Var,Factored_Eqs),
        solve_equations(Factored_Eqs?,Ss).
solve_by_method((Eq,Var),isolate,Ss) ←
        pos(Var,Eq,[Side|Posn]),
        maneuver_sides(Side,Eq,Eq1),
        isolate(Posn?,Eq1?,Ss).
solve_by_method((Lhs=Rhs,Var),polynomial,Ss) ←
        polynomial_normal_form(Lhs–Rhs,Var,Poly),
        choose_poly_method(Poly?,PolyMethod),
        apply_poly_method(Poly?,Var,PolyMethod?,Ss).
solve_by_method((Eq,Var),MOS,Ss) ←
        otherwise |
        homogenize(Eq,Var,MOS,NewEq,NewVar),
        slve_equations([(NewEq?,NewVar?)],Ss1),
        filter_equations(Ss1?,Var,Feqns),
        solve_equations(Feqns?,Ss).
```

/ Choosing a method */*

```
choose(EqVar,Method)←
        condition_factorize(EqVar,Method),
        condition_isolation(EqVar,Method),
        condition_polynomial(EqVar,Method),
        condition_homogenization(EqVar,Method).

condition_factorize((Lhs=0,_),Method) ←
        mulbag(Lhs?,Method).
condition_factorize(_,Method) ←
        otherwise | true.

condition_isolation((Eq,Var),Method) ←
        single_occ(Var,Eq,Method).

condition_polynomial((Lhs=Rhs,Var),Method)←
        is_polynomial(Var,Lhs–Rhs,Method).

condition_homogenization(EqVar,Method) ←
        multiple_offender_set(EqVar,Method).
```

II. The methods

/* *Predicates for factorisation* */

% The condition:

mulbag(A*B,factorize).
mulbag(_,_) ← otherwise | true.

% The method:

factorize(Lhs,X,Feqs) ←
    make_stream(Lhs,X,Flow),
    remove_trivial_and_duplicate(Flow?,Feqs).

make_stream(A*B,X,[(B=0,X)|Flow]) ←
    make_stream(A?,X,Flow).
make_stream(A,X,[(A=0,X)]) ← A ≠ _*_ | true.

/* *Predicates for isolation* */

% condition for isolation is single occurrence, appears later.
% The Method:

isolate([ ],Eq,[Eq|Ss]–Ss).
isolate([N|Position],Eq,IsolatedEquations) ←
    isolax(N,Eq,Equation1),
    isolate(Position?,Equation1?,IsolatedEquations).

maneuver_sides(1,Lhs = Rhs,Lhs = Rhs).
maneuver_sides(2,Lhs = Rhs,Rhs = Lhs).

% Some axioms for isolation

isolax(1,–Lhs = Rhs,Lhs = –Rhs).
isolax(1,Term1+Term2 = Rhs,Term1 = Rhs–Term2).
isolax(2,Term1+Term2 = Rhs,Term2 = Rhs–Term1).
isolax(1,Term1–Term2 = Rhs,Term1 = Rhs+Term2).
isolax(2,Term1–Term2 = Rhs,Term2 = Term1–Rhs).
isolax(1,Term1*Term2 = Rhs,Term1 = Rhs/Term2) ←
    Term2 ≠ 0 | true.
isolax(2,Term1*Term2 = Rhs,Term2 = Rhs/Term1) ←
    Term1 ≠ 0 | true.
isolax(1,Term1/Term2 = Rhs,Term1 = Rhs*Term2) ←
    Term2 ≠ 0 | true.
isolax(2,Term1/Term2 = Rhs,Term2 = Term1/Rhs) ←
    Rhs ≠ 0 | true.
isolax(1,Term1↑Term2 = Rhs,Term1 = Rhs↑(–Term2)).

isolax(2,Term1↑Term2 = Rhs,Term2 = log(base(Term1),Rhs)).

% position

pos(Sub,Term,Path) ← pos(Sub,Term,Path,H).
pos(Sub,Term,[kill],H) ← H =?= halt | true.
pos(Term,Term,[ ],halt).
pos(Sub,Term,[kill],H) ← atomic(Term), Sub ≠ Term | true.
pos(Sub,Term,Path,H) ← structure(Term) |
    functor(Term,_,N), pos(N?,Sub,Term,Path,H).
pos(N,Sub,Term,[kill],H) ← H =?= halt | true.
pos(N,Sub,Term,Path,H) ← N > 1 |
    M := N–1, arg(N,Term,Arg),
    pos(M?,Sub,Term,P1,H), pos(Sub,Arg?,P2,H),
    merge_pos_results(N,P1,P2,Path).
pos(N,Sub,Term,Path,H) ← N =?= 1 |
    arg(N,Term,Arg),
    pos(Sub,Arg?,P1,H),
    merge_pos_results(N,[kill],P1,Path).

merge_pos_results(N,[kill],P2,[N|P2]) ←
    P2 ≠ [kill] | true.
merge_pos_results(_,P1,[kill],P1) ←
    P1 ≠ [kill] | true.
merge_pos_results(_,P1,P2,[kill]) ←
    P1 =?= [kill], P2 =?= [kill] | true.

/* Predicates for polynomials */

% The condition:

is_polynomial(Var,Term,Method)←
    is_polynomial(Var,Term,Method,H).
is_polynomial(_,_,_,H) ← H =?= halt | true.
is_polynomial(_,_,M,halt) ← nonvar(M) | true.
is_polynomial(Var,Term1+Term2,Method,H) ←
    is_polynomial(Var,Term1?,M1,H),
    is_polynomial(Var,Term2?,M2,H),
    poly_merge_results(M1,M2,Method,H).
is_polynomial(Var,Term1–Term2,Method,H) ←
    is_polynomial(Var,Term1?,M1,H),
    is_polynomial(Var,Term2?,M2,H),
    poly_merge_results(M1,M2,Method,H).
is_polynomial(Var,Term1*Term2,Method,H) ←
    is_polynomial(Var,Term1?,M1,H),

```
        is_polynomial(Var,Term2?,M2,H),
        poly_merge_results(M1,M2,Method,H).
is_polynomial(Var,Term↑N,Method,H) ←
        integer(N), N ≥ 0 |
        is_polynomial(Var,Term?,Method,H).
is_polynomial(Var,Var,polynomial,H).
is_polynomial(Var,Term,M,H) ← otherwise |
        free_of(Var,Term,Ans), base_is_polynomial(Ans?,M).

base_is_polynomial(yes,polynomial).
base_is_polynomial(_,_) ←
        otherwise | true.

poly_merge_results(_,_,_,H) ←
        H =?= halt | true.
poly_merge_results(M1,M2,polynomial,H) ←
        M1 =?= polynomial, M2 =?= polynomial | true.
poly_merge_results(_,_,_,halt) ←
        otherwise | true.
```

% The method: (only quadratic method implemented)

```
choose_poly_method([(_,2)|_],quadratic).

apply_poly_method(Poly,Var,quadratic,Ss) ←
        find_coefficients(Poly,Coeffs),
        discriminant(Coeffs?,Discriminant),
        roots(Var,Coeffs?,Discriminant?,Ss).

find_coefficients([(A,2)|Poly],(A,B?,C?)) ← find2(Poly?,B,C).

find2([(B,1),(C,0)],B,C).
find2([(B,1)],B,0).
find2([(C,0)],0,C).
find2([ ],0,0).

discriminant((A,B,C),Discriminant?) ← Discriminant := B*B−4*A*C.

roots(Var,(A,B,_),0,[Var = Root?|Rs]\Rs) ←
        Root := −B/(2*A).
roots(Var,(A,B,C),Discr,[Var = Root1?,Var = Root2?|Rs]\Rs) ←
        Discr ≠ 0 |
        Root1 := (−B + sqrt(Discr))/(2*A),
        Root2 := (−B − sqrt(Discr))/(2*A).
```

% Polynomials are converted to a normal form consisting of a list of the form
% [(Ck,Nk), ..., (C0,0)]. Terms with zero coefficients are removed

polynomial_normal_form(Polynomial,Var,NormalForm) ←
    polynomial_to_list(Var,Polynomial,List),
    remove_zero_terms(List?,NormalForm).
polynomial_to_list(Var,Var,[(1,1)]).
polynomial_to_list(Var,Var↑N,[(1,N)]).
polynomial_to_list(Var,Poly1+Poly2,List) ←
    polynomial_to_list(Var,Poly1,List1),
    polynomial_to_list(Var,Poly2,List2),
    add_polynomials(List1?,List2?,List).
polynomial_to_list(Var,Poly1−Poly2,List) ←
    polynomial_to_list(Var,Poly1,List1),
    polynomial_to_list(Var,Poly2,List2),
    subtract_polynomials(List1?,List2?,List).
polynomial_to_list(Var,Poly1∗Poly2,List) ←
    polynomial_to_list(Var,Poly1,List1),
    polynomial_to_list(Var,Poly2,List2),
    multiply_polynomials(List1?,List2?,List).
polynomial_to_list(Var,Poly↑N,List) ←
    polynomial_to_list(Var,Poly,List1),
    binomial(List1?,N,List).
polynomial_to_list(Var,Term,[(Term,0)]) ←
    otherwise |
    free_of(Var,Term,yes).

add_polynomials([ ],Poly,Poly).
add_polynomials(Poly,[ ],Poly).
add_polynomials([(C1,N1)|Ps],[(C2,N2)|Qs],[(C1,N1)|Rs]) ←
    N1 > N2 |
    add_polynomials(Ps,[(C2,N2)|Qs],Rs).
add_polynomials([(C1,N)|Ps],[(C2,N)|Qs],[(C?,N)|Rs]) ←
    C := C1+C2, add_polynomials(Ps,Qs,Rs).
add_polynomials([(C1,N1)|Ps],[(C2,N2)|Qs],[(C2,N2)|Rs]) ←
    N1 < N2 |
    add_polynomials([(C1,N1)|Ps],Qs,Rs).

subtract_polynomials(Poly1,Poly2,Poly) ←
    multiply_single(Poly2,(−1,0),Poly3),
    add_polynomials(Poly1,Poly3?,Poly).

multiply_polynomials([ ],−,[ ]).

multiply_polynomials([(C,N)|Ps],Qs,Rs) ←
    multiply_single(Qs,(C,N),Rs1),
    multiply_polynomials(Ps,Qs,Rs2),
    add_polynomials(Rs1?,Rs2?,Rs).

multiply_single([ ],_,[ ]).
multiply_single([(C1,N1)|Ps],(C,N),[(C2?,N2?)|Qs]) ←
    N2 := N+N1, C2 := C*C1,
    multiply_single(Ps,(C,N),Qs).

binomial(_,0,[(1,0)]).
binomial(Bag,1,Bag).
binomial(Sbag,N,Ebag) ←
    N > 1 |
    N1 := N–1,
    binomial(Sbag,N1?,Ebag1),
    multiply_polynomials(Sbag,Ebag1?,Ebag).

remove_zero_terms([ ],[ ]).
remove_zero_terms([(0,N)|Ps],Qs) ←
    remove_zero_terms(Ps?,Qs).
remove_zero_terms([(C,N)|Ps],[(C,N)|Qs?]) ←
    C ≠0 |
    remove_zero_terms(Ps?,Qs).

/* Predicates for homogenization */

% condition is multiple offender set:

multiple_offender_set((Eq,Var),Method) ←
    prse(Eq,Var,Offs),
    remove_duplicates(Offs?,Foffs),
    mult_members(Foffs?,Method).

prse(E,Var,L)←parse(E,Var,L\[ ]).

parse(A*B,Var,L1\L2)←
    parse(A?,Var,L1\L3),parse(B?,Var,L3\L2).
parse(A/B,Var,L1\L2)←
    parse(A?,Var,L1\L3),parse(B?,Var,L3\L2).
parse(A–B,Var,L1\L2)←
    parse(A?,Var,L1\L3),parse(B?,Var,L3\L2).
parse(A+B,Var,L1\L2)←
    parse(A?,Var,L1\L3),parse(B?,Var,L3\L2).
parse(A=B,Var,L1\L2)←
    parse(A?,Var,L1\L3),parse(B?,Var,L3\L2).

```
parse(A↑B,Var,L) ←
    integer(B) |
    parse(A?,Var,L).
parse(Var,Var,[Var|L]\L).
parse(A,Var,L,M) ←
    otherwise |
    free_of(Var,A,YorN), base_parse(A,YorN?,L).

base_parse(A,yes,L\L).
base_parse(A,no,[A|L]\L).

mult_members(_,M) ← nonvar(M) | true.
mult_members([X|Xs],M) ← mult_members2([X|Xs?],M).

mult_members2(_,M) ← nonvar(M) | true.
mult_members2([X|[Y|Ys]],[X|[Y|Ys]]).
mult_members2(_,_) ← otherwise | true.
```

% The method:

```
homogenize(Eq,X,Offs,NewEq?,Subterm?) ←
    reduced_term(Eq,X,Offs,Type,Subterm),
    rewrite(Offs,Type?,Subterm?,Substitutions),
    substitute(Substitutions?,Eq,NewEq).

reduced_term(_,_,[2↑(2*x),2↑(x+1)],expo,2↑ x).
reduced_term(_,_,[2↑(x+1),2↑(2*x)],expo,2↑ x).

rewrite([Term|Rest],Type,Subterm,[Term=Rw?|Rws?]) ←
    rewrite_rule(Term,Type,Subterm,Rw),
    rewrite(Rest,Type,Subterm,Rws).
rewrite([ ],_,_,[ ]).
rewrite_rule(A↑(N*X),expo,A↑X,(A↑X)↑N).
rewrite_rule(A↑(−X),expo,A↑X,1/(A↑X)).
rewrite_rule(A↑(X+B),expo,A↑X,A↑B*A↑X).

substitute(Subs,A=B,(NewA?)=(NewB?)) ←
    substitute(Subs,A,NewA),
    substitute(Subs,B,NewB).
substitute(Subs,A*B, (NewA?)*(NewB?)) ←
    substitute(Subs,A,NewA),
    substitute(Subs,B,NewB).
substitute(Subs,A/B,(NewA?)/(NewB?)) ←
    substitute(Subs,A,NewA),
    substitute(Subs,B,NewB).
substitute(Subs,A+B,(NewA?)+(NewB?)) ←
```

substitute(Subs,A,NewA),
    substitute(Subs,B,NewB).
substitute(Subs,A–B,(NewA?)–(NewB?)) ←
    substitute(Subs,A,NewA),
    substitute(Subs,B,NewB).
substitute(Subs,A↑B,NewA?) ←
    integer(B) |
    substitute(Subs,A,NewA).
substitute(Subs,A,NewA?) ←
    otherwise |
    ground_substitute(Subs?,A?,NewA).

ground_substitute([ ],A,A).
ground_substitute([Some = Thing|Subs],A,NewA) ←
    Some ≠ A |
    ground_substitute(Subs?,A,NewA).
ground_substitute([Some = Thing|Subs],A,Thing) ←
    Some =?= A | true.

III. Occurrence predicates

occs(_,_,_,H) ← ground(H) | true.
occs(Sub,Term,[ ],H) ← Term ≠ Sub, atomic(Term) | true.
occs(Sub,Term,[ ],H) ← Term ≠ Sub, var(Term) | true.
occs(Sub,Term,[pulse],H) ← Term =?= Sub | true.
occs(Sub,Term,Ps,H) ←
    structure(Term) |
    functor(Term,F,A),
    occs(A?,Sub,Term,Ps,H).
occs(_,_,_,_,H) ← ground(H) | true.
occs(0,Sub,Term,[ ],H).
occs(N,Sub,Term,Ps,H) ←
    N > 0 |
    M := N–1, arg(N,Term,Arg),
    occs(Sub,Arg?,Ps1,H),
    occs(M?,Sub,Term,Ps2,H),
    haltable_merge(Ps1?,Ps2?,Ps,H).

free_of(Sub,Term,Answer) ←
    occs(Sub,Term,Pulses,_),
    no_pulse(Pulses?,Answer).

no_pulse([ ],yes).
no_pulse(_,no) ← otherwise | true.

single_occ(Sub,Term,Method) ←
    occs(Sub,Term,Pulses,Method),
    single_pulse(Pulses?,Method).

single_pulse([pulse],isolate).
single_pulse(_,_) ← otherwise | true.

IV. Filtering processes

% filtering can be done onto a *blackboard*. A closed circuit method is used */
% removing duplicates from a stream:

remove_duplicates(In,Out) ←
    close_outstream(Out?,Out,Ground?),
    remove_duplicates(In,Out,Ground).
remove_duplicates([X|Xs],Out,Left) ←
    copy(X,Out,Left,Right),
    remove_duplicates(Xs?,Out,Right).
remove_duplicates([ ],Out,power).

% removing duplicates and trivial floating objects from a stream:

remove_trivals_and_duplicates(In,Out) ←
    close_outstream(Out?,Out,Ground?),
    remove_trivals_and_duplicates(In,Out,Ground).
remove_trivals_and_duplicates([(A=0,X)|Eqs],Out,Left) ←
    free_of(X,A,Answer),
    copy_if_not_trivial(Answer?,(A=0,X),Out,Left,Right),
    remove_trivals_and_duplicates(Eqs?,Out,Right).
remove_trivals_and_duplicates([ ],Out,power).

% filtering intermediate results into a stream of non redundant equations:

filter_equations(InterResults,X,Feqs) ←
    pack_eqs(InterResults?,Eqs),
    remove_duplicates(Eqs?,Feqs).

% copying onto a blackboard

copy(X,[X|Out],Done,Done) ←
    ground(X) | true.
copy(X,[Y|Out],Left,Right) ←
    X ≠ Y |
    copy(X,Out,Left,Right).

copy_if_not_trivial(no,X,Out,Left,Right) ←
    copy(X,Out,Left,Right).

copy_if_not_trivial(yes,_,_,Done,Done).

% A process who closes the *Blackboard*. Before the circuit has been closed it
% cdr's along the instantiated part of the blackboard. After circuit has been
% closed cuders along but when uninstantiated part is reached it is closed.

close_outstream(_,Out,power) ←
    close_outstream(Out).
close_outstream([_|Out],_,Ground) ←
    close_outstream(Out?,Out,Ground).
close_outstream([ ]).
close_outstream([_|Xs]) ←
    close_outstream(Xs).

V. Merge utility

haltable_merge(_,_,_,H)← H=?=halt | true.
haltable_merge([X|Xs],Ys,[X|Zs?],H)←
    haltable_merge(Ys,Xs?,Zs,H).
haltable_merge(Xs,[Y|Ys],[Y|Zs?],H)←
    haltable_merge(Xs,Ys?,Zs,H).
haltable_merge([ ],Ys,Ys,_).
haltable_merge(Xs,[ ],Xs,_).

Chapter 32

Compiling Or-Parallelism into And-Parallelism

Michael Codish and Ehud Shapiro

The Weizmann Institute of Science

Abstract

This paper suggests a general method for compiling Or-parallelism into And-parallelism. An interpreter for an And/Or-parallel language written in the And-parallel subset of the language induces a source-to-source transformation from the full language into the And-parallel subset. This transformation can be identified and implemented as a special purpose compiler or applied using a general purpose partial evaluator.

The method is demonstrated to compile a variant of Concurrent Prolog into an And-parallel subset of the language called Flat Concurrent Prolog (FCP). This variant is identified and called Safe Concurrent Prolog. A formal definition of Safe Concurrent Prolog provides the basis for its implementation as an interpreter written in FCP. The interpreter is shown to induce a simple and efficient transformation from the And/Or-parallel variant to FCP. The method is also shown to be applicable to the compilation of Or-parallel Prolog into FCP. The performance of the method is discussed in the context of programming examples. These compare well with conventionally compiled Prolog programs.

32.1 Introduction

Concurrent Prolog (Shapiro, Chapter 2), PARLOG (Clark and Gregory, Chapter 3), Guarded Horn Clauses (GHC) (Ueda, Chapter 4) and Flat Concurrent Prolog (FCP) (Mierowsky et al., 1985; Shapiro, Chapter 5) are examples of concurrent logic programming languages. The common aspects of these languages are that they support parallel and committed choice non-deterministic semantics. In addition they use a single assignment convention, communication via shared variables and simple data flow synchronization. The computational model of these languages allows two forms of parallelism to be exploited And-parallelism and Or-parallelism. These correspond to the two forms of non-determinism in the model: process selection and clause selection respectively.

A number of difficult implementation problems must be solved in order to support Or-parallelism in a language. These involve management of multiple environments and communication between environments as well as the management of hierarchical process structures. Experience has shown that the And-parallel subset of a language is sufficient for most applications; it is easier to implement and more efficient as well. The problem with implementing only the And-parallel subset of a language is that the expressiveness of the language is restricted.

This paper suggests a general method to compile Or-parallelism into And-parallelism. An interpreter for an And/Or-parallel language written in the And-parallel subset of the language induces a source-to-source transformation from the full language into the And-parallel subset.

The method is demonstrated by presenting a simple and efficient transformation from a nontrivial variant of Concurrent Prolog to FCP. This variant, called Safe Concurrent Prolog (SCP), is identified, defined by operational semantics and implemented. Membership in SCP is shown to be undecidable. However, syntactic conditions are defined and shown to identify a subset of SCP.

The implementation of Safe Concurrent Prolog written in Flat Concurrent Prolog includes three components: a syntactic safety checker, a precompiler and an interpreter. The interpreter simulates Or-parallelism using And-parallel processes and a mechanism for mutual exclusion. It is shown to induce a simple and efficient transformation from SCP into FCP. The transformation produces a speed-up of two orders of magnitude over interpreted programs. An optimized transformation is achieved by the combination of the interpreter and a partial evaluator developed by Safra (1986).

Several compilation examples are presented. An Or-parallel Prolog interpreter due to Kahn is used to provide for the compilation of various Prolog programs into FCP. The results compare well with similar programs written in GHC (Levy, 1986) and Prolog (Quintus, 1985).

32.2 Safety

An initial implementation of Concurrent Prolog was sufficient to explore the new formalism but was slow, inadequate for large applications and did not correctly implement Or-parallelism (Saraswat, 1986; Ueda, 1985). A full implementation of Concurrent Prolog proved to be a nontrivial task. Problems encountered in the context of Concurrent Prolog suggest that it may be difficult to provide efficient implementation of concurrent logic programming languages which support general hierarchical computations. In languages such as PARLOG, Concurrent Prolog and GHC a guard computation must not effect the global environment until commit time.

In Concurrent Prolog guards are executed in local environments. Guard systems are defined to have access to global variables only via read-only occurrences (Shapiro, Chapter 2). This model is difficult to implement efficiently since variables may become read-only dynamically. A model in which the relationship between variables in a guard system can be determined statically is more amenable to efficient implementation. Such a model can be defined and implemented in terms of a single global environment. A restriction must be imposed on guard computations to enforce the static definition regarding the relationship between variables. Such a restriction is imposed on PARLOG programs and is called a *safety* restriction.

32.2.1 Safety in PARLOG

The notion of *safety* first arises in the context of PARLOG (Gregory, 1987). A fundamental difference between PARLOG and Concurrent Prolog is a safety restriction imposed on the Or-parallel part of a PARLOG computation. Another Difference between the two languages is that in PARLOG each procedure includes a *mode-declaration* which declares the mode of each argument to be *input* or *output*. The mode-declaration also provides a synchronization mechanism. PARLOG does not support general unification but rather provides several term-matching primitives depending on the modes of the terms involved.

The safety restriction of PARLOG prohibits the guards invoked in a computation from instantiating variables in the global environment of the computation. A guard is defined to be *potentially-unsafe* if its evaluation might bind an input variable; a program is defined to be *potentially-unsafe* if one or more of its guards are so (Gregory, 1987). The language employs a compile-time check which detects potentially-unsafe programs. A program which is found to be not potentially-unsafe is claimed to be safe.

The definition of PARLOG (Clark and Gregory, 1985) presents several problems. Programs which are potentially-unsafe are rejected by a syntactic compile-time check. The syntactic restrictions imposed on a program are defined in terms of a complex recursive algorithm on its structure. It is not clear how to write syntactically legal PARLOG programs. Also, there is no proof that programs which are not rejected as potentially unsafe are indeed safe. Clark and Gregory (1985) point out that the suggested safety analysis is not sufficiently fine so that safe programs may be rejected as potentially-unsafe. We claim below that the problem of detecting safe programs is undecidable. Any syntactic algorithm which determines safety is therefore not "sufficiently fine".

We suggest below several possible approaches to provide a more refined safety restriction.

32.2.2 Safety and Concurrent Prolog

In order to discuss safety in the context of Concurrent Prolog, there must be a distinction between input and output variables in a program. We assume an annotation ('↑') annexed to terms in the head of a clause. Two types of terms are distinguished in a clause head: *input* and *output*. Output terms are terms which are annotated; input terms are those which are not. This specification is similar to the mode declarations of PARLOG (Clark and Gregory, Chapter 3) but is more flexible since it applies to terms rather than to arguments.

Annotated Concurrent Prolog

The main design choice of Annotated Concurrent Prolog (ACP) was to add an annotation to the syntax of Concurrent Prolog and to apply a safety restriction to well defined executions. The added annotation defines an asserted statement about the executions of a program and provides a static definition of which variables a guard may instantiate. It also determines which variables in the global environment are accessible from a guard system. Input variables appearing in a guard are defined to be accessible during the computation of that guard; output variables are defined to be inaccessible. The guard of a procedure is not allowed to write on an input variable.

The distinction between input and output variables enables an alternative to the hierarchical environments necessary in Concurrent Prolog. For input variables we take one extreme: as different Or-parallel environments are restricted from writing on input variables they may occur in a single global environment. For output variables we take the opposite extreme: we forfeit the communication with the Or-parallel environments regarding output variables by allocating distinct temporary variables for them until commitment. These temporary variables may occur in a single global environment as they are distinct. The combination of these two strategies allows a non hierarchical environment structure.

Syntax

An Annotated Concurrent Prolog program is a finite set of guarded Horn clauses. Variables in a clause may be marked *read-only* ('?'). Terms in the head of a clause may be marked *writable* ('↑').

Definition. An *input (output) term* of a clause is a term which occurs unannotated (annotated) in the clause head. A position I in a goal G is an *input (output) position* if there is a clause for G which contains an unannotated (annotated) term at position I in its head. A variable occurring in an input (output) position of a goal is called an *input (output) variable* in that goal. Note that a position can be both input and output.

Computational model

The read-only annotation imposes a restriction on the unification of terms and provides a synchronization mechanism. A read-only variable is 'protected' from being instantiated in unification.

Definition. Let T_1 and T_2 be terms unifiable with substitution θ. We say that the unification of T_1 and T_2 via θ *suspends* if θ contains a substitution element $X = T$, for which X occurs in T_1 or in T_2 as read-only and T is a non-variable term. We say that the reduction of a goal A using a clause $A_1 \leftarrow B_1$, B_2, $\ldots$, B_n *suspends* if the unification of A and A_1 suspends. (Note that this definition should be refined, e.g., as done by Shapiro (Chapter 5), in case a variable occurs both as read-only and non-read-only in T_1 or T_2.)

This section defines the operational semantics of Annotated Concurrent Prolog. The computation of an initial goal G with respect to a program P is a sequence of configurations. The initial configuration is defined by G and other configurations are derived from their predecessors using axioms in P and the elementary transition rules of the computational model. A *configuration* is either an ordered pair consisting of a *continuation* and a *data state* or a special state called *abort*. A computation is associated with a single global environment. If a guard attempts to write on an input variable, the computation enters a special state called *abort* and execution is aborted.

A continuation is an And/Or tree in which nodes correspond to processes. An Or-node corresponds to a goal; an And-node, to a clause. These are called also *goal-nodes* and *clause-nodes* respectively. The data state D of a configuration is a mapping which assigns bindings to terms. It models a single global environment shared by the nodes of the continuation. This is not a standard substitution, as it also assigns values to annotated terms.

The initial configuration S_0, of a computation for a goal A, consists of an initial continuation C_0 and an initial data state D_0. The continuation C_0 is a tree consisting of a goal-node A corresponding to the initial goal.

$$S_0 = \langle\ C_0, D_0\ \rangle$$
where $D_0(X) =$ initial binding of X.

A computation is *successful* if it is finite and ends in a configuration $\langle C_f, D_f \rangle$ where C_f consists of a single goal-node *true*. The computation is *unsafe* if it is finite and ends in *abort*; it is *failed* if it is finite and neither of the above; it is divergent if it is infinite.

'The result of a successful computation is the mapping:

$$\text{Res: Vars}(A) \rightarrow \text{Bindings}$$
$$\text{Res} = D_f \setminus \text{Vars}(A)$$

where A is the initial goal of the computation.

Intuitively, active nodes in a continuation are at the leaves. The possible sequences of configurations are defined by the axioms of the program and by three elementary transition rules which are applied at the active nodes. The three transition rules of the model are: *goal-reduction*, for reducing a goal using the clauses in the program; *clause-reduction*, for spawning computations for the guards in a clause; and *commit*, for committing a computation to the body of a clause whose guard has reduced to *true*. Concurrency is modeled by *interleaving* though a weaker restriction may be imposed and is described in the context of an implementation presented in the next section.

Goal-reduction

An active goal-node, corresponding to a goal A, may reduce *spawning* a clause-node for each clause for A in program P. Each such clause-node contains a renamed copy of a clause C. Output variables in the clause are copied to temporary local variables.

$$\langle \triangle \,;\, D \rangle \longrightarrow \langle \qquad \triangle \qquad ;\, D \rangle$$

$$
\begin{array}{cc}
| & | \\
A & A \\
 & | \\
 & C_1 \; C_2 \;\cdots\; C_n
\end{array}
$$

$C_1, \ldots, C_n$ are clause-nodes corresponding to the clauses in P.

Clause-reduction

Each active clause-node corresponds to a clause C and is associated with a parent goal-node A. An active clause-node may reduce if the head of C and the goal A are unifiable. This reduction may result in one of two possible outcomes depending on the result of this unification. If the unification does not cause a *safety violation*, then the reduction involves spawning goal-nodes for the goals in the guard of C. Otherwise it results in the *abort* state.

The mgu θ of a goal A and the head of a clause C causes a *safety violation* in either of two cases: if it binds a variable which has an input occurrence in C or in any of C's ancestor clause-nodes or if it binds an unannotated nonvariable term to a variable.

$$\langle\ \triangle\ ;\ D\ \rangle \longrightarrow \langle\qquad \triangle \qquad ;\ D\theta\ \rangle$$

$$\begin{array}{ccc} | & & | \\ A & & A \\ | & & | \\ C & & C \\ & & | \\ & & G_1\ \ G_2\ \ \cdots\ \ G_n \end{array}$$

if A and H are unifiable and there is no safety violation; where C corresponds to $(H \leftarrow G \mid B)$ and $G_1, \ldots, G_n$ are goal-nodes corresponding to guard calls.

Commit

If all the sons of a clause-node C are *true*, we say that the guard of C has reduced to *true*. A clause-node C associated with a parent goal A, whose guard has reduced to *true* may commit if the associated goal and temporary environments are unifiable. Commitment involves replacing the entire subtree rooted at A by new goal-nodes corresponding to the the body of C. The unifier is applied to these body goals and to the brother goal-nodes of A.

$$\langle\qquad \triangle \qquad ;\ D\ \rangle \longrightarrow \langle\qquad \triangle \qquad ;\ D\theta\ \rangle$$

$$\begin{array}{ccc} | & & | \\ A & & B_1\ \ \cdots\ \ B_n \\ | & & \\ C & & \\ | & & \\ \text{true}\ \cdots\ \text{true} & & \end{array}$$

if the goal and temporary environments for C are unifiable with substitution θ where $C = (H \leftarrow G \mid B_1, \ldots, B_n)$.

Safe Concurrent Prolog

Definition. A goal G is *safe* if each variable in an input position of G is a read-only occurrence.

Definition. An execution of an Annotated Concurrent Prolog program is *safe* if it is not *unsafe* (i.e., it does not end in an abort state).

An Annotated Concurrent Prolog program is *safe with respect to a goal* if all executions of that goal are safe executions.

An Annotated Concurrent Prolog program is *safe* if it is safe with respect to all safe goals.

Safe Concurrent Prolog (SCP) is the set of safe Annotated Concurrent Prolog programs.

32.2.3 Verifying safety

We have defined a computational model for Annotated Concurrent Prolog. An implementation of this model must include an expensive runtime check to abort computations which violate the safety restriction. We have identified a subset of ACP called SCP which contains safe programs. An execution of a SCP program does not violate the safety restriction and therefore does not require a run-time safety check. The remaining question is how to identify the safe subset (SCP) of ACP.

In this section we prove that membership in SCP is undecidable and therefore in the general case compile-time analysis cannot replace the runtime check. We identify a subset of SCP called Syntactic Safe Concurrent Prolog (SSCP) which can be syntactically determined. The syntactic conditions are defined and are shown to imply membership in SCP. The subject of enlarging the set of programs which can be proven safe is discussed.

Membership in SCP is undecidable

Lemma. Membership in SCP is undecidable.

Proof. Shapiro (1984) has shown a technique for simulating a Turing machine by a logic program. This simulation can be expressed as an Annotated Concurrent Prolog program which can be proven safe. Let $tm_M(Halt)$ be a Safe Concurrent Prolog simulation of a Turing machine M which accepts a language L. Assume that $tm_M(Halt)$ halts and instantiates $Halt$ to M halts on the empty input tape.

Let P_M be the following Annotated Concurrent Prolog program:

$$\mathrm{p}_M(\mathrm{X}) \leftarrow \mathrm{tm}_M(\mathrm{X}) \mid \mathrm{true}.$$

Predicate $p_M/1$ is defined such that X will be instantiated to *halt* if the simulation of Turing machine M halts. But X is an input variable and any execution of $p_M(X)$ which instantiates X is not a safe execution.

Assume that SCP was decidable. Then, given any Turing machine M, write an Annotated Concurrent Prolog program P_M and decide if P_M is safe. If it is, then M does not halt, otherwise M halts. Therefore SCP is undecidable. ∎

Although the general problem of identifying if an Annotated Concurrent Prolog program is safe is undecidable, many programs can be proven safe. A model for programs which are safe can be efficiently implemented because the run-time check can be omitted.

A syntactic subset of Safe Concurrent Prolog

We suggest a syntactic restriction on ACP programs that implies membership in SCP. This provides a usable language which is a subset of SCP and can therefore be implemented efficiently.

Syntactic safety

Definition. An Annotated Concurrent Prolog program is *consistent* if no input position of a goal G is also an output position.

Definition. An Annotated Concurrent Prolog program P is *syntactically safe* if it is *consistent* and for every clause C in P.

(a) variables occur only once in the head of C and once in each goal.

(b) an input variable in C occurs only in input positions of calls and is read-only annotated.

We now prove that programs which are syntactically safe are Safe Concurrent Prolog programs. In the context of this discussion we assume that the structures appearing in the head of a clause have only one level of nesting. Note that a trivial transformation can be shown to transfer any general SCP program to one of this form by adding appropriate equalities in the guard. A variable is said to be *protected* if it is read-only or it appears only as a subterm of a term in an input position.

Lemma. Let P be a SSCP program, A a safe goal and E an execution of A; then for each configuration which is not *abort* in E the following is true:
For each goal node in the continuation each variable which is an input variable or a subterm of an input variable in one of its ancestors is *protected*.
Proof. By induction on the execution sequence E.

- Initially: The continuation contains a single goal node A which is safe and therefore every variable in an input position is read-only.

- Each of the transition rules of the model preserves the claim:

  (1) goal-reduce: Does not add new goal nodes to the continuation.

  (2) Clause reduce: The goal nodes spawned for the guard of the clause contain only protected occurrences of variables which are conveyed from the head. New variables which occur in input positions are protected as well (from syntactic safety).

  (3) Commit: The goal nodes spawned for the body of the clause contain only protected occurrences of variables conveyed from the head. New variables which occur in input variables are protected as well (from syntactic safety). No variable can become a non-read-only occurrence of another variable thus no variable can become unprotected (variables may occur only once in the goal and the head). ∎

Theorem. No execution of an SSCP program and a safe goal is unsafe.

Proof. Only a clause-reduce transition can lead to an *abort* configuration. If all the input variables are protected, the substitution cannot violate the safety condition (read-only unification and one level of nesting).   ∎

The computational model presented for Annotated Concurrent Prolog in this section involves a complex check to determine violations of safety. The syntactic safety conditions defined above ensure that programs will not violate the safety condition. However there are Safe Concurrent Prolog programs which are not syntactically safe. In particular the proof of the above theorem does not differ between safety violations occurring in guard computations and others. The syntactic safety condition may be relaxed to enlarge the subset of programs which can be determined safe syntactically.

32.2.4 Refined safety verification

The syntactic safety condition described above provides an inductive proof of the semantic safety condition of SCP. It requires the initial safety of a goal and ensures that each resolution step preserves this condition. This is done by imposing sufficient syntactic conditions on the program. The advantage of this approach is the simplicity of the syntactic conditions which imply the safety of all executions of the program. Its disadvantage is that it determines a limited subset of SCP. Several possible approaches to provide a refined safety verification and to extend the determinable subset of SCP are listed below:

- A refined algorithm based on a relaxation of the syntactic conditions defined above is conceivable. Note that in a SCP computation goals which are not invoked in a guard may write on input variables. The algorithm described above ignores this aspect.

- The current algorithm involves a local analysis which considers possible computation steps by considering all combinations of safe goals and clause heads. A refined safety verification based on a global analysis of computation paths could consider each step in the context of the bindings created in previous steps. The techniques of abstract interpretation (Cousot and Cousot, 1977) may prove useful in the development of such an algorithm.

- A program may be safe with respect to some goals and unsafe with respect to others. Instead of proving the safety of a general program, we may consider a refined safety algorithm which determines a program safe with respect to a specific goal or set of goals. A refined analysis which verifies each step of a computation path in the context of its previous steps should in particular allow for the safety verification a program only with respect to those goals with which it may be invoked.

- A simple and practical way to provide for refined safety verification relies not on a refinement of the safety verifying algorithm but rather on a refinement of the program to be determined safe. Partial evaluation may be applied to restrict a program with respect to a given goal and to eliminate useless sections of code. The refined program can then be verified using the syntactic safety conditions described above. The examples in Section 32.5 demonstrate the usefulness of this approach. The Or-parallel Prolog interpreter (Program 32.4) is not a syntactically safe program; however, its restriction to specific Prolog programs is syntactically safe.

32.3 A Safe Concurrent Prolog Interpreter

A working implementation for Safe Concurrent Prolog has been written in FCP. It is a two-stage process consisting of three components: a syntactic safety checker, a precompiler and an interpreter. The first stage involves a syntactic safety check and the precompilation of a program. The second stage involves the interpretation of the precompiled program. A more detailed description of the implementation was given by Codish, 1985).

The safety verifier implements an algorithm which verifies if a given program is a Syntactic Safe Concurrent Prolog program. The algorithm is based on the definitions presented in the previous section. The precompiler provides facilities for the implementation of the commit operator and allocates local copies of global output variables. It sets up the communication between global and local environments that will be needed at run-time. Each clause *Head* ← *Guard* | *Body* of an annotated program is precompiled to a *clause triplet* consisting of:

- a unique identifier to support mutual exclusion at commitment.

- a modified copy of the clause, *NewHead* ← *Guard* | *Body*, in which annotated terms of *Head* are replaced by new variables.

- a copy of the original head.

A procedure *number_of_clauses/2* which defines the number of clauses in each procedure of the program is added to the precompiled program.

32.3.1 The interpreter

The interpreter is a direct implementation of the operational model described in the previous section. It contains three procedures: *solve_and* for solving conjunctions (spawning And-parallelism), *solve_or* for applying the clauses of a program to a goal (spawning Or-parallelism) and *commit* for simulating commit. The operational model allows concurrent execution of these procedures but requires the commit operation to be atomic.

To solve a unit goal, each of the precompiled clauses for that goal are applied to it. This involves unifying the head of the modified clause with the goal and spawning subgoals for the guards of each modified clause. If the computation of a guard terminates successfully, then the corresponding clause may commit. At most one clause may commit for a given goal. The other components of a clause triplet, the unique identifier and the original copy of the clause head are used to simulate the commit operation. The former is used for mutual exclusion, the latter for unification of local and global environments at commit time. The correct implementation of the commit operation is conceptually difficult but can be expressed as a concise and elegant three-line FCP program.

Guard systems instantiate only output variables and have direct access to input variables in the global environment. This is due to annotated terms in the original clause heads having been copied to new variables in the modified clauses and to the safety restriction.

The computation of a (conjunctive) goal G is initialized by spawning *solve_and* processes for the subgoals of G. If all the subgoals reduce to *true*, then the computation succeeds. The *short circuit technique* due to Takeuchi (1983) is used to detect successful termination of a computation. The processes of a computation are chained in a circuit, each process acting as an open switch. A process which terminates closes the switch. When all of the processes have terminated, the entire circuit is shortened and successful termination can be detected.

Logical variables are used to represent links connecting processes in a circuit. A process is invoked with two variables *Left* and *Right* connecting it to the neighbor left and right processes in the circuit. Two processes that are connected share a common link variable. Each process that terminates unifies its *Left* and *Right* variables. When all the processes have terminated, the entire chain becomes one variable. The leftmost and rightmost processes contain the circuit *ends*. One of the circuit ends is instantiated to a constant. When the circuit is short, the other circuit end becomes instantiated to this constant.

Program 32.1a implements the *solve_and* process. A *solve_and* process is invoked with two variables *Left* and *Right* connecting it to the neighbor left and right processes in the circuit. Each process that reduces to *true* unifies its *Left* and *Right* variables. One of the circuit ends is instantiated to *true* and the other to the result variable of the computation. When the circuit is short, the result variable becomes instantiated to *true*. A process *solve_and(A, L, R)* for a unit goal A spawns *solve_or* processes corresponding to each of the clauses for goal A. Note that the *otherwise* predicate in the guard of the third clause is an FCP kernel predicate which succeeds if all the other guards in the procedure fail (Mierowsky et al., 1985). An *otherwise* kernel may be replaced with the negation of the other guards of the procedure.

```
solve(Goal, Result) ←
    solve_and(Goal, true, Result).

solve_and(true, Link, Link).
solve_and((A, B), Left, Right) ←
    solve_and(A, Left, Middle),
    solve_and(B, Middle, Right).
solve_and(A, Left, Right) ←
    otherwise |
    number_of_clauses(A, N),
    solve_or(A, N?, ME, Left, Right).
```

Program 32.1a: Spawning And-parallelism

Each *solve_or* process, *solve_or(A, N, ME, L, R)*, attempts to solve the guard of a clause for *A* and to commit the computation to the body of this clause. Two processes are spawned: a *solve_and* process to solve the guard and an associated commit process. All of the *solve_or* processes for a given goal operate concurrently and may attempt to commit if the computation of their guard reduces to *true*. At most one *solve_or* process may succeed to commit.

Program 32.1b implements the *solve_or* process. Each process receives a variable representing the goal *A*, a unique identifier *N* from the clause triplet, an occurrence of a mutual exclusion variable *ME* and occurrences of the left and right links of its parent *solve_and* process.

```
solve_or(_, 0, _, _, _).
solve_or(A, N, ME, Left, Right) ←
    N > 0 |
    clause(N, (A ← G | B), A1),
    solve(G?, Result),
    commit(Result?, N, ME, A1, A, B, Left, Right),
    N1 := N - 1,
    solve_or(A, N1?, ME, Left, Right).
```

Program 32.1b: Spawning Or-parallelism

A commit process succeeds if the associated guard computation has reduced to *true*, no other commit process for the same goal has committed and the respective global and local environments unify. It *suspends* until there is sufficient information to succeed, and if any of the above conditions do not hold it terminates, having *failed to commit*.

A commit process that succeeds commits the computation to the body of the corresponding clause. A system of *solve_and* processes corresponding to the body is inserted to the circuit between the left and right links of the reducing *solve_and* process.

Program 32.1c implements the commit process. A commit process *commit(Result?, N, ME, Local, Global, Body, Left, Right)* contains: a result variable for the associated guard computation, an identifier from the clause triplet, a mutual exclusion variable, a copy of the local environment from the clause triplet, a copy of the global environment, the body of the modified clause and the left and right links of the parent *solve_and* process.

> commit(true, N, N, Head, Head, Body, L, R) ←
>   solve_and(Body, L, R).
> commit(_, _, _, _, _, _, _, _) ← otherwise | true.

Program 32.1c: Commit Processes

The result variable *Result* of the guard computation will become instantiated to *true* if this guard computation is successful. The unique identifier *N* of a committing clause is unified with the mutual exclusion variable *ME* preventing other clauses from committing.

Properties of the commit operator

The atomicity of the commit operator relies upon the atomicity of unification and commitment in FCP. A commit goal succeeds if it unifies with the head of the first clause in the commit procedure. This unification is an atomic action which does four things. It verifies that the associated guard computation reduced to *true* and that no other clause has committed. It unifies the global and local environments and prevents other clauses from committing by instantiating the mutual exclusion variable. Reduction to the body of the committing clause need not be part of this atomic action.

Two main strategies are generally used to detect the failure of a clause to commit; *early detection* and *late detection* (Miyazaki et al., Chapter 37). The first strategy requires that the inability of a clause commit be detected as early as possible. This can be difficult to implement as complex mechanisms are required to repeatedly check the consistency of environments. For this reason late detection, which delays the consistency checks until termination of the associated guard computation, is generally implemented.

In the above implementation a process may fail to commit either because another process instantiates the mutual exclusion variable or because the local and global environments become inconsistent. In extended versions of the interpreter which differentiate between suspension and failure a process may fail to commit also in the case that its associated guard computation fails. The implementation relies on the order independence of unification in FCP to achieve an elegant solution for early detection. This allows immediate failure if either the environments become inconsistent or the mutual exclusion variable becomes instantiated.

In a distributed implementation the processes associated with a computation may reside on different processors. The algorithms for distributed unification and distributed commit are relatively simple in FCP (Taylor et al., Chapter 39); thus the above program also specifies a distributed commit operator for Safe Concurrent Prolog.

32.4 Compiling SCP to FCP

The convenience of implementing an And/Or language using the flat subset has been demonstrated above. A simple interpreter for SCP has been implemented in FCP. There remains the problem of efficiency; a level of meta-interpretation normally may cost a factor of $4 - 20$ in execution time (Shapiro, Chapter 5). In the case of an interpreter which simulates Or-parallelism one could expect this factor to be much larger. The results below indicate an overhead of two orders of magnitude over compilation.

An interpreter $I_{L_1}^{L_2}$ written in a language L_1 for a language L_2 induces a transformation $T: L_2 \rightarrow L_1$. For a given interpreter this source-to-source transformation can be identified and applied to programs in L_2 to produce programs in L_1. Such transformations can be identified and implemented automatically using a technique called *partial evaluation* (Futamura, 1971; Jones et al., 1985; Kahn, 1984a).

32.4.1 The source-to-source transformation

The SCP interpreter written in FCP induces the simple source-to-source transformation shown in Figure 32.1. A Safe Concurrent Prolog procedure:

$$\{\text{Clause}_i\}_{i=1}^n$$

is transformed into a Flat Concurrent Prolog program:

$$\{\text{Procedure}_i\}_{i=0}^n$$
$$\{\text{Commit}_i\}_{i=1}^n.$$

A procedure is invoked by calling *Procedure$_n$*. Each *Procedure$_i$* process tries to solve the guard of *Clause$_i$*, to commit the computation to the body of that clause and invokes *Procedure$_{i-1}$*.

Clause$_i$:   Head(Global) $\leftarrow$ Guard(Global) | Body(Global).

Procedure$_i$:   Head$_i$(Global, ME, Res)$\leftarrow$
            Guard$_i$(Local, ME1, Res1),
            Commit$_i$(Res1?, ME, Global, Local, Res),
            Head$_{i-1}$(Global, ME, Res).
          Head$_i$(Global, ME, Res) $\leftarrow$
            otherwise | Head$_{i-1}$(Global, ME, Res).

Procedure$_0$:   Head$_0$($\_$, $\_$, $\_$) $\leftarrow$ true | true.

Commit$_i$:   Commit$_i$(true, $\underline{i}$, Head, Head, Res) $\leftarrow$ Body$_i$(ME, Res).
          Commit$_i$($\_$, $\_$, $\_$, $\_$, $\_$) $\leftarrow$ otherwise | true.

Figure 32.1: The transformation to FCP induced by the SCP
            interpreter

32.4.2 Partial evaluation

Partial evaluation is an important program transformation technique which
has recently received increased attention. It involves a specialization of a general
function with respect to a partial description of its input to derive a residual
function in the remaining variables. This technique can be applied to generate
compilers from interpreters (Futamura, 1971; Jones et al., 1985; Kahn, 1984a).
An interpreter corresponds to the general function; a given program to a partial
description of its input. A specialization of the interpreter to the given program
corresponds to a residual function. Given an interpreter $I_{L_1}^{L_2}$ and a partial evaluator PE for L_1, then the transformation T induced by the interpreter $I_{L_1}^{L_2}$ can
be applied authomatically using the partial evaluator.

$$\text{T: L}_2 \rightarrow \text{L}_1$$
$$\text{T}(\text{P}_{L_2}) = \text{PE}(\text{I}_{L_1}^{L_2}, \text{P}_{L_2})$$

The combination of an FCP partial evaluator developed by Safra (1986) with the
interpreter presented above has been applied to compile SCP to FCP. This is
shown to provide an optimization of the transformation in Figure 32.1 which was
identified manually.

Another application of partial evaluation involves a refinement of the syntactic safety check. A general program P which is not syntactically safe can be
specialized with respect to a specific goal G (using the techniques of partial evaluation). Often the specialized program is syntactically safe. In this case we say
that the program P is *syntactically safe with respect to goal G*. The Or-parallel
Prolog interpreter presented in Program 32.4 is an example of a program which

is syntactically safe with respect to some goals (i.e., some Prolog programs).

32.4.3 Example 1

Program 32.2 is a Safe Concurrent Prolog program which determines if two binary trees are isomorphic. Two trees are isomorphic if their corresponding subtrees are isomorphic in either order. Leaves are isomorphic if they are identical. The isotree program is an example of a program whose execution depends on Or-parallelism. It is not immediately expressed as a *flat* program (i.e., a program with simple guards). Program 32.2 is a restriction of the more general Concurrent Prolog program which could also output an isomorphic tree for a given input tree.

```
isotree(leaf(X), leaf(X)).
isotree(tree(A, B), tree(C, D)) ←
    isotree(A, C) | isotree(B, D).
isotree(tree(A, B), tree(C, D)) ←
    isotree(A, D) | isotree(B, C).
```

Program 32.2:   SCP isotree

The isotree program was compiled to FCP using the transformation in Figure 32.1 and using Safra's partial evaluator. The optimized transformation produced by the latter is shown in Program 32.3.

```
isotree3(tree(A, B), tree(C, D), MEV, Res) ←
    isotree3(A, D, MEV1, Res1),
    commit(Res1?, 3, MEV, B, C, Res),
    isotree2(A, B, C, D, MEV, Res).
isotree3(T1, T2, MEV, Res) ← otherwise |
    isotree1(T1, T2, MEV, Res).

isotree2(A, B, C, D, MEV, Res) ←
    isotree3(A, C, MEV1, Res1),
    commit(Res1?, 2, MEV, B, D, Res).

isotree1(leaf(A), leaf(A), 1, true).
isotree1(_, _, _, _) ← otherwise | true.

commit(true, N, N, T1, T2, Res) ←
    isotree3(T1, T2, MEV, Res).
commit(_, _, _, _, _, _) ← otherwise | true.
```

Program 32.3:   FCP isotree from partial evaluation

In Program 32.3 the first clause for *isotree3* calls *isotree2*. The structures in the head of *isotree3* are eliminated and only the variables are conveyed to *isotree2*.

The information regarding the removed structures is implicitly conveyed. It is for this reason that *isotree2* contains only one clause; any goal is sure to unify with the head of this clause. It is also for this reason that the second clause for *isotree3* calls *isotree1* instead of *isotree2*; a goal that did not unify with the head of *isotree3* will not unify with the head of *isotree2*.

Another optimization performed by the partial evaluator involves the simplification of the *commit* procedures. In this example it is known at compile time that the local and global environments are consistent as they are identical. The *commit* procedures have been generalized to a single *commit* procedure with an additional argument.

The Flat Concurrent Prolog isotree program shown in Program 32.3 will return a result *true* in the case that the original SCP program succeeds. It returns no result in the case that the original program were to fail or suspend.

The derived FCP isotree program was run for several example goals and compared with similar programs in other languages (see Table 32.1). In general the FCP program derived by the transformation in Figure 32.1 introduced an improvement of two orders of magnitude over interpretation for these examples. Other optimization introduced by the partial evaluator provided an additional speed-up of 25%.

32.4.4 Example 2

Program 32.4 contains an Or-parallel Prolog interpreter written in Concurrent Prolog which is due to Ken Kahn. To simplify the interpreter, it is assumed that each Prolog clause $A \leftarrow B_1,\ldots,B_n$ is represented as $A \leftarrow [B_1,B_2,\ldots,B_n \mid Bs] \setminus Bs$, i.e., the clause body is a difference-list. A predicate *clauses(A,Cs)* is assumed which instantiates *Cs* to the set of clauses which are potentially unifiable with *A*.

```
solve([ ]).                                            %1
solve([A | As]) ←                                      %2
        clauses(A?, Cs), resolve(A?, Cs?, As?).

resolve(A, [(A←Bs \ As) | Cs], As) ←                   %3
        solve(Bs?) | true.
resolve(A, [C | Cs], As) ←                             %4
        resolve(A, Cs?, As) | true.
```

Program 32.4: Or-parallel Prolog interpreter

The interpreter maintains a continuation of goals *As* to be solved. It attempts, in Or-parallel, to unify its first goal with the heads of the clauses in the program (clause 2). If successful, it concatenates the goals in the body of the clause in front of the continuation, and recurses with the new continuation (clause 3). The interpreter terminates when the continuation is empty (clause 1), and commits.

Program 32.4 is an incomplete program as it calls an unspecified predicate *clauses/2*. It is completed by adding to it the *clauses* form of a Prolog program. Unfortunately, any completion of Program 32.4 is not syntactically safe. Therefore the correctness of the transformation to FCP depends on prior verification that it is being applied to an SCP program. The completion of the Or-parallel Prolog interpreter with respect to a Prolog program which only tests variables is in particular always an SCP program.

Program 32.5 is an FCP isotree program derived by applying partial evaluation to the completion of the Or-parallel Prolog interpreter with respect to a Prolog isotree program. Notice that the implicit append call has been partially evaluated away and that similar optimizations to that in Program 32.3 have been introduced.

> isotree3(tree(A, B), tree(C, D), As, ME, Res) ←
>   isotree3(A, D, [isotree(B, C) | As], ME1, Res1),
>   commit(Res1?, 3, ME, Res),
>   isotree2(A, B, C, D, As?, ME, Res).
> isotree3(T1, T2, As, ME, Res) ←
>   otherwise |
>   isotree1(T1, T2, As?, ME, Res).
>
> isotree2(A, B, C, D, As, ME, Res) ←
>   isotree3(A, C, [isotree(B,D) | As], ME1, Res1),
>   commit(Res1?, 2, ME, Res).
> isotree1(leaf(X), leaf(X), [isotree(T1,T2) | As], ME, Res) ←
>   isotree3(T1, T2, As?, ME1, Res1),
>   commit(Res1?, 1, ME, Res).
> isotree1(leaf(X), leaf(X), [ ], 1, true).
> isotree1(_, _, _, _, _) ← otherwise | true.
>
> commit(true, N, N, true).
> commit(_, _, _, _) ← otherwise | true.

Program 32.5: FCP Or-parallel isotree

Program 32.5, like the Or-parallel Prolog interpreter, maintains a continuation of goals which are yet to be solved. Each *isotree* goal contains a current goal to be reduced and a continuation of other goals to be reduced. A successful reduction of *isotree3* or *isotree2* reduces the current goal to two subgoals. One of these is the new current goal and the other is added to the continuation. A successful reduction of *isotree1* removes a goal from the continuation. A computation is successful if the current goal reduces to *true* and the continuation is empty. If a goal from the continuation fails, the entire continuation is discarded. This provides an optimization which prunes the search tree.

32.4.5 Example 3

The Prolog interpreter may also be safe with respect to a Prolog program which contains output variables. Program 32.6 is a Prolog program applying generate and test to find an element in the intersection of two given lists. The program defines an element *X* to be on the intersection of two lists *L1* and *L2* if it is a member of each list. The first goal in the clause defining this relation chooses an element *X* from *L1*. The second goal tests if this element is a member of *L2*. The program has been annotated to specify input/output variables. There are two versions of the member procedure, each with a different annotation.

intersect(X↑, L1, L2) ← member1(X, L1), member2(X, L2).

member1(X↑, [X|Xs]).
member1(X↑, [Y|Ys]) ← member1(X, Ys).

member2(X, [X|Xs]).
member2(X, [Y|Ys]) ← member2(X, Ys).

Program 32.6: Annotated Prolog intersection program

Program 32.7 contains a specialization of the Prolog interpreter with respect to Program 32.6. This is a syntactically safe program which can be further transformed to FCP. It was derived by manual partial evaluation of the Or-parallel Prolog interpreter with respect to Program 32.6.

intersect(X↑, L1, L2) ←
    member_member(X, L1, L2) | true.

member_member(X↑, [X|Xs], L2) ←
    member(X, L2) | true.

member_member(X↑, [Y|Ys], L2) ←
    member_member(X, Ys, L2) | true.

member(X, [X|Xs]) ← true | true.
member(X, [Y|Ys]) ← member(X, Ys) | true.

Program 32.7: A safe specialization for intersect

The partially evaluated intersect program is given as Program 32.8; it has the same basic structure and contains optimizations as in the previous examples.

The comparison of results for the intersect programs is similar to those for the isotree examples and is discussed below.

```
intersect(X, L1, L2, ME, Res) ←
    member_member2(X1, L1, L2, ME1, GR),
    commit(GR?, 1, ME, X1, X, Res).

member_member2(X, [Y| Ys], L2, ME, Res) ←
    member_member2(X1, Ys, L2, ME1, GR),
    commit(GR?, 2, ME, X1, X, Res),
    member_member1(X, Y, L2, ME, Res).
member_member2(X, L1, L2, ME, Res) ←
    otherwise |
    true.

member_member1(X, Y, L2, ME, Res) ←
    member2(Y, L2, ME1, GR),
    commit(GR?, 1, ME, Y, X, Res).

member2(X, [Y| Ys], ME, Res) ←
    member2(X, Ys, ME1, GR),
    commit(GR?, 2, ME, _, _, Res),
    member1(X, Y, ME, Res).
member2(X, Ys, ME, Res) ←
    otherwise |
    true.

member1(X, X, 1, true).
member1(_, _, _, _) ← otherwise | true.

commit(true, N, N, X, X, true).
commit(_, _, _, _, _, _) ← otherwise | true.
```

Program 32.8: FCP intersect program

The basic transformation (Figure 32.1) provides a general technique for compiling any SCP program into FCP. For some Prolog programs, the Or-parallel Prolog interpreter is safe, and in such a case the compilation of Or-parallel Prolog to FCP is defined. We have shown that the technique can be optimized using partial evaluation.

32.5 Optimizations and Extensions

The above SCP interpreter is a basic implementation of the computational model for Safe Concurrent Prolog. It models correctly the semantics but does not consider efficiency. Also, there is no distinction in the model between failing and suspending computations. A series of extensions and optimizations of the model and its interpreter have been implemented. These include an interpreter which reports failure, extensions for interpretation of kernel predicates and several optimizations to the basic model.

32.5.1 An interpreter which reports failure

This interpreter represents a slight extension to the computation model. A goal is said to *fail* if none of the clauses in the program can be used to reduce it. In terms of the basic interpreter this means that all of the commit processes spawned for the goal terminated, having failed to commit the computation.

An extended interpreter is defined such that the *Result* variable is instantiated to *true* or *false* if the goal succeeds or fails respectively. The interpreter will *suspend* if the corresponding computation suspends.

Determining the failure of a goal is implemented using the same technique used to determine the success of a computation. A goal process is defined to fail if all of the corresponding commit processes failed to commit the computation. All of the commit processes corresponding to a goal are connected in a circuit. One end of the circuit is instantiated to the constant *false*. The other end of the circuit is instantiated to the result variable of the computation. Each commit process that fails to commit the computation closes a switch. If all of the commit processes fail to commit the computation, the result variable becomes instantiated to *false* signifying that the corresponding goal fails.

Figure 32.2 shows the structure of the processes in a computation. And-processes are spawned in And-circuits, Or-processes in Or-circuits. The *Result* variable can be instantiated to either *true* or *false* depending on which circuit closes.

If the And-circuit closes, then each *solve_and* process in the circuit must have reduced to *true*. This implies that, for each *solve_and* process, one of the processes in its Or-circuit succeeded to commit. This Or-process prevents the Or-circuit in which it resides from ever closing. If one of the Or-circuits closed, then all of the clauses for some goal in the And-circuit failed to commit. This goal prevents the And-circuit from closing. Hence an attempt may be made to unify the *Result* variable with either *true* or *false* but never with both.

Program 32.9 contains an SCP interpreter which reports failure. The result of partially evaluating the SCP isotree program with respect to this interpreter

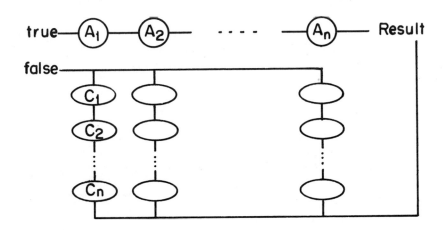

Figure 32.2: The process structure of a computation

solve_and(true, Link, Link, Res).
solve_and((A, B), Left, Right, Res) ←
    solve_and(A, Left, Middle, Res),
    solve_and(B, Middle, Right, Res).
solve_and(A, Left, Right, Res) ←
    otherwise |
    number_of_clauses(A, N),
    solve_or(A, N?, ME, Left, Right, Res, false, Res).

solve_or(_, 0, _, L, R, Link, Link, _).
solve_or(A, N, ME, Left, Right, OrL, OrR, Res) ←
    N > 0 | clause(N, (A ← G | B), Local),
    solve(G?, GR),
    commit(GR?, N, ME, Local, A, B, Left, Right, OrL, OrM, Res),
    N1:=N − 1,
    solve_or(A, N1?, ME, Left, Right, OrM, OrR, Res).

commit(true, N, N, Head, Head, Body, L, R, OrL, OrR, Res) ←
    solve_and(Body, L, R, Res).
commit(_, _, _, _, _, Link, Link, _) ← otherwise | true.

Program 32.9: Extended SCP Interpreter: Reports failure

is shown as Program 32.10. The structure is similar to the isotree program derived from the previous transformation but has the additional functionality that it reports failure. Program 32.10 runs with speed similar to that of the restricted version shown in Program 32.3. No additional reductions are added to a computation but each reduction is slightly more complex since arguments have been added.

isotree(T1, T2, Res) ← isotree3(T1, T2, ME, Res).

isotree3(t(A, B), t(C, D), ME, Res) ←
    isotree3(A, D, ME1, Res1),
    commit3(Res1?, ME, B, C, Res, OrL),
    isotree2(A, B, C, D, ME, Res, OrL).
isotree3(T1, T2, ME, Res) ← otherwise | isotree1(T1, T2, ME, Res).

commit3(true, 3, B, C, Res, _) ←
    isotree3(B, C, ME1, Res).
commit3(_, _, _, _, G, G) ← otherwise | true.

isotree2(A, B, C, D, ME, Res, OrL) ←
    isotree3(A, C, ME1, Res1),
    commit2(Res1?, ME, B, D, Res, OrL).

commit2(true, 2, B, D, Res, _) ←
    isotree3(B, D, ME1, Res).
commit2(_, _, _, _, _, false) ← otherwise | true.

isotree1(leaf(A), leaf(A), 1, true).
isotree1(_, _, _, false) ← otherwise | true.

Program 32.10: Extended FCP isotree program from partial
evaluation

32.5.2 Kernel predicates

Two additional extensions provide interpretation of programs which contain kernel predicates. Kernel predicates are simple nonrecursive tests from a predefined set which may appear in the guards of an FCP program. Their evaluation is immediate and does not require spawning of a subcomputation. There is one special kernel called *otherwise*, whose interpretation requires additional attention.

The interpretation of kernel predicates (except otherwise) is demonstrated in Program 32.11. Kernel predicates are executed in the guard of a *solve_and* process. If this guard reduces to *true*, the process unifies its left and right links (clause 3); otherwise failure is handled by the *solve_or* procedure.

```
solve_and(true, Link, Link).                              %1
solve_and((A, B), Left, Right) ←                          %2
    solve_and(A, Left, Middle),
    solve_and(B, Middle, Right).
solve_and(Goal, Link, Link) ← kernel(Goal), Goal | true.  %3
solve_and(A, Left, Right) ←                               %4
    otherwise |
    number_of_clauses(A, N),
    solve_or(A, N?, ME, Left, Right).
```

Program 32.11: Solving kernel predicates.

In many cases kernel predicates can be evaluated at compile time and thus disappear during partial evaluation.

Due to the lack of meta kernel calls in Logix, the actual implementation of Program 32.11 (clause 3) was slightly more complex. It involved defining a predicate *reduce_kernel(Kernel, L, R)* which unifies L and R if and only if the kernel *kernel* reduces to *true*.

32.5.3 Interpretation of otherwise

In SCP as in FCP, the last clause in a procedure may contain an *otherwise* guard. The meaning of an *otherwise* clause as defined here is that the current goal may reduce to the body of the *otherwise* clause if all other clauses have failed to commit. The implementation of *otherwise* does not depend on stability as defined by Mierowsky et al. (1985) and is a simple extension to the basic interpreter. The implementation will also support a definition of SCP extended to allow procedures which contain any number of *otherwise* clauses. In this case an *otherwise* clause is defined to reduce if all of the clauses which textually precede it fail to commit. Although this definition imposes a textual ordering on the clauses of a program, it is fully concurrent and does not depend on stability.

Or-processes corresponding to the clauses of a procedure are spawned according to textual order. When all clauses preceding an *otherwise* clause have failed to commit, the constant *false* of the Or-circuit will have propagated to this Or-process. The interpretation of the kernel *otherwise* is thus defined to be true if *false* has propagated along the Or-circuit. Program 32.12 demonstrates part of an interpreter which implements *otherwise*. In Program 32.12 when an Or-process spawns the computation of its guard it includes a read-only occurrence of its right link (clause 7). If this is an *otherwise* guard, it will suspend until *false* has propagated to the link (clause 3).

solve(A, OtherwiseLink, Result) ←   %1
    solve_and(A, OtherwiseLink, true, Result, Result).

solve_and(true, _, Link, Link, _).   %2
solve_and(otherwise, false, Link, Link, _).   %3
solve_and((A, B), _, Left, Right, Res) ←   %4
    solve_and(A, _, Left, Middle, Res),
    solve_and(B, _, Middle, Right, Res).
solve_and(A, _, Left, Right, Res) ←   %5
    otherwise | num_clauses(A, N),
    solve_or(A, N?, ME, Left, Right, Res, false, Res).

solve_or(_, 0, _, _, _, OrL, OrL, _).   %6
solve_or(A, N, ME, Left, Right, OrL, OrR, Res) ←   %7
    N > 0 |
    clause(N, (A←G|B), Local),
    solve(G?, OrM?, GR),
    commit(GR?, N, ME, Local, A, B, Left, Right, OrL, OrM, Res),
    N1:=N−1,
    solve_or(A, N1?, ME, Left, Right, OrM, OrR, Res).

Program 32.12: Interpreting *otherwise*

32.5.4 Optimizing the SCP interpreter

During the execution of the SCP interpreter various processes may become irrelevant to the rest of the computation but continue to execute. There are several general cases in which groups of processes whose abortion would not affect the continuation of the computation can be identified.

A trivial example concerns the set of all processes which have not terminated when the interpreter has finished solving the initial goal. Clearly any such processes are irrelevant to the computation and can be aborted. Program 32.13 demonstrates the result of partially evaluating the intersect program with respect to a SCP interpreter which performs such an optimization. Each process spawned contains an occurrence of a common Halting variable. A computation is invoked in conjunction with a *trigger* process. When the result variable of the computation becomes instantiated, this process *triggers* the abortion of any remaining active processes by instantiating the Halting variable to *abort*.

There are two additional cases in which processes may be aborted. These are termed And-abort and Or-abort.

A conjunction of goals is defined to fail if any one of its conjuncts fails. In this case all of the other goals in the conjunction may be aborted. A conjunc-

intersect1(X, L1, L2, ME, Res) ←
    mem_mem2(Halt?, X1, L1, L2, ME1, Res1),
    commit_intersect1(Res1?, ME, X1, X, Res, false),
    trigger(Res?, Halt)

commit_intersect1(true, 1, X, X, true, OrL).
commit_intersect1(_, _, _, _, OrL, OrL) ← otherwise |

mem_mem2(H, _, _, _, _, _) ← H = =abort | true.
mem_mem2(Halt, X, [Y| Ys], L2, ME, Res) ←
    mem_mem2(Halt?, X1, Ys, L2, ME1, Res1),
    commit_mem_mem2(Res1?, ME, X1, X, Res, OrL),
    mem_mem1(Halt?, X, Y, L2?, ME, Res, OrL).
mem_mem2(_, _, _, _, _, false) ← otherwise | true.

commit_mem_mem2(true, 2, X, X, true, OrL).
commit_mem_mem2(_, _, _, _, OrL, OrL) ← otherwise | true.

mem_mem1(H, _, _, _, _, _, _) ← H = = abort | true.
mem_mem1(Halt, X, Y, L2, ME, Res, H) ←
    member2(Halt?, Y, L2, ME1, Res1),
    commit_mem_mem1(Res1?, ME, Y, X, Res, H).

commit_mem_mem1(true, 1, X, X, true, _).
commit_mem_mem1(_, _, _, _, _, _, false) ← otherwise | true.

member2(H, _, _, _, _) ← H = = abort | true.
member2(Halt, X, [Y|Ys], ME, Res) ←
    member2(Halt?, X?, Ys?, ME1, Res1),
    commit_member2(Res1?, ME, Res, OrL),
    member1(X?, Y, ME, Res, OrL).
member2(_, _, _, _, false) ← otherwise | true.

commit_member2(true, 2, true, OrL).
commit_member2(_, _, OrL, OrL) ← otherwise | true.

member1(H, _, _, _, _) ← H = = abort | true.
member1(X, X, 1, true, OrL).
member1(_, _, _, _, false) ← otherwise | true.

trigger(true, abort).
trigger(false, abort).

Program 32.13: Optimized FCP Intersect Program

solve(H, A, Result) ←
    solve_and(H, A, true, Result, Result),
    trigger(Result?, H).

solve_and(H, _, _, _, _, _) ← H? = = abort | true.
solve_and(_, true, Link, Link, Res).

solve_and(H, (A, B), Left, Right, Res) ←
    solve_and(H, A, Left, Middle, Res),
    solve_and(H, B, Middle, Right, Res).

solve_and(H, A, Left, Right, Res) ←
    otherwise |
    num_clauses(A, N),
    solve_or(H, LH, A, N?, ME, Left, Right, Res, false, Res).

solve_or(_, _, _, 0, _, _, _, OrL, OrL, _).
solve_or(H, LH, A, N, ME, Left, Right, OrL, OrR, Res) ←
    N>0 |
    clause(N, (A←G|B), Local),
    solve(LH, G?, GR),
    commit(H, GR?, N, ME, Local, A, B, Left, Right, OrL, OrM, Res),
    link(H?, LH), trigger(ME?, LH),
    N1:=N−1,
    solve_or(H, LH1, A, N1?, ME, Left, Right, OrM, OrR, Res).

commit(H, true, N, N, Head, Head, Body, L, R, OrL, OrR, Res) ←
    solve_and(H, Body, L, R, Res).
commit(_, _, _, _, _, _, _, _, _, OrL, OrL, _) ← otherwise | true.

link(abort, abort).

trigger(true, abort).
trigger(false, abort).
trigger(ME, abort) ← integer(ME) | true.

Program 32.14: An Interpreter Which Aborts Insignificant
                      Computations

tion of processes is implemented as a circuit of *solve_and* processes. Since failure of any single *solve_and* process instantiates the result variable of the circuit to a constant *false*, And-abort can be implemented as a generalization of the previous optimization. Each Or-parallel subcomputation is provided with a local variable to trigger an abort of the local subcomputation. Local abort variables are necessary to prevent the failure of one Or-parallel computation from affecting other environments. The local abort variables must be linked to their global counterparts so that abortion of a global computation can be propagated.

A disjunction of *solve_or* processes is defined to succeed if any one *solve_or* process succeeds. In this case all other processes in the disjunction may be aborted. A disjunction of processes is implemented as a circuit which includes a mutual exclusion variable common to all processes. The implementation of Or-abort uses this variable which becomes instantiated when any one *solve_or* process has succeeded to commit. A trigger is used to instantiate the local halting variable whenever the associated mutual exclusion variable becomes instantiated.

Program 32.14 is a SCP interpreter which performs both And-abort and Or-abort.

32.6 Performance Results

The basic program transformation identified in Figure 32.1 provides a speed-up of two orders of magnitude over interpretation for nontrivial examples. Partial evaluation optimizes this transformation and provides an additional speed-up of 25%. The basic interpreter can be extended to differentiate between failure and suspension inducing an extended transformation. The loss of speed is 10%. An interpreter which aborts insignificant computation may often provide additional optimization. The FCP programs were executed on the Logix (Silverman et al., Chapter 21) FCP system. For comparison, Prolog programs were run on Quintus Prolog and a result from Levy (1986) is used to compare with GHC. The comparison is made on the cpu run time, the number of logical reductions and the number of process creations. All probrams were run on a Sun workstation.

Table 32.1 presents performance results of the *isotree* example. The generic example used to compare the different programs is *isotree*(T, T), where T is a balanced tree with 128 distinct leaves. The FCP isotree examples (interpreted and compiled) traverse the entire search space in parallel. The Prolog program used for comparison searches the space using a depth first strategy with backtracking. The results quoted for this program measure the time and number of reductions it took to traverse the entire search space, including backtracking.
The following are compared:

Basic Int   The SCP interpreter executing the SCP isotree program.

Basic Tra   The FCP isotree program produced by the basic transformation.

Basic Pev   The partially evaluated FCP program, derived from the isotree program.

FCP OPP   The program derived by partial evaluation of FCP Or-parallel Prolog interpreter and the Prolog isotree program.

Ext Int   An extended SCP interpreter which reports failure executing the isotree program.

Ext Pev   An extended FCP isotree program which reports failure derived by partial evaluation of the isotree program.

GHC   A GHC isotree program run on Levy's (1986) GHC abstract machine.

Qprolog   A Prolog isotree program run on Quintus Prolog (results include backtracking).

	CPU (secs)	Process reductions	Process creations
Basic Int	470.00	300,000	40,000
Basic Tra	3.00	3,280	1,800
Basic Pev	**2.35**	2,300	1,300
FCP OPP	2.80	2,350	1,500
Ext Int	670.00	300,000	40,000
Ext Pev	2.70	3,000	1,300
GHC	**3.80**	3,700	2,000
Qprolog	1.00	1,025	

Table 32.1: Results For *isotree* Programs

Various examples were used to test the efficiency of the different intersect programs. The examples used were *intersect(X, L1, L2)* where $L2 = [a]$ and $L1$ is a list of 20 b elements with a single a element inserted at different places in the list. Figure 32.3 contains the results of running these tests. The X-axis denotes the number of b elements preceding the a element in $L2$ in the different test cases. Figure 32.3a compares the basic SCP interpreter with the optimized inter-

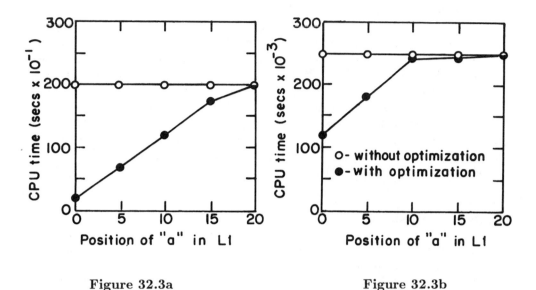

Figure 32.3a   **Figure 32.3b**

preter and demonstrates the speed-up achieved for the various examples. Figure 32.3b compares the respective transformed FCP programs, with and without the abort-optimization. The speed gained from the abort optimization depends on the time it takes to find a successful computation path. Execution of the aborting itself also takes time. For this reason the FCP programs gain less from this optimization than their interpreted counterparts. The basic interpreter and the respective FCP program always complete the entire computation, even after a successful branch has been found. This is represented by the horizontal lines in the two graphs. The speed-up provided by the transformation to FCP in these examples is between 20 and 80 times in run time. The examples run on Quintus Prolog were about 10 times faster than the programs compiled to FCP.

32.7 Related Work

A method to eliminate Or-parallelism from PARLOG programs is suggested by Clark and Gregory, (1984). This method involves calling a conjunction of meta-calls for the guards of a procedure. Each meta-call contains additional *result* and *abort* variables. The first *meta-guard* to succeed causes the computation to reduce to the appropriate clause's body and triggers the abortion of the other. This provides a transformation conceptually similar to the one suggested in this paper but is less efficient, less general, and requires the definition and implementation of a complex system predicate.

Ueda's Guarded Horn Clauses (Chapter 4) also supports a restricted form of Or-parallelism. The main decision choice of GHC was to eliminate multiple Or-parallel environments from Concurrent Prolog. The language involves a runtime-check which replaces PARLOG's compile-time safety check to prevent guards from writing on global variables. This also provides a synchronization mechanism; a guard that attempts to write on a global variable is suspended until the variable is sufficiently instantiated. Nevertheless, GHC seems to be no more expressive than SCP. Programs which are excluded from PARLOG or SCP appear to have no useful meaning in GHC. The method of compilation presented in this paper is in particular applicable to GHC.

32.8 Conclusions

A general method to compile Or-parallelism to And-parallelism has been demonstrated. An interpreter written in the And-parallel subset of a language can be defined to interpret Or-parallelism. This interpreter induces a transformation which can be identified and implemented as a special purpose compiler or applied using a general purpose partial evaluator.

The method is demonstrated for the case of SCP, an And/Or-parallel variant of Concurrent Prolog. An operational semantics for SCP provide a basis for its implementation in FCP. A simple interpreter for SCP written in FCP is described. This interpreter induces a transformation from SCP to FCP, which is shown to be simple and efficient. A FCP partial evaluator is shown to further optimize this transformation. The partial evaluator is applied also to provide the transformations induced by several extended and optimized versions of the basic SCP interpreter.

The compilation method suggested in this paper is applicable, in particular, both to PARLOG and to GHC. The Or-parallelism supported by these languages is restricted from creating multiple environments. Thus it can always be eliminated using the techniques presented in this paper. The results presented suggest that a good way to implement PARLOG and GHC is to first implement their And-parallel subsets. The full languages may then be compiled into these subsets.

Acknowledgements

Many thanks are due to Steve Taylor and Shmuel Safra for helpful discussions and suggestions.

Chapter 33

Translation of Safe GHC and Safe Concurrent Prolog to FCP

Jacob Levy and Ehud Shapiro

The Weizmann Institute of Science

Abstract

An efficient source-to-source transformation from the safe subset of Guarded Horn Clauses (GHC) to Flat Concurrent Prolog (FCP) is described. An implementation based on this approach allows GHC programs to rely on the computation control and protection tools of the Logix system, which are expressible in FCP but not in GHC.

The source-to-source transformation is conceptually composed of two stages: transformation of Safe GHC to Safe Concurrent Prolog (SCP), and translation of SCP to FCP. Thus, in effect, an implementation of SCP is also obtained. The same technique can also be used to obtain a PARLOG-to-FCP compiler. The paper describes the theory underlying a novel clause indexing technique which aids in the efficient compilation of SCP to FCP.

33.1 Introduction

33.1.1 Background

Three major parallel logic programming languages are currently being investigated: Concurrent Prolog (Shapiro, Chapter 2, Chapter 5), PARLOG (Clark and Gregory, Chapter 3; Gregory, 1987) and Guarded Horn Clauses (Ueda, Chapter 4, 1986a,b). In these languages, clauses are tried in parallel and goals in a conjunction are also solved in parallel. The first form of parallelism is called *Or-parallelism* and the second *And-parallelism*. The antecedent of a clause is divided into two parts: the *guard* and the *body*. When the head of a clause unifies with the goal and the guard goals are solved successfully, the computation *commits* to this clause, the original goal is reduced to the conjunction of body goals in the committing clause and the computations of other clauses for the goal are discarded. If two or more clauses attempt to commit for a goal, one is non-deterministically chosen.

Since the publication of these proposals, much research has been devoted to the realization of the languages, and many implementation problems have been uncovered (Saraswat, 1986; Ueda, 1985). As a result of these difficulties, subsets of the original languages have been defined. Recent implementation efforts were limited to the "flat" subset of the languages (Foster and Taylor, 1987; Fuchi and Furukawa, 1987; Houri and Shapiro, Chapter 38; Mierowsky et al., 1985). In these subsets, the guard of a clause consists only of calls to predefined system predicates. The resultant sub-languages are called Flat Concurrent Prolog (FCP), Flat Guarded Horn Clauses (FGHC) and Flat PARLOG, respectively. Clause selection in these languages can be implemented sequentially, and this yields a simpler and more efficient implementation than possible for the full language.

PARLOG is based on the concept of *safety* (Clark and Gregory, 1985): a PARLOG program is semantically legal if it is safe. A PARLOG program consists of procedures accompanied by input-output mode declarations. The argument positions in the head of clauses in a procedure are separated into input and output argument positions. A guard is safe if no computation of it can bind variables appearing in an input argument position in the head of the clause. A PARLOG procedure is safe if every guard in it is safe. A PARLOG program is safe if every procedure in it is safe. Furthermore, a transformation technique from safe PARLOG programs into a language which contains only And-parallelism called Kernel PARLOG was shown (Clark and Gregory, 1985). The PARLOG compiler first checks program safety, and if the program passes this test, it compiles it to Kernel PARLOG. Since safety is an undecidable property (Codish and Shapiro, Chapter 32), the PARLOG compiler rejects some safe programs as being unsafe. All PARLOG programs can also be translated to Flat PARLOG programs with equivalent behavior (Foster and Taylor, 1987).

Codish and Shapiro (Chapter 32) defined the language Safe Concurrent Prolog (SCP) and showed how programs in the language can be translated to equivalent programs in FCP. The translation can be realized by application of partial evaluation (Futamura, 1971; Safra, 1986; Safra and Shapiro, Chapter 25) to an interpreter of SCP written in FCP. The definition of safety in SCP is different from that in PARLOG. Annotated Concurrent Prolog (ACP) is defined by augmenting Concurrent Prolog with an annotation in the head of a clause denoting that the corresponding position in the goal may be instantiated by commitment to this clause. There is no guarantee that all executions of a program conform to the output pattern defined in it. Safe Concurrent Prolog is defined as all ACP programs for which all possible executions only instantiate positions in a goal corresponding to annotated positions in the head of a clause.

Miyazaki (personal communication) defines Safe GHC as all GHC programs for which in all possible computations there are no suspensions of unification goals in the body. Our transformation implements Safe GHC.

33.1.2 Implementing Safe GHC and SCP as translators to FCP

The research reported herein addresses the question of how to implement Safe GHC and Safe Concurrent Prolog via translation to FCP programs with equivalent behavior. The reasons for pursuing this approach are enumerated below. In order to realize this transformation, two problems have to be addressed. First, the synchronization mechanism of GHC must be modelled using read-only annotations. Second, the And/Or parallelism of GHC must be transformed into the And-parallelism available in FCP.

It is convenient to classify all possible goals of a program into three possibly intersecting sets: the *success set*, containing all goals having successful computations, the *failure set*, containing all goals having failing computations, and the *suspension set*, which contains all goals having computations which do not terminate because of deadlock (Lichtenstein et al., Chapter 27; Lloyd and Takeuchi, 1986; Takeuchi, Chapter 26). Safe GHC programs can be transformed into SCP programs with behavior which is equivalent to the original GHC programs with respect to the input-output characteristics: for the same input, the Safe GHC and SCP programs produce the same output. Also, the success set of a Safe GHC program and the success set of the resulting SCP program are identical. The translation of GHC to Safe Concurrent Prolog solves the first problem, how to model GHC's synchronization mechanism using read-only annotations.

The translation can be applied to all Safe GHC programs. Section 33.2, describing GHC and Safe GHC, has an example of two unsafe GHC programs, in order to give an intuitive understanding of the kind of programs which can and which cannot be compiled by the current transformation.

The second stage of the transformation involves application of an optimized form of the source-to-source transformation developed by Codish and Shapiro (Chapter 32) to translate SCP programs to FCP. This solves the question of modelling GHC's And/Or parallelism in a language which contains only And-parallelism. As a side product, an efficient implementation of SCP is also obtained. The two-stage source-to-source transformation is applied directly, with the use of a compiler, rather than through partial evaluation.

The advantages of this implementation technique for Safe GHC and SCP are:

The deficiencies of GHC as a systems programming language are well-known.

KL-1, a language based on GHC, attempts to solve this problem by incorporating a primitive meta-call facility. However, FCP is sufficiently expressive so that it does not need extensions to provide the same functionality (Hirsch et al., Chapter 20). Therefore, by embedding GHC in FCP, these disadvantages are alleviated, and GHC programs can make use of the computation control and protection tools provided by Logix.

- By embedding GHC in FCP, the program development tools present in the Logix system (Silverman et al., Chapter 21), are also available in GHC. Also, an implementation of GHC for all media supporting an implementation of FCP is automatically obtained.

- Most interesting applications of GHC use only its safe subset. By concentrating on implementing the safe subset, many implementation problems which must be tackled when attempting to implement the full language. As a result, a more efficient implementation can be obtained. Safe computations of unsafe programs, e.g., the GHC-in-GHC debugger (Takeuchi, Chapter 26) when run on a Safe GHC program, can also be executed on such an implementation.

- Implementations of several languages as translators to FCP have been reported: CFL, a non-deterministic concurrent functional language (Levy and Shapiro, Chapter 35), Vulcan, an object-oriented language (Kahn et al., Chapter 30), and a Hardware Description Language (Weinbaum and Shapiro, Chapter 36). The runtime linking mechanism of Logix allows a program in GHC or SCP to call programs written in any of the other languages embedded within Logix, with the correct behavior generated by a system interface.

- By dividing the transformation into two distinct stages, an implementation of SCP is also obtained with little additional effort. The structure of the implementation of GHC and SCP reflects the underlying transformations and the problems they address.

33.1.3 The structure of the paper

Guarded Horn Clauses and Safe Guarded Horn Clauses are briefly described in Section 33.2. Section 33.3 introduces Safe Concurrent Prolog and shows the transformation from Safe Guarded Horn Clauses to Safe Concurrent Prolog. The naive source-to-source transformation from SCP to FCP as described by Codish and Shapiro (Chapter 32) is also surveyed. Section 33.4 develops the idea of partial variants, which is used in the optimized translation from SCP to FCP. Section 33.5 presents this optimized translation and shows several examples. Section 33.6 presents an analysis of the transformed code. Several claims about the size of the code and the computational overhead introduced by the translation mechanism are derived. A comparison of the efficiency of the implementation of GHC described here and of an emulator-based implementation of GHC (Levy, 1986) is also given.

33.2 Guarded Horn Clauses and Safe Guarded Horn Clauses

33.2.1 Syntax

A GHC program is a finite set of guarded Horn clauses. Each clause is of the following form:

$$H \leftarrow G_1 \dots G_n \mid B_1 \dots B_m \qquad (n, m \geq 0).$$

H, the Gi's and the Bi's are atomic formulae. H is the clause's head, the Gi's are the guard goals and Bi's are the body goals.

Ueda (Chapter 4) proposed the following names for the parts of the clause. The part before the "|" is the *passive* part, and the part following it is the *active* part. Ueda proposed the name *trust* operator for the "|" sign. This paper will use the Concurrent Prolog name, *commit* operator.

The set of all clauses with heads of the same arity and main functor is a *procedure*. A procedure *matches* the structure of a goal if the goal and the heads of clauses in the procedure have the same arity and main functor.

33.2.2 Operational semantics

Ueda (Chapter 4) describes the semantics of GHC in detail. Here an informal introduction to its operational semantics is given.

To solve a goal G, all clauses in the procedure matching the structure of the goal are tried in parallel. For all clauses C_i, the unifications of the head H_i with the goal and the solution of the guard conjunction G_i are done in parallel. Once the passive part of one of the clauses (e.g., G_j) is solved successfully, the computation reduces the original goal to the active part B_j of the committing clause.

In order to allow synchronization between goals, some limitations are imposed by the following rule. A unification which attempts to instantiate variables in the goal before the clause invoking this unification has committed is suspended. A suspended unification can only resume when the value of the variable causing the suspension is determined by some other goal. At that time, the unification may proceed, if the value determined for the variable is compatible with its expectation, or it fails. The solution of goals in the active part of a clause may be started before that clause commits, provided that unifications do not instantiate variables appearing the passive part of the clause before commitment. Such unifications are also suspended until they can be resumed without requiring these instantiations.

33.2.3 Safe guarded Horn clauses

Safe GHC is the safe subset of GHC, defined by Miyazaki (personal communication) as follows: a GHC program is safe if in all its possible computations there are no suspensions of body unification goals.

Below we give two examples of unsafe GHC programs and explain why they are unsafe. The program:

> Clause 1 – $g1(X) \leftarrow g2(X) \mid$ true.
> Clause 2 – $g2(Y) \leftarrow$ true $\mid Y = 3$.

is unsafe, since in the computation of *g1(W)* the goal *W = 3* in the body of clause 2 suspends. The next example shows a more subtle manifestation of unsafety:

Goal   – g1(A), g2(A)

Clause 1 – $g1(A) \leftarrow r1(A) \mid$ true.
Clause 2 – $g2(A) \leftarrow$ true $\mid A = f(I)$.
Clause 3 – $r1(f(I)) \leftarrow$ true $\mid I = 3$.

This program is unsafe since the computation of *I = 3* in the body of clause 3 suspends. This is equivalent to the variable importation problem (Lindstrom, 1984).

It is easy to see (Codish and Shapiro, Chapter 32) that recognizing safe programs is undecidable. In the compiler described here no effort is devoted to analyzing whether an input program is safe. Instead, the safety of the input program is assumed. To enhance the usability of the compiler, a safety checking algorithm such as that reported by Clark and Gregory (1985) may be included as a preprocessing stage, to reject potentially unsafe GHC programs.

33.3 Safe Concurrent Prolog

Safe Concurrent Prolog (SCP) was defined by Codish and Shapiro (Chapter 32). The definition of safety in SCP is different from that in PARLOG and GHC, and makes use of an annotated form of Concurrent Prolog called ACP. Annotated Concurrent Prolog (ACP) is defined as Concurrent Prolog augmented with annotations in the head of a clause denoting the corresponding positions. Upon violation of the specified annotations, the computation enters a terminal error state. Safe Concurrent Prolog is defined as all ACP programs for which all possible executions instantiate only positions in a goal corresponding to annotated positions in the head of a clause. The definition of safety in SCP reflects the fact that synchronization in Concurrent Prolog is done at the data level, rather than at the procedure level as in GHC and PARLOG.

A Safe GHC program can be transformed into an equivalent SCP program while preserving the success-set of the program. Saraswat showed that this property also holds when GHC programs are translated to $\mathbf{CP}[\downarrow,\|]$ (Saraswat, 1987b). An intuitive justification for our claim is given. Development of a formal proof, as done in (Saraswat, 1987b), is beyond the scope of this paper.

33.3.1 Translation from Safe GHC to SCP

The transformation from Safe GHC to SCP is simple. The GHC program is transformed into an ACP program. To show that an SCP program results, it must be shown that the ACP program is safe.

Assuming that the GHC program is safe, two modifications are necessary:

Output unifications are moved from the body of the clause into the commit operation. This is done by replacing each occurrence of an output variable in the head of the clause by an annotated occurrence of the term it is instantiated to in the body.

Input unifications in the head of the GHC clause are unfolded into read-only unifications in the guard of the transformed ACP clause. Special handling is necessary if a variable occurs several times in an input position. In this case the subsequent occurrences are replaced by new variables and a call to $=?=$ is added to the guard. The definition of $=?=$ specifies that it suspends until its two arguments are identical or until their unification is known to fail (Silverman et al., Chapter 21).

The transformation is shown schematically in Figure 33.1.

$$h(T_1, \ldots, T_n, V_1, \ldots, V_m) \leftarrow$$
$$g_1, \ldots, g_k \mid$$
$$V_1 = T_l, \ldots, V_m = T_{l+m},$$
$$b_1, \ldots, b_k.$$

$$\downarrow$$

$$h(V_1, \ldots, V_n, T_l\uparrow, \ldots, T_{l+m}\uparrow) \leftarrow$$
$$V_1? = T_1, \ldots, V_n? = T_n,$$
$$g_1, \ldots, g_k \mid$$
$$b_1, \ldots, b_k.$$

Figure 33.1: Transformation from GHC to ACP

Positions in the head marked with "$\uparrow$" are output positions, and all other positions are input positions. All terms appearing at input positions in the head of the clause are replaced by new variables and each term is unfolded to a series of read-only unifications in the guard of the clause.

It must now be shown that a Safe GHC program, with safety as defined for GHC, is converted into an SCP program, with safety as defined for SCP, by this transformation. A full proof of this claim is beyond the scope of this paper, but the following informal arguments can be presented to support it:

- Moving the output unifications from the body into the commit operation does not affect the success-set of the program. This is based on Ueda's observation (Ueda, Chapter 4) that only the value a variable is instantiated to determines the success or failure of a goal in GHC, not the time at which the instantiation is done. Therefore, making the instantiations occur early does not affect the success of a computations. Conversely, the intent of the output annotations in the ACP program is fulfilled: only those terms appearing in an output-annotated position in the head of a clause may be written (output) on a variable in the goal. Thus, this leads to an SCP program.

- Moving the output unifications from the body into the commit operation. Unfolding GHC head input unifications to ACP read-only unifications in the guard guarantees that the ACP program cannot instantiate any structure in the goal except those in positions annotated with an output annotation. This is the intent of input unifications in the original GHC program. Therefore this transformation also leads to an SCP program.

While the success-set of Safe GHC programs is preserved by the first transformation, the failure-set is subtly changed: some goals which appear in the GHC program's failure set are not present in the SCP program's failure set. This change may be understood if it is observed that now commitment of a clause may fail for two reasons:

- An input head unification or a guard computation may have failed.

- An output unification fails.

Whereas in GHC the second kind of failure leads to a goal failure, in the modified SCP program this leads to a clause failure. Thus, some other clause may successfully commit later, leading to the eventual success of the original goal. In effect this is equivalent to elimination of the computation leading to the goal failure from the set of possible computations.

To summarize, the transformations produce an SCP program, given a Safe GHC program. The success-set and suspension-set of a Safe GHC program are preserved in the translated SCP program. The failure-set of the SCP program is smaller than that of the original GHC program, because some goal failures are converted into clause failures.

Saraswat (1987b) proposes a similar translation from GHC to **CP**[↓,|] and formally shows that by going from GHC to **CP**[↓,‖] the success-set is preserved and the failure-set becomes smaller. We conjecture that translation of the safe subset of **CP**[↓,‖] to SCP by a similar transformation is possible. This research direction has not yet been pursued.

33.3.2 Translation from Safe Concurrent Prolog to Flat Concurrent Prolog

The translation mechanism employed here is a modification of that described by Codish and Shapiro (Chapter 32). For completeness, the latter is surveyed here, and shown in Figure 33.2.

Clause_i: Head(Args) ← Guard(Args) | Body(Args).

Procedure_i: Head_i(Global, ME, Res) ←
         Guard_i(Local, ME1, Res1),
         Commit_i(Res1?, ME, Global, Local, Res),
         Head_{i-1}(Global, ME, Res).
     Head_i(Global, ME, Res) ←
         otherwise | Head_{i-1}(Global, ME, Res).

Procedure_0: $\text{Head}_0(\_,\_,\_)$ ← true | true.

Commit_i: Commit_i(true, i, Global, Local, Res) ←
         Local = Global |
         Body_i(ME, Res).
     $\text{Commit}_i(\_,\_,\_,\_,\_)$ ← otherwise | true.

Figure 33.2: Transformation from SCP to FCP

An SCP procedure:

     $\{\text{Clause}_i\}_{i=1}^n$

is transformed into an FCP program:

     $\{\text{Procedure}_i\}_{i=1}^n$
     $\{\text{Commit}_i\}_{i=1}^n.$

A goal G invokes a conjunctive And-parallel set of processes:

     $\{\text{Procedure}_i, \text{Commit}_i\}_{\text{Clause}_i}$ applicable to G

by invoking $Procedure_n$. Each $Procedure_i$ process tries to solve the guard of $Clause_i$, to commit the computation to the body of that clause and in parallel invokes $Procedure_{i-1}$.

If the head unification of several clauses is similar or even identical, the work involved will be repeated uselessly. It would be much more efficient to try each specific head unification only once. By collecting clauses for which input head unification is similar, much repeated work can be avoided. Also, by thus clustering clauses, attention can be focused efficiently on the group of clauses from which candidate clauses for commitment are finally obtained.

An alternative method for translating SCP to FCP, which avoids this redundant work and allows, in most cases, a selection of the group of clauses which contains the committing clause, is presented below. The solution is achieved by analyzing the requirements for input unification of each clause and collecting all clauses for which these requirements are similar to a certain degree. For these clauses, the collected input unification is done only once. For the class of SCP procedures in which clause selection is determined only by input unification, this allows immediate identification of the group of clauses containing potential candidate clauses. All other groups are discarded efficiently.

In some SCP procedures, clause selection is not solely determined by head input unification. For these procedures, two or more groups of clauses may remain as candidates after head input unification has been performed. Therefore, two forms of the translation method are defined. One form is applicable to procedures in which clause selection is determined solely by head input unification, and another, slightly less efficient, form is applicable to all other SCP procedures.

The theory of partial variants which is the basis of the clause indexing used in the translation algorithm is presented in the next section. The clause indexing scheme based on the idea of partial variants is also the basis of an efficient compiler from FCP to machine language (Kliger, 1987). There, a procedure is translated to a "decision tree"

33.4 Partial Variants

Intuitively, variant terms are terms which, when unified with each other, are not further instantiated. Thus unification of two variant terms requires only a consistent renaming of variables appearing in them. A substitution obtained from such a unification is called a *renaming* (Lloyd, 1984).

The purpose of this section is to introduce the idea of "partial variance" among terms. This means informally that if the unification between two terms is carried out only part of the way, the substitution obtained so far is a renaming. This notion is useful for efficient compilation of Horn logic languages in general. Another version of this idea is described by Kliger (1987), where it is used in compilation of FCP to machine code, to construct a "decision tree" for distinguishing, when given a goal, between candidate and non-candidate clauses for reduction.

In this paper, the idea is applied to compilation of non-flat SCP procedures.

33.4.1 Definitions and proofs

The following definitions show a stepwise construction of a method for efficient indexing on sets of terms.

Definition. We associate trees with terms in the natural way. Edges in the tree are labeled with indices of the term's argument, and vertices with the main functor of the corresponding term.

Definition. A *position* is a series of tree labels.

Definition. Let T be a term with a subterm T'. The *position of T' in T* is the sequence of labels in the tree corresponding to T from its root to the vertex corresponding to the root of the tree of T', inclusive. A position is *terminal* if its last label is a constant or a variable. Otherwise it is *non-terminal*.

Now the concept of *partial most general unifier* is defined. A partial mgu of two terms with respect to a set of positions is an mgu obtained by unifying the terms only for positions which are proper prefixes of positions in the set.

Definition. Given a set of positions S, the *minimal covering set of S*, is obtained by removing all $p' \in S$ such that $\exists\, p \in S$, p' is a proper prefix of p. Let T be a term and S a set of positions with a minimal covering set S'. Then T/S is the term obtained by replacing all subterms in T denoted by a non-terminal position in S' with distinct variables not occurring elsewhere in T. T/ϕ denotes a variable.

Definition. A *partial mgu* of two terms T_1 and T_2, denoted by $mgu(T_1,\, T_2)/S$, is defined as:

$$mgu(T_1,\, T_2)/S \equiv mgu(T_1/S,\, T_2/S)$$

Definition. Two terms T_1 and T_2 are *partial variants* with respect to S if $mgu(T_1,\, T_2)/S$ is a renaming. Let *pvar* be a predicate $T \times T \times 2^p$ so that:

$$pvar(T_1,\, T_2,\, S) = \begin{cases} true, & \text{if } T_1 \text{ and } T_2 \text{ are partial variants} \\ & \text{with respect to } S; \\ false, & \text{otherwise.} \end{cases}$$

This predicate can be easily extended to accept a set of terms instead of two terms.

We present an example, to lend concreteness to the above definitions. A term $a(b(X),\, c(1))$ is associated with the tree shown in Figure 33.3. We denote a position as a series of indices, separated by ".". Thus, the position of $b(X)$ in $a(b(X),\, c(1))$ is *1.1*. The partial mgu of $a(b(X),\, c(1))$ and $a(b(3),\, c(1))$ with respect to the set of positions $S = \{1,1.1,1.2,1.2.1\}$ is computed as follows. The minimal covering set of S is $S' = \{1.1,1.2.1\}$. T_1/S is $a(X1,c(1))$, and T_2/S

is $a(Y,c(1))$. The partial mgu of these terms is $\{X=Y\}$, which is a renaming. Therefore, $a(b(X),\ c(1))$ and $a(b(3),\ c(1))$ are partial variants with respect to S.

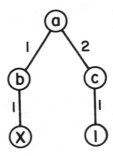

Figure 33.3: Tree associated with $a(b(X),\ c(1))$

The above definitions formalize the concept of partial variants. This concept is used below to define how to separate a set of terms into partial variants with respect to a set of positions.

Definition. Let U a set of terms, and p a position. Let *sep* be a function $2^T \times p \to 2^{2^T}$ that partitions U into a set of maximal sets of terms, such that each set contains partial variants with respect to $\{p\}$.

Lemma. The *sep* function is well-defined.
Proof. Renaming is an equivalence relation, and therefore *sep* computes the equivalence classes of U with respect to renaming on the position denoted by p. These equivalence classes always exist and are unique.   ■

Lemma. If T_1 and T_2 are partial variants with respect to a set of positions S and with respect to $\{p\}$, then T_1 and T_2 are also partial variants with respect to $S \cup \{p\}$.
Proof. Let θ be $mgu(T_1/S,\ T_2/S)$. Let X_1 and X_2 be the variables in position p in $T_1/S \cup \{p\}$ and $T_2/S \cup \{p\}$. Assume that the same variables are introduced for non-terminal positions in T_1/S and $T_1/S \cup \{p\}$, and also in T_2/S and $T_2/S \cup \{p\}$. It follows that $\theta' = \theta \cup \{X_1 = X_2\}$ is a renaming, and that it is the mgu of $T_1/S \cup \{p\}$ and $T_2/S \cup \{p\}$.   ■

Note that the above lemma implies that if U is a set of partial variants with respect to S, then $sep(U,\ p)$ defines a set of sets of terms, where each is a set of partial variants with respect to $S \cup \{p\}$.

$\{p(a(X)),\ p(a(1)),\ p(a(2)),\ p(a(Y))\}$ is a set of partial variants with respect to the set of positions $\{1\}$. The set separates into three sets of partial variants with respect to the set of positions $\{1,1.1,1.1.1\}$: $\{p(a(X)), p(a(Y))\}$, $\{p(a(1))\}$ and $\{p(a(2))\}$.

The tools needed for stepwise decomposition of a set of terms into sets of partial variants have now been defined. This corresponds to the concept of general indexing on arguments. What is lacking is a way to obtain the common structure in all terms in a set of partial variants. For this purpose, the concept of maximal intersection is defined. An intersection of two terms is a set of positions for which these terms are partial variants. The maximal intersection is the largest such set of positions.

Definition. Let *covers* be a predicate $p \times p$ so that $covers(p_1, p_2)$ is *true* or *false* depending on whether p_2 is a proper prefix of p_1.

Definition. Let $\prec$ be a partial ordering relation between sets of positions S_1 and S_2, defined as:

$$S_1 \prec S_2 \equiv \exists p_2 \in S_2, \forall p_1 \in S_1, \neg covers(p_1, p_2),$$
$$\wedge \; \forall p_1 \in S_1, \exists p_2 \in S_2, covers(p_2, p_1).$$

Definition. A set of positions S is an *intersection* of T_1 and T_2 if $pvar(T_1, T_2, S)$ is true. S is a *maximal intersection* of T_1 and T_2 iff:

$$pvar(T_1, T_2, S) \wedge \forall S', S \prec S', \neg \; pvar(T_1, T_2, S')$$

Definition. Let max be a function $T \times T \rightarrow 2^p$ returning the maximal intersection of T_1 and T_2. This function can easily be extended to accept a set of terms instead of two terms.

Lemma. The max function is well-defined.

Proof. An intersection always exists, e.g., ϕ. Assume that S_1 and S_2 are two different maximal intersections of two terms T_1 and T_2. Let S' be the common positions of S_1 and S_2. Then $pvar(T_1, T_2, S')$, since $S' \subseteq S_1$ and $S' \subseteq S_2$. Contradiction, since $S' \prec S_1$ and $S' \prec S_2$, but $pvar(T_1, T_2, S_1)$ and $pvar(T_1, T_2, S_2)$. Hence, the maximal intersection of two terms is unique. ∎

Definition. Let T_1 and T_2 be two terms. The *maximal intersection term* of T_1 and T_2 is defined as $T_1/max(T_1, T_2)$. This definition can be generalized in the natural way for a set of terms.

The maximal intersection of $\{p(a(X)), p(a(1)), p(a(2)), p(a(Y))\}$ is the set of positions $\{1,1.1\}$. However, the maximal intersection of $\{p(a(X)), p(a(Y))\}$ is $\{1,1.1,1.1.1\}$ which covers both terms.

The definitions for an incremental indexing scheme have been given above. The idea of partial variants has been formalized, and two central functions have been defined:

- The *sep* function, which, given a set of terms and a position, separates the set into sets of partial variants with respect to that position.

- The *max* function, which, given a set of terms, returns the set of positions covering the common sub-term of the terms in the set.

A clause indexing algorithm using these tools is shown in the next subsection.

Note the close relationship between the maximal intersection of a set of terms and the least general generalization of a set of terms, as defined by Plotkin (1969, 1970). A generalization of a set of terms U is a term T such that all terms in U are instances of T. The *least general* generalization of a set of terms U is a term T such that there exists no instance of T, T', such that all terms in U are instances of T'. The difference between least general generalizations and maximal intersections can be traced to the definition of partial variants. The least general generalization of $p(a)$ and $p(b)$ is $p(Z)$. This corresponds to the set of positions $\{1,\ 1.1\}$. However, the maximal intersection of these terms is $\{1\}$.

33.4.2 Indexing using partial variants

The above definitions provide the tools for designing an algorithm which separates a group of terms into sets of partial variant terms. The algorithm presented below is designed to expose the iterative nature of the indexing process. As such, it is not the most efficient one possible, and a real implementation could benefit from a more optimized design:

> pvars(U) = {
>   Comment: pvars returns a set of sets of partial variants, given
>   a set of terms U.
>
>   return pvars(U, {[ ]}).
> }
> pvars(U, S) = {
>   Comment: pvars returns a set of sets of partial variants, given
>   a set of positions S and a set of terms U which are partial variants
>   with respect to S.
>
>   if (U is a set of variants) or (termination_condition(U))
>   return {U}
>   else {
>   choose a position p so that $S \prec S' = S \cup \{p\}$.
>   V = sep(U, p).
>   return $\bigcup_{v \in V}$ pvars(v, S').
>   }
> }

Two important components of the algorithm are purposely left unspecified. First, the termination condition, and second, how to choose a position by which to further divide U. This can be any heuristic, such as the cardinality of U.

The question of how to choose a position p is more important, and will have a major effect on the quality of the separation achieved. For example, given $U = \{p(a,\ b),\ p(b,\ c),\ p(b,\ d)\}$, choosing the first argument of p divides U into two subsets: $\{p(a,\ b)\}$ and $\{p(b,\ c),\ p(b,\ d)\}$. However, choosing the second argument yields a complete separation: $\{p(a,\ b)\}$, $\{p(b,\ c)\}$ and $\{p(b,\ d)\}$. Generally, choosing at each stage a position at which the largest number of different values occur seems like a good heuristic.

Note that variants are just a special case of partial variants, when the set of positions covers every position in every term in the set. This is reflected in the algorithm above. Another special case is the case of partial variants covering the part of the head in all clauses which is not output-annotated. These are called *input-covering partial variants*.

The algorithm specified above can be used to construct a decision tree from the heads of clauses in a procedure, to allow clause selection to proceed in a stepwise manner. This is what is done by Kliger (1987). In the compiler presented here, input-covering partial variants are used throughout, and it never uses stepwise clause selection. A procedure is separated into sets of clauses whose heads are variant terms with respect to the input parts.

Definition. Let U_1 and U_2 be two sets of partial variants with respect to a set of positions S, such that $U_1 \cup U_2$ is not a set of partial variants with respect to S. U_1 and U_2 are *dependent* if $mgu(U_1/max(U_1),\ U_2/max(U_2))/S$ exists and is not a renaming. If the partial mgu does not exist the sets are *independent*.

The above definition provides a criterion for deciding whether the selection of a candidate clause is entirely controlled by head input unifications. If the sets of input-covering partial variants constructed from the heads of the clauses in a procedure are independent, then the selection of a candidate clause is determined only by head input unification.

The relationship between dependency of sets of variants and the clause selection process can be understood by studying the example below. The example shows the clauses of an SCP procedure in the GHC meta-interpreter. Each set is presented with its maximal intersection term, as defined in the previous subsection.

```
solve(A = B) ← A = B.
solve(true).
solve((A, B)) ←
    solve(A), solve(B).
solve(G) ←
    clauses(G?, Cs),
    reduce(G?, Cs, B) |
```

solve(B).

This procedure separates into the following sets of clauses, with their associated maximal intersection term:

Set	Maximal Intersection Term
{solve(A = B) ← ...}	solve(A = B)
{solve(true).}	solve(true)
{solve((A,B)) ← ...}	solve((A, B))
{solve(G) ← ...}	solve(G)

Clearly, the maximal intersection term of the fourth set is unifiable with the maximal intersection term of all other sets, producing substitutions which are not renamings.

The problem with this code is that input unification is not sufficient to determine which group of clauses contains candidates for commitment. Even when the argument of *solve/2* is known to be of the form (A, B), two sets of partial variants still remain as candidates. Selection of one of these sets is dependent on the result of guard computations.

The next section shows two forms of the translation process. One form is suitable for procedures which can be separated into sets of clauses whose heads form independent sets of variants. The other form is for procedures which separate into sets of clauses whose heads yield dependent sets of variants.

33.5 Translation from SCP to FCP

The translation of SCP to FCP involves several issues:

- The Or-parallel clause search of SCP must be converted to And-parallel solution in FCP.

- Only one clause in a procedure must be allowed to commit.

- The transformation must guarantee that the effects of guard computations on the goal, as specified by the output annotations in the head of the clause, are evident only at this clause's commitment.

- As an optimization, the transformation must guarantee the efficient "garbage collection" of unneeded branches of the computation tree once a clause is committed to.

As mentioned above, two forms of the transformation are presented. The first is suitable for translation of procedures which can be decomposed into sets of clauses which yield independent sets of variants for the heads, and another for procedures which cannot be decomposed in this manner. The first class of procedures is called *independent* procedures. Procedures for which the decomposition produces dependent sets of variants are called *dependent*.

When the translation starts from an SCP program instead of from a Safe GHC program, the head input unification unfolding transformation is applied, after computation of the sets of input-covering partial variants. Thus, the translation procedures described below also yield an implementation of SCP.

33.5.1 Translation of independent procedures

This section starts with an example, the translation of *isotree/2*, a program for determining isomorphism of two binary trees. This code separates into independent sets of partial variants, and its translation is quite simple. After this, the principles of the translation process are presented, with reference to the example.

The GHC code for *isotree/2* is:

```
isotree(leaf(X), leaf(X)) ← true | true.
isotree(tree(A,B), tree(C,D)) ←
     isotree(A, C) | isotree(B, D).
isotree(tree(A,B), tree(C,D)) ←
     isotree(A, D) | isotree(B, C).
```

The SCP code for this procedure is:

```
isotree(V1, V2) ←
     V1? = leaf(X1), V2? = leaf(X2), X1 =?= X2 | true.
isotree(V1, V2) ←
     V1? = tree(A,B), V2? = tree(C,D),
     isotree(A?,C?) |
          isotree(B?, D?).
isotree(V1, V2) ←
     V1? = tree(A,B), V2? = tree(C,D),
     isotree(A?,D?) |
          isotree(B?, C?).
```

An SCP procedure:

$$\{\text{Clause}_i\}_{i=1}^n$$

which can be decomposed into m independent sets of variants and their associated maximal intersection terms:

$$\{(P_j, \ maxterm_j)\}_{j=i}^m$$

is transformed into an FCP program:

$$P',$$
$$\{Commit_j\}_{j=1}^m.$$

The P' procedure is the top-level procedure: it is responsible for execution of the computation of P. The *Commit* procedures ensure that only one clause from a set of partial variants can commit.

The FCP code generated for the above example is shown with the full definitions of each class of procedure. In the above example, P is *isotree/2* and P' is *isotree/7*. There is one *Commit* procedure, *isotree_commit/7*.

The definition of the generated procedures is shown below:

P': $(n+5)$-ary, where n was the arity of the original procedure P of the SCP program. The meaning of:

$$P'(\sigma, \text{Abort}, S_1, S_2, F_1, F_2)$$

is that invoking it runs the clauses of the original procedure P. σ represents the n original arguments of the procedure. If the invocation succeeds and some clause commits, S_1 and S_2 are unified. If the invocation failed, F_1 and F_2 are unified. If *Abort* is instantiated by a goal running in parallel with the invocation, the computations of this procedure and of all subgoals it created are aborted. The P' procedure contains $m + 2$ clauses, as follows: the first m clauses correspond to selection of each of the m sets of partial variants. The guard of each clause contains a sequence of read-only unifications corresponding to the input-unification requirements defined by the maximal intersection term associated with this set. The body of each clause contains the original guard goals of all clauses in the set of partial variants, suitably modified to invoke the $n + 5$ argument version, and a call to $Commit_i$, if this is the ith clause. Calls to primitive kernels are translated to FCP library procedures, as explained below. The $m + 1^{th}$ clause corresponds to a failure to select one of the m sets of partial variants. The last clause aborts the computation if *Abort* becomes instantiated.

The code generated for P' from the above example is:

```
isotree(V1, V2, _, S, S, _, _) ←
    V1? = leaf(X1), V2? = leaf(X2), X1 =?= X2 | true.
isotree(V1, V2, Abort, S1, S2, F1, F2) ←
    V1? = tree(A,B), V2? = tree(C,D) |
        isotree(A?, C?, Commit, 1, Commit, failure, FV1),
        isotree(A?, D?, Commit, 2, Commit, FV1, Commit),
        isotree_commit(Commit, Abort, {B,C,D}, S1, S2, F1, F2),
isotree(_, _, _, _, _, F, F) ← otherwise | true.
isotree(_, _, Abort, _, _, _, _) ← known(Abort) | true.
```

{Commit$_j$}$_{j=1}^{m}$: 7-ary, one procedure for each of m sets of partial variants of the original SCP procedure. The meaning of:

$$Commit_j(\text{LC}, \text{Abort?}, \text{Env}, S_1, S_2, F_1, F_2)$$

is that invoking it runs the body goals of at most one of the clauses in the jth set of partial variants. If *Commit* is instantiated to n, the body goals of the nth clause in this set are invoked, with additional arguments S_1, S_2, F_1, F_2 and *Abort*. S_1 and S_2 are unified if all goals in the body succeed. They are part of a short-circuit which is threaded "in series" through the body goals. F_1 and F_2 are unified if any of the body goals fail. They are part of a short circuit which is threaded "in parallel" through the body goals. If *Commit* is instantiated to *failure*, then all guards have failed. In this case, F_1 and F_2 are unified to indicate the failure of the invoking goal. *Env* serves for bidirectional communication of the body goals with other goals running in parallel. It serves both to pass values of variables computed elsewhere into the body goals, and for output unifications. The procedure has $l + 2$ clauses, where l is the number of clauses in this set. The first l clauses correspond to a commitment of the respective clause, and the body of each clause contains the suitably modified body goals of the original SCP clause. The $l + 1^{th}$ clause is committed to when all l clauses of the set fail to commit. The last clause aborts the computation if *Abort* is instantiated by another goal running in parallel with the invocation of P'. It instantiates *Commit* to a value which can not be produced by commitment of any of the l clauses, thus in effect blocking attempts to commit in these clauses.

The above example shows that the *Commit* variable is used both as the terminal of the success and failure short-circuits connecting the recursive invocations of *isotree/7*, and as their local *Abort* variable. If an abort signal arrives through the *Abort* variable, the last clause of *isotree_commit/7* instantiates *Commit*. This causes the last clause of *isotree/7* to be selected, if none has committed already. Otherwise, the recursive *isotree_commit/7* causes the *Abort* signal to be propagated further down into the computation tree. If *Commit* becomes instantiated because one of the recursive calls to *isotree/7* has committed, its instantiation will cause the other recursive call to receive an *Abort* signal. This useless branch of the computation tree is therefore automatically discarded. Instantiation of *Commit* also causes the selection of one of the clauses in *isotree_commit/7*.

Although the code for *isotree/2* separated into two sets of partial variants, the compiler optimized away one of the *Commit* procedures, and produced only one:

```
isotree_commit(Commit, Abort, {B, _, D}, S1, S2, F1, F2) ←
    Commit? = 1 |
        isotree(B?, D?, Abort, S1, S2, F1, F2).
isotree_commit(Commit, Abort, {B, C, _}, S1, S2, F1, F2) ←
    Commit? = 2 |
        isotree(B?, C?, Abort, S1, S2, F1, F2).
isotree_commit(Commit, _, _, _, _, F, F) ←
    Commit? = failure | true.
```

```
isotree_commit(abort, Abort, _, _, _, _, _) ←
    known(Abort) | true.
```

Another example of the translation of a procedure which separates into independent sets of partial variants is given below. The *resolve/3* procedure of the GHC meta-interpreter is translated to FCP. The GHC code of *resolve/3* is:

```
resolve(_, [ ], _).
resolve(H, [I|Is], B) ←
    clause(I, (H ← G | B1)),
    solve(G) |
        B = B1.
resolve(H, [I|Is], B) ←
    resolve(H, Is, B1) | B1 = B.
```

The SCP code is:

```
resolve(_, L, _) ← L? = [ ] | true.
resolve(H, L, B1↑) ←
    L? = [I|Is],
    clause(I?, (H? ← G | B1)),
    solve(G?) |
        true.
resolve(H, L, B1↑) ←
    L? = [I|Is],
    resolve(H?, Is?, B1) |
        true.
```

The FCP code generated for this example is:

```
resolve(_, L, _, _, S, S, _, _) ← L? = [ ] | true.
resolve(H, L, B1, Abort, S1, S2, F1, F2) ←
    L? = [I|Is] |
        clause(I?, (H? ← G | B11), Commit, 1, S1, failure, FV1),
        solve(G?, Commit, S1, Commit, failure, FV1),
        resolve(H?, Is?, B12, Commit, 2, Commit, FV1, Commit),
        resolve_commit(Commit, Abort, {B1,B11,B12},
                S1, S2, F1, F2).
```

```
resolve_commit(Commit, _, {B1,B1,_}, S, S, _, _) ←
    Commit? = 1 | true.
resolve_commit(Commit,, _, {B1,_,B1}, S, S, _, _) ←
    Commit? = 2 | true.
resolve_commit(Commit, _, _, _, _, F, F) |
    Commit? = failure | true.
resolve_commit(abort, Abort, _, _, _, _, _) ← known(Abort) | true.
```

Note that there is no need to copy H, since the GHC code to be interpreted is assumed to be safe. Note also that *resolve_commit* does the output unification and the closing of the success short-circuit in one reduction, as part of its commitment.

33.5.2 Translation of dependent procedures

The translation of procedures separating into dependent sets of partial variants is examined next. Again, the section starts with an example, the translation of the *solve/1* procedure in the GHC meta-interpreter. Note that the GHC meta-interpreter is unsafe, since the first clause of *solve/1* is unsafe. However, assuming that the interpreted program is safe, the meta-interpreter operates correctly. The translation of code separating into dependent sets of partial variants generates three procedures.

The GHC code for *solve/1* is:

```
solve(A = B) ← A = B.
solve(true).
solve((A, B)) ← solve(A), solve(B).
solve(G) ←
    clauses(G, ClIndexes),
    resolve(G, ClIndexes, B) |
        solve(B).
```

The SCP code is:

```
solve(X) ← X? = (A = B) | A = B.
solve(X) ← X? = true | true.
solve(X) ← X? = (A, B) | solve(A?), solve(B?).
solve(G) ←
    clauses(G?, ClIndexes),
    resolve(G?, ClIndexes?, B) |
        solve(B?).
```

An SCP procedure:

$$\{\text{Clause}_i\}_{i=1}^{n}$$

which can be decomposed into m dependent sets of partial variants and their associated maximal intersection term:

$$\{(P_j,\ maxterm_j)\}_{j=i}^{m}$$

is transformed into an FCP program:

P',
Commit,

PVar

The purpose of P' and the *Commit* procedure is the same as for independent procedures. The *PVar* procedure executes the guards of the clauses in one of the sets of partial variants in parallel.

The FCP code for the above example is shown with the description of each class of generated procedure. In the current example, P is *solve/1*, P' is *solve/6*, *PVar* is *solve_variant/6* and *Commit* is *solve_commit/7*.

The definition of the generated procedures is:

P′: $(n+5)$-ary, where n was the arity of the original procedure P of the SCP program. The meaning of:

$$P'(\sigma, \text{Abort}, S_1, S_2, F_1, F_2)$$

is as for the case of independent variants. The P' procedure contains a single clause, whose head is the maximal intersection term of the heads of all clauses in the original procedure. The body of the clause invokes *Commit* and m invocations of *PVar* in And-parallel, where m is the number of dependent sets of partial variants the original SCP procedure separates into. The invocations of *PVar* are connected by a failure short-circuit which is threaded through them "in series". Thus, failure of all of them closes the failure short-circuit.

The FCP code for *solve/6* is:

```
solve(X, Abort, S1, S2, F1, F2) ←
    solve_variant(0,{X,A1,B1}, Commit, Commit, failure, FV1),
    solve_variant(1,{X}, Commit, Commit, FV1, FV2),
    solve_variant(2,{X,A2,B2}, Commit, Commit, FV2, FV3),
    solve_variant(3,{X,B3}, Commit, Commit, FV3, Commit),
    solve_commit(Commit, Abort, {A2,B2,B3,A1,B1}, S1, S2, F1, F2).
```

Commit. 7-ary. The meaning of:

$$\text{Commit}(\text{Commit}, \text{Abort}, \text{Env}, S_1, S_2, F_1, F_2)$$

is that invoking it runs the body goals of at most one of the clauses of the original SCP procedure. The purpose of the *Commit* procedure is the same as in the case of independent sets of partial variants. The only difference is that here there is only one *Commit* procedure, which invokes one of the n clauses of the entire procedure, as opposed to m *Commit* procedures, one for each set of partial variants.

The code generated for the *Commit* procedure in this example is:

```
solve_commit(Commit, Abort, {_, _, _, A, B}, S1, S2, F1, F2) ←
    Commit? = 0 | unify(A, B, S1, S2, F1, F2, Abort).
solve_commit(Commit, _, _, S, S, _, _) ←
```

Commit? = 1 | true.
solve_commit(Commit, Abort, {A,B,_}, S1, S2, F1, F2) ←
    Commit? = 2 |
        solve(A?, Abort, S1, SM, F1, F2),
        solve(B?, Abort, SM, S2, F1, F2).
solve_commit(Commit, Abort, {_, _, B}, S1, S2, F1, F2) ←
    Commit? = 3 |
        solve(B?, Abort, S1, S2, F1, F2).
solve_commit(Commit, _, _, _, _, F, F) ←
    Commit? = failure | true.
solve_commit(abort, Abort, _, _, _, _, _) ← known(Abort) | true.

Note that propagation of the *Abort* signal operates in the same way as shown for independent procedures. This is a crucial aspect of the translation mechanism, since all aspects of the control of the computation must work in the same way for dependent and independent procedures.

PVar: 6-ary. The meaning of:

$$PVar(i, Env, Commit, Abort, F_1, F_2)$$

is that invoking it attempts to commit the computation to one of the clauses of the ith set of partial variants. If this is successful, *Commit* is instantiated to the number of the selected clause. If none of the clauses in this set of partial variants can commit, F_1 and F_2 are unified. If *Abort* is instantiated by a goal running in parallel with this invocation, all attempts to commit to one of the clauses are aborted. The procedure contains $m + 2$ clauses, where m is the number of dependent sets of partial variants the SCP procedure separates into. The ith clause ($i \leq m$), in its guard, contains a sequence of read-only unifications corresponding to the input-unification requirements common to all the clauses in this set of partial variants. The body of this clause contains the original guard goals of all clauses in the set of partial variants, suitably modified to invoke the $n + 5$ argument version. If an SCP guard or body contains calls to primitives, these are translated into calls to the FCP library procedures for primitive kernels. This is explained in the next subsection. The guard goals of each clause are connected by a short-circuit, initialized at one end with the number of this clause and ending with *Commit*. The guard goals of all clauses are connected by a short-circuit, initialized at one end with F_1 and ending with F_2. Thus, failure of one goal in each guard suffices to close the failure short-circuit. The $m + 1^{th}$ clause corresponds to a failure of the input unification required to select one of the clauses in the ith set of partial variants for commitment. It unifies F_1 and F_2. The last clause succeeds when *Abort* is instantiated. It aborts the computation of this procedure.

In the above example, the guards of all SCP clauses must be executed in parallel. The guard of the third clause for *solve/1* must be executed in any case, since it contains no input unification conditions.

The code for the *PVar* procedure is shown below:

solve_variant(0, {X, A, B}, 0, _, _, _) ← X? = (A = B) | true.
solve_variant(1, {X}, 1, _, _, _) ← X? = true | true.
solve_variant(2, {X,A,B}, 2, _, _, _) ← X? = (A,B) | true.
solve_variant(3, {X,B}, Commit, Abort, F1, F2) ←
       clauses(X?, ClIndexes, Abort, 3, Commit1, F1, F2),
       resolve(X?, ClIndexes?, B, Abort, Commit1, Commit, F1, F2).
solve_variant(_, _, _, _, F, F) ← otherwise | true.
solve_variant(_, _, _, Abort, _, _) ← known(Abort) | true.

An alternative method, used in an earlier version of the translator, is to generate individual *PVar* procedures for each set of partial variants. Each procedure had three clauses. The first clause solved the guards of all clauses in this set of partial variants, in parallel. The second clause was selected if none of the guards was solved successfully. The last clause was used to terminate execution if an *Abort* signal arrived before any of the guards was solved. However, the size of the generated code using the method shown here is much smaller, and the number of clause tries performed in the average case is also reduced. We therefore chose to use the more efficient method, shown here.

33.5.3 Translation of kernel primitives

We assume that the implementation provides a library of FCP procedures, one for each kernel. Each library procedure is of arity $k + 5$, where k is the arity of the primitive. The meaning of the arguments is as follows: the first k arguments are the arguments to the primitive. The next two arguments are part of a success short-circuit, and success of the kernel causes the unification of these two arguments. The next two arguments are part of a failure short-circuit, and failure of the kernel causes their unification. The last argument, if it becomes instantiated before the kernel succeeds or fails, causes the computation of the kernel to be aborted without waiting for it to succeed or fail.

Each FCP library procedure has three clauses. The first clause executes the appropriate kernel in its guard, passing it the first k arguments. If the kernel computation succeeds, the clause commits, unifying the two arguments following the kth argument. The next clause commits if the kernel computation fails. Its guard contains a call to *otherwise*. When it commits, it closes the failure short-circuit by unifying the appropriate arguments. The last clause commits without any further instantiations when the last argument is instantiated. It suspends until its value is known.

As an example, we show the FCP library procedure for the *integer/1* kernel:

integer(I, S, S, _, _, _) ← integer(I) | true.
integer(_, _, _, F, F, _) ← otherwise | true.
integer(_, _, _, _, _, Abort) ← known(Abort) | true.

Note that in some cases it is possible to optimize and translate primitive kernels inline. This approach has not been taken here, in order to keep the presentation simple.

33.6 Analysis of Translated Code

This section starts by a static analysis of the size of the generated FCP code, and a worst-case analysis of the computational overhead introduced by the translation. Then, the performance of translated GHC programs is compared with equivalent FCP programs. Last, the performance of the translated GHC procedures on the FCP implementation is compared with their efficiency on an emulator-based GHC implementation (Levy, 1986).

33.6.1 Theoretical analysis

Four aspects of the translation process are quantified in this subsection. First, we analyze the size of the generated FCP code and show that it is linear in the size of the original GHC code. Second, we compute worst-case and best-case estimates on the number of FCP reductions performed for every GHC or SCP reduction. Third, the number of FCP clause tries is related to the number of SCP clauses tried. Last, the cost of unification in the FCP program is compared with the cost in the original SCP or GHC program. These facets of the translation mechanism are also compared with the naive translation method proposed by Codish and Shapiro (Chapter 32), in order to estimate the improvement obtained in our scheme.

It is easy to show that the code size of the resultant FCP program is linear in the code size of the original GHC program. First, it is obvious that the SCP program generated from a Safe GHC program is of the same size (up to a constant) as the original GHC program. In fact, the number of clauses is the same, and the only additional code introduced is the read-only unifications in the guard. This overhead is balanced by the reduction in the size of the structures in the heads of clauses. The number of arguments of the SCP procedure is the same as that of the original GHC procedure.

First, the case of independent SCP procedures is examined. The number of clauses in the P' procedure is determined by the number of sets of partial variants into which the SCP procedure separates. The maximum number of sets possible is n, and thus the maximum number of clauses in P' is $n + 2$, which is linear in n. The number of arguments of P' is increased by five over the number of arguments of the SCP procedure. The number of *Commit* procedures is the same as the number of sets of partial variants, and this number is bounded by n. The maximum total number of clauses in all *Commit* procedures is $3 \times n$. Hence, for the case of independent procedures, the maximum number of FCP clauses generated for an SCP or GHC procedure with n clauses is $4 \times n + 2$, which is linear in n.

To show the same for the case of dependent procedures is also straightforward. The P' procedure always has only one clause. The size of this clause is determined by the number of sets of partial variants into which the SCP procedure separates (the number of invocations of $PVar$). This number is bounded by n, the number of clauses in the original SCP procedure. The number of arguments of P' is increased by five over the number of arguments of the original SCP procedure. There is only one *Commit* procedure, which always contains $n + 2$ clauses. There is also only one $PVar$ procedure, which contains $m + 2$ clauses where m is the number of sets of partial variants the original SCP procedure separates into. This number is bounded by n. Therefore, for the case of dependent procedures, the maximum number of FCP clauses generated for an SCP or GHC procedure with n clauses is $2 \times n + 5$, which is also linear in n. Note that if the translation employs individual $PVar$ procedures for each set of partial variants, then the maximum number of clauses generated is $4 \times n + 3$.

The naive translation mechanism of SCP to FCP presented by Codish and Shapiro (Chapter 32) also generates FCP code which is linear in the size of the SCP program. For an SCP procedure with n clauses, $2 \times n$ FCP procedures with two clauses each are produced. Therefore the number of generated clauses is $4 \times n$. The number of arguments of the translated procedures is also increased by a constant over the number of arguments in the SCP procedure.

The number of reductions performed by the generated FCP code for every SCP or GHC reduction is also easily estimated. For the case of independent procedures, for every GHC or SCP reduction exactly two FCP reductions are performed: one P' reduction, and one *Commit* reduction. The number of clauses tried is dependent on the size of the set of partial variants selected for commitment. In the worst case, when the SCP procedure separates into one set of n clauses, the guards of all n clauses have to be executed.

For the case of dependent procedures, the number of FCP reductions per one SCP or GHC reduction depends on the degree of separation into sets of partial variants. We can compute worst-case and best-case estimates. In the worst case, an SCP procedure with n clauses separates into n sets of partial variants, each containing a single clause. In this case, n invocations of $PVar$ are necessary. The maximum number of reductions is therefore $n + 2$, computed as follows: n

reductions of *PVar*, and one reduction each for P' and for *Commit*. In the best case, the SCP procedure separates into one set of n clauses. In this case, the number of reductions is three: one P' reduction, one *Commit* reduction and one *PVar* reduction.

In the worst case, an SCP reduction may require n SCP clause tries. If the SCP procedure separates into one set of partial variants containing n clauses, the *PVar* procedure contains exactly $n + 2$ clauses, and therefore the total number of FCP clause tries is $2 \times n + 3$. If the translation uses individual *PVar* procedures for each set of partial variants, then each reduction of a *PVar* procedure involves a maximum of three clause tries. The worst-case number of *PVar* procedures is n, and therefore the part of the selection process encoded as *PVar* may require up to $3 \times n$ FCP clause tries. Hence, the total number of FCP clause tries in this case would be $4 \times n + 3$. In the translation method used here, the size of the *PVar* and *Commit* procedures is linear in n, and therefore the number of clause tries is in the worst case $2 \times n$. This number can be even further improved if an efficient indexing scheme is used in the FCP implementation.

In the naive translation mechanism proposed by Codish and Shapiro (Chapter 32), an SCP reduction results in $2 \times n + 1$ FCP reductions, where n is the number of clauses in the SCP procedure. The number of FCP clause tries is at most $4 \times n$.

The overall cost of unification in our scheme is less than the cost in the original GHC or SCP program, if the SCP procedure separates in a useful way into sets of partial variants. This is the case in the majority of Safe GHC programs. The reduced cost of unification is a result of the elimination of redundant input unifications. The added cost of unification on the additional arguments is negligible, since these arguments are always instantiated to simple structures of bounded size, or to constants. It is complicated to estimate the exact improvement as a result of the reduction in the amount of unification done, and we can again only provide best-case and worst-case estimates. The best case is when an n-clause, m-argument SCP procedure can be separated into n sets of partial variants on the basis of unification of a single head position. In this case we have avoided unification on $n \times m - 1$ head positions. The worst case is when an SCP procedure does not separate at all into sets of partial variants on the basis of head input unification. In this case, we have to unify with $m \times n$ head positions. This is also the number of unifications which would be performed in the naive translation (Codish and Shapiro, Chapter 32).

33.6.2 Performance of Safe GHC

The performance of the translated code was measured, and the results are summarized in Table 33.1. The data gathered shows the performance of the compiled GHC code on Logix 1.21, with eight MBytes of heap space (Silverman et al., Chapter 21) on a Sun 3/50. The following benchmarks were run: naive reverse of a list of a 1000 elements, *append* and *merge* of two lists of 10000 elements, matrix multiplication of two 25 by 25 matrices, the towers of Hanoi with 13 disks, and *isotree* with a complete binary tree of depth 9. Because it is difficult to determine the actual number of FCP reductions into which any specific GHC reduction translates into, global execution times were measured instead, in milliseconds. All execution times are of examples compiled in trust mode.

Benchmark	GHC-T	FCP-T	G-RPC
Nrev10000	216360	101220	214
Append10000	4220	2005	1
Merge10000	4520	2130	1
Mm25 × 25	33160	27580	332
Hanoi13	36100	24505	1202
Isotree9	43620	–	42

Table 33.1: GHC execution runtimes

The meaning of the columns is as follows. The column marked *Benchmark* denotes the specific benchmark run. The column marked *GHC-T* denotes the execution time of GHC code compiled with the compiler to FCP, and from FCP to the abstract machine instructions of Logix. The column marked *FCP-T* denotes the execution time of equivalent hand-written FCP code. For the *isotree* example this measurement was impossible, since *isotree* requires Or-parallelism. The column marked *G-RPC* denotes the reductions per cycle measured for the specific benchmark. This indicates the average number of processors which could be utilized in solving this problem.

Table 33.1 shows that execution of GHC is about two times slower than execution of equivalent FCP code. The reasons for this are two:

- FCP code uses general unification in the head, whereas GHC code compiles into input unification operations in the guard. Each input unification requires a call to a guard kernel in the implementation of FCP used (Houri and Shapiro, Chapter 38). This is an expensive operation. Thus, the size of the structures on which input unification is done in GHC determines the overhead of GHC code over equivalent FCP code, since it determines the number of calls to guard kernels needed.

- FCP code has fewer arguments, which reduces the number of instructions executed. The additional arguments are required in code generated from GHC in order to correctly model the Or-parallelism available in GHC. Thus, this aspect of the overhead can be attributed to the presence of Or-parallelism in GHC.

In order to assess the relative importance of these two causes, the following experiment was done. Taking the code translated from GHC benchmarks which do not require Or-parallelism, the additional arguments were removed, and the execution times were measured. Table 33.2 summarized the results. Note that in general, it is impossible for the compiler to generate the resultant FCP code directly from Flat GHC programs. The additional arguments are required for correct interface with GHC programs using these predicates in their guards.

Benchmark	GHC-T	GHC-OT	FCP-T	G-RPC
Nrev10000	210105	216360	101220	214
Append10000	4010	4220	2005	1
Merge10000	4200	4520	2130	1
Mm25 × 25	29420	33160	27580	332
Hanoi13	32050	36100	24505	1202

Table 33.2: GHC execution runtimes without Or-parallelism

The meaning of the columns is the same as in Table 33.1, except for the column marked *GHC-OT* which measures the execution time of the original code translated from GHC.

These results show that the main factor causing overhead is the inefficient handling of input unification by the current Logix implementation. Kliger (1987) and Taylor and Shapiro (1987) report on advanced FCP compilation techniques which, among other things, produce much better code for input unification than the current compiler. Initial measurements on Kliger's compiler indicate that for FCP code which has no guards, a speedup of ten is generally obtained. It is therefore reasonable to expect an even greater speedup for the code generated by the GHC compiler, since calls to guard kernels are compiled inline in Kliger's compiler. Code produced by the CFL compiler (Levy and Shapiro, Chapter 35) also uses explicit input unification. Measurements of CFL code compiled using Kliger's compiler show an improvement by a factor of twenty-five over the same code when compiled by the current FCP compiler.

Table 33.3 summarizes the operation of the GHC compiler. The columns have the following meaning. The column marked *Mode* denotes the mode of the FCP compilation. The column marked *Redns (Total)* measures the total number of reductions in compilation of the meta-interpreter from GHC to abstract machine instructions. The column marked *Redns (GHC)* measures only the number of reductions needed to compile the GHC code to FCP. The column marked *RPC* denotes the reductions-per-cycle measurement of the compilation in each mode. This number indicates the average number of processors which could be utilized for this task. The column marked *RPC (GHC)* denotes the reductions-per-cycle measured when only the GHC-to-FCP compilation was carried out.

Mode	Redns (Total)	Redns (GHC)	RPC	RPC (GHC)
Trust	35477	19234	25	38
Failsafe	43501	19234	24	38
Interruptible	52931	19234	23	38
Controlled	65223	19234	24	38

Table 33.3: Compilation of the GHC meta-interpreter

As can be seen, the compiler is built so that large amounts of parallelism can be obtained. In compilation of the GHC-in-GHC debugger (Takeuchi, Chapter 26), even larger measurements of RPC were observed. This is caused by the structure of the compiler, which handles GHC code in small, procedure-sized chunks. Thus, in compilation of a program with many procedures, very large RPC numbers may be observed.

33.6.3 Comparison with an emulator-based GHC implementation

We now compare the efficiency of the translation scheme with an emulator-based GHC implementation described in (Levy, 1986). This emulator correctly implements a subset of GHC which includes Safe GHC and a large subset of all unsafe GHC programs. The exact characterization of the subset of GHC implemented was not done in (Levy, 1986), but the original intent was to implement the full language. As a result, mechanisms which can be used to improve efficiency in an implementation specifically geared for execution of Safe GHC were not utilized.

The benchmarks reported in the previous subsection were also executed on the GHC emulator, on a Sun 3/50. The results are summarized in Table 33.4.

All times shown are in milliseconds. The columns have the following meaning. The first column shows the name of the benchmark. The column marked *GHC-T* shows the execution time of the translated FCP program on this benchmark, and the column marked *EGHC-T* denotes the execution time of the GHC emulator.

Benchmark	GHC-T	EGHC-T
Nrev10000	216360	329450
Append10000	4220	6905
Merge10000	4520	7505
Mm25 × 25	33160	60750
Hanoi13	36100	72005
Isotree9	43620	92300

Table 33.4: Comparison with emulator-based GHC implementation

Table 33.4 shows that for programs which use only the flat subset of GHC, the FCP implementation improves execution speed by a factor of 1.5. When guard tests are used, as in matrix multiplication or in the Towers of Hanoi, the ratio is somewhat better for the FCP implementation. For programs using the Or-parallel component of GHC, for example, *isotree*, the improvement of the FCP implementation over the emulator-based scheme is even more pronounced: an improvement by a factor of two or more is obtained.

It is difficult to attribute these results to any specific feature of the two implementations. However, one can conjecture that the mechanisms for managing the Or-parallelism used in the emulator-based implementation are less efficient than those employed in the FCP implementation. Another possible reason is the smaller number of reductions performed in the FCP implementation, and the more optimized implementation of the FCP emulator. The fact that we specifically restrict ourselves in the FCP implementation to the safe subset of GHC, while the emulator-based implementation was intended to be a full realization of the language, may also influence the results.

33.7 Discussion

A compiler from Safe GHC to FCP is described in this paper. As a side product, a compiler for SCP is also obtained. The compiler is a practical tool: it produces efficient FCP code with equivalent behavior. Several large examples such as the GHC debugger, written in GHC (Takeuchi, Chapter 26), have been successfully compiled with it. The translation technique presented for Safe GHC and SCP is also applicable to PARLOG.

The paper also presents the theory underlying a novel clause indexing mechanism which is used as the basis of an optimized source-to-source transformation from SCP to FCP. This clause indexing mechanism is developed independently by Kliger (1987), where it is used to aid in the efficient compilation of FCP to machine language. There, the structure of the heads of all clauses in the procedure is examined, and a tree-like structure is constructed to allow the implementation to choose one or a group of clauses. In (Kliger, 1987), every position in the head of a clause must be in one of two modes, either input or output. In GHC adding these mode declarations is unnecessary, since structures appearing in the head of clauses are always "input". Therefore, this information is known at compile time, and can be inferred by the compiler without help from the programmer.

The current compiler always uses input-covering partial variants for compilation from SCP to FCP. Conceivably, general partial variants could be used, and a decision-tree of choices could be constructed as in (Kliger, 1987). This approach was not taken here, since every decision in the tree requires an additional reduction, thus raising the execution overhead of the translated code. Instead, some translated guards contain redundant input unifications. Generally the price of a reduction is much higher than the price of a unification on a constant or term. Therefore this design decision is justified for the current research. However, the decision-tree approach *is* justified in (Kliger, 1987), since there on the one hand there is only a very small overhead associated with each choice in the decision tree, and on the other hand the redundant unifications are avoided.

The work described here supports the view that FCP can be considered as the "machine language" of future parallel computers (Shapiro, Chapter 5). It shows that FCP is a suitable target language for compilation of other languages and demonstrates the versatility of Logix in supporting several different languages within the same environment.

Acknowledgements

Eyal Yardeni's assistance with the development of the theory of partial variants is gratefully acknowledged. Without the help of Bill Silverman and Michael Hirsch with the internals of Logix this work would not have been realized.

Chapter 34

Or-Parallel Prolog
in Flat Concurrent Prolog

Ehud Shapiro

The Weizmann Institute of Science

Abstract

We describe a simple Or-parallel execution algorithm for Prolog that naturally collects all solutions to a goal. For a large class of programs the algorithm has $O(\log n)$ overhead and exhibits $O\left(\frac{n}{(\log n)^2}\right)$ parallel speedup over the standard sequential algorithm. Its constituent parallel processes are independent, and hence the algorithm is suitable for implementation on non-shared-memory parallel computers.

The algorithm can be implemented directly in Flat Concurrent Prolog. We describe a simple interpreter-based FCP implementation of the algorithm, analyze its performance under Logix, and include crude estimates of its parallel speedup. The implementation is easily extended. We show an extension that performs parallel demand-driven search. We define two parallel variants of cut, cut-clause and cut-goal, and describe their implementation. We discuss the execution of the algorithm on a parallel computer, and describe implementations of it that perform centralized and distributed dynamic load balancing.

Since the FCP implementation of the algorithm relies on full test-unification, the algorithm does not seem to have a similarly natural implementation in GHC or PARLOG.

34.1 Introduction

Concurrent Prolog was developed with the goal of being a general-purpose high-level concurrent programming language. Being well-aware of the advantages of Prolog as a high-level programming language, one of our design goals was to properly include Prolog as a sublanguage of Concurrent Prolog. Since the initial design of the language did not seem to fulfill this design goal, the reported language was called "A Subset of Concurrent Prolog" (Shapiro, Chapter 2). The same design goal was shared by PARLOG (Clark and Gregory, Chapter 3). Not seeing a method for tightly integrating the capabilities of Prolog with the concurrent component of PARLOG, the designers simply defined two sublanguages — the single-solution sublanguage, and the all-solutions sublanguage — which interact with each other at arms length. An interface was defined which allows a single-solution process to invoke an all-solutions process, and obtain from it a stream of solutions.

Although applicable to Concurrent Prolog as well, we have not adopted this solution. We wanted to view Concurrent Prolog as a future high-level parallel machine language. As such, all systems programs, higher-level languages, and applications should be implemented in terms of its basic computation model. Simply putting two sublanguages side by side, each with its own properties, machine requirements, and implementation problems, seemed to us to defer the problem of identifying a uniform fundamental computational model, rather than to solve it.

Further investigation into the computation model of (the subset of) Concurrent Prolog revealed that the initial assumption — that this language is not capable of implementing Prolog rather directly — was wrong. Kahn (see Shapiro, Chapter 5), showed how an Or-Parallel Prolog interpreter can be easily expressed in Concurrent Prolog. His interpreter (Program 5.8) used deep recursion into Or-parallel guards in Concurrent Prolog to simulate the parallel search in Or-Parallel Prolog. This mechanism exploited the full unification and multiple-environments mechanism of Concurrent Prolog, and hence could not be implemented in PARLOG (or in the more recent language GHC).

The simplicity of the interpreter attested to the expressive power of Concurrent Prolog. However, since it implied that implementing Concurrent Prolog was even more complex than implementing Or-parallel Prolog, it was also a sort of pragmatic counter-example to the implementability of Concurrent Prolog, especially to its multiple-environments mechanism.

Indeed, the main focus of our research turned into Flat Concurrent Prolog, a subset of Concurrent Prolog with simple guards, and we were left with the original problem: How to embed Prolog in a machine whose language is Flat Concurrent Prolog?

One approach to the problem was developed by Ueda (1987). He showed how, given sufficient information on the mode of unification of a Prolog program, it can be converted into a Flat GHC program. His solution is applicable also to FCP. Codish and Shapiro (Chapter 32) describe a different approach to the problem, with similar results: if sufficient mode information of a Prolog program can be determined statically, then it can be transformed into an FCP program.

These results are encouraging, since they seem to give a practical solution for a large class of Prolog programs. Nevertheless, they do not solve the entire problem.

This paper describes an Or-parallel execution algorithm for Prolog that has a very simple realization in Flat Concurrent Prolog. Unlike the previous proposals, the algorithm does not require mode information. Unlike Kahn's Or-parallel interpreter in Concurrent Prolog or the standard all-solutions predicates in Prolog, the FCP implementation does not require side-effects to collect all solutions. For a large class of Prolog programs the algorithm has constant or logarithmic overhead over the standard sequential execution algorithm, and in these cases its parallel execution with $O(n)$ processors exhibits an $O\left(\frac{n}{(\log n)^2}\right)$ speedup over a sequential Prolog computation that requires n steps. In the worst case its overhead is linear and it shows no speedup over the standard algorithm.

Several similar algorithms have been recently proposed, independently and with a different motivation (Ali, 1986a, 1986b; Clocksin and Alshawi, 1986).

These algorithms are different from most proposals for implementing Or-parallel Prolog, which attempt to share as much information as possible between the Or-parallel processes. The mainstream approach concentrates on providing an efficient representation of the binding environment to allow sharing when possible and support splitting when necessary (Crammond, 1985). By contrast, in our algorithm, as well as in the similar algorithms mentioned, there is no sharing of environments or logical variables between the constituent parallel processes. As a result, the algorithm is very simple, and can use the standard structure-sharing or structure-copying representation of terms. Furthermore, since the constituent parallel processes are independent, the algorithm is most suitable for implementation on non-shared-memory parallel computers.

The algorithm is simple enough to be implemented in any conventional language rather directly. We estimate the effort in constructing an interpreter-based implementation of the algorithm to be comparable to constructing a standard sequential interpreter for Prolog. However, the algorithm can be implemented even more easily in Flat Concurrent Prolog, using read-only unification to implement Prolog's unification and goal reduction, and using And-parallel FCP processes to implement the Or-parallel Prolog search processes. Such an implementation has the advantage of flexibility: it can be extended in many different ways quite easily. It also has the advantage of being embedded in a sophisticated development environment for concurrent programming (Silverman et al., Chapter 21), and in an operating system with powerful tools for implementing process and code mapping algorithms (Taylor et al., Chapter 22), as well as dynamic load balancing.

If this algorithm and its FCP implementation prove to be practical, as our present results suggest, it will solve one of the remaining questions about the general applicability of a Flat Concurrent Prolog based system: how to embed Prolog in it. Since its implementation requires full test-unification, I do not see, at present, how to implement it directly in GHC or PARLOG.

34.2 The Algorithm and its Complexity

Abstractly, the algorithm searches all paths in the Prolog search tree of the given goal in parallel. Each path is explored by a separate process that has its own copy of the goal and does not share logical variables with other processes. If the path explored by a process is successful, the process adds its (appropriately instantiated) copy of the goal to the set of solutions. The key problem is how to organize the search so that every path in the search tree is explored exactly once.

Assume that the clauses in the program are indexed. There is a one-to-one correspondence between a path in the Prolog search tree for a goal, and the list of indices of clauses used in this path. Hence a path in the search tree can be represented by a list of indices.

The Algorithm. The algorithm is composed of a dynamically changing set of parallel processes, each with its own resolvent and copy of the goal. Each process is invoked with the resolvent initialized to its copy of the goal and with some prefix of a path in the tree, and is responsible for finding all solutions obtained from paths which extend this prefix. There are two types of processes: a *tracer* and an *explorer*. The algorithm begins by invoking an explorer with the empty prefix.

En explorer operates as follows. If its resolvent is empty, then it returns its instantiated goal as a solution, and halts. If the resolvent is the special constant *fail*, then it halts. Otherwise, it computes the set of indices $C_1, C_2, \ldots C_n$ of clauses that potentially unify with the left-most goal in the resolvent. It picks one clause, say with index C_1, and for every remaining alternative clause index C_i, $i=2, \ldots, n$, $n \geq 1$, it spawns a tracer with the prefix $(P.C_i)$ and a new copy of the goal, where P is the prefix explored by the process so far. It reduces the resolvent using the clause with index C_1, and iterates with the new resolvent and the prefix $(P.C_1)$.

A tracer reduces its resolvent sequentially, using the clauses specified by its prefix, and then becomes an explorer. If a tracer or an explorer attempts a reduction that fails, it replaces its resolvent by the constant *fail*. ∎

It it easy to see that every path in the search tree is explored by the algorithm exactly once. In addition, observe that only the last reduction of a tracer can fail, and this is handled once the process becomes an explorer.

In the following we analyze the overhead and parallel speedup of the algorithm. To measure the overhead, we compare a standard sequential implementation of Prolog, with a sequential (timesharing) implementation of the Or-parallel execution algorithm. For this analysis we assume that in a concurrent implementation a deterministic goal reduction can be implemented with the same efficiency as in sequential Prolog, and that the cost of spawning a process is similar to the cost of allocating a choice point in sequential Prolog. Both assumptions are substantiated by the performance of FCP implementations (Houri and Shapiro, Chapter 38). To measure parallel speedup, we assume sufficient processors. If there are not enough processors, then each processor timeshares between several processes; the algorithm's performance with one processor is according to the overhead calculated.

Let G be a goal with a search tree T, whose size is n, height is h, and number of leaves is l. Let p be the sum of the lengths of the paths in T. From the abstract description of the algorithm it should be evident that the total number of reductions performed by the algorithm is p, and that given l processors, the algorithm can compute all solutions in $O(h^2)$ parallel reductions. Since the sequential execution algorithm of Prolog performs only $O(n)$ reductions (ignoring the overhead of creating choice-points and backtracking) the overhead of the parallel algorithm over the sequential one, in terms of the number of reductions performed, is $O(p/n)$. Since the sequential algorithm executes in time $O(n)$, the speedup of the parallel algorithm over the sequential one using ℓ processors is $O(n/h^2)$.

This implies that for thick search trees, i.e., search trees whose height is logarithmic in their size, the overhead of the algorithm is $O(\log n)$, and its parallel speedup is $O\left(\frac{n}{(\log n)^2}\right)$. For deterministic (linear) trees both the overhead and the parallel speedup are $O(1)$. The worst performance is obtained for nondeterministic thin trees (nonlinear trees whose height is linear in their size): the overhead is $O(n)$, and the speedup is $O(1)$.

The parallel speedup analysis ignores communication costs. These are nil in theoretical shared-memory machine models, such as the PRAM (Fortune and Wyllie, 1978). Below we describe implementations of the algorithm for non-shared memory models; an analysis of the communication costs of these implementations for concrete non-shared memory architectures requires further study.

The analysis above ignores the additional work required by the sequential Prolog algorithm to construct multiple solutions, which may reduce the overhead of the parallel algorithm to $O(1)$ even for thin nondeterministic trees. An example is the goal $append(X, Y, [1, 2, \ldots, n])$, whose overhead is $O(1)$, and speedup is $O(n^{1/2})$ in case the *append* clauses are ordered with the recursive clause first.

The algorithm involves two major operations besides reductions: generating alternative prefixes, and creating new copies of the original goal for every such prefix. A prefix can be generated in time linear in its length. The work to generate it can be apportioned to the first process that explores this prefix, increasing its time by a constant factor.

If the original goal is frozen (Nakashima et al., 1984), one can create a new melted copy of a frozen goal G in constant time if structure sharing is used, and in time linear in $\sum depth(V,G)$, if structure copying is used (where V is a variable occurrence in G and $depth(V,G)$ is the distance of the occurrence V from the root in the tree representing the term G). Most Prolog programs can be written so that this number is bound by a small constant for all useful top-level goals.

Most Prolog programs do not perform general unifications of unbounded input data-structures. Hence for the majority of programs the number of primitive operations required to perform one reduction can be bound by a constant, which is program dependent, and thus 'reductions' can be substituted by 'operations' in the analysis above.

34.3 An FCP Implementation

The FCP implementation assumes that the program is accessible via two predicates. One is *clauses(G,Cs)* that returns the list of indices Cs of the clauses applicable to the reduction of a goal G; *clauses* can use sophisticated indexing mechanisms to reduce the size of this list. The other is *clause($C,A,Bs\backslash As$)* that returns in $Bs\backslash As$ a difference-list of the goals of the body of the clause C, after unifying its head with A. If the clause does not unify, then $Bs=fail$. It also assumes a procedure *melt(Frozen,Melted)*, that can efficiently melt goals for that program.

For example, Program 34.2 includes the FCP clausal representation of the Prolog program for generating a permutation, shown in Program 34.1 of the algorithm. For the purpose of this paper, the FCP guard predicate *unknown* can be considered similar to Prolog's *var*.

```
perm(Xs,[X|Ys]) ←
    select(X,Xs,Xs1), perm(Xs1,Ys).
perm([ ],[ ]).

select(X,[X|Xs],Xs).
select(X,[X1|Xs],[X1|Ys] ) ←
    select(X,Xs,Ys).
```

Program 34.1: A Prolog permutation program

clauses(perm(A1,A2),[2]) ←
    A1? = [ ] | true.
clauses(perm(A1,A2),[1]) ←
    A1? = [_|_] | true.
clauses(perm(A1,A2),[1,2]) ←
    unknown(A1) | true.
clauses(select(A1,A2,A3),[3,4]) ←
    A2? = [_|_] | true.
clauses(select(A1,A2,A3),[3,4]) ←
    unknown(A2) | true.
clauses(_,[ ]) ←
    otherwise | true.

clause(1,perm(Xs,[Y|Ys]),[select(Y,Xs,Xs1), perm(Xs1,Ys)|As]\As).
clause(2,perm([ ],[ ]),As\As).
clause(3,select(X,[X|Xs],Xs),As\As).
clause(4,select(X,[X1|Xs],[X1|Ys]),[select(X,Xs,Ys)|As]\As).
clause(N,A,fail\As) ←
    otherwise | true.

melt(perm(L,_),perm(L,_)).

Program 34.2: FCP representation of the Prolog Program 34.1

The FCP implementation directly matches the description above. The Prolog proof tree is searched by a pool of FCP processes. Each process is invoked with some prefix, and is responsible for exploring all solutions, whose proof is found by first traversing the prefix. The first process is invoked with the empty prefix. Each process carries a path, a trail, a resolvent, a frozen copy of the goal, a melted copy of it, and an output channel.

There are two types of processes: a tracer and an explorer. The initial process is an explorer with an empty path and trail, a frozen goal, a freshly melted copy of the goal, and a resolvent containing that copy.

An explorer inspects its resolvent. If its resolvent is *fail* then it halts. If its resolvent is empty, then it sends the instantiated melted goal on its output channel and halts. If its resolvent is not empty, then it computes the set of applicable clauses for the first goal in the resolvent, and becomes *explore1*. If the set of applicable clauses is empty, then *explore1* terminates. Otherwise, it reduces its resolvent using the first clause, adds the clause index to the trail, and forks into two parallel processes: *explore*, with the updated resolvent and trail, and *explore_rest*, with the rest of the applicable clauses. For every clause index C in the list of clause indices, the *explore_rest* process appends C to the path traversed

solve(Program,FrozenGoal,Sols) ←
    Sols are the provable instances of the melted FrozenGoal.

solve(Program,FrozenGoal,Sols) ←
    Program#melt(FrozenGoal?,Goal),
    explore([Goal?],[ ],[ ],FrozenGoal?,Goal?,Sols\[ ],Program).

explore(Resolvent,Path,Trail,FG,G,Sols,P) ←
    Sols are the instances of FG whose proof has a prefix
    append(Path,reverse(Trail)), given that Resolvent and G
    are the resolvent and the goal obtained by reducing melt(FG)
    using the clauses specified by that prefix.

explore([ ],Path,Trail,FG,G,[G|Sols]\Sols,P).
explore(fail,Path,Trail,FG,G,Sols\Sols,P).
explore([A|As],Path,Trail,FG,G,Sols,P) ←
    P#clauses(A?,Cs),
    explore1(Cs?,[A|As],Path,Trail,FG,G,Sols,P).

explore1([ ],As,Path,Trail,FG,G,Sols\Sols,P).
explore1([C|Cs],[A|As],Path,Trail,FG,G,Sols\Sols2,P) ←
    P#clause(C?,A?,Bs\As),
    explore(Bs?,Path,[C|Trail],FG,G,Sols\Sols1,P),
    explore_rest(Cs?,Path,Trail,FG?,Sols1\Sols2,P).

explore_rest([ ],Path,Trail,FG,Sols\Sols,P).
explore_rest([C|Cs],Path,Trail,FG,Sols\Sols2,P) ←
    append_reverse(Path?,[C|Trail],NewPath),
    P#melt(FG?,G),
    trace(NewPath?,[G?],NewPath?,FG,G,Sols\Sols1,P),
    explore_rest(Cs?,Path,Trail,FG,Sols1\Sols2,P).

trace(Cs,Resolvent,Path,FG,G,Sols) ←
    Sols are the instances of FG whose proof has a prefix
    Path, given that Resolvent and G are the resolvent
    and the goal obtained by reducing melt(FG)
    using the clauses specified by Path\Cs.

trace([C|Cs],[A|As],Path,FG,G,Sols,P) ←
    P#clause(C?,A?,Bs\As?),
    trace(Cs?,Bs?,Path,FG,G,Sols,P).
trace([ ],As,Path,FG,G,Sols,P) ←
    explore(As?,Path,[ ],FG?,G?,Sols,P).

Program 34.3: An Or-parallel Prolog interpreter

append_reverse([X|Xs],Ys,[X|Zs]) ←
    append_reverse(Xs?,Ys,Zs).
append_reverse([ ],Ys,Zs) ←
    reverse(Ys?,[ ],Zs).

reverse([ ],Ys,Ys).
reverse([X|Xs],Ys,Zs) ←
    reverse(Xs?,[X|Ys],Zs).

Program 34.3: Continued

so far (represented for efficiency reasons by *append(Path,reverse(Trail))*), and spawns a *trace* process with this path and a freshly melted copy of the goal.

A tracer performs the proof according to the given path, and then becomes an explorer.

The FCP implementation of the algorithm is shown in Program 34.3. *Program#Goal* is the Logix notation for solving *Goal* using the axioms in the program module named *Program*.

34.4 Performance Analysis of Overhead and Parallel Speedup

The interpreter shown is not the most efficient way to implement the algorithm in FCP. The algorithm is best implemented by a compiler, which can either be derived from the interpreter using techniques of partial evaluation (Safra, 1986) or be constructed manually. Furthermore, programs (or subprograms) whose mode of unification can be determined at compile time are better implemented using Ueda's Or-to-And transformation (Ueda, 1987). Such an implementation can be easily interfaced to our execution algorithm, in case only some self-contained subsets of the program are amenable to such analysis. The construction of a compiler-based implementation of the algorithm is a subject of further research, as well as the execution of the algorithm on the parallel implementation of FCP on the iPSC hypercube (Taylor et al., Chapter 39).

To measure the overhead of the parallel algorithm over the standard sequential execution algorithm for Prolog, one can compare the uniprocessor performance of the FCP implementation with the performance of a good Prolog implementation, e.g., Quintus Prolog. Quite accurate figures can be obtained, if the differences in implementation technologies are taken into account (remember we are trying to compare the algorithms, not their particular implementations). First, the Prolog programs should be run under a Prolog meta-interpreter, to factor out the FCP interpretation overhead. Second, the difference between the implementation technologies should be factored out. For example, when comparing Quintus Prolog to Logix on the same machine, the Logix time should be divided by about 3 or 4, to factor the difference between the highly optimized assembly language emulator of Quintus, and the C based emulator of Logix.

An alternative is to run the Prolog programs under a normal interpreter. We have taken the second approach, and used the C-Prolog interpreter (Pereira, 1983) for benchmarking.

Logix contains a crude mechanism to measure the amount of parallelism available in a computation: the number of reductions performed in one queue cycle. Since several dependent reductions might be performed in a single cycle, this measure should be considered only an upper bound on the available parallelism. However, since most of the parallel processes in our algorithm are independent, the effect of these 'hidden pipelines' should be marginal.

We have performed several simple benchmarks, and obtained the following results. C-Prolog is about three to four times faster on combinatorial problems, such as generating all permutations or the N-queens problem. It is twice as fast for deterministic naive reverse. It is about twice as slow for nondeterministic append.

The amount of parallelism found was abundant. The number of processors and the number of parallel machine cycles required to solve the problem were of the same order of magnitude.

The results are summarized in Appendix 34.1.

34.5 Demand-Driven Parallel Search

The algorithm as described performs an all-out parallel search for all solutions. Sometimes only a few solutions to a goal are needed, and in some cases the need for additional solutions is determined by the previous solutions.

We describe a variant of the basic algorithm that performs demand-driven search. The modified algorithm is composed of a centralized monitor and several search processes. The monitor maintains two queues: one of unsatisfied requests for solutions, the other of unexplored prefixes. At any time one queue at the most is not empty. As in the classical solutions to demand-driven computations (Takeuchi and Furukawa, Chapter 18), unsatisfied requests are represented by terms containing uninstantiated logical variables and requests are satisfied by instantiating these variables.

If the monitor receives a request for a new solution, and the prefixes queue is not empty, it dequeues a prefix and starts a search process with the request and the prefix. Otherwise it enqueues the request to the requests queue.

If the monitor receives a new prefix from some of the search processes, and

```
solve(Program,FrozenGoal,Sols) ←
    stream#merger([path([ ]),merge(Sols?),merge(ToMerger?)],FromMerger),
    monitor(FromMerger?,[ ],[ ],ToMerger,FrozenGoal,Program).
```

monitor(In?,Paths,Sols,ToSelf,FrozenGoal,P) ←
    In is a stream of:
        solution(X) – get another solution
        path(X) – *X* is an unexplored path.
    Paths is a list of unexplored paths.
    Sols is a list of unsatisfied requests for solutions.
    ToSelf is a stream to the merger to self.

```
monitor([solution(Sol)|In],[Path|Paths],Sols,[merge(ToMonitor)|ToSelf],FG,P) ←
    P#melt(FG,G),
    trace(Path?,[G?],Path,G,Sol,ToMonitor,P),
    monitor(In?,Paths?,Sols?,ToSelf,FG,P).
monitor([solution(Sol)|In],[ ],Sols,ToSelf,FG,P) ←
    monitor(In?,[ ],[Sol|Sols],ToSelf,FG,P).
monitor([path(Path)|In],Paths,[Sol|Sols],[merge(ToMonitor?)|ToSelf],FG,P) ←
    P#melt(FG,G),
    trace(Path?,[G?],Path,G,Sol,ToMonitor,P),
    monitor(In?,Paths?,Sols?,ToSelf,FG,P).
monitor([path(Path)|In],Paths,[ ],ToSelf,FG,P) ←
    monitor(In?,[Path|Paths],[ ],ToSelf,FG,P).

trace([C|Cs],[A|As],Path,G,Sol,ToMonitor,P) ←
    P#clause(C?,A?,Bs\As?),
    trace(Cs?,Bs?,Path?,G,Sol,ToMonitor,P).
trace([ ],As,Path,G,Sol,ToMonitor,P) ←
    explore(As,Path,[ ],G,Sol,ToMonitor,P).

explore([ ],Path,Trail,G,G,[ ],P).
explore(fail,Path,Trail,G,Sol,[solution(Sol)],P).
explore([A|As],Path,Trail,G,Sol,ToMonitor,P) ←
    P#clauses(A?,Cs),
    explore1(Cs?,[A|As],Path,Trail,G,Sol,ToMonitor,P).

explore1([ ],As,Path,Trail,G,Sol,[solution(Sol)],P).
explore1([C|Cs],[A|As],Path,Trail,G,Sol,ToMonitor,P) ←
    P#clause(C,A?,Bs\As),
    return_rest(Cs?,Path?,Trail?,ToMonitor,ToMonitor1),
    explore(Bs?,Path,[C|Trail],G?,Sol,ToMonitor1,P).
```

Program 34.4: A demand-driven Or-parallel Prolog interpreter

```
return_rest([ ],Path,Trail,Out,Out).
return_rest([C|Cs],Path,Trail,[path(NewPath)|Out],Out1) ←
    append_reverse(Path?,[C|Trail],NewPath),
    return_rest(Cs?,Path,Trail,Out,Out1).
```

Program 34.4: (Continued)

the requests queue is not empty, it dequeues a request and starts a search process with the request and the prefix. Otherwise it enqueues the prefix in the prefixes queue.

The monitor is initialized with the prefixes queue containing the empty prefix. It terminates when all search processes terminate and the prefixes queue is empty.

A search process operates like the tracer and explorer of the basic algorithm, with two major differences. If it reaches the end of a path and the resolvent is empty, it satisfies the request by instantiating it to the current goal and halts. If no solution was found, it returns the request back to the monitor and halts. If several extensions to the prefix are found, the process chooses one to explore by itself and returns the remaining prefixes to the monitor.

Note that as long as there are at least n unsatisfied requests and n unexplored prefixes, there would be at least n search processes operating in parallel.

The FCP implementation of the algorithm is shown in Program 34.4. For simplicity, it does not detect termination of the search processes, and it ends in deadlock rather than in proper termination. Distributed termination can easily be incorporated in it using the standard short-circuit technique (Takeuchi, 1983). Also, the program maintains stacks rather than queues.

34.6 Parallel Cut

The standard definition of cut is asymmetric and relies on the sequential execution model of Prolog. Cut still makes sense and can be useful in a parallel context. However, its semantics should be made symmetric, lest its correct implementation should require a considerable reduction in the available parallelism.

To simplify both the definition and implementation of cut, we break its functionality into two control constructs, *cut-clause* and *cut-goal*. Cut-clause, denoted $!_c$, cuts alternative clauses, and is a symmetric version of what has been called *soft-cut*. Cut-goal, denoted $!_g$, cuts alternative solutions from goals preceding the cut in the clause, and has been called sometimes *snip*. The full effect of (parallel) cut can be achieved by the conjunction of cut-goal and cut-clause: the symmetric version of the standard cut, denoted $!$, is defined to be the result of textually substituting it by the conjunction $(!_g,!_c)$.

More precisely, the operational semantics of cut-clause and cut-goal is as follows. Let G be a node in the search tree with path P from the root, with clauses indexed $C_1, C_2, \ldots, C_n$ as immediate extensions. Let G' be a goal in the clause C_i. If G' is a cut-clause goal, the execution of G' aborts all computations that search a path that is an extension of $(P.C_j)$, $j \neq i$. If G' is a cut-goal goal, the execution of G' aborts all computations that search a path that is an extension of $(P.C_i)$ except the one in which G' participates.

The effect of cut-clause and cut-goal is shown in Figure 34.1.

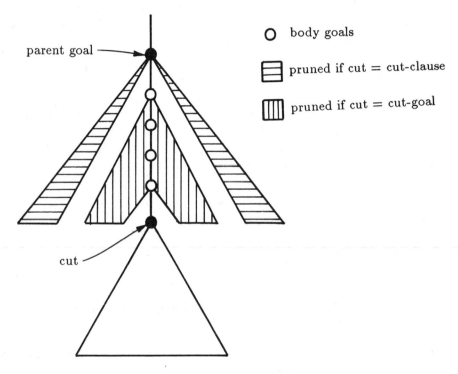

Figure 34.1: The effect of cut-clause and cut-goal

Given this operational semantics, one can distinguish between red cuts and green cuts. Green cuts abort computations that may not contribute additional solutions. Red cuts abort computations that include additional solutions. Green cuts do not change the logical semantics of the program, and the Or-parallel execution algorithm remains a complete and correct deduction mechanism. Red cuts reduce the completeness of the algorithm. Nevertheless, their use may be justifiable in certain cases on practical grounds. Note that both cut-clause and cut-goal can be either red or green.

Note also that both cut-clause and cut-goal are subject to race conditions, and the time in which a cut is executed determines whether alternative solutions are found or not. Hence, unlike sequential cut, the parallel cuts cannot be used to implement negation as failure, and in this sense are closer to the commit operator of concurrent logic programming languages.

Our implementation of the parallel cuts requires no modification to the interpreter and puts the burden on the program representation. (We do not have an explanation of why this mixture of compilation and interpretation turns out to be the simplest.) We implement the cuts as follows. We associate with every goal an interrupt variable, which is used by the goal to sense if the path it is involved in has been aborted.

34.6.1 Cut-clause

A nondeterministic goal G, whose potentially unifiable clauses $C_1, C_2, \ldots, C_n$ contain cut-clause, is reduced as follows. For each clause C_i a new abort variable $AbortCi$ is allocated. A *Cut* variable is allocated, which is shared by all clauses, and a *cut_clause/3* process is spawned connecting the abort variable of G, *ParentAbort*, with *Cut* and the *AbortCi* variables, as shown in Figure 34.2.

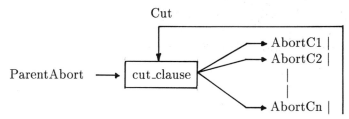

Figure 34.2: A *cut_clause* process connecting the *ParentAbort*, *Cut*, and clause *Abort* variables

In addition, the cut-clause goal in the ith clause is replaced by a goal that unifies the variable *Cut* with the integer i.

The *cut_goal* process operates as follows. If it receives an abort signal from its parent (i.e., *ParentAbort* is instantiated to *abort*), it aborts all its children processes by instantiating the clause abort variables $AbortCi$, $i=1,\ldots,n$ to *abort* and terminates. If a cut was executed, that is, *Cut* was instantiated to some clause index i, then the *cut_clause* process instantiates all other $AbortCj$ variables, $j \neq i$, to *abort*, unifies *ParentAbort* with *AbortCi*, and terminates. Its implementation is shown in Program 34.5.

Computations are aborted by the *clauses/2* procedure, which returns an empty list of alternatives when an abort interrupt is sensed.

cut_clause(ParentAbort,Cut,Children) ←
    known(Cut) | abort(Cut?,ParentAbort,Children?).
cut_clause(ParentAbort,Cut,Children) ←
    ParentAbort? = abort | abort(0,abort,Children?).

abort(C,Abort,[{C,Abort}|Cs]) ←
    abort(C,Abort,Cs?).
abort(C,Abort,[{C1,abort}|Cs]) ←
    C=\=C1 | abort(C,Abort,Cs?).
abort(C,Abort,[ ]).

Program 34.5: An implementation of the cut-clause process

Program 34.6 is a Prolog program for computing whether one of two lists has
an element in common with a third list.

intersect(X,L1,L2,L3) ← member(X,L1), member(X,L3), !$_c$.
intersect(X,L1,L2,L3) ← member(X,X2), member(X,L3), !$_c$.

member(X,[X|Xs]).
member(X,[Y|Ys]) ← member(X,Ys).

Program 34.6: A Prolog program with cut-clause

The FCP representation of Program 34.6 is shown as Program 34.7. Note
that *melt/2* is defined to share the abort variable of the original goal between all
computation paths. This is necessary for implementing cut-clause in the clauses
unifiable with the top-level goal. It has the added benefit that the user can abort
the computation at will by instantiating that variable to *abort*.

34.6.2 Cut-goal

Cut-goal is implemented as follows. Call the part of the clause to the left of
cut-goal the *prunable* part of the clause. When a goal is reduced with a clause
that contains cut-goal, a new *Abort* variable is allocated for aborting amongst the
computations attempting to solve the prunable part of the clause. A *cut_goal/3*
process is spawned for passing the abort signal from the parent goal to the prunable part of the body. In addition, the cut-goal goal is replaced by a goal that
unifies the abort variable of the prunable part with *abort*.

The implementation of the *cut_goal* process is shown in Program 34.8.

The Prolog Program 34.9 for computing intersection has the FCP representation shown in Program 34.10.

One of the consequences of this implementation is that an abort interrupt

melt(intersect(X,L1,L2,L3,Abort),intersect(_,L1,L2,L3,Abort)) ←
    unknown(X) | true.
melt(intersect(X,L1,L2,L3,Abort),intersect(X,L1,L2,L3,Abort)) ←
    known(X) | true.

clauses(member(X,L,Abort),[{1,Abort},{2,Abort}]) ←
    unknown(Abort) | true.
clauses(intersect(X,L1,L2,L3,Abort),[{3,Cut,Abort3},{4,Cut,Abort4}]) ←
    unknown(Abort) | cut_clause(Abort?,Cut?,[{3,Abort3},{4,Abort4}]).
clauses('='(X,X,Abort),[true]) ←
    unknown(Abort) | true.
clauses(Goal,[ ]) ←
    otherwise | true.

clause(1,Abort,member(X,[X|Xs],Abort),As\As).
clause(2,Abort,member(X,[Y|Ys],Abort),[member(X,Ys,Abort)|As]\As).
clause({3,Cut,Abort},intersect(X,L1,L2,L3,Abort),
    [member(X,L1,Abort),member(X,L3,Abort),'='(3,Cut,Abort)|As]\As).
clause({4,Cut,Abort},intersect(X,L1,L2,L3,Abort),
    [member(X,L2,Abort),member(X,L3,Abort),'='(4,Cut,Abort)|As]\As).
clause(true,A,As\As).
clause(N,A,fail\As) ←
    otherwise | true.

Program 34.7: An FCP representation of a program with cut-clause

cut_goal(From,To) ←
    From? = abort | To=abort.
cut_goal(From,To) ←
    To? = abort | true.

Program 34.8: An implementation of the *cut_goal* process

intersect(X,L1,L2) ←
    member(X,L1), member(X,L2), !g.

Program 34.9: A Prolog program with cut-goal

melt(intersect(X,L1,L2,Abort),intersect(_,L1,L2,Abort)) ←
    unknown(X) | true.
melt(intersect(X,L1,L2,Abort),intersect(X,L1,L2,Abort)) ←
    known(X) | true.

clauses(intersect(X,L1,L2,Abort),[{5,Abort}]) ←
    unknown(Abort) | true.
clauses(member(X,L,Abort),[{1,Abort},{2,Abort}]) ←
    unknown(Abort) | true.
clauses('='(X,X,Abort),[true]) ←
    unknown(Abort) | true.
clauses(Goal,[ ]) ←
    otherwise | true.

clause({5,Abort},intersect(X,L1,L2,Abort),
    [member(X,L1,Abort1),
    member(X,L2,Abort1),
    '='(Abort1,abort,Abort)|As]\As
) ←
    cut_goal(Abort?,Abort1).
clause({1,Abort},member(X,[X|Xs],Abort),As\As).
clause({2,Abort},member(X,[Y|Ys],Abort),[member(X,Ys,Abort)|As]\As).
clause(true,A,As\As).
clause(N,A,fail\As) ←
    otherwise | true.

Program 34.10: An FCP representation of a Prolog program with
                    cut-goal

may "chase" a computation that is exploring a path, without ever reaching its frontier. To prevent this, processes that propagate the abort signal need to be given higher priority then normal computations.

Several straightforward optimizations are applicable. If there are no cuts in the set of clauses used to reduce a goal, then neither new processes nor new variables need to be allocated. Neck-cuts can be handled specially by first attempting to reduce using clauses with neck cuts, and only if these reductions have failed when trying the other paths. Our implementation of cut easily accommodates such optimizations.

34.7 Mixing Tracing with Environment Freezing

For every node N in the search tree, define *environment*(N) to be the pair containing the resolvent and the instantiated goal in that node, and *depth*(N) to be the depth of that node in the tree.

Using the standard DAG representation of terms, there is a program-dependent constant c_1 such that

$$|\text{environment}(N')| - |\text{environment}(N)| < c_1$$

for any two consecutive nodes N and N' in the tree.

Also, there is a program dependent constant $c_2 > 0$, such that every program reduction takes at least c_2 steps. Hence there is a constant c, such that for every node N for which

$$|\text{environment}(N)| < c \cdot \text{depth}(N)$$

it is cheaper to copy the environment by freezing it and melting it than to trace the computation of N from the root of the tree. Furthermore, if, when freezing the environment, a multiset of subterms whose total size is g is discovered to be ground, the cost of melting the environment can be reduced to $|environment(N)|-g$. In addition, if subterms of the environment are known before freezing to be ground, the cost of freezing can be reduced similarly. This can be done, for example, by recording such information at the time the environment was last frozen and/or using additional marking propagation techniques (DeGroot, 1984).

Another factor to be considered is communication costs. In non-shared memory implementations of the algorithm, such as the ones discussed below, the cost of communicating environments would be greater than the cost of communicating prefixes, since the latter have a very compact representation. Finding a good strategy for mixing tracing with freezing, and the effect of communication costs on such a strategy, is a subject of further research. When found, the interpreter shown above can be enhanced to accommodate such a strategy. Each process, instead of maintaining just a frozen copy of the goal, would maintain a frozen copy of an environment. Its path would be the path from the node in the search tree where the environment was frozen, rather than from the root. An explorer that encounters a branch in the search tree can either melt its inherited frozen environment and spawn a tracer that traces the alternative path from the point in which the environment was frozen, or freeze its own environment and spawn an explorer with a melted copy of that environment and a path containing just the alternative clause, whichever is dictated by the strategy chosen.

34.8 Dynamic Load Balancing in a Parallel Implementation

The algorithm as described does not address issues of process and code mapping. One possible realization of it on a non-shared-memory computer is as follows. Initialize each processor to contain a copy of the program and a frozen copy of the goal. Connect all processors to a centralized queue. Initialize the queue to contain the empty prefix.

Each processor performs the following cycle: Dequeue a prefix from the queue, explore it to completion, returning unexplored branches to the queue. If a solution is found, return it. Iterate.

The only data-structures communicated at runtime between processors (besides solutions) are prefixes. Prefixes can be encoded very efficiently as vectors of integers, whose range can be restricted to the number of clauses in the program.

This implementation of the algorithm can be realized on a parallel computer directly, using its native operating system and programming language. One would have to implement the many-to-one and one-to-many communication mechanism required by the queue, and implement unification and indexing on the processors. It seems that developing such an interpreter-based implementation in a low level language (e.g., C) should not be more difficult than developing a sequential Prolog interpreter, since the mechanisms associated with backtracking (trail, choice points) are not needed.

In addition, one can simply connect multiple Prolog implementations (whether interpreter or compiler based), and let each execute code similar to Program 34.11. This approach is a bit of an overkill, since the backtracking capabilities of Prolog would not be exploited. However, it might be easier to construct, given a Prolog implementation with interface to a low-level language such as C.

An alternative approach is to implement the algorithm on top of a parallel implementation of FCP, such as the iPSC implementation developed at the Weizmann Institute (Taylor et al., Chapter 39). The benefits of this approach, of course, are that in addition to using FCP unification to implement the Prolog unification, it can also rely on the powerful communication mechanism of FCP to implement the queue and the communication between it and the processors, as well as use its process and code mapping mechanisms to map the processes implementing the algorithm, the Prolog program, and the frozen goal, onto the physical processors. Such an implementation is described below.

Program 34.11 contains the code of the process executed within each processor. The basic cycle of this process is: dequeue a prefix from the queue and trace it. Explore one extension of it, returning unexplored branches to the queue. When the end of the explored path is reached, iterate.

processor([dequeue(Path,_)|ToQueue],FG,P) ←
    P#melt(FG,G),
    trace(Path?,[G?],Path?,G,ToQueue,FG,P).

trace([C|Cs],[A|As],Path,G,ToQueue,FG,P) ←
    P#clause(C?,A?,Bs\As?),
    trace(Cs?,Bs?,Path,G,ToQueue,FG,P).
trace([ ],As,Path,G,ToQueue,FG,P) ←
    explore(As?,Path,[ ],G,ToQueue,FG,P).

explore([ ],Path,Trail,G,[solution(G)|ToQueue],FG,P) ←
    processor(ToQueue,FG,P).
explore(fail,Path,Trail,G,ToQueue,FG,P) ←
    processor(ToQueue,FG,P).
explore([A|As],Path,Trail,G,ToQueue,FG,P) ←
    P#clauses(A?,Cs),
    explore1(Cs?,[A|As],Path,Trail,G,ToQueue,FG,P).

explore1([ ],As,Path,Trail,G,ToQueue,FG,P) ←
    processor(ToQueue,FG,P).
explore1([C|Cs],[A|As],Path,Trail,G,ToQueue,FG,P) ←
    P#clause(C?,A?,Bs\As),
    return_rest(Cs?,Path?,Trail?,ToQueue\ToQueue1),
    explore(Bs?,Path,[C|Trail],G?,ToQueue1,FG,P).

return_rest([ ],Path,Trail,Out\Out).
return_rest([C|Cs],Path,Trail,[enqueue(NewPath?,_)|Out]\Out1) ←
    append_reverse(Path,[C|Trail],NewPath),
    return_rest(Cs?,Path,Trail,Out\Out1).

append_reverse(Xs,Ys,Zs) ←
    See Program 34.4.

Program 34.11: The process executing in each processor

34.8.1 · Centralized dynamic load balancing

Assume that processors are ordered and that the mapping annotation *P@next* is interpreted by a processor as a request to execute the process *P* on the next processor. Using such a mapping notation, the processes executing in each processor can be mapped and connected to a centralized queue using the FCP Program 34.12.

Similar to the previous implementation, Program 34.12 deadlocks instead of detecting termination. It can be enhanced to terminate properly by testing that

solve(*N,Program,FrozenGoal,Sols*) ←
    N is the number of processors to be used.

solve(N,Program,FrozenGoal,Sols) ←
    queue([enqueue([ ],_)|FromProcessors?],Q\Q,Sols),
    processors(N,FrozenGoal,Program,ToQueue),
    stream#merger(ToQueue?,FromProcessors).

queue([dequeue(X,_)|In],[X|H]\T,Sols) ←
    queue(In?,H\T,Sols).
queue([enqueue(X,_)|In],H\[X|T],Sols) ←
    queue(In?,H\T,Sols).
queue([solution(X)|In],H\T,[X|Sols]) ←
    queue(In?,H\T,Sols).

processors(0,FG,P,[ ]).
processors(N,FG,P,[merge(Out)|Out1]) ←
    N>0 |
    processor(Out,FG,P),   % @here
    N1:=N–1,
    processors(N1?,FG,P,Out1)@next.

Program 34.12: Mapping processes to processors, and connecting them to a centralized queue

the top-level queue has n unsatisfied dequeue requests, where n is the number of processors spawned.

It is interesting to observe that even though the FCP interpreter performs dynamic load balancing of the underlying Prolog execution, its constituent processes are mapped statically. In addition, once the process network is in place, no FCP remote process spawn is performed during the entire computation. This corroborates an earlier claim (Shapiro, Chapter 7) that one of the better ways to implement dynamic load balancing is via statically mapped interpreters.

Note that copying of the Prolog program and the frozen goal to each processor is specified implicitly by the FCP program, and is performed by the underlying FCP implementation on a demand driven basis. Furthermore, the prefixes are not really sent to the queue; rather, a reference to the prefix is sent by the enqueueing processor and obtained by the dequeing processor. The actual prefix is transmitted directly between the enqueuer and dequeuer, not via the queue.

The algorithm has been tried on the iPSC implementation of FCP. Performance analysis results are yet to be compiled.

Note that extending this implementation to support a mixed strategy that

combines tracing with environment freezing increases the communication overhead; the frozen environment has to be sent together with a (partial) prefix, in
contrast to just the (full) prefix in the pure algorithm. More detailed analysis is
required to determine the exact tradeoffs between a mixed and a pure strategy.

34.8.2 Distributed dynamic load balancing

The centralized queue shown above could be a communication bottleneck
in a parallel computer with a local-connections interconnection network, such as
a mesh or a hypercube. Even in a globally connected computer network the
centralized queue is far from ideal, since it does not give priority to satisfying
requests locally, within a processor.

We describe below a distributed queue, which alleviates these problems somewhat. The distributed queue is composed of a tree of queue processes. It can be
mapped on a tree or hypercube-connected computer using standard techniques. It
can be mapped on a mesh using the $\aleph$-tree mapping technique (Shapiro, Chapter
7).

The leaves of the queue-tree are connected to the processors. Processors send
to the queues enqueue and dequeue requests as well as solutions. Each queue
process operates as follows. When it receives an enqueue or dequeue request, it
attempts to satisfy it using a matching unsatisfied request from its local queue.
If it cannot satisfy the request locally, it enqueues it, and sends a copy of it to its
parent. Solutions are simply forwarded to the parent. The root of the queue-tree
is connected to a filter process that ignores enqueue and dequeue requests and
forwards the solutions it receives to the user.

The key problem in this approach is to ensure that even though multiple
copies of the same request are spread throughout the tree, a request will be
satisfied once at the most.

This is guaranteed using a mutual exclusion mechanism that relies on the
atomicity of unification in FCP, and on the property that the unification of two
distinct read-only variables suspends. The idea is as follows. Each enqueue and
dequeue request is sent with an additional argument, which is initially uninstantiated. A queue that wants to serve a request using a matching request, attempts
atomically to instantiate the mutual-exclusion variables in both requests to the
term $served(\_?)$, where $\_?$ is an anonymous read-only variable. If it succeeds,
then no other queue can serve either of these requests, since the unification of
their mutual exclusion variable with another such term will not succeed. If a
queue process ever discovers that a mutual exclusion variable of a request is instantiated to $served(X)$, for any X, then it can conclude that the request has
already been served and discard it from the queue.

This idea is implemented in Program 34.13. The process-to-processor mapping notation is omitted.

solve(N,Program,FrozenGoal,Sols) ←
    queue_tree(1,N,FrozenGoal,Program,[enqueue([ ],Served)],Out),
    filter(Out?,Sols).

queue_tree builds a binary tree of queues.
    Unsatisfied requests are both queued locally and forwarded up
    the tree. Mutual exclusion on requests guarantees that each
    request is served at most once.

queue_tree(N,N,FG,P,Q,Out) ←
    queue(ToQueue?,Q,Out),
    processor(ToQueue,FG,P).
queue_tree(N1,N4,FG,P,Q,Out) ←
    N1<N4 | N2:=(N1+N4)/2, N3:=N2+1,
    queue(ToQueue?,Q,Out),
    merge(Out1?,Out2?,ToQueue),
    queue_tree(N1?,N2?,FG,P,[ ],Out1),
    queue_tree(N3?,N4?,FG,P,[ ],Out2).

queue([Req|In],Q,Out) ←
    Req=\=solution(_) |
    serve(Req,Q?,Q1,Out,Out1),
    queue(In?,Q1?,Out1).
queue([solution(Sol)|In],Q,[solution(Sol)|Out]) ←
    queue(In?,Q,Out).
queue([ ],_,[ ]).

serve(Req,Q,Q1,Out,Out1) ←
    The result of serving *Req* with respect to *Q* and *Out* is *Q1* and
    Out1. *Q* is the queue of unserved enqueue and dequeue requests.
    There are three basic cases:
    1. The *Request* was already served, so ignore it (Clause 1).
    2. The *Request* can be served locally, so mark the *Request* and
       the matching queue entry as served, and update the queue
       (Clause 2).
    3. The *Request* cannot be served locally: add it to the local queue,
       and also send it to the parent queue (Clauses 3,4).
       In addition, if served requests are found in the queue, then
       remove them (Clause 5).

    Queue invariant: the queue always contains requests of one type
    only. Hence if the first queue entry is of the wrong type (same as
    the request), then conclude that the request cannot be served
    locally.

Program 34.13: Spawning a distributed queue

```
serve({Type,Path,Served},Q,Q,Out,Out) ←                    % 1
    Served? = served(_) | true.
serve( {Type,Path,served(_?)},                             % 2
    [{Type1,Path,served(_?)}|Q],Q,
    Out,Out
) ←
    Type=\=Type1 | true.
serve( {Type,Path,Served},                                 % 3
    [ ],[{Type,Path,Served}],
    [{Type,Path,Served}|Out],Out
) ←
    unknown(Served) | true.
serve( {Type,Path,Served},                                 % 4
    [Req|Q],[{Type,Path,Served},Req|Q],
    [{Type,Path,Served}|Out],Out
) ←
    Req={Type,_,Served1},
    unknown(Served1),
    unknown(Served) | true.
serve( Req,[{Type,Path,Served}|Q],Q1,Out,Out1) ←           % 5
    Served? = served(_) | serve(Req,Q?,Q1,Out,Out1).

filter([{_,_,_}|In],Out) ←
    filter(In?,Out).
filter([solution(Sol)|In],[solution(Sol)|Out]) ←
    filter(In?,Out).
filter([ ],[ ]).

merge([X|Xs],Ys,[X|Zs]) ←
    merge(Ys?,Xs?,Zs).
merge(Xs,[Y|Ys],[Y|Zs]) ←
    unknown(Xs) |
    merge(Ys?,Xs?,Zs).
merge([ ],Xs,Xs).
```

Program 34.13: (Continued)

34.9 Conclusions

We have presented a simple Or-parallel execution algorithm for Prolog, and
have analyzed its overhead and amenability to parallel execution. The theoretical
analysis indicates that the algorithm may be practical for a large class of Prolog

programs. The algorithm can be easily interfaced to more specialized execution schemes for Prolog, such as the one proposed by Ueda (1987), which are applicable in case additional mode information can be derived.

We have demonstrated an FCP implementation of the algorithm, which preserves its complexity. The implementation uses FCP read-only unification to implement Prolog's unification. Languages that have a weaker notion of unification, such as GHC and PARLOG, might not have such a direct implementation of the algorithm. The FCP implementation can be extended quite easily in several useful ways, and in this sense is preferable over a direct implementation of the algorithm. Its performance on a uni-processor indicates that the approach has acceptable execution overhead.

Further research, both theoretical and experimental, is required to investigate the parallel speedup and communication overhead of non-shared memory parallel implementations of the algorithm. Other research directions include the development of an effective strategy for mixing tracing and freezing, and the construction of an Or-parallel Prolog to FCP compiler, based on the interpreters shown.

The paper has not addressed the issue of side-effects in Prolog. We feel that in the scheme we have proposed of embedding Or-parallel Prolog in FCP, problems whose implementation in Prolog requires side-effects, i.e., interaction with the environment and maintenance of updatable data, are best left to FCP. FCP can express their solution in a much cleaner way, using pure logic programs without side-effects. Which capabilities of the underlying FCP system should be provided to Prolog and how, are yet to be determined. We suspect they may be quite different from the ones provided by current Prolog systems.

The algorithm described is suitable for small programs with a lot of search. An extension, or a different algorithm, may be required for handling large Prolog programs whose code can be distributed across several processors, e.g., database applications.

Acknowledgements

The development of the algorithm was inspired by an enumeration technique for FCP computations, developed jointly with Yossi Lichtenstein and Michael Codish (Chapter 27). Thanks to John Gallagher, Ken Kahn, Vinet Singh, Jeff Ullman, Moshe Vardi and the anonymous referees for their comments.

Part of this research was carried while the author was at Stanford University, Department of Computer Science.

Appendix 34.1: Preliminary Performance Analysis

The benchmarks were run under Logix and C-Prolog on a VAX 8650.

Prolog is the C-Prolog time in miliseconds. The C-Prolog collected all solutions using *bagof*. *Orpp* is the time, in miliseconds, of the Or-parallel Prolog interpreter in FCP. The interpreter in Program 34.2 was compiled with the clause representation in the same module, to eliminate the overhead of Logix's remote procedure calls. Trust-mode compilation was used.

Ln represents the list $[1,2,...,n]$. Time is in milliseconds. *Creations* is the numbers of processes created during the computation, *Reductions* is the number of process reductions performed. *RPC* stands for reductions per queue cycle and is a crude measure of the available parallelism. *Cycles* (when available) is the total number of queue cycles. They were obtained by setting the process time-slice of Logix to 1 (breadth-first scheduling). The line marked *FCP* indicates the performance of naive reverse in FCP. The programs used are shown in Appendix 34.2.

Note: These numbers should be taken as indicative figures and are not a result of a serious performance analysis. Several system factors were taken into account slightly differently in different columns, and as a result some of the numbers don't add (e.g., rpc × cycles = reductions does not always hold).

Note: The code in the paper was cleaned up a bit after benchmarking was finished. This resulted in about 10-20% performance improvement.

Goal	Prolog	Orpp	Creations	Reductions	RPC	Cycles
reverse(L30,_)	166	350	1500	2500	2	
(FCP)		40	31	500	10	
reverse(L60,_)	416	1150	5700	9700	2	
(FCP)		110	61	1900	26	
append(X,Y,L30)	466	190	670	2055	14	
append(X,Y,L60)	1150	690	2550	6200	25	
perm(L4,_)	100	320	1200	2800	19	157
perm(L5,_)	550	2250	7300	17800	70	257
perm(L6,_)	4000	16500	52600	133100	313	425
queens(L4,_)	80	260	750	1700	12	154
queens(L5,_)	250	1100	3100	7150	29	256
queens(L6,_)	800	5100	13600	33000	73	453
queens(L7,_)	3800	24700	63250	158100	214	738
queens(L8,_)	17600	123700	313000	802000	746	1074

Appendix 34.2: Benchmark Programs

rev([X|Xs],Ys) ← rev(Xs,Zs), append(Zs,[X],Ys).
rev([ ],[ ]).

append([X|Xs],Ys,[X|Zs]) ← append(Xs,Ys,Zs).
append([ ],Xs,Xs).

perm(Xs,[X|Ys]) ←
    select(X,Xs,Xs1), perm(Xs1,Ys).
perm([ ],[ ]).

select(X,[X|Xs],Xs).
select(X,[X1|Xs],[X1|Ys]) ←
    select(X,Xs,Ys).

queens(Ns,Qs) ←
    queens(Ns,[ ],Qs).

queens(Ns,Ss,Qs) ←
    select(Q,Ns,Ns1),
    safe(Q,1,Ss),
    queens(Ns1,[Q|Ss],Qs).
queens([ ],Ss,Ss).

safe(Q,N,[X|Xs]) ←
    Y1 is Q+N, Y2 is Q–N, X\==Y1, X\==Y2, N1 is N+1,
    safe(Q,N1,Xs).
safe(Q,N,[ ]).

Chapter 35

CFL — A Concurrent Functional Language Embedded in a Concurrent Logic Programming Environment

Jacob Levy and Ehud Shapiro

The Weizmann Institute of Science

Abstract

This paper describes CFL, a concurrent functional language. The implementation of the language is based on a source-to-source transformation of a CFL program to an equivalent Flat Concurrent Prolog program. The resulting Flat Concurrent Prolog program is then compiled and executed directly.

The approach taken in this paper has several advantages over conventional implementations of concurrent functional languages. First, concurrency is obtained at no extra cost by exploiting the parallel implementation of Flat Concurrent Prolog. Second, CFL can be used as a front-end language for novice Flat Concurrent Prolog programmers, since it alleviates the need to consider synchronization. Third, functional languages cannot realize global state information without side effects. By embedding CFL within FCP, this problem is alleviated, since FCP is able to realize global state information through perpetual processes.

35.1 Introduction

Recently, the combination of logic and functional languages has received much attention (DeGroot and Lindstrom, 1986). The relationship between the two disciplines is clearly exposed by Reddy (1986), and the greater expressive power of logic languages is shown. The increased expressive power of logic languages stems from the following characteristics —

- Logic languages do not specify a rigid input-output configuration on their arguments whereas in functional languages, all arguments are input and the result of a call is the only output. A con of this feature is that when an input-output configuration between goals must be expressed in a logic language, this may necessitate introduction of dummy variables. A pro is that a single specification in a logic language may be used for all input-output configurations, whereas in a functional language each input-output configuration requires its own specification.

- Because of the relational nature of logic programming, concurrent logic languages allow the formation of general communication graphs. This property is absent from standard functional programming languages, where the natural communication structure is a tree.

- Logic languages provide the ability to delay determination of a data structure in an arbitrary manner. Pure functional languages do not provide the concept of uninstantiated variables. A function cannot return a variable which will be later instantiated to some value, without a special extention such as the "futures" of Multilisp (Halstead, 1985).

- Logic languages use *resolution* as the basic computation mechanism, whereas functional languages use *reduction* (Darlington et al., 1986).

- Because functional languages specify a direction on all communications, the execution of calls must be done in a certain order to achieve best performance. This leads to less opportunities for utilizing parallelism. If a program needs forward references to as-yet undetermined data, in functional languages this has to be programmed explicitly. The above restrictions are not present in logic languages, and therefore the execution order can be determined at runtime by the specific input-output configuration used.

- Functional languages are inherently deterministic, following from the mathematical definition of functions. On the other hand, logic programming languages provide relations and thus incorporate non-determinism. Extending functional languages to incorporate don't-care non-determinism, as done in (Henderson, 1980), requires modification and extension of the semantics of functional language. One possible approach in this direction is the work done by Plotkin (1976).

Narrowing (Goguen and Meseguer, 1984; Lindstrom, 1985) is an attempt to recapture this additional expressive power within the framework of functional languages. Other researchers have attempted to unify the logic and functional frameworks to obtain a system which supports both (Subrahmanyam and You, 1984a, 1986; Robinson and Sibert, 1982; Mellish and Hardy, 1984). Embedding of a logic programming system within a functional environment has also been attempted (McCabe, 1986; Carlsson and Kahn, 1984). Lastly, interpretation of a functional language in a logic programming framework is described by Cohen (1986).

The current paper suggests that a functional program can be compiled by a simple source-to-source transformation to a logic program. The logic program is then executed directly by the logic programming system in which the translator is written. This approach has been used for translation to Prolog by Buettner and Bowen (1987). The translation of a functional language to intentional logic is described by (Yaghi, 1983). Here, the translation is to Flat Concurrent Prolog (Mierowsky et al., 1985; Shapiro, Chapter 5), a concurrent logic programming language, thus allowing the exploitation of the inherent concurrency of functional languages.

The translation of a functional language to Prolog as described by Buettner and Bowen (1987) results in a deterministic program. Introducing nondeterminacy into a functional language produces code which may yield one of a set of solutions. However, the translated code always finds the "first" solution according to the search rule employed by Prolog.

Flat Concurrent Prolog belongs to a group of committed-choice concurrent logic programming languages (Shapiro, Chapter 5). The semantics of the commit operator in these languages is similar to cut in Prolog, but it is cleaner due to its symmetrical nature. Thus, committed-choice logic languages are suitable as translation targets for functional languages incorporating nondeterminism. However, as discussed above, incorporation of nondeterminism into functional languages requires a major revision of the semantics.

Darlington et al. (1986) contend that logic languages are inherently first-order (Warren, 1982c). Below it is shown how, by a simple source-to-source transformation, higher-order functions and lexical closure expressions can be compiled into logic programs. The translator is capable of handling both "downward" and "upward" closures (Allen, 1978). The translation of these constructs to Flat Concurrent Prolog is natural, and the translated code does not use any extra-logical features. Thus, this claim is not applicable to the work reported here.

The embedding of a functional programming system within a concurrent logic programming environment has several advantages. Flat Concurrent Prolog has a comprehensive programming environment, Logix (Silverman et al., Chapter 21). The environment provides a compiler and various tools for debugging, program-development aids and a host of predefined utilities. Thus, programs in CFL, if embedded within this system, have access to all these facilities.

Development of concurrent functional systems is being actively pursued in various research programs around the world (Vegdahl, 1984; Keller, 1980a, 1980b; Hudak, 1985; Hudak and Smith, 1985; Holmstrom , 1983; Fahlman et al., 1983;

Darlington and Reeve, 1981; Steinberg, 1986; Halstead, 1985; Harrison, 1986; Gottlieb et al., 1983). However, given a parallel implementation of Flat Concurrent Prolog (Taylor et al., Chapter 39), programs translated from CFL can be run on this implementation and obtain parallelism almost for free. Sequential implementations (Houri and Shapiro, Chapter 38; Kliger, 1987) can also run the same translated program, allowing the simulation of concurrency at the level of CFL even on a serial computer.

The next section introduces CFL and surveys its syntax and semantics. Section 35.3 shows how CFL expressions are transformed into equivalent Flat Concurrent Prolog expressions. Section 35.4 discusses the translation of higher-order functions and lexical closure expressions. Section 35.5 discusses the evaluation strategy used by the translated code, eager evaluation. Alternative evaluation strategies are examined. Section 35.6 shows how CFL can be transformed into GHC, and discusses the relationship between these two languages. Section 35.7 presents some benchmarks of translated CFL programs and compares them with results obtained from executing programs written directly in FCP, where possible. Lastly the virtues and shortcomings of CFL as a user front-end language for programming in Flat Concurrent Prolog are surveyed in Section 35.8.

35.2 The Concurrent Functional Language

CFL is a lexically scoped functional language (Steele and Sussman, 1978a; Sussman and Steele, 1975; White, 1979; Steele, 1984). Its syntax is somewhat reminiscent of Pascal (Jensen and Wirth, 1974). Appendix 35.1 contains a full BNF grammer describing the syntax. Here, the syntax of each construct is introduced briefly, and the main emphasis is on the semantics. In the examples of syntax shown below, non-terminals are printed in *italics* and reserved words are shown in roman.

A CFL program consists of a set of *function definitions*. A *function definition* has the following syntax —

> *head* ← *body*.

The *head* of the definition is either a symbol, denoting a function without formal parameters, or a symbol followed by a list of parameter specifications. Each parameter specification is either a symbol starting with an upper-case letter or with "_", or a quoted term. A quoted term has the following structure —

> '*term*

where *term* can be a general term, possibly containing parameter names.

The semantics of the head of a definition are that the parameter names specify the creation of named variables which will be bound at runtime to structures passed in the call to this function. Named variables declared in the *head* of a definition may be used in the *body* of the definition. At runtime, the parameter names in the *body* will be substituted with the actual parameters passed in the call. Quoted terms in the head must match the call at runtime or the call will fail. Since quoted terms may contain parameter names, this provides an automatic form of *destructuring* (Bawden et al., 1981). mti Bawden A.

The *body* of a definition can be of one of the forms listed in Appendix 35.1. Below, the different forms and their semantics are examined.

An *if* expression is of the following form —

> if *condition* then *expression*
>
>   or
>
> if *condition* then *expression* also *expression*
>
>   or
>
> if *condition* then *expression* else *expression*

The *condition* can be a predicate or a series of predicates separated by *and*. Disjunction of predicates, using *or*, is currently not supported. This is not a loss of expressive power, since disjunctions can be transformed into conjunctions.

CFL provides a rich set of predefined test predicates, listed in Appendix 35.2. In addition, a predicate may be user-defined. A *condition* may also be a *destructuring* expression —

> *expression* = *expression*

The arguments of this form may be any *expression*s. The *expression*s are evaluated, and the results matched against each other. The resulting values may contain new variables, and these variables are added to the lexical scope of the *condition* and the *expression* following the *then*. If the matching fails, no new variables are created.

The semantics of the *if* expression are that if the *condition* succeeds (evaluates to *true*), then the *expression* following the *then* is evaluated. Otherwise the *expression* (if any) following the *also* or *else* is evaluated.

If an *also* is followed by another *if* expression, the *conditions* are performed in parallel. If both *conditions* succeed, one of the *expression*s following the two *then*s will be non-deterministically selected for evaluation. In a sequence of *if* expressions separated by *also*s, all *expression*s following successful *conditions* are candidates for evaluation, and one will be chosen non-deterministically.

Using *else* in place of *also* guarantees that all tests before the *else* will have failed before the branch of the *if* expression following it will be tried. Thus, it introduces an ordering in the execution of the different branches of the *if* expression. CFL programmers are encouraged to use *also* wherever possible, since it leads to more concurrency in the translated program.

Adding *also* to the language extends it beyond being a pure functional language, since now it non-deterministically computes one of a set of solutions. Henderson (1980) defines another primitive for incorporating non-determinism into functional languages, an *or* operator. Its form is

> expression *or* expression

and its semantics are that the value of an *or* expression is the value of one of its sub-expressions. Both sub-expressions are evaluated, and the value of one of them is non-deterministically returned. Henderson shows precise semantics for the *or* expression and discusses the loss of substitutivity following from incorporation of this primitive. Plotkin (1976) also shows how don't-care nondeterminism can be incorporated into a deterministic language.

It is clear that *also* can be easily represented using only *else* and *or*. Specifically, an expression of the form

> if test then expr_a also expr_b

can be rewritten using *or* and *else* as

> if test then expr_a or expr_b else expr_b.

Wherever the word *expression* was used above, an *if* expression or one of the following forms can appear. A *let* expression is of the following form —

> let *definitions* in *expression*
>
> or
>
> *expression* where *definitions*

The two forms are equivalent. The *definitions* can be a pair —

> *parameter name* = *expression*

or a sequence of such pairs separated by *and*.

The semantics of the *let* expression are that the parameter names defined in the *definitions* create new named variables, which are added to the context of the *expression* and bound to the values of the corresponding defining *expression*. The *expression*s used in the *definitions* to compute values for the parameter names may use only variables which are bound in the environment lexically enclosing the *let* expression — they cannot use variables newly created by other definitions in this *let* expression. The *expression* following the *in* is evaluated in the augmented environment.

A quoted term is also a legal CFL *expression* and can appear anywhere a CFL *expression* is accepted. Its semantics are that evaluating it results in a term of the same structure but with all named variables occurring in it substituted with their values.

A variable name is also a legal CFL *expression*. Its value is the value of the variable when it becomes bound.

An *expression* can be enclosed in curly brackets, to indicate grouping when operator priorities would cause a mis-parsing. The rule is that if the *expression* contains operators or reserved words of lower priority than the last preceding operator or reserved word, it should be enclosed in curly brackets. Appendix 35.3 contains a list of the operators and their priorities.

The last form explained here is the *call* expression. It represents a function call. Its form is —

> *symbol*
>
> > or
>
> *symbol (list-of-expressions)*

where *list-of-expressions* is either an *expression* or a sequence of *expression*s separated by commas. *Call* expressions may be composed. Some calls such as arithmetic functions and comparison operators may be used in an infix notation, to denote a call to the respective function with the left-hand and right-hand *expression*s as arguments.

A *call* expression is a function application. The function specified by the outermost symbol and the number of arguments supplied is applied to the values of the arguments. The value returned by this application is the value of the *call* expression.

Two more forms, the *lambda* expression and the *application* expression, are also legal CFL forms. These are explained in Section 35.5.

The semantics of CFL do not restrict the value of an *expression* to be ground. A value may contain variables, which may be bound by other computations. Since CFL is lexically scoped the computations which will bind these variables are recursively descended from computations which occur within the lexical scope producing the value. However, there is no guarantee that the value will be produced only when all computations participating in its construction have terminated. Rather, the value may become accessible outside the lexical scope producing it as soon as its top-level structure is determined. CFL provides dataflow synchronization (Arvind et al., 1978; Ackerman, 1982; Davis and Keller, 1982; Wise, 1982b) to ensure correct operation — computations which attempt to examine an as-yet undetermined part of a value suspend until the value becomes available.

CFL does not specify an order in which tests in a *condition* of an *if* expression are evaluated. Any ordering, and in particular a completely parallel one, is acceptable. CFL also does not specify an order in which compound *call* expressions are evaluated. Thus, various evaluation strategies may be implemented. The current CFL translator produces code which implements eager evaluation

(Allen, 1978). In this method, arguments and sub-arguments are evaluated in parallel, and a call can be started as soon as enough data is available to operate upon. Different evaluation strategies and their possible implementation within Flat Concurrent Prolog are examined in Section 35.5.

This section closes with some examples of CFL code. The aim is to familiarize the reader with the syntax and semantics of CFL and to introduce some applications for which CFL is suitable.

Merging of two lists is to concurrent programming what appending two lists is to sequential programming. The code below implements this function in CFL.

```
merge(S1,S2) ←
    if list(S1)
        then cons(car(S1),merge(cdr(S1),S2))
    also if list(S2)
        then cons(car(S2),merge(S1,cdr(S2)))
    also if null(S1)
        then S2
    also if null(S2)
        then S1.
```

Using *destructuring* expressions, the above program can be coded as follows —

```
merge(S1,S2) ←
    if S1 = [H|T]
        then cons(H, merge(T, S2))
    also if S2 = [H|T]
        then cons(H, merge(S1, T))
    also if S1 = [ ]
        then S2
    also if S2 = [ ]
        then S1
```

Matrix multiplication is a task eminently suited for parallel execution. Systolic algorithms (Kung, 1979, 1982; Shapiro, Chapter 7) which operate on matrices have been published. A matrix is represented as a list of lists, where each sublist represents a column. The code for matrix multiplication is shown below —

```
mm(M1, M2) ←
    if M1 = [ ]
        then [ ]
    also if M1 = [H|T]
        then cons(vm(H, M2), mm(T, M2)).

vm(V1, M2) ←
    if M2 = [ ]
```

```
            then [ ]
        also if M2 = [H|T]
            then cons(ip(V1, H), vm(V1, T)).

   ip(V1, V2) ←
        if V1 = [ ] and V2 = [ ]
            then 0
        also if V1 = [H1|T1] and V2 = [H2|T2]
            then (H1 * H2) + ip(T1, T2).
```

A canonical example in parallel programming is that of determining whether two binary trees are isomorphic (Lamport, 1982). The code below performs this task —

```
   isotree(T1, T2) ←
        if T1 = 'leaf(X) and T2 = 'leaf(X)
            then true
        also if T1 = 'tree(A,B) and T2 = 'tree(C,D) and isotree(A,C)
            then isotree(B,D)
        also if T1 = 'tree(A,B) and T2 = 'tree(C,D) and isotree(A,D)
            then isotree(B,C)
        else false.
```

Note the use of *destructuring* expressions to create new variables, and the use of these variables in tests in the same *condition*.

The last example shows a use of *let*. It computes the sequence of moves needed in a game of the Towers of Hanoi —

```
   free(A, B) ← car(delete(A, delete(B, '[a,b,c]))).

   delete(E, L) ←
        if L = [ ]
            then [ ]
        also if L = [E|T]
            then T
        else
            cons(car(L), delete(E, cdr(L))).

   hanoi(N, A, B) ←
        if N = 0
            then cons(A, B)
        also if N > 0
            then {
                let C = free(A, B) and N1 = N – 1 in
                    cons(hanoi(N1, A, C),
```

$$\text{cons(cons(A, B), hanoi(N1, B, C)))}$$
$$\}.$$

The *let* expression is used to avoid recomputing *free(A, B)* and *N – 1* twice. *Let* expressions are context boundaries. The values for the new variables are computed in the old environment, and all new variables are bound at once. Thus it is impossible to use the value of some new variable in a subsequent *definition*. In the above *let* expression, the *definitions* —

> let C = free(A, B) and N1 = N – 1 in
> ...

could also have been coded as —

> let C = free(A, B) and N = N – 1 in
> ...

The two uses of *N* refer to different variables, and thus this represents no difficulty.

35.3 Translation of CFL to Flat Concurrent Prolog

This section shows how CFL code is translated to Flat Concurrent Prolog. The actual translation process is not explained here, and only the resultant Flat Concurrent Prolog code is shown.

First, the translation of *merge* is examined, to provide a concrete example. The resultant Flat Concurrent Prolog code is —

```
merge([H|T], S2, [H|Result]) ←
    merge(T?, S2?, Result).
merge(S1, [H|T], [H|Result]) ←
    merge(S1?, T?, Result).
merge([ ], S2, S2).
merge(S1, [ ], S1).
```

The convention of translating CFL code to Flat Concurrent Prolog is that generated clauses have *N + 1* arguments, where *N* is the number of arguments in the CFL definition. The additional argument serves to communicate the result of the computation.

An *if* expression is translated into a series of clauses. Each clause contains the tests which are required by this branch of the *if* expression in its guard. The variables declared in the head of the CFL definition are common to all branches of the *if* expression. Therefore the heads of all clauses in the translated program contain the same set of variable names

Notice how the destructuring expressions are compiled away. Calls to *cons*, *list*, *null*, *car* and *cdr* are recognized specially so that a unification is generated instead of a goal-call. Thus, the respective head position of each translated clause is pre-unified with the result of the destructuring expression.

When *else* is used instead of *also* to separate branches of an *if* expression, the guard of the next clause contains a call to the Flat Concurrent Prolog predicate *otherwise*. This predicate succeeds only when all previous clauses have failed, and suspends otherwise. Thus, inserting this predicate at the beginning of the next guard ensures that this branch of the *if* expression will be evaluated only once all previous branches have failed.

An example of a use of *else* is shown below —

```
test_type(Expr) ←
    if compound(Expr)
        then test_compound_type(Expr)
    also if string(Expr)
        then 'symbol
    also if integer(Expr)
        then 'integer
    else
        error('cant_determine_type_of(Expr)).
```

This is translated to –

```
test_type(Expr, Result) ←
    compound(Expr) | test_compound_type(Expr?, Result).
test_type(Expr, symbol) ←
    string(Expr) | true.
test_type(Expr, integer) ←
    integer(Expr) | true.
test_type(Expr, Result) ←
    otherwise |
        error(cant_determine_type_of(Expr?), Result).
```

Compound *call* expressions are open-coded. Dummy variables are added to communicate results from argument expressions to calls which use the value. An example of this can be seen in the code for *mm*. The resultant Flat Concurrent Prolog code is —

```
mm([ ], M2, [ ]).
mm([H|T], M2, [V1|V2]) ←
    vm(H?, M2?, V1), mm(T?, M2?, V2).
```

Note how read-only annotations are added to arguments passed to calls, in order to ensure dataflow synchronization.

An example showing how compound arithmetic calls are translated is depicted below. The code for *ip* results in the Flat Concurrent Prolog code —

```
ip([ ], [ ], 0).
ip([H1|T1], [H2|T2], Result) ←
     times(H1?, H2?, V1),
     ip(T1?, T2?, V2),
     plus(V1?, V2?, Result).
```

Let expressions are a way for the programmer to help the translation process to perform folding of common sub-expressions. No code is generated for the *let* expression itself, since its only purpose is to introduce dummy variables. The code for *hanoi* is —

```
hanoi(0, A, B, [A|B]).
hanoi(N, A, B, [V1, [A|B], V2]) ←
     N > 0 |
          free(A?, B?, C),
          plus(N1, 1, N?),
          hanoi(N1?, A?, C?, V1),
          hanoi(N1?, B?, C?, V2).
```

When the guard contains compound tests, it is important to translate the tests in the right order, since guards in the current implementation of Flat Concurrent Prolog are executed from left to right. If this is neglected, a suspension may occur where otherwise the guard computation would have succeeded. For example, in —

```
test(N, M) ←
     if N * 3 > M * 4
          then log(N, M)
     also if N + M > 50
          then sin(M, N)
```

the translation must ensure that the value of sub-expressions such as $N * 3$ is computed before the > test —

```
test(N, M, Result) ←
     times(N?, 3, V1), times(M?, 4, V2),
     V1 > V2 | log(N?, M?, Result).
test(N, M, Result) ←
     plus(N?, M?, V1), V1 > 50 |
          sin(M?, N?, Result).
```

Below are the main principles of the translation process —

- *If* expressions are translated into a series of clauses, each with the same set of variables in the head of the generated clause.

- When *else* is used instead of *also*, the guard of the next clause contains a call to *otherwise*. This ensures that all previous clauses have failed before this clause is tried.

- Destructuring expressions are translated into head position unifications whenever possible. This can be done automatically for quoted terms and for tests involving calls to *cons*, *list*, *null*, *car* and *cdr*.

- Compound tests are translated in such a way as to avoid suspension when executed from left to right. This conforms to the implemented guard evaluation strategy of Flat Concurrent Prolog.

- *Let* expressions do not generate code, but only introduce new dummy variables.

- Read-only annotations are added to all occurrences of variables except when they appear in the last position of a goal. This occurrence is a producer of the variable's value and the other occurrences consume its value. Thus, correct data-flow synchronization is obtained.

35.4 Higher-Order Functions and Lexical Closures

CFL recognizes two additional types of expressions, namely the *lambda* expression and the *application* expression.

A *lambda* expression has the following form —

lambda ({*parameter names*}, *expression*)

The *parameter names* are either a symbol or a sequence of symbols separated by commas.

The semantics of the *lambda* expression are that its evaluation returns a lexical closure (Allen, 1978). This closure contains an environment binding all variables used by *expression* and which are not declared in *parameter names* to the values they had at the time the closure was created. The closure also contains the *expression*, in this environment.

A closure created by a *lambda* expression can be applied to values in an *application* expression. An *application* expression comes in two forms. The first form of this expression is —

expression-evaluating-to-closure : {*list-of-expressions*}

The *expression* on the left side of the colon must evaluate to a lexical closure. The *list-of-expressions* is either an *expression* or a sequence of *expressions* separated by commas. The number of *expressions* in *list-of-expressions* must match the number of *parameter names* declared in the *lambda* expression which created the closure.

The semantics of this form of the *application* expression are as follows. The *expression* on the left side of the colon and the *expressions* in *list-of-expressions* are evaluated. The *expression* closed in the lexical closure is evaluated in the closed environment, augmented with bindings of the *parameter names* to the values of *expressions* in the *list-of-expressions*. The result of this last evaluation is returned as the result of the *application* expression. If the *expression* on the left-hand side of the colon does not evaluate to a lexical closure, or if the number of values produced by *list-of-expressions* does not match the number of *parameter names*, the evaluation of the *application* expression returns *nil*.

The second form of the *application* expression is —

expression-evaluating-to-closure :: *tuple-of-values*

Its semantics are similar to those of the first form, except that *tuple-of-values* is evaluated and must produce a tuple with the expected arity. The arguments of this tuple are used as the parameter values in the application of the *expression-evaluating-to-closure*.

The classical mapping functions of Weinreb and Moon (1983) and of Moon (1974) can be coded in CFL. Below, the code for *mapcar* is shown —

```
mapcar(Func, List) ←
    if List = [ ]
        then [ ]
    also if List = [H|T]
        then cons(Func : {H}, mapcar(Func, T)).
```

This function can be used in code as follows —

```
square_list(Ints) ←
    mapcar(lambda({I}, I * I), Ints).
```

CFL allows closures to be returned as the value of a call. Thus, both "downward" closures, as shown in the example above, and "upward" closures (Allen, 1978) are allowed. The following function returns a closure, which when applied to an integer, will add the value *5* to it —

```
add_five_closure ←
    lambda({I}, I + 5).
```

A more sophisticated example, producing a closure which contains an expression using values of variables in the closure-producing expression, is depicted below. The closure, when applied to an integer, will multiply it by the value of X in its environment —

```
multiply_X_closure(X) ←
    lambda({I}, X * I).
```

When called as —

```
multiply_X_closure(15)
```

it produces a closure which when applied to an integer will multiply it by *15*.

The last example shows how a closed environment may be augmented with new bindings, to create nested lexical closures. The principle is to create a new closure which contains the new bindings, and apply the original closure in this environment —

```
augment_environment(Closure,X) ←
    lambda({RestOfArgs}, Closure :: make_arguments(X, RestOfArgs)).
```

The new closure applies the old closure in an environment closed over a value for *X*. The application of the new closure should be called with *RestOfArgs* bound to a list or tuple (as expected by *make_arguments*) of the other parameter values.

To see how *lambda* expressions are translated to Flat Concurrent Prolog, the translation of *multiply_X_closure* is shown below —

```
multiply_X_closure(X,
                closure(1, ID, {X})).

call_closure(ID, {X}, {I}, Result) ←
    times(I?, X?, Result).
```

The first clause is used to create the lexical closure. It returns a structure which is recognized in the context of an *application* expression as representing a closure. The sub-arguments of the structure have the following meaning — *1* denotes that the closure expects one value to be passed when applied, *ID* is a unique, generated, identifier which will be used when the closure is applied to locate the code for the closed *expression*, and {*X*} is a tuple containing the closed values. The second *call_closure/4* clause evaluates the closed *expression* in the closed environment. This method was first proposed by Warren.

Application expressions are translated to a call to a runtime library procedure, *apply*, which checks the validity of the closure, identifies the specific *call_closure/4* clause to use and calls it. The translation of the *mapcar* function is shown below —

```
mapcar(Func, [ ], [ ]).
mapcar(Func, [H|T], [V1|V2]) ←
    apply(Func?, {H?}, V1),
    mapcar(Func?, T?, V2).
```

The second form of the *application* expression evaluates the right-hand side *expression* at runtime. The code generated for *augment_environment* is —

> augment_environment(Closure,X,closure(1, *ID*, {Closure,X}).

> call_closure(*ID*, {Closure,X}, {RestOfArgs}, Result) ←
>   make_arguments(X?,RestOfArgs?,V1),
>   apply(Closure?,V1?,Result).

The code for *apply* is as follows (only the legal case is shown) —

> apply(closure(N, ID, Closed), Parameters, Result) ←
>   tuple(Parameters), arity(Parameters, N?) |
>   call_closure(ID?, Closed?, Parameters?, Result).

Thus, if a closure is supplied and the number of expected and passed parameters match, the correct clause for *call_closure/4* is selected with the use of *ID* and the result of evaluating it is returned.

Dataflow synchronization works correctly for closures produced by *lambda* expressions as well. If a closure is applied before all variables it requires access to are bound, the evaluation will correctly suspend. Therefore, closure-returning functions work as expected.

The ease with which both "downward" and "upward" closures are incorporated into Flat Concurrent Prolog should be contrasted with the difficulty of direct implementation (Burke et al., 1984; Rees and Adams, 1982), even in a sequential environment. The translated code in Flat Concurrent Prolog makes no use of extra-logical features and seems very natural, and this contrasts with the claim (Darlington et al., 1986) that logic languages are inherently first-order. The clean integration of lexical closures, higher-order functions and lexical scoping with dataflow synchronization and the elegance of the translation show that this approach has merit. We are not aware of any other system which provides all these features as well as concurrency.

A CFL program cannot create completely new functional expressions at runtime; it can only create "clones" of predefined ones, as is done in the code of *multiply_X_closure*. Thus, the implementation presented here is not a complete higher-order functional system. The reason for this deficiency stems from the separation of data and program in FCP — the only executable object is compiled code. An approach, not currently implemented due to its high overhead, is to run CFL under a meta-interpreter which supports dynamically created clauses as executable objects.

Dixon (Dixon, M., personal communication) describes another method for implementing lexical closures and functional arguments in FCP. In his scheme, a lexical closure is an object, and an application of a lexical closure to arguments is equivalent to sending a message on a stream to the object representing the closure. This is an elegant concept, but implementing it requires knowing at compile-time whether an argument of a function is data or represents a functional object. Thus, functions accepting lexical closures must have a special annotation on the arguments representing streams to these objects. This is necessary also for functions which do not use the functional arguments but simply pass them on. Therefore, this in effect requires knowing at compile-time the calling graph of the program.

35.5 Evaluation Strategies for CFL

The current CFL translator generates code which implements eager evaluation of calls — calls and arguments to these calls are evaluated in parallel, and when a call requires access to an as-yet uncomputed value, its computation suspends. This is but one of the many possible evaluation strategies. This section discusses the different approaches and sketches how each could be implemented in Flat Concurrent Prolog.

Sequential Lisp implementations evaluate arguments before the call which uses the value of these arguments. The arguments are evaluated in a predetermined order, e.g., from left to right. This is a *top-down sequential* strategy. In Flat Concurrent Prolog, using this method would lead to virtually no parallelism. Thus, a concurrent implementation would probably not employ it. Nevertheless, a method for its implementation is shown here.

The easiest way to sequentialize a computation in Flat Concurrent Prolog is to add a synchronization argument to each goal and to pass a synchronization token. This method is due to Kusalik (1984b). The technique is demonstrated on the example of *ip* —

```
ip(S–S, [ ], [ ], 0).
ip(start–End, [H1|T1], [H2|T2], Result) ←
      times(start–M1, H1?, H2?, V1),
      ip(M1?–M2, T1?, T2?, V2),
      plus(M2?–End, V1?, V2?, Result).
```

When the *start* token reaches this invocation of *ip*, it allows the computation of *times*, the recursive call to *ip* and *plus* to proceed sequentially.

Another evaluation strategy which yields significant amounts of parallelism is to allow argument evaluation to proceed in parallel, but to start calls only after all arguments have been computed (Cohen, 1983). This is the *top-down parallel* strategy. It can be implemented with a variation on the synchronization token method —

```
ip(S–S, [ ], [ ], 0).
ip(start–End, [H1|T1], [H2|T2], Result) ←
     times(start–M1, H1?, H2?, V1),
     ip(M1–M2, T1?, T2?, V2),
     plus(M2?–End, V1?, V2?, Result).
```

The recursive call to *ip* and the call to *times* are done in parallel, but they must terminate before the call to *plus* is started.

Eager evaluation and the evaluation strategies shown above all compute an argument's value irrespective of whether it will be used in a subsequent computation or not. It is desirable to avoid a computation if its value will never be used. A method which does this is to start the outermost call in a compound call expression first, and to evaluate its arguments only when their values are needed. This is the *lazy evaluation* technique (Cohen, 1983; Henderson and Morris, 1976; Henderson, 1980; Friedman and Wise, 1976b; Turner, 1979; Kahn, 1982b; Subrahmanyam and You, 1984b). This technique can be implemented in Flat Concurrent Prolog using a variation of the bounded buffer method developed by Takeuchi and Furukawa (Chapter 18). The idea is that the consumer of a stream produces "boxes" for the producer to put values into. When the producer temporarily exhausts the supply of boxes, it suspends. In CFL only a single value is produced by a producer and therefore the consumer produces only one box, instead of a stream of boxes —

```
ip({V1}, {V2}, {Result}) ←
     ip1(V1?, V2?, Result).

ip1([ ], [ ], 0).
ip1([H1|T1], [H2|T2], Result) ←
     times(H1, H2, V1?),
     ip(T1, T2, V2?),
     plus(V1, V2, Result).

plus({I1}, {I2}, Result) ←
     real_plus(I1?, I2?, Result).

times({I1}, {I2}, Result) ←
     real_times(I1?, I2?, Result).
```

All calls receive a read-only annotated instance of their result variable and wait until it is instantiated to a tuple containing a new variable. This new variable is unified with the result of this call. At that time, "boxes" for the required values of the arguments are sent to the producers.

The compiler can easily recognize when an argument is not used in a call, and not generate code to request its value. A problem with this is that it leaves behind suspended computations for those arguments whose value is not used. This can be remedied with a simple enhancement —

```
ip(abort, abort, abort).
ip({V1}, {V2}, {Result}) ←
      ip1(V1?, V2?, Result).

ip1([ ], [ ], 0).
ip1([H1|T1], [H2|T2], Result) ←
          times(H1, H2, V1?),
          ip(T1, T2, V2?),
          plus(V1, V2, Result).

plus({I1}, {I2}, Result) ←
      real_plus(I1?, I2?, Result).

times({I1}, {I2}, Result) ←
      real_times(I1?, I2?, Result).
```

Each procedure is augmented with another clause which waits for an *abort* message, in place of a "box" to put the value in. When this message arrives, the call sends the same message to the computations waiting to produce the values of the arguments, and terminates.

Lazy evaluation is useful when the body of a function is an *if* expression, and not all branches require the values of all arguments. However, since normally all branches of an *if* expression are evaluated in parallel in CFL, lazy evaluation can save work only if an argument is ignored by all branches. Therefore, the coupling of lazy evaluation with unrestricted Or-parallelism is of limited value.

Recently, another method for implementing lazy evaluation in Prolog was proposed by Narain (1986). This method works by passing the computation needed to produce a value as a continuation to the value's consumer. The consumer must explicitly call the continuation in order to obtain the delayed value. The technique published by Narain has not yet been tested for Flat Concurrent Prolog.

35.6 Relationship Between CFL And GHC

Sometimes, the code generated by compiling CFL is not FCP, since user test predicates are used in an *if* expression. For example, the code compiled from the *isotree* example is —

```
isotree(leaf(X), leaf(Y), true) ←
    X =?= Y | true.
isotree(tree(A,B), tree(C,D), R) ←
    isotree(A?, C?, true) | isotree(B?, D?, R).
```

```
isotree(tree(A,B), tree(C,D), R) ←
    isotree(A?, D?, true) | isotree(B?, C?, R).
isotree(_, _, false) ←
    otherwise | true.
```

This code is in Concurrent Prolog, and therefore not legal FCP. However, since it does not use the multiple environments mechanism of Concurrent Prolog, it is simple to convert it to GHC, as shown below —

```
isotree(leaf(X), leaf(Y), R) ←
    X = Y | R = true.
isotree(tree(A,B), tree(C,D), R) ←
    isotree(A, C, true) | isotree(B, D, R).
isotree(tree(A,B), tree(C,D), R) ←
    isotree(A, D, true) | isotree(B, C, R).
isotree(_, _, R) ←
    otherwise | R = false.
```

In general, there is a simple transformation from CFL code to GHC. The GHC programs produced from CFL code are always *safe*, and they always use at most a single output unification in the body. Safe GHC programs (see Levy and Shapiro, Chapter 33) which have only a single output unification in the body of each clause can also easily be transformed to CFL. This is not true for general safe GHC programs, where more than one output unification in each body is allowed.

35.7 Performance

All CFL code can be translated to GHC, and thence to FCP, using the GHC-to-FCP compiler (Levy and Shapiro, Chapter 33). This technique removes the restriction on the use of nested *if* expressions and on the use of user predicates in *if* expressions in CFL code, but it imposes a large overhead for code which does not utilize these features. Therefore, whenever possible, CFL code is translated directly to FCP, and only when necessary is the two-stage translation, using GHC intermediate code, employed.

Below we show measurements on the efficiency of the translated code. All measurements were done on a Sun-3/50 with four MBytes of main memory, using Logix 1.21, with a heap size of eight MBytes (Silverman et al., Chapter 21). Since the number of execution steps of FCP code has no simple relation to the number of execution steps of the original CFL program, execution times (in milliseconds) were measured instead. The columns of the table have the following meaning. The first column contains the name of the benchmark. The column marked *CFL-T* denotes the execution time of code translated directly from CFL to FCP, where applicable. The column marked *C-RPC* contains the reductions per cycle measured, which gives an upper bound on the number of concurrently executing processes. The column marked *FCP-T* denotes the execution time of code hand-written in FCP, where applicable. The column marked *GHC-T* denotes the execution time of code first translated to GHC, and thence to FCP. The column marked *G-RPC* contains the RPC measurement for code first translated to GHC and from it to FCP. The column marked *GD-T* denotes the execution time of code hand-written in GHC and translated to FCP.

Benchmark	CFL-T	C-RPC	FCP-T	GHC-T	G-RPC	GD-T
Nrev1000	102215	223	101220	216360	214	206035
Append10000	2110	1	2005	4220	1	4100
Merge10000	2360	1	2130	4520	1	4220
Mm25 × 25	27580	337	26450	3316	332	31600
Hanoi13	26320	1239	24505	36100	1202	35240
Isotree9	–	–	–	43620	42	42035

The benchmarks used were *Nrev1000*, naive reverse on a list of 1000 elements; *Append10000*, appending a list of 10000 elements; *Merge10000*, merging two lists of 10000 elements; *Mm25 × 25*, matrix multiplication of two 25 by 25 matrixes of small integers; *Hanoi13*, the towers of Hanoi with 13 disks, and *Isotree9*, determining tree isomorphism on two identical complete binary trees of depth 9.

As can be seen from the above table, the hand-coded FCP code and the directly-translated CFL code achieve nearly the same efficiency. When translation through intermediate GHC code is employed, a large overhead is incurred. The reasons for this inefficiency is a result of the inefficient handling of input unification by the instruction set of the emulator used, and not an inherent inefficiency of the code. This is explained in (Levy and Shapiro, Chapter 33). Also, the CFL code, when translated to GHC, produces code of the same efficiency as hand-written GHC code. This shows that the overhead in the two-step translation process is entirely due to the translation of GHC to FCP.

The RPC measurement indicates the maximal number of concurrently executing processes. It gives an upper bound on the number of processors which could be utilized to solve this problem. For example, for naive reverse this number approaches the limit of a quarter of the length of the list being reversed, which is the expected result from analysis of the parallelism available in the program. For append and merge, there is always only a single executing process.

The RPC obtained for the example of the towers of Hanoi shows the large degree of parallelism inherent in the FCP formulation. A large degree of parallelism is also obtained for systolic code such as the matrix multiplication example. The small degree of parallelism obtained for the tree isomorphism example deserves explanation. It is a result of the translation technique used by the GHC-to-FCP compiler, coupled with tail-recursion optimization done by the emulator. Specifically, the translated code aborts unneeded branches of the computation tree as soon as another branch has committed, and this pruning is done very efficiently. Tail-recursion optimization guarantees that the computation of *isotree* will continue with a chosen branch of the tree as long as possible, and this will lead to a fast commitment to one of the two alternative branches. From this analysis we see that the low RPC measured for this example is an artifact of its execution on a uni-processor, and that we may expect higher utilization rates in a multi-processor environment. However, this also implies that the amount of unnecessary work done on a multi-processor will be larger.

A user of CFL should not be penalized for using the language even if he is interested only in its sequential component. Therefore, a comparison between the efficiency of CFL and of compiled Franz Lisp (Foderaro et al., 1983) on a Sun-3/50 was done. The results are summarized in the table below (all times are in milliseconds). The columns have the following meaning. The first column contains the name of the specific benchmark executed. The column marked CFL-T contains the execution time of CFL on this problem. The column marked CL-T shows the execution time of an equivalent compiled Lisp program.

Benchmark	CFL-T	CL-T
Nrev1000	102215	122830
Append10000	2110	1600

The above results demonstrate that the current CFL implementation is comparable in efficiency to that of Franz Lisp on a Sun 3/50. It is interesting to note that naive reverse in CFL is faster than in compiled Lisp. A possible explanation for this is that the Lisp code is very cons-intensive, and thus executes a large number of function calls. The CFL code uses unification for the creation of the list, which generates only a few simple instructions for the emulator. The results of running these examples show that the Franz Lisp compiler performs some tail-recursion optimizations. For example, this is probably the reason that the Lisp *append* is more efficient than naive reverse, when compiled.

Kliger (1987) reports on an advanced compilation technique from FCP directly to native code of the 68000 family of processors. Initial measurements indicate that a speedup of about twenty times is experienced when the output of the CFL compiler is compiled by that compiler. For example, naive reverse of a list of 600 elements, taking 75 seconds for CFL-generated FCP code executed on the emulator, executes in 1.9 seconds in native code. Appending a list of 40000 elements, taking 16.5 seconds on the emulator, executes in 0.65 seconds in native code.

35.8 CFL as a Front End for Programming in FCP

Flat Concurrent Prolog was developed as the kernel language of future parallel computer systems (Shapiro, Chapter 5). As such, it is deemed too low-level to be used as a user-level programming language. In addition, it is sometimes criticized as being too bulky and verbose, or as having a too-opaque syntax which obscures the program's meaning. The one feature which was the target of the most concentrated criticism is the fact that specifying correct synchronization is the onus of the programmer. A user-level language which relieves the programmer from this chore and which can be translated efficiently is thus a contribution towards the wider applicability of a Flat Concurrent Prolog based system.

CFL is an attempt to provide such a user-level language. It has several attractive features —

- It relieves the programmer from having to be concerned with synchronization. The translated Flat Concurrent Prolog code is automatically augmented with read-only annotations so as to provide correct dataflow synchronization between value-producing and value-consuming computations.

- Different evaluation strategies can be incorporated in the translated code. This is transparent to the programmer. Thus, an implementation of CFL is free to choose one of the many possible evaluation strategies, in order to provide the best performance. This choice can even be made dynamically, if the translator is able to produce several different behaviors.

- CFL provides a functional interface to logic programming. This is an advantage for programmers accustomed to Lisp and other functional dialects — it provides a painless introduction to logic programming for novice programmers and for experienced functional programmers alike. Destructuring expressions can be seen as a gently couched introduction to unification.

- CFL is not a toy functional language — it is a lexically scoped language which has many advanced features, such as both "downward" and "upward" closures. In addition, it has a compiler which produces efficient code, and provides a rich runtime environment.

Some programs cannot be easily expressed in CFL but can be coded in Flat Concurrent Prolog. Thus, programs written in CFL do not make use of the full power of Flat Concurrent Prolog. Since CFL is a functional language, it is impossible to write many-valued relations. For example, a function which returns both the modulu and the divisor of two integers can be easily written in Flat Concurrent Prolog but not in CFL. Some programming techniques, e.g., the short-circuit technique for detection of global termination (Takeuchi, 1983), cannot be expressed in CFL. It is also difficult to write code which manipulates difference lists (Clark and Tärnlund, 1977) explicit calls to *append* must be used. Thus, the elegant Flat Concurrent Prolog coding of *quicksort* shown by Shapiro (Chapter 5) cannot be easily programmed in CFL.

In practice, this is not a real impediment to using CFL. In Logix, functions written in CFL can call procedures written in Flat Concurrent Prolog, and vice-versa. Modules written in CFL and in Flat Concurrent Prolog are compiled separately and can be linked at runtime. This "late binding" is a feature of the Logix module system (Silverman et al., Chapter 21).

CFL is the first language which was embedded in the Logix programming environment. Other languages for which compilers to Flat Concurrent Prolog are currently being constructed are GHC and Safe Concurrent Prolog (Levy and Shapiro, Chapter 33). Weinbaum and Shapiro (1986) describe a hardware description language which is also embedded in the Logix environment. Kahn et al. (Chapter 30) describe an object-oriented language called Vulcan, for which a compiler to Flat Concurrent Prolog is being developed.

35.9 Discussion

This paper described CFL, a concurrent functional language, and its translation to Flat Concurrent Prolog. In order to simplify the language, CFL provides only minimal constructs for control of concurrency, such as the use of *else* instead of *also*. As a result, the programmer is free to write his program in a functional style, without concern for synchronization and concurrency.

Deterministic and non-deterministic programs can be mixed and coexist peacefully within CFL. When *also* is exclusively used instead of *else*, a non-deterministic program results. When the programmer only uses *else*, a deterministic program is obtained.

The translation to Flat Concurrent Prolog produces very efficient code, which implements correctly the semantics of the original CFL program. The Flat Concurrent Prolog code automatically takes care of dataflow synchronization.

CFL provides higher-order functions and closure-producing expressions. It has been shown how these features can be naturally integrated into a logic programming system, without using any meta-logical facilities. Thus, CFL is not a toy functional language.

Since CFL does not provide mechanisms for the user to control concurrency, implementations must choose an evaluation strategy for ordering execution of compound calls. Several different methods such as eager evaluation, two top-down evaluation strategies and lazy evaluation were surveyed. The eager evaluation method is the easiest to implement and provides much opportunity for exploiting parallelism. Therefore the current CFL translator implements this strategy.

Using CFL as a front-end language for programming in FCP has several advantages. The foremost amongst these is that it frees the programmer from having to consider synchronization issues. Correct coding of synchronization is of paramount importance in any Flat Concurrent Prolog program. If this chore can be automated, at least in some cases, programming in Logix becomes an order of magnitude easier.

The concurrency of CFL is a result of its translation to Flat Concurrent Prolog. Since a parallel implementation of Flat Concurrent Prolog on an Intel iPSC hypercube system is available (Taylor et al., Chapter 39), this translation in effect provides a concurrent implementation of CFL. The effort invested in this implementation is much smaller than needed for a direct implementation of concurrent functional systems on parallel hardware (Vegdahl, 1984; Keller, 1980a, 1980b; Hudak, 1985; Hudak and Smith, 1985; Holmstrom, 1983; Fahlman et al., 1983; Darlington and Reeve, 1981; Steinberg, 1986; Halstead, 1985; Harrison, 1986; Gottlieb et al., 1983). Flat Concurrent Prolog has an efficient uni-processor implementation (Houri and Shapiro, Chapter 38; Kliger, 1987), and CFL code translated to Flat Concurrent Prolog also runs on this system, allowing the simulation of functional concurrency even on a sequential computer.

CFL is the first concurrent functional language to provide a clean integration of higher-order functions, closure-producing expressions and dataflow synchronization, all in a concurrent environment. The ease with which all these features are combined in this system, together with real concurrency, should be contrasted with the difficulty of direct implementation.

The embedding of CFL in Logix shows the viability of the "embedded language" approach. Compilers for other languages such as GHC and Safe Concurrent Prolog to Flat Concurrent Prolog are currently being constructed (Levy and Shapiro, Chapter 33). Logix allows mixing of languages in the coding of a program — some parts of a program may be coded in CFL while other parts can be coded in Flat Concurrent Prolog, and calls from one language to another are mediated at runtime by a system routine. This paper therefore supports the claim (Shapiro, Chapter 5) that Flat Concurrent Prolog should be considered as a kernel language for programming of parallel computers, and that other languages should be translated into it.

Acknowledgements

This work is based on many useful discussions with Ken Bowen and Kevin Buettner of Syracuse University. Special thanks are due to Kevin Buettner for donating the code for FLIP and explaining its intricacies and "hacks". We wish also to thank Bill Silverman and Michael Hirsch for help in extending Logix to accept the CFL syntax and for various other hooks into the system.

Appendix 35.1: BNF of CFL

⟨statement⟩   := ⟨definition⟩. | ⟨expr⟩. ;

⟨definition⟩   := ⟨head⟩ ← ⟨top_level_expr⟩ ;

⟨head⟩   := CONSTANT | ⟨head_tuple⟩ ;

⟨head_tuple⟩   := CONSTANT (⟨head_args_list⟩) ;

⟨head_args_list⟩   := ⟨head_arg⟩ , ⟨head_args_list⟩
                       | ⟨head_arg⟩
                       ;

⟨head_arg⟩   := VAR | ⟨quoted_constant⟩ ;

⟨quoted_constant⟩ := ' ⟨general_term⟩ ;

⟨general_term⟩   := VAR | CONSTANT | ⟨general_tuple⟩ ;

⟨general_tuple⟩   := { ⟨general_terms⟩ } ;

⟨general_terms⟩   := ⟨general_term⟩ , ⟨general_terms⟩
                       | ⟨general_term⟩
                       ;

⟨top_level_expr⟩   := ⟨if_expr⟩ | ⟨expr⟩ ;

⟨if_expr⟩   := if ⟨condition⟩ then ⟨expr⟩
                       | if ⟨condition⟩ then ⟨expr⟩ also ⟨expr⟩
                       | if ⟨condition⟩ then ⟨expr⟩ else ⟨expr⟩
                       ;

⟨condition⟩   := ⟨cond⟩ and ⟨condition⟩
                       | ⟨cond⟩
                       ;

⟨cond⟩   := ⟨primitive_test⟩ | ⟨application⟩ ;

⟨primitive_test⟩   := shown in Appendix 35.2

⟨expr⟩   :— ⟨let_expr⟩
                    | ⟨where_expr⟩
                    | ⟨lambda_expr⟩
                    | ⟨application⟩
                    ;

⟨let_expr⟩   := let ⟨vardefs⟩ in ⟨expr⟩ ;

⟨where_expr⟩   := ⟨expr⟩ where ⟨vardefs⟩ ;

⟨vardefs⟩   := ⟨vardef⟩ and ⟨vardefs⟩
                    | ⟨vardef⟩
                    ;

⟨vardef⟩   := VAR = ⟨application⟩ ;

⟨lambda_expr⟩   := lambda (⟨params⟩ , ⟨top_level_expr⟩) ;

⟨params⟩   := { ⟨params_list⟩ } ;

⟨params_list⟩   := VAR , ⟨params_list⟩ | VAR ;

⟨application⟩   := ⟨general_term⟩
                    | ⟨expr⟩ : ⟨parameters⟩
                    ;

⟨parameters⟩   := { ⟨parameter_list⟩ } ;

⟨parameter_list⟩   := ⟨expr⟩ , ⟨parameter_list⟩
                    | ⟨expr⟩
                    ;

Appendix 35.2: CFL Test Predicates

Type Tests —

integer(⟨expr⟩)   – succeeds if ⟨expr⟩ evaluates to integer.
string(⟨expr⟩)   – succeeds if ⟨expr⟩ evaluates to string.

constant(⟨expr⟩)   – succeeds if ⟨expr⟩ evaluates to constant.
tuple(⟨expr⟩)   – succeeds if ⟨expr⟩ evaluates to tuple.
list(⟨expr⟩)   – succeeds if ⟨expr⟩ evaluates to list.
compound(⟨expr⟩)   – succeeds if ⟨expr⟩ evaluates to tuple or list.

Comparison Operators —

⟨exprA⟩ == ⟨exprB⟩   – succeeds if values are unifiable.
⟨exprA⟩ =? = ⟨exprB⟩ – succeeds if values are RO-unifiable (Foster et al., 1986).

⟨exprA⟩ =\= ⟨exprB⟩ – succeeds if values are not unifiable.
⟨exprA⟩ =:= ⟨exprB⟩ – succeeds if numeric values are equal.
⟨exprA⟩ ⟩ ⟨exprB⟩ – succeeds if 1st value is large than 2nd.
⟨exprA⟩ >= ⟨exprB⟩ – succeeds if 1st value is larger or equal to 2nd.
⟨exprA⟩ ⟨ ⟨exprB⟩ – succeeds if 1st value is less than 2nd.
⟨exprA⟩ =< ⟨exprB⟩ – succeeds if 1st value is less or equal to 2nd.
⟨exprA⟩ @ < ⟨exprB⟩ – succeeds if 1st value is ordered less than 2nd.

Meta Logical Tests —

unknown(⟨expr⟩) – succeeds if value of ⟨expr⟩ is variable.
known(⟨expr⟩)   – succeeds if value of ⟨expr⟩ is non-variable.
true   – always succeeds.

Appendix 35.3: Operator Precedences

Infix Operators —

X : Y   – xfy, 741.
X :: Y   – xfy, 741.
X and Y   – xfy, 750.
X then Y   – xfx, 780.
X also Y   – yfx, 785.
X else Y   – yfx, 785.
X in Y   – yfx, 975.
X where Y – yfx, 975.

Prefix Operators —

'X   – fx, 100.
if X – fy, 775.
let X – fy, 990.

The arithmetic operators and comparison operators have the same priorities as in Prolog and in Flat Concurrent Prolog (Silverman et al., Chapter 21).

Chapter 36

Hardware Description and Simulation Using Concurrent Prolog

David Weinbaum and Ehud Shapiro

The Weizmann Institute of Science

Abstract

This paper describes the use of Concurrent Prolog for hardware description and simulation. We discuss some major aspects of hardware description and how they fit into the programming model of Concurrent Prolog. Examples which demonstrate the effectiveness of Concurrent Prolog as a hardware description language are given and discussed.

A hardware description in Concurrent Prolog is an executable program. Two phases of the execution of such programs are identified. The first is the structural decomposition of a hierarchical description to a canonical form. The second is functional simulation.

We discuss further some aspects of distributed simulation mechanisms. We show an implementation of a distributed clock-driven mechanism and outline a method for implementing a distributed event-driven mechanism. We conclude with a brief description of a simulator we have implemented and some directions for future research.

36.1 Introduction

Concurrent Prolog supports recursive, hierarchical and object oriented programming styles as well as communication and synchronization between concurrent processes. This makes Concurrent Prolog a candidate language for hardware description and hardware simulation.

As a hardware description language, the parallelism of hardware is naturally expressed in Concurrent Prolog. By using recursive and hierarchical programming styles, high level of abstraction can be achieved in describing complex hardware systems in a relatively compact and comprehensive code (Shapiro and Takeuchi, Chapter 29; Shapiro, Chapter 7). Furthermore, not only can Concurrent Prolog express parallelism, but it can also be executed in parallel (Shapiro and Takeuchi, Chapter 29). This makes it a suitable implementation language for distributed hardware simulation algorithms that can be executed on a parallel computer.

This paper reports on the present state of our work in this direction. The goal of this research effort is to develop a parallel hardware design environment based on Concurrent Prolog. Our work follows and extends the initial direction of Suzuki (1986). We extend the above work, emphasizing the ability to specify hardware at different levels of abstraction, the ability to open hierarchical descriptions into canonical representations, and the implementation of distributed simulation mechanisms.

The paper is organized as follows: The next section describes the conceptual method of hardware description in Concurrent Prolog. The third section deals with the execution of hardware description. The fourth section outlines the simulation mechanism we use. The fifth section describes the implementation of a simulator based on the methods mentioned. The sixth is a brief comparison to related work. Finally we conclude the paper with directions for our future research.

36.2 Hardware Description in Concurrent Prolog

36.2.1 A concept of hardware description

Two aspects can be identified in hardware description:

1. Behavior – Description of a component in terms of its I/O relationships.
2. Structure – Description of a component in terms of interconnected subcomponents.

We use several common terms as follows:

By a *primitive component* we mean a hardware object which is described in terms of its I/O relationships. An I/O description entails the legal inputs to the component and the kind of outputs it can produce. A description in terms of I/O relationships is also called a *behavioral model*. A *composite component*, or *component* for short, is a hardware object which is described in terms of interconnected subcomponents. Subcomponents may themselves be components or primitive components. Such a description is also called a *structural model*. An *interconnection* is a communication channel which carries information between components. A *hierarchical description* is a hardware object description which includes composite subcomponents. A *canonical description* is a hardware object description in terms of interconnected primitive components.

A description is termed a *complete description* if it is defined in terms of I/O relationships, or it is canonical, finite, and all primitive components are defined, or it is hierarchical but can be transformed into canonical description using some terminating procedure.

A description is termed a *valid description* if and only if it is complete and for any ordered pair of interconnected primitive components c_1, c_2 in the canonical description every message that c_1 can output is a legal input to c_2.

The term *design level* entails what part of the information in the hardware description is given as behavior and what part of the information is given as a structure of behavioral entities (i.e., primitive components). High level description is characterized by simple structures of complex behavioral entities. Low level description is characterized by complex structures of very simple behavioral entities.

Whenever the set of messages exchanged by the behavioral entities during simulation reflects the complexity of those entities, it can be used to identify (and classify) different design levels.

Examples.

(1) The message set {*0, 1, unknown*} defines a simplistic logic level design.

(2) The message set {*0, 1, unknown, rising, falling*} defines a gate level design with notion of timing.

(3) The message set {*forcing 1, forcing 0, forcing unknown, resistive 1, resistive 0,*
resistive unknown, hi_impedance} defines a more realistic gate level design.

(4) The message set {*read(address,contents), write(address,contents), fetch(adress,op-code), input(i/o_address,contents), . . .*} defines abstraction level used to specify computer architectures.

A hardware description may be a multilevel description. We can indicate such a description by decomposing its set of messages into several distinguishable subsets, using a criteria meaningful to the designer. For example the set {*0,1,unknown,read,write,fetch,. . .*} indicates a mixed level description: Parts of the model are abstract, while others are already realized in logic level design.

Let us now specify a methodology for hardware description:

(1) *Abstraction*: Choose an appropriate abstraction level.

(2) *Behavior*: Write a behavioral description of the primitive components to be

used at this level.

(3) *Structure*: Specify the structural reduction rules which describe the hierarchical decomposition of the design into primitive components.

In case of a mixed level design, several sets of primitive components are used. Special components may be required to interface parts of the design which are defined at different levels.

This description methodology is mapped almost directly into the method of programming in Concurrent Prolog. A primitive component is mapped into an iterative process, and a composite component description is mapped into a general recursive process in Concurrent Prolog. An interconnection pattern is expressed via communication streams between processes. Following this mapping, the canonical description is actually a network of communicating processes, and the hierarchical description is a set of structural reduction rules. In the next section we discuss in more detail the relationships between hierarchical and canonical descriptions.

36.2.2 Behavior description

The behavior of a primitive component is defined as a Concurrent Prolog asynchronous iterative process. The process realizes the following general mechanism: It is suspended until it receives a message on one or more of its input channels. It is then activated, and using the input information and its internal state, evaluates the output and its new internal state. The process then sends the calculated values over its output channels and iterates with a new internal state. This cycle of events defines an atomic simulation step of a primitive component (Figure 36.1).

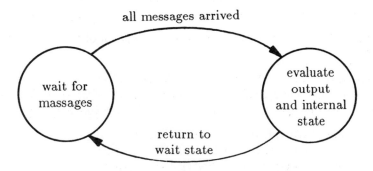

all messages arrived

wait for massages

evaluate output and internal state

return to wait state

Figure 36.1: State diagram of the primitive component mechanism

The transition from a suspended to an active state upon input on some channel, as well as state change and output communication, are all mechanisms supported by the language. A communication stream is a shared variable. Within the receiving process it is annotated with as read-only. In the transmitting process the variable's name appears with no special annotation, i.e., write enabled.

Example 1. The behavioral description of an *and* gate.

An *and* gate is modeled as a primitive component using three logic levels $\{0, 1, unknown\}$. No delay is introduced. The procedure defines the relation *and(In1,In2,Out)* between two input streams *In1* and *In2* and an output stream *Out*. Clauses *1*, *2* express the fact that when one of the inputs is 0 the output is 0. Clause *5* expresses the fact that when both inputs are 1 the output is 1. Clauses *3*, *4* express the fact that when at least one of the inputs is in the unknown state and the other one is not zero the output state is unknown. When input messages arrive, the procedure iterates using one of the clauses. It produces the appropriate output value and suspends waiting for the next set of input messages.

1. and([0|In1],[_|In2],[0|Out])← and(In1?,In2?,Out).

2. and([_|In1],[0|In2],[0|Out])← and(In1?,In2?,Out).

3. and([X|In1],[unknown|In2],[unknown|Out])←
    X ≠ 0 | and(In1?,In2?,Out).

4. and([unknown|In1],[X|In2],[unknown|Out])←
    X ≠ 0 | and(In1?,In2?,Out).

5. and([1|In1],[1|In2],[1|Out])← and(In1?,In2?,Out).

36.2.3 Structure description

A structural description is set of general clauses. Each clause defines a reduction rule which decomposes a component to its subcomponents.

Example 2. Behavioral versus Structural description of 2-input multiplexer.

2a. *Behavioral description*

The procedure defines the relation *mux(In1,In2,Select,Out)* between three input ports *In1, In2, Select*, and an output port *Out*: If *Select=1*, then *Output=In1*, if *Select=0*, then *Output=In2*. It uses only 0,1 logic levels for simplicity.

1. mux([X|In1],[_|In2],[1|Select],[X|Out])←
    mux(In1?,In2?,Select?,Out).

2. mux([_|In1],[X|In2],[0|Select],[X|Out])←
    mux(In1?,In2?,Select?,Out).

2b. *Structure description*

Let us use a predefined primitive component set which includes the behavioral description of an *and* gate, (Example 1) an *or* gate, and *inverter* gate. The following is a general clause which defines the decomposition of 2-input multiplexer to primitive components (Figure 36.2). It is also an example of a canonical description.

> mux(In1,In2,Select,Out)←
>   and(In1,Select,O1),
>   inv(Select,Inv_sel),
>   and(In2,Inv_sel?,O2),
>   or(O1?,O2?,Out).

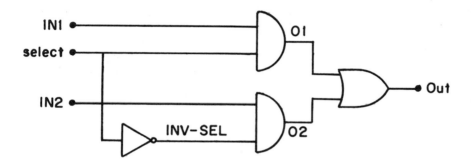

Figure 36.2: 2-input multiplexer

Example 3. Specifying structural rules hierarchically.

The following example demonstrates the use of recursion and hierarchical programming in describing a word adder.

The relation *word_adder(As,Bs,Cin,Outs,Cout)* is a relation between words *As* and *Bs*, a carry input port, *Cin* and a word *Out* and a carry output port *Cout* (see Figure 36.3c). The words *As*, *Bs* and *Out* are represented by lists of bit-streams of identical length. The word length is a parameter in this description.

> 1.1 word_adder([A|As],[B|Bs],Cin,[O|Os],Cout)←
>   full_adder(A,B,Cin,O,Ctemp),
>   word_adder(As?,Bs?,Ctemp?,Os,Cout).

> 1.2 word_adder([ ],[ ],Carry,[ ],Carry).

full_adder(In1,In2,Cin,Out,Cout) is a relation between three input ports *In1*, *In2*, *Cin* and two output ports *Out* and *Cout* (see Figure 36.3b).

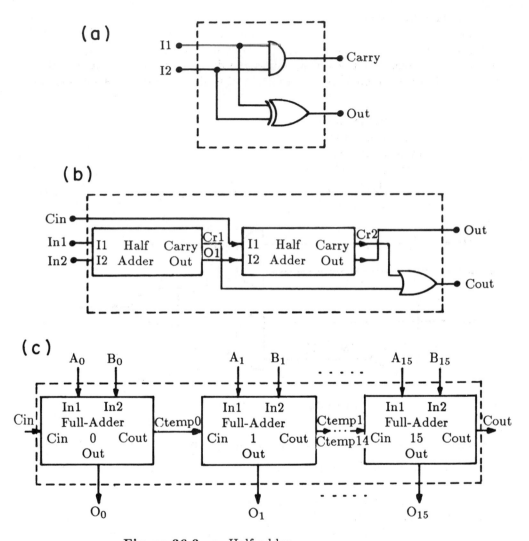

Figure 36.3: a. Half-adder
b. Full-adder
c. Expansion of 16 bit word_adder

2. full_adder(In1,In2,Cin,Out,Cout)←
      half_adder(In1,In2,O1,Cr1),
      half_adder(Cin,O1?,Out,Cr2),
      or(Cr1?,Cr2?,Cout).

half_adder(I1,I2,Out,Carry) is a relation between two input ports *I1*, *I2* and two output ports *Out* and *Carry* (see Figure 36.3a).

3. half_adder(I1,I2,Out,Carry)←
      xor(I1,I2,Out),
      and(I1,I2,Carry).

Example 3 demonstrates the effectiveness and compactness of hardware description in Concurrent Prolog. If *and*, *xor*, and *or* are defined primitives, this is a complete description in the sense defined above.

Example 4. Specification level design.

The concluding example refers to the specification level design. The following is a high level specification of a simple facsimile. A facsimile is a device which is used to transmit pictures or text via a telephone line.

We use a block diagram to specify a decomposition of the facsimile to lower level functional blocks:

(1) A scanner, which transforms optical information to a bit stream.

(2) A data compressor, which encodes its input bit stream to a compressed output bit stream to achieve lower transmission rate.

(3) A modem, which is capable of dialing a given phone number, establishing a link to another facsimile, and transmitting the bits in its input stream over the link.

(4) A controller unit, which controls the rest of the system.

In the following code examples { } are used to separate input channels from output channels.

4a. *A block diagram specification of a facsimile, coded in Concurrent Prolog*:

    Control_in, is a control port for human interface.
    Optic_in, is the optical scanner input port.
    Ack_in, is a remote handshake input port.
    Data_out, is the modem output port for information.
    Status_out, is an output port which indicates the machine state.
        (busy,ready,wait).
    Request_out,is a remote handshake output port.
        etc. . . . (Figure 36.4).

facsimile({Optic_in,Control_in,Ack_in},
      {Data_out,Status_out,Request_out})←
controller({Control_in,Modem_ack?},
      {Modem_cntrl,Scanner_cntrl,Status_out},Status),
optical_scanner({Scanner_control?,Optic_in},{Bit_stream}),
data_compressor(Bit_stream?,Compressed_stream),
modem({Modem_control?,Compressed_stream?,Ack_in},
      {Request_out,Data_out,Modem_ack}).

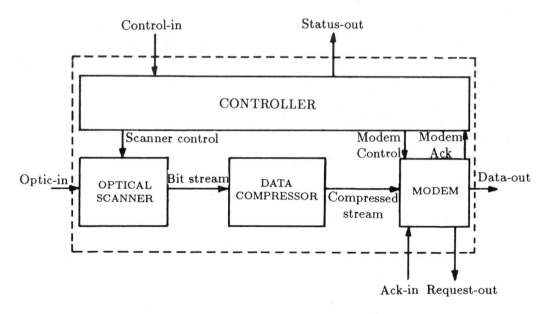

Figure 36.4: Facsimile block diagram

4b. *A state diagram specification of a facsimile controller coded in Concurrent Prolog*:

    The controller functional definition is expressed in terms of the state diagram (in Figure 36.5).

        Cin is a control input port which could be realized using two push buttons: one for *reset* and one for *start*.

        M is an input port from the modem. A *pos_ack* message indicates that a remote link has been established.

        A *neg_ack* message indicates failure to establish the link.

        Cntrl1 and *Cntrl2* are the optical scanner control port, and modem con-

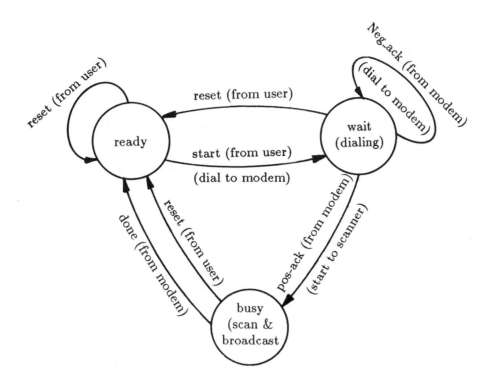

Figure 36.5: Facsimile controller state diagram

trol port respectively.

Stat is an output port which indicates the internal status of the machine (ready,wait,busy). *Status* is an internal state variable.

controler({[reset|Cin],M},{[reset|Cntrl1],[reset|Cntrl2],[ready|Stat]},Status)←
  controler({Cin?,M},{Cntrl1,Cntrl2,Stat},ready).

controler({[start|Cin],M},{Cntrl1,[dial(Number)|Cntrl2],[wait|Stat]},ready})←
  controler({Cin?,M},{Cntrl1,Cntrl2,Stat},wait).

controler({[start|Cin],M},{Cntrl1,Cntrl2,Stat},Status)←
  Status ≠ ready |
  controler({Cin?,M},{Cntrl1,Cntrl2,Stat},Status).

controler({Cin,[pos_ack|M]},{[start|Cntrl1],Cntrl2,[busy|Stat]},wait)←
  controler({Cin,M?},{Cntrl1,Cntrl2,Stat},busy).

controler({Cin,[neg_ack|M]},{Cntrl1,[dial(Number)|Cntrl2],[wait|Stat]},wait)←
   controler({Cin,M?},{Cntrl1,Cntrl2,Stat},wait).

controler({Cin,[done|M]},{Cntrl1,Cntrl2,[ready|Stat]},busy)←
   controler({Cin,M?},{Cntrl1,Cntrl2,Stat},ready)}.

4c. *Definition of a data compressor coded in Concurrent*
    Prolog:
    The data compressor encoding is done according to Table 36.1.

Input bits	Output bits
1	000
01	001
001	010
0001	011
00001	100
000001	101
0000001	110
0000000	111

Table 36.1: *run_zero* encoding method

The following is the data compressor procedure coded in Concurrent Prolog:

```
data_compressor(In,Out)←
    encode(In?,Out).

encode([1|In],[0,0,0|Out])← encode(In?,Out).
encode([0,1|In],[0,0,1|Out])← encode(In?,Out).
encode([0,0,1|In],[0,1,0|Out])← encode(In?,Out).
encode([0,0,0,1|In],[0,1,1|Out])← encode(In?,Out).
encode([0,0,0,0,1|In],[1,0,0|Out])← encode(In?,Out).
encode([0,0,0,0,0,1|In],[1,0,1|Out])← encode(In?,Out).
encode([0,0,0,0,0,0,1|In],[1,1,0|Out])← encode(In?,Out).
encode([0,0,0,0,0,0,0|In],[1,1,1|Out])← encode(In?,Out).
```

Example 4 demonstrates the effectiveness of Concurrent Prolog as a high
level specification language.

36.3 Execution of Hardware Descriptions

36.3.1 Phases of execution

An hardware description in Concurrent Prolog is executable. Two phases of execution are identified: structural reduction and functional simulation.

Structural reduction

The hierarchical description is a collection of structural reduction rules that define relations between components and subcomponents. This description is a program in Concurrent Prolog, and the reduction rules are general Concurrent Prolog clauses. As mentioned earlier, a primitive component is a process that activates upon receiving messages on its input. In the absence of such messages, the execution of the description is carried on to a stage where all clauses are reduced to goals associated with primitive components. It then suspends waiting for messages. Up to this stage of execution, the hierarchical description is transformed to a network of primitive components, i.e., the canonical description. A necessary condition for the program to reach this stage of suspension is that the description be complete in the sense defined in Section 36.2.1.

One should note that hierarchical description of hardware is very flexible since the reduction rules may be parametric (e.g., *word_adder*) or conditional. For this reason the transformation from hierarchical to canonical description possesses some basic properties of a silicon compiler. This subject is one of our future research issues.

Functional simulation

The canonical description of the hardware is the basis for functional execution. It is a network of asynchronously communicating processes; each of them is a functional simulator of a (primitive) component. The functional behavior of the hardware is simulated in terms of message exchange between processes. A method of introducing stimulus messages via stimulus injection ports, and monitoring the resulting message flow over points of interest, is used to verify the correct functional behavior of a design. A necessary condition for the execution of simulation is that the model under simulation be a valid description in the sense defined in Section 36.2.1.

As the network of processes is asynchronous, it does not include any explicit notion of time. The delays associated with components and other aspects of the temporal behavior of the model are meaningless unless we attach to the network some synchronization mechanism along with explicit modeling of time.

It is clear that the synchronization mechanism must be reflected in the behavior (and code) of the the processes which form the model. Integrating this aspect of behavior into the description of primitive components via a source-to-source transformation in a way transparent to the user is one of our present implementation efforts.

36.3.2 Synchronization mechanisms

Clock-driven mechanism

In a clock-driven mechanism there is a clock process which distributes clock ticks to all the processes in the network. On every clock tick every process in the model inputs messages and evaluates its output and new internal state. It then suspends until the next clock tick. Synchronization is achieved if a clock tick is issued only when all evaluations associated with the previous clock tick have completed. The clock process simulates a consistent time axis for the model despite the fact that different process evaluations of the same tick may take different periods of real time, and the interval between clock ticks may vary in terms of real time.

Once the network of processes is synchronized, a time unit can be defined, and a consistent time stamp can be associated to each event (message). Delay times associated with components are expressed in terms of time units, also set-up times, hold times, rising and falling times, etc.

The resolution of time axis during simulation is decided by association of a real time unit to the simulation time unit. For example we decide that each time unit is one micro-second. All the components' timing parameters are expressed in micro-seconds, and stimulation events one millisecond apart from each other will be introduced to the model with intervals of 1000 simulation time units.

The clock-driven mechanism is simple to implement in a distributed environment. It imposes low overhead on every process in terms of execution time and size of code. Generally it is poor in performance, because on every clock tick all processes are activated regardless of the state of their inputs. In an average simulation session only a small percentage of the channels indicate input changes; therefore most of the clock-driven evaluations do not provide any new information.

Event-driven mechanism

The event-driven mechanism is an optimization to the clock-driven one. Messages between processes are associated with events rather then with states. A process is activated and does evaluation only upon receiving at least one event. The redundancy of the clock-driven mechanism is eliminated since evaluation takes place only in case it might produce new information.

Implementing distributed event-driven mechanism is more difficult than clock-driven mechanism. For example: A process with a delay time T encounters an event in time T_0 and produces an output event to be output in time $T_0 + T$.

After T_0 no events are introduced to that certain component and it is suspended. There is no straightforward method for updating the internal delay counter of the process, without activating it each clock tick, or without centralizing time-dependent functions of the distributed process.

We are investigating an algorithm that can overcome the above problem and others.

36.4 Distributed Simulation Mechanism

36.4.1 A distributed clock-driven simulation mechanism using the short circuit

Method

This section describes in detail the distributed clock-driven mechanism. The execution model of the simulator is a network of concurrent communicating processes. The processes are asynchronous. We present a mechanism to synchronize the execution of these processes using a clock process attached to the network. The clock process generates clock ticks. Global synchronization is achieved if the following holds:

(1) Upon each clock tick every process in the model receives inputs and evaluates its outputs and internal states once.

(2) Only when all evaluations of the present clock tick have completed is another clock tick issued.

We use the term *simulation step* as a synonym for all the events associated with a clock tick.
It can be shown that condition 1 is implied by the following assumptions:

(1) Each process has at least one input port.

(2) All input ports in the network are connected either to output ports within the network or to stimulus injection ports.

(3) Each process is activated only when all its input ports receive messages.

(4) When activated, each process produces messages on all its output ports.

(5) At least one communication channel in the graph is a stimulus injection port.

(6) Introduction of messages to the stimulus injection ports is triggered by a clock tick (one message per channel per clock tick).

Assumptions *1*, *2* and *5* are properties of the hardware description. Assumptions *3* and *4* are properties of the mechanism of a primitive component.

Assumption *6* is a technical property of the simulator implementation.

For the second condition to be true, the clock process must detect the global termination of all process evaluations of the previous simulation step before it initiates a new simulation step.

The following is a description of a method for detecting global termination of distributed processes. It is called the "short circuit" method and was proposed by Takeuchi (1983). Our version of the method uses only existing communication channels in the model and thus preserves the inherent locality of communication.

The short circuit principle

Assume a collection of m communicating processes that run concurrently, and an attached clock process.

(a) Let us define a list of pairs of variables,

$$(R,X_1),(X_1,X_2),(X_2,X_3),\ldots,(X_n,L). \qquad n \geq m.$$

(b) The clock process is the global termination detector. It can write on variable R and read variable L. When initiating a simulation step, it writes a message on R and waits to receive the same message in L.

(c) Assume we posses a technique to distribute the above pairs of variables, at least one for each process.

(d) As part of each process evaluation, a process unifies the two variables of each received pair. (If we treat a variable as a pointer to some memory location, the unification of two variables is to make them point to the same location.)

The above statements imply that L is instantiated to the value written on R if and only if all process evaluations have been terminated. Therefore reading the message written on R from L actually indicates global termination. We have still to show how we create the synchronization variables and how they are distributed.

The distribution and creation of synchronization variables is done locally. Every process gets a pair of variables with every message it receives. All the pairs except one are unified as a part of the evaluation. The pair which is not unified (it can be chosen arbitrarily) is split into a number of pairs as the number of output channels of the process. Each pair is sent along with the appropriate information via one of the output channels to the input of another component. Splitting a variable pair is done as follows:

$$(V_1,V_2) \rightarrow (V_1,M_1),(M_1,M_2),(M_2,M_3),\ldots,(M_n,V_2).$$

If the pair (V_1, V_2) is part of a short circuit, it implies that all its descendents are part of the same short circuit whereas (V_1, V_2) disappears.

The initiation of the short circuit distribution is done via the input channels used for stimulus injection. The clock process which drives the simulation is connected to the model via these channels. Every simulation step the clock creates a pair of variables (R,L) which is split (as shown above) into pairs, one for each stimulus injection channel. These pairs are sent along with stimulus messages to the connected processes. Each process incorporates all the processes attached to its output ports into the circuit (Figure 36.6).

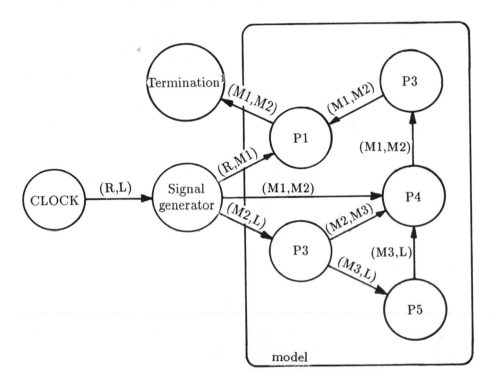

[1] The termination process sinks dangling output ports of components to ensure proper function of the short circuit mechanism.

Figure 36.6: Distribution of synchronization variables

Following the assumption that all input ports are connected, all the processes are attached to the circuit. So R and L are not unified unless every process has completed its evaluation.

Example 5. *and* gate behavioral description including synchronization mechanism.

1. and($\{[(0,L,R)|In1],[(\_,X,X)|In2]\},[(0,L,R)|Out])\leftarrow$ and($\{In1?,In2?\},Out$).

2. and({[(,L,R)|In1],[(0,X,X)|In2]},[(0,L,R)|Out])← and({In1?,In2?},Out).
3. and({[(X,L,R)|In1],[(unknown,Y,Y)|In2]},[(unknown,L,R)|Out])←
       X ≠ 0 | and({In1?,In2?},Out).
4. and({[(unknown,L,R)|In1],[(X,Y,Y)|In2]},[unknown|Out])←
       X ≠ 0 | and({In1?,In2?},Out).
5. and({[(1,L,R)|In1],[(1,X,X)|In2]},[(1,L,R)|Out])← and({In1?,In2?},Out).

36.4.2 Towards an event-driven simulation algorithm

An event-driven mechanism is currently being developed using a more sophisticated version of the short circuit method. We associate messages with events. As in the clock-driven mechanism, short circuit variables are distributed along with the messages. Only processes which have event in the input receive synchronization variables and participate in the global termination mechanism of a certain simulation step. Processes which were not activated by an event do not receive any synchronization variables.

The general mechanism of a primitive component is more complicated: Internal states are allocated to save the present state of each input and output port. Input event messages may arrive to an input port only during an input phase. Two kinds of events drive the component mechanism. The first is an input event that can occur on any of the input ports (more than one may occur). The second is an acknowledge message to notify the termination of an input phase. Upon receiving an acknowledge message, evaluation takes place. The evaluation does not necessarily produce any output. Upon termination of evaluation the component returns to input phase mode.

A suspended process may have a notion of time if the following method is used. Clock ticks are distributed via event messages. Upon any event, a process can capture the tail of the ticks stream and suspend itself on the Nth tick from now. By this method a process points now to the event upon which it will activate in the future.

The exact mechanism of global synchronization is yet to be worked out and implemented. The overhead imposed on any one of the processes will be higher than in clock-driven simulation mechanism, but the number of process activations per simulation step will be reduced dramatically, even by orders of magnitude, as compared to the clock-driven simulation mechanism.

36.5 Implementation of the Simulation Environment

A simulator based on a clock-driven mechanism has been implemented and can be used to simulate hardware designs.

Following the programming model of Concurrent Prolog, the simulator is best described in terms of concurrent communicating processes (Figure 36.7).

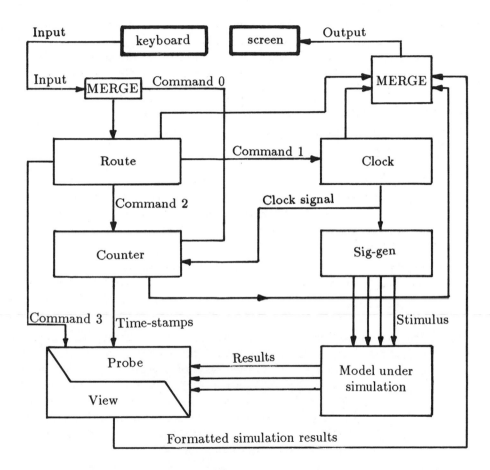

Figure 36.7: Simulator block diagram

The simulator is an interactive program. The user can activate the simulator, stop it, abort it, define how many simulation steps are to be carried out, define what is the resolution of the simulator output sampling (how many simulation steps per sample), and inspect the simulation results on the screen.

The simulator is divided into functional subprocesses which execute concurrently:

clock: This process is responsible for synchronization of the simulation process. It is the global termination detector. It can start, suspend, resume, or abort the simulation process. It is controlled by a control input stream.

counter: This process performs the time calculations. It supplies time stamps for the probe process. It also monitors the number of simulation steps. It can issue a command to the clock process to stop the simulation after a predefined number of steps. Three parameters of the counter are user-defined:

(1) Total number of simulation steps in a session.

(2) Resolution factor, i.e., how many simulation steps per output sample.

(3) Start point of data sampling.

route: This process is the traffic controller. It receives messages from the user or any processes within the simulator and distributes them to their destination. The distribution is according to an address which is part of the message. An illegal message produces an error message on the user's terminal and is then discarded.

sig_gen: This process is a signal generator. Stimulation patterns are read by this process from a user-defined file. The process constructs messages including synchronization information received from the clock process and sends these messages to the input channels of the hardware model.

probe: This process collects the simulation results. Communication channels are attached to points of interest in the model. Via these channels, the messages flowing through the points of interest are sampled in constant time intervals. The interval between samples is controlled by time stamps supplied by the counter process. The receiving side of these channels is in the probe process. The sampled messages are saved in a special buffer together with an absolute time stamp. Results can be viewed on the user's terminal or stored in a file.

view: This process is an independent utility. Its input is a buffer of raw data collected by the probe process. This buffer is formatted and processed to produce a display of the simulation results on the user's screen. The view utility has two versions. The first is a runtime version. It is attached to the probe process and makes it possible to view simulation results on the fly. The second version is a batch version, and reads its input from a file.

36.6 Comparison to Other Hardware Description Languages

Three major aspects can be identified as a basis for comparing our work to other hardware description languages; namely, the description methodology, the expressiveness, and the implementation technique.

The proposed methodology is based on the separation of the behavioral aspect of a description from its structural aspect. The first decision that must be made using this methodology is to choose an abstraction level. This decision defines the scope of the behavioral description and places a strict borderline between the behavioral and structural aspects of a description. Several other languages were developed based on a similar methodology, e.g., VHDL (Shahdad et al., 1985).

In VHDL a hardware object is composed of a *body* which may have either structural or behavioral definition, and an *interface* which defines certain information items such as I/O declarations and physical parameters. We see the method of integrating all physical properties into the behavioral description to be more natural.

Another language which separates behavior from structure is ZEUS (German and Lieberherr, 1985). However in ZEUS the separation is not so strict as behavior and structure aspects of a description can be mixed in the code.

On the question of expressiveness and suitability for hardware description, the need for an ability to describe concurrent activities is clear. In contrast to many languages, including those mentioned above, expressing concurrency in Concurrent Prolog is natural and elegant. Other languages such as Occam have tools to express concurrency naturally, but can use only primitive message types. This restricts the usage of a language for hardware description only to low abstraction levels. In contrast, Concurrent Prolog as a symbolic language does not have any limitation on massage types; therefore it is not restricted to any specific abstraction level.

Yet another aspect of expressive power is demonstrated by ZEUS: The ability to generate representations of abstract algorithms, which are transformable to hardware. This can be done using Concurrent Prolog, too (Shapiro, Chapter 7).

A paper by Noda et al. (1985) presents work close in direction to ours. Noda's paper discusses the potential use of Concurrent Prolog for hardware description and simulation, which emphasizes parallel simulation strategies. Our work emphasizes more the methodological aspects of hardware description in Concurrent Prolog.

The simulation mechanism presented above is termed by Noda as Global-type, Non-event-type strategy. Compared to Noda's simulation method, our method uses only communication channels which already exist in the model. This has the advantage of preserving the inherent locality of communication in the model under simulation.

O'Donnell (1987), describes the application of functional programming to hardware description. His paper discusses a few aspects of hardware description not mentioned in this paper, such as netlist extraction and placement. O'Donnell's approach to hardware description is similar to the methodology introduced in this paper. Defining a primitive component, as shown in this paper, corresponds to assigning a component a "meaning" in O'donnel's terminology. Under both approahces this "meaning" can include, in addition to a pure functional description, also information about size, fan-in, fan-out, critical timing relationships, etc.

We can use functional programming techniques within our methodology. However, not all hardware components are easily expressed as functions. Some require the full power of a relational language such as Concurrent Prolog. A simple example is modeling a pass transistor, which has no direct functional representation, but has a simple relational one.

Considering implementation issues, Concurrent Prolog cannot compete, as yet, with the performance of sequential languages on a sequential machine. The natural environment to execute Concurrent Prolog programs is a parallel machine. This fact is reflected in the development of distributed simulation mechanisms.

It should be pointed out that Concurrent Prolog may not be suitable for the execution of intensive simulation even in a distributed environment due to its relative poor performance as compared to special purpose parallel simulation machines. Still the automatic reduction mechanism to canonical description can be used to generate code for special purpose simulation machines. Also, simulation in high abstraction levels which can be executed only by a high level language, cannot be executed on special purpose machines, and here the parallel execution of Concurrent Prolog may be advantageous over other high level languages.

36.7 Future Research

The full potential of hardware description in Concurrent Prolog is yet to be explored. Present research efforts are aimed at the following issues:

- Development of source to source transformation from functional descriptions into executable code, including synchronization mechanism.

- Development and implementation of a distributed event-driven simulation algorithm.

- Definition of a rigorous formalism for hardware description.

- Using the formalism for automatic design validation (see Section 36.2).

- Using the structural description in Concurrent Prolog as a basis for silicon compiler.

Part VII

Implementation

Introduction

A precondition for the success of a kernel language is efficient implementation. Unlike the belief of early enthusiasts of parallelism, we do not expect that a slow language, or a bad algorithm, will suddenly become practical when run on a parallel computer. On the contrary, given our current understanding we believe that the basic building blocks of a parallel computer system should be a fast processor, an efficient concurrent programming language, and good parallel algorithms. One criterion we would like our computer architecture, language, and algorithms to fulfill is scalability: that their performance would increase linearly with the number of processors employed. An equally important criterion, and perhaps in the short run even more important, is that in the limiting case of one processor, our processor, language, and algorithms must not have substantially inferior performance compared to their conventional sequential counterparts.

Many parallel algorithms possess this second property. The Transputer is an example of a building block for parallel computers which is also an efficient uniprocessor. The remaining component is an efficient implementation of the concurrent programming language. The first two papers in this part report on initial attempts to develop efficient uniprocessor implementations of Concurrent Prolog and Flat Concurrent Prolog.

Sequential implementations

Chapter 37, "A Sequential Implementation of Concurrent Prolog Based on the Shallow Binding Scheme", by Miazaki, Takeuchi, and Chikayama, reports on an effort to implement Concurrent Prolog efficiently on a uniprocessor. The approach was one of three investigated; the other two were deep binding (Sato et al., 1984) and lazy copying (Levy and Friedman 1986; Tanaka et al., 1984). Shallow binding proved to be the fastest on a uniprocessor. However, it was not clear how it could scale to a multiprocessor. The difficulties with all the schemes proposed led to the switch to Flat Concurrent Prolog, as reported in Chapter 5.

Chapter 38, "A Sequential Abstract Machine for Flat Concurrent Prolog", by Houri and Shapiro, reports on the implementation of FCP presently incorporated in the Logix system. The paper describes an abstract machine for Flat Concurrent Prolog, its implementation via a compiler to an abstract instruction set, and an emulator for these instructions. The compiler is written in FCP, and the emulator in C. The design of the abstract machine is strongly influenced by the Warren Abstract Machine (Warren, 1983), but deviates from it in fundamental ways, in order to support the concurrent semantics of Flat Concurrent Prolog.

The basic operation of FCP is process reduction: a process is unified with the head of some clause, whose instantiated guard is found to be true, and replaced by the instantiated body of that clause. Operationally, a process reduction corresponds to termination, iteration, or forking, depending on whether the body of the clause has zero, one, or more goals, respectively.

Process iteration corresponds to tail-recursive call in sequential recursive programming languages. Process forking is similar in frequency and granularity to, and subsumes the functionality of, general recursive calls in such languages. The design of the abstract machine for FCP ensures that process iteration is implemented with efficiency comparable to that of iteration in conventional sequential languages, and that process forking is implemented with efficiency comparable to that of recursive procedure calling in such languages. It thus debunks the "expensive process spawn myth".

Most of the overhead of this implementation is not related to process management, but rather to unification. Better compilation techniques for unification have been developed (Kliger, 1987; Taylor and Shapiro, 1987) but have not ripen in time to be included in this volume. Kliger (1987) reports on a native code compiler for a subset of FCP which achieves more than a ten-fold speed up compared with the emulator-based implementation.

When studying the present paper it is useful to distinguish between the concrete instruction set used, which is tailored for emulation, and the more abstract concepts of the machine architecture, notably the process and memory management techniques employed. These carry over to the more efficient implementations of the language.

The performance of the sequential implementation of Flat Concurrent Prolog suggests that the language can fulfill the second requirement presented above: that is, not to have a substantially inferior uniprocessor performance compared with its sequential counterparts. The performance of FCP on a uniprocessor is comparable with that of sequential Prolog. The uniprocessor performance of CFL (Chapter 35), embedded in Flat Concurrent Prolog, is comparable to that of conventional Lisp systems. In addition, we find the uniprocessor performance of Logix acceptable for FCP program development.

Parallel implementation

The other criterion suggested, scalability, is relevant only to parallel implementations. Scalability implies that the fundamental barrier in exploiting parallelism effectively is communication costs. Therefore, architectures, programming languages, and algorithms that can exploit locality of communication should be investigated. The concern for scalability is the major motivation behind the systolic programming approach (Chapter 7, Chapter 8). Because of this concern, our implementation efforts concentrate on non shared-memory architectures based on local interconnection.

Chapter 39, "A Parallel Implementation of Flat Concurrent Prolog", by Taylor, Safra, and Shapiro, reports on a parallel execution algorithm for Flat Concurrent Prolog for such an architecture. The algorithm is embodied in an interpreter based implementation of Flat Concurrent Prolog for the iPSC hypercube. The algorithm, however, does not depend on the topology of the network, and is suitable for any non-shared memory architecture, including a loosely coupled network of computers. The performance of a specific algorithm implemented in FCP depends, of course, on the match between its communication requirements, including topology and bandwidth, and the communication capabilities of the underlying architecture.

Our experience with the parallel execution of Flat Concurrent Prolog is still preliminary. The parallel interpreter of Flat Concurrent Prolog was designed mostly for testing the correctness of the parallel execution algorithm for FCP, and the methods of process and code mapping described in Chapter 22, and not for performance. Initial benchmarking showed close to linear speed-up in some instances, but since the overall performance was low, it is hard to reach definite conclusions from these results. Recently, a compiler/emulator based implementation has been developed based on a more advanced compilation technique (Taylor and Shapiro, 1987) but its performance is yet to be analyzed.

Chapter 39 reports on the parallel execution algorithm for Flat Concurrent Prolog, which underlies this parallel interpreter. It describes how logical variables can be shared between processors, and how a unification which requires writing and/or reading on several shared variables can be executed as an atomic action. (The paper uses an earlier definition of read-only unification; however, most of its ideas and techniques are applicable to the current definition as well.) The paper suggests a locking mechanism to achieve this atomicity, and describes a method to prevent deadlock in case several unifications compete for writing on the same variables. Reading occurs much more often than writing and single-writer variables are much more frequent than multiple-writer variables, hence the algorithm is optimized for these cases.

The scalability criterion and the resulting emphasis on locality of communication are controversial. Indeed, most of the theoretical research on parallel algorithms and complexity centers on the PRAM model of computation, which abstracts away communication costs and hence is "scalable" by definition. There is also experimental research along the same path. Several concrete architectures, which attempt to provide approximations to this abstract computation model, are being constructed, including NYU's Ultracomputer, BBN's Butterfly, and IBM's RP3. Nevertheless, due to scalability considerations for large-scale parallel computers and to simplicity and uniformity considerations for small-scale parallel computers, we presently believe that non shared-memory parallel computers will eventually win across the board.

This position on the future direction of parallel computers, however, is not directly related to concurrent logic programming. It seems that concurrent logic programming languages in general, and Flat Concurrent Prolog in particular, do not take a stand on the issue. Obviously, the non shared-memory execution algorithm of FCP is applicable directly to shared-memory parallel computers, simply by implementing some communication protocol between processors, and ignoring more sophisticated ways of sharing memory. Although not fully investigated yet, it seems that an execution algorithm for Flat Concurrent Prolog which relies on, and better exploits, a shared memory, might be even simpler than the non shared-memory one.

We believe that the same programming techniques and operating system concepts should be applicable to both kinds of parallel computers, and to networks of (sequential or parallel) computers as well. We find the prospects of programming all types of computers and their networks in a uniform way enticing.

The last two papers in this part describe first steps towards efficient implementation of Flat Concurrent Prolog. Further progress is required before FCP can be used as a genuine general purpose parallel machine language. The previous parts of the book provided evidence that achieving this goal is worthwhile and desirable. The papers in this part suggest that achieving this goal is possible.

Chapter 37

A Sequential Implementation
of Concurrent Prolog
Based on the Shallow Binding Scheme

Toshihiko Miyazaki, Akikazu Takeuchi and Takashi Chikayama

Institute for New Generation Computer Technology

Abstract

This paper presents an efficient implementation scheme on sequential computers of Concurrent Prolog. The key issues of the implementation are (1) the scheduling of suspended computations and (2) Or-parallel evaluation of clauses in order to select one clause for the goal resolution. The solution to the first problem is briefly explained, and we will focus on the solution to the second problem. The second problem is divided into two sub-problems: (2.1) realization of multiple environments for clauses executed in parallel and (2.2) realization of value access control which is necessary when guards are deeply nested.

The proposed implementation technique is based on the so-called shallow binding scheme and introduces two new low level constructs, a trail cell and a local environment number. The former realizes multiple environments and the latter realizes value access control.

37.1 Introduction

Recently many logic programming languages based on stream-and-parallelism have been proposed, and it has become clearer that these languages are very powerful for parallel programming. Some of these languages are Relational Language

(Clark and Gregory, Chapter 1), Concurrent Prolog (Shapiro, Chapter 2), PAR-LOG (Clark and Gregory, Chapter 3) and Guarded Horn Clauses (Ueda, Chapter 4). The common features of these languages are:

- And-parallelism,

- communication through shared logical variables, and

- don't-care nondeterminism based on committed choices.

Implementations of these languages were and are being performed by several researchers (Clark and Gregory, 1985; Levy, 1984; Nitta, 1984; Shapiro, Chapter 2). The key issues of such implementations are

(1) the scheduling of suspended computations.

(2) Or-parallel evaluation of clauses in order to select one clause for the goal resolution.

In this paper we present a new sequential algorithm implementing for an interpreter for Concurrent Prolog, which solves the above problems efficiently. The implementation scheme is based on the so-called shallow binding scheme, which is a well-known scheme for implementing the variable-value binding environment in LISP (Baker, 1978b).

The structure of the paper is as follows. In Section 37.2, a general computational model for Concurrent Prolog is presented. In Section 37.3, the key issues of the implementation are described. In Section 37.4, the shallow binding scheme is described in detail. In Section 37.5, advantages and disadvantages of the scheme are discussed and compared with other schemes.

37.2 Computation Model

As in the case of Prolog, the computation model of Concurrent Prolog can be represented by an *And-Or* tree. In the following discussion, *And* nodes and *Or* nodes are referred to as *And*-processes and *Or*-processes, respectively. An *And*-process and an *Or*-process correspond to a literal and a guarded clause in Concurrent Prolog respectively.

Figure 37.1 shows a slightly modified *And-Or* tree which illustrates a snapshot of the state of a Concurrent Prolog computation (Shapiro, 1983c).

A loop formed by $\longleftrightarrow$ is called an *And*-loop, and a loop formed by $\leftarrow\,\text{-}\,\text{-}\,\rightarrow$ is called an *Or*-loop. Each loop has one parent process and several child processes.

In an *And*-loop, the parent process is an *Or*-process and the child processes are *And*-processes which correspond to conjunctive goals in the guard part of the

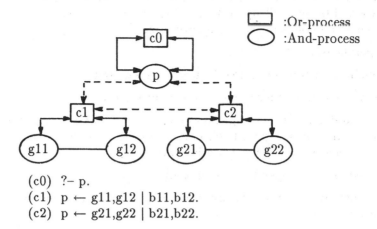

(c0) ?– p.
(c1) p ← g11,g12 | b11,b12.
(c2) p ← g21,g22 | b21,b22.

Figure 37.1: An And-Or tree

Or-process. In an *Or*-loop, the parent process is an *And*-process and the child processes are *Or*-processes which are candidate clauses of the *And*-process. The clauses which may resolve a goal are called the candidate clauses of the goal. Without loss of generality, we assume the top level goal statement always consists of a single goal, which means that the root of the tree is always an *Or*-loop, including this goal as a parent *And*-process.

If one of the *And*-processes in an *And*-loop fails, then the parent *Or*-process fails. If all the *And*-processes succeed, then the parent *Or*-process succeeds. Similarly since the child *Or*-processes in *Or*-loop represent disjunctive clauses, if one such *Or*-process succeeds then the parent *And*-process succeeds, and if all the *Or*-processes fail then the parent *And*-process fails.

When all the *And*-processes in an *And*-loop succeed, that is, the computation of the guard part of the clause represented by the parent *Or*-process in the *And*-loop successfully terminates and reaches the commit operator, then the *Or*-process succeeds and commits. During commitment, the *Or*-process kills all the other *Or*-processes in the *Or*-loop to which it belongs and replaces its parent *And*-process by the literals in its body part. In other words, the selection of the clause (the *Or*-process) which resolves the goal is established and all the other choices are discarded (See Figure 37.2).

Generally, in an *And-Or* tree, every leaf process is ready and every other process is waiting for the completion of the computation of its child processes. In this sequential implementation, the system scheduler serves enabled processes one by one according to the scheduling algorithm. This implementation provides

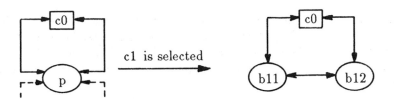

Figure 37.2: Commitment

several scheduling algorithms: breadth-first, depth-first and bounded depth-first.

37.3 Key Issues of the Implementation

The two key issues of an efficient implementation of Concurrent Prolog are:

(1) The scheduling of suspended computations.

(2) The management of multiple computation environments for Or-parallel evaluation of clauses.

There is a reasonable solution to the first problem (Shapiro, 1983c). In this paper, we will concentrate on the second issue. However, before the second problem is specified in more detail, we briefly summarize the first problem and a solution.

Since Concurrent Prolog provides a read-only annotation as the synchronization primitive, when a goal cannot be resolved without instantiating a variable annotated as read-only to a non-variable term, the computation suspends. The problem is how to schedule these suspended computations.

Since a computation suspends when it tries to instantiate a read-only variable to a non-variable term and it can resume when the read-only variable becomes instantiated to a non-variable term by another computation, it is natural to associate suspended computations with variables which caused suspensions. For this purpose, a suspension queue is introduced. A suspension queue is a queue which can keep suspended computation. The suspension queue is attached to an uninstantiated variable and it keeps only suspended computation which have read-only access to the variable and have tried to instantiate it to non-variable terms. The suspended computation kept in the suspension queue of some uninstantiated variable becomes ready when the variable is instantiated to a non-variable term by another computation which has non-read-only access to the variable.

The second problem, the management of multiple environments, is demonstrated by the following simple examples.

In Program 37.1, during the parallel evaluation of two clauses, *clause1* tries to unify the variable X in the goal $p(X)$ with *1*, while *clause2* tries to unify the same variable X with *2*. These two bindings to the same variable must be kept independently in their own local environment until one of the clauses is selected, and must be made invisible from other environments such as the environment for the goal $q(X)$.

> goal1: ?– p(X), q(X).
>
> clause1: p(1) ← guard1 | body1.
> clause2: p(2) ← guard2 | body2.

Program 37.1

> goal2: ?– p(f(A)), r(A).
>
> clause3: p(X) ← q1(X), q2(X) | . . . .
> clause4: q1(f(1)) ← . . . | ⌣. . .
> clause5: q1(f(2)) ← . . . | . . . .
> clause6: q2(f(B)) ← . . . | . . . .

Program 37.2

In Program 37.2, the goal $p(f(A))$ invokes the guard part $q1(X)$, $q2(X)$, of *clause3*, and $q1(X)$ invokes *clause4* and *clause5*. During the parallel evaluation of *clause4* and *clause5*, the two inconsistent bindings to the same variable A will be made and they must be kept independently, as in the case of Program 37.1. When either clause is selected, the value of A which is kept in the selected environment is exported to the environment of *clause3*, and now the goal $q2(X)$ can access the value of A. However it must not be exported to the environment of environment of *goal2*, because *clause3* has not yet been selected. In other words, although the variable A first appeared in *goal2*, it is instantiated in either *clause4* or *clause5* and it is still kept in the local environment of *clause3*. Therefore *goal2* does not have access to the value of A until *clause3* is selected.

Generally, in Concurrent Prolog, when the candidate clauses for a goal are executed concurrently (Or-parallel), head unification and guard computation of each candidate clause must be executed in its own local environment until one of the clauses is selected. When one of the clauses reaches the commit operator, computation of other clauses are abandoned and the local environment of the selected clause is exported to the environment of the goal. The essential difficulty in Or-parallel evaluation of candidate clauses is in the realization and the management of multiple environments corresponding to independent computations of candidate clauses and the control of the value access illustrated by Program 37.2.

37.4 Implementation

We employ the shallow binding scheme for the realization of multiple environments. The differences among the multiple environments come only from different instantiations to the variables in the goal. Therefore, in order to realize multiple environments, it is enough to keep multiple bindings for each variable in the goal. The shallow binding scheme implements this idea. In what follows, the details of this scheme is described.

37.4.1 Shallow binding and environment switching

When an *Or*-process is invoked, the variable cells for the variables appearing in the clause are allocated first in its environment. These cells will have values or reference pointers to other cells (Warren, 1977; Yokota, 1984).

In the local environment, when an uninstantiated variable appearing in a goal is unified with a non-variable term during the head unification or guard computation, the pair of the address of the variable cell and its current content is saved in the local environment and the non-variable term is written into the variable cell itself. The pair is called the "trail cell" and plays a central role in the realization of multiple environments. Since the value written into the variable cell must be transparent to other processes, when another process is scheduled, the local value must be saved in the local environment and the original value must be restored to the cell.

goal: ?– p(X), q(X).

clause1: p(1) ← guard | body.

Program 37.3

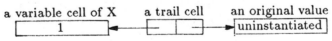

(a) The trail cell is used for saving original value

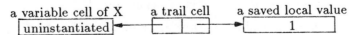

(b) The trail cell is used for restoring the local value

Figure 37.3: The trail cell

In Program 37.3, when the head unification is performed for the goal $p(X)$ and *clause1*, the pair shown in Figure 37.3 is produced. However, since *clause1* has not been selected yet, X must be uninstantiated for the goal $q(X)$. This means that in the resolution of the goal $q(X)$, the value of X must be recovered using the trail cell, as shown in Figure 37.3. When the computation of the guard of *clause1* is resumed, the local binding is recovered again using the trail cell. This procedure is called an environment switch. In general, the head unification and the execution of the guard of each clause may require trail cells.

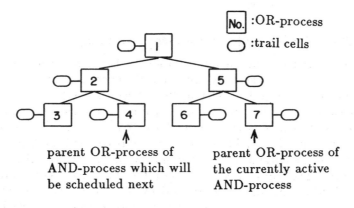

parent OR-process of
AND-process which will
be scheduled next

parent OR-process of
the currently active
AND-process

Figure 37.4: An Or-tree

Assume that we have the *Or*-tree of the form shown in Figure 37.4. (Each *Or*-process is assumed to have one or more trail cells, and *Or*-process 7 is the parent process of the currently active *And*-process and *Or*-process 4 will be scheduled next.) In order to activate *Or*-process 4 next, the trail cells attached to *Or*-processes on the way between process 7 and process 4 (i.e., *Or*-process 7, 5, 2, and 4) are used to recover the local environment of *Or*-process 4 in the following way (notice that since the environment for *Or*-process 1 is shared between *Or*-processes 4 and 7, the trail cells in *Or*-process 1 are not used for this environment switch):

(1) If trail cells are used for saving the original bindings, then their global bindings are restored and their local bindings are saved.

(2) Otherwise the local bindings are restored and the original bindings are saved.

In order to perform environment switching, the path between the *Or*-process of the current active process and the *Or*-process of the *And*-process scheduled next must be identified quickly. Therefore, an environment pointer is introduced in order to enable a process to know the way to the current active process. An environment pointer points to either a parent or a child. When a pointer points to a child, there must be an active *And*-process in the descendants. See Figure 37.5 for an example.

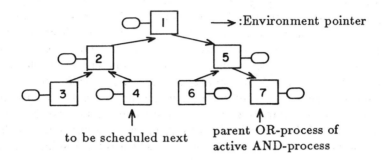

Figure 37.5: The Or tree with environment chain

Environment switching is described as follows:

(1) Starting from the *Or*-process scheduled next, follow the environment pointers until the currently active process is reached, reversing the direction of pointers.

(2) Follow the environment pointers in reverse order until the *Or*-process scheduled next is found. Exchange values if there are any trail cells in the Or-process.

(3) When the process is found, change its pointer to nil (the environment pointer of the active process is always nil).

Figure 37.6 shows the directions of pointers after environment switching has been completed.

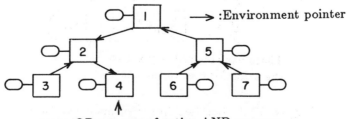

Figure 37.6: The Or tree after environment switching

37.4.2 Value access control

The trail cell of the variable must be kept in the local environment if the variable does not belong to the local environment. Hence it is necessary to determine whether a variable belongs to the local environment of the currently active process or not. For determining this, a unique number (called a local environment number) is assigned to each local environment for identification. When an *Or*-process is created, a new local environment number is allocated and assigned to the associated environment. At the same time, a pointer to the cell containing the number is stored in all the variable cells which are allocated in the environment, so that one can decide whether an uninstantiated variable belongs to some environment or not by comparing the environment numbers. We show a simple example in Figure 37.7. All cells of uninstantiated variables point to the local environment number cell of the environment to which the variables belong.

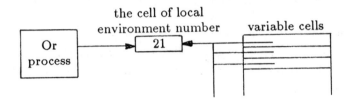

Figure 37.7: The local environment number cell

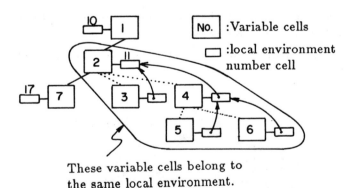

These variable cells belong to the same local environment.

Figure 37.8: Local environment management

During commitment, the content of this local environment number cell is changed to a reference pointer to its parent (in the Or tree) local environment number cell. Figure 37.8 shows the situation in which variable cells 2, 3, 4, 5 and 6 belong to the same local environment after several commitments. However, in Figure 37.8, we must follow two reference pointers in order to get the local environment number of the variable cell belonging to 5. In general, a variable may have a chain of pointers to its local environment number, the length of which is N after N commitments. When unifying such a variable, we must follow N reference pointers. To avoid this overhead, once a reference chain is detected, it is replaced by a direct reference pointer to the current local environment number cell.

37.4.3 Dereferencing and head unification

When a writable variable is unified with another writable variable, a reference pointer is set up from one variable to another. When a read-only variable and a writable variable are unified, the read-only reference pointer to the cell of the read-only variable is assigned to the cell of the writable variable. Thus, an attribute of "read-only" is represented by a read-only reference pointer. A variable cell consists of two fields, a tag field and a value field. The tag field of a cell indicates the attribute of the value field.

In general, a unified variable either refers to another variable via one or more reference pointers (or read-only reference pointers) or has its own value. The value obtained through dereferencing is either an uninstantiated variable cell or a non-variable term (atom, integer, list, or tuple). Figure 37.9 shows the algorithm for dereferencing.

```
dereference(VarCell)
    begin:
        case( tag(VarCell) )
            undef:
                return( VarCell );
            susp:
                return( VarCell );
            non-variable term:
                return( VarCell );
            reference:
                dereference( value(VarCell) );
            read-only-reference:
                F := on;
                dereference( value(VarCell) )
    end;
```

Figure 37.9: Dereferencing algorithm

The unification algorithm is summarized in Table 37.1. Here, *X or Y* means either X or Y may be used. If F is on after the execution of the *dereference* procedure, a read-only reference pointer was found in the reference pointer chain.

In this case, the value X obtained by dereferencing is represented by $X\text{-}ro$ in Table 37.1. The tag *undef* is used to represent an uninstantiated variable. The tag *susp* is used to represent a pointer to a suspension record which has a pointer to a suspension queue and a pointer to a local environment number cell. These two tags indicate that the variable is uninstantiated.

P C	undef	susp	undef-ro	susp-ro	term
undef	C:=REF(P) or P:=REF(C)	C:=REF(P) or P:=REF(C)*	C:=ROREF(P)	C:ROREF(P)	C:=P
susp	C:=REF(P)* or P:=REF(C)	C:=REF(P)** or P:=REF(C)**	C:=ROREF(P)*	C:ROREF(P)**	C:=P
undef-ro	P:=ROREF(C)	P:=ROREF(C)*	SUSPEND	SUSPEND	SUSPEND
susp-ro	P:=ROREF(C)	P:=ROREF(C)**	SUSPEND	SUSPEND	SUSPEND
term	P:=C	P:=C	SUSPEND	SUSPEND	unify(P,C)

X-ro : means that the flag F is on.
P,C   : result values of dereference.
  *   : the suspension record moves to the other cell.
  **   : concatenate two suspension queues.

Table 37.1: Outline of unification

In the unification of two uninstantiated variables A and B, if both cells have the same data type *susp*, both suspension queues are concatenated and stored in the suspension record. The suspension record is stored in one of the cells and the other cell refers to it. If the data type of A is *susp* and that of B is *undef-ro*, the suspension record of A is stored in B, the tag of B is changed to *susp* and the read-only reference pointer to B is stored in A.

SUSPEND means that the unification is to be suspended. In this case, the tag of the variable causing the suspension is changed to "susp" if it is uninstantiated, and a suspension queue is produced. A suspended goal is put into the suspension queue. If the tag of the variable is *susp*, the goal is added to the end of the suspension queue.

A detailed description of the unification algorithm used for a variable and a term is shown in Figure 37.10.

```
X : variable cell
X↑ : address of variable cell
T : term

if instantiated(X) then
      unify(X, T);
elseif belongs-to-the-current-env(X) then
      X := T;
else
      allocate-trail-cell(C);
      save-trail-cell(C, X↑, X);
endif;
```

Figure 37.10: The unification algorithm

37.4.4 Commitment

The commit operation is performed by a selected *Or*-process. The procedure is as follows:

(1) Abandon other *Or*-processes in the same *Or*-loop

(2) Export the binding information in the local environment to the parent environment.

(3) Create *And*-processes for the goals in the body part of the clause, and replace the parent *And*-process by a doubly-linked list consisting of them.

The export operation consists of two stages. In the first stage, for each trail cell kept in the local environment, the global value in the trail cell is unified with the current local value of the corresponding variable. In the second stage, if the first stage ends successfully, the content of the local environment number cell of the local environment is changed to a reference pointer to that of the parent environment as described in Section 37.4.2.

In Program 37.4, the value *1* of the variable *A* is made visible only within the guard of *clause1* when *clause2* is selected. It is never seen from the *goal*. That is, when *clause2* is selected, the trail cell for *A* is moved to the *Or*-process corresponding to *clause1*.

       goal: ?– p(f(A)).

       clause1: p(X) ← q(X), ... | ....
       clause2: q(f(1)) ← ... | ....

Program 37.4

Unification performed in the exportation process differs from head unification in the following two points:

(1) When a variable, the tag of which is "susp", is instantiated to a non-variable term, all the entries in its suspension queue are moved to the ready queue.

(2) If unification suspends during commitment, the *Or*-process is put in the corresponding suspension queue.

The algorithm is shown in Figure 37.11.

> $X\uparrow$: Pointer to the cell of the
> variable X in the trail cell
> V : Value saved in the trail cell
> (the current global value of
> the variable X)
>
> if (The variable cell pointed to by
> $X\uparrow$ belongs to the environment
>   of the parent *Or*-process)
> then
>   The current value of X and V are unified;
> else (* the variable does not belong to it *)
>   The trail cell is moved to the
>   environment of the parent *Or*-process;
> endif;

Figure 37.11: Export

37.5 Comparison

There are several methods by which multiple environments can be implemented. In this section, we will characterize some of them, the copying scheme and the binding scheme, and compare the performance of the shallow binding scheme with that of the others.

(1) Copying scheme

Conceptually in this scheme, local copies of arguments of the goal are produced for each candidate clause. Head unification and guard computation can freely instantiate these local copies, without affecting the computation of other clauses. During commitment, the local copies are unified with the arguments in the goal. The scheme can be further subdivided into two sub-schemes, the eager copying scheme and the lazy copying scheme, according to the time at which local copies are made.

(a) Eager copying scheme

In the eager copying scheme, local copies of all arguments of the goal are made when the goal is invoked. This scheme is simple; however, it introduces a large copying overhead, and it may copy terms not necessary for computation.

(b) Lazy copying scheme

The lazy copying scheme was proposed by Levy (1984) and Tanaka et al. (1984). In the lazy copying scheme, terms are copied when trying to instantiate them. However, it needs a complicated mechanism to ensure that goals in the same environment share locally instantiated terms.

(2) Binding scheme

In this scheme, instead of making a local copy for each candidate clause, local bindings are made in an environment when variables in the goal are instantiated during the execution of a candidate clause. The scheme is further subdivided into two subschemes, the deep binding scheme and the shallow binding scheme, according to the implementation details. In both schemes, local bindings for a clause are kept in the *Or*-process corresponding to the clause.

(a) Deep binding scheme

In this scheme, local bindings for variables in the goal are kept as an association list in each environment (Sato et al., 1984). During commitment, local values kept in the association list are unified with the current values of variables in the goal. This scheme requires a linear search for the association lists residing in the ancestor *Or*-processes in order to get the value of a variable when guard computations are deeply nested, because there is no way to know in which guard the variable is bound to a term. Figure 37.12 shows a simple example environment representation of the deep binding scheme.

(b) Shallow binding scheme

This is the scheme described in this paper.

The shallow binding scheme proposed here is similar to the scheme proposed by D.S. Warren (1984). Basically, Warren's scheme can be regarded as a deep binding scheme. However, it has achieved the same efficiency as the shallow binding scheme, with respect to the cost of getting a value of a variable, by introducing the Binding Array. The main difference between our scheme and his scheme is in the environment switching. When switching environment, in Warren's scheme, the whole Binding Array is initialized to 'unknown' and is reconstructed upon demand. On the other hand, in our scheme, the new environment can be obtained by slightly modifying part of the old environment using trail cells on the way from the old to the new.

goal : ?– p(X).
clause: p(1) ⟵ ··· .

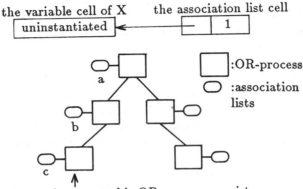

The environment this OR-process consist
of tree association lists, a, b, c.

Figure 37.12: Deep binding scheme

37.5.1 Advantages of the shallow binding scheme

Unification is fast compared with the eager copying scheme, because shallow binding does not need copying of goals.

Dereferencing is clear and very fast compared with the deep binding scheme, because in the deep binding scheme it is always necessary to search association lists linearly for the value of a variable. The cost of getting values in the worst case is the order of the number of ancestor *Or*-processes.

In the lazy copying scheme, the first dereferencing of a variable is as expensive as in the deep binding scheme. Once a term is accessed, it must be copied into all the environments between the environment of the currently active process and the environment to which the term belongs.

37.5.2 Disadvantages of the shallow binding scheme

The expensive operation of the shallow binding scheme is the environment switching which occurs when the next process is scheduled from the ready queue. The cost of environment switching depends on the distance between the currently active process and the process which should be scheduled next on the *Or*-tree. One possible remedy for this disadvantage is to employ a bounded depth-first scheduling method. We illustrate this by a simple example.

In Program 37.5, the number of reduction is $(M * 4)/2$. Predicate *ap* in

Program 37.5 recursively calls itself in its guard. The number of recursive calls is specified by the first argument of *ap*. A new trail cell is created for each recursive call. In breadth-first scheduling method, environment switching takes place on each recursive call. In bounded depth-first scheduling, it takes place once every N times, where N is the bound of the depth.

goal: ?– ap(M,A,A), ap(M,B,B).

```
ap(N,[a|X],XX) ←
     ap(N, N > 0, N1 is N–1,
     ap(N, m(XX?),
     ap(N, ap(N1,X,XX) | true.
ap(0, [ ], –).
m([_|_]).
```

Program 37.5

37.6 Conclusion

In Figure 37.13 the timings of the Program 37.5 measured on different interpreters are shown. The bounded depth-first scheduling was effective for Program 37.5 in our interpreter, because environment switches are scarce.

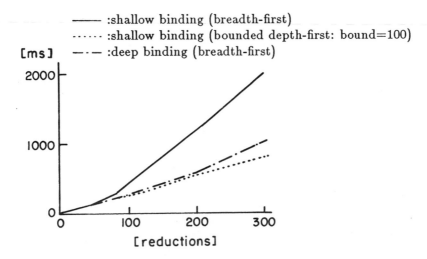

Figure 37.13: Results of Program 37.5

The features of this shallow binding implementation are summarized below:

(1) The realization of multiple environments by trail cells.

(2) The realization of the value access control by the local environment numbers.

Acknowledgements

We thank Kazunori Ueda, Jirou Tanaka, Nobuyuki Ichiyoshi, Hitoshi Aida and other members of KL1 implementation group for their valuable suggestions.

We also thank Kazuhiro Fuchi, Koichi Furukawa and all the other members of ICOT, both for helping this research and for providing a stimulating place in which to work.

Daniel Szoke assisted in editing this paper.

Chapter 38

A Sequential Abstract Machine for Flat Concurrent Prolog

Avshalom Houri and Ehud Shapiro

The Weizmann Institute of Science

Abstract

This paper describes a uniprocessor implementation of Flat Concurrent Prolog, based on an abstract machine and a compiler for it. The machine instruction set includes the functionality necessary to implement efficiently the parallel semantics of the language. In addition, the design includes a novel approach to the integration of a module system into a language.

Both the compiler and the emulator for the abstract machine have been implemented and form the basis of Logix, a practical programming environment for Flat Concurrent Prolog. Its performance suggests that a process-oriented language need not be less efficient then a procedure-oriented language, even on a uniprocessor. In particular, it shows that a process queue and process spawning can be implemented as efficiently as an activation stack and procedure calling, and thus debunks the "expensive process spawn myth".

38.1 Introduction

Compilation techniques for implementing logic programming languages have been investigated extensively. The most important techniques were developed by Warren (1977, 1983) for the compilation of Prolog. Each clause in the source program is compiled into a set of abstract machine instructions. These instructions compile away much of the run-time overhead of unification and provide the basic control flow required by the language. The methods have significantly improved performance in both time and space; as a result, Prolog is widely accepted to be of performance comparable to Lisp. To test the compilation process and to give a level of portability an emulator for the abstract machine can be built. This emulator is generally written in a lower level implementation language.

However, Prolog does not provide explicitly the notion of concurrency. To add this capability to logic programming, a family of languages have evolved which originated in the Relational Language of Clark and Gregory (Chapter 1, Chapter 3; Shapiro, Chapter 2; Ueda, Chapter 4). These languages have a parallel semantics and use dataflow synchronization with stream-oriented communication.

Flat Concurrent Prolog (FCP) (Mierowsky et al., 1985; Shapiro, Chapter 5) is a simple concurrent logic programming language. Its simplicity lies in the non-hierarchical structure of its process and data environment. The language, like the concurrent logic languages mentioned above, incorporates nondeterministic goal selection, committed-choice nondeterminism in clause selection, dataflow synchronization and stream-based communication.

The guards of FCP clauses are only primitive actions in contrast to most of the other languages. This provides two major benefits; only a single environment needs to exist during execution and there is no need to distribute the commit operation. These simplifications allow nondeterminism to be simulated by a simple iterative deterministic algorithm. This algorithm was originally designed and developed in an interpreter based implementation of FCP (Mierowsky et al., 1985); however, this implementation was too slow for practical use. The algorithm admits a simple transformation from the source code to abstract machine code and provides an opportunity for efficient compilation.

The abstract machine described in this paper utilizes a number of novel techniques to compile the parallel semantics and provides a novel approach to the implementation of modules. Its instruction set implements the parallel and nondeterministic features of the language.

The implementation has been compared to one of the fastest commercially available Prolog compiler. Although slower in absolute terms, it should be recognized that the emulator is written in C and a variety of straightforward optimizations are not yet utilized. In contrast, the Prolog emulator is written largely in machine code and uses a heavily optimized compiler.

The implementation forms the lower-end of the Logix system (Silverman et al., Chapter 21), an FCP program development environment. Logix is in regular use at the Weizmann Institute and several other places. It has been used to develop several applications, including the Logix system itself, whose total size exceeds 30,000 lines of FCP source code at the time of writing the paper.

38.2 Language Description

This section provides a brief description of the language syntax and informal semantics.

38.2.1 Definitions

An FCP *clause* is a guarded Horn clause of the form:

$$H \leftarrow G_1, G_2, \ldots G_n \mid B_1, B_2, \ldots, B_m \qquad m, n \geq 0.$$

Where H is the *head* of the clause, each G_i is a system defined test called a *guard* and each B_i is a general *body goal*.

An FCP *program* is a finite set of clauses.

An FCP *term* is either a variable or a structure. A *variable* is a single assignment variable which may have two types of occurrences: a *writable* occurrence by which the variable can be assigned and a *read-only* occurrence that cannot be used for assigning the variable.

A *structure* is either a *constant* or a *compound* structure which is a composition of terms.

38.2.2 Semantics

An informal operational semantics for FCP is described in (Shapiro, Chapter 5). A general overview follows.

Each state of the computation consists of a multiset of processes which form the resolvent and a program.

A possible state transition involves rewriting *some* process from the resolvent using *some* clause of the program. Rewriting a process using a clause consists of the following operations:

(a) Unifying the process with the head of the clause.

(b) Evaluating the guards with respect to terms in the goal.

(c) After the unification and guard evaluation succeed, the process is replaced in the resolvent by the processes in the body of the clause, and variables in the resolvent are assigned in accordance with the unifying substitution.

The language employs read-only unification as the basic operation. Read-only unification is an extension of standard unification to read-only variables. The read-only unification of two terms containing read-only variables can either succeed, fail, or suspend. A suspended unification may succeed or fail later, as new bindings are produced by concurrently executing unifications. For a full definition of read-only unification see (Shapiro, Chapter 5; Silverman et al., Chapter 21).

A *success* state is a state in which the resolvent is empty.

A *deadlock* state is a state in which no reduction transition is possible.

A *failure* state is a terminal state reached when a failing process is encountered.

The computation is just hence when a process is continuously enabled it will be eventually reduced.

No order is imposed on the processes to be reduced; thus computation proceeds by nondeterministic process selection. If there are independently reducible goals, this nondeterminism enables the reduction of processes in parallel; the resolvent may be regarded as *And-parallel*. In addition, all attempts to perform rewriting using a clause may be carried out in any arbitrary order; thus clause selection is based on *Or-nondeterministic* choice.

38.3 Abstract Machine Concepts

The abstract machine description is derived below from the semantic properties of the language, and its basic properties are outlined.

38.3.1 Realizing non-deterministic process selection

The set of active processes is realized by a queue of processes. Nondeterministic process selection can be realized by a number of process reduction attempts. Each reduction attempt may have one of three possible outcomes:

- success — The process is replaced in the process queue by the clause body.

- suspension — The process should be retried later.

- failure — The process can never be reduced. The abstract machine enters a terminal failure state.

The abstract machine cannot guess which processes can reduce in a given state thus the first process in the queue is dequeued and a reduction attempt is made. If the process cannot be reduced at this point it can be enqueued again and tried later. This scheme, called busy waiting, achieves the correct behavior but is inefficient.

To avoid processes from being repeatedly dequeued and enqueued to the process queue a suspension mechanism is used. When a reduction attempt suspends, the process is associated with the variables whose instantiation can cause it to succeed later. Upon instantiation of any of these variables the process is enqueued to the process queue.

The abstract machine does not handle process failure. A method for containing and handling process failure within FCP is described by Hirsch et al. (Chapter 20).

38.3.2 Realizing non-deterministic clause selection

Non-deterministic clause selection can be achieved by any arbitrary clause try sequence. For simplicity the clauses are tried in textual order. Upon success of any clause try the process commits and the clause body is enqueued to the process queue. When a clause try is unsuccessful no changes to the global environment should be made. This is achieved by recording global changes in a stack called the *trail*; upon suspension or failure of a clause try the trail is used to undo global changes.

38.3.3 Tail recursion optimization

Upon commitment of a reduction attempt to one of the clauses, the process record of the committed process becomes available for reuse; moreover, the execution may proceed with any one of the processes being spawned. Instead of enqueuing the process to the process queue, execution may proceed with some chosen process. This scheme reduces process switching and process record management. To ensure the justice of the scheduling policy the number of times that this optimization can be employed must be bounded. A *time slice* is used to bound the number of times this optimization is employed. When a process is dequeued from the process queue its time slice is initialized to a compiler constant. The time slice is decremented each time the execution iterates and when the time slice is exhausted (i.e., becomes zero) the tail recursion optimization is not carried out; instead, the process is enqueued into the process queue.

The above optimization leads to a bounded depth-first control strategy. The method is particularly useful for tight iterative loops since process switching does not impact their efficiency, and process reduction can be implemented by a simple *goto*.

38.3.4 Clause encoding

Each clause in the source program is individually encoded by the compiler into a sequence of abstract machine instructions. The code corresponding to a single clause contains two parts: the *clause try* and *body spawning*; the later is executed upon commitment.

Clause try

Each clause try consists of instructions which perform unification of the process with the head of the clause and calls for each guard test, similar to Warren (1983). The instructions are extended to implement read-only unification. If a read-only unification suspends, the address of the first variable it suspends upon is stored in the suspension table, and the clause try fails. Upon failure of all the clause tries, the process is suspended if the suspension table is not empty, and fails if it is.

Unification is a recursive algorithm that executes operations corresponding to different data states. Part of the execution of the algorithm is known at compile-time due to the clause structure. This knowledge is used to advantage by encoding unification instructions at compile-time instead of interpreting data-structures at run-time. This leads to a view of the execution as a tree whose vertices are known; unknown parts of the execution tree occur at the leaves. Figure 38.1 shows the tree of operations which must be carried out in order to unify the clause head $p(\{f,X\}^1, \{g,Y,X\})$ with a goal.

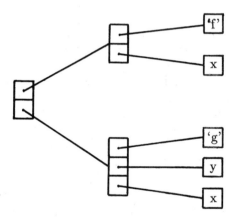

Figure 38.1: A tree of unification operations

A depth-first walk on the tree of execution can be flattened to produce a sequence of abstract machine instructions. Each node of the tree corresponds to one or more instructions that execute the needed operation of the unification algorithm. Thus the known part of the unification algorithm is executed by using static structures rather than using dynamic stack. The needed operations are implicitly encoded in the abstract machine instructions and need not be analyzed at run-time. Figure 38.2 illustrates the depth-first walk on the execution tree.

---

[1] Note that *tuples* rather then *functors* are used to represent compound terms, thus the term $f(X_1,X_2,\ldots,X_n)$ is equivalent to $\{f,X_1,X_2,\ldots,X_n\}$.

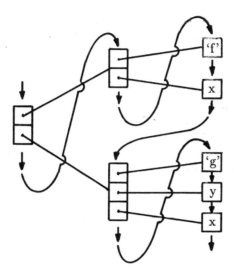

Figure 38.2: Depth-first traversal of the unification tree

Flattening the tree of execution must preserve the mode in which the unification operations are executed. Each vertex in the tree (instruction in the sequence) can be reached either when structures needed previously were available in the global environment (*read-mode*) or when a variable was encountered (*write-mode*). In the former case the instruction is executed in read-mode which causes it to analyze the global data. In the latter case a variable assignment has been carried out previously; thus the instruction is carried out in write-mode causing structures corresponding to the clause structure to be allocated. The clause structure is implicitly encoded in the instructions.

Body spawning

The abstract instructions for spawning of the clause body may perform some combination of the following operations:

- Allocate a process record.
- Create process arguments.
- Enqueue a process into the process queue.
- Iterate on one of the body processes if the time slice is not exhausted.
- Halt the execution of the current process and return control to the scheduler.

38.3.5 Module system

To facilitate a distributed implementation of the language, global data objects such as a global symbol table or a global code area were avoided. Instead, each program is represented as a single unit containing all the data needed for its execution, called a *module*. Since there is no central symbol table, string comparison may need to be carried during unification. Due to the use of a hash code in a string representation, the resulting overhead is negligible.

Different modules should be able to communicate and execute remote procedure calls. The machine supports a module system (Safra, 1986) which provides this functionality. The module system is viewed as a set of communicating code segments. The approach taken is to handle the different aspects of the module system at the language level where possible. A design decision was made to utilize the inherent stream communication mechanism of FCP, and use incomplete messages (Shapiro, Chapter 2) between modules to implement remote procedure calls. When a module is activated, an associated process, called the *module manager*, is spawned, and is given two streams; an input stream for incoming requests and an output stream for requests to other modules. A convention was adopted that the procedure for the module manager is the first procedure of the module; its code is produced automatically by the compiler.

The module manager can easily handle input procedure calls by recognizing messages on the input stream and calling the appropriate local procedures. For each procedure with name p and arity n in the module which does not perform, directly or indirectly, remote procedure calls, the module manager includes one clause:

$$\text{module\_manager}([p(X_1,X_2,\ldots,X_n)|\text{In}],\text{Out}) \leftarrow$$
$$p(X_1,X_2,\ldots,Xn),$$
$$\text{module\_manager}(\text{In?},\text{Out}).$$

Remote procedure calls are handled by merging them onto the module manager's output stream. The above method enables the programming environment to organize inter-module communication simply by merging and distributing the appropriate streams to various modules. This methodology is incorporated in the Logix system.

The above scheme differentiates between the *code* of a module and its *activation*. The module code is a special data structure representing the compiled program. An activation is an abstract notion corresponding to the set of processes whose code resides in the module. The module code is a result of the compilation process and does not represent an active object. The system defined call *activate* accepts as its arguments a module and two streams for input and output; it spawns a process which inherits these arguments and whose procedure is the first procedure of the module.

To show the elegance of this solution consider an operating system. Modules may be compiled and debugged; due to the chosen representation modules can be replaced without a need for complex linking operations. The processes of a module activation continue running with the code of the old module but the streams can be redirected to the new module when replaced. All these operations can be written in the language and do not require additional support in the abstract machine. When the system closes the input stream of a module activation and all its processes terminate, the module's code is garbage collected automatically.

The viability of this approach is shown also in a parallel implementation of the language, where code management is a much more complex problem. The ability to define in the language processes that maintain and activate code in each processor and communicate code between processors is an essential basis for the code management mechanisms described in (Taylor et al., Chapter 22).

38.4 Abstract Machine Implementation

38.4.1 Execution algorithms and structures

The main loop of the execution proceeds in the following steps:

(1) The first process in the process queue is dequeued and a reduction attempt is made by trying the clauses in the associated procedure one after another.

(2) If a clause try succeeds the clause body is enqueued into the process queue and any processes that were suspended on variables which have been changed are woken up. If a clause try fails the variables that the process needs to be suspended upon are recorded in the suspension table and the next clause is tried.

(3) If all clause tries fail the process is suspended on the variables recorded in the suspension table. If the table is empty when trying to suspend a process, the abstract machine enters a terminal failure state.

The compiler generates abstract instructions which perform the correct control for the clause tries as explained in Appendix 38.6.

Processes

A process record is a compound structure containing the following:

- The address of a procedure.

- The arguments of the process.

- A reference to the next process record in the process queue.

The procedure address corresponds to a saved program counter, and the process arguments correspond to saved registers of conventional operating system processes. In a direct implementation of the abstract machine this correspondence can be used to advantage, especially if the process model of the underlying processor and that of the abstract machine are similar.

Read-only unification

Recall from the semantics of the language that at unification time writing on a writable variable and reading its corresponding read-only variable cannot be done at the same unification. Hence a read-only variable has to be distinct from its corresponding writable variable, and the fact that a writable variable has been instantiated should not be observable from its read-only counterpart prior to the completion of the unification.

A pair of writable and read-only variables are represented as two distinct data-objects, whose type is *writable* and *read-only*, respectively. The writable variable contains the address of its counterpart read-only variable, if it has been allocated, otherwise it is null. The read-only variable points, indirectly, to the processes suspended on it, as explained below. The following diagram illustrates the representation of a pair of writable and read-only variables. Note that the writable variable can not be accessed from its read-only counterpart, a fact which might be useful when we are concerned with security.

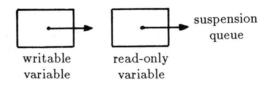

Figure 38.3: A pair of writable and read-only variables

During unification writable variables are instantiated and this fact is trailed. Only if the unification completes, the clause commits and the read-only variables are bound to the value that their corresponding writable variables were bound to. This is done by scanning the trail.

Suspension queues

Processes suspend upon a set of variables waiting for one of them to be instantiated. More than one process may suspend on a single variable. When any variable is instantiated all the processes suspended on it must be woken up, i.e., enqueued to the process queue. In order to perform these operations, suspension notes are used to record which processes have suspended on a given variable. These suspension notes are held as a suspension queue, the most recently suspended process first. A pointer to the beginning of the suspension queue is associated with the read-only variable. When a note is added it is placed at the start of the suspension queue and the pointer is updated.

A process may attempt to reduce more then once, and each reduction attempt may suspend on some variables. When a process is woken up due to the instantiation of a variable, a mechanism is required to ensure that the process is not rewoken when any of the other variables are instantiated. This is achieved by a level of indirection from a suspension note to a process. All the suspension notes for a single reduction attempt point to a pointer, called a *hanger*, which points to the actual process. When a process is woken up via a suspension note the hanger is nulled. Subsequent attempts to wake up the process via this hanger perform no operation.

Figure 38.4 illustrates how a process is suspended on two variables.

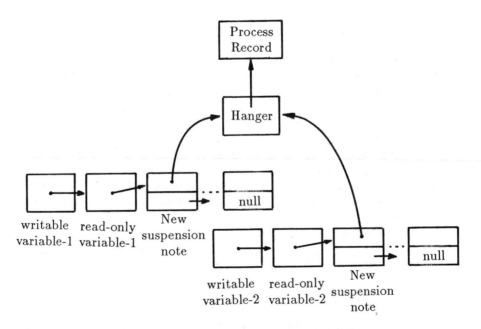

Figure 38.4: Suspending a process on two variables

In a single reduction attempt different clause tries may cause suspension on the same variable. If a note is produced for each entry in the suspension table, more than one note to the same process may be associated with the same variable. This scheme is correct but producing multiple notes is inefficient both in time and in space. To prevent the same reduction attempt from producing multiple notes on the same variable, the first element of a suspension queue is inspected before adding a new note to the list. If this note references the same hanger as the suspension note about to be added, no operation is carried out. Thus no duplicate notes for a single reduction attempt can occur in a single suspension queue.

When a clause try succeeds, suspended processes need to be woken up. All writable variables which have been instantiated during the clause try are recorded in the trail and thus their corresponding read-only variables and their suspension queues are accessible. By scanning the trail at commit time the values of read-only variables are updated to those of their corresponding writable ones, and the necessary process activations are carried out. The order of processes in a suspension queue is the reverse of the order in which they were suspended. At the time of activation, the suspension queue is enqueued in reverse order to the active queue. Hence the most recently suspended processes are enqueued last.

Free lists

When a process is reduced, tail recursion optimization is carried out and the process record is reused for one of the body goals. If the body of the clause is empty the process halts, and the record cannot be reused. A free list of process records is maintained and the process record is added to this free list. When a process record needs to be allocated for a newly created process, the free list is checked and if it is non-empty a process record from the free list is used. If the free list is empty a new process record is allocated from the heap. For efficiency all process records are of identical size, and there is one process free list. Some processes may require more arguments then available in the process record; they are transformed by the compiler to conform to the bound. Since structures are used to hold the extra arguments, tail recursion optimization on such processes may be less effective.

The same technique is used for allocation of suspension records. This scheme reduces the number of process records and suspension records allocated from the heap and thus reduces the frequency of garbage collection.

38.4.2 Heap and registers

All system runtime structures are constructed from tagged data objects thus there is no need to allocate runtime structures from separate areas. A single data area, the *heap*, is used for terms, programs and processes. The heap grows when objects are allocated, and shrinks only by garbage collection.

In addition to the heap, two data structures are required to support run time algorithms: the *trail* and the *suspension table*. The trail is a stack which is empty at the beginning of a clause try. When a heap word is changed an entry containing the address of the word and its previous value is pushed onto the trail. If the clause try fails the trailed changes are undone, resetting the global environment to its previous state. The suspension table is empty at the beginning of a process try and when a clause try needs the value of a variable to proceed, the writable or the read-only variable is added to the suspension table.

The current state of the machine is defined by the contents of its heap, trail, suspension table and registers. The registers can be divided into three groups according to the time in which their value is significant:

- The general registers which are significant throughout all the machine's operation.

- The process try registers which are significant only during a reduction attempt.

- The clause try registers which are significant only during a clause try.

General registers

HB Heap Backtrack, contains the value of the top of the heap prior to a process try.

HP Heap Pointer, points at the current top of the heap.

QF Queue Front, points at the first process in the process queue.

QB Queue Back, points at the last process in the process queue.

PFL Process Free List, the address of the first process in the process free list, or null.

SFL Suspension Free List, the address of the first suspension note in the suspension free list, or null.

Process try registers

CP Current Process, points at the process currently being tried.

TS Time Slice, the remaining number of times that the current process may use tail recursion optimization.

PC Program Counter, the address of the next instruction to be executed.

STP Suspension Table Pointer, points at the top of the suspension table.

Clause try registers

FL Failure Label, the address of the instruction to branch to in case of failure of the clause try.

TRP TRail Pointer, points at the top of the trail.

A   Argument pointer, points at an argument of a process or of a guard. This register is used by the *get* and *put* instructions.

SP   Structure Pointer, points at an argument of a compound structure. This register is used by the *unify* instructions.

Mode   Mode register, can specify either *read* or *write* mode. This register is used by the *unify* instructions.

X_i X registers, a set of temporary registers used for holding intermediate values during a clause try.

38.4.3 Garbage collection

Since FCP programs tend to generate a large amount of garbage relative to the amount of useful data, stop-and-copy garbage collection (Mierowsky et al., 1985) is used in the machine. Even though stop-and-copy requires two heaps for its operation it is more suitable for the machine since its complexity is linear with respect to the useful data rather then the total memory.

Since the machine can access data only through processes residing in the process queue the only data which need to be copied is that accessible from the current process and the process queue. Both free lists are discarded when a garbage collection is started. Any suspension note whose hanger is null is not copied.

Processes which are suspended only on inaccessible variables are not copied during garbage collection. By maintaining a count of the number of existing processes and comparing it with the number of processes that are copied during garbage collection it is possible to detect if processes are lost. As mentioned before, unreferenced code is also garbage collected; no special code-management mechanism is necessary to support interactive program development.

38.5 Encoding

The encoding scheme follows largely that of Warren (1983). Since there is no backtracking, no environments should be handled and the encoding of a clause becomes much simpler. Indexing instructions were not implemented as well.

38.5.1 Encoding scheme

This section provides an overview of the encoding scheme; the set of abstract instructions is described in the following section.

Procedure encoding

The code for a procedure is a sequence of abstract instructions. When a clause try fails execution should proceed in the next clause try. This is achieved by the instruction *try_me_else Failure_Label*; when the clause try following the instruction fails execution proceeds from *Failure_Label*.

Upon failure of all the clause tries, the process is to be suspended on the variables in the suspension table. After the last clause try of a procedure a *suspend* instruction is planted to suspend the process. The failure-label of the last clause refers to this instruction.

P: (label of the procedure)
        try_me_else C2
        (code for first clause)
C2:

        try_me_else C3
        (code for second clause)

        . . .

Cn:

        try_me_else S:
        (code for last clause)
S:

        suspend

Clause encoding

The code for a single clause try is constructed from abstract instructions for head unification and guard execution, followed by instructions for commit and spawning of the body processes.

A clause is encoded as followed:

        (code for head unification and guard execution)
        commit
        (code for body spawn)

Head unification

Recall the unification algorithm presented in Section 38.3. Flattening of the execution tree could be carried out using a stack of pairs. Each pair corresponds to an argument in the clause and an argument in the goal which is to be unified. Apart from the values of bound variables, flattened structure is known at compile-time; as a result a stack is not required but rather a set of registers can be used to hold values and pointers to the arguments. Since the data type of the clause argument is also known at compile-time the clause part of the pair can be omitted and can be represented by different abstract instructions.

Some optimizations can be carried out before the final encoding. When a constant appears in the clause, the goal argument would be pushed onto the stack and later popped either to match or assign a goal variable. These push and pop operations can be carried out together and encoded into a single instruction. When a variable appears in the clause which does not require general unification the operation succeeds trivially thus can be omitted.

The following primitive instruction types, form the basic operations on the above stack and encode the structure of the data required. The dynamic stack is replaced by the set of X_i registers and the goal argument is pointed to by an argument register which is advanced upon a successful completion of the instruction.

compound Arity

Corresponds to a pop of the stack and match or assignment of a compound structure.

constant Value

Corresponds to a match or assignment of a constant.

var X_i

Corresponds to push onto the stack of an argument.

val X_i

Corresponds to general unification for subsequent occurrences of a variable in a clause.

ro_var X_i

Corresponds to push onto the stack of an argument when the clause argument is a read-only variable.

ro_val X_i

Corresponds to general unification for subsequent occurrences of a variable in a clause when annotated read-only.

The abstract machine uses more than one instruction for each of the above primitive instruction types. The different instructions correspond to the primitive data types in the language (See Appendices 38.1 and 38.3). In addition different instructions are used to distinguish the first and subsequent levels in the execution tree.

There are two types of head instructions: *get* and *unify*. Unify instructions correspond to the actions that would normally be executed by the unification algorithm and may thus execute in either read or write mode. The get instructions occur only at the first level of the head structure and thus always operate in read mode.

Most clause heads have some compound structure as an argument. Pushing and popping the argument at this level would have been an overhead. In order to avoid this overhead a different argument register is used by the get instructions. Thus the encoding of a compound structure appearing at the first level of the head is a *get_compound* instruction immediately followed by the unify instructions for its arguments.

The encoding of the arguments of the clause head $p(f(X, X?),X)$ is:

```
get_compound 3
unify_constant 'f'      % f
unify_var Xn            % X
unify_ro_val Xn         % X?
get_val Xn              % X
```

A nested compound structure is encoded by a *push X_i* instruction which loads the mode on which the current sequence of unify instructions operate and the continuation of the current compound structure into the X_i register. A corresponding *pop X_i*, following the next unify sequence, will get the mode and continuation of the current compound structure, enabling the current sequence of unify instructions to continue. Thus the encoding of the arguments of the clause head $p(f(1, f(X?), X),1)$ is:

```
get_compound 4
unify_constant 'f'      % f
unify_constant 1        % 1
push Xm                 % (save ",X)")
unify_compound 2
unify_constant 'f'      % f
unify_ro_var Xn         % X?
pop Xm                  % (load ",X)")
unify_val Xn            % X
get_constant 1          % 1
```

Note that when the nested compound structure is the last argument of the current compound structure there is no need to save the continuation, thus the pop and push instructions are not needed.

Argument creation

An argument creation in the guard or in the body of the clause cannot be executed in read-mode. Thus another type of argument instruction *put* is added which corresponds to the operation of the unify instructions in write-mode. The justification for having these instructions explicitly is similar to that of get instructions. The put and get instructions use the same argument register for their operation. The put instructions also correspond to the arguments in the first level of the clause. The instructions for creating the arguments for the goal $q(a,g(1,\ g(X)))$ are:

```
put_constant 'a'        % a
put_compound 3
unity_constant 'g'      % g
unify_constant 1        % 1
unify_compound 2
unify_constant 'g'      % g
unify_var Xn            % X
```

Guard

The encoding of a guard call is composed of two parts: creating the arguments for the guard and an instruction which calls the guard.

In order to enable optimizations of the arguments allocation for a guard, the X registers are used for transferring arguments to the guard. If the arguments the guard needs have already been loaded into X registers, no arguments allocation is needed.

Two additional instructions are used for guard encoding: *set* X_i sets the argument register to the X_i register. The following put and unify instructions will create arguments starting at X_i. The actual call to the guard is carried out by the *call Index, Args* instruction where *Index* is the guard's internal number and *Args* is a list of X registers which refer to the arguments for the guard. The encoding of the clause $p(X,Y) \leftarrow guard(Y,X) \mid q(X,Y).$ is:

```
try_me_else Label
get_var X0              % X
get_var X1              % Y
call Index X1 X0
commit
(code for body)
```

The encoding of the clause $p(X,Y) \leftarrow guard(1,X,Y) \mid true.$ is:

```
try_me_else Label
get_var X0              % X
get_var X1              % Y
set X2                  % start creating arguments for the guard.
put_constant 1
call Index X2 X0 X1
commit
halt
```

Body

An empty body is encoded into a single instruction called *halt*; this instruction frees the current process record for future use and returns control to the scheduler. A non-empty body is encoded to do the following operations:

- Allocate process records for body goals.

- Create the arguments for each process.

- Enqueue the body processes into the process queue.

- Iterate on one of the body processes if the time slice is not exhausted.

The allocation and enqueuing of new processes is carried out by the *spawn* instruction. The creation of arguments is carried out by the put and unify instructions. Since the current process record is used for tail recursion optimization there is no need to allocate a process record for the iterated goal. By convention this is the first goal in the body. The commit instruction is followed by the instructions which create arguments for the first goal in the body. The last instruction in the encoding of a non-empty body is an *execute* or *iterate* instruction which tries to iterate on the first body goal.

The body of a general clause is encoded as follows:

(code for args of first goal)	% put arguments of the first % goal in the current process.
spawn $Proc_2$	% $Proc_2$ is the procedure of % the second goal.
(code for args of second goal)	% put arguments % of second goal in the process.
...	
spawn $Proc_n$	% $Proc_n$ is the procedure for % the last goal.
(code for args of last goal) execute $Proc_1$	% $Proc_1$ is the procedure for % the first goal.

38.5.2 Abstract instructions

The abstract instruction set can be divided into four types: *clause* (or *indexing*), *argument*, *guard* and *process*. A description of each type of instruction is given below.

Clause (indexing) instructions

Clause instructions are concerned with the flow of control through a procedure. Currently there is only one clause instruction "*try_me_else Label*". The code section following this instruction corresponds to a clause try. Upon failure of the clause try execution proceeds at the point labeled by *Label*. More clause instructions can be added as in (Warren, 1983) to perform clause selection according to the arguments of a process.

Argument instructions

The argument instructions are used for two purposes: execution of the known part of the unification algorithm and allocation of data structures. For the verification of the global data state *get* and *unify* instructions are used. Allocation of arguments of processes and guards is performed using *put* and *unify* instructions. The data structure to be verified or allocated is implicitly encoded into the different instructions. The get and put instructions use the A register which refers to the arguments of the process record while the unify instructions use the SP register which refers to general data structures. Each of the argument instructions increments the register it uses upon successful completion. Some of the instructions explicitly use the set of X registers to write or read values.

There are two main differences in the format of the argument instructions between Warren's instructions and ours. The first is the use of an implicit argument register A for the put and the get instructions instead of using a set of explicit argument registers (A_i) in Warren's instructions. The other difference is the use of the *push* and *pop* instructions for the encoding of nested substructures.

Since most of the instructions are similar to those of Warren, their explicit description is omitted. Only the completely new instructions are shown:

get_ro_var X_i

> This instruction encodes the first occurrence of a variable in the clause when annotated read-only. If the argument given by A contains a writeable variable, that variable is bound to a read-only variable while X_i is set to its writable counterpart. Otherwise, the argument given by A is stored in X_i.

get_ro_val X_i

> This instruction encodes subsequent occurrences of a variable when annotated read-only. General unification is applied with the read-only counter part of this variable and the current argument.

put_ro_var X_i

> This instruction encodes the first occurrence of a variable in the clause when annotated read-only. A new writeable variable is allocated; A reference to it is stored in X_i while a reference to its read-only counterpart is stored in the argument referenced by A.

put_ro_value X_i

This instruction encodes subsequent occurrences of a variable in the clause when annotated read-only. If the argument given by X_i is a writable variable its read-only counterpart is stored in the argument referenced by A. Otherwise a reference to the argument given by X_i is stored in the argument given by A.

push X_i

This instruction starts the encoding of a nested substructure. The state in which the next unify instruction would have operated is saved in the X_i register. This state consists of the value of the *SP* register incremented by one and the value of the *Mode* register which is either read or write.

pop X_i

This instruction ends the encoding of a nested substructure and it corresponds to a previous push instruction. The state of the higher sequence of unify instructions is loaded from the X_i register.

set X_i

This instruction starts the creation of arguments such that they will be referred by a consecutive X registers starting at X_i. The A register is initialized to X_i. Recall that the put instructions will create arguments at the place pointed to by the A register.

Guard instruction

The guard instruction provides the mechanism for calling a guard. The instruction is:

call Index, Args

Call the guard procedure whose internal number is *Index* and its arguments are the X registers specified by *Args*.

Process instructions

The process instructions correspond to the possible outcomes of a process try. The instructions are:

commit

Commit to the current clause; this instruction appears after the instructions for the head and guards of the clause. The instruction scans the trail while binding read-only variables to the value of their bounded writable counterparts and activates suspended processes which are reachable from the trail. In addition tail recursion optimization is employed and the current process record is prepared for reuse.

spawn Proc

This instruction creates a process record and enqueues it to the process queue. The procedure that is attached to this process is indicated by *Proc*. In addition the *A* register is initialized such that the following put and unify instructions will create the arguments of the process.

execute Proc

This instruction iterates on the procedure indicated by *Proc* if the time-slice is not exhausted. Otherwise the current process is enqueued to the process queue and control is given back to the scheduler.

iterate

This instruction is similar to the execute instruction but iterates on the procedure of the current process.

halt

This instruction halts the execution of the current process. The process record is freed for future use. Control is given back to the scheduler.

suspend

This instruction is executed when all the clause tries fail. The process is suspended on all the variables in the suspension table and control is given back to the scheduler. If the suspension table is empty, the machine enters a terminal failure state.

38.6 Data Objects

In representing data objects we have used the method of *tagged objects* rather than *tagged pointers* used by the Warren abstract machine. The difference between the two is implied by their name, in tagged pointers the tag which tells the type of the data object is stored in a pointer to the data object while in tagged objects the tag is stored with the object itself.

Detailed description of the various data objects is given in Appendix 38.1. Here we describe only the important points.

38.6.1 Strings

Strings are consecutive bytes of memory. There are several types of strings: character strings, modules, procedures, and frozen terms. A module is the result of compiling an FCP program and it contains a series of smaller strings which correspond to procedures, character strings, and frozen terms in the program. A procedure may appear only within a module and it represents the encoding of a single procedure in the program. A frozen term is the result of freezing an FCP term (Nakashima et al., 1984).

During a computation many string unifications are carried out, in particular clause selection is often based on the value of a string argument. Strings created at run time may cause redundant string unifications since they may be equal to existing strings. To avoid this overhead the following method is used.

When comparing two strings, the machine checks that the two strings are not from the same module. Since strings in a module are unique, two strings from the same module are known to be different. If the strings are not from the same module, the hash and the length of the two strings are compared before comparing the characters. This method saves full string comparisons in most of the cases where the strings are different.

After two strings are compared and found identical, if one of the strings is a "free" string (not within a module) this string becomes a reference to the other string. In this way redundant occurrences of strings are canceled and time and space are saved.

38.6.2 Tuples and lists

The machine uses two main types of compound objects for representing compound terms, namely *tuples* and *lists*. Tuples are used for representing a finite compound object as $a(b)$ or $\{X, Y\}$ while lists represent a list of terms which is not always of a bounded length.

There are two important things to mention about tuples and lists: unification and car-coding.

Unification

When unifying two compound objects (tuples or list-cells) the machine starts the unification by changing the first word of one of the compound objects to a reference to the other. There are two reasons why this is done:

(1) The space of the compound object is saved when garbage collection occurs.

(2) Since the occur check is not performed during unification, circular terms may be created. The method proposed avoids infinite loops when unifying two circular terms.

Car-coding

Lists and streams are used often in FCP, therefore optimizations of list representation and manipulation is very important. In this implementation a method called *car*-coding is used in order to reduce the space needed for list representation. This method is the tagged-object counterpart of the *cdr*-coding technique found in tagged-pointer implementations of Lisp.

In *car*-coding the tag of the list-cell is condensed into the tag of the *car*, saving one heap word for each list cell. Furthermore, since the *cdr* is generally a reference to another list-cell this next list-cell is put at the place where the *cdr* would have been. This method can be applied inductively. Hence, the list $[1,2,3]$ can be represented by four consecutive heap words (the fourth is [ ]) instead of using three separate list-cells.

Lists can be created using separate *car*-coded list-cells and be condensed at garbage collection. Condensed lists can also be created by recursive procedures which produce only one list-cell at every iteration. For example:

merge([X|Xs],Ys,[X|Zs]) ← merge(Ys?, Xs?,Zs).
merge(Xs,[Y|Ys],[Y|Zs]) ← merge(Ys?, Xs?,Zs).

Since *merge* iterates during its time-slice, and allocates only one list-cell per reduction, the list-cell created by the previous reduction is at the top of the heap; the variable *Zs* will be its *cdr*. Checking whether a variable is at the top of the heap before instantiating it to a new list-cell enables the machine to create the list-cell at the location of the variable itself instead of instantiating the variable to a reference to the list-cell. Hence the sublist created by *merge* during one time slice is condensed.

In addition to condensing lists cells, this scheme allows any one word object, including variables, to be an immediate argument of a tuple. Furthermore any data object can appear as the last argument of a tuple or as the *cdr* of a list cell.

38.7 Performance

Appendix 38.5 contains a number of performance measurements and compares the results to that of Quintus Prolog (Quintus, 1985). Although slower in absolute terms, FCP has not undergone the extensive optimizations used in the Quintus implementation. In addition, the emulator is written in C rather than assembly language. Quintus Prolog is one of the faster commercially available Prolog compilers; the results demonstrate that the FCP compiler is both practical and efficient despite its simplicity. The benchmarks were run on a VAX-11/750.

The results indicate that Quintus Prolog is at best four times faster than the FCP emulator. In more complex Prolog programs the speedup is much smaller, unless a cut is used in every Prolog clause.

In absolute terms, the emulator achieves a speed of 2K LIPS (logical inferences, or reductions per second) on the standard naive reverse benchmark. On real life programs the average speed is much smaller, about 500 LIPS. Iteration of an empty procedure

p ← p.

achieves a peak performance of 10K LIPS. Iterative process spawning, defined by

p ← q, p.
q.

runs at a rate of 5K LIPS, generating about 2500 processes per second.

The entire FCP compiler, including the tokenizer, parser, code generator and assembler are written in FCP. It compiles about 100 line of source code per CPU minute. During the compilation of 100 lines of code, about 10,000 processes are created, and 30,000 process reductions occur.

More detailed measurements of the cost of different operations are yet to be carried.

38.8 Future research

The main drawback of the instruction set defined is that each clause must be compiled individually. Better performance can be achieved if all clause tries of a procedure are compiled as one unit, into a decision tree. Such a compiler is being developed presently (Kliger, 1987).

Another direction pursued is the parallel implementation of the language (Taylor et al., Chapter 39). The abstract machine described is extended to execute in each processor in a parallel implementation. It must preserve the atomicity of process reduction in spite of the environment being distributed across several memories, and allow several processors to attempt to reduce simultaneously.

38.9 Conclusions

The abstract machine described in this paper uses a similar approach to that of Warren (1977) in compiling Prolog. The instruction set for FCP uses a number of the Warren instructions to compile unification but enhances them to handle read-only variables. Additional instructions are required, and have been described, to handle process control and execution of guard predicates.

Although it would appear that due to the overhead for suspending and activating processes, FCP is less efficient then Prolog, this is not the case, as it is compensated for by the lack of backtracking in the language. There is no need to keep backtrack information, and it is not necessary to maintain two different global areas (i.e., heap and stack).

The methods used to compile FCP are of general interest and can be applied to other concurrent logic programming languages. Some of the ideas in this work have already been applied to the compilation of Guarded Horn Clauses (Ueda, Chapter 4) by Levy (1986).

The methods described have been used to provide the first efficient and practical implementation of a concurrent logic programming language.

Acknowledgements

The design of the abstract machine and the implementation of its emulator were part of a group project, and ideas of many are incorporated in this work. We would like to thank Jim Crammond, Michael Hirsch, Jacob Levy, Colin Mierowsky, William Silverman, and Steve Taylor for their contributations in general, and Shmuel Safra's contribution to the idea of modules in particular. Shmuel, Steve, and Michael Codish helped with the organization and the writing of this paper.

Appendix 38.1: Data Types

FCP data objects are represented as words in memory. The tag of the object is stored in the six least significant bits of its first word. Objects can be atomic or compound.

The following is a BNF definition of FCP data-objects:

⟨data-object⟩ = ⟨atomic-object⟩ | ⟨compound-object⟩.

<u>Atomic objects</u>

⟨atomic-object⟩ =
    ⟨reference⟩ |
    ⟨writable⟩ |
    ⟨read-only⟩ |
    ⟨integer⟩ |
    ⟨real⟩ |
    ⟨string⟩.
    ⟨nil⟩.

<u>Reference</u>

⟨reference⟩ = ⟨address⟩⟨ref⟩.

The reference is used as a general reference to other data objects.

<u>Writable variable</u>

⟨writable⟩ = ⟨address⟩⟨var⟩.

The address is null if the corresponding read-only variable has not been allocated. Otherwise, it is the address of the read-only variable.

Read-only variable

> ⟨read-only⟩ = ⟨address⟩⟨ro⟩.

The address is null if the read-only variable does not have a suspension queue. Otherwise, it is the address of the last suspension note which was entered to the queue.

Integer

> ⟨integer⟩ = ⟨integer-value⟩⟨int⟩.

An integer-value is negative if its left most bit is set. Sign extension can be used to create the full negative value.

Real

> ⟨real-object⟩ =
>   ⟨zero-value⟩⟨real⟩
>   ⟨real-value⟩
>   ⟨real-value⟩

A real-value is composed from two word and its internal representation is machine dependent.

String

> ⟨string⟩ =
>   ⟨string-type⟩⟨string-offset⟩⟨str⟩
>   ⟨string-hash⟩⟨string-length⟩
>   ⟨characters⟩
>   ⟨padding-nulls⟩
>
> ⟨string-type⟩ = 0 ... 15
> ⟨string-offset⟩ = 0 | positive number
> ⟨string-hash⟩ = hash(characters)
> ⟨string-length⟩ = number of characters
> ⟨characters⟩ = ⟨character⟩ | ⟨character⟩⟨characters⟩
> ⟨padding-nulls⟩ = 4 − (string-length mod 4) ⟨zero-bytes⟩

The string-type which consists of 4 bits determines the type of the string. The current types are character string, module, procedure and frozen term. A module is the result of compiling an FCP program, and it contains a series of smaller strings which correspond to procedures, character strings, and frozen terms in the program. A procedure may appear only within a module, and it represents the encoding of a single procedure in the program. A frozen term is the result of freezing an FCP term.

The string-offset is used for garbage collection for deciding whether the referred string is part of a module.

Nil

$$\langle \text{nil} \rangle = \langle \text{null-value} \rangle \langle \text{nil} \rangle.$$

Nil represens the symbol [ ].

Compound objects

$$\langle \text{compound-object} \rangle =$$
$$\langle \text{list-object} \rangle \mid$$
$$\langle \text{tuple-object} \rangle \mid$$
$$\langle \text{vector-object} \rangle.$$

List

$$\langle \text{list-object} \rangle = \langle \text{car} \rangle \langle \text{cdr} \rangle.$$

Lists are time and space optimization. They are used in FCP programs for stream-like structures. They could be represented by a binary tuple but since they are the most heavily used data type they are optimized extensively.

$$\langle \text{car} \rangle =$$
$$\langle \text{car reference} \rangle \mid$$
$$\langle \text{car integer} \rangle \mid$$
$$\langle \text{car nil} \rangle.$$

$$\langle \text{car reference} \rangle = \langle \text{address} \rangle \langle \text{l\_ref} \rangle.$$

$$\langle \text{car integer} \rangle = \langle \text{integer-value} \rangle \langle \text{l\_int} \rangle.$$

$$\langle \text{car nil} \rangle = \langle \text{null-value} \rangle \langle \text{l\_nil} \rangle.$$

$$\langle \text{cdr} \rangle = \langle \text{data-object} \rangle.$$

Any data object can appear as list-cdr and in particular a car.

Tuple

$$\langle \text{tuple-object} \rangle =$$
$$\langle \text{tuple-length} \rangle \langle \text{tpl} \rangle$$
$$\langle \text{tuple-arguments} \rangle.$$

$$\langle \text{tuple-length} \rangle = \text{number of arguments}$$
$$\langle \text{tuple-arguments} \rangle =$$
$$\langle \text{data-object} \rangle \mid$$
$$\langle \text{tuple-argument} \rangle \langle \text{tuple-arguments} \rangle$$
$$\langle \text{tuple-argument} \rangle =$$

⟨reference⟩ |
⟨writable⟩ |
⟨read-only⟩ |
⟨integer⟩ |
⟨nil⟩.

Note that $f(X)$ and $\{f, X\}$ both have the same representation which is a tuple of arity 2. Any data object can appear as the last argument of a tuple.

Vector

⟨vector-object⟩ =
  ⟨vector-length⟩⟨vctr⟩
  ⟨vector-arguments⟩.

⟨vector-length⟩ = number of arguments
⟨vector-arguments⟩ =
  ⟨vector-argument⟩ |
  ⟨vector-argument⟩⟨vector-arguments⟩
⟨vector-argument⟩ =
  ⟨reference⟩ |
  ⟨integer⟩ |
  ⟨nil⟩.

The third type of compound data object, used internally by the machine, is called *vector*. It is used for representing finite compound objects and is similar in structure to tuples. However a vector cannot contain variables, which are address dependent objects, as an immediate argument. Vectors are used for representing data structures such as process records, hangers, and mutual-references (Shapiro and Safra, Chapter 15). These data structures can be destructively changed during the computation, and hence cannot be condensed like tuples.

Appendix 38.2: Bootstrap and Control Flow of the Machine

Conventions

If R is a register, then $*R$ is the value of the memory location pointed by R.
beginning_of_heap, *boot*, *null*, *time_slice*, *trail*, and *suspension_table*, are emulator constants. $pc\_of(PR){=}PR{+}1$, $next\_of(PR){=}PR{+}2$, $args\_of(PR){=}PR{+}3$ are addresses of words inside the process record with address PR.

Utility procedures

The following procedures are used in the machine description:

procedure Enqueue(Process)
    if QF=null
           % process queue is empty
    then QF:=QB:=Process
           % initialize queue to contain the new process
    else *next_of(QB):=Process; QB:=Process
           % add new process to the process queue

procedure Dequeue
    if QF=null
           % process queue is empty
    then stop
           % stop the machine
    else
        CP:=QF
           % current process is first process
        QF:=*next_of(QF)
           % update *QF* register to point to the next process
    A:=args_of(CP)
           % set argument register to point to
           % first argument of current process
    PC:=*pc_of(CP)
           % set program counter to procedure of current process
    TS:=time_slice

Machine operation

Initially the process queue contains a single process, the booting process, at address 'boot'. The initial values of the registers are as follows:

HB=top of heap
HP=top of heap
QF=boot
QB=boot
PFL=null
SFL=null
STP=suspension_table
TRP=trail.

Initial values of other registers are unimportant.

    Start:

Dequeue
> % dequeue booting process.

Next:

Fetch next instruction
Case instruction of:

get(Arg):
> unify(*A,Arg)
>> % get *A, the current argument,
>> % and unify it with *Arg*
>
> A:=A+1
>> % Advance argument register

put(Arg):
> create(*A,Arg)
>> % initialize *A, the
>> % current argument, to be *Arg*.
>
> A:=A+1
>> % Advance argument register

unify(Arg):
> if Mode=0
>> % value of Mode register is "read"
>
> then unify(*SP,Arg)
>> % unify *SP, the current structure
>> % argument, with *Arg*.
>
> elseif Mode=1
>> % value of *Mode* register is "write"
>
> then create(*SP,Arg)
>> % initialize *SP, the current
>> % structure argument, to be *Arg*.
>
> SP:=SP+1
>> % Advance structure pointer register

set(Xn):
> Set A to point to register Xn.

call(Index, Xi, Xj, ...):
> Call guard guard number Index, with the arguments
> Xi, Xj, ...

commit:
> Bind read-only counterparts of trailed writable variables.
> Activate processes in suspension queues which are
> reachable from the trail.

```
        TRP:=trail
            % reset trail pointer register
        STP:=suspension_table
            % reset suspension table pointer register
        A:=args_of(CP)
            % set argument register to first argument
            % of current process
  spawn(Proc):
        Allocate a new process record, store its address in NPR.
        *pc_of(NPR):=Proc
            % initialize the program counter
            % of the process to Proc
        Enqueue(NPR)
            % enqueue process NPR
        A:=args_of(NPR)
            % set argument register to first
            % argument of NPR
  execute(Proc):
        *pc_of(CP):=Proc
            % change procedure of current
            % process to Proc.
        If TS>0
            % time-slice not exhausted
        then TS:=TS-1;
            % decrement time-slice
        A:=args_of(CP)
            % set argument register to point to
            % first argument of current process
        PC:=Proc
            % set program counter to Proc
        else
        Enqueue(CP)
            % enqueue current process
        Dequeue
            % dequeue next process
  halt:
        *next_of(CP):=PFL; PFL:=CP
            % return current process to process free list
        Dequeue
  suspend:
        Suspend current process on the variables in the
```

suspension table. If the suspension table is empty
then fail the computation.
STP:=suspension_table
        % reset suspension table
Dequeue

goto Next

Appendix 38.3: List Of Instructions

Procedural instructions

commit
spawn *Proc*
execute *Proc*
iterate
halt
suspend

Clause instruction

try_me_else *Label*.

Guard instruction

call *Index*, X_i, X_j, ...

Argument instructions:

set X_i
push X_i
pop X_i
void

Put instructions:

put_var X_i
put_val X_i
put_ro_var X_i
put_ro_val X_i
put_int *Integer-Value*
put_real *Real-Value*
put_str *Address*
put_nil
put_tpl *Arity*

> put_car_var X_i
> put_car_val X_i
> put_car_ro_var X_i
> put_car_ro_val X_i
> put_car_int *Integer-Value*
> put_car_real *Real-Value*
> put_car_str *Address*
> put_car_nil
> put_car_list X_i
> put_car_tpl X_i, *Arity*

The Xi register in *put_car_list* and *put_car_tpl* instructions is used for pushing into it the *Mode* of unification and the address of the next argument. The same applies to the get and unify instructions.

Get instructions:

> get_var X_i
> get_val X_i
> get_ro_var X_i
> get_ro_val X_i
> get_int *Integer-Value*
> get_real *Real-Value*
> get_str *Address*
> get_nil
> get_tpl *Arity*
>
> get_car_var X_i
> get_car_val X_i
> get_car_ro_var X_i
> get_car_ro_val X_i
> get_car_int *Integer-Value*
> get_car_real *Real-Value*
> get_car_str *Address*
> get_car_nil
> get_car_list X_i
> get_car_tpl X_i, *Arity*

Unify instructions:

> unify_var X_i
> unify_val X_i
> unify_ro_var X_i
> unify_ro_val X_i
> unify_int *Integer-Value*

unify_real *Real-Value*
unify_str *Address*
unify_nil
unify_tpl *Arity*

unify_car_var X_i
unify_car_val X_i
unify_car_ro_var X_i
unify_car_ro_val X_i
unify_car_int *Integer-Value*
unify_car_real *Real-Value*
unify_car_str *Address*
unify_car_nil
unify_car_list X_i
unify_car_tpl X_i, *Arity*

Appendix 38.4: Encoding Examples

The examples below were produced by the Logix compiler and relate to the data types used in the implementation. The examples were adjusted by hand to remove unneeded information and to make them readable. Note that X registers are allocated only as long as they are needed and an attempt is made to reduce the use of X registers as much as possible. This will be most important when part of the X registers reside in real registers.

Compiling read-only variables in the head and in the body

merge([X|Xs],Ys,[X|Zs?]) ← merge(Xs?,Ys,Zs).

A0:

```
try_me_else A1      % merge(
get_car_var X0      % X|
unify_var X2        % Xs],
get_var X1          % Ys,
get_car_val X0      % X|
unify_ro_var X0     % Zs?])
commit              % ← merge(
put_ro_val X2       % Xs?,
put_val X1          % Ys,
put_val X0          % Zs).
iterate             %
```

A1:

suspend.

Compiling a complete procedure, with process spawning

```
qsort([X|Xs],S1,L2) ←
    part(X,Xs?,S,L), qsort(S?,S1,[X|L1]), qsort(L?,L1,L2).
qsort([ ],X,X).
```

B0:

try_me_else B1	% qsort(
get_car_var X1	% X|
unify_var X4	% Xs],
get_var X3	% S1,
get_var X0	% L2)
commit	% ← part(
put_val X1	% X,
put_ro_val X4	% Xs?,
put_var X4	% S,
put_var X2	% L),
spawn B0	% qsort(
put_ro_val X4	% S?,
put_val X3	% S1,
put_car_val X1	% X|
unify_var X1	% L1]),
spawn B0	% qsort(
put_ro_val X2	% L?,
put_val X1	% L1,
put_val X0	% L2).
execute C0	%

B1:

try_me_else B2	% qsort(
get_nil	% [ ]
get_var X0	% X,
get_val X0	% X,
commit	%).
halt	

B2:

suspend.

Compilation of non empty guard

```
part(X,[Y|Ys],[Y|S?],L) ← X>Y | part(X,Ys?,S,L).
part(X,[Y|Ys],S,[Y|L?]) ← X≤Y | part(X,Ys?,S,L).
part(X,[ ],[ ],[ ]).
```

```
C0:
        try_me_else C1      % part(
        get_var X3          % X,
        get_car_var X4      % Y|
        unify_var X2        % Ys],
        get_car_val X4      % Y|
        unify_ro_var X1     % S?],
        get_var X0          % L) ←
        call >, X3, X4      % X>Y
        commit              % | part(
        put_val X3          % X,
        put_ro_val X2       % Ys?,
        put_val X1          % S,
        put_val X0          % L).
        iterate             %
C1:
        try_me_else C2      % part(
        get_var X3          % X,
        get_car_var X4      % Y|
        unify_var X2        % Ys],
        get_var X1          % S,
        get_car_val X4      % Y|
        unify_ro_var X0     % L?]) ←
        call ≤, X3, X4      % X≤Y
        commit              % | part(
        put_val X3          % X,
        put_ro_val X2       % Ys?,
        put_val X1          % S,
        put_val X0          % L).
        iterate             %

C2:
        try_me_else C3      % part(
        get_var X0          % X,
        get_nil             % [ ],
        get_nil             % [ ],
        get_nil             % [ ]).
        commit
        halt
C3:
        suspend.
```

Compiling complex structures in the head

```
d(U*V,X,(DU*V)+(U*DV)) ←
    d(U,X,DU), d(V,X,DV).
```

D0:

```
try_me_else D1      % d(
get_tuple 3
unify_string '*'
unify_var X4        % U*
unify_var X2        % V,
get_var X1          % X,
get_tpl 3
unify_string '+'
push X0             % (save "(U*DV)")
unify_tpl 3
unify_string '*'
unify_var X3        % (DU*
unify_val X2        % V)+(
pop X0              % (load "(U*DV)")
unify_tpl 3
unify_string '*'
unify_val X4        % U*
unify_var X0        % DV))
commit              % ← d(
put_val X4          % U,
put_val X1          % X,
put_val X3          % DU),
spawn D0            % d(
put_val X2          % V,
put_val X1          % X,
put_val X0          % DV).
iterate             %
```

D1:

```
suspend.
```

Compiling complex structures in the body

```
test ← do(parse(s(np,vp),[birds,fly],[ ])).
```

E0:

```
try_me_else E1          % test
commit                  % ← do(
put_tuple 4
```

```
        unify_string 'parse'         % parse(
        push X0                      % (save "[birds,fly], [ ]")
        unify_tuple 3
        unify_string 's'             % s(
        unify_string 'np'            % np,
        unify_string 'vp'            % vp),
        pop X0                       % (load "[birds,fly], [ ]")
        push X0                      % (save "[ ]")
        unify_car_string 'birds'     % birds,
        unify_car_string 'fly'       % fly
        unify_nil                    % ]
        pop X0                       % (load "[ ]")
        unify_nil                    % [ ]
        execute (offset to do)       %
E1:
        suspend.
```

Appendix 38.5: Benchmarks

Note: Benchmarks were carried on a slightly older version of the abstract machine.

Naive reverse

```
        % FCP (C emulator)

        Call: rev(100)

        rev(N) ← list(N?,X), rev(X?,_).

        list(N,[N|Xs?])←
              N > 0, N1:=N-1 | list(N1,Xs).
        list(0,[ ]).

        rev([X|Xs],Ys) ←
              rev(Xs?,Zs), append(Zs?,[X],Ys).
        rev([ ],[ ]).

        append([X|Xs],Ys,[X|Zs]) ←
              append(Xs?,Ys,Zs).
        append([ ],Xs,Xs).
```

Without tail recursion optimization (time-slice is 1)

Creations:	102
Suspensions:	101
Process Switches:	5152
Reductions:	5254
Speed:	1616.62 LIPS
Time:	3250 ms.

With tail recursion optimization (time-slice is 26)

Creations:	102
Suspensions:	100
Process Switches:	149
Reductions:	5254
Speed:	1843.51 LIPS
Time:	2850 ms.

```
% Prolog (Quintus)

run(T) ←
    statistics(runtime,[T1,_]),
    rev(100),
    statistics(runtime,[T2,_]),
    T is T2–T1.

rev(N) ← list(N,X), rev(X,_).

list(N,[N|Xs])←
    N > 0, N1 is N–1, list(N1,Xs).
list(0,[ ]).

rev([X|Xs],Ys) ←
    rev(Xs,Zs), append(Zs,[X],Ys).
rev([ ],[ ]).

append([X|Xs],Ys,[X|Zs]) ←
    append(Xs,Ys,Zs).
append([ ],Xs,Xs).
```

Time is 717 ms (4.5–4.0 times speed up)

Quick sort

```
%FCP (C emulator)

Call: list(100,X), qsort(X?,_).

qsort([X|List],Sorted-Tail) ←
```

```
        partition(X?,List?,Small,Large),
        qsort(Small?,SSorted-Tail),
        qsort(Large?,Sorted-[X|SSorted]).
qsort([ ],X-X).

partition(X,[Y|List],[Y|Small],Large) ←
    X > Y |
    partition(X,List?,Small,Large).
partition(X,[Y|List],Small,[Y|Large]) ←
    X ≤ Y |
    partition(X,List?,Small,Large).
partition(_,[ ],[ ],[ ]).
```

Without tail recursion optimization (time-slice is 1)

Creations:	202
Suspensions:	201
Process Switches:	5152
Reductions:	5354
Speed:	634.36 LIPS
Time:	8440 ms.

With tail recursion optimization (time-slice is 26)

Creations:	202
Suspensions:	153
Process Switches:	79
Reductions:	5354
Speed:	707.27 LIPS
Time:	7570 ms.

```
% Prolog (Quintus)

run(T) ←
    statistics(runtime,[T1,_]),
    qsort(100),
    statistics(runtime,[T2,_]),
    T is T2-T1.

qsort(N) ← list(N,X), qsort(X,_).

list(N,[N|Xs])←
    N > 0, N1 is N-1, list(N1,Xs).
list(0,[ ]).

qsort([X|List],Sorted-Tail) ←
    partition(X,List,Small,Large),
```

```
        qsort(Small,SSorted-Tail),
        qsort(Large,Sorted-[X|SSorted]).
qsort([ ],X-X).

partition(X,[Y|List],[Y|Small],Large) ←
    X > Y,
    partition(X,List,Small,Large).
partition(X,[Y|List],Small,[Y|Large]) ←
    X ≤ Y,
    partition(X,List,Small,Large).
partition(_,[ ],[ ],[ ]).
```

Time is 5150 ms (1.64–1.47 times speed up)

However, if cuts are added after the first goal in the first partition clauses, the speed of Quintus Prolog is increased by a factor of 3.

Hanoi towers

```
% FCP (C emulator)

boot(_,_) ← hanoi(10).

hanoi(N) ←
    hanoi(N,_).

hanoi(N,X) ←
    hanoi(N,a,c,X).

hanoi(N,From,To,(Before,(From,To),After))←
    N > 0, diff(N,1,N1) |
    free(From,To,Free),
    hanoi(N1,From,Free,Before),
    hanoi(N1,Free,To,After).
hanoi(0,From,To,(From,To)).

free(a,b,c).
free(a,c,b).
free(b,a,c).
free(b,c,a).
free(c,a,b).
free(c,b,a).
```

Without tail recursion optimization (time-slice is 1)

Creations:	2047
Suspensions:	0
Process Switches:	1026

Reductions: 3073
Speed: 532.58
Time: 5770

With tail recursion optimization (time-slice is 26)

Creations: 2047
Suspensions: 0
Process Switches: 0
Reductions: 3073
Speed: 555.70
Time: 5530

% Prolog (Quintus)

```
run(T) ←
    statistics(runtime,[T1,_]),
    hanoi(10),
    statistics(runtime,[T2,_]),
    T is T2–T1.

hanoi(N) ←
    hanoi(N,_).

hanoi(N,X) ←
    hanoi(N,a,c,X).

hanoi(N,From,To,(Before,(From,To),After))←
    N > 0, N1 is N–1,
    free(From,To,Free),
    hanoi(N1,From,Free,Before),
    hanoi(N1,Free,To,After).
hanoi(0,From,To,(From,To)).

free(a,b,c).
free(a,c,b).
free(b,a,c).
free(b,c,a).
free(c,a,b).
free(c,b,a).
```

Time is 2716 (2.12–2.00 times speed up)

Appendix 38.6: Code Of The Encoder

Following is the FCP code for an encoder which transforms an FCP program into an executable binary module. This encoder forms the back end of the FCP compiler and is part of the Logix system. It assumes the program is error free since it has already been checked by other parts of the compiler. The encoder given here is not the current encoder which Logix uses but an older one. However it is simpler for reading.

The encoder works in two phases: code generation and assembly. Code generation is responsible for converting an FCP program to a symbolic sequence of instructions. Parts of the instructions which can not be determined during the code generation phase are represented by variables and are instantiated at a latter stage (e.g., the destination for an execute instruction).

The assembler accepts the instruction stream produced by code generation and fills in the missing parts of the instructions. It also converts the symbolic instructions into opcodes and produces the binary module.

The encoder is based upon the compiler construction methods described by Warren (1980). In FCP the process is considerably simplified by using suspended processes which wait for the necessary information and insert it into the instruction stream. This prevents additional passes or table construction which would be required in Prolog or other sequential languages.

Note: The encoder is from an earlier version of Logix, and uses an instruction set slightly different from the one described in this paper.

Dictionary

```
% Compiler's Dictionary Server
boot(Input,Output) ←
    dictionary_server(Input?,Output).

dictionary_server(
        [dictionary(Input,Strings)|In],
        [guardtable#dictionary(Input1?)|Out]
) ←
    module_dictionary(Input?,Strings,Input1),
    dictionary_server(In?,Out).
dictionary_server([ ],[ ]).

module_dictionary(In,Strings,Out) ←
    module_dictionary(In,Procedures,Strings,done,Out).
module_dictionary(
        [clause_dictionary(Input,Output)|In],
```

```
            Procedures,
            Strings,
            Done,
            Out
) ←
    clause_dictionary(Input?,Output),
    module_dictionary(In?,Procedures,Strings,Done,Out).
module_dictionary(
            [lookup_procedure(Name/Arity,Label)|In],
            Procedures,
            Strings,
            Done,
            Out
) ←
    member(procedure(Name,Arity,Label),Procedures,_,_),
    module_dictionary(In?,Procedures,Strings,Done,Out).
module_dictionary(
            [lookup_string(String,Label)|In],
            Procedures,
            Strings,
            Left,
            Out
) ←
    member(string(String,Label),Strings,Left,Right),
    module_dictionary(In?,Procedures,Strings,Right,Out).
module_dictionary(
            [X|In],
            Procedures,
            Strings,
            Done,
            [X|Out]
) ←
    module_dictionary(In?,Procedures,Strings,Done,Out).
module_dictionary([ ],Procedures,Strings,Done,[ ]) ←
    close_list(Done?,Strings).

member(X,[X|Xs],Done,Done).
member(X,[Y|Xs],Left,Right) ←
    otherwise |
    member(X,Xs,Left,Right).

close_list(done,L) ←
```

close_list(L).
close_list([ ]).
close_list([X|Xs]) ← close_list(Xs).

% Clause dictionary augmented to optimize register allocation.

clause_dictionary(In,Out) ←
    clause_dictionary(In?,[guards_base(GsB)],GsB,Out).
clause_dictionary([allocate_temporary(Register)|In],D,GsB,Out) ←
    clause_dictionary(In?,[allocate(Register)|D],GsB,Out).
clause_dictionary([deallocate_temporary(Register)|In],D,GsB,Out) ←
    clause_dictionary(In?,[deallocate(Register)|D],GsB,Out).
% Anonymous var.
clause_dictionary([lookup_var('_',var(Register))|In],D,GsB,Out) ←
    clause_dictionary(In?,[var('_',Register)|D],GsB,Out).
clause_dictionary([lookup_var(X,CompiledX)|In],D,GsB,Out) ←
    wait(X), X\='_' |
    lookup_var(X,D?,D_Entry,CompiledX),
    clause_dictionary(In?,[D_Entry?|D],GsB,Out).
clause_dictionary([guards_base(GsB)|In],D,GsB,Out) ←
    clause_dictionary(In?,D,GsB,Out).
clause_dictionary([X|In],D,GsB,[X|Out?]\Out1) ←
    otherwise |
    clause_dictionary(In?,D,GsB,Out\Out1?).
clause_dictionary([ ],D,GsB,Out\Out) ←
    allocate_registers(D).

lookup_var(
        Name,
        [var(Name,Register)|D],
        value(Name,Register),
        value(Register?)
).
lookup_var(Name,[value(Name,Register)|D],
    value(Name,Register),value(Register?)).
lookup_var(Name,[ ],var(Name,Register),var(Register?)).
lookup_var(Name,[Y|Ys],D_Entry,CompiledX) ←
    otherwise |
    lookup_var(Name,Ys?,D_Entry,CompiledX).

allocate_registers(Dictionary) ←
    allocate_registers(Dictionary,0,[ ]).

% Already allocated.

allocate_registers([var(_,N)|D],Max_Reg,Frd_Regs) ←
    integer(N) |
    N1 := N+1,
    allocate_registers(D?,N1?,[N]).
% Anonymous var, not allocated. No freed register.
% *MaxReg* is incremented to avoid overwriting on guard args.
allocate_registers([var(_,N)|D],N,[ ]) ←
    integer(N) |
    N1 := N+1,
    allocate_registers(D?,N1?,[N]).
% Anonymous var, not allocated. There is freed register.
allocate_registers(
        [var(_,Frd_Reg)|D],
        MaxReg,[Frd_Reg|Frd_Regs]
) ←
    integer(Frd_Reg) |
    allocate_registers(D?,MaxReg,[Frd_Reg|Frd_Regs]).
% Already allocated.
allocate_registers([value(_,N)|D],Max_Reg,Frd_Regs) ←
    integer(N) |
    allocate_registers(D?,Max_Reg,Frd_Regs).
% Not allocated. No freed register.
allocate_registers([value(_,N)|D],N,[ ]) ←
    integer(N) |
    N1 := N+1,
    allocate_registers(D?,N1?,[ ]).
% Not allocated. There is freed register.allocate_registers(
        [value(_,Frd_Reg)|D],
        MaxReg,
        [Frd_Reg|Frd_Regs]
) ←
    integer(Frd_Reg) |
    allocate_registers(D?,MaxReg,Frd_Regs).
% Already allocated.
allocate_registers([allocate(N)|D],Max_Reg,Frd_Regs) ←
    integer(N) |
    allocate_registers(D?,Max_Reg,[N|Frd_Regs]).
% Temporary var. Not allocated. No freed·register.
allocate_registers([deallocate(N)|D],N,[ ]) ←
    integer(N) |
    N1 := N+1,

```
      allocate_registers(D?,N1?,[ ]).
% Temporary var. Not allocated. There is freed register.
allocate_registers(
        [deallocate(Frd_Reg)|D],
        MaxReg,
        [Frd_Reg|Frd_Regs]
) ←
    integer(Frd_Reg) |
    allocate_registers(D?,MaxReg,Frd_Regs).
% Base case. Give value to the base register for guards.
allocate_registers([guards_base(Max_Reg)],Max_Reg,Frd_Regs).
```

<u>Code generator</u>

```
% Flat Concurrent Prolog Code Generator

boot(Input,Output) ←
    encoder(Input?,Output).

encoder(
        [encode(module(FileName,Procedures),
        module(Instructions?,Strings?))|In],
        [dictionary#dictionary(Requests?,Strings)|Out]
) ←
    encode(Procedures?,Instructions,Requests),
    encoder(In?,Out).
encoder([ ],[ ]).

encode(Procedures,Instructions,Requests) ←
    encode_procedures(Procedures?,Instructions,Requests\[ ]).

% Encode module
encode_procedures(
        [Procedure|Ps],
        (EncodedProcedure?;CPs?),
        Rqs\Rqs2
) ←
    encode_procedure(Procedure?,EncodedProcedure,Rqs\Rqs1?),
    encode_procedures(Ps?,CPs,Rqs1\Rqs2).
encode_procedures([ ],skip,Rqs\Rqs).

% Encode procedure
encode_procedure(
        procedure(Name/Arity,Clauses),
        procedure(
```

```
            (Name?)/(Arity?),
            Label,
            (EncodedClauses?;suspend(Label))
        ),
        [
            lookup_procedure((Name?)/(Arity?),Label),
            lookup_string(Name?,Label1)|Rqs?
        ]\Rqs1
) ←
    encode_clauses(Clauses?,EncodedClauses,Rqs\Rqs1?).

% Encode clauses
encode_clauses(
        [Clause|Cs],
        (EncodedClause?;CCs?),
        [clause_dictionary(ClauseRqs?,Rqs\Rqs1?)|Rqs?]\Rqs2
) ←
    encode_clause(Clause?,EncodedClause,ClauseRqs\[ ]),
    encode_clauses(Cs?,CCs,Rqs1\Rqs2?).
encode_clauses([ ],skip,Rqs\Rqs).

% Encode clause
encode_clause(
        (Head←Guard|Body),
        (
            try_me_else(Label);
            EncodedHead?;
            EncodedGuard?;
            commit;
            EncodedBody?;
            label(else,Label)
        ),
        Rqs\Rqs3
) ←
    encode_head(Head?,EncodedHead,Rqs\Rqs1?),
    encode_guard(Guard?,EncodedGuard,Rqs1\Rqs2?),
    encode_body(Body?,EncodedBody,Rqs2\Rqs3?).
encode_clause(
        (Head←Body),
        (
            try_me_else(Label);
            EncodedHead?;
```

```
                    commit;
                    EncodedBody?;
                    label(else,Label)
            ),
            Rqs\Rqs2
    ) ←
        otherwise |
        encode_head(Head?,EncodedHead,Rqs\Rqs1?),
        encode_body(Body?,EncodedBody,Rqs1\Rqs2?).
encode_clause(
            Head,
            (
                    try_me_else(Label);
                    EncodedHead?;
                    commit;
                    halt;
                    label(else,Label)
            ),
            Rqs
    ) ←
        otherwise |
        encode_head(Head?,EncodedHead,Rqs).

% Encode Head.
encode_head(Head,EncodedHead,Rqs) ←
        encode_args(get,Head?,EncodedHead,Rqs).

% Encode guard
encode_guard(true,skip,D\D).
encode_guard(skip,skip,D\D).
encode_guard((Goal,Gs),(EncodedGoal?;CGs?),D1\D3) ←
        encode_guard(Goal?,EncodedGoal,D1\D2?),
        encode_guard(Gs?,CGs,D2\D3?).
encode_guard(Goal,EncodedGoal,D1\D3) ←
        otherwise |
        functor(Goal?,Name,Arity),
        encode_args(put, Goal?, ArgsCode, D1\D2?),
        optimize_guard(ArgsCode?, (Name?)/(Arity?), EncodedGoal, D2\D3?).

% Encode body
encode_body(true,halt,D\D).
encode_body(
            (Goal,Gs),
```

```
        (EncodedArgs?;CGs?;execute((Name?)/(Arity?),Label)),
        [lookup_procedure((Name?)/(Arlty?),Label)|D1]\D3
) ←
    functor(Goal?,Name,Arity),
    encode_args(put,Goal?,EncodedArgs,D1\D2?),
    encode_other_goals(Gs?,CGs,D2\D3?).
encode_body(
        Goal,
        (EncodedArgs?;execute((Name?)/(Arity?),Label)),
        [lookup_procedure((Name?)/(Arity?),Label)|D1?]\D2
) ←
    otherwise |
    functor(Goal?,Name,Arity),
    encode_args(put,Goal?,EncodedArgs,D1\D2?).

encode_other_goals(
        (Goal,Gs),
        (spawn((Name?)/(Arity?),Label);EncodedArgs?;CGs?),
        [lookup_procedure((Name?)/(Arity?),Label)|D1?]\D3
) ←
    functor(Goal?,Name,Arity),
    encode_args(put,Goal?,EncodedArgs,D1\D2?),
    encode_other_goals(Gs?,CGs,D2\D3?).
encode_other_goals(
        Goal,
        (spawn((Name?)/(Arity?),Label);EncodedArgs?),
        [lookup_procedure((Name?)/(Arity?),Label)|D1?]\D2
) ←
    otherwise |
    functor(Goal?,Name,Arity),
    encode_args(put,Goal?,EncodedArgs,D1\D2?).

% Compiling general (head, guard, body) goal arguments
encode_args(Type,Goal,ArgsCode,D) ←
    goal_arity(Goal?,Arity),
    encode_args(Arity?,Type?,Goal?,ArgsCode,D).

encode_args(N1, Type, Goal, (ArgsCode?;ArgCode?;SubArgCode?), D1\D4) ←
    N1>0 | N:=N1−1,
    encode_args(N?, Type?, Goal?, ArgsCode, D1\D2?),
    goal_arg(N1?,Goal?,Arg),
    encode_arg(Arg?, Type?, ArgCode, SubArgCode, D2\D3?, D3\D4?).
encode_args(0, Type, Goal, skip, D\D).
```

```
% Encode arguments
encode_arg(
        S,
        Type,
        string(Type?,Label),
        skip,
        [lookup_string(S?,Label)|D]\D,
        SD\SD
) ←
    string(S?) | true.
encode_arg(
        I,
        Type,
        integer(Type?,I?),
        skip,
        D\D,
        SD\SD
) ←
    integer(I?) | true.
encode_arg(
        _VX,
        Type,
        var(Type?,EncodedX?),
        skip,
        [lookup_var(X?,EncodedX)|D]\D,
        SD\SD
) ←
    arg(1,_VX,T1), T1 = '_var',
    arg(2,_VX,T2), X = T2 | % patch instead of _var(X)
    true.
encode_arg(
        _RX,
        Type,
        ro(Type?,EncodedX?),
        skip,
        [lookup_var(X?,EncodedX)|D]\D,
        SD\SD
) ←
    arg(1,_RX,T1), T1 = '_ro',
    arg(2,_RX,T2), X = T2 | % patch instead of _ro(X)
    true.
```

```
encode_arg(
        [Car|Cdr],
        Type,
        ArgsCode,
        SubArgsCode,
        D,
        SD
) ←
    in_structure(Type?,InStructure),
    encode_list(InStructure?,Car?,Cdr?,Type?,ArgsCode,SubArgsCode,D,SD).
encode_arg(
        Tuple,
        Type,
        ArgsCode,
        SubArgsCode,
        D,
        SD
) ←
    tuple(Tuple), arity(Tuple,Arity), Arity>0 |
    in_structure(Type?,InStructure),
    encode_tuple(InStructure?,Tuple?,Type?,ArgsCode,SubArgsCode,D,SD).
encode_arg(
        [ ],
        Type,
        ArgsCode,
        SubArgsCode,
        D,
        SD
) ←
    in_structure(Type?,InStructure),
    encode_nil(InStructure?,Type?,ArgsCode,SubArgsCode,D,SD).

in_structure(get,false).
in_structure(put,false).
in_structure(unify,true).
in_structure(unify_list,true).

% Encode structures
encode_tuple(
        true,
        Tuple,
        Type,
```

```
            var(Type?,var(Z?)),
            (tuple(unify,Z?,Ta?);ArgsCode?;SubArgsCode?),
            [allocate_temporary(Z)|D]\D,
            [deallocate_temporary(Z)|SD1?]\SD3
) ←
        arity(Tuple?,Ta),
        encode_tuple_args(
            Ta?,
            Tuple?,
            ArgsCode,
            SubArgsCode,
            SD1\SD2?,
            SD2\SD3?
            ).
encode_tuple(
        false,
        Tuple,
        Type,
        (tuple(Type?,Ta?);ArgsCode?),
        SubArgsCode,
        D,
        SD
) ←
        arity(Tuple?,Ta),
        encode_tuple_args(Ta?,Tuple?,ArgsCode,SubArgsCode,D,SD).

encode_tuple_args(0,Tuple,skip,skip,D\D,SD\SD).
encode_tuple_args(
        N1,
        Tuple,
        (ArgsCode?;ArgCode?),
        (SubArgsCode?;SubArgCode?),
        D1\D3,
        SD1\SD3
) ←
        N1>0 | N:=N1−1,
        encode_tuple_args(
            N?,
            Tuple?,
            ArgsCode,
            SubArgsCode,
            D1\D2?,
```

```
                SD1\SD2?
        ),
        arg(N1?,Tuple?,Arg),
        encode_arg(Arg?,unify,ArgCode,SubArgCode,D2\D3?,SD2\SD3?).
encode_list(
        true,
        Car,
        Cdr,
        Type,
        var(Type?,var(Z?)),
        (list(unify,Z?);CarCode?;CdrCode?;SubCarCode;SubCdrCode?),
        [allocate_temporary(Z)|D]\D,
        [deallocate_temporary(Z)|SD1?]\SD5
) ←
        encode_arg(
        Car?,
        unify_list,
        CarCode,
        SubCarCode,
        SD1\SD2?,
        SD3\SD4?
        ),
        encode_arg(
        Cdr?,
        unify,
        CdrCode,
        SubCdrCode,
        SD2\SD3?,
        SD4\SD5?
        ).
% The Cdr is treated like tuple-argument
encode_list(
        false,
        Car,
        Cdr,
        Type,
        (list(Type?);CarCode?;CdrCode?),
        (SubCarCode?;SubCdrCode?),
        D1\D3,
        SD1\SD3
) ←
```

```
    encode_arg(Car?,unify_list,CarCode,SubCarCode,D1\D2?,SD1\SD2?),
    encode_arg(Cdr?,unify,CdrCode,SubCdrCode,D2\D3?,SD2\SD3?).
encode_nil(
        true,
        Type,
        var(Type?,var(Z?)),
        tuple(unify,Z?,0),
        [allocate_temporary(Z)|D]\D,
        [deallocate_temporary(Z)|SD]\SD).
encode_nil(
        false,
        Type,
        tuple(Type?,0),
        skip,
        D\D,
        SD\SD).

% Utilities
functor(Term,Functor,Arity) ←
    tuple(Term),
    arg(1,Term,Functor),
    arity(Term,Arity1) |
    Arity:=Arity1-1.
functor(Term,Term,0) ←
    string(Term) |
    true.

goal_arity(Goal,Arity) ←
    tuple(Goal),
    arity(Goal,Arity1) |
    Arity:=Arity1-1.
goal_arity(Goal,0) ←
    string(Goal) |
    true.

goal_arg(N,Goal,Arg) ←
    N1:=N+1, arg(N1,Goal,Arg) |
    true.

% Guard Optimizing
optimize_guard(
        ArgsCode,
        GuardName,
```

```
                (ArgsCode1?;call(BaseReg?,GuardIndex?)),
                [
                    guard_index(GuardName?,GuardIndex),
                    guards_base(GuardsBase)|D?
                ]\D
) ←
        guard_optimizing(ArgsCode?,GuardsBase?,BaseReg,ArgsCode1).
guard_optimizing(ArgsCode,GuardsBase,BaseReg,NewArgsCode) ←
        check_vars(ArgsCode?,ArgsBase,ThrownAble),
        new_guard_code(
                ThrownAble?,
                ArgsCode?,
                ArgsBase?,
                GuardsBase?,
                BaseReg,
                NewArgsCode
        ).
new_guard_code(true,ArgsCode,ArgsBase,GuardsBase,ArgsBase,skip).
new_guard_code(
                false,
                ArgsCode,
                ArgsBase,
                GuardsBase,
                GuardsBase,
                (guard(GuardsBase?);ArgsCode?)
).
check_vars(skip,0,true).
check_vars(skip,N,true) ←
        integer(N) |
        true.
check_vars((var(Type,value(N));Args),N,Opt) ←
        N1 := N+1,
        check_vars(Args?,N1?,Opt).
check_vars((skip;Args),N,Opt) ←
        check_vars(Args?,N,Opt).
check_vars(((A1;A2);Args),N,Opt) ←
        check_vars((A1?;(A2?;Args?)),N,Opt).
check_vars((Arg;Args),N,false) ←
        otherwise |
        true.
```

<u>Assembler</u>

% FCP Assembler

boot(Input,Output) ←
    assembler_server(Input?,Output).

assembler_server([assemble(CompiledModule,AssembledModule)|In],Out) ←
    assemble(CompiledModule,AssembledModule),
    assembler_server(In?,Out).
assembler_server([ ],[ ]).

assemble(module(Procedures,StringsDictionary),AssembledModule) ←
    assemble_procedures(
        Procedures,
        2,
        EndOfProcs,
        ProcsAndStrings\Strings?
    ),
    % 2 for module header.
    assemble_strings(StringsDictionary?,EndOfProcs?,Strings),
    grounded_list(ProcsAndStrings?,Grounded),
    strings_to_module(Grounded?,ProcsAndStrings?,AssembledModule).

assemble_procedures(
        (procedure(Name,IC1,Instructions);Ps),
        IC1,
        IC3,
        [AssembledProcedure|ProcsAndStrings?]\Strings
) ←
    assemble_procedure(
        Instructions?,
        IC1?,
        IC2,
        AssembledProcedure
    ),
    assemble_procedures(Ps?,IC2?,IC3,ProcsAndStrings\Strings).
assemble_procedures(skip,IC,IC,Strings\Strings).

assemble_strings(
        [string(String,IC)|StringsDictionary],
        IC,
        [String|Strings]
) ←
    string_length_in_words(String?,Length),

```
        IC1:=IC+Length+2,
        assemble_strlngs(StrlngsDlctlonary?,IC1?,Strlngs).
assemble_strings([ ],_,[ ]).
```

% Assembling procedures
```
assemble_procedure(Instructions,IC1,IC4,Procedure) ←
        IC2:=IC1+2,      % for string header
        assemble_procedure1(Instructions,IC2?,IC3,AssembledProcedure\[ ]),
        IC4:=IC3+1,      % list_to_string will always pad with null word.
        grounded_list(AssembledProcedure?,Grounded),
        integers_to_string(Grounded?,AssembledProcedure?,Procedure).
```

```
assemble_procedure1(skip,IC,IC,Bs\Bs).
assemble_procedure1((skip;Is),IC,IC1,Bs) ←
        assemble_procedure1(Is?,IC,IC1,Bs).
assemble_procedure1((Is1;Is2),IC1,IC3,Bs1\Bs3) ←
        otherwise |
        assemble_procedure1(Is1?,IC1?,IC2,Bs1\Bs2?),
        assemble_procedure1(Is2?,IC2?,IC3,Bs2\Bs3).
assemble_procedure1(I,IC,IC1,Bs) ←
        otherwise |
        instruction(I,IC,IC1,Bs).
```

% Label
```
instruction(label(Name,IC),IC,IC,Bs\Bs).
```

% Procedural instructions
```
instruction(guard(BaseRegister),IC,IC1,[N,BaseRegister|Bs]\Bs) ←
        IC1:=IC+2,
        instruction_number(guard,N).
instruction(void,IC,IC1,[N|Bs]\Bs) ←
        IC1:=IC+1,
        instruction_number(void,N).
instruction(
        call(BaseRegister,Index),
        IC,
        IC1,
        [N,BaseRegister,Index|Bs]\Bs
) ←
        IC1:=IC+3,
        instruction_number(call,N).
        % assuming Guard kernel functors are integers
instruction(commit,IC,IC1,[N|Bs]\Bs) ←
```

```
    IC1:=IC+1,
    instruction_number(commit,N).
instruction(halt,IC,IC1,[N|Bs]\Bs) ←
    IC1:=IC+1,
    instruction_number(halt,N).
instruction(spawn(Name,Label),IC,IC1,[N,Offset|Bs]\Bs) ←
    IC1:=IC+2,
    instruction_number(spawn,N),
    offset(IC?,Label?,Offset).
instruction(execute(Name,Label),IC,IC1,[N,Offset|Bs]\Bs) ←
    IC1:=IC+2,
    instruction_number(execute,N),
    offset(IC?,Label?,Offset).

% Indexing and glue instructions
instruction(suspend(Label),IC,IC1,[N,Offset|Bs]\Bs) ←
    IC1:=IC+2,
    instruction_number(suspend,N),
    offset(IC?,Label?,Offset).
instruction(try_me_else(Label),IC,IC1,[N,Offset|Bs]\Bs) ←
    IC1:=IC+2,
    instruction_number(try_me_else,N),
    offset(IC?,Label?,Offset).

% Head Instructions
instruction(var(Type,var(Xn)),IC,IC1,[N,Xn|Bs]\Bs) ←
    IC1:=IC+2,
    instruction_number(var(Type,var),N).
instruction(var(Type,value(Xn)),IC,IC1,[N,Xn|Bs]\Bs) ←
    IC1:=IC+2,
    instruction_number(var(Type,value),N).
instruction(ro(Type,var(Xn)),IC,IC1,[N,Xn|Bs]\Bs) ←
    IC1:=IC+2,
    instruction_number(ro(Type,var),N).
instruction(ro(Type,value(Xn)),IC,IC1,[N,Xn|Bs]\Bs) ←
    IC1:=IC+2,
    instruction_number(ro(Type,value),N).

instruction(integer(Type,I),IC,IC1,[N,I|Bs]\Bs) ←
    IC1:=IC+2,
    instruction_number(integer(Type),N).
instruction(string(Type,S),IC,IC1,[N,Offset|Bs]\Bs) ←
    IC1:=IC+2,
```

```
    instruction_number(string(Type),N),
    offset(IC?,S?,Offset).
instruction(tuple(Type,Ta),IC,IC1,[N,Ta|Bs]\Bs) ←
    IC1:=IC+2,
    instruction_number(tuple(Type),N).
instruction(tuple(Type,Xn,Ta),IC,IC1,[N,Xn,Ta|Bs]\Bs) ←
    IC1:=IC+3,
    instruction_number(tuple(Type),N).
instruction(list(Type),IC,IC1,[N|Bs]\Bs) ←
    IC1:=IC+1,
    instruction_number(list(Type),N).
instruction(list(Type,Xn),IC,IC1,[N,Xn|Bs]\Bs) ←
    IC1:=IC+2,
    instruction_number(list(Type),N).

% Instruction Numbers
instruction_number(stop,0).
instruction_number(guard,1).
instruction_number(void,2).
instruction_number(call,3).
instruction_number(commit,4).
instruction_number(spawn,5).
instruction_number(execute,6).
instruction_number(suspend,7).
instruction_number(halt,8).
instruction_number(try_me_else,9).

instruction_number(var(put,var),10).
instruction_number(var(put,value),11).
instruction_number(ro(put,var),12).
instruction_number(ro(put,value),13).
instruction_number(string(put),14).
instruction_number(integer(put),15).
instruction_number(tuple(put),16).
instruction_number(list(put),17).

instruction_number(var(get,var),20).
instruction_number(var(get,value),21).
instruction_number(string(get),22).
instruction_number(integer(get),23).
instruction_number(tuple(get),24).
instruction_number(list(get),25).
```

```
% crunch get_list and unify_list instructions
instruction_number(var(unify,var),30).
instruction_number(var(unify,value),31).
instruction_number(ro(unify,var),32).
instruction_number(ro(unify,value),33).
instruction_number(string(unify),34).
instruction_number(integer(unify),35).
instruction_number(tuple(unify),36).
instruction_number(list(unify),40).

instruction_number(var(unify_list,var),41).
instruction_number(var(unify_list,value),42).
instruction_number(ro(unify_list,var),43).
instruction_number(ro(unify_list,value),44).
instruction_number(string(unify_list),45).
instruction_number(integer(unify_list),46).

% 37 instructions so far.

% Utilities
offset(From,To,Offset) ←
      Offset:=To-(From+1).
% 1 is the length of instruction.

string_length_in_words(String,Length) ←
      string_length(String,Length1) |
      Length:=(Length1+4)/4.      % assuming word size is 4 bytes.

grounded_list([X|Xs],Grounded) ←
      wait(X) |
      grounded_list(Xs?,Grounded).
grounded_list([ ],grounded).

strings_to_module(grounded,Strings,Module) ←
      strings_to_module(Strings,Module) | true.

integers_to_string(grounded,List,String) ←
      list_to_string(2,List,String) |
      true
```

Chapter 39

A Parallel Implementation of Flat Concurrent Prolog

Stephen Taylor, Shmuel Safra and Ehud Shapiro

The Weizmann Institute of Science

Abstract

Flat Concurrent Prolog is a simple, practical, concurrent programming language which has an efficient uni-processor implementation. This paper describes an initial parallel implementation of the language; it consists of an interpreter implemented on an Intel iPSC Hypercube.

The parallel execution of concurrent logic programming languages involves many non-trivial implementation problems. Some of these problems are well known and have been treated extensively in the literature. The most difficult task is to integrate problem solutions in a coherent and efficient manner. The algorithm presented has been useful in providing insights into the major problems and includes a number of novel ideas to simplify implementation. It does not attempt to solve all the problems involved but rather provides a workable basis for current and future research. The algorithm is under ongoing refinement, simplification and improvement.

39.1 Introduction

Flat Concurrent Prolog (FCP) is a simple, process oriented, single assignment language (Ackerman, 1982). This paper describes an initial parallel interpreter for the language which is operational on the Intel iPSC Hypercube. The primary goals which have been maintained in designing a parallel implementation of FCP are:

- To achieve a correct implementation supporting applications which use general logic programming techniques. This requires support for multiple writers on a single variable and variable to variable bindings.

- To maintain uni-processor performance.

- To provide efficient support for the major parallel programming techniques. Those of primary importance in parallel applications are producer/consumer relations, pipelining, incomplete messages and the short circuit technique.

The algorithm for parallel implementation is an extension of the uni-processor algorithm for FCP described by Mierowsky et al. (1985). It It extends unification to allow reading and writing on remote terms. These operations are distinguished, as in database systems (Ullman, 1982), for efficiency; reading occurs most often and requires less overhead for synchronization. The ability for multiple processes to write on a single variable is implemented via a locking scheme. The algorithm favours single writer programs since these occur more frequently than multiple writer ones.

39.2 Language Overview

An FCP program comprises a set of rules of the following form:

$$H \leftarrow G \mid B.$$

where H is the head, G is the guard consisting of simple test predicates and B is the body. A process whose data state unifies (matches) with the head may be re-written to the processes described by the body if the guard predicates are true.

The semantics of FCP is based on non-deterministic process and clause selection. Each state of a computation consists of a multi-set of processes (which form the resolvent), a program and the data state. A *reduction* transition involves non-deterministically selecting a process from the resolvent and a clause from the program. The transition involves the following operations:

- Making a new copy of the selected clause.

- Unifying the process with the head of the clause copy and solving the clause guard.

- Replacing the process by the body of the clause copy in the resolvent and applying the unifying substitution to the resolvent.

The computation must be *just*, i.e., a process whose reduction is continuously enabled is eventually taken; no other restrictions on the order of process selection exist.

Non-deterministic process selection can be realized by a number of deterministic process reduction attempts. Each reduction attempt may result in either success or suspension.

Non-deterministic clause selection is described by the following parallel algorithm. Each clause is copied and a set of processes, which run in parallel on a local environment, are spawned for each clause copy. Each set consists of a unification process, which attempts to unify the selected process with the clause head and a guard process for each guard call. A unification process may compare the function symbol of its arguments and may spawn a set of unification processes, which run in parallel, to unify the arguments of the terms under consideration. A unification process may not write on a variable via a read-only occurrence of it and must wait for the variable to be assigned; this provides the synchronization mechanism. Each guard process may test its arguments and may spawn a set of parallel unification processes. When all the unification and guard processes for a clause terminate successfully, the clause commits; no other clause is able to commit for this process.

The notions of process, communication and synchronization are supported directly in the language. Software processes communicate via shared streams, and read-only variable annotations provide a means to specify data-flow synchronization. The use of parallel semantics does not imply that processes and operations *must* be performed in parallel; this provides the compiler with considerable flexibility for optimization but there are instances where parallel execution may not be beneficial, e.g.,

- when tail recursion optimization can be applied;

- when the *granularity* of operations is too small to offset the overhead of starting a remote process and communicating with it.

39.3 Problems

A parallel implementation of FCP requires that a number of non-trivial problems be solved. Most of the problems are familiar and have been treated extensively in the literature on database systems, operating systems, data-flow languages and distributed systems. The most difficult task is to integrate solutions for solving these problems in a coherent, simple and efficient algorithm. In summary, the major problems are:

Mutual exclusion

Processes must be mutually excluded when updating shared variables (Coffman, 1973).

Deadlock prevention

Deadlock (Havender, 1968) may occur when multiple processes attempt to access shared variables; these may be viewed as shared resources, e.g.,

$$f(X,Y), \; g(Y,X)$$

in this example f may gain access to variable X and prevent other processes from accessing it while attempting to access variable Y. If process g does likewise then deadlock occurs.

Infinite structures

Infinite structures (e.g., streams) require special consideration when involved in communication (Weng, 1975; Keller and Lindstrom, 1981).

Circular references

It is possible to generate circular references within terms, e.g.,

$$X = f(Y), \; X = Y$$

Unification may never terminate if this term is unified with a similar term. On a uni-processor the problem may be solved using a technique involving pointer comparison. On a parallel machine variables and structures may exist on different processors making pointer comparison difficult (Keller and Lindstrom, 1981).

Data-flow synchronization

To implement data-flow synchronization on a uni-processor is relatively simple. Consider the process:

$$X? = a$$

If X is unbound the unification process is simply suspended using a data structure associated with the variable X; when the variable is bound by some other process, the unification process may be woken up to attempt reduction again. The situation is more complex on a parallel machine; the variable X may reside on another machine and may be bound by a process executing on it.

Housekeeping overheads

Maintaining the status of inter-processor requests can require complex algorithms and data structures. Minimizing the overheads involved presents a significant problem. In order to maintain uni-processor performance, if many processes access variables that reside locally there should be no overhead incurred by the parallel algorithm.

Starvation

A process may recurse infinitely while holding access to variables and never writing on them; other processes will as a result never obtain access.

39.4 Concepts

Some simple concepts can be applied in order to attack the above problems:

Order independent unification

An order independent semantics for unification is used. For example, the goal:

f(X?,X)

when matched against the clause head:

f(a,a).

will succeed irrespective of the order in which subparts of the unification are executed. This provides an elegant semantics for unification involving read-only occurrences of variables; it has been an important conceptual tool in reasoning about the parallel algorithm.

Variable occurrences

The implementation ensures that only a single instance of each variable exists; all occurrences are represented by either local or remote references to it. A remote reference includes both the notion of processor and location within a processor. This effectively implements a global address space; it circumvents the problem of maintaining consistency between multiple copies of variable bindings.

Reading

It is possible to distinguish two operations performed during unification: reading the value of a term and attempting to write the value of a term onto a variable. Consider the following unifications:

X? = a, Y = a

The first unification requires the *value* of X when it becomes bound even if X resides in a remote processor. The second must access the variable Y in order to write the value a on it even if Y resides on a remote processor.

Reading of remote values occurs more frequently than binding remote terms. The following table shows the percentage out of the total number of messages transmitted (for both reading and writing) which were concerned with reading and transferring values. The tests were conducted on some simple initial parallel algorithms using the implementation described in this paper:

Program	% Reading
Virtual Machines	87.2
Matrix Multiplication	95.8
Insertion Sort	95.9
Symbolic Differentiation	96.6
Naive Reverse	98.8

Of the programs examined, matrix multiply, insertion sort and naive reverse are simple, regular, systolic applications. The symbolic differentiation application uses a dynamic load balancing algorithm. The virtual machines program is highly dynamic and comprises a number of different applications running concurrently on three virtual machines.

It is possible to determine locally at a processor whether reading or writing on a remote term is required. This is achieved by:

- Not allowing variables in the environment of the process to bind with read-only occurrences of a variable in the same environment.

- Ensuring that data structures copied between processors are fully dereferenced and passed with the correct access mode.

In general, reading requires less synchronization and can be implemented more efficiently. When data is needed in several processors, the data can be replicated (with remote references to unbound parts of the terms) and sent to each reading processor; this operation is legal because of the single assignment rule employed by the language.

Variable migration

When a process needs to write on a variable which resides in another processor, the variable is brought locally; this operation is termed *variable migration* since variables migrate between processors. The operation involves transforming a remote reference into a variable at the processor where writing is needed and transforming the variable into a remote reference at the original location of the variable. This is achieved using communication, i.e.,

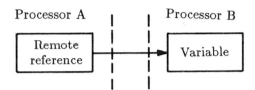

after variable migration becomes:

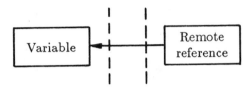

Replicating structures and bringing variables locally provides the opportunity to detect circular references using pointer comparison; moreover, the algorithm may attain uni-processor performance when all structures and variables are held locally.

Localization

Chains of remote references can occur through processors. Messages are always forwarded through these chains until the destination is found to be either a variable or a value. If a message is received at its source processor after being forwarded through a remote chain, a technique termed *localization* is applied. This operation effectively dereferences a chain of remote references and replaces it by a local reference.

When a message is received at its source processor, if the localization operation has not already been carried out and the source of the message is a remote reference, then the destination is inspected. If it is a value or variable, processes suspended on the the source remote reference are woken up and the source is overwritten with a local reference to the destination; if the destination is a remote reference, the message is forwarded[1] . Figure 39.1 illustrates the idea; remote chain A is replaced by local reference B.

If the source of the message is not a remote reference, then a number of bogus cases exist which, if they can occur, do so via unusual and complex message sequences. In all these cases no action is required, and we choose to make no optimizations for simplicity.

---

[1] Some other housekeeping information needs to be manipulated but this description captures the idea

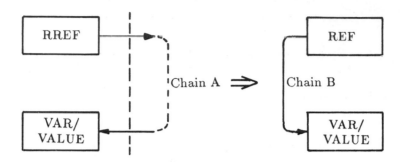

Figure 39.1

Atomicity of unification

Processes are mutually excluded when updating shared variables by ensuring that reduction is implemented as an atomic action. To achieve atomicity, no communication is carried out during a reduction attempt; any *necessary* structures which must be read and variables to be written upon are brought locally (variable migration). These techniques ensure that all required data structures needed are local and that nothing can affect them during unification other than the actions of unification. This reduces the problem of multiprocessor atomicity to that of uni-processor atomicity solving it trivially.

Demand copying

In order to deal with infinite structures, a demand copying scheme (Treleaven et al., 1982; Arvind and Thomas, 1978) can be employed. If unification requires access to a term which resides on another processor, the term is accessed incrementally by sending some constant number of levels in the structure at a time. Remote pointers can be used to access unbound variables. Demand copying copies only the *necessary* information to allow a process to commit; this is performed in response to demands generated by unification.

Relative references

All structures which may be transferred between processors are implemented using relative references. As a result, messages must be packed for sending to other processors but at the receiving processor can be simply loaded onto the heap and used immediately. Runable compiled code may be transferred between secondary storage and processors directly.

Broadcast notes

A simple technique can be used to achieve data-flow synchronization. When a remote processor attempts to read the value of an unbound variable, a note is attached to it. This note can be used when the variable becomes bound to copy the value to the requesting processor.

Deadlock prevention

Naive implementations of variable migration result in livelock; it is necessary to employ some form of locking when processes access shared variables. Unfortunately, deadlock may occur when processes lock some variables while requesting locks on others. Since deadlock may occur only in rare occasions involving multiple writers on multiple variables, we seek a solution which requires little overhead for single writer programs.

A simple but effective prevention algorithm (Havender, 1968) is often used in operating systems; resources are numbered in an arbitrary manner and processes are required to acquire their resources in order. This technique denies the circular wait condition and therefore prevents deadlock. Unfortunately the resources (variables) in FCP programs are distinctly dynamic objects since it is not known a priori which path of execution will be taken by a running program and which clauses will be executed.

Instead we choose to use an alternative technique. A priority is assigned to processors which is used to determine which processor obtains access to a variable in the event of competition. This is simpler and more efficient since processors are known statically. Locks are pooled (i.e., jointly owned by all local processes) at a processor for simplicity; this prevents competition for local locks since the atomicity of reduction ensures that only one process accesses a variable at a time. Each variable must have an associated number which specifies the processor locking it and each processor must hold a count of how many of its processes jointly require a lock. The following policy is used when a process p in processing element P of priority i requests a lock on variable X:

(1) If no processor owns the lock, then p is granted ownership of the lock.

(2) If a process (or processes) in another processing element P' with priority number h, where $h < i$, already owns the lock, then p is refused the lock and gives up ownership of all the locks that it currently owns, jointly or independently.

(3) If another process in P has already been granted the lock, p is given joint ownership of the lock.

(4) If a process (or processes) in another processing element P' with priority number j, where $j > i$, already owns the lock, then the request is temporarily

deferred and p must wait for the lock until no processes in P' own the lock.

Locks are granted immediately if the variable is unlocked. If the variable is locked and the priority of a lock request is lower than the locking processor, then the lock is refused and must be re-requested. Locks are granted within one queue cycle if the variable is locked and the incoming request is from a higher priority processor. If remote locks are required, all local variables required by the process are also locked; this prevents low priority processors from stealing locks until the process has gained sufficient locks to either commit or suspend. The algorithm ensures that there is always one processor in the system which will eventually gain all its locks, reduce and release locks to other processors; this prevents deadlock. A proof of correctness is presented in Appendix 39.1.

Since variables are always brought locally to be locked (variable migration), the processor number associated with a variable is implied and need not be included in the representation of a variable.

Integration of reading and writing

Consider an interrupt handling process which may modify some global structure and waits on an interrupt stream. The handler may never be executed; thus it is imperative that the process does not hold locks on the global structure while waiting. Reading and writing are thus integrated such that processes hold their locks only while requesting locks that they have not yet obtained. Eventually all the necessary locks are granted and the process is re-scheduled. At this time the process either commits or still requires data to be read. In the latter case the process suspends releasing its locks. If the necessary data arrives, the process must regain the locks it requires in order to commit.

Busy-waiting

In the initial approach described in this paper, processes busy-wait for locks. This substantially reduces the overheads associated with maintaining the status of inter-processor lock availablity.

Priority rotation

A number of ideas have been ventured to deal with the problem of starvation. One such suggestion is to allow each processor to become the highest priority processor. The processor must be highest priority for long enough to ensure that processes which require locks have the opportunity to obtain them and attempt reduction. It is not yet clear how much complexity this solution adds; the problem may occur only in contrived examples.

39.5 An Overview of the Algorithm

We assume the following model of computation.

- Processors are connected via a regular interconnection topology, e.g., mesh, ring, etc.

- There is no global storage; each processor has access to local storage.

- Processors may communicate with some small number of neighboring processors via message passing.

- Computations are described as a set of communicating processes in FCP.

- Dynamic process mapping allows processes to be assigned to neighboring processors.

Every processor executes an identical algorithm and may communicate with any other processor in the network via a simple routing algorithm. Each logical variable resides in a single processor; all other processors may access it via remote references using communication.

Each processor maintains two communication queues; one for incoming messages and one for outgoing messages. The algorithm executed at each processor consists of three sections; reduction, communication and buffering. Figure 39.2 illustrates the organization.

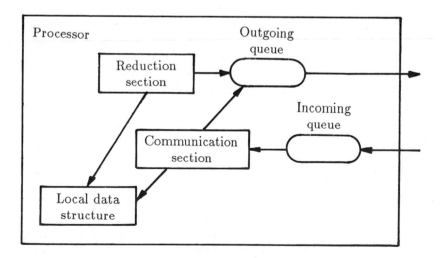

Figure 39.2

The buffering section accepts messages from other processors, deposits them into the incoming queue and transmits requests placed in the outgoing queue. It runs continually and is implicit in the discussions that follow.

The communication section processes messages in the incoming queue and may modify local data structures. The operation of the communication section occurs between process reductions to preserve atomicity of reduction.

The reduction section maintains a queue of active processes and performs reduction attempts. Each *reduction_attempt* involves choosing a process from the active queue and attempting a *clause_try* for each clause in an associated procedure. Each clause try involves making a new copy of the selected clause, unifying the process with the head of the clause copy and solving the clause guard. If unification and guard execution succeed, the process is replaced by the body of the clause copy in the active queue. If either unification or guard execution fails, the process may suspend or busy-wait.

The unification algorithm treats remote references as references to unknown terms which must be either read or written upon. If unification requires the *value* of an unknown term (e.g., $X? = a$), an attempt is made to *read* the remote term by placing a *READ* message in the outgoing communication queue. If unification requires binding of an unknown term via a remote reference (e.g., $Y = a$), it is assumed that the remote term is a variable; an attempt is made to *lock* the variable by placing a *LOCK* communication message in the outgoing communication queue.

Individual clause tries may independently require reading and/or locking. If unification and guard execution both succeed without needing reading or locking, the clause try commits and no communication is necessary. If either unification or guard execution fails no communication is necessary for the clause try. Otherwise, the clause try either attempts to bind a variable via a read-only reference (data-flow synchronization) or some communication is required for the clause try to commit.

It cannot be known a-priori if a clause will commit; thus no communication is transmitted until the outcome of a reduction attempt is known. Instead, communication required is logged (in a *suspension table*) during each clause try and actually transmitted only if no clause commits. When a clause try fails, any entries it deposits in the suspension table are discarded. Since all the necessary communication will be logged during each clause try, all communication messages are issued together at the completion of a reduction attempt for simplicity.

If no clause commits, the process may have some collection of read and/or write requests entered into the suspension table. If only read requests have been logged, all read communication is issued and the process suspends on the disjunction of the requests. The requests include attempts to bind a read-only occurrence of a variable locally. If both read and write requests are present in the suspension table, all communication is issued and the process busy-waits. Eventually the process will obtain all the locks it requires and will either commit or suspend on outstanding read requests.

39.6 Implementation of Reading

When unification requires the value of a remote term, a *READ* communication request is sent via the appropriate remote reference. At the receiving processor, if the value is not yet known, a *broadcast note* is attached to the variable. When the variable is eventually bound, a *WRITE_VALUE* message is used to copy the value to each processor referenced by a broadcast note. Figure 39.3 shows the protocol.

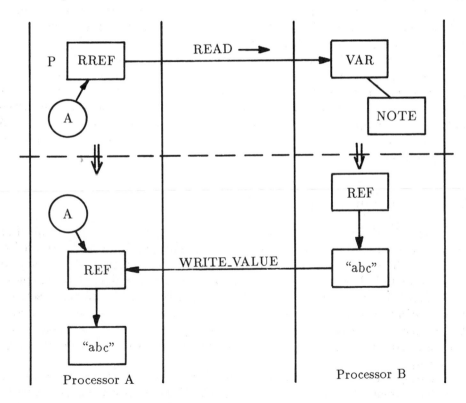

Figure 39.3

Process A requests the value of a remote variable via remote reference P using a *READ* communication request and suspends on P. At the receiving processor B a broadcast note is attached to the variable. Eventually, the variable is bound by another process to the string *abc*. The value is returned to each sender referenced by a broadcast note using a *WRITE_VALUE* message. This causes the original remote reference to be overwritten by a local reference to the communicated value and processes suspended on the remote reference to be woken up; eventually they will be re-scheduled and access the value.

The above protocol is implemented using a simple extension to the uni-processor suspension mechanism. A process may be suspended on some number of variables. Each variable has an associated queue (possibly empty) of suspension records. Each suspension record references the process indirectly via a *hanger* (Houri and Shapiro, Chapter 38). The hanger is invalidated when the process is woken up so that subsequent attempts to wake up the process have no effect. This structure is shown in Figure 39.4; process A is suspended on variables X and Y while process B is suspended on Y and Z.

If a process requires the value of a remote term in order to reduce, it may suspend on a remote reference in the same way it suspends waiting for the value of a variable. Only the first process to suspend on a remote reference causes a *READ* communication message to be sent. Eventually the value will be returned and will cause suspended processes to wake up. In the above diagram process A has suspended on remote reference P in addition to variables X and Y; process C is suspended on remote references P and Q.

39.7 Implementation of Locking

The reduction section of the scheme may cause a process to busy-wait if an attempt is made to bind a term via a remote reference. Two counts are used to control the busy-waiting of processes; and the *owner_count* reflects the number of owners for a locked variable, the *request_count* reflects the number of local requests for ownership of a remote variable. When a lock is granted to a processor, the remote reference in question becomes a local locked variable (variable migration). The *owner_count* of the locked variable is initialized to the *request_count* in the remote reference since this represents the number of processes requesting joint ownership.

A busy-waiting process carries a list of the lock requests made on its last reduction attempt. This list is non-empty only if the process is busy-waiting for locks. At each reduction attempt the process withdraws joint ownership of its locks by undoing all lock requests made on the previous reduction attempt. It then requests all the required locks independently of previous requests.

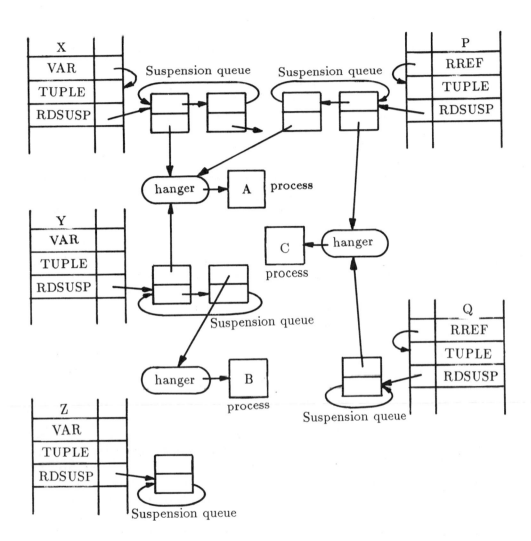

Figure 39.4

Lock requests can either fail (and do nothing) or succeed. If a lock request succeeds, either the variable is already local and the *owner_count* may be incremented or the variable is not local (i.e., a remote reference) and the *request_count* may be incremented. Successful requests are recorded in the list of requests assigned to a process for its next reduction.

A lock request for a variable fails if a higher priority processor is waiting for the lock; this causes locks to be physically released within one processor queue cycle. All processes which requested a lock are busy-waiting and will be re-scheduled. When re-scheduled they will logically release each lock but fail when trying to re-request it if a higher priority processor is waiting; thus the *owner_count* will be decremented but not incremented. Locks are physically released when the *owner_count* is decremented to zero (i.e., when all owners have logically released the lock).

The deadlock prevention scheme described previously requires that when a lock is refused, all processes which have requested joint ownership of the variable release all their locks. This may cause some variables to be unlocked allowing other remote processes to gain locks that they require. The crucial action is the physical release of locks to other processors because this allows high priority processors to obtain locks held by low priority processors. The time required to perform the action after it is initiated is unimportant but must be bounded; in the following algorithm it will take one processor queue cycle.

If a lock is refused, the status of the remote reference becomes *refused*. A lock request for a lock that has been refused fails; thus subsequent requests for the lock leave the *request_count* unchanged. Processes which previously made requests for the lock will decrement but not increment the *request_count* by virtue of the reduction algorithm. When a *request_count* is decreased to zero, the status of the remote reference is set to *not_requested*. This indicates that all processes which previously requested the refused lock have now withdrawn joint ownership of their locks (some locks may have been physically released). A process may re-request a lock the next time it is scheduled; the first such re-request may cause a physical *LOCK* communication request.

The set of variables which are physically released in each processor queue cycle includes as a subset those variables which should have been released because a lock was refused. This satisfies, indirectly, the critical requirement for deadlock prevention under joint ownership.

Locked variables which do not have a higher priority processor waiting will be released and then re-requested, maintaining the *owner_count* correctly. Remote references which have not been refused will be released and then re-requested, maintaining the *request_count* correctly.

Figure 39.5 outlines the protocol involved in locking.

Process A requests a lock on variable X and busy waits. Eventually the request arrives to either a higher priority or lower priority processor. If X is already bound then the value is copied to the sending processor using a *WRITE_VALUE* message; this copying operation is legal due to the single assignment rule (see situation A above). If X is unbound and unlocked, the lock is granted to the requesting processor. If it is locked and the priority of the sending processor is

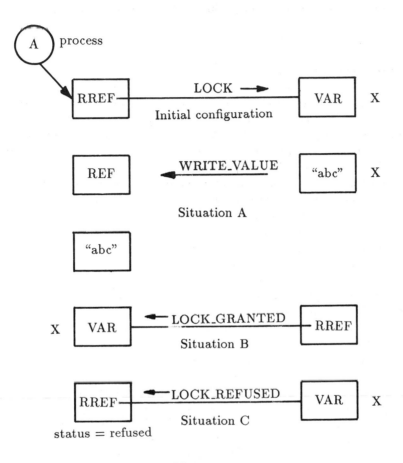

Figure 39.5

higher than that of the receiver, then the request is held at the receiver until the variable is unlocked; the variable is then granted to the requesting processor. Granting a lock involves *variable migration*; the variable is modified to be a remote reference to the sender and a *LOCK_GRANTED* message is used to transfer the variable to the sender (see situation *B* above). If *X* is locked and the priority of the receiving processor is highest, then a *LOCK_REFUSED* message is sent in reply causing the sender to release its locks (see situation *C* above).

Eventually a process will obtain all the variables it requires in order to commit. Provided that all the necessary values have also been obtained, the busy waiting process will eventually be re-scheduled and reduce; no communication is executed during a reduction attempt; thus with all locks held locally reduction is achieved as an atomic action.

39.8 Data Structures

Three primary data structures are used by the implementation: the heap, suspension table and trail. The heap is a global area used for allocation of dynamic structures. The suspension table is a static table used for recording variables and remote references on which to suspend or busy wait; it is reset at every reduction attempt. The suspension table is updated during unification and inspected if no clause commits at the end of a reduction attempt. The trail is used by unification to record bindings made to variables in the global environment. If a clause try fails, the environment may be reset to its original state using the entries in the trail. The trail is reset at every clause try.

All run time structures are represented by tagged words on the heap. This includes processes, suspension records, broadcast notes, etc. Variables and remote references are represented by a heap word with the appropriate tag and a pointer to a tuple of housekeeping information; this representation allows compact entries on the trail of the form: $\langle$ *pointer_to_variable, pointer_to_tuple* $\rangle$.

The housekeeping information required for a variable involved in inter-processor communication involves a suspension list, broadcast list, *owner_count* and high priority request. The suspension list is a list of processes suspended locally waiting for the variable to be bound. The broadcast list contains notes used for transmitting the value of the variable to other processors when it becomes bound. The owner count is used by the deadlock prevention algorithm and the high priority request is used to allow a remote high priority processor to wait for a lock on the variable.

A remote reference also requires considerable housekeeping information; a suspension list, remote pointer, *request_count* and status entry. The remote pointer is comprised of a processor identifier and a location within the processor. The request count is used by the deadlock prevention algorithm, and the status entry reflects whether a lock has been requested or refused.

39.9 The Parallel Interpreter

The main control algorithm of the parallel interpreter consists of the reduction and communication sections described previously. The communication section is executed between process reduction attempts for atomicity of unification. It services messages from remote processors by accessing the incoming queue.

```
control =
{ repeat
    { reduction_attempt          % do a reduction
      communication              % service incoming messages
    } forever
}

communication =
{ for each request in incoming_queue do
    execute(request)
}
```

39.9.1 Messages

Only five message types are used by the implementation; the following list describes each and its effects.

READ(To,From)

The *READ* message is received when a remote processor requests the value of a variable via some remote reference. *To* indicates the processor to receive the message and the variable to be read. *From* represents the sending processor and the location of the source remote reference. If the message is received at the source processor, *localization* is performed; otherwise the *To* location is inspected. If it is a variable, a broadcast note is attached to the variable; when the variable becomes bound, the note is used to return the value to the requesting processor. If there is a remote reference at the *To* location, the message is forwarded with the *To* field in the message replaced by the address in the remote reference. If the *To* location is a value, it is copied to the requesting processor using a *WRITE_VALUE* message. Constants are copied verbatim and demand driven coping is used for tuples (i.e., the top level of the structure is copied; if any argument of the tuple is a constant, it is copied verbatim but remote references are sent to the other arguments).

LOCK(To,From)

This message requests a lock on a variable. *To* indicates which processor receives the message and which variable must be locked. *From* indicates the processor which sent the message and the location of the source remote reference.

If the message is received at the source processor *localization* applied; otherwise the location at *To* is inspected. If it is a value or remote reference, a similar action is taken to that described above for *READ*. If the location at *To* is a variable, the deadlock prevention algorithm is invoked.

The deadlock prevention algorithm uses processor priority to decide which action to take. If the variable is unlocked, the lock can be granted immediately. If it is locked and the priority of the sending processor is lower than that of the local processor, a *LOCK_REFUSED* message is sent to the sending processor; this forces the sending processor to release its locks. The variable may also be locked when a request from a higher priority processor is received. If no previous high priority request was received, the request can simply be associated with the variable; otherwise the highest of the two requests is associated with the variable and the other is requested to try later by sending a *LOCK_REFUSED* message.

Granting a lock involves *variable migration*. A *LOCK_GRANTED* message is used to transmit the variable together with its broadcast list; the variable is replaced by a remote reference. A number of processes may be suspended waiting to read the variable. These processes remain suspensed upon the new remote reference, but it is necessary to ensure that they are woken up if the variable becomes bound. To do this, a broadcast note to the local processor is added to the list of broadcast notes sent in the *LOCK_GRANTED* message. Since locks are only granted to other processors when there are no owners, the *request_count* for the remote reference is initialized to zero.

LOCK_GRANTED(To,Broadcast_list)

This message grants ownership of a variable to a processor which requested a lock via the remote reference specified by *To*. It carries the broadcast list for the variable. The remote reference at the receiver is transformed into a local variable with the number of owners initialized to be the number of requests made; processes waiting on the remote reference are woken up. It is impossible for the value at *To* to be anything other than a remote reference because this message effectively carries the unbound variable.

If any of the destinations specified in the *Broadcast_list* are local to the receiver, then the remote references in question can be changed to local references immediately (a form of localization).

LOCK_REFUSED(To)

This message indicates that the remote processor from which a lock was requested is either higher priority than the local processor and is using the variable, or has a higher priority processor waiting for the variable and is using the variable.

To specifies the address of the remote reference via which the lock request was issued; the message causes a *lock_refused* flag is set in this remote reference. This causes processes to release their locks during reduction.

WRITE_VALUE(To,Value)

This message is responsible for copying values between processors. If a *READ* or *LOCK* request is issued via a remote reference and the end of the remote chain is a value, a *WRITE_VALUE* message is received in answer to the request. The argument *Value* is a term and *To* specifies the location of a remote reference via which the request originated.

The *WRITE_VALUE* message causes the remote reference at *To* to be bound to the value *Value*. If a process is suspended on the remote reference, by virtue of having issued a read request, it is activated. Busy-waiting processes may be waiting for a lock on the location; in this case they simply use the value when they are scheduled.

39.9.2 Unification

The parallel execution algorithm uses the order independent semantics for unification. If all variables and values required for unification are local to the processor, then unification proceeds normally. The uni-processor algorithm treats an unbound variable as an unknown term; when attempting to read an unknown term via a read-only reference, suspension occurs. In the parallel algorithm remote references simply refer to unknown terms which must be either read or written upon; there are only two modifications to the normal unification algorithm. If an attempt is made to bind an unknown term via a remote reference, a write request is logged in the suspension table. This informs the control algorithm to *LOCK* the remote term for writing. Any attempt to read an unknown term (locally or remotely) causes a read request to be logged in the suspension table. This informs the control algorithm to suspend until the value is known and to read the term via a *READ* communication message if it is not local.

The unification algorithm distinguishes between variables in the clause and variables or remote references in the goal environment. It never writes on remote references; when the variable or value is local, unification will be carried out. Since remote references can only occur in the goal environment and only instantiations to goal variables are trailed, all requests generated in the suspension table will be to goal variables or remote references; moreover, goal variables can never be bound to remote references.

A function *wait* is used to log a read request in the suspension table; its argument is a read-only variable or remote reference to wait upon. A function *bind* is used to bind terms in the goal environment; it enters write requests in the suspension table and sets a flag (LWF) which is local to the clause try to indicate that write requests are required.

The symmetric Table 39.1 describes the unification algorithm.
Unification either succeeds (returning True) or fails (returning False). A successful unification may make entries in the suspension table.

horizontal – term 1, vertical – term 2

1 / 2	clause variable	goal	ro	value
clause variable	$T1 :=$ REF(T2)			
goal	$T1 :=$ REF(T2)	bind (T1,T2)		
ro	$T1 :=$ RO(T2)	wait (T2)	wait (T1)	
value	$T1 :=$ REF(T2)	bind (T1,T2)	wait (T1)	UnifyTerms (T1,T2)

RO — read-only reference, REF — reference

Table 1

39.9.3 Reduction attempt

Reduction of a process using the clauses in an associated procedure involves unifying the process with the head and solving the guard of each clause. The first clause which can commit, commits. Each clause try may either fail or succeed; failure may cause read and/or write requests to be placed in the suspension table. These requests indicate either that an unknown term is to be read or written upon.

Recall that a process may commit, busy-wait or suspend. If no clause commits and failure does not occur, then either:

(a) The process must busy-wait because there are write requests in the suspension table.

or:

(b) The process must suspend because there are no write requests in the suspension table.

In the former case all read and write requests are issued and the process is put back into the active queue. In the latter case all read requests are sent and the process is suspended to await a value.

```
reduction_attempt =
{ if (AQ != Null)
    { success := WF := FALSE
      pid := dequeue(AQ)                              % get process
      release_locks(pid.requests)
      while (not success) and (not end of procedure) do    % reduce
      { success :=
            clause_try(goal(pid),head(clause),guards(clause))
          if (not success) clause := next_clause
      }
      if (success) commit(pid,body(clause))           % commit
          else process_suspension_table(pid)          % suspend/busy-wait
    }
}
```

When a process releases its locks, the algorithm described under "Implementation of Locking" is executed. Appendix 39.2 gives abstract code which implements the algorithm.

If no clause commits, the suspension table is processed. A global flag (WF) is set by any clause try that suspends and makes write entries in the suspension table. This flag is used to determine whether to busy-wait or suspend.

Clause try

A clause try may either succeed (returning TRUE), fail (returning FALSE) or suspend (returning FALSE). Success indicates that there are no entries in the suspension table and that the reduction attempt may commit. Failure causes the environment to be reset to its original state prior to the clause try; this involves resetting variables by undoing instantiations entered in the trail, resetting the heap and suspension tables. Since failed clause tries generate no effects external to the clause try algorithm, they will not generate communication traffic. If a clause try suspends, the entries in the suspension table are saved but the environment and heap are reset.

The clause try uses both a table-driven unification algorithm and a method for solving guard predicates. Two pointers are required to manipulate the suspension table: one marks the suspension table position when a clause try begins (STB); the other marks the top of the suspension table (STP). A flag, local to the clause try (LWF), is set by the unification algorithm if a write entry is placed in the suspension table. If the clause try does not fail, this flag is used to set a global write flag (WF) which informs the control algorithm that the process should busy wait if no clause commits.

```
clause_try(goal,head,guards) =
{ LWF := FALSE
```

```
    success :=
      unify(goal,head) and do_guards(guards) and    % logical and
              order_check
    if (success)
      { if (STP = SBP) return(True)                  % commit
          if (LWF) Undo_and_log                      % lock local variables
            else Undo_trail                          % reset global environment
          SBP := STP                                 % save suspensions
          WF := WF or LWF                            % signal WF by logical or
      }
    else                                             % unification failed
      { Undo_trail                                   % reset global environment
          STP := SBP                                 % discard suspensions
      }
    reset_heap                                       % try another clause
    return(False)                                    % do not commit
}
```

An *order_check* is applied to discover if any read-only occurrences of a variable, which were suspended upon, were later bound; if so, unification and guard evaluation are repeated, thus providing an order-independent algorithm.

During unification only instantiations to variables in the goal environment are trailed; failure or suspension causes these instantiations to be undone. If write requests are being issued, additional requests are entered into the suspension table for each goal variable that has been bound (c.f. Undo_and_log). This prevents variables held locally from being stolen by low priority processors. It allows processors to keep locks they have obtained until either they write on them or a high priority processor needs them.

Commit

When unification binds a goal variable, its value (a pointer to a tuple containing a suspension queue and broadcast list) is saved in the trail. If a clause try commits, the trail is scanned. Each process referenced from a suspension queue in the trail is woken up and values are sent to processors referenced by broadcast notes. The body of the clause is spawned and each body process is enqueued into the active queue.

Suspension

When a read request is detected, a check must be made to decide if a message must be sent. To minimize communication, *READ* messages are only sent if no previous *READ* message has been sent and no *LOCK* message has been sent for a given remote reference. The process is suspended to await a reply using a suspension record as described previously (in: "Implementation of Reading"). Abstract code which describes this operation is given in Appendix 39.2.

Busy-waiting

When a process must busy-wait for locks, a list of lock requests is accumulated while processing the suspension table and all necessary communication is performed. The list of lock requests is then attached to the process and the process is put back into the active queue.

If a read entry is found while processing the suspension table, an attempt is made to send the necessary read communication. If the entry is a write request, it may indicate that either a local variable or remote variable needs to be locked. In the former case the *owner_count* in the local variable is incremented; in the latter the *request_count* in the remote reference is incremented and an attempt is made to send the necessary *LOCK* communication message. This attempt only succeeds if the remote reference does not indicate that the lock was refused and that a *LOCK* message has not already been sent earlier. The procedure is described more fully in "Implementation of Locking" and abstract code is given in Appendix 39.2.

39.10 Correctness and Complexity

Unfortunately, the complexity of the algorithm and the lack of a formal language definition prevents a formal proof of the algorithm; it is possible to make some intuitive comments.

When all the data structures are local, the algorithm performs the uniprocessor algorithm for FCP; the additional complexity is required to ensure that needed data is brought locally. For reading, the algorithm ensures that only *necessary* structures are copied and that copying is performed as soon as the data is available. For writing, in the event that no conflicts occur or single writer programs are used, variables and values are brought locally immediately.

The algorithm does not involve areas of major computational complexity; there are only three places in the code where a loop exists within a loop. These areas all arise from actions that are fundamentally part of the uni-processor reduction algorithm such as waking up processes suspended on a variable. Most of the actions added for parallel execution are simple straight line code segments involving a few tests and assignments. Hand timings indicate that the cost of a simple producer/consumer relation between two processors is approximately twice that of the same program executed on a single processor. An incomplete message requires an overhead of three times the uni-processor cost.

39.11 Related Work

Some early work in this area (Bar-On, 1986) was an experiment to test the feasibility of implementing FCP under simulated multiprocessing. A major goal of this work was to assess the suitability of Occam for implementing FCP. The scheme implemented a restrictive subset of FCP, did not prevent livelock and could not deal with multiple writers or variable to variable binding; however it produced a number of interesting insights.

Tamaki (1985) has investigated parallel unification for a subset of Concurrent Prolog. This scheme enforces local communication, does not specify how communication primitives operate, makes no attempt to solve the deadlock problem and disregards non-local communication. Non-local communication can be beneficial in some applications (Taylor et al., Chapter 8). The scheme does not allow variable to variable binding or multiple writers and as a result cannot support the short circuit technique. In addition the scheme cannot properly utilize partially bound input. Slight variations to a program causes Tamaki's scheme not to work (Taylor et al., Chapter 8).

39.12 Conclusion

The algorithm presented has been useful for providing insights into the major problems and includes a number of novel ideas. The implementation has been demonstrated on a range of applications including the code and process mapping techniques described by Taylor et al. (Chapter 22). It represents the first parallel implementation of FCP and provides a workable basis for current and future research. Garbage collection and detection of global termination are discussed by Av-Ron and Taylor (1986); system bootstrapping is discussed by Taylor et al. (Chapter 22).

Unfortunately, the data structures required to support the scheme are cumbersome; moreover the deadlock prevention scheme seems complex although it is by far the most simple of many proposed schemes. Perhaps most concerning is that the algorithm is sufficiently complex that it is difficult to reason about its correctness

The algorithm has some known deficiencies which may occur in atypical applications. A high priority process may recurse infinitely while holding locks on variables and never writing on them; other processes will as a result never obtain access thus starvation occurs. Two processes may cooperate to prevent messages from accessing a variable; both processes recurse infinitely, sharing a variable; each takes a turn to lock it but never writes on it.

Each of the above problems has proposed solutions; each solution increases the level of complexity in an algorithm which is already far too complex. Current research thus focuses primarily on simplifying the algorithm. A number of significant improvements are under consideration but have not yet been implemented. These improvements substantially decrease the complexity of the locking scheme and data-structures.

Finally, the requirement that communication occurs between process reductions can be relaxed substantially if more flexible hardware is available. In particular, *READ* and *LOCK* messages arriving at a destination which is either a value or remote reference can be served immediately.

Acknowledgements

The authors wish to acknowledge the various contributions of Lisa Hellerstein in early versions of the parallel algorithm described in this paper. In addition, the work of Uri Bar-on has had considerable impact on this work.

Appendix 39.1 Proof of correctness for deadlock prevention

The necessary and sufficient conditions for deadlock to occur are:

(1) Resources cannot be pre-empted while being used.

(2) Resources cannot be shared.

(3) Processes hold resources while requesting others.

(4) A circular wait exists in which each process holds resources requested by other processes.

Deadlock, as defined earlier, is a state of execution where there is a list of processes, $[p0, p1, \ldots, pn]$, $n \geq 1$, such that each process pi has ownership of a distinct resource ri. Moreover, each process pi has requested resource $r(i+1)mod(n+1)$ and is being forced to wait for the resource until after such time that process $p(i+1)mod(n+1)$ gives up its ownership of the resource. The important point is mutual wait. Joint ownership of resources does not alter the fact that mutual wait is required in order to have deadlock.

We prove by contradiction that circular wait is impossible and that the policies described above prevent deadlock:

Assume a situation of circular wait, that is, a list of processes $[p0, p1, \ldots, pn]$, $n \geq 1$, such that each process pi has ownership of a distinct lock ri, and has requested lock $r(i+1)mod(n+1)$, but is being forced to wait for the resource at least until after such time that process $p(i+1)mod(n+1)$ has given up its ownership of the resource. For the above scenario to happen, the following must be true:

Assume process pi belongs to processor Pi, and process $p(i+1)mod(n+1)$ belongs to processor Pj. Then the priority of Pi must be higher than the priority of Pj, because otherwise process Pi would either have been granted joint ownership of the lock ($Pi = Pj$), or its lock request would have been denied altogether (priority of Pi lower than priority of Pj).

Thus the priority of *P1* must be higher than the priority of *P2*, the priority of *P2* higher than the priority of *P3*, and, by transitivity and induction, the priority of *P0* is therefore higher than the priority of *Pn*. However, the priority of *Pn* must be higher than the priority of $P(n+1)mod(n+1)$. But $P(n+1)mod(n+1)$ is just *P0*, so that it has been now shown that the priority of *P0* is higher than the priority of *Pn*, and the priority of *Pn* is higher than the priority of *P0*; a contradiction. ∎

Appendix 39.2

```
release_locks(requests) =
{ for each request in requests do
   { lock := request.lock_ptr
     case lock↑ .tag of
     { VAR :
          { tp := lock↑ .value                          % get tuple pointer
            decrement(tp↑ .owner_count)                 % withdraw ownership
            if (tp↑ .owner_count = 0) and               % no owners
               (tp↑ .priority_req != Null)              % priority req. waiting
            grant_lock(lock,tp↑ .priority_req)          % physically release
          }
     } RREF :
          { tp := lock↑ .value                          % get tuple pointer
            decrement(tp↑ .request_count)               % withdraw ownership
            if (tp↑ .request_count = 0) and             % no requests made
               (tp↑ .state = refused)                   % lock was refused
            tp↑ .state := not_requested                 % allow re-request
          }
       Default :                                        % do nothing
   }
}
```

```
}
read_and_suspend(hangerp,rref_tp) =
{ if ((rref_tp↑ .rd_susps=Null) and                      % no reads sent
        (rref_tp↑ .state=not_requested))                 % no lock req sent
    { from.pe := my_pe_num
      from.location := rref_tp
      to := rref_tp↑ .ptr
      send_read(to,from)                                 % send read msg
    }
  queue_put(rref_tp↑ .rd_susps, hangerp)                 % suspend process
}

busy_wait(pid) =
{ requestq := Null
  hangerp := allocate_hanger(0)                          % dummy hanger
  for each entry in suspension_table do
  { case entry.tag of
    { RD :
        if (entry.ptr↑ .tag = RREF)
            read_and_suspend(hangerp,entry.ptr↑ .value)
      WR :
        { tp := entry.ptr↑ .value                        % get tuple ptr
          if (entry.ptr↑ .tag = VAR)
            { if (tp↑ .priority_req = null)               % no priority req
                { increment(tp↑ .owner_count)            % joint ownership
                  rec := allocate_request_rec(entry.ptr)
                  add_to_queue(requestq,rec)
                }
            }
        }
        else                                             % RREF
          { if (not tp↑ .state = refused)                % not refused
              { if (tp↑ .state = not_requested)          % no prev req
                { from.pe_num := my_pe_num
                  from.location := lockp
                  to := tp↑ .ptr
                  send_lock(to,from)                     % issue request
                  tp↑ .state := requested
                }
                increment(tp↑ .request_count)            % joint ownership
                rec := allocate_request_rec(entry.ptr)
                add_to_queue(requestq,rec)
```

```
                    }
                }
            }
        }
    pid.requests := requestq                    % process gets requests
    add_to_queue(AQ, pid)                       % busy wait
}
```

References

Ackerman, W.B., Data flow languages, *IEEE Computer* **15**(2), pp. 15–25, 1982.

Adobe Systems Inc., *PostScript Language Manual*, Addison-Wesley, 1985.

Aho, A.V., Hopcroft, J.E., and Ullman, J.D., *The Design and Analysis of Computer Algorithms*, Addison-Wesley, 1974.

Ahuja, S., Carriero, N., and Gelernter, D., Linda and Friends, *IEEE Computer* **19**(8), pp. 26–34, August 1986.

Ali, K.A.M., Object-Oriented Storage Management and Garbage Collection in Distributed Processing Systems, Ph.D. Thesis, Royal Institute of Technology, Stockholm, 1984.

Ali, K.A.M., Or-parallel execution of Prolog on a multi-sequential machine, SICS Tech. Report, 1986a.

Ali, K.A.M., Or-parallel execution of Horn clause programs based on the WAM and shared control information, SICS Tech. Report, November 1986b.

Allen, J., *The Anatomy of Lisp*, McGraw-Hill, 1978.

Anderson, J.M., Coates, W.S., Davis A.L., Hon, R.W., Robinson, I.N., Robison, S.V. and Stevens, K.S., The architecture of FAIM1, *Computer* **20**(1), pp. 55–66, 1987.

Andrews, G.R., Synchronizing resources, *ACM Trans. on Programming Languages and Systems* **3**(4), pp. 405–430, 1981.

Andrews, G.R., The distributed programming language SR — mechanisms, design and implementation, *Software — Practice and Experience* **12**(8), pp. 719–754, 1982.

Andrews, G.R., and Olsson, R., The evolution of the SR programming language, Tech. Report 85-22, Department of Computer Science, Univ. of Arizona, 1985.

ANSI PL/I, ANS X3.53–1976, American National Standards Institute, 1976.

Apt, K.R., and van Emden, M.H., Contributions to the theory of logic programming, *J. ACM* **29**(3), pp. 841–863, 1982.

Arvind, K., and Brock, J.D., Streams and managers, in Maekawa, M., and Belady, L.A. (eds.), *Operating Systems Engineering, LNCS* **143**, pp. 452–465, Springer-Verlag, 1982.

Arvind, K., Gostelow, K.P., and Plouffe, W., Indeterminacy, monitors and dataflow, *Proc. 6th ACM Symposium on Operating Systems Principles, Operating Systems Reviews* **11**(5), pp. 159–169, 1977.

Arvind, K., Gostelow, K.P., and Plouffe, W., An asynchronous programming language and computing machine, Tech. Report TR114a, University of California at Irvine, 1978.

Arvind, K., and Thomas, R.E., I-structures: An efficient data type for functional languages, Tech. Mem. TM-178, Laboratory for Computer Science, MIT, Cambridge, Massachusetts, 1978.

Av-Ron, E., and Taylor, S., A distributed garbage collector for FCP, Department of Computer Science, The Weizmann Institute of Science, Rehovot, 1986.

Baker, H., Actor systems for real-time computation, Tech. Report TR-197, Laboratory for Computer Science, MIT, Cambridge, Massachusetts, 1978a.

Baker, H., Shallow binding in LISP 1.5, *Comm. ACM*, **21**(7), 1978b.

Baker, H., and Hewitt, C., The incremental garbage collection of processes, *ACM Conference on Artificial Intelligence and Programming Languages*, Rochester, *SIGPLAN Notices* **12**(8), pp. 55–59, New York, 1977.

Bar-on, U., A distributed implementation of Flat Concurrent Prolog, M.Sc. Thesis, Department of Computer Science, The Weizmann Institute of Science, Rehovot, 1986.

Bawden, A., Burke, G.S., and Hoffman, C.W., MacLISP extensions, Tech. Report TM-203, Laboratory for Computer Science, MIT, Cambridge, Massachusetts, 1981.

Beckman, L., Haraldson, A., Oskarsson, O., and Sandewall, E., A partial evaluator and its use as a programming tool, *Artificial Intelligence* **7**(4), pp. 319–357, 1976.

Berman, F., and Snyder, L., On mapping parallel algorithms into parallel architectures, *Proc. IEEE International Conference on Parallel Processing*, 1984.

Bloch, C., Source-to-source transformations of logic programs, Tech. Report

CS84-22, Department of Computer Science, The Weizmann Institute of Science, Rehovot, 1984.

Bobrow, D.G., What it takes to support AI programming paradigms or, if Prolog is the answer, what is the question?, *IEEE Trans. on Software Engineering*, **11**, pp. 1401–1408, 1985.

Bobrow, D.G., and Hayes, P.J., Artificial intelligence: Where are we? *Artificial Intelligence* **25**, pp. 375–415, 1985.

Bobrow, D.G., Kahn, K., Kiczles, G., Masinter, L., Stefik, M., and Zdybel, F., CommonLoops: Merging Common Lisp and object-oriented programming, *ACM Conference on Object-Oriented Programming Systems, Languages and Applications*, pp. 17–29, Portland, Oregon, 1986.

Bobrow D.G., and Stefik, M., *The LOOPS Manual* (Preliminary version), Memo KB-VLSI-81-13, Xerox Parc, 1983.

Bokhari, S.H., On the mapping problem, *IEEE Trans. on Computers*, **C-30**(3), pp. 207–214, 1981.

Borning, A., The programming language aspects of ThingLab, a constraint-oriented simulation laboratory, *ACM Trans. on Programming Languages and Systems* **3**(4), pp. 353–387, 1981.

Bowen, D.L., Byrd, L., Pereira, L.M., Pereira, F.C.N., and Warren, D.H.D., PRO-LOG on the DECSystem-10 User's Manual, Tech. Report, Department of Artificial Intelligence, University of Edinburgh, 1981.

Bowen, K.A., and Kowalski, R.A., Amalgamating language and metalanguage in logic programming, in Clark, K.L., and Tärnlund, S.-Å. (eds.), *Logic Programming*, pp. 153–172, Academic Press, London, 1982.

Brock, J.D., and Ackerman, W.B., Scenarios: A model of non-determinate computations, in Dias and Ramos (eds.), *Formalization of Programming Concepts*, *LNCS* **107**, pp. 252–259, Springer-Verlag, 1981.

Broda, K., and Gregory, S., PARLOG for discrete event simulation, Tärnlund, S.-Å. (ed.), *Proc. 2nd International Conference on Logic Programming*, pp. 301–312, Uppsala, 1984.

Bruynooghe, M., Adding redundancy to obtain more reliable and more readable Prolog programs, *Proc. 1st International Conference on Logic Programming*, pp. 129–134, ADDP-GIA, Faculte des Sciences de Luminy, Marseille, 1982.

Bryant, R.E., and Dennis, J.B., Concurrent programming, in Maekawa, M., and Blady, L.A. (eds.), *Operating Systems Engineering*, *LNCS* **143**, pp. 426–452, Springer-Verlag, 1982.

Buettner, K., and Bowen, K.A., FLIP — a functional language in Prolog, Tech. Report CIS-86-12, Syracuse University, 1986.

Bundy, A., and Silver, B., Homogenization: Preparing equations for change of unknown, *Proc. 7th International Joint Conference on Artificial Intelligence*, pp. 551–553, 1981.

Bundy, A., and Welham, B., Using meta-level inference for selective applicaiton of multiple rewrite rules in algebraic manipulation, *Artificial Intelligence* **16**, pp. 189–212, 1981.

Burke, G.S., Carrette, G.J., and Eliot, C.J., The NIL reference Manual, Tech. Report 311, Laboratory for Computer Science, MIT, Cambridge, Massachusetts, 1984.

Burkimsher, P.C., PRISM — A DSM multiprocessor reduction machine for the parallel implementation of applicative languages, *Proc. Declarative Programming Workshop*, pp. 189–202, London, 1983.

Ciepielewski, A., Towards a computer architecture for Or-parallel execution of logic programs, Ph.D. Thesis, TRITA-CS-8401, Department of Computer Systems, Royal Institute of Technology, Stockholm, 1984.

Clark, K.L., Negation as failure, in Gallaire, H., and Minker, J. (eds.), *Logic and Data Bases*, pp. 293–322, Plenum Publishing Co., New York, 1978.

Clark, K.L., Predicate logic as a computational formalism, Research Monograph 79/59 TOC, Department of Computing, Imperial College, London, 1979.

Clark, K.L., and Gregory, S., A relational language for parallel programming, *Proc. ACM Conference on Functional Languages and Computer Architecture*, pp. 171–178, 1981. Also Chapter 1, this volume.

Clark, K.L., and Gregory, S., Notes on systems programming in PARLOG, *Proc. International Conference on Fifth Generation Computer Systems*, pp. 299–306, Tokyo, 1984.

Clark, K.L., and Gregory, S., Notes on the implementation of PARLOG, Research Report DOC84/16, 1984. Also in *J. Logic Programming* **2**(1), pp. 17–42, 1985.

Clark, K.L., and Gregory, S., PARLOG: Parallel programming in logic, *ACM TOPLAS* **8**(1), pp. 1–49, 1986. Also Chapter 3, this volume.

Clark, K.L., and McCabe, F.G., *micro-PROLOG: Programming in Logic*, Prentice-Hall, New Jersey, 1984.

Clark, K.L., McCabe, F.G., and Gregory, S., IC-PROLOG — language features, in Clark, K.L., and Tärnlund, S.-Å. (eds.), *Logic Programming*, pp. 253–266,

Academic Press, London, 1982.

Clark, K.L., and S.-Å. Tärnlund, A first-order theory of data and programs, in Gilchrist, B. (ed.), *Information Processing* **77**, pp. 939–944, North-Holland, 1977.

Clinger, W., Foundations of actor semantics, Tech. Report TR-633, Artificial Intelligence Laboratory, MIT, Cambridge, Massachusetts, 1981.

Clocksin, W.R., and Alshawi, H., A method for efficiently executing Horn clause programs using multiple processors, Tech. Report, Department of Computer Science, Cambridge University, Cambridge, May 1986.

Clocksin, W.F., and Mellish, C.S., *Programming in Prolog*, 2nd Edition, Springer-Verlag, New York, 1984.

Codish, M., Compiling Or-parallelism into And-parallelism, M.Sc. Thesis, Department of Computer Science, The Weizmann Institute of Science, Rehovot, 1985.

Codish, M., and Shapiro, E., Compiling Or-parallelism into And-parallelism, *New Generation Computing* **5**(1), pp. 45–61, 1987. Also Chapter 32, this volume.

Coffman, E.G., and Denning, P.J., *Operating Systems Theory*, Prentice-Hall, New Jersey, 1973.

Cohen, S., Parallel computation, Ph.D. Thesis, The Hebrew University of Jerusalem, 1983.

Cohen, S., The APPLOG language, in DeGroot, D., and Lindstrom, G. (eds.), *Logic Programming — Functions, Relations and Equations*, pp. 239–276, Prentice-Hall, New Jersey, 1986.

Colmerauer, A., Kanui, H., and van Kanegham, M., Last steps towards an ultimate Prolog, *Proc. 7th International Joint Conference on Artificial Intelligence*, pp. 947–948, 1981.

Colmerauer, A. et al., *PROLOG II: Reference Manual and Theoretical Model*, Groupe d'Intelligence Artificielle, Faculte des Sciences de Luminy, Universite d'Aix-Marseille II, 1982.

Conery, J.S., The AND/OR process model for parallel interpretation of logic programs, Ph.D. Thesis, Tech. Report 204, Department of Information and Computer Science, University of California, Irvine, 1983.

Conery, J.S., and Kibler, D.F., Parallel interpretation of logic programs, *Proc. ACM Conference on Functional Programming Languages and Computer Architecture*, pp. 163–170, 1981.

Cousot, P., and Cousot, R., Abstract interpretation: A unified lattice model for static analysis of programs by construction or approximation of fixpoints, *Proc. ACM Symposium on Principles of Programming Languages*, pp. 238–252, 1977.

Crammond, J., A comparatie study of unification algorithms for Or-parallel execution of logic languages, *Proc. IEEE International Conference on Parallel Processing*, pp. 131–138, 1985.

Darlington, J., Field, A.J., and Pull, H., The unification of functional and logic languages, in DeGreeot, D., and Lindstrom, G. (eds.), *Logic Programming — Functions, Relations and Equations*, pp. 37–70, Prentice-Hall, New Jersey, 1986.

Darlington, J., and Reeve, M.J., ALICE: A multi-processor reduction machine, *Proc. ACM Conference on Functional Programming Languages and Computer Architecture*, pp. 65–75, Portsmouth, New Hampshire, 1981.

Dausmann, M., Persch, G., and Winterstein, G., Concurrent logic, *Proc. 4th Workshop on Artificial Intelligence*, Bad Honnef, 1979.

Davis, A.L., and Keller, R.M., Data flow graphs, *Computer* **15**(2), pp. 26–41, 1982.

DeGroot, D., Mapping Computation Structures onto SW-Banyan Networks, Ph.D. Thesis, University of Texas at Austin, 1981.

DeGroot, D., Restricted And-parallelism, *Proc. International Conference on Fifth Generation Computer Systems*, pp. 471–478, Tokyo, 1984.

DeGroot, D., and Lindstrom, G. (eds.), *Logic Programming — Functions, Relations and Equations*, Prentice-Hall, New Jersey, 1986.

Dennis, J.B., First version of a data flow procedure language, in Rodiner, B. (ed.), *Programming Symposium: Proceedings, Colloque sur la Programmation*, *LNCS* **19**, pp. 362–376, Springer Verlag, 1974.

Dennis, J.B., *A language design for structured concurrency*, Williams, J.H., and Fischer, D.A. (eds.), *LNCS* **54**, pp. 231–242, Springer-Verlag, 1976.

Dijkstra, E.W., Guarded commands, nondeterminacy and formal derivation of programs, *Comm. ACM* **18**(8), pp. 453–457, 1975.

Dijkstra, E.W., *A Discipline of Programming*, Prentice-Hall, New Jersey, 1976.

Dijkstra, E.W., Feijen, W.H., and van Gasteren, A.J.M., Derivation of a termination algorithm for distributed computation, *Inf. Proc. Lett.* **16**, pp. 217–219, 1983.

Dinic, E.A., Algorithm for solution of maximum flow in a network with power estimation, *Soviet Math. Dokl.* **II**, pp. 1277–1280, 1970.

Dolev, D., Klawe, M., and Rodeh, M., An $O(N \log N)$ unidirectional distributed algorithm for extrema finding in a circle, *J. of Algorithms* **3**, pp. 245–260, 1982.

Dubitzki, T., Wu, A., and Rosenfeld, A., Parallel region property computation by active quadtree networks, *IEEE Trans.*, **PAMI-3**, pp. 626–633, 1981.

Dyer, C., and Rosenfeld, A., Parallel image processing by memory-augmented cellular automata, *IEEE Trans.*, **PAMI-3**, pp. 29–41, 1981.

Foderaro, J.K., Sklower, K.L., and Layer, K., *The Franz Lisp Manual*, Unix Programmer's Manual, Supplementary Documents, 1983.

Edelman, S., Line connectivity algorithms for an asynchronous pyramid computer, *Computer Vision, Graphics and Image Processing*, 1987 (to appear).

Edelman, S., and Shapiro, E., Quadtrees in Concurrent Prolog, *Proc. IEEE International Conference on Parallel Processing*, pp. 544–551, 1985.

Edelman, S., and Shapiro, E., Image processing with Concurrent Prolog, Chapter 12, this volume.

Ellis, J.R., Mishkin, N., van Leunen, M., and Wood, S.R., Tools: An environment for timeshared computing and programming, Research Report 232, Department of Computer Science, Yale University, 1982.

van Emden, M.H., and Kowalski, R.A., The semantics of predicate logic as a programming language, *J. ACM* **23**(4), pp. 733–742, 1976.

van Emden, M.H., and de Lucena, G.J., Predicate logic as a language for parallel programming, in Clark, K.L., and Tärnlund, S.-Å. (eds.), *Logic Programming*, pp. 189–198, Academic Press, London, 1982.

Ershov, A., On the partial evaluation principle, *Inf. Proc. Lett.* **6**(2), pp. 38–41, 1977.

Even, S., *Graph Algorithms*, Computer Science Press, 1979.

Fages, F., Associative-commutative unification, *Proc. 7th Conference on Automated Deduction*, *LNCS* **170**, pp. 194–208, Springer-Verlag, 1984.

Fahlman, S.E., Hinton, G.E., and Sejnowski, T.J., Massively parallel architecture for AI — NETL, THISTLE and Boltzmann machines, *Proc. National Conference on Artificial Intelligence*, pp. 109–113, 1983.

Ferrand, G., Error diagnosis in logic programming: An adaptation of E.Y. Shapiro's method, Rapport de Recherche 375, INRIA, 1985.

Fiat, A., Shamir, A., and Shapiro, E., Polymorphic arrays: An architecture for a programmable systolic machine, *Proc. IEEE International Conference on Parallel Processing*, pp. 112–117, 1985.

Fisher, A.F., Kung, H.T., Monier, M., and Yasunori, D., Architecture of the PSC: A programmable systolic chip, *Proc. 10th IEEE Annual International Symposium on Computer Architecture*, pp. 48–58, 1983.

Fortune, S., and Wyllie, J., Parallelism in random access machines, *Proc. 10th ACM Annual Symposium on Theory of Computing*, pp. 114–118, 1978.

Foster, I., Gregory, S., and Ringwood, G.A., A sequential implementation of PARLOG, in Shapiro, E. (ed.), *Proc. 3rd International Conference on Logic Programming*, *LNCS* **225**, pp. 149–156, Springer-Verlag, 1986.

Foster, I., and Taylor, S., Flat PARLOG: A basis for comparison, Tech. Report, Department of Computer Science, The Weizmann Institute of Science, Rehovot, 1987.

Friedman, D.P., and Wise, D.S., The impact of applicative programming on multiprocessing, *Proc. IEEE International Conference on Parallel Processing*, pp. 263–272, 1976a.

Friedman, D.P., and Wise, D.S., CONS should not evaluate its arguments, in Michaelson, D., and Milner, R. (eds.), *Automata, Languages and Programming*, Edinburgh University Press, 1976b.

Friedman, D.P., and Wise, D.S., Aspects of applicative programming for parallel processing, *IEEE Trans. on Computers* **C-27**(4), pp. 289–296, 1978.

Friedman, D.P., and Wise, D.S., An approach to fair applicative multiprogramming, in Kahn, G. (ed.), *Semantics of Concurrent Computation*, *LNCS* **70**, pp. 203–226, Springer-Verlag, 1979.

Friedman, D.P., and Wise, D.S., An indeterminate constructor for applicative programming, *Conference Record 7th ACM Symposium on Principles of Programming Languages*, pp. 245–250, 1980.

Fuchi, K., Revisiting original philosophy of fifth generation computer systems project, *Proc. International Conference on Fifth Generation Computer Systems*, Tokyo, 1984.

Fuchi, K., Aiming for knowledge information processing systems, in van Canegham, M., and Warren, D.H.D. (eds.), *Logic Programming and its Applications*, pp. 279–305, Ablex Publishing Co., 1986.

Fuchi, K., and Furukawa, K., The role of logic programming in the Fifth Generation Computer Project, *New Generation Computing* **5**(1), pp. 3–28, 1987.

Furukawa, K., Kunifuji, S., Takeuchi, A., and Ueda, K., The conceptual specification of the Kernel Language version 1, ICOT Tech. Report TR-054, Institute for New Generation Computer Technology, Tokyo, 1984a.

Furukawa, K., Nakajima, R., and Yonezawa, A., Modularization and abstraction in logic programming, *New Generation Computing* **1**(2), pp. 169–177, 1983.

Furukawa, K., Takeuchi, A., Kunifuji, S., Yasukawa, H., Ohki, M., and Ueda, K., Mandala: A logic based knowledge programming system, *Proc. International Conference on Fifth Generation Computer Systems*, pp. 613–622, Tokyo, 1984b.

Futamura, Y., Partial evaluation of computation process — an approach to a compiler-compiler, *Systems, Computers, Controls* **2**(5), pp. 721–728, 1971.

Futo, I., and Szeredi, J., *T-Prolog: A Very High Level Simulation System*, Tech. Report, SZKI, Budapest, 1981.

Gallager, R.G., Humblet, P.A., and Spira, P.M., A distributed algorithm for minimum weight spanning trees, Tech. Report LIDS-P-906-A, MIT, Cambridge, Massachusetts, 1979.

Gallagher, J., An approach to the control of logic programs, Ph.D. Thesis, Department of Computer Science, Trinity College, Dublin, Ireland, 1983.

Gallagher, J., Transforming logic programs by specialising interpreters, *Proc. 7th European Conference on Artificial Intelligence*, pp. 109–122, Brighton, 1986.

Gelernter, D., A note on systems programming in Concurrent Prolog, *Proc. IEEE International Symposium on Logic Programming*, pp. 76–82, Atlantic City, New Jersey, 1984.

Gentleman, M., Some complexity results for matrix computations on parallel processors, *J. ACM* **25**, pp. 112–115, 1978.

German, S.M., and Lieberherr, K.J., Zeus: A language for expressing algorithms in hardware, *IEEE Computer*, **18**(2), pp. 55–65, 1985.

Gettys, J., Newman, R., and Della Fera T., Xlib — C language X interface protocol version 10, 1986.

Goguen, J.A., and Meseguer, J., Equality, types, modules and generics for logic programming, Tärnlund, S.-Å. (ed.), *Proc. 2nd International Conference on Logic Programming*, pp. 115–125, Uppsala, 1984. Also in *J. Logic Programming* **1**(2), pp. 179–210, 1984.

Gosling, J., SunDew, A Distributed and Extensible Window System, in Hopgood F.R.A., et al. (eds.), *Methodology of Window Management*, Springer-Verlag, 1986.

Gottlieb, A., Grishman, R., Kruskal, C.P., McAuliffe, K.P., Rudolph, L., and Snir, M., The NYU ultracomputer — designing an MIMD shared memory parallel computer, *IEEE Trans. on Computers* **C-32**(2), pp. 175–190, 1983.

Green, C.C., Theorem proving by resolution as a basis for question answering, in B. Meltzer and D. Michie (eds.), *Machine Intelligence* **4**, pp. 183–205, Edinburgh University, 1969.

Gregory, S., Implementing PARLOG on the Abstract PROLOG Machine, Research Report DOC 84/23, Department of Computing, Imperial College, London, 1984a.

Gregory, S., How to use PARLOG, Unpublished report, Department of Computing, Imperial College, London, 1984b.

Gregory, S., *Parallel Logic Programming in PARLOG*, Addison-Wesley, 1987.

Gregory, S., Foster, I.T., Burt, A.D., and Ringwood, G.A., An abstract machine for the implementation of PARLOG on uniprocessors, Research report, Department of Computing, Imperial College, London, 1987.

Gregory, S., Neely, R., and Ringwood, G.A., PARLOG for specification, verification and simulation, *Proc. 7th International Symposium on Computer Hardware Description Languages and their Applications*, pp. 139–148, Tokyo, 1985.

Gullichsen, E., BiggerTalk: Object-oriented Prolog, Tech. Report STP-125-85, MCC-STE, Austin, Texas, 1985.

Hagiya, M., On lazy unification and infinite trees, *Proc. Logic Programming Conference '83*, Institute for New Generation Computer Technology, Tokyo, 1983 (in Japanese).

Halstead, R.H., MultiLisp – A language for concurrent symbolic computation, *ACM Trans. on Programming Languages and Systems* **7**(4), pp. 501–538, 1985.

Halstead, R.H., and Loaiza, J.R., Exception handling in multilisp, *Proc. IEEE International Conference on Parallel Processing*, pp. 822–830, 1985.

Hansen, P.B., The programming language Concurrent Pascal, *IEEE Trans. on Software Engineering* **SE-1**(2), pp. 199–207, 1975.

Hansson, A., Haridi, S., and Tärnlund, S.-Å., Properties of a logic programming language, in Clark, K.L., and Tärnlund, S.-Å. (eds.), *Logic Programming*, pp. 267–280, Academic Press, London, 1982.

Harel, D., and Nehab, S., Concurrent And/Or programs: Recursion with communication, Tech. Report CS82-09, Department of Comptuer Science, The

Weizmann Institute of Science, Rehovot, 1982.

Harel, D., and Pnueli, A., On the development of reactive systems, Tech. Report CS85-02, Department of Computer Science, The Weizmann Institute of Science, Rehovot, 1985.

Harrison, W.L., Compiling Lisp for evaluation on a tightly coupled multiprocessor, Ph.D. Thesis, University of Illinois at Urbana-Champain, 1986.

Havender, J.W., Avoiding deadlock in multitasking systems, *IBM Systems J.* **7**(2), pp. 74–84, 1968.

Hellerstein, L., A Concurrent Prolog based region finding algorithm, Honors Thesis, Computer Science Department, Harvard University, 1984. Also Chapter 10, this volume.

Hellerstein, L., and Shapiro, E., Implementing parallel algorithms in Concurrent Prolog: The MAXFLOW experience, *J. Logic Programming* **3**(2), pp. 157–184, 1984. Also Chapter 9, this volume.

Henderson, P., *Functional Programming — Application and Implementation*, Prentice-Hall, New Jersey, 1980.

Henderson, P., Purely functional operating systems, in Darlington, J., Henderson, P., and Turner, D. (eds.), *Functional Programming and Its Applications*, Cambridge University Press, 1982.

Henderson, P., and Morris, J.H., A lazy evaluator, *Proc. 3rd ACM Symposium on Principles of Programming Languages*, pp. 95–103, 1976.

Hewitt, C., Description and theoretical analysis (using schemata) of PLANNER: A language for proving theorems and manipulating models in a robot, Tech. Report TR-258, Artificial Intelligence Laboratory, MIT, Cambridge, Massachusetts, 1972.

Hewitt, C., A universal, modular Actor formalism for artificial intelligence, *Proc. International Joint Conference on Artificial Intelligence*, 1973.

Hewitt, C., Viewing control structures as patterns of passing messages, *Artificial Intelligence* **8**, pp. 323–363, 1977.

Hewitt, C., The Apiary network architecture for knowledgeable systems, *Proc. IEEE Conference on Lisp and Functional Programming*, pp. 107–117, 1980.

Hewitt, C., The challenge of open systems, *Byte Mag.*, pp. 223–242, April 1985.

Hewitt, C., Atardi, G., and Lieberman, H., Specifying and proving properties of guardians for distributed systems, in Kahn, G. (ed.), *Semantics of Concurrent Computations*, *LNCS* **70**, pp. 316–336, Springer-Verlag, 1979.

Hewitt, C., and Lieberman, H., Design issues in parallel architectures for artificial intelligence, *Proc. IEEE Computer Conference*, pp. 418–422, 1984.

Hirakawa, H., Chart parsing in Concurrent Prolog, ICOT Tech. Report TR-008, Institute for New Generation Computer Technology, Tokyo, 1983.

Hirakawa, H., Chikayama, T., and Furukawa, K., Eager and lazy enumerations in Concurrent Prolog, Tärnlund, S.Å. (ed.), *Proc. 2nd International Logic Programming Conference*, pp. 89–101, Uppsala, 1984.

Hirakawa, H., Onai, R., and Furukawa, K., Implementing an Or-Parallel Optimizing Prolog System (POPS) in Concurrent Prolog, ICOT Tech. Report TR-020, Institute for New Generation Computer Technology, Tokyo, 1983.

Hirata, M., Self-description of Oc and its applications, *Proc. 2nd National Conference of Japan Society on Software Science and Technology*, pp. 153–156, 1985 (in Japanese).

Hirsch, M., The Logix system, M.Sc. Thesis, Department of Computer Science, The Weizmann Institute of Science, 1987.

Hirsch, M., Silverman, W., and Shapiro, E., Layers of protection and control in the Logix system, Tech. Report CS86-19, Department of Computer Science, The Weizmann Institute of Science, Rehovot, 1986. Revised as Chapter 20, this volume.

Hoare, C.A.R., Monitors: An operating system structuring concept, *Comm. ACM* **17**(10), pp. 549–557, 1974.

Hoare, C.A.R., Communicating sequential processes, *Comm. ACM* **21**(8), pp. 666-677, 1978.

Hoare, C.A.R., *Communicating Sequential Processes*, Prentice-Hall, New Jersey, 1985.

Hogger, C.J., Concurrent logic programming, in Clark, K.L., and Tärnlund, S.-Å. (eds.), *Logic Programming*, pp. 199–211, Academic Press, London, 1982.

Hogger, C.J., *Introduction to Logic Programming*, Academic Press, London, 1984.

Holt, R.C., Graham, G.S., Lazowska, E.D., and Scott, M.A., *Structured Programming with Operating Systems Applications*, Addison Wesley, 1979.

Hopcroft, J.E., and Ullman, J.D., *Introduction to Automata Theory, Languages, and Computation*, Addison-Wesley, 1979.

Hopgood, F.R.A., Duce, D.A., Fielding, E.V.C., Robinson, K., and William, A.S., *Methodology of Window Management*, Springer-Verlag, 1986.

Houri, A., and Shapiro, E., A sequential abstract machine for Flat Concurrent

Prolog, Tech. Report CS86-20, Department of Computer Science, The Weizmann Institute of Science, Rehovot, 1986. Also Chapter 38, this volume.

Hudak, P., Functional programming on multiprocessor architectures, Research Report 447, Department of Computer Science, Yale University, 1985.

Hudak, P., and Smith, L., Para-functional programming — A paradigm for programming multiprocessor systems, Research Report 448, Department of Computer Science, Yale University, 1985.

Huet, G., Confluent reductions: Abstract properties and applications to term rewriting systems, *J. ACM*, **27**(4), pp. 797–821, 1980.

Hwang, K., and Briggs, F.A., *Computer Architecture and Parallel Processing*, McGraw-Hill, 1984.

Ingalls, D.H., The Smalltalk-76 programming system: Design and implementation, *Conference Record 5th Annual ACM Symposium on Principles of Programming Languages*, pp. 9–16, 1978.

INMOS Ltd., *IMS T424 Transputer Reference Manual*, INMOS, 1984a.

INMOS Ltd., *OCCAM Programming Manual*, Prentice-Hall, New Jersey, 1984b.

Jefferson, D., and Sowizral, H., Fast Concurrent simulation using the time warp mechanism, Part 1: Local control, N-1906-AS Rand Corporation, 1982.

Jensen, K., and Wirth, N., *Pascal User Manual and Report*, Springer-Verlag, Berlin, 1974.

Johnson, S.D., Circuits and systems: Implementing communications with streams, Tech. Report 116, Computer Science Department, Indiana University, 1981.

Jones, N.D., Sestoft, P., and Sondergaard, H., An experiment in partial evaluation: The generation of a compiler generator, DIKU Report 85/1, University of Copenhagen, 1985.

Kahn, G., and MacQueen, D., Coroutines and networks of parallel processes, in Gilchrist, B. (ed.), *Information Processing* **77**, *Proc. IFIP Congress*, pp. 993–998, North-Holland, 1977.

Kahn, K., Uniform — a language based upon unification which unifies (much of) Lisp, Prolog, and Act 1, *Proc. 7th International Joint Conference on Artificial Intelligence*, pp. 933–939, Vancouver, Canada, 1981.

Kahn, K., A partial evaluator of Lisp written in Prolog, *Proc. 1st International Conference on Logic Programming*, pp. 19–25, Marseille, 1982a.

Kahn, K., Intermission — Actors in Prolog, in Clark, K.L., and Tärnlund, S.-Å.

(eds.), *Logic Programming*, pp. 213–228, Academic Press, London, 1982b.

Kahn, K., The compilation of Prolog programs without the use of a Prolog compiler, *Proc. International Conference on Fifth Generation Computer Systems*, pp. 348–355, Tokyo, 1984a.

Kahn, K.M., A primitive for the control of logic programs, *Proc. IEEE International Symposium on Logic Programming*, pp. 242–251, Atlantic City, New Jersey, 1984b.

Kahn, K.M., and Carlsson, M., How to implement Prolog on a LISP machine, in Campbell, J.A. (ed.), *Implementations of Prolog*, pp. 117–134, Ellis Horwood, 1984.

Kahn, K., Tribble, E.D., Miller, M.S., and Bobrow, D.G., Objects in concurrent logic programming languages, *Proc. ACM Conference on Object Oriented Programming Systems, Languages, and Applications*, Portland, Oregon, *SIGPLAN Notices* **21**(11), pp. 242–257, 1986.

Kahn, K., Tribble, E.D., Miller, M., and Bobrow, D.G., Vulcan: Logical concurrent objects, in Shriver, B., and Wegner, P. (eds.), *Research Directions in Object-Oriented Programming*. Also Chapter 30, this volume.

Kasif, S., Kohli, M., and Minker, J., PRISM: A parallel inference system for problem solving, *Proc. Logic Programming Workshop '83*, pp. 123–152, Algarve, Portugal, 1983.

Katzenellenbogen, D., A distributed window system in Flat Concurrent Prolog, M.Sc. Thesis, Department of Computer Science, The Weizmann Institute of Science, Rehovot, 1987.

Katzenellenbogen, D., Cohen, S., and Shapiro, E., An architecture of a distributed window system and its FCP implementation, Tech. Report CS87-09, Department of Computer Science, The Weizmann Institute of Science, Rehovot, 1987. Also Chapter 23, this volume.

Keller, R.M., Data structuring in applicative multiprocessing systems, *Proc. IEEE Conference on Lisp and Functional Programming*, pp. 196–202, 1980a.

Keller, R.M., Some theoretical aspects of applicative multiprocessing, *Proc. Conference on Mathematical Foundations of Computer Science*, pp. 58–74, 1980b.

Keller, R.M., and Lindstrom, G., Applications of feedback in functional programming, *ACM Conference on Functional Languages and Computer Architecture*, pp. 123–130, 1981.

Keller, R.M. et al., Rediflow: A multiprocessing architecture combining reduction with data-flow, Unpublished Manuscript, Department of Computer Science,

University of Utah, 1983.

Kleene S., *Introduction to Metamathematics*, Van Nostrand, New York, 1952.

Kliger, S., Towards a native-code compiler for Flat Concurrent Prolog, M.Sc. Thesis, Department of Computer Science, The Weizmann Institute of Science, Rehovot, 1987.

Knuth, D.E., *The Art of Computer Programming*, Vol. 3: *Searching and Sorting*, Addison-Wesley, 1973.

Komorowski, H.J., Partial evaluation as a means for inferencing data-structures in an applicative language: A theory and implementation in the case of Prolog, *Conference Record 9th Annual ACM Symposium on Principles of Programming Languages*, pp. 255–268, 1982.

Kornfeld, W.A., The use of parallelism to implement a heuristic search, *Proc. International Joint Conference on Artificial Intelligence*, pp. 575–580, 1981.

Kornfeld, W.A., Equality for Prolog, *Proc. 7th International Joint Conference on Artificial Intelligence*, pp. 514–519, 1983.

Kornfeld, W.A., and Hewitt, C., The scientific community metaphor, *IEEE Trans. on Systems, Man, and Cybernetics* **SMC-11**, pp. 24–33, 1981.

Kowalski, R.A., Predicate logic as programming language, *Proc. IFIP Congress* **74**, pp. 569–574, North-Holland, Stockholm, 1974.

Kowalski, R.A., *Logic for Problem Solving*, Elsevier, North-Holland, 1979.

Kowalski, R.A., Logic programming, *Proc. IFIP Congress*, pp. 133–145, 1983.

Kung, H.T., Let's design algorithms for VLSI systems, *Proc. Conference on Very Large Scale Integration: Architecture, Design, Fabrication*, pp. 65–90, Caltech, 1979a.

Kung, H.T., The structure of parallel algorithms, Tech. Report 79-143, Carnegie-Mellon University, 1979b.

Kung, H.T., Why systolic architectures?, *IEEE Computer* **15**(1), pp. 37–46, 1982.

Kung, H.T., The warp processor: A versatile systolic array for very high speed signal processing, Tech. Report, Department of Computer Science, Carnegie-Mellon University, Pittsburgh, Pennsylvania, 1984.

Kung, H.T., Memory requirements for balanced computer architectures, Tech. Report CMU-CS-85-158, Department of Computer Science, Carnegie-Mellon University, Pittsburgh, Pennsylvania, 1985.

Kung, H.T., and Leiserson, C.E., Algorithms for VLSI processor arrays, in Mead,

C.A., and Conway, L. (eds.), *Introduction to VLSI Systems*, pp. 271–292, 1980.

Kusalik, A.J., Bounded-wait merge in Shapiro's Concurrent Prolog, *New Generation Computing* **1**(2), pp. 157–169, 1984a.

Kusalik, A.J., Serialization of process reduction in Concurrent Prolog, *New Generation Computing* **2**(3), pp. 289–298, 1984b.

Lam, M., and Gregory, S., PARLOG and ALICE: A marriage of convenience, Lassez, J.-L. (ed.), *Proc. 4th International Conference of Logic programming*, MIT Press, 1987.

Lamport, L., A recursive concurrent algorithm, 1982 (unpublished note).

Lampson, B.W., and Redell, D.D., Experience with processes and monitors in Mesa, *Comm. ACM* **23**(2), pp. 105–117, 1980.

Leiserson, C.E., *Area-Efficient VLSI Computation*, The MIT Press, 1983.

Lenat, D.B., The role of heuristics in learning by discovery: Three case studies, in Michalski, R.S., Carbonnel, J.G., and Mitchell, T.M. (eds.), *Machine Learning: An Artificial Intelligence Approach*, pp. 243–305, Tioga Publishing Company, Palo Alto, 1983.

Levi, G., Logic programming: The foundations, the approach and the role of occurrency, in de Bakker, J.W., de Roever, W.P., and Rozenberg, G. (eds.), *Current Trends in Concurrency, Overviews and Tutorials*, *LNCS* **224**, pp. 396–441, Springer-Verlag, 1986.

Levi, G., and Palamidessi, C., The declarative semantics of logical read-only variables, *IEEE Symposium on Logic Programming*, pp. 128–137, Boston, 1985.

Levy, J., A unification algorithm for Concurrent Prolog, Tärnlund, S.-Å. (ed.), *Proc. 2nd International Conference on Logic Programming*, pp. 333–341, Uppsala, 1984.

Levy, J., A GHC abstract machine and instruction set, in Shapiro E. (ed.), *Proc. 3rd International Conference on Logic Programming*, *LNCS* **225**, pp. 157–171, Springer-Verlag, 1986.

Levy, J., CFL — A concurrent functional language embedded in a concurrent logic programming environment, Tech. Report CS86-28, Department of Computer Science, The Weizmann Institute of Science, Rehovot, 1986. Revised as Chapter 35, this volume.

Levy, J., and Friedman, N., Concurrent Prolog implementations — two new schemes, Tech. Report CS86-13, Department of Computer Science, The Weizmann Institute of Science, Rehovot, 1986.

Levy, J., and Shapiro, E., Translation of Safe GHC and Safe Concurrent Prolog to FCP, Tech. Report CS87-08, Department of Computer Science, The Weizmann Institute of Science, Rehovot, 1987. Also Chapter 33, this volume.

Lichtenstein, Y., Codish, M., and Shapiro, E., Representation and enumeration of Flat Concurrent Prolog Computations, Chapter 27, this volume.

Lieberman, H., A preview of Act 1, Tech. Report AIM-625, Artificial Intelligence Laboratory, MIT, Cambridge, Massachusetts, 1981.

Lieberman, H., Using prototypical objects to implement shared behavior in object-oriented systems, *Proc. ACM Conference on Object Oriented Programming Systems, Languages, and Applications*, Portland, Oregon, *SIGPLAN Notices* **21**(11), pp. 214–223, 1986.

Lindstrom, G., Or-parallelism on applicative architectures, Tärnlund, S.-Å. (ed.), *Proc. 2nd International Conference on Logic Programming*, pp. 159–170, Uppsala, 1984.

Lint, B., and Agerwala, T., Communication issues in the design and analysis of parallel algorithms, *IEEE Trans. on Software Engineering*, **SE-7**(2), pp. 174–188, 1981.

Liskov, B., Atkinson, R., Bloom, D., Moss, E., Schaffert, J.C., Scheifler, R., and Snyder, A., *CLU Reference Manual*, *LNCS* **114**, Springer-Verlag, 1981.

Liu, C.L., *Introduction to Combinatorial Mathematics*, McGraw-Hill, 1968.

Lloyd, J.W., *Foundations of Logic Programming*, Springer-Verlag, 1984.

Lloyd, J.W., Declarative error diagnosis, Tech. Report 86/3, Department of Computer Science, University of Melbourne, 1986.

Lloyd, J.W., and Takeuchi, A., A framework for debugging GHC, ICOT Tech. Report TR-186, Institute for New Generation Computer Technology, Tokyo, 1986.

MacQueen, D.B., Models for distributed computing, Rapport de Recherche 351, INRIA, France, 1979.

Mago, G.A., A cellular computer architecture for functional programming, *Proc. IEEE Computer Conference*, pp. 179–187, 1984.

Martin, A.J., The Torus: An exercise in constructing a processing surface, *Proc. Conference on Very Large Scale Integration: Architecture, Design, Fabrication*, pp. 52–57, California Institute of Technology, 1979.

Matsumoto, Y., A parallel parsing system for natural language analysis, *New Generation Computing* **5**(1), pp. 63–78, 1987.

McCabe, F.G., Abstract PROLOG machine — a specification, Research Report DOC 83/12, Department of Computing, Imperial College, London, 1984.

McCabe, F.G., Lambda Prolog, Internal Report, Department of Computing, Imperial College, London, 1986.

McCarthy, J., A basis for a mathematical theory of computation, in Brafford P., and Hirchberg, D. (eds.), *Computer Programming and Formal Systems*, pp. 33–70, North-Holland, 1963.

McCarthy, J., Abrahams, P.W., Edwards, D.J., Hart, T.P., and Levin, M.I., *LISP 1.5 Programmer's Manual*, The MIT Press, 1965.

Mellish, C., and Hardy, S., Integrating Prolog in the POPLOG environment, in Campbell, J.A. (ed.), *Implementation of Prolog*, pp. 147–162, Ellis Horwood, 1984.

Mierowsky, C., Taylor, S., Shapiro, E., Levy J., and Safra, S., The design and implementation of Flat Concurrent Prolog, Tech. Report CS85-09, Department of Computer Science, The Weizmann Institute of Science, Rehovot, 1985.

Miller, M.S., Merge filters, 1987 (in preparation).

Miller, M.S., Bobrow D.G., Tribble, E.D., and Levy, J., Logical Secrets, Lassez, J.-L. (ed.), *Proc. 4th International Conference on Logic Programming*, pp. 704–728, MIT Press, 1987. Also Chapter 24, this volume.

Miller, R., and Stout, Q., Convexity algorithm for pyramid computers, *Proc. IEEE Conference on Parallel Processing*, pp. 177–184, 1984.

Milne, G., and Milner, R., Concurrent processes and their syntax, *J. ACM* **26**(2), pp. 302–321, 1979.

Milner, R., A theory of type polymorphism in programming, *J. Computer and System Sciences* **17**(3), pp. 348–375, 1978.

Milner, R., A Calculus of Communicating Systems, *LNCS* **92**, Springer-Verlag, 1980.

Milner, R., A complete inference system for a class of regular behaviours, *J. Computer and System Sciences*, **28**, pp. 439–466, 1984.

Minsky, M., *Society of Mind*, Simon and Schuster, 1986.

Mishra, P., Towards a theory of types in Prolog, *Proc. IEEE International Symposium on Logic Programming*, pp. 289–298, 1984.

Miyazaki, T., Takeuchi, A., and Chikayama, T., A sequential implementation of Concurrent Prolog based on the shallow binding scheme, *IEEE Symposium on Logic Programming*, pp. 110–118, 1985. Also Chapter 37, this volume.

Moens, E., and Yu, B., Implementation of PARLOG on the Warren machine, Tech. Report, Department of Computer Science, University of British Columbia, Vancouver, 1985.

Moon, D., MacLISP reference manual, revision 0, Artificial Intelligence Laboratory, MIT, Cambridge, Massachusetts, 1974.

Moss, C.D.S., Computing with sequences, *Proc. Logic Programming Workshop '83*, pp. 623–630, Algarve, Portugal, 1983.

Morris, J.H., et al., Andrew: A distributed personel computing environment, *Comm. ACM* **29**(3), pp. 184–201, 1986.

Moto-Oka, T., et al., Challenge for knowledge information processing systems (Preliminary Report on Fifth Generation Computer Systems), *Proc. International Conference on Fifth Generation Computer Systems*, pp. 1–85, Tokyo, 1981.

Moto-Oka, T., Tanaka, H., Aida, H., Hirata, K., and Maruyama, T., The architecture of a parallel inference engine – PIE, *Proc. International Conference on Fifth Generation Computer Systems*, pp. 479–488, Tokyo, 1984.

Mycroft, A., and O'Keefe, R., A polymorphic type system for Prolog, *Proc. Logic Programming Workshop '83*, pp. 107–121, Algarve, Portugal, 1983.

Naish, L., *MU-Prolog 3.1db Reference Manual*, Internal Memorandum, Department of Computer Science, University of Melbourne, 1984.

Nakashima, H., Tomura, S., and Ueda, K., What is a variable in Prolog?, *Proc. International Conference on Fifth Generation Computer Systems*, pp. 327–332, Tokyo, 1984.

Narain, S., A technique for doing lazy evaluation in logic, *J. Logic Programming* **3**(3), pp. 259–276, 1986.

Nelson, T.H., *Literary Machines*, Ted Nelson, Box 128, Swarthmore, Pennsylvania 19081, 1981.

Nievergelt, J., and Preparata, J.P., Plane sweep algorithms for intersecting geometric figures, *Comm. ACM* **25**, p. 10, 1982.

Nitta, K., On a Concurrent Prolog interpreter, Preprint of the 8th WGSF Meeting, Information Processing Society of Japan, 1984 (in Japanese).

Noda, Y., Kinoshita, T., Okumura, A., Hirano, T., and Hiruta, N., A parallel logic simulator based on Concurrent Prolog, *The Logic Programming Conference '85*, pp. 353–363, Tokyo, 1985 (in Japanese).

O'Donnel, J.T., Hardware description with recursion equations, *Proc. of CHDL-87*, pp. 363-382, Elsevier Science Publishing, 1987.

Panangaden, P., Abstract interpretation and indeterminacy, Seminar on Concurrency, Carnegie-Mellon University, Pittsburgh, Pennsylvania, *LNCS* **197**, pp. 497–511, Springer-Verlag, 1984.

Papert, S., *Mindstorms: Children, Computers, and Powerful Ideas*, Basic Books, New York, 1980.

Park, D., On the Semantics of fair parallelism, in Bjorner, D. (ed.), *LNCS* **86**, pp. 504–526, Springer-Verlag, 1980.

Pereira, F.C.N., *C-Prolog User's Manual*, EdCAAD, University of Edinburgh, 1983.

Pereira, L.M., Logic control with logic, *Proc. 1st International Conference on Logic Programming*, pp. 9–18, Marseille, 1982.

Pereira, L.M., Rational debugging in logic programming, in Shapiro, E. (ed.), *Proc. 3rd International Conference on Logic Programming*, *LNCS* **225**, pp. 203–210, Springer-Verlag, 1986.

Pereira, L.M., and Monteiro, L., The semantics of parallelism and coroutining in logic programming, *Proc. Colloquium on Mathematical Logic in Programming*, Salgotarjan, 1978.

Pereira, L.M., and Nasr, R., Delta-Prolog: A distributed logic programming language, *Proc. International Conference on Fifth Generation Computer Systems*, pp. 283–291, Tokyo, 1984.

Pike, R., Graphics in overlapping bitmap images, *ACM Trans. in Graphics* **2**(2), pp. 133–150, 1983.

Plotkin, G.D., A note on inductive generalization, in Melzer, B., and Michie, D. (eds.), *Machine Intelligence* **5**, pp. 153–164, 1969.

Plotkin, G.D., A further note on inductive generalization, in Melzer, B., and Michie, D. (eds.), *Machine Intelligence* **6**, pp. 101–124, 1970.

Plotkin, G.D., A powerdomain construction, *SIAM J. Computing* **5**(3), pp. 452-487, 1976.

Pnueli, A., Applications of temporal logic to the specification and verification of reactive systems: A survey of current trends, in de Bakker, J.W., de Roever, W.P., and Rozenberg, G. (eds.), *Current Trends in Concurrency, Overviews and Tutorials*, *LNCS* **224**, pp. 510–584, Springer-Verlag, 1986.

Pollard, G.H., Parallel execution of Horn clause programs, Ph.D. Thesis, Department of Computing, Imperial College, London, 1981.

Pratt, V.R., On the composition of processes, *Conference Record 9th ACM Symposium on Principles of Programming Languages*, pp. 213–223, 1982.

Quintus Prolog Reference Manual, Quintus Computer Systems Ltd., 1985.

Ramakrishnan, R., and Silberschatz, A., Annotations for Distributed Programming in Logic, *Conference Record 13^{en} ACM Symposium on Principles of Programming Languages*, pp. 255–262, 1986.

Reddy, U.S., On the relationship between logic and functional languages, in DeGroot, D., and Lindstrom, G. (eds.), *Logic Programming — Functions, Relations and Equations*, pp. 3–36, Prentice-Hall, New Jersay, 1986.

Rees, J.A., and Adams, IV, N.I., T: A dialect of Lisp or, Lambda: The ultimate software tool, *Proc. ACM Symposium on Lisp and Functional Programming*, pp. 114–122, 1982.

Reeve, M.J., A BNF description of the ALICE compiler target language, Department of Computing, Imperial College, London, 1985 (unpublished report).

Richie, D.M., and Thompson, K., The Unix time-sharing system, *Comm. ACM* **17**(7), pp. 365–375, 1974.

Rivest, R., Shamir, A., and Adleman, L., A method for obtaining digital signatures and public-key cryptosystems, *Comm. ACM* **21**(2), pp. 120–126, 1978.

Roberts, G., *The Waterloo Prolog Reference Manual, Version 1.3*, 1979.

Robinson, J.A., A machine oriented logic based on the resolution principle, *J. ACM* **12**(1), pp. 23–41, 1965.

Robinson, J.A., and Sibert, E.E., LOGLISP — motivation, design and implementation, in Clark, K.L., and Tärnlund, S.-Å. (eds.), *Logic Programming*, pp. 299–314, Academic Press, London, 1982.

Roussel, P., *Prolog: Manual de Reference et d'Utilisation*, Groupe d'Intelligence Artificielle, Marseille-Luminy, 1975.

Safra, S., Partial evaluation of Concurrent Prolog and its implications, Tech. Report CS86-24, Department of Computer Science, The Weizmann Institute of Science, Rehovot, 1986.

Safra, S., and Shapiro, E., Meta-interpreters for real, *Information Processing 86*, pp. 271–278, North-Holland, 1986. Also Chapter 25, this volume.

Samet H., Connected component labeling using quadtrees, *J. ACM* **28**(3), pp. 487–501, 1981.

Samet H., The quadtree and related hierarchical data structures, *ACM Computing surveys* **16**(2), pp. 187–260, 1984.

Sandewall, E., Programming in an interactive environment: The Lisp experimence, *ACM Computing Surveys*, pp. 35–72, 1978.

Saraswat, V.A., Partial Correctness Semantics for CP[↓,|,&], *Proc. 5th Conference on Foundations of Software Technology and Theoretical Computer Science, LNCS* **206**, pp. 347–368, New Delhi, 1985.

Saraswat, V.A., Problems with Concurrent Prolog, Tech. Report 86-100, Carnegie-Mellon University, 1986.

Saraswat, V.A., Merging many streams efficiently: The importance of atomic commitment, Chapter 16, this volume.

Saraswat, V.A., Concurrent Logic Programming Languages, Ph.D. Thesis, Carnegie-Mellon University, 1987 (in preparation).

Saraswat, V.A., The concurrent logic programming language CP: Definition and operational semantics, *Proc. ACM SIGACT-SIGPLAN Symposium on Principles of Programming Languages*, pp. 49–63, 1987a.

Saraswat, V.A., The language GHC: Operational semantics, problems and relationship with CP[↓,|], *Proc. IEEE Symposium on Logic Programming*, San Francisco, 1987b.

Sato, M., and Sakurai, T., Qute: A functional language based on unification, *Proc. International Conference on Fifth Generation Computer Systems*, pp. 157–165, Tokyo, 1984.

Sato, H., Ichiyoshi, N., Dasai, T., Miyazaki, T., and Takeuchi, A., A sequential implementation of Concurrent Prolog — based on deep binding scheme, *The 1st National Conference of Japan Society for Software Science and Technology*, pp. 299–302, 1984 (in Japanese).

Schlichting, R.D., and Purdin, T.D.M., Failure handling in distributed programming languages, Tech. Report 85-14, Department of Computer Science, University of Arizona, 1985.

Schwans, K., Tailoring software for multiple processor systems, Ph.D. Thesis, Tech. Report CMU-CS-82-137, Department of Computer Science, Carnegie-Mellon University, 1982.

Schwarz, J., Using annotations to make recursion equations behave, Research Report 43, Department of Artificial Intelligence, University of Edinburgh, 1977.

Sejnowiski, M.C., Upchurch, E.T., Kapur, R.N., Charlu, D.P.S., and Lipovski,

G.J., An overview of the Texas reconfigurable array computer, *Proc. AFIPS Conference*, pp. 631–641, 1980.

Sequin, C.H., Doubly twisted torus networks for VLSI processor arrays, *Proc. 8th IEEE International Conference on Computer Architecture*, pp. 471–480, 1981.

Shafrir, A., and Shapiro, E., Distributed programming in Concurrent Prolog, Tech. Report CS83-12, Department of Computer Science, The Weizmann Institute of Science, Rehovot, 1983. Also Chapter 11, this volume.

Shahdad, M., Lipsett, R., Marschner, E., Sheehan, K., Cohen, H., Waxman, R., Ackley, D., VHSIC hardware description language, *IEEE Computer* **18**, pp. 94–102, 1985.

Shamir, A., and Fiat, A., Polymorphic arrays: A novel VLSI layout for systolic computers, *J. Computer and System Sciences* **33**(1), pp. 47–65, 1986.

Shapiro, E., *Algorithmic Program Debugging*, The MIT Press, 1982.

Shapiro, E., A subset of Concurrent Prolog and its interpreter, ICOT Tech. Report TR-003, Institute for New Generation Computer Technology, Tokyo, 1983. Revised as Chapter 2, this volume.

Shapiro, E., Lecture notes on the Bagel: A systolic Concurrent Prolog machine, ICOT TM-0031, Institute for New Generation Computer Technology, Tokyo, 1983a.

Shapiro, E., Logic programs with uncertainties: A tool for implementing rule-base systems, *Proc. 8th International Joint Conference on Artificial Intelligence*, pp. 529–532, Kalsruhe, 1983b.

Shapiro, E., Notes on sequential implementation of Concurrent Prolog, Summary of Discussions in ICOT, 1983c (unpublished).

Shapiro, E., Systolic programming: A paradigm of parallel processing, *Proc. International Conference on Fifth Generation Computer Systems*, pp. 458–471, 1984. Revised as Chapter 7, this volume.

Shapiro, E., Alternation and the computational complexity of logic programs, *J. Logic Programming* **1**(1), pp. 19–33, 1984.

Shapiro, E., Systems programming in Concurrent Prolog, in van Canegham, M., and Warren, D.H.D. (eds.), *Logic Programming and its Applications*, pp. 50–74, Ablex Publishing Co., 1986. Also Chapter 19, this volume.

Shapiro, E., Concurrent Prolog: A progress report, *IEEE Computer*, **19**(8), pp. 44–58, August 1986. Also Chapter 5, this volume.

Shapiro, E., On evaluating the adequacy of a language for an architecture, Tech. Report CS86-01, Department of Computer Science, The Weizmann Institute of Science, Rehovot, 1986. Revised as Chapter 13, this volume.

Shapiro, E., An Or-parallel execution algorithm for Prolog and its FCP implementation, Lassez, J.-L. (ed.), *Proc. 4th International Conference of Logic programming*, pp. 311–337, MIT Press, 1987. Revised as Chapter 34, this volume.

Shapiro, E., and Mierowsky, C., Fair, biased, and self-balancing merge operators: Their specification and implementation in Concurrent Prolog, *New Generation Computing* **2**(3), pp. 221–240, 1984. Also Chapter 14, this volume.

Shapiro, E., and Safra, S., Multiway merge with constant delay in Concurrent Prolog, *New Generation Computing* **4**(2), pp. 211–216, 1986. Also Chapter 15, this volume.

Shapiro, E., and Takeuchi, A., Object-oriented programming in Concurrent Prolog, *New Generation Computing* **1**(1), pp. 25–49, 1983. Also Chapter 29, this volume.

Shiloach, Y., and Vishkin, U., Finding the maximum, merging and sorting in a parallel computation model, *J. Algorithms* **2**(1), pp. 88–102, 1981.

Shiloach, Y., and Vishkin, U., An $O(log\ n)$ parallel connectivity algorithm, *J. Algorithms* **3**, pp. 57–67, 1982a.

Shiloach, Y., and Vishkin, U., An $O(n^2 log n)$ parallel MAX-FLOW algorithm, *J. Algorithms* **3**, pp. 128–146, 1982b.

Silverman, W., Houri, A., Hirsch, M., and Shapiro, E., The Logix system user manual, Tech. Report CS86-21, Department of Computer Science, The Weizmann Institute of Science, Rehovot, 1986. Also Chapter 21, this volume.

Smith, B.C., Reflection and semantics in a procedural language, Ph.D. Dissertation, MIT, 1982.

Smyth, M.B., Finitary relations and their fair merge, Internal Report CSR-107-82, Department of Computer Science, University of Edinburgh, 1982.

Snyder, A., Encapsulation and inheritance in object-oriented programming, *ACM Conference on Object-Oriented Programming Systems, Languages and Applications*, pp. 38–45, Portland, Oregon, 1986.

Snyder, L., Parallel programming and the Poker programming environment, *IEEE Computer* **17**(7), pp. 55–62, 1984.

Steele, C.S., Placement of Communicating Processes on Multiprocessor Networks, Ph.D. Thesis, California Institute of Technology, 1985.

Steele, G.L., The definition and implementation of a computer programming language based on constraints, Tech. Report TR-595, Artificial Intelligence Laboratory, MIT, Cambridge, Massachusetts, 1980.

Steele, G.L., *Common Lisp: The Language*, Digital Press, 1984.

Steele, G.L., Jr., and Sussman, G.J., The revised report on scheme, a dialect of Lisp, AI Memo 379, Artificial Intelligence Laboratory, MIT, Cambridge, Massachusetts, 1978a.

Steele, G.L., Jr., and Sussman, G.J., The art of the interpreter or, the modularity, complex, Tech. Memorandum AIM-453, Artificial Intelligence Laboratory, MIT, Cambridge, Massachusetts, 1978b.

Stefik, M., The next knowledge medium, *AI Mag.* **7**(1), pp. 34–46, 1986.

Steinberg, S.A., The butterfly Lisp system, *Proc. National Conference on Artificial Intelligence*, pp. 730–742, 1986.

Sterling, L.S., Expert System = Knowledge + Meta-interpreter, Tech. Report CS84-17, Department of Computer Science, The Weizmann Institute of Science, Rehovot, 1984.

Sterling, L.S., Bundy, A., Byrd, L., O'Keefe, R., and Silver, B., Solving symbolic equations with PRESS, in *Computer Algebra*, *LNCS* **144**, pp. 109–116, Springer-Verlag, 1982.

Sterling, L.S., and Codish, M., PRESSing for parallelism: A Prolog program made concurrent, *J. Logic Programming* **3**(1), pp. 75–92, 1986. Also Chapter 31, this volume.

Sterling, L.S., and Shapiro, E., *The Art of Prolog*, The MIT Press, 1986.

Stone, H., Multiprocessor scheduling with the aid of network flow algorithms, *IEEE Trans. on Software Engineering* **SE-3**, pp. 85–93, 1977.

Stone, H., and Bokhari, S.H., Control of distributed processes, *Computer* **11**, pp. 97–106, July 1978.

Subrahmanyam, P.A., and You, J.H., FUNLOG = Functions + Logic: A computational model integrating functional and logic programming, *Proc. IEEE International Symposium on Logic Programming*, pp. 144–153, Atlantic City, New Jersey, 1984a.

Subrahmanyam, P.A., and You, J.H., Conceptual basis and evaluation strategies for integrating functional and logic programming, *Proc. IEEE International Symposium on Logic Programming*, Atlantic Ciry, New Jersey, 1984b.

Subramahnyam, P.A., and You, J.H., FUNLOG — a computational model integrating logic programming and functional programming, in DeGroot, D., and Lindstrom, G. (eds.), *Logic Programming — Functions, Relations and Equations*, pp. 157–198, Prentice-Hall, New Jersey, 1986.

Sun Microsystems Inc., *NeWS Preliminary Technical Overview*, 2550 Garcia Avenue, Mountain View, California 94043, October 1986.

Sun Microsystems Inc., *User's Manual for the SUN Unix System*, 2550 Garcia Avenue, Mountain View, California 94043.

Sussman, G.J., and Steele, G.L., Scheme — An interpreter for extended lambda calculus, AI Memo 349, Artificial Intelligence Laboratory, MIT, Cambridge, Massachusetts, 1975.

Sussman, G.J., and Steele, G.L., Constraints — A language for expressing almost-hierarchical descriptions, *Artificial Intelligence* **14**, p. 39, 1980.

Suzuki, N., Experience with specification and verification of complex computer using Concurrent Prolog, in Warren, D.H.D., and van Caneghem, M. (eds.), *Logic Programming and Its Applications*, pp. 188-209, Ablex Pub. Co., New Jersey, 1986.

Takahashi, N., and Ono, S., Strategic bug location method for functional programs, *Proc. 6th RIMS Symposium on Mathematical Methods in Software Science and Engineering*, RIMS, Kyoto University, 1985.

Takeuchi, A., How to solve it in Concurrent Prolog, 1983 (unpublished note).

Takeuchi, A., Algorithmic debugging of GHC programs and its implementation in GHC, ICOT Tech. Report TR-185, Institute for New Generation Computer Technology, Tokyo, 1986. Also Chapter 26, this volume.

Takeuchi, A., and Furukawa, K., Bounded-buffer communication in Concurrent Prolog, *New Generation Computing* **3**(2), pp. 145–155, 1985. Also Chapter 18, this volume.

Takeuchi, A., and Furukawa, K., Partial evaluation of Prolog programs and its application to meta-programming, ICOT Tech. Report TR-126, Institute for New Generation Computer Technology, Tokyo, 1985. Also in *Information Processing 86*, pp. 415–420, North-Holland, 1986.

Takeuchi, A., and Furukawa, K., Parallel logic programming languages, in Shapiro, E. (ed.), *Proc. 3rd International Conference on Logic Programming*, *LNCS* **225**, pp. 242–255, Springer-Verlag, 1986. Also Chapter 6, this volume.

Takeuchi, I., Okuno, H., and Osato, N., A list processing language TAO with multiple programming paradigms, *New Generation Computing* **4**, pp. 401–444, 1986.

Tamaki, H., A distributed unification scheme for systolic logic programs, *Proc.*

IEEE International Conference on Parallel Processing, pp. 552–559, 1985.

Tamaki, H., and Sato, T., A transformation system for logic programs which preserves equivalence, ICOT Tech. Report TR-018, Institute for New Generation Computer Technology, Tokyo, 1983.

Tanaka, J., Miyazaki, T., and Takeuchi, A., A sequential implementation of Concurrent Prolog — based on lazy copying scheme, *The 1ˢᵗ National Conference of Japan Society for Software Science and Technology*, pp. 303–306, 1984 (in Japanese).

Tarski, A., A lattice-theoretical fix-point theorem and its application, *Pacific J. Mathematics* **5**, pp. 285–309, 1955.

Taylor, S., and Shapiro, E., Compiling concurrent logic programs into decision graphs, Tech. Report, Department of Computer Science, The Weizmann Institute of Science, Rehovot, 1987.

Taylor, S., Av-Ron, E., and Shapiro, E., A layered method for process and code mapping, *J. New Generation Computing*, (in press). Also Chapter 22, this volume.

Taylor, S., Hellerstein, L., Safra, S., and Shapiro, E., Notes on the complexity of systolic programs, *J. Parallel and Distributed Computing*, (in press). Also Chapter 8, this volume.

Taylor, S., Safra, S., and Shapiro E., A parallel implementation of Flat Concurrent Prolog, *J. Parallel Programming* **15**(3), pp. 245–275, 1987. Also Chapter 39, this volume.

Thompson, C.D., and Kung, H.T., Sorting on a mesh-connected parallel computer, *Comm. ACM* **20**(4), 1977.

Treleaven, P.C., Brownbridge, D.R., and Hopkins, R.P., Data-driven and demand-driven computer architecture, *Computing Surveys* **14**(1), pp. 93–143, 1982.

Tribble, E.D., Miller, M.S., Kahn, K., Bobrow, D.G., and Abbott, C., Channels: A generalization of streams, Lassez, J.-L. (ed.), *Proc. 4ᵗʰ International Conference of Logic Programming*, pp. 839–857, MIT Press, 1987. Also Chapter 17, this volume.

Turchin, V., Semantics definitions in REFAL and the automatic production of compilers, in Jones, N.D. (ed.), *Semantics-Directed Compiler Generation*, *LNCS* **94**, pp. 441–474, Springer-Verlag, 1980.

Turner, D.A., A new implementation technique for applicative languages, *Software Practice and Experience* **9**, pp. 31–49, 1979.

Turner, D.A., The semantic elegance of applicative languages, *Proc. of the ACM*

Conference on Functional Programming Languages and Computer Architecture, pp. 85–92, Portsmouth, New Hampshire, 1981.

Uchida, S., Towards a new generation computer architecture: Research and development plan for computer architecture in the Fifth Generation Computer project, ICOT Tech. Report TR-001, Institute for New Generation Computer Technology, Tokyo, 1982.

Uchida, S., Inference machine: From sequential to parallel, *Proc. 10th Annual International Symposium on Computer Architecture*, pp. 410–416, Stockholm, 1983.

Ueda, K., Concurrent Prolog re-examined, ICOT Tech. Report TR-102, Institute for New Generation Computer Technology, Tokyo, 1985.

Ueda, K., Guarded Horn Clauses, ICOT Tech. Report TR-103, Institute for New Generation Computer Technology, Tokyo, 1985. Also in Wada, E. (ed.), *Logic Programming*, *LNCS* **221**, pp. 168–179, Springer-Verlag, 1986. Also Chapter 4, this volume.

Ueda, K., Guarded Horn Clauses — A parallel logic programming language with the concept of a guard, ICOT Tech. Report TR-208, Institute for New Generation Computer Technology, Tokyo, 1986a.

Ueda, K., Introduction to Guarded Horn Clauses, ICOT Tech. Report TR-209, Institute for New Generation Computer Technology, Tokyo, 1986b.

Ueda, K., Making exhaustive search programs deterministic, *New Generation Computing* **5**(1), pp. 29–44, 1987.

Ueda, K., and Chikayama, T., Efficient stream/array processing in logic programming languages, *Proc. International Conference on Fifth Generation Computer Systems*, pp. 317–326, Tokyo, 1984.

Ueda, K., and Chikayama, T., Concurrent Prolog compiler on top of Prolog, *Proc. IEEE Symposium on Logic Programming*, pp. 119–126, 1985.

Ullman, J.D., *Principles of Database Systems*, Computer Science Press, Maryland, 1982.

Vegdahl, S.R., A survey of proposed architectures for the execution of functional languages, *IEEE Trans. on Computers* **33**(12), pp. 1050–1071, 1984.

Viner, O., Distributed constraint propagation, Tech. Report CS84-24, Department of Computer Science, The Weizmann Institute of Science, Rehovot, 1984.

Wadge, W.W., An extensional treatment of dataflow deadlock, in Kahn, G. (ed.), *Semantics of Concurrent Computations*, *LNCS* **70**, pp. 283–299, Springer-Verlag, 1979.

Warren, D.H.D., Implementing Prolog — compiling predicate logic programs, Tech. Report DAI 39/40, Department of Artificial Intelligence, University of Edinburgh, 1977.

Warren, D.H.D., Logic programming and compiler writing, *Software-Practice and Experience* **10**, pp. 97–125, 1980.

Warren, D.H.D., MegaLIPS now!, 1982a (unpublished note).

Warren, D.H.D., Perpetual processes: An unexploited Prolog programming technique, *Proc. Prolog Programming Environments Workshop*, Datalogi, Linkoping, 1982b.

Warren, D.H.D., Higher order extensions to Prolog — are they needed?, *Machine Intelligence* **10**, pp. 441–454, 1982c.

Warren, D.H.D., An abstract Prolog instruction set, Tech. Report 309, Artificial Intelligence Center, SRI International, 1983.

Warren, D.H.D., Pereira, L.M., and Pereira, F.C.N., PROLOG — The language and its implementation compared with Lisp, *SIGPLAN Notices* **12**(8), pp. 109–115, 1977.

Warren, D.S., Efficient Prolog memory management for flexible control strategies, *New Generation Computing* **2**(4), pp. 361–369, 1984.

Weinbaum, D., and Shapiro, E., Hardware description and simulation using Concurrent Prolog, *Proc. CHDL '87*, pp. 9–27, Elsevier Science Publishing, 1987. Also Chapter 36, this volume.

Weinreb, D., and Moon, D., Flavors: Message passing in the Lisp machine, Memo 602, Artificial Intelligence Laboratory, MIT, Cambridge, Massachusetts, 1980.

Weinreb, D., and Moon, D., Lisp machine Lisp, Artificial Intelligence Laboratory, MIT, Cambridge, Massachusetts, 1983.

Weiser, U., and Davis, A.L., A wavefront notation tool for VLSI array design, in Kung, H.T., Sproull, R.F., and Steele, G.L., Jr. (eds.), *VLSI Systems and Computations*, pp. 226–364, Carnegie-Mellon University, Computer Science Press, 1981.

Weng, K.S., Stream-oriented computation in recursive data flow schemes, Tech. Report MTMM-68, MIT, Cambridge, Massachusetts, 1975.

White, J.L., NIL — A perspective, *Proc. Macsyma Users Conference*, 1979.

Wise, M.J., A parallel Prolog: The construction of a data driven model, *ACM Symposium on Lisp and Functional Programming*, pp. 56–67, 1982a.

Wise, M.J., Epilog = Prolog + data flow — arguments for combining Prolog with a data driven mechanism, *SIGPLAN Notices* **17**(12), pp. 80–86, 1982b.

The XEROX Learning Research Group, The Smalltalk-80 System, *BYTE* **6**(8), pp. 36–48, August 1981.

Yaghi, A.A.G., The compilation of a functional language into intensional logic, Theory of Computation Report 56, Department of Computer Science, University of Warwick, 1983.

Yardeni, E., A type system for logic programs, M.Sc. Thesis, Department of Computer Science, The Weizmann Institute of Science, Rehovot, 1987.

Yardeni, E., and Shapiro, E., A type system for logic programs, Chapter 28, this volume.

Yokota, M., Yamamoto, A., Taki, K., Nishikawa, H., Uchida, S., Nakajima, K., and Mitsui, M., A microprogrammed interpreter for the personal sequential inference machine, *Proc. International Conference on Fifth Generation Computer Systems*, pp. 410–418, Tokyo, 1984.

Index

Note: Page numbers in roman type refer to Volume 1; page numbers in italic type refer to Volume 2.

The MIT Press, with Peter Denning, general consulting editor, and Brian Randell, European consulting editor, publishes computer science books in the following series:

ACM Doctoral Dissertation Award and Distinguished Dissertation Series

Artificial Intelligence, Patrick Winston and Michael Brady, editors

Charles Babbage Institute Reprint Series for the History of Computing, Martin Campbell-Kelly, editor

Computer Systems, Herb Schwetman, editor

Exploring with Logo, E. Paul Goldenberg, editor

Foundations of Computing, Michael Garey, editor

History of Computing, I. Bernard Cohen and William Aspray, editors

Information Systems, Michael Lesk, editor

Logic Programming, Ehud Shapiro, editor; Fernando Pereira, Koichi Furukawa, and D. H. D. Warren, associate editors

The MIT Electrical Engineering and Computer Science Series

Scientific Computation, Dennis Gannon, editor